EDUGORILLA™
PUBLICATION

NTA PM Yasasvi

Entrance Test Class XI

Latest Edition
Practice Kit

15 Tests

15 Practice Test

Based On Real Exam Pattern

✓ Thoroughly Revised and Updated

✓ Detailed Analysis of all MCQs

Title   : NTA PM Yasasvi Entrance Test Class XI

Author Name   : Mr. Rohit Manglik

Published By   : EduGorilla Community Pvt. Ltd.

Publishers Address : 12/651, First Floor Opp. Arvindo Park, Near Jama Masjid,
                         Indira Nagar, Lucknow, Uttar Pradesh-226016, India

Copyright EduGorilla

ISBN : 978-93-55569-18-9

First Edition

Disclaimer EduGorilla

Compiled and created by EduGorilla Community Pvt. Ltd

Printed By EduGorilla Community Pvt. Ltd.

TABLE OF CONTENTS

Mathematics

1. To divide a line segment AB in the ratio $3 : 4$, first, a ray AX is drawn so that $\angle$BAX is an acute angle and then at equal distances points are marked on the ray AX such that the minimum number of these points is:
   (a) 5
   (b) 7
   (c) 9
   (d) 11

2. To divide a line segment AB of length 7.6 cm in the ratio $5 : 8$, a ray AX is drawn first such that $\angle$BAX forms an acute angle and then points $A_1, A_2, A_3, \ldots$ are located at equal distances on the ray AX and the point B is joined to:
   (a) A_5
   (b) A_6
   (c) A_{10}
   (d) A_{13}

3. A survey was conducted by a group of students as a part of their environment awareness programme, in which they collected the following data regarding the number of plants in 20 houses in a locality. Find the mean number of plants per house.

Number of plants	0–2	2–4	4–6	6–8	8–10	10–12	12–14
Number of houses	1	2	1	5	6	2	3

   (a) 8.1
   (b) 8.5
   (c) 10.5
   (d) 12.3

4. A metallic sphere of radius $10.5 cm$ is melted and thus recast into small cones, each of radius $3.5 cm$ and height $3 cm$. Find how many cones are obtained.
   (a) 123
   (b) 124
   (c) 125
   (d) 126

5. A wooden article was made by scooping out a hemisphere from each end of a solid cylinder, as shown in figures. If the height of the cylinder is $10 cm$ and its base is of radius $3.5 cm$, find the total surface area of the article.

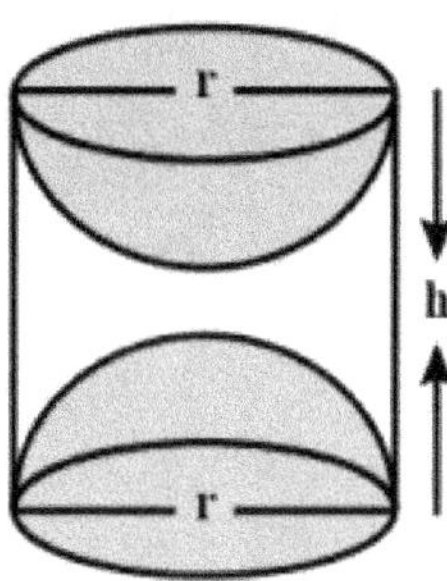

   (a) $375 cm^2$
   (b) $374 cm^2$
   (c) $376 cm^2$
   (d) $377 cm^2$

6. If $(x - 4)$ and $(x + 6)$ are the factors of equation $x^2 + ax + b = 0$ then find the value of $(a - b)$?
   (a) 22
   (b) -34
   (c) 17
   (d) 26

7. If the roots of the quadratic equation $(\log 5k)x^2 - 2x + 1 = 0$ are real and equal, then the value of k is:
   (a) 2
   (b) 4
   (c) 5
   (d) 3

8. The wheels of a car are of diameter 80 cm each. How many complete revolutions does each wheel make in 10 minutes when the car is traveling at a speed of 66 km per hour?
   (a) 3375
   (b) 4375
   (c) 4475
   (d) 4575

9. If the perimeter and the area of a circle are numerically equal, then the radius of the circle is:
   (a) 2 units
   (b) π units
   (c) 4 units
   (d) 7 units

10. In a right triangle ABC, right-angled at $B, \cot^2 A = \dfrac{9}{16}$. What is the value of $\cos A$?
    (a) $\dfrac{3}{5}$
    (b) $\dfrac{5}{3}$
    (c) $\dfrac{4}{5}$
    (d) $\dfrac{4}{3}$

11. What is the value of $\cot^2 A \times \tan^2 A$?
    (a) 0
    (b) 1
    (c) 2
    (d) 3

12. In a right triangle ABC, right angled at $B, \sin A = \dfrac{1}{\sqrt{2}}$. What is the value of $\tan A$?
    (a) 1
    (b) 2
    (c) $\dfrac{1}{\sqrt{2}}$
    (d) $\dfrac{2}{\sqrt{2}}$

13. The angle of elevation of the top of the building from the foot of the tower is 30 and the angle of the top of the tower from the foot of the building is 60. If the tower is 50 m high, find the height of the building.
    (a) $16.66 m$
    (b) $18 m$
    (c) $18.66 m$
    (d) $20 m$

14. Solve the following pairs of linear equations.
    $3x - 5y - 4 = 0$ and $9x = 2y + 7$
    (a) $x = \dfrac{19}{13}$ and $y = -\dfrac{15}{13}$
    (b) $x = \dfrac{10}{13}$ and $y = -\dfrac{6}{13}$
    (c) $x = \dfrac{9}{13}$ and $y = -\dfrac{5}{13}$
    (d) $x = \dfrac{5}{13}$ and $y = -\dfrac{9}{13}$

15. Five years ago, Nuri was thrice as old as Sonu. Ten years later, Nuri will be twice as old as Sonu. How old are Nuri and Sonu?
    (a) 60 years, 40 years
    (b) 30 years, 10 years
    (c) 60 years, 20 years
    (d) 50 years, 20 years

16. The decimal expansion of the rational number $\dfrac{33}{2^2 \times 5}$ will terminate after:
    (a) One decimal place
    (b) Two decimal places
    (c) Three decimal places
    (d) More than 3 decimal places

17. For some integer m, every even integer is of the form:
    (a) m
    (b) $m + 1$
    (c) $2m$
    (d) $2m + 1$

18. The least number that is divisible by all the numbers from 1 to 10 (both inclusive) is:
    (a) 10
    (b) 100
    (c) 504
    (d) 2520

19. Three alarm clocks ring their alarms at regular intervals of 20 min, 25 min and 30 min respectively. If they first beep together at 12 noon, at what time will they beep again for the first time?
    (a) $4 : 00$ pm
    (b) $4 : 30$ pm
    (c) $5 : 00$ pm
    (d) $4 : 30$ pm

20. The zeroes of $x^2 - 2x - 8$ are:
    (a) $(2, -4)$
    (b) $(4, -2)$
    (c) $(-2, -2)$
    (d) $(-4, -4)$

21. What is the quadratic polynomial whose sum and the product of zeroes is $\sqrt{2}, \dfrac{1}{3}$ respectively?

(a) $3x^2 - 3\sqrt{2}x + 1$

(b) $3x^2 + 3\sqrt{2}x + 1$

(c) $3x^2 + 3\sqrt{2}x - 1$

(d)   None of the above

22. An unbiased die is thrown once. The probability of getting a prime number is:

(a) $\dfrac{1}{4}$ (b) $\dfrac{1}{2}$

(c) $\dfrac{1}{5}$ (d) $\dfrac{1}{3}$

23. Find the sum of all three-digit natural numbers, which are multiples of 11 :

(a)   56550   (b)   55550

(c)   45550   (d)   44550

24. The 8th term of an AP is half its 2nd term and the 11th term exceeds $\dfrac{1}{3}$ of its fourth term by 1 . Find the 15th term:

(a) -1 (b)   1

(c) -2 (d)   0

25. A vertical pole of length $6\,m$ casts a shadow $4\,m$ long on the ground and at the same time a tower casts a shadow $28\,m$ long. Find the height of the tower.

(a)   42 meter   (b)   52 meter

(c)   62 meter   (d)   72 meter

26. Let $\triangle ABC \sim \triangle DEF$ and their areas be, respectively, 64 cm^2 and 121 cm^2. If $EF = 15.4 \text{ cm}$, find BC.

(a) $BC = 9.2 \text{ cm}$

(b) $BC = 10.2 \text{ cm}$

(c) $BC = 11.2 \text{ cm}$

(d) $BC = 15.2 \text{ cm}$

27. In the given figure, O is the center of the circle, $AM = PQ$ and $\angle POQ = 45°$. The measure of $\angle AOM$ is:

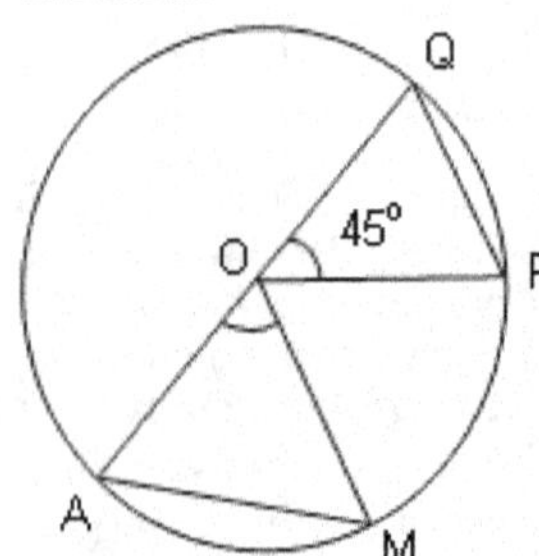

(a) $45°$

(b) $90°$

(c) $60°$

(d)   Cannot be determined

28. In the given circle, O is the centre and length of chord $XY =$ length of chord ZW . If $\angle\ XOY = 60°$, then what is the measure of $\angle ZOW$?

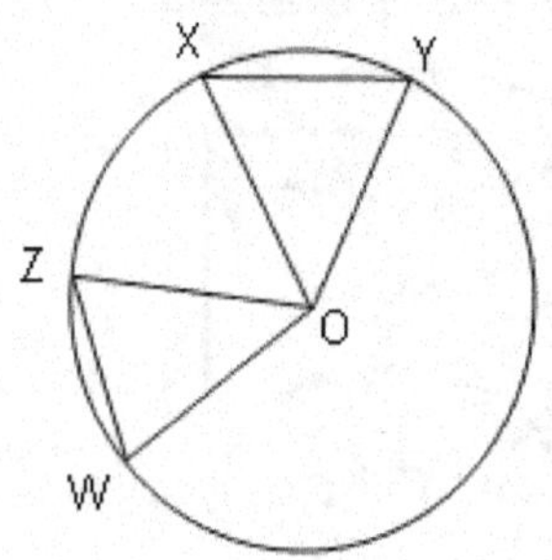

(a) $120°$

(b) $60°$

(c) $30°$

(d)   None of these

29. The distance between the points $(a\cos\theta + b\sin\theta, 0)$ and $(0, a\sin\theta - b\cos\theta)$, is:

(a) $a^2 + b^2$ (b) $a^2 - b^2$

(c) $\sqrt{a^2 + b^2}$ (d) $\sqrt{a^2 - b^2}$

30. If the distance between the points $(4, p)$ and $(1, 0)$ is 5 , then the value of p is:

(a)   4   (b) ± 4

(c)   0   (d)   2

Science

31. A food chain starts with__________.

(a)   Respiration

(b)   Decomposers

(c)   Nitrogen fixation organisms

(d)   Photosynthesising organisms

32. Every food chain in the ecosystem begins with __________ which are the original source of food.

(a)   Herbivores   (b)   Parasites

(c)   Producers   (d)   Saprophytes

33. A student added dilute HCl to a test tube containing zinc granules. Which of the following observations are correct?

I. Zinc surface became dull and black.

II. A gas was evolved which burnt with a pop sound.

III. The solution remained colourless.

(a)   I and II   (b)   I and III

(c)   II and III   (d)   I, II and III

34. A metal gives lilac colour in bunsen flame and the solution of its oxide turns red litmus paper blue. The metal is:

(a)   Na   (b) K

(c) Ca (d)   Li

35. Geotropism is the movement of plant parts in response to __________ as stimulus.

(a)   light   (b)   gravity

(c)   water   (d)   contact

36. Which one of the following statements is correct?

(a)   Endocrine glands regulate neural activity, but not vice versa

(b)   Neurons regulate endocrine activity, but not vice versa

(c)   Endocrine glands regulate neural activity, and nervous system regulates endocrine glands

(d)   Neither hormones control neural activity nor the neurons control endocrine activity

37. You mix two colourless solutions and the resulting mixture becomes cloudy. What type of reaction is observed?

(a)   A physical reaction

(b)   A redox reaction

(c)   A precipitation reaction

(d)   An acid base reaction

38. Solution of lead nitrate turn yellow when potassium iodide is added to it becuase:

(a)   Due to the formation of potassium nitrate

(b)   Due to the formation of lead iodide

(c)   Due to the formation of lead

(d)   Due to the formation of iodine

39. Oils on treating with hydrogen in the presence of palladium or nickel catalyst form fats. This is an example of ______.

(a)   addition reaction

(b)   substitution reaction

(c)   displacement reaction

(d)   oxidation reaction

40. Buckminsterfullerene is an allotropic form of:

(a)   phosphorus   (b)   sulphur

(c)   carbon   (d)   tin

41. In human beings, fertilization takes place in the:

(a)   Uterus

(b)   Fallopian tube

(c)   Ovary

(d)   Vagina

42. ______ acts as a platform where the pollen grains lands.

(a)   Anther   (b)   Style

(c)   Ovary   (d)   Stigma

43. From an evolutionary point of view, what was the function of feathers

before they were used for flight?
- (a) Obtaining nutrition
- (b) Protection from predators
- (c) Providing insulation
- (d) Camouflaging

44. Fossil records suggest that birds are closely related to ;
- (a) fishes
- (b) amphibians
- (c) reptiles
- (d) mammals

45. The refraction of light is commonly known as:
- (a) Bending
- (b) Scattering
- (c) Reflection
- (d) Interference

46. If a ray of light goes from a rarer medium to a denser medium, will it bend towards the normal or away from it?
- (a) Bends away from the normal
- (b) Bends towards from the normal
- (c) Goes undeviated
- (d) Is reflected back

47. Which of the following is a vector quantity?
- (a) Magnetic field
- (b) Velocity, force and magnetic field
- (c) Force
- (d) Velocity

48. Which of the following organs in the human body where the magnetic field produced is significant?
- (a) Heart, brain
- (b) Heart, lung
- (c) Lungs, brain
- (d) Liver, heart

49. Urine leaves the kidney through the:
- (a) urethra
- (b) ureter
- (c) collecting duct
- (d) renal vein

50. Waste products are stored as ______ in old xylem plants.
- (a) sucrose
- (b) glucose
- (c) resins
- (d) water

51. To prepare an indicator from red cabbage leaves, these are boiled in ____.
- (a) Benzene
- (b) Water
- (c) Chloroform
- (d) Ethyl alcohol

52. In which of the following solutions does vanilla essence lose its flavour?
- (a) HCl
- (b) H_2SO_4
- (c) HNO_3
- (d) NH_4OH

53. The far point of a healthy person is:
- (a) Infinity
- (b) 100m.
- (c) 15cm
- (d) 0.15m

54. A bulb rated at ($100\,W, 200\,V$) is used on a $100\,V$ line. The current in the bulb is:
- (a) $0.25\,A$
- (b) $4\,A$
- (c) $0.5\,A$
- (d) $2\,A$

55. A copper wire of resistance R is cut into ten parts of equal length. Two-piece are joined in series and then five such combinations are joined in parallel. The new combination will have resistance.
- (a) R
- (b) $\dfrac{R}{4}$
- (c) $\dfrac{R}{5}$
- (d) $\dfrac{R}{25}$

56. Why is water scarcity mainly caused?
- (a) Water pollution
- (b) Excessive use and unequal access to water
- (c) Water management
- (d) Using to utility

57. Which animals in India are on the verge of extinction?
- (a) Kangaroo
- (b) Cheetah, Pink-Headed Duck
- (c) Jaguar
- (d) Mountain bear

58. Gold, silver and platinum are examples of ________.
- (a) Ferrous minerals
- (b) Non-ferrous minerals
- (c) Precious minerals
- (d) Non-metallic minerals

59. When we produce a good by exploiting natural resources it is called:
- (a) Tertiary sector
- (b) Primary sector
- (c) Service sector
- (d) Public sector

60. Development of a country can generally be determined by its:
- (a) per capita income
- (b) average literacy level
- (c) health status of its people
- (d) All of the above

61. By whom was the Estates General elected?
- (a) Men and Women
- (b) Active Citizens
- (c) Women
- (d) Senior Citizens

62. How much of India's population is engaged in Agricultural activities?
- (a) Two-third
- (b) Half
- (c) One third
- (d) Almost all

63. What do the banks do with the deposits which they accept from the customers?
- (a) Banks use these deposits for charitable activities.
- (b) Banks use a major portion of deposits to extend loans.
- (c) Banks use deposits to give bonus to their employees.
- (d) Banks use deposits to set up more branches in the country.

64. Which body supervises the functioning of formal sources of loans?
- (a) Finance Ministry
- (b) Head Office of each Bank
- (c) Reserve Bank of India
- (d) Cooperative Societies

65. Which one of the following organisations lay stress on liberalisation of foreign trade and foreign investment?
- (a) International Monetary Fund
- (b) International Labour Organisation
- (c) World Health Organisation
- (d) World Trade Organisation

66. Which one of the following refers to investment?
- (a) The money spent on religious ceremonies
- (b) The money spent on social customs
- (c) The money spent to buy asset such as land
- (d) The money spent on household goods

67. ISI mark is given to:
- (a) Product's compliance with the country standards
- (b) Product's compliance with the manufacture standards
- (c) Product's compliance with the required standards
- (d) Product's compliance with the customer standards

68. The Consumer Protection Act or COPRA was enacted in the year:
- (a) 1989
- (b) 1986
- (c) 1990
- (d) 1991

69. Where did the development of print first begin?

(a) East Asia   (b) Europe
(c) India   (d) America

70. **How were the books in China printed?**
(a) Printing by seals
(b) By rubbing paper, against the inked surface of woodblocks
(c) Machine printing
(d) Rust printing

71. **What is the percentage of German speaking people in Belgium?**
(a) 30   (b) 59
(c) 10   (d) 01

72. **SriLanka emerged as an independent nation in ____.**
(a) 1948   (b) 1943
(c) 1953   (d) 1958

73. **Which of the following allowed the British Government to restrict the import of corn?**
(a) Food Act   (b) Corn Act
(c) Corn Laws   (d) Import Act

74. **Federalism is a system of government in which the power is:**
(a) Divided
(b) Concentrated
(c) Centralised
(d) None of these

75. **What is the opposite of federal government?**
(a) Authoritarian Government
(b) Monarchical Government
(c) Democratic Government
(d) Unitary Government

76. **What is proto-industrialization?**
(a) Industry based on heavy factory production
(b) First and early form of Industrialization
(c) Industry based on modern technology
(d) Rural Industry

77. **Which one of the following soils is ideal for growing cotton?**
(a) Regular soil
(b) Laterite soil
(c) Desert soil
(d) Mountainous soil

78. **Which of the following statements are true about Democratic Government?**
(a) Democratic Government is a legitimate Government.
(b) Democratic Government may be slow, less efficient, and not always very responsive or clean.
(c) Democratic Government is the people's own Government.
(d) All the above given statements are true.

79. **Democracy is preferred over dictatorship in South Asia except ____.**
(a) India   (b) Bhutan
(c) Pakistan   (d) Nepal

80. **What did the idea of Satyagraha emphasise?**
(a) The power of truth and the need to search for truth, and physical force was not necessary to fight the oppressor
(b) Need to search for truth, and use physical force
(c) Fight with arguments and violence
(d) Agitation and violence

General Awareness/ Knowledge

81. **'Gunning for the Godman' book was written by:**
(a) Nand Bhardwaj
(b) IPS Ajaypal Lamba
(c) Vikram Seth
(d) Amitav Gosh

82. **Which of the following is the salient feature of Indian Constitution?**
(a) Directive Principles
(b) CJI
(c) President of India
(d) None of the above

83. **Which among the following countries is not a member of "BRICS"?**
(a) India   (b) South Africa
(c) Russia   (d) Canada

84. **Who among the following has the right to establish the bench of the Supreme Court elsewhere in the country?**
(a) The Chief Justice of the Supreme Court
(b) The President of India
(c) The Parliament
(d) The bench of the Supreme Court of Judges

85. **Which of the following is a major element of the Earth's crust?**
(a) Aluminum   (b) Oxygen
(c) Iron   (d) Silicon

86. **A device used for listening the sound of heart is:**
(a) odometer   (b) CT scanner
(c) MRI   (d) Stethoscope

87. **Which of the following is the first State in India formed on the basis of languages?**
(a) Kerala
(b) Madhya Pradesh
(c) Andhra Pradesh
(d) Uttar Pradesh

88. **Kathakali dance style belongs to:**
(a) Karnataka
(b) Kerala
(c) Tamil Nadu
(d) Andhra Pradesh

89. **The Hundru Fall lies along the course of which of the following rivers?**
(a) Damodar
(b) Sone
(c) Mahanadi
(d) Subarnarekha

90. **The fear of the Phallus worship was replaced in the ____ by its recognition as an official ritual.**
(a) Rig Veda
(b) Sama Veda
(c) Yajur Veda
(d) Atharva Veda

91. **Which of the following Mughal emperors wrote their own autobiography?**
(a) Shah Alam and Farrukhsiyar
(b) Babur and Jahangir
(c) Jahangir and Shahjahan
(d) Akbar and Aurangzeb

92. **Where did the first freedom struggle begin in 1857?**
(a) Lucknow   (b) Jhansi
(c) Meerut   (d) Kanpur

93. **Major source of formation of soil is:**
(a) Rocks
(b) Snow covered mountains
(c) Rivers beds
(d) Volcanoes

94. **Read the following statements:**
(a) First State to offer 50% reservation for women in Panchayati Raj Institutions is Bihar.
(b) The number of seats reserved for scheduled caste members in Lok Sabha is 84.
(c) The number of seats reserved for scheduled tribe members in Lok Sabha is 41.
(a) (c) is correct but (a) and (b) are

wrong

(b) (c) and (a) are correct, but (b) is wrong

(c) (a) and (b) are correct, but (c) is wrong

(d) All (a), (b) and (c) are wrong

95. Who won the National Hockey Championship 2023 ?

(a) ITBP   (b) BSF

(c) Bhopal   (d) Haryana

96. Who was the first man who climb Mount Everest?

(a) Edmund Hillary

(b) George Leigh Mallory

(c) Tenzing Norgay

(d) Both (A) and (B)

97. Which of the following induces souring of milk?

(a) Acetic Acid

(b) Citric Acid

(c) Ascorbic Acid

(d) Lactic Acid

98. Which of the following is an excretory organ of cockroach?

(a) Malphigian Tubules

(b) Nephridia

(c) Coxal Gland

(d) Green Gland

99. During which time period was the First World War fought?

(a) Sep, 1911 - Apr, 1914

(b) Sep, 1913 - Dec, 1917

(c) July, 1914 - Nov, 1918

(d) Feb, 1909 - Apr, 1913

100. Who among the following cricketers has won the ESPNcricinfo 'Captain of the Year' awards 2022?

(a) Kane Williamson

(b) KL Rahul

(c) Virat Kohli

(d) Babar Azam

// Hints and Solutions //

1(B). We know that to divide a line segment in the ratio m : n , we draw AX which makes an acute angle BAX , then we mark m + n points at equal distances from each other.

Here, m = 3, n = 4

So, the minimum number of these points $= m + n = 3 + 4 = 7$

2(D). We know that to divide a line segment in the ratio m : n , first draw a ray AX which makes an acute angle $\angle BAX$, then we are required to mark $(m + n)$ points at equal distances from each other.

So, the minimum points located in the ray AX is $5 + 8 = 13$. Hence, point B will join point A_{13} .

3(A). The number of houses denoted by x_i

The mean can be found as given below:

$$\bar{X} = \frac{\sum f_i x_i}{\sum f_i}$$

Class mark (x_i) for each interval is calculated as follows:

$$x_i = \frac{(\text{Upper class limit} + \text{Lower class limit})}{2}$$

x_i and $f_i x_i$ can be calculated as follows:

Number of plants	Number of houses f_i	x_i	$f_i x_i$
0 − 2	1	1	$1 \times 1 = 1$
2 − 4	2	3	$2 \times 3 = 6$
4 − 6	1	5	$1 \times 5 = 5$
6 − 8	5	7	$5 \times 7 = 35$
8 − 10	6	9	$6 \times 9 = 54$
10 − 12	2	11	$2 \times 11 = 22$
12 − 14	3	13	$3 \times 13 = 39$
Total	20		162

From the table, it can be observed that

$\sum f_i = 20$

$\sum f_i x_i = 162$

Substituting the value of $f_i x_i$ and f_i in the formula of mean we get:

Mean number of plants per house $(\bar{X})$:

$$\bar{X} = \frac{\sum f_i x_i}{\sum f_i}$$

$$\bar{X} = \frac{162}{20} = 8.1$$

Therefore, mean number of plants per house is 8.1 .

4(D). Given,

Radius of metallic sphere $(R) = 10.5 cm$

Radius of circular base of smaller cone $(r) = 3.5 cm$

Height of cone $(h) = 3 cm$

Volume of metallic sphere $V = \frac{4}{3}\pi R^3$

$$= \frac{4}{3} \times \frac{22}{7} \times (10.5)^3$$

$$= \frac{4}{3} \times \frac{22}{7} \times 1157.625$$

$$= \frac{88}{21} \times 1157.625$$

$$= 88 \times 55.125$$

$$= 4851 cm^3$$

Volume of metallic sphere $(V) = 4851 cm^3$

Volume of one cone $(v) = \frac{1}{3}\pi r^2 h$

$$= \frac{1}{3} \times \frac{22}{7} \times (3.5)^2 \times 3$$

$$= \frac{22}{7} \times 12.25$$

$$= 38.5 cm^3$$

Number of cones formed

$$(n) = \frac{\text{Volume of sphere } (V)}{\text{Volume of one cone } (v)}$$

$$= \frac{4851 cm^3}{38.5 cm^3}$$

$$= 126$$

Therefore, 126 smaller cones are obtained from the melted metallic sphere.

5(B). Given,

Height of cylinder $= 10 cm$

Radius of base $= 3.5 cm$

As we know,

Curved surface area of the cylinder $= 2\pi rh$

Curved surface area of a hemisphere $= 2\pi r^2$

Total surface area of the article = Curved surface area of the cylinder $+2$ Curved surface area of a hemisphere

$$= 2\pi rh + 2(2\pi r^2)$$

$$= 2\pi r(h + 2r)$$

$$= 2 \times \frac{22}{7} \times 3.5(10 + 2 \times 3.5)$$

$$= 2 \times \frac{22}{7} \times 3.5(10 + 7)$$

$$= 2 \times \frac{22}{7} \times 3.5 \times 17$$

$$= 374 cm^2$$

So, the total surface area of the article is $374 cm^2$.

6(D). Given:

$(x - 4)$ and $(x + 6)$ are the factors of equation $x^2 + ax + b = 0$

If $(x - p)$ is the factors equation $x^2 + ax + b = 0$ then ' p ' will be the root of the equation.

Roots of equation $x^2 + ax + b = 0$ will be: 4 and -6 .

Putting the values of the roots we will get two equations as follows:

$16 + 4a + b = 0$

$\Rightarrow 4a + b = -16 \quad - (1)$

And

$36 - 6a + b = 0$

$\Rightarrow -6a + b = -36 - (2)$

Solving these two equations we get

$\Rightarrow a = 2$ and $b = -24$

So,

$(a - b) = 2 - (-24) = 26$

7(C). Given,

Roots of the quadratic equation $(\log 5k)x^2 - 2x + 1 = 0$ are real and equal.

To Find: Value of k

For real roots: Discriminant $= 0$

$\Rightarrow (-2)^2 - 4 \times \log_5 k \times 1 = 0$

$\Rightarrow 4 - 4 \times \log_5 k = 0$

$\Rightarrow 1 - \log_5 k = 0$

$\Rightarrow \log_5 k = 1$

$\therefore k = 5$

Therefore, the value of k is 5 .

8(B). Given,

Diameter of the wheel of the car $= 80$ cm

Radius $= \dfrac{\text{Diameter}}{2}$

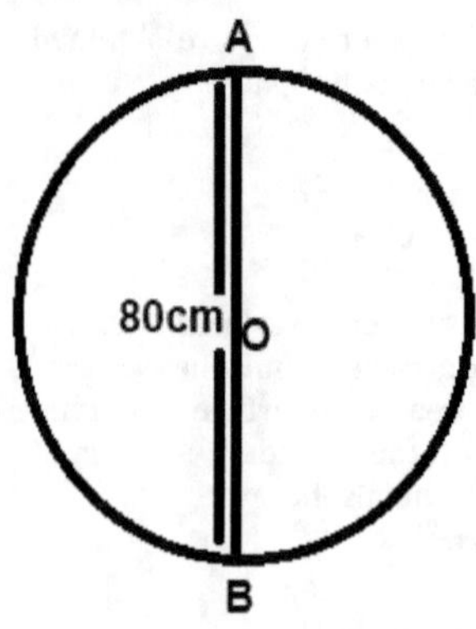

Thus, radius of the wheel of the car
$= r = 40$ cm
Speed of car $= 66$ km/hour
We know that,
Circumference of wheel $= 2\pi r$
$= 2\pi(40)$
$= 80\pi$ cm
Speed of car $= \frac{66 \times 100000}{60}$ cm/min
$= 1,10,000$ cm/min
1 km $= 1000$ m
1 m $= 100$ cm
1 h $= 60$ min
Now, distance travelled by the car in 10 minutes
$= 110000 \times 10 = 11,00,000$ cm
Let the number of revolutions of the wheel of the car be n.
We know that,
Distance travelled in 10 minutes $= n \times$ Distance travelled in 1 revolution (i.e., circumference).
$\Rightarrow 1100000 = n \times 80\pi$
$\Rightarrow n = \frac{1100000 \times 7}{22 \times 80}$
$= \frac{35000}{8}$
$= 4375$
Therefore, each wheel of the car will make 4375 revolutions.

9(A). Given,
the circumference and the area of the circle are numerically equal.
Let the radius (to be found) of the circle be r

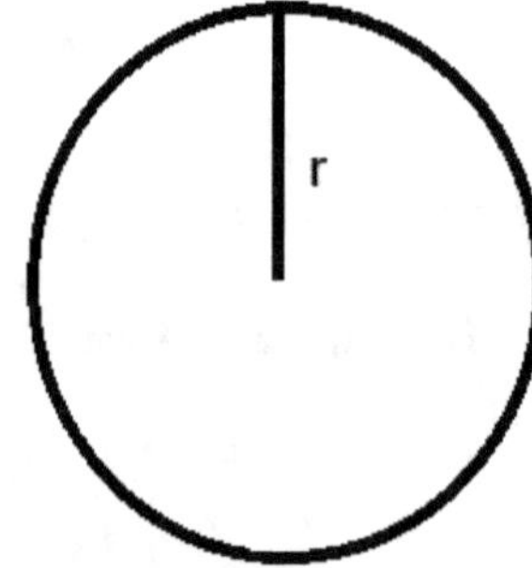

As we know,
Circumference of circle $= 2\pi r$ and
Area of circle $= \pi r^2$
According to given condition,
$2\pi r = \pi r^2$
$\Rightarrow r = 2$
Therefore, the radius of the circle is 2 units.

10(A). Given,
$\cot^2 A = \frac{9}{16}$
$\Rightarrow \cot A = \frac{3}{4} = \frac{\text{Base}}{\text{Perpendicular}}$
We know that,
$(\text{Hypotenuse})^2 = (\text{Base})^2 + (\text{Perpendicular})^2$
$\Rightarrow H^2 = (3)^2 + (4)^2$
$\Rightarrow H^2 = 25$
$\Rightarrow H = \sqrt{25}$
$\Rightarrow H = 5$
Now,
$\cos A = \frac{\text{Base}}{\text{Hypotenuse}} = \frac{3}{5}$

11(B). We know that,
$\cot^2 A = \frac{(\text{Base})^2}{(\text{Perpendicular})^2} \cdots\cdots (1)$
$\tan^2 A = \frac{(\text{Perpendicular})^2}{(\text{Base})^2} \cdots\cdots (2)$
By multiply equation (1) and equation (2) we get,
$\cot^2 A \times \tan^2 A = \left(\frac{(\text{Base})^2}{(\text{Perpendicular})^2} \times \frac{(\text{Perpendicular})^2}{(\text{Base})^2} \right)$
$= 1$

12(A). Given:
$\sin A = \frac{1}{\sqrt{2}}$
squaring it we get,
$\sin^2 A = \frac{(1)^2}{(\sqrt{2})^2} = \frac{1}{2}$
$\sin^2 A = \frac{(\text{Perpendicular})^2}{(\text{Hypotenuse})^2} = \frac{1}{2}$
We know that,
$(\text{Hypotenuse})^2 = (\text{Base})^2 + (\text{Perpendicular})^2$
$(\text{Base})^2 = (\text{Hypotenuse})^2 - (\text{Perpendicular})^2$
$= 2 - 1$
$= 1$
Now,
$\tan A = \frac{\text{Perpendicular}}{\text{Base}}$
$= \frac{1}{1}$
$= 1$

13(A).

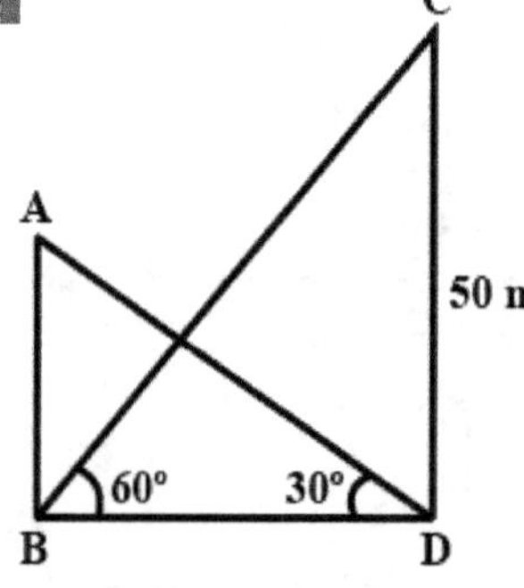

Given,
Height of tower $(CD) = 50$ m
Let h be the height of the building (AB).
In right angled $\triangle BDC$,
$\tan 60° = \frac{CD}{BD}$

$\Rightarrow \sqrt{3} = \frac{50}{BD}$
$\Rightarrow BD = \frac{50}{\sqrt{3}}$ m
In right angled $\triangle ABD$,
$\tan 30° = \frac{AB}{BD}$
$\Rightarrow \frac{1}{\sqrt{3}} = \frac{h}{\frac{50}{\sqrt{3}}}$
$\Rightarrow \frac{1}{\sqrt{3}} = \frac{\sqrt{3}h}{50}$
$\Rightarrow h = \frac{50}{\sqrt{3} \times \sqrt{3}}$
$\Rightarrow h = \frac{50}{3}$
$\Rightarrow h = 16.66$ m
$\therefore$ The height of the building is 16.66 m.

14(C). Given,
$3x - 5y - 4 = 0$
$3x - 5y = 4 \quad \cdots\cdots (1)$
$9x = 2y + 7$
$9x - 2y = 7 \quad \cdots\cdots (2)$
Now, we multiply first equation by 3
$3(3x - 5y) = 3 \times 4$
$9x - 15y = 12 \quad \cdots\cdots (3)$
We use elimination method with equations (3) and (2)
$9x - 2y = 7$
$9x - 15y = 12$
$(-) \quad (+) \quad (-)$
$\overline{13y = -5}$
$13y = -5$
$y = \frac{-5}{13}$
Putting $y = \frac{-5}{13}$ in equation (2)
$9x - 2y = 7$
$9x - 2 \times \left(\frac{-5}{13}\right) = 7$
$9x + \frac{10}{13} = 7$
$9x = 7 - \frac{10}{13}$
$9x = \frac{7 \times 13 - 10}{13}$
$9x = \frac{91 - 10}{13}$
$9x = \frac{81}{13}$
$x = \frac{81}{13} \times \frac{1}{9}$
$x = \frac{9}{13}$
Therefore,
$x = \frac{9}{13}$ and $y = -\frac{5}{13}$ are the solutions of the given equations.

15(D). Let Present age of Nuri $= x$ years
Present age of Sonu $= y$ years
Five years ago,
Nuri's age $= x - 5$ years
Sonu's age $= y - 5$ years
Given,
Nuri was thrice as old as Sonu
$x - 5 = 3(y - 5)$
$x - 5 = 3y - 15$
$x - 3y = -10 \quad \cdots\cdots (1)$
Ten years later,
Nuri's age $= x + 10$ years
Sonu's age $= y + 10$ years
Given,
Nuri will be twice as old as sonu.

$x + 10 = 2(y + 10)$
$x + 10 = 2y + 2(10)$
$x + 10 = 2y + 20$
$x - 2y = 20 - 10$
$x - 2y = 10 \quad \ldots\ldots(2)$
So, our equations are
$x - 3y = -10 \quad \ldots\ldots(1)$
$x - 2y = 10 \quad \ldots\ldots(2)$
Using elimination method with equation (1) and 2).
$y - 3y = -10$
$x - 2y = 10$
$\underline{(-)(+) \quad (-)}$
$\overline{-y = -20}$
$-y = -20$
$y = 20$
Putting $y = 20$ in (1),
$x - 3y = -10$
$x - 3(20) = -10$
$x - 60 = -10$
$x = -10 + 60$
$x = 50$
Therefore,
Present age of Nuri $= x = 50$ years.
Present age of Sonu $= y = 20$ years.

16(B). Given,
$\frac{33}{2^2 \times 5}$
So,
$\Rightarrow \frac{33}{2^2 \times 5} \times \frac{5}{5}$
$\Rightarrow \frac{33 \times 5}{(2^2 \times 5^2)}$
$\Rightarrow \frac{33 \times 5}{(2 \times 5)^2}$
$\Rightarrow \frac{33 \times 5}{10^2}$
So, the number will terminate after 2 decimal places

17(C). Every even integer is a multiple of 2.
$\therefore 2m$ is an even integer

18(D). The least number Divisible by all numbers 1 to 10 is:
LCM of all number 1 to 10

2	1, 2, 3, 4, 5, 6, 7, 8, 9, 10
2	1, 1, 3, 2, 5, 3, 7, 4, 9, 5
2	1, 1, 3, 1, 5, 3, 7, 2, 9, 5
3	1, 1, 3, 1, 5, 3, 7, 1, 9, 5
3	1, 1, 1, 1, 5, 1, 7, 1, 3, 5
5	1, 1, 1, 1, 5, 1, 7, 1, 1, 5
7	1, 1, 1, 1, 1, 1, 7, 1, 1, 1
	1, 1, 1, 1, 1, 1, 1, 1, 1, 1

Thus,
$LCM = 2 \times 2 \times 2 \times 3 \times 3 \times 5 \times 7$
$\Rightarrow 2520$

19(C). Here,
Time when they next ring together $=$ LCM of 20, 25 and 30

2	20, 25, 30
2	10, 25, 15
3	5, 25, 15
5	5, 25, 5
5	1, 5, 1
	1, 1, 1

$\therefore$ LCM $= 2 \times 2 \times 3 \times 5 \times 5$
$= 4 \times 3 \times 25$
$= 300$
Thus, the three bells ring together after 300 minutes, i.e. after 5 hours.
So, Time when the three bells ring together is 5 : 00 pm

20(B). $x^2 - 2x - 8$
$= x^2 - 4x + 2x - 8$
$= x(x - 4) + 2(x - 4)$
$= (x - 4)(x + 2)$
Therefore, $x = 4, -2$.

21(A). Sum of zeroes $= \alpha + \beta = \sqrt{2}$
Product of zeroes $= \alpha\beta = \frac{1}{3}$
$\therefore$ If α and β are zeroes of any quadratic polynomial, then the polynomial is;
$x^2 - (\alpha + \beta)x + \alpha\beta$
$= x^2 - (\sqrt{2})x + (\frac{1}{3})$
$= 3x^2 - 3\sqrt{2}x + 1$

22(B). Possible event when a die is thrown: $1, 2, 3, 4, 5, 6$
$\therefore n(S) = 6$
Probability of getting a Prime number: $2, 3, 5$
$n(A) = 3$
$\therefore P(A) = \frac{n(A)}{n(S)} = \frac{3}{6} = \frac{1}{2}$

23(D). All three-digit natural numbers, multiples of 11 are $110, 121, 132, \ldots, 990$
Here, common difference,
$121 - 110 = 132 - 121 = \ldots = 11$.
So, it is an AP with first term,
$a = 110$,
Common difference, $d = 11$ and
Last term, $i = 990$
Let,
$i = a_n = a + (n - 1)d$
$\therefore 990 = 110 + (n - 1) \times 11$
$\Rightarrow 990 = 110 + 11n - 11$
$\Rightarrow 11n = 891$
$\Rightarrow n = 81$
$S_n = \frac{n}{2}[a + i]$
$\therefore S_{81} = \frac{81}{2}[110 + 990]$
$= \frac{81}{2} \times 1100 = 81 \times 550 = 44550$

24(B). Let a and d be the first term and last term of an AP.
Then,
$a_s = \frac{1}{2}a_2$ and $a_{11} = \frac{1}{3}a_4 + 1$

$\Rightarrow a + (S - 1)d = \frac{1}{2}[a + (2 - 1)d]$
And $a + (11 - 1)d = \frac{1}{3}[(a + (4 - 1)d) + 1]$
$\Rightarrow a + 7d = \frac{1}{2}(a + d)$
And $a + 10d = \frac{1}{3}[(a + 3d) + 1]$
$\Rightarrow 2a + 14d - a - d = 0$
And $3a + 30d = a + 3d + 1$
$\Rightarrow a + 13d = 0 \ldots\ldots\ldots\ldots(i)$
And $2a + 27d - 1 = 0 \ldots\ldots\ldots(ii)$
On solving Eqs. (i) and (ii), we get
$\therefore a = -13, d = 1$
$\therefore a_{15} = a + (15 - 1)(1)$
$= -13 + 14 = 1$

25(A). Given:
Height of pole $= AB = 6m$
Length of pole of shadow $= BC = 4m$
Length of shadow of tower $= EF = 28$

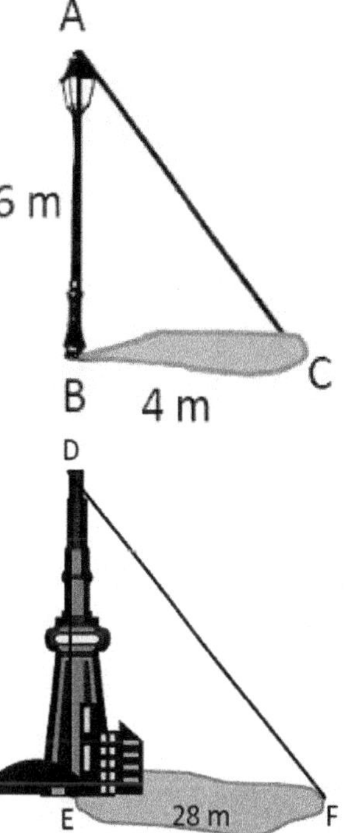

To Find: Height of tower i.e., ED
In $\triangle ABC$ and $\triangle DEF$
$\angle B = \angle E = 90°$ (Both 90° as both are vertical to ground)
$\angle C = \angle F$ (Same elevation in both the cases as both shadows are cast at the same time)
$\therefore \triangle ABC \sim \triangle DEF$ (AA similarity criterion)
$\triangle ABC \sim \triangle DEF$
We know that if two triangles are similar, ratio of their sides are in proportion.

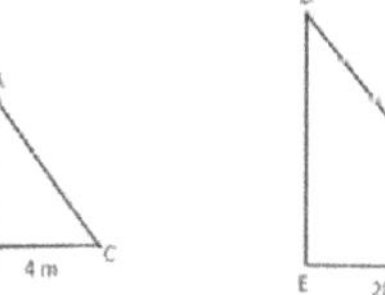

So, $\frac{AB}{DE} = \frac{BC}{EF}$
$\frac{6}{DE} = \frac{4}{28}$

$6 \times 28 = DE \times 4$

$\dfrac{6 \times 28}{4} = DE$

$6 \times 7 = DE$

$DE = 42$

So, the height of the tower is 42 meters.

26(C). Given:

$\triangle ABC \sim \triangle DEF$

ar $\triangle ABC = 64 \text{ cm}^2$

ar $\triangle DEF = 121 \text{ cm}^2$

$EF = 15.4 \text{ cm}$

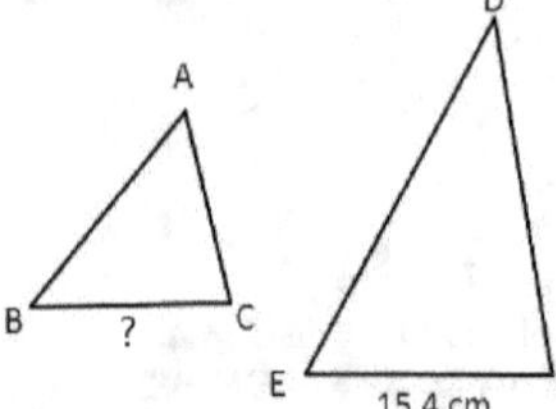

To find: BC

Since, $\triangle ABC \sim \triangle DEF$

We know that if two triangle are similar,

Ratio of areas is equal to square of ratio of its corresponding sides

So, $\dfrac{\text{ar } \triangle ABC}{\text{ar } \triangle DEF} = \left(\dfrac{BC}{EF}\right)^2$

Putting the values,

$\dfrac{64}{121} = \left(\dfrac{BC}{15.4}\right)^2$

$\dfrac{64}{121} = \dfrac{BC^2}{(15.4)^2}$

$\dfrac{64}{121} \times (15.4)^2 = BC^2$

$\left(\dfrac{8 \times 8}{11 \times 11}\right) \times (15.4)^2 = BC^2$

$\dfrac{8^2}{11^2} \times (15.4)^2 = BC^2$

$\left(\dfrac{8}{11} \times 15.4\right)^2 = BC^2$

$\dfrac{8}{11} \times 15.4 = BC$

$BC = \dfrac{8}{11} \times 15.4$

$BC = 8 \times 1.4$

$BC = 11.2$

So, $BC = 11.2 \text{ cm}$

27(A). Given,

$\angle POQ = 45°$, AM=PQ

In $\triangle AOM$ and $\triangle POQ$ OA, OM and OP, OQ are radius of circle.

$\therefore \triangle AOM$ and $\triangle POQ$ are Congruent triangles

Since, two Congruent triangles have all three sides and angles equal in measurement, we conclude that $\angle AOM = 45°$

28(B). Given,

$\angle XOY = 60°$, XY = ZW

In $\triangle WOZ$ and $\triangle XOY$ OZ, OW and OX, OY are radius of circle.

$\therefore \triangle WOZ$ and $\triangle XOY$ are Congruent triangles

Since, two Congruent triangles have all three sides and angles equal in measurement, we conclude that $\angle ZOW = 60°$

29(C). The given points are $(a\cos\theta + b\sin\theta, 0)$ and $(0, a\sin\theta - b\cos\theta)$

Here,

$x_1 = a\cos\theta + b\sin\theta, y_1 = 0$

$x_2 = 0, y_2 = a\sin\theta - b\cos\theta$

$\therefore$ Required distance

$= \sqrt{(x_1 - x_2)^2 + (y_1 - y_2)^2}$

$= \sqrt{(a\cos\theta + b\sin\theta - 0)^2 + (0 - a\sin\theta + b\cos\theta)^2}$

$= \sqrt{(a\cos\theta + b\sin\theta)^2 + (b\cos\theta - a\sin\theta)^2}$

$= \sqrt{a^2\cos^2\theta + b^2\sin^2\theta + 2ab\cos\theta\sin\theta + b^2\cos^2\theta + a^2\sin^2\theta - 2ab\sin\theta\cos\theta}$

$= \sqrt{\cos^2\theta\,(a^2 + b^2) + \sin^2\theta\,(a^2 + b^2)}$

$= \sqrt{(a^2 + b^2)\,(\cos^2\theta + \sin^2\theta)}$

$= \sqrt{a^2 + b^2} \quad [\because \cos^2\theta + \sin^2\theta = 1]$

30(B). According to the question, the distance between the points $(4, p)$ and $(1, 0) = 5$

$\because$ distance between the points (x_1, y_1) and (x_2, y_2)

$d = \sqrt{(x_2 - x_1)^2 + (y_2 - y_1)^2}$

$\sqrt{(1 - 4)^2 + (0 - p)^2} = 5$

$\Rightarrow \sqrt{(-3)^2 + p^2} = 5$

$\Rightarrow \sqrt{9 + p^2} = 5$

On squaring both the sides, we get

$9 + p^2 = 25$

$\Rightarrow p^2 = 16$

$\Rightarrow p = \pm 4$

So, the required value of p is ± 4

31(D). A food chain starts with the primary energy source, usually the sun or boiling-hot deep-sea vents. The next link in the chain is an organism, that makes its own food from the primary energy source - an example is photosynthetic plants, that make their own food from sunlight (using photosynthesis), and chemosynthetic bacteria, that make their food energy from chemicals in hydrothermal vents. These are called as autotrophs or primary producers.

32(C). All green plants and few blue-green algae which can produce food by photosynthesis are called the producers. Producers, also known as autotrophs, make their own food. They make up the first level of every food chain. Autotrophs are usually plants or one-celled organisms. Nearly all autotrophs use a process called photosynthesis to create "food" (a nutrient called glucose) from sunlight, carbon dioxide, and water.

33(D). $Zn + 2HCl \rightarrow ZnCl_2 + H_2$

Due to the reaction of zinc with the acid, zinc loses its shiny appearance and became dull and black.

H_2 gas is evolved during the reaction. We can identify the gas with a burning match stick. A pop sound indicates its presence. Zinc chloride formed in the reaction is colourless, so, the solution does not change its colour.

34(B). Potassium metal (K) gives lilac (pink) colour in bunsen flame. Its oxide dissolves in water to form potassium hydroxide, which is an alkali. So, the solution of its oxide turns red litmus paper blue.

$K_2O + H_2O \rightarrow 2KOH$

Sodium metal (Na) gives yellow flame, calcium (Ca) gives orange red flame and lithium (Li) gives red flame.

35(B). Geotropism is the movement of plant parts in response to gravity as stimulus.

Primary roots always grow downward in the direction of gravity and thus are positively geotropic, whereas the main shoots grow upward away from the gravity and are thus negatively geotropic.

36(C). Endocrine system, like the nervous system, is meant for internal communication and regulation of the animal body. These two systems operate in a coordinated way on many occasions. Many important functions of the endocrine system are infact, under the control of nervous system. Therefore, the two systems are often collectively called as neuroendocrine system

37(C). When we first start by taking two colourless solution into two different beakers. We then pour each of the two separate solutions into one common test tube. It is observed that there is there is a cloudy mixture which has formed in the test tube. This type of reaction are precipitation reaction.

For example:

$Na_2SO_4 + BaCl_2 \rightarrow BaSO_4 + 2NaCl$

In this reaction, $BaSO_4$ is the precipitate.

38(B). Lead nitrate solution contains particles of lead, potassium iodide contains particles of iodide. When the solutions mix, the lead particles and iodide particles combine to form a new substance, lead iodide, which is a yellow solid. So, the chemical equation for the reaction is:

$Pb(NO_3)_2(aq) + 2KI(aq) \rightarrow PbI_2(s) + 2KNO_3(aq)$

The reaction takes place between lead nitrate and potassium iodide, the lead and potassium exchange their anions to give lead iodide and potassium nitrate.

39(A). Hydrogenation of oils in presence of palladium or nickel catalyst to form fat is an addition reaction.

During hydrogenation, vegetable oils are reacted with hydrogen gas at about 60°C . A nickel catalyst is used to speed up the reaction. The double bonds are converted to single bonds in the reaction. In this way unsaturated fats can be made into saturated fats - they are hardened.

40(C). Buckminsterfullerene is an allotropic form of carbon with formula C_{60} . It has carbon atoms arranged in the form of a football. It is soft, slippery, brittle, electrical insulator, and insoluble in water. They are known as buckyballs due to their resemblance with football.

41(B). In humans, the process of fertilization takes place in the fallopian tube. During this process, semen comprising thousands of sperms are inseminated into the female vagina during coitus. The sperms move towards the uterus and reach the opening of the fallopian tube.

42(D). Stigma acts as a platform where the pollen grains lands.
Stigma is the topmost part of carpels in the gynoecium of a flower. In all flowering plants, stigma functions as a receptive tip, which collects pollen grains.

43(C). Feather provides many functions to birds like flying, controlling body temperature, floating etc., but the primary function of feathers in birds is to insulate birds from water and cold temperatures, thereby prevents loss of heat from the body for thermoregulation.

44(C). Feather provided insulation to dinosaurs in cold weather. Later in the evolutionary process, feathers were used for flight in birds. Because dinosaurs were reptiles, it means that birds are closely related to reptiles.

45(A). The refraction of light is commonly known as bending.
The refracted rays bend towards the normal when they enter from rarer medium to denser medium.

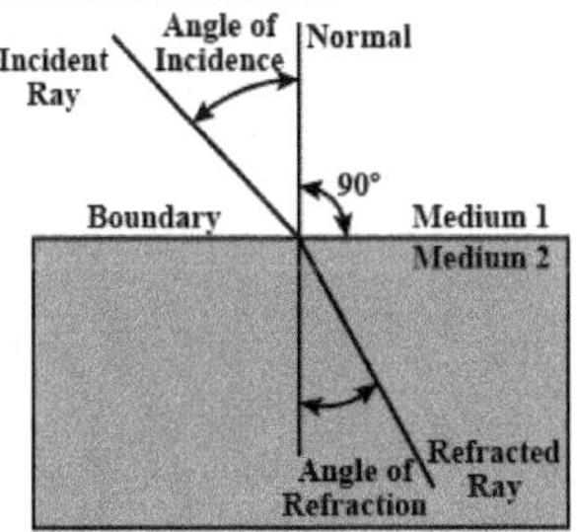

The refracted rays bend away from the normal when they enter from a denser to rarer medium.

46(B). Refraction is the bending of light rays after entering a medium where its speed is different. Due to the refraction of light, when a ray of light passes from a rarer medium to a denser medium, bends the normal toward to the boundary between the two media. The amount of bending depends on the indices of refraction of the two media. Therefore, when a ray of light from the air enters a denser medium, it bends towards the normal.

47(B). Velocity, force, and the magnetic field are vector quantities.
Vector is the quantity which has both magnitude and direction. Velocity is a vector quantity because it is the speed of an object in a particular direction. Force is a vector quantity because it actually does depend on which direction you apply the force. Magnetic field is a vector quantity as it is specified by both magnitude and direction.

48(A). The heart and brain are the two main organs in the human body where this magnetic field is quite significant.
The human body is an electromagnetic organism. In human body, small electric currents travels along the nerve cells due to ions, same way as electricity flows through an electric wire. This current produces a very weak magnetic field in the human body.

49(B). Urine leaves the kidney through the ureter.
From the calyxes, pee travels out of the kidneys through the ureters to be stored in the bladder (a muscular sac in the lower belly). When a person urinates, the pee exits the bladder and goes out of the body through the urethra, another tube-like structure.

50(C). Waste products are stored as resins in old xylem plants.
The resins and gums are stored in the plant part called Old Xylem. Other than that, the by-products of metabolism like gums, latex, resins, and oils that are not useful to the plant are stored in plant parts like barks, stems, leaves, etc. Eventually, these parts are shed off, getting rid of the waste.

51(B). To prepare an indicator from red cabbage leaves, these are boiled in water.
Red cabbage contains a pigment molecule called flavin (an anthocyanin). This water-soluble pigment is also found in apple skins, plums, poppies, cornflowers, and grapes. Very acidic solutions will turn anthocyanin into a red color. Neutral solutions result in a purplish color. Basic solutions appear in greenish-yellow.

52(D). In NH_4OH solutions vanilla essence lose its flavour.
The characteristic smell of vanilla is destroyed by basic solutions. So in basic solutions, we cannot detect the smell of vanilla. Whereas, it is retained in an acidic solution. So the given solution is a basic solution.

53(A). The farthest point upto which the eye can see objects clearly is called the far point of the eye. As we can see the distance object such as sun, planets, stars etc. we consider the far point of the eye as the infinity. Normal eye can see objects clearly that are between 25 cm and infinity.

54(A). Given,
Power of the bulb $(P) = 100\ W$
Voltage rating $(V) = 200\ V$
As we know,

$P = \dfrac{V^2}{R}$

$R = \dfrac{V^2}{P}$

$R = \dfrac{200^2}{100}$

$R = 400\ \Omega$

Now applied voltage changes to $100\ V$, So current passing through the resistance:

$I = \dfrac{V}{R}$

$I = \dfrac{100}{400}$

$I = \dfrac{1}{4}\ A$

$I = 0.25\ A$

Hence, the correct option is (A)

55(D). Given:
Resistance of copper wire $= R$
Now,
When it is cut in to lo equal parts, each resistance will be $\dfrac{R}{10}$
When 2 piecess are joined in series then

$R_S = \dfrac{R}{10} + \dfrac{R}{10} = \dfrac{R}{5}$

when 5 such $\dfrac{R}{5}$ combination are connected in parallel, then

$\dfrac{1}{R_p} = \dfrac{1}{\frac{R}{5}} + \dfrac{1}{\frac{R}{5}} + \dfrac{1}{\frac{R}{5}} + \dfrac{1}{\frac{R}{5}} + \dfrac{1}{\frac{R}{5}}$

$= \dfrac{5}{\frac{R}{5}}$

$= \dfrac{25}{R}$

$R_p = \dfrac{R}{25}\ \Omega$

56(B). Water scarcity in most cases is caused by over-exploitation, excessive use and unequal access to water among different social groups.
Water scarcity may be an outcome of a large and growing population and consequent greater demands for water, and unequal access to it. A large population means more water not only for domestic use but also to produce more food.
So, to facilitate higher food-grain production, water resources are being over-exploited to expand irrigated areas and dry-season agriculture.

57(B).
Cheetah and Pink headed Duck animals in India are on the verge of extinction.
Among the mammals, two animals Acinonyx jubatus and Dicerorhinus sumatrensis are considered to be extinct from India where the former one is commonly known as Indian Cheetah or Asiatic Cheetah and the later one as Sumatran rhinoceros. As per the Ministry of India, the main causes behind the extinction of these animals are factors like predation, natural selection, competition, and some human-induced factors like habitat destruction, hunting, etc. The Asiatic Cheetah is currently found only in Iran and is in the list of critically endangered species of the world.
In India, many more animal species are on the verge of extinction and currently have

been listed in the critically endangered species. Over the past years, more than 30% of the land area in our country has been damaged due to deforestation, over-cultivation, soil erosion, and similar reasons. Currently, Hangul, Great Indian Bustard, Sangai, and Dugong are on the verge of extinction in India.

58(C). Gold, silver and platinum are examples of Precious minerals.

Precious metals are metals that are rare and have a high economic value due to various factors, including their scarcity, use in industrial processes, hedge against currency inflation, and role throughout history as a store of value. The most popular precious metals with investors are gold, platinum, and silver.

59(B). When we produce a good by exploiting natural resources it is called Primary sector.

The primary sector of the economy includes any industry involved in the extraction and production of raw materials, such as farming, logging, hunting, fishing, and mining. The primary sector tends to make up a larger portion of the economy in developing countries than it does in developed countries.

60(D). The country's development depends on the following factors:

- A country's growth is decided by its per capita income, its average level of literacy as well as the health status of the people in the nation.
- A country's growth is a general concept that improves people's per capita income and living standards.
- It also lowers the poverty, the rate of crimes as well as the illiteracy of individuals.

Development not just depends on the economic factors of a country but are also dependent on resources that are available for the people of a country to use.

Two aspects of development are:
- Economic growth or increase in people's income.
- Social progress includes literacy, health and the provision of public services.

61(B). The Estate General was elected by Active Citizens.

The Estates General was elected by the body of active citizens and renamed the National Assembly. The lay lords and the ecclesiastical lords (bishops and other high clergy) who made up the Estates General were not elected by their peers, but directly chosen and summoned by the king. Only representatives of the Third Estate were chosen by election.

62(A). Two-thirds of India's population is still dependent on agriculture.

Agriculture is a primary activity because many regions in India have fertile land that is favourable for agriculture. Two-thirds of the Indian population still depend on agriculture. This is mainly because of the lack of literacy among the people.

63(B). Banks use a major portion of deposits to extend loans.

When you deposit money into your account at a financial institution , you give the institution use of your money to make loans in exchange for its promise to pay you back. In short, banks don't take the money that you deposit, turn around and loan it at a higher interest rate. But they do use the money you deposit to balance their books and meet the necessary cash reserves that make those loans possible .

64(C). The Reserve Bank of India supervises the functioning of formal sources of loans.

A loan is a form of debt incurred by an individual or other entity. The lender usually a corporation, financial institution, or government advances a sum of money to the borrower. In return, the borrower agrees to a certain set of terms including any finance charges, interest, repayment date, and other conditions. The advantage of taking loan from formal sector.
- These institutions are regulated by the Reserve Bank of India.
- There is no exploitation by the lenders.
- Everyone can take a loan that includes big businessmen as. well as the small cultivators or borrowers.
- The cost of borrowing is usually less.

65(D). World Trade Organisation lay stress on liberalisation of foreign trade and foreign investment.

The World Trade Organization (WTO) is the only global international organization dealing with the rules of trade between nations. At its heart are the WTO agreements, negotiated and signed by the bulk of the world's trading nations and ratified in their parliaments. The goal is to ensure that trade flows as smoothly, predictably and freely as possible. The WTO has over 160 members representing 98 per cent of world trade. Over 20 countries are seeking to join the WTO. To join the WTO, a government has to bring its economic and trade policies in line with WTO rules and negotiate its terms of entry with the WTO membership. India has been a WTO member since 1 January 1995.

66(C). Investment refers to the money spent to buy asset such as land.

Investment or investing means that an asset is bought, or that money is put into a bank to get a future interest from it. Investment is total amount of money spent by a shareholder in buying shares of a company. In economic management sciences, investments means longer-term savings. For companies, assets are things of value that sustain production and growth. For a business, assets can include machines, property, raw materials, and inventory as well as intangibles such as patents, royalties, and other intellectual property.

67(C). ISI mark is given to product's compliance with the required standards.

The ISI mark is a standards-compliance mark for industrial products in India since 1955. The mark certifies that a product conforms to an Indian standard (IS) developed by the Bureau of Indian Standards (BIS), the national standards body of India.

68(B). The Consumer Protection Act or COPRA was enacted in the year 1986.

The Consumer Protection Act,1986 (COPRA) was an Act of the Parliament of India enacted to protect the interests of consumers in India. It was replaced by the Consumer Protection Act, 2019. It was made for the establishment of consumer councils and other authorities for the settlement of consumer's grievances and matters connected with it. This Act is regarded as the 'Magna Carta' in the field of consumer protection for checking unfair trade practices, 'defects in goods' and 'deficiencies in services' as far as India is concerned. It has led to the establishment of a widespread network of consumer forums and appellate courts all over India. It has significantly impacted how businesses approach consumers and have empowered consumers to a greater extent.

69(A). The development of print first begin in East Asia.

It originated in China in antiquity as a method of printing on textiles and later on paper. As a method of printing on cloth, the earliest surviving examples from China date to before 220 A.D.

70(B). The books in China were printed by rubbing paper, against the inked surface of woodblocks.

Books were first printed in China by using wooden blocks in which letters and designs were carved. Ink was applied to these blocks and was pressed against paper. The letter or design would then get printed on the paper.

71(D). Less than one percent of the German-speaking people live in Belgium.

German is one of the least common languages in Belgium, and only 1% of the population speaks German. It is confined only to the East cantons part of Belgium, where mainly german-speaking people reside. Of the country's total population, 59 per cent lives in the Flemish region and speaks Dutch language. Another 40 per cent people live in the Wallonia region and speak French. Remaining 1 per cent of the Belgians speak German.

72(A). Sri Lanka emerged as an independent country in 1948.

The leaders of the Sinhala community sought to secure dominance over government by virtue of their majority. As a result, the democratically elected government adopted a series of MAJORITARIAN measures to establish Sinhala supremacy.

73(C). The laws allowing the British Government to restrict import of corn is known as "Corn Law".

These laws were abolished because the industrialists and urban dwellers were unhappy with high food prices; as a result of which they forced the abolition of the Corn Laws.The laws which allowed the government to restrict the import of corn were commonly known as the Corn Laws. Soon, the corn laws had to be abolished as the urban dwellers who are industrialists were unhappy with the rising food prices. After this, food could be imported more cheaply than its production cost.

74(A). Federalism is a system of government in which the power is divided between a central authority and various constituent units of the country.

Usually, a federation has two levels of government. One is the government for the entire country that is usually responsible for a few subjects of common national interest. The others are governments at the level of provinces or states that look after much of the day-to-day administering of their state. Both these levels of governments enjoy their power independent of the other.

75(D). Federations are contrasted with unitary governments.

Under the unitary system, either there is only one level of government or the sub-units are subordinate to the central government. The central government can pass on orders to the provincial or the local government. But in a federal system, the central government cannot order the state government to do something. State government has powers of its own for which it is not answerable to the central government. Both these governments are separately answerable to the people.

Let us look at some of the key features of federalism :

- There are two or more levels (or tiers) of government.
- Different tiers of government govern the same citizens, but each tier has its own JURISDICTION in specific matters of legislation, taxation and administration.
- The jurisdictions of the respective levels or tiers of government are specified in the constitution. So the existence and authority of each tier of government is constitutionally guaranteed.
- The fundamental provisions of the constitution cannot be unilaterally changed by one level of government.

Such changes require the consent of both the levels of government.

- Courts have the power to interpret the constitution and the powers of different levels of government. The highest court acts as an umpire if disputes arise between different levels of government in the exercise of their respective powers.
- Sources of revenue for each level of government are clearly specified to ensure its financial autonomy.

76(B). Proto-industrialization is First and early form of Industrialization.

The regional development, alongside commercial agriculture, of rural handicraft production for external markets. Proto-industrialization is also a term for a specific theory about proto-industries' role in the emergence of the Industrial Revolution.

Proto-Industrialisation was the phase of industrialization in Europe when industrial production was not exclusively factory based. By producing for the merchants, the peasants could cultivate their own small patches of land and yet could earn some supplementary income.

77(B). Laterite soil is ideal for growing cotton.

When wet, laterite soil is soft, but when dried, it becomes hard and cloddy. The Western Ghats, RajMahal Hills, Eastern Ghats, Satpura, Vindhya, Odisha, Chhattisgarh, Jharkhand, West Bengal, North Cachar Hills, and Garo Hills are the most common locations.

Organic matter, nitrogen, potassium, lime, and potash are all in short supply. These soils, which are rich in iron and aluminium, are ideal for culturing. Laterite soil is a sandy form of soil with a higher water absorption capacity.

Laterite soil is ideal for cotton production since cotton requires more water. In moist areas, laterite soil is accessible, which is ideal for cotton production. Black soil is also known as regur soil. These soils are rich in calcium carbonate, magnesium carbonate, potash and lime. Regur soil has high water retention capacity and in summer it gets cracked which makes it more oxygen rich. Hence it is good for growing cotton.

78(D). All the above given statements are true about Democratic Government.

Democracy is a form of government in which the rulers are elected by the people. Democracy is suitable for large countries with wide diversities. Democracy is most suitable to accommodate social diversities. Democracy doesn't creates social division among political parties. Democracy provides scope for dissent. Every government that holds an election are democratic government.

Democracy is supposed to be a people's

government. In a democratic country, citizens are granted fundamental rights. They are granted the right to express themselves, to organise, to protest and to vote. Dissent is an essential element of a democracy. People must have the freedom to criticise the ruling government.

79(C). Democracy is preferred over dictatorship in South Asia except Pakistan.

Democracy is a system of government in which the citizens exercise power directly or elect representatives from among themselves to form a governing body. Democracy is sometimes referred to as a rule of the majority. On the other hand, dictatorship is a form of government in which a country is ruled by one person (a dictator). In the political history of Pakistan, dictatorship is seen preferred over democracy as many military dictators have ruled that country till date.

80(A). The idea of satyagraha basically emphasised the power of truth and the demand to search for truth.

It suggested that if the cause was true, if the struggle was against injustice, then the physical force was not necessary to fight the oppressor. By this huge and great struggle, the truth was bound to ultimately triumph.

81(B). Gunning for the Godman:

It is a true account of the life of Asaram Bapu.

It is written by IPS Ajaypal Lamba.

This book presents the capture of Asaram Bapu.

Asaram Bapu was considered to be Godman by his followers.

This book narrates the incident of rape of a minor girl and the trial that followed after that.

82(A). Directive Principles of the state Policy:

Part IV of the constitution deals with Economic and cultural Rights. However, they are not justifiable in the court of law. The idea of a 'welfare state' envisaged in our constitution can only be achieved if the states try to implement them with a high sense of moral duty.

Salient Features of the constitution are as follows:

- Lengthiest constitution in the world.
- Sovereignty resides in the people
- Parliamentary form of Government.
- Unique blend of rigidity and flexibility.
- Fundamental Rights.
- Directive principles of the state policy.
- Quasi – federal in nature.
- Adult suffrage.
- Independence of Judiciary
- Judicial Review.
- Fundamental duties
- Sovereign.
- Democracy.
- Republic.
- Secular.

- Single citizenship.
- Uniformity in Basic Administration.
- Revolutionary.
- Lawyer's paradise.
- Judicial Review and parliament sovereignty.

83(D). Canada is not a member of "BRICS".
BRICS is the acronym coined to associate five major emerging economies: Brazil, Russia, India, China, and South Africa. The BRICS members are known for their significant influence on regional affairs. Since 2009, the governments of the BRICS states have met annually at formal summits. Originally the first four were grouped as "BRIC" (or "the BRICs") before the induction of South Africa in 2010. The BRICS have a combined area of 39,746,220 km2 (15,346,101.0 sq mi) and an estimated total population of about 3.21 billion, or about 26.7% of the world land surface and 41.5% of the world population. Four out of five members are among the world's ten largest countries by population and by area, except for South Africa which is twenty-third in both.

84(D). The Chief Justice of the Supreme Court has the right to seek the permission of the President before setting up the Supreme Court bench elsewhere in the country.

85(B). Oxygen is a major element of the Earth's crust.
Oxygen (46.6%) is the most abundant element in the Earth's crust, followed by silica (27.7%) aluminum (8.1%) and iron is (5%) present. Apart from this, elements like calcium, sodium, potassium, magnesium etc. are also present.

86(D). A stethoscope is a medical instrument used for listening to sounds produced within the body, mainly in the heart or lungs.
The sound reaches the doctor's ear by multiple reflections through the stethoscope tube.

87(C). Andhra Pradesh was the first state of Independent India formed on a linguistic basis.
It was formed on October 1, 1953.
This state was formed for Telugu-speaking people after prolonged agitations.

88(B). Kathakali is a major form of classical Indian dance. It is a "story play" genre of art, but one distinguished by the elaborately colorful make-up, costumes and face masks that the traditionally male actor-dancers wear. Kathakali is a Hindu performance art in the Malayalam-speaking southwestern region of Kerala.

89(D). The Hundru Fall lies along the course of Subarnarekha river.
Subarnarekha is a rain-fed river flowing in the eastern part of India. It flows in the state of Jharkhand, West Bengal, and Orissa. It originates near Nagri village in the Ranchi district. It runs through some major industrial towns and cities: Jamshedpur, Chaibasa, Ranchi, and Bhadrak before joining to the Bay of Bengal at Kirtania port in Orissa.
Hundru Falls is the 34th highest waterfall in India. It falls from a height of 98 meters (322 ft) creating which is one of the highest waterfalls in Ranchi district of Jharkhand state.

90(C). The fear of the Phallus worship was replaced in the Yajur Veda by its recognition as an official ritual.
Harappans worshipped Mother Goddess but the female deities played a minor part in the Vedic religion.

91(B). Babur and Jahangir themselves wrote their own autobiography.
Babur wrote his autobiography 'Baburnama' and his poetry collection 'Diva' in Turkish. Babur was the first Mughal emperor of the Mughal dynasty. Jahangir wrote his autobiography Tujuke Jahangiri in Persian by the 17th year of his reign, later completed by Motamid Khan.

92(C). The first freedom struggle started from Meerut in 1857. Later, this revolution spread like fire all over the country. This created the role of uprooting the British from India and finally India got independence in 1947.

93(A). The parent material is the substance by which the soil is formed, these are generally rocks.
Soil is a thin layer of sediments and fine particles covering the earth's surface. It is mainly formed from weathering and natural erosion.
Water, wind, temperature change, gravity, chemical interaction, living organisms and pressure differences all help break down parent material(rocks).

94(C). Statement (a): First State to offer a 50% reservation for women in Panchayati Raj Institutions is Bihar.
'Panchayat', being "Local government", is a State subject and part of the State List of the Seventh Schedule of the Constitution of India.
Clause (3) of Article 243D of the Constitution ensures participation of women in Panchayati Raj Institutions by mandating not less than one-third reservation for women out of a total number of seats to be filled by direct election and number of offices of chairpersons of Panchayats.
Statement (b): As per the order issued by the Delimitation Commission in 2008, 412 are general, 84 seats are reserved for Scheduled Castes.
Statement (c): As per the order issued by the Delimitation Commission in 2008, 47 seats are reserved for the Scheduled Tribes.

95(A). The central ice hockey team of the Indo-Tibetan Border Police (ITBP) won the 12th edition of the National Ice Hockey Championship for men 2023 organized in Leh, Ladakh for the third time in a row. ITBP team defeated Ladakh Scouts 1-0 in the final match.

96(D). Both Edmund Hillary and Tenzing Norgay are the first to climb Mount Everest. Edmund Hillary of New Zealand and Tenzing Norgay, a Sherpa of Nepal, become the first explorers to reach the summit of Mount Everest, which at 29,035 feet above sea level is the highest point on earth.
Hence the correct option is (D).

97(D). Lactic acid induces souring of milk.

98(A). Malphigian Tubules is an excretory organ of cockroach.

99(C). World War I or The First World War, often abbreviated as WWI or WW1, began on the 28th of July, 1914 and ended on the 11th of November, 1918. Referred to by contemporaries as the "Great War", belligerents included much of Europe, Russia, the United States and Turkey, with fighting also expanding into the Middle East, Africa and parts of Asia. One of the deadliest conflicts in history, an estimated 9 million were killed in combat, while over 5 million civilians died from occupation, bombardment, hunger or disease. Millions of additional deaths resulted from genocides within the Ottoman Empire and the 1918 Spanish flu pandemic, which was exacerbated by the movement of combatants during the war.

100(A). New Zealand skipper Kane Williamson was adjudged 'Captain of the Year' at the 15th Annual ESPNcricinfo awards 2022.
Williamson won it for leading his side to the World Test Championship win and a runners-up place at the T20 World Cup. he jury picked the best performances in the three men's international formats, and performances in women's cricket at large, in the 2021 calendar year.

Mathematics

1. To divide a line segment AB in the ratio $3:4$, first, a ray AX is drawn so that $\angle BAX$ is an acute angle and then at equal distances points are marked on the ray AX such that the minimum number of these points is:
   (a) 5
   (b) 7
   (c) 9
   (d) 11

2. To divide a line segment AB of length 7.6 cm in the ratio $5:8$, a ray AX is drawn first such that $\angle BAX$ forms an acute angle and then points A_1, A_2, A_3, ...are located at equal distances on the ray AX and the point B is joined to:
   (a) A_5
   (b) A_6
   (c) A_{10}
   (d) A_{13}

3. Consider the following distribution of daily wages of 50 worker of a factory.

Daily wages (in Rs)	100–120	120–140	140–160	160–180	180–200
Number of workers	12	14	8	6	10

   Find the mean daily wages of the workers of the factory by using an appropriate method.
   (a) 200.50
   (b) 150.20
   (c) 145.20
   (d) 100.10

4. A solid piece of iron in the form of a cuboid of dimensions $49cm \times 33cm \times 24cm$ is moulded to form a solid sphere. The radius of the sphere is:
   (a) $21cm$
   (b) $23cm$
   (c) $25cm$
   (d) $19cm$

5. A cylindrical container of radius $6cm$ and height $15cm$ is full with ice cream. The whole ice cream has to be distributed to 10 children in equal cones with hemispherical tops. If the height of the conical portion is four times the radius of its base, find the radius of the ice cream cone.
   (a) $3cm$
   (b) $1cm$
   (c) $4cm$
   (d) $2cm$

6. Find the integer value of k for which the equation $x^2 - 5(k-1)x + (8k+1) = 0$ has equal roots.
   (a) 8
   (b) 3
   (c) 16
   (d) 24

7. If $\cot \alpha$ and $\cot \beta$ are the roots of the equation $x^2 - 5x + 4 = 0$, then what is $\cot(\alpha + \beta)$ equal to?
   (a) $\frac{1}{3}$
   (b) $\frac{1}{4}$
   (c) $\frac{3}{5}$
   (d) $\frac{2}{5}$

8. Find the area of a sector of a circle with radius 6 cm if angle of the sector is $60°$. $(\pi = \frac{22}{7})$
   (a) $\frac{132}{7}$ cm^2
   (b) $\frac{136}{7}$ cm^2
   (c) $\frac{143}{7}$ cm^2
   (d) $\frac{146}{7}$ cm^2

9. Find the area of a quadrant of a circle whose circumference is 22 cm. $(\pi = \frac{22}{7})$
   (a) $\frac{77}{8}$ cm^2
   (b) $\frac{87}{8}$ cm^2
   (c) $\frac{77}{3}$ cm^2
   (d) $\frac{88}{3}$ cm^2

10. In a right triangle ABC, right-angled at B, $\sin A = \frac{1}{\sqrt{2}}$. The value of $\tan A$ is ___ .
    (a) 1
    (b) 2
    (c) $\frac{1}{\sqrt{2}}$
    (d) $\frac{2}{\sqrt{2}}$

11. In a right triangle MNO, right angled at N, $\sin M = \frac{4}{4\sqrt{2}}$. What is the value of $\cos M$?
    (a) $\frac{1}{\sqrt{2}}$
    (b) $\frac{1}{2}$
    (c) 1
    (d) 2

12. If $\operatorname{cosec} \theta = \frac{5}{4}$, the value of $\sin^2 \theta$ is:
    (a) $\frac{9}{16}$
    (b) $\frac{9}{25}$
    (c) $\frac{9}{6}$
    (d) $\frac{16}{25}$

13. The angles of elevations of the top of the tower from two points in the same straight line and at a distance of 9 m and 16 m from the base of the tower are complementary. The height of the tower is:
    (a) 18 m
    (b) 16 m
    (c) 10 m
    (d) 12 m

14. Solve the linear equations by using substitution method.
    $x + y = 14$
    $x - y = 4$
    (a) $x = 9, y = 5$
    (b) $x = 9, y = 8$
    (c) $x = 5, y = 8$
    (d) $x = 6, y = 5$

15. Ten students of class X took part in Mathematics quiz. If the number of girls is 4 more than the number of boys. Represent this situation algebraically.
    (a) $x + y = 10$ and $x - y = 4$
    (b) $x = y - 12$ and $y = 6 + x$
    (c) $x - y = 10$ and $x + y = 4$
    (d) None of the above

16. For some integer q, every odd integer is of the form:
    (a) q
    (b) $q + 1$
    (c) $2q$
    (d) $2q + 1$

17. The product of a non-zero rational and an irrational number is:
    (a) always irrational
    (b) always rational
    (c) rational or irrational
    (d) 1

18. The decimal expansion of the rational number $\frac{14587}{1250}$ will terminate after:
    (a) one decimal place
    (b) two decimal places
    (c) three decimal places
    (d) four decimal places

19. The greatest number which when divided by 1251, 9377 and 15628 leaves remainder 1, 2 and 3 respectively is:
    (a) 575
    (b) 450
    (c) 750
    (d) 625

20. If the zeroes of the quadratic polynomial $ax^2 + bx + c, c \neq 0$ are equal, then:
    (a) c and b have opposite signs
    (b) c and a have opposite signs
    (c) c and b have same signs
    (d) c and a have same signs

21. If one of the zeroes of cubic polynomial is $x^3 + ax^2 + bx + c$ is -1, then product of other two zeroes is:
    (a) $b - a - 1$
    (b) $b - a + 1$
    (c) $a - b + 1$
    (d) $a - b - 1$

22. A die is thrown once. The probability of getting an even number and a multiple of 3 is:
    (a) $\frac{1}{2}$
    (b) $\frac{1}{5}$
    (c) $\frac{1}{6}$
    (d) $\frac{1}{3}$

23. An AP consists of 50 terms of which the third term is 12 and the last term is 106. Find the 29th term.
    (a) 64
    (b) 68
    (c) 74
    (d) 78

24. The 26 th, 11 th and the last term of an AP are $0, 3$ and $-\frac{1}{5}$ respectively. Find the common difference and the number of terms.

(a) $-\frac{1}{5}, 27$ (b) $-\frac{2}{5}, 29$

(c) $-\frac{1}{10}, 17$ (d) $-\frac{3}{5}, 37$

25. Diagonals of a trapezium $ABCD$ with $AB \| DC$ intersect each other at the point O. If $AB = 2CD$, find the ratio of the areas of triangles AOB and COD.

(a) $4 : 1$ (b) $6 : 1$

(c) $8 : 1$ (d) $10 : 1$

26. D, E and F are respectively the mid-points of sides AB, BC and CA of $\triangle ABC$. Find the ratio of the areas of $\triangle DEF$ and $\triangle ABC$.

(a) $\frac{1}{3}$ (b) $\frac{1}{4}$

(c) $\frac{3}{5}$ (d) $\frac{5}{3}$

27. In the given figure, O is the centre of the circle. The length of chord BC is:

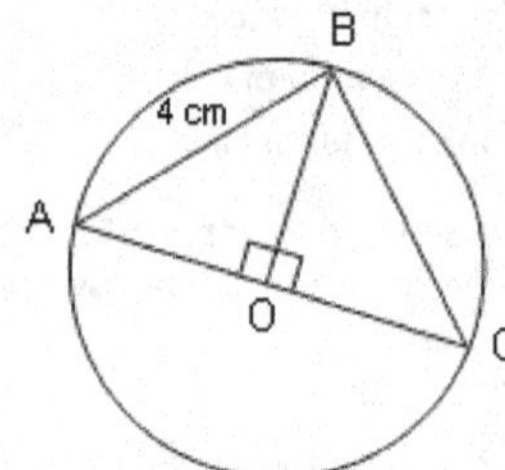

(a) 2 cm   (b) 8 cm

(c) 4 cm   (d) 16 cm

28. In the given circle with centre X, XY $\perp$ AB. Which of the following options is always true?

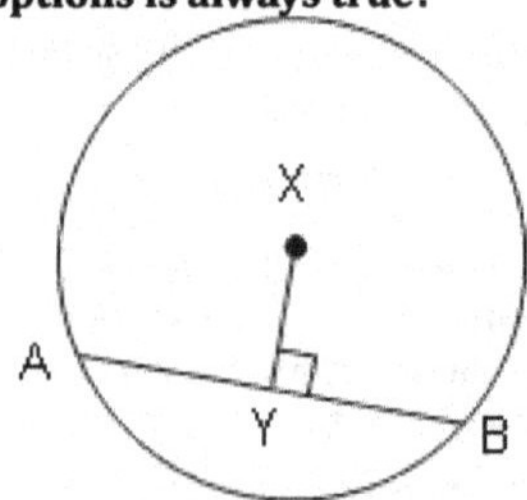

(a) YA = XY   (b) YB = XY

(c) AB = XY   (d) AY = BY

29. If $AOBC$ is a rectangle whose three vertices are $A(0, 3), O(0, 0)$ and $B(5, 0)$, then the length of its diagonal is:

(a) 5 units   (b) 3 units

(c) $\sqrt{34}$ units   (d) 4 units

30. The perimeter of a triangle with vertices $(0, 4), (0, 0)$ and $(3, 0)$ is:

(a) 5 units

(b) 12 units

(c) 11 units

(d) $(7 + \sqrt{5})$ units

31. What is the fourth trophic level called?

(a) Producer

(b) Primary consumer

(c) Secondary consumer

(d) Tertiary consumers

32. From the Autotrophs, the energy goes to the _______ and then finally to the_______.

(a) heterotrophs and producers

(b) carnivores and omnivores

(c) heterotrophs and decomposers

(d) producers and decomposers

33. Choose the correct statement.

(a) Non-metals have higher ionisation enthalpies and higher electronegativity then the metals

(b) non metals and metalloids exist only in the p-block of the periodic table.

(c) change of non-metallic to metallic character can be illustrated by the nature of oxide they form

(d) all are correct,

34. Which of the following metal evolves hydrogen on reacting with cold dilute HNO_3 ?

(a) Mg   (b) Al

(c) Fe   (d) Cu

35. The nervous system in humans can be divided into three main parts, find the odd out.

(a) Central Nervous System

(b) Peripheral Nervous System

(c) Autonomous Nervous System

(d) Sympathetic nervous system

36. Axon transmits impulse ______ cell body and dendrites transmit impulse ______ cell body.

(a) away from, towards

(b) towards, away from

(c) away from, away from

(d) towards, towards

37. Which of the following is a balanced chemical equation of the reaction between carbon monoxide gas and hydrogen gas?

(a) $3CO(g) + 2H_2(g) \xrightarrow{340 \text{ atm}} CH_3OH(l)$

(b) $CO(g) + 3H_2(g) \xrightarrow{340 \text{ atm}} CH_3OH(l)$

(c) $CO(g) + 2H_2(g) \xrightarrow{340 \text{ atm}} 2CH_3OH(l)$

(d) $CO(g) + 2H_2(g) \xrightarrow{340 \text{ atm}} CH_3OH(l)$

38. Exposure of silver chloride to sunlight for a long duration turns grey due to:

(a) Decomposition of chlorine gas from silver chloride

(b) Sublimation of silver chloride

(c) The formation of silver by decomposition of silver chloride

(d) Oxidation of silver chloride

39. The molecules of soap are ______ salts of higher ______.

(a) magnesium or barium, fatty acids

(b) magnesium or barium, aldehydes

(c) sodium or potassium, fatty acids

(d) sodium or potassium, aldehydes

40. Homologue of C_3H_4 is:

(a) C_4H_6 (b) C_2H_6

(c) CH_3OH (d) $HCHO$

41. Which of the following animals has the ability to regenerate its broken body parts?

(a) Cockroach   (b) Frog

(c) Sparrow   (d) Starfish

42. A narrow waistline, wide hip and oily skin are the secondary signs of puberty in:

(a) Males

(b) Females

(c) Both A and B

(d) Not gender-based

43. What is the gene ratio of F_2 generation in a monohybrid cross?

(a) $3 : 1 : 1$ (b) $1 : 2 : 1$

(c) $2 : 3$ (d) $3 : 1$

44. Which of the following experimental plants was used by Mendel?

(a) Wild pea   (b) Edible pea

(c) Garden pea   (d) Chick pea

45. The two light rays will undergo interference phenomenon only when:

(a) The source of two light rays must be coherent

(b) The rays must be of single

    wavelength

(c) Both (A) and (B) are wrong

(d) Both (A) and (B) are correct

46. In the case of refraction of light:

a. Frequency changes

b. Speed changes

c. Wavelength changes

(a) a is correct

(b) b and c are correct

(c) a, b and c are correct

(d) a and b are correct

47. 'An electric current always produces a magnetic field' , the above statement is:

(a) Partially false

(b) False

(c) Partially true

(d) True

48. Which of the following sentences is correct about overloading?

(a) Overloading can occur due to an accidental hike in the supply voltage

(b) Overloading is caused by connecting too many appliances to a single socket

(c) Overloading can occur when the live wire and the neutral wire wire come into direct contact

(d) All of the above

49. Chief function of HCl is:

(a) To maintain a low pH to prevent growth of microorganisms.

(b) To facilitate absorption.

(c) To facilitates the action of the enzyme pepsin.

(d) To dissolve enzyme secreted in stomach.

50. Mammal excretes nitrogenous wastes in the form of:

(a) Ammonia   (b) Amino acids

(c) Urea   (d) Uric acid

51. Why is tartaric acid added to baking powder?

(a) For flavour enhancement

(b) For making the cake fluffy

(c) For neutralization of the effect of carbon dioxide produced

(d) For neutralization of the bitter taste of base produced by baking powder

52. Why is vinegar added while preparing beetroot soup?

(a) To preserve it

(b) To add flavour to it

(c) To neutralise the basic nature of beetroot soup

(d) To make it acidic

53. ________ lens is used to correct the defect of vision termed as presbyopia.

(a) Convex   (b) Concave

(c) Bi-focal   (d) Contact

54. A hollow cylinder $\left(\rho = 2.2 \times 10^{-8}\,\Omega - m\right)$ of length $3\,m$ has inner and outer diameter as $2\,mm$ and $4\,mm$ respectively. The resistance of the cylinder is:

(a) $0.35 \times 10^{-3}\,\Omega$

(b) $3 \times 10^{-3}\,\Omega$

(c) $7 \times 10^{-3}\,\Omega$

(d) None of these

55. An electric heater kept in a vacuum is heated continuously by passing an electric current. Its temperature:

(a) It will go on rising with time

(b) It will stop after some time as it will lose heat to the surroundings by conduction

(c) It will rise for sometime and thereafter will starts falling

(d) It will become constant after sometime because of loss of heat due to radiation

Social Science

56. According to the hydrological cycle, how can freshwater be obtained?

(a) Snow

(b) Rainwater

(c) Groundwater

(d) Drainage

57. Under which category of species does the Andaman wild pig come?

(a) Extinct   (b) Rare

(c) Vulnerable   (d) Endemic

58. Cobalt is an example of ________ .

(a) Ferrous minerals

(b) Non-ferrous minerals

(c) Energy minerals

(d) Non-metallic minerals

59. Where are the employment and non-employment figures taken from to study the data?

(a) Real-Time Handbook of Statistics on Indian Economy.

(b) National Statistical Office (NSO)

(c) NITI Aayog

(d) Statistics information Bureau

60. Which is/are not the method of measuring economic development?

(a) Profit loss

(b) Sales

(c) Import-export

(d) None of the above

61. What was the new name of the Estates General?

(a) Federal Assembly

(b) States Assembly

(c) National Assembly

(d) Peoples Assembly

62. Which symbol is used for classified agricultural produce?

(a) ISI   (b) FSSAI

(c) AGMARK   (d) BSI

63. Which among the following options will be the cheapest source of credit in rural areas?

(a) Bank

(b) Cooperative Society

(c) Money-lender

(d) Finance Company

64. Which of the following is not an informal source of credit?

(a) Money-lender

(b) Relatives and Friends

(c) Commercial Banks

(d) Traders

65. Special Economic Zones (SEZs) are being set up to attract:

(a) Foreign tourists

(b) Foreign investment

(c) Foreign goods

(d) Foreign policies

66. Ford Motors set up its first plant in India at:

(a) Kolkata   (b) Mumbai

(c) Chennai   (d) Delhi

67. Who can seek information under the RTI Act, 2005?

(a) A group of persons

(b) An individual citizen

(c) A registered company

(d) An association / society

68. What is Consumers International?

(a) Charity

(b) An NGO

(c) Civil Society

(d) None of the above

69. Which country was a major producer of print material for a long time?

(a) Korea   (b) China

(c) Japan   (d) India

70. How did the candidates prepare for this examination in 16th century?

    (a) Studying textbooks printed for the preparation of this exam

    (b) Tutorials through teachers

    (c) Self research

    (d) Home tutoring

71. Which type of social diversity or division do we find in Belgium?

    (a) Religious   (b) Linguistic

    (c) Regional   (d) Gender

72. Which types of social differences are in SriLanka?

    (a) Linguistic and regional

    (b) Linguistic and religious

    (c) Physical appearance and class

    (d) Caste and tribe

73. In which one of the following cities did the European powers meet in 1885 to divide Africa between themselves?

    (a) London   (b) New York

    (c) Berlin   (d) Amsterdam

74. If it is desired in India to switch over to unitary system of government from the present federal structure such a change can be brought about by __________.

    (a) A simple majority of the members of the Parliament

    (b) A two-third majority of members present and voting, provided it is not less than the majority of the total members

    (c) A two-third majority of the total membership of the Parliament

    (d) A special procedure in Parliament and ratification by a majority of Sates in the Indian Union

75. The main feature of India as a Federal State is __________.

    (a) Decentralization

    (b) Three-tier government

    (c) Theory of separation of powers

    (d) Sovereignty

76. London in fact came to be known as a ______ before the cloth was sold in the international market.

    (a) Trade centre

    (b) Finishing Centre

    (c) Work centre

    (d) Manufacturing centre

77. Soil is formed by the process of:

    (a) Denudation   (b) Gradation

    (c) Weathering   (d) Erosion

78. Among the below given countries, which country has the highest support for democracy?

    (a) India   (b) Nepal

    (c) Bangladesh   (d) Pakistan

79. Which of these factors play a role in the economic development of a country?

    (a) Cooperation from other countries.

    (b) Size of the population

    (c) Economic priorities adopted by the Government.

    (d) All of the above

80. Which areas did Gandhi organise the satyagraha?

    (a) Champaran in Bihar and Ahmedabad

    (b) Champaran in Bihar, Kheda district of Gujarat, Ahmedabad

    (c) Kheda district of Gujarat, Ahmedabad

    (d) Champaran in Bihar, Kheda district of Gujarat

General Awareness/ Knowledge

81. Famous musician Shakoor Khan was associated with which of the following musical instruments?

    (a) Santoor   (b) Sarangi

    (c) Sitar   (d) Sarod

82. ______ has/have the power to implement the Fundamental Right.

    (a) The Supreme Court and High Courts

    (b) Members of Parliament

    (c) The President

    (d) None of these

83. What is India's rank among the top milk producing countries for the year 2014-15?

    (a) 1st (b) 2nd

    (c) 3rd (d) 5th

84. Patna High Court exercised jurisdiction over the territories of the Province of Bihar & Orissa till ______.

    (a) 1947   (b) 1948

    (c) 1972   (d) 2000

85. Which one of the following earthquakes occurred in India was highly devastating and destructive?

    (a) Kangra Earthquake of 1905

    (b) Bihar earthquake of 1934

    (c) Gujarat earthquake of 2001

    (d) Koyna earthquake of 1967

86. Linear momentum is defined as the product of:

    (a) Acceleration and velocity

    (b) Mass and Velocity

    (c) Mass and Temperature

    (d) Mass and Pressure

87. Which one among the following Union Territories of India is the smallest in geographical area?

    (a) Chandigarh

    (b) Puducherry

    (c) Dadra and Nagar Haveli and Daman and Diu

    (d) Lakshadweep

88. Who among the following was associated with Vaisheshika School of Philosophy?

    (a) Kanada   (b) Patanjali

    (c) Gautama   (d) Jaimini

89. Which of the following rivers ends in the Arabian Sea?

    (a) Narmada   (b) Godavari

    (c) Krishna   (d) Kaveri

90. Which of the following is also called Chalcolithic Age?

    (a) Old stone age

    (b) New stone age

    (c) Copper age

    (d) Iron age

91. Who among the following did Babur defeat in the year 1528 at Chanderi?

    (a) Muhammad Lodhi

    (b) Ibrahim Lodi

    (c) Bappa Rawal

    (d) Medini Rai

92. Direction : Read the passage carefully and answer the following questions.

The sepoys in the East India Company's army had a number of grievances, which led to the Revolt of 1857. The sepoys of the Bengal army, were mostly Brahmins and Rajputs having grievances of their own. Among them were unsatisfactory conditions of service, encroachment upon their religious customs and offences against their dignity and self-respect. They had a strong sense of resentment, as their salary scale was very low compared to their English counterparts. There was discrimination in matters of promotion and pension also.

In the guise of enforcing discipline, the British authorities prohibited the Hindus and the Muslim sepoys displaying their religious marks. These restrictions harmed the religious sentiments of the sepoys.

The sepoys realised that their service conditions, at times impinged upon their religious beliefs. For example at Vellore, there was a mutiny by the sepoys due to the replacement of the turban they wore, by a leather cockade.

The Indian soldiers also had grievances against the British as they were forced to go for the military expeditions to abroad. In order to prevent any kind of resistance from the sepoys against their deployment abroad, Lord Canning's government passed an act in 1856.

The sepoys of Bengal Army around 1857 were mainly consisted of:
(A) Brahmins
(B) Sikhs
(C) Rajputs
Choose the correct option.
(a)   A and C are correct
(b)   A and B are correct
(c)   B and C are correct
(d)   A, B and C are correct

93. Solar radiation heat-up:
(a)   Land faster than the water bodies.
(b)   Land slower than the water bodies.
(c)   Equally both land and water bodies.
(d)   Neither land nor water bodies.

94. The ninth Schedule to the Indian Constitution was added by:
(a) 21st Amendment
(b)   Sixth Amendment
(c)   First Amendment
(d)   Ninth Amendment

95. Which country has won the Women's Doubles and Mixed Doubles Squash titles held in Glasgow in April 2022?
(a)   China   (b)   Thailand
(c)   India   (d)   Malaysia

96. Rajinder Singh was the _________ recipient of Mahavir Chakra.
(a)   First   (b)   Second
(c)   Third   (d)   Fourth

97. Which of the following is/are correctly matched pairs concerning Newton's Law of Motion?
1. First Law of Motion: Everybody continues to be in its state of rest or of uniform motion in a straight line unless compelled by some external force to act otherwise.
2. Second Law of Motion: To every action, there is always an equal and opposite reaction.
3. Third Law of Motion: The rate of change of momentum of a body is directly proportional to the applied force and takes place in the direction in which the force acts.
(a)   1 only   (b)   2 and 3 only
(c)   2 only   (d)   1, 2 and 3

98. Consider the following statements about Fast Radio Burst (FRB)
A. FRB's are a bright burst of radio waves
B. The duration of FRB is very small that's why it is difficult to detect them.
Choose correct statement:
(a)   Only A
(b)   Only B
(c)   Both A and B
(d)   Neither A nor B

99. Which of the following statements is not correct about the French Revolution?
(a)   It gave birth to ideas of liberty, freedom, and equality
(b)   It led to the end of monarchy in France
(c)   The event which marked the beginning of the French revolution was taking of Bastille fortress on July 14, 1789
(d)   The French revolution was fought between 1775 and 1783

100. Which actor has been awarded "the Golden Visa" by The United Arab Emirates (UAE) government in July 2022 ?
(a)   Amitabh Bachchan
(b)   Rajnikanth
(c)   Rana Daggubati
(d)   Kamal Haasan

// Hints and Solutions //

1(B). We know that to divide a line segment in the ratio m : n , we draw AX which makes an acute angle BAX , then we mark m + n points at equal distances from each other.

Here, $m = 3, n = 4$

So, the minimum number of these points $= m + n = 3 + 4 = 7$

2(D). We know that to divide a line segment in the ratio m : n , first draw a ray AX which makes an acute angle $\angle BAX$, then we are required to mark $(m + n)$ points at equal distances from each other.

So, the minimum points located in the ray AX is $5 + 8 = 13$. Hence, point B will join point A_{13} .

3(C). Let the class size of the data be h . The mean can be found as given below:

$$\bar{X} = a + \left(\frac{\sum f_i u_i}{\sum f_i}\right) h$$

Take the assured mean (a) of the given data $a = 150$

Class mark (x_i) for each interval is calculated as follows:

$$x_i = \frac{\text{Upper class limit} + \text{Lower class limit}}{2}$$

Class size (h) of this data is:
$h = 120 - 100$
$h = 20$
d_i, u_i , and $f_i u_i$ can be evaluated as follows:

Daily wages (In Rs)	Number of Workers (f_i)	x_i	$d_i = x_i - 150$	$u_i = \dfrac{d_i}{20}$	$f_i u_i$
100 – 120	12	110	−40	−2	−24
120 – 140	14	130	−20	−1	−14
140 – 160	8	150	0	0	0
160 – 180	6	170	20	1	6
180 – 200	10	190	40	2	20
Total	50				−12

From the table, it can be observed that
$\sum f_i = 50$
and
$\sum f_i u_i = -12$
Substituting the value of u_i , and $f_i u_i$ in the formula of mean we get:
The required mean:

$$\bar{X} = a + \left(\frac{\sum f_i u_i}{\sum f_i}\right) h$$

$\bar{X} = 150 + \left(\frac{-12}{50}\right) 20$

$\bar{X} = 150 - \frac{24}{5}$

$\bar{X} = 150 - 4.8$

$\bar{X} = 145.2$

So, the mean daily wage of the workers of the factory is Rs. 145.20 .

4(A). Given,
Length $(l) = 49 cm$
Breadth $(b) = 33 cm$
Height $(h) = 24 cm$
Let r be the radius of the sphere.
As we know,
Volume of sphere $= \frac{4}{3} \pi r^3$
Volume of cuboid $= l \times b \times h$
Volume of cuboid = Volume of sphere molded

$l \times b \times h = \frac{4}{3} \pi r^3$

$\Rightarrow 49 \times 33 \times 24 = \frac{4}{3} \times \frac{22}{7} r^3$

$\Rightarrow \dfrac{49 \times 33 \times 24 \times 3 \times 7}{4 \times 22} = r^3$

$\Rightarrow 9261 = r^3$

$\Rightarrow (21)^3 = r^3$

$\therefore r = 21 cm$

So, the radius of sphere is $21 cm$.

5(A).

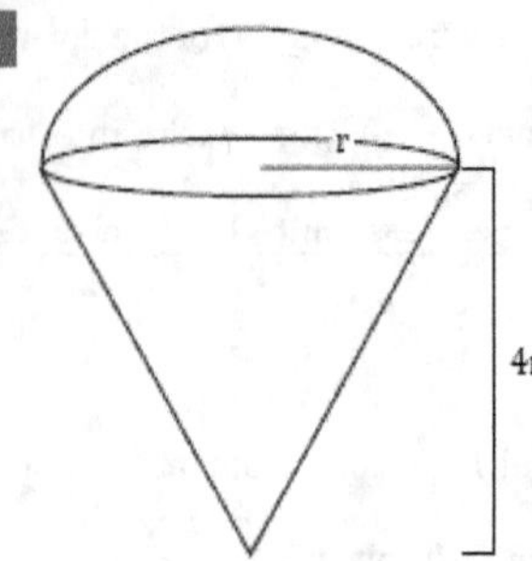

Given,
Radius of cylindrical container $= 6cm$
Height of cylindrical container $= 15cm$
As we know,
Volume of cone $= \frac{1}{3}\pi r^2 h$

Volume of hemisphere $= \frac{2}{3}\pi r^3$

Volume of cylinder $= \pi r^2 h$
Volume of cylindrical container
$= \pi \times (6)^2 \times 15 = 540\pi cm^3$
As it has to be divided among 10 children,
$\therefore$ Dividing volume by $10 = \frac{540}{10} = 54\pi cm^3$
Volume of cone + Volume of hemispherical
top = Volume of ice cream in it
$\frac{1}{3}\pi r^2 h + \frac{2}{3}\pi r^3 = \pi r^2 h$
$\Rightarrow \frac{1}{3}\pi r^2 (4r) + \frac{2}{3}\pi r^3 = 54\pi$
$\Rightarrow \frac{4}{3}\pi r^3 + \frac{2}{3}\pi r^3 = 54\pi$
$\Rightarrow \frac{1}{3}\pi r^3 (4 + 2) = 54\pi$
$\Rightarrow \frac{6}{3}\pi r^3 = 54\pi$
$\Rightarrow 2r^3 = 54$
$\Rightarrow r^3 = \frac{54}{2}$
$\Rightarrow r^3 = 27$
$\Rightarrow r^3 = (3)^3$
$\therefore r = 3$
So, the radius of ice cream cone is $3cm$.

6(B). As given,
$x^2 - 5(k - 1)x + (8k + 1) = 0$ has equal
roots.
$b^2 - 4ac = 0$
$\Rightarrow \{5(k - 1)\}^2 - 4(8k + 1) = 0$
$\Rightarrow \{5(k - 1)\}^2 = 4(8k + 1)$
$\Rightarrow 25 (k^2 - 2k + 1) = 32k + 4$
$\Rightarrow 25k^2 - 82k + 21 = 0$
$\Rightarrow 25k^2 - 75k - 7k + 21 = 0$
$\Rightarrow 25k(k - 3) - 7(k - 3) = 0$
$\Rightarrow (k - 3)(25k - 7) = 0$
$\Rightarrow k = 3$ is the integer value.

7(C). The given equation is,
$x^2 - 5x + 4 = 0$
We need to find out the roots of the given
equation. So, for that, we can write the
equation as,
$x^2 - 4x - x + 4 = 0$
$\Rightarrow x(x - 4) - (x - 4) = 0$
$\Rightarrow (x - 4)(x - 1) = 0$
$\therefore x = 1, 4$
$\cot\alpha$ and $\cot\beta$ are the roots of the equation
$x^2 - 5x + 4 = 0$
$\cot\alpha = 1$ and $\cot\beta = 4$

$\cot(\alpha + \beta) = \frac{(\cot\alpha\cot\beta - 1)}{(\cot\alpha + \cot\beta)}$
Putting the value of the roots we get,
$\cot(\alpha + \beta) = \frac{(1 \times 4 - 1)}{(1 + 4)}$
$\therefore \cot(\alpha + \beta) = \frac{3}{5}$

8(A).

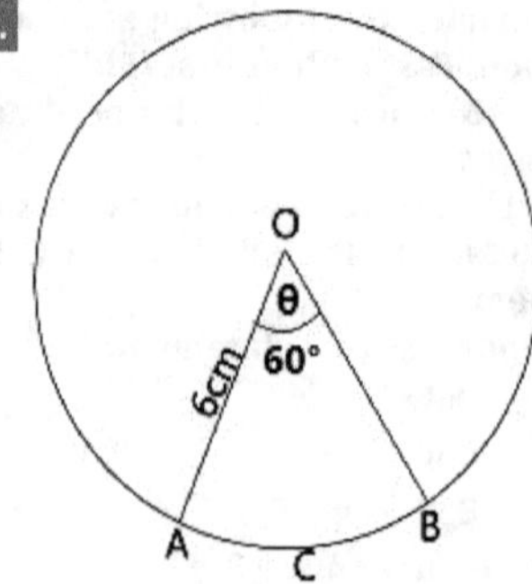

Given that,
Radius of the circle $r = 6$ cm
Angle made by the sector with the center,
$\theta = 60°$
Let $OACB$ be the sector of the circle
making $60°$ angle at center O of the circle.
We know that area of sector $= \frac{\theta}{360°} \times \pi r^2$
Thus, Area of sector $OACB$
$= \frac{60°}{360°} \times \frac{22}{7} \times (6)^2$
$= \frac{1}{6} \times \frac{22}{7} \times 6 \times 6$
$= \frac{132}{7}$ cm^2
Therefore, the area of the sector of the
circle making $60°$ at the center of the circle
is $\frac{132}{7}$ cm^2.

9(A).

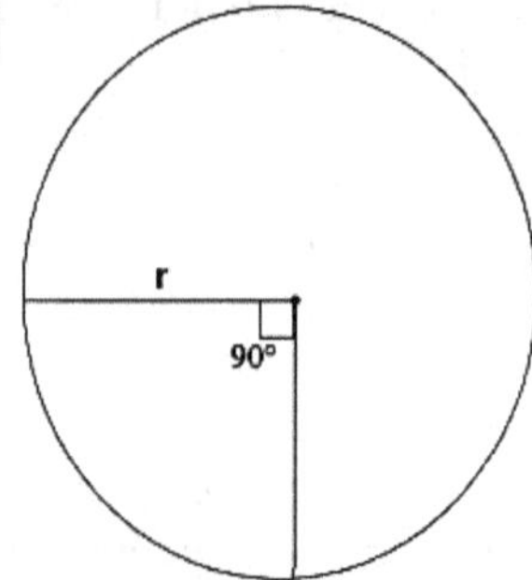

Given that,
Circumference $= 22$ cm
Let the radius of the circle be r.
According to the given condition,
$2\pi r = 22$
$\Rightarrow r = \frac{22}{2\pi}$
$= \frac{11}{\pi}$
We know that, quadrant of circle subtends
$90°$ angle at the center of the circle.
Thus,
Area of such quadrant of the circle
$= \frac{90°}{360°} \times \pi \times r^2$
$= \frac{1}{4} \times \pi \times \left(\frac{11}{\pi}\right)^2$
$= \frac{121}{4\pi}$
$= \frac{121 \times 7}{4 \times 22}$

$= \frac{77}{8}$ cm^2
So, the area of a quadrant of a circle whose
circumference is 22 cm is.
$= \frac{77}{8}$ cm^2

10(A). Given,
$\sin A = \frac{1}{\sqrt{2}} = \frac{\text{Perpendicular}}{\text{Hypotenuse}}$
As we know,
$(\text{Hypotenuse})^2 = (\text{Perpendicular})^2 + (\text{Base})^2$
$(\sqrt{2})^2 = (1)^2 + (\text{Base})^2$
$(\text{Base})^2 = (\sqrt{2})^2 - (1)^2$
$= 2 - 1$
$= 1$
$\tan A = \frac{\text{Perpendicular}}{\text{Base}}$
$= \frac{1}{1}$
$= 1$

11(A). Given,
$\sin M = \frac{4}{4\sqrt{2}} = \frac{\text{Perpendicular}}{\text{Hypotenuse}}$
As we know,
$(\text{Hypotenuse})^2 = (\text{Perpendicular})^2 + (\text{Base})^2$
$MN = 4$
$MO = 4\sqrt{2}$
$NO = ?$
$NO^2 = MO^2 - MN^2$
$= (4\sqrt{2})^2 - (4)^2$
$NO^2 = 32 - 16 = 16$
$NO = \sqrt{16}$
$NO = 4$
$\cos M = \frac{\text{Base}}{\text{Hypotenuse}} = \frac{NO}{MO}$
$= \frac{4}{4\sqrt{2}}$
$= \frac{1}{\sqrt{2}}$

12(D). $\csc\theta$ is the reciprocal of $\sin\theta$ i.e.,
$\csc\theta = \frac{1}{\sin\theta} = \frac{\text{Hypotenuse}}{\text{Perpendicular}}$
So, $\sin\theta$ will be $\frac{\text{Perpendicular}}{\text{Hypotenuse}} = \frac{4}{5}$
$\therefore \sin^2\theta = \frac{(\text{Perpendicular})^2}{(\text{Hypotenuse})^2}$
$= \frac{(4)^2}{(5)^2}$
$= \frac{16}{25}$

13(D).

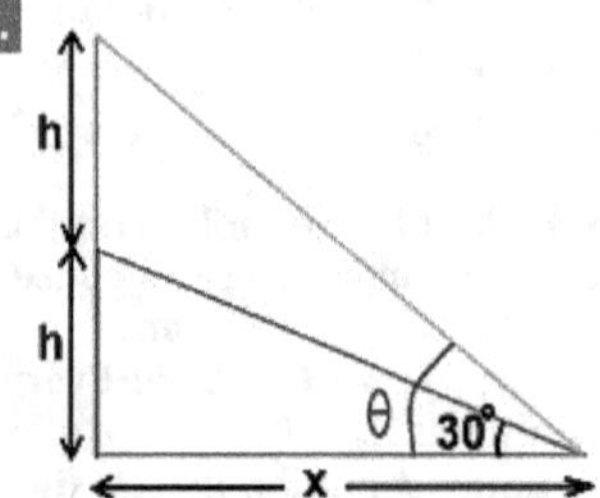

In $\triangle ABC$
$\tan\theta = \frac{h}{9}$ ...(i)
In $\triangle ABD$
$\tan(90° - \theta) = \frac{h}{16}$

Multiplying the equations (i) and (ii), we get

$\tan\theta \times \tan(90° - \theta) = \dfrac{h}{9} \times \dfrac{h}{16}$

$\Rightarrow \tan\theta \times \cot\theta = \dfrac{h^2}{9\times16}$ $[\because \tan(90° - \theta) = \cot\theta]$

$\Rightarrow \tan\theta \times \dfrac{1}{\tan\theta} = \dfrac{h^2}{9\times16}$ $[\because \cot\theta = \dfrac{1}{\tan\theta}]$

$\Rightarrow 1 = \dfrac{h^2}{9\times16}$

$\Rightarrow 9 \times 16 = h^2$

$\Rightarrow 144 = h^2$

$\Rightarrow \sqrt{144} = h$

$\therefore h = 12$

So, the height of the tower is $12m$.

14(A). Given,

$x + y = 14$

or, $x = 14 - y \ldots \ldots (1)$

$x - y = 4 \ldots \ldots \ldots (2)$

Now substituting the value of x from (1) in (2) we get, $14 - 2y = 4$

or, $2y = 10$

or, $y = 5$.

Now substituting the value of y in (1) we get, $x = 9$

So $x = 9, y = 5$.

15(A). Let the number of girls be x and the number of boys be y. It is given that a total of ten students took part in the quiz.

$\therefore$ Number of girls + Number of boys = 10

i.e., $x + y = 10$

It is also given that the number of girls is 4 more than the number of boys.

$\therefore$ Number of girls = Number of boys $+4$

i.e., $x = y + 4$

or, $x - y = 4$

Algebraic Representation:

Thus, the algebraic representation of the given situation is

$x + y = 10$

$x - y = 4$

16(D). As we know,

Every odd integer is not divisible by 2.

$\therefore$ Only option we have is $2q + 1$.

17(A). The product of a non-zero rational with and an irrational number is always irrational.

Example:

$2 \times \sqrt{3} = 2\sqrt{3}$ is an irrational number.

18(D). Given,

$\dfrac{14587}{1250}$

$= \dfrac{14587}{2^1 \times 5^4}$

$= \dfrac{14587}{2^1 \times 5^4} \times \dfrac{2^3}{2^3}$

$= \dfrac{14587 \times 2^3}{(2^4 \times 5^4)}$

$= \dfrac{14587 \times 2^3}{(2\times5)^4}$

$= \dfrac{114587 \times 2^3}{10^4}$

So, the number will terminate after 4 decimal places.

19(D). Subtract the remainders from the numbers

$1251 - 1 = 1250$

$9377 - 2 = 9375$

$15628 - 3 = 15625$

So, we need to find largest number which divides 1250, 9375 and 15625, and leaves remainder 0.

Thus, we need largest number which divides 1250, 9375, and 15625.

$\therefore$ We need to find HCF of 1250, 9375, and 15625.

Finding HCF of 1250, 9375 and 15625

2	1250		3	9375		5	15625
5	625		5	3125		5	3125
5	125		5	625		5	625
5	25		5	125		5	125
5	5		5	25		5	25
	1		5	5		5	5
				1			1

Thus,

$1250 = 2 \times 5 \times 5 \times 5 \times 5$

$9375 = 3 \times 5 \times 5 \times 5 \times 5 \times 5$

$15625 = 5 \times 5 \times 5 \times 5 \times 5 \times 5$

$\therefore$ HCF of $1250, 9375$, and $15625 = 5 \times 5 \times 5 \times 5 = 625$.

20(D). For equal roots, discriminant will be equal to zero.

$b^2 - 4ac = 0$

$b^2 = 4ac$

$ac = \dfrac{b^2}{4}$

$ac > 0$ (as square of any number cannot be negative)

So, c and a have same signs.

21(B). Since one zero is -1, hence;

$P(x) = x^3 + ax^2 + bx + c$

$P(-1) = (-1)^3 + a(-1)^2 + b(-1) + c$

$0 = -1 + a - b + c$

$c = 1 - a + b$

Product of zeroes, $\alpha\beta\gamma = \dfrac{-\text{constant term}}{\text{coefficient of } x^3}$

$(-1)\beta\gamma = \dfrac{-c}{1}$

$c = \beta\gamma$

$\beta\gamma = b - a + 1$

22(C). even outcomes = $2, 4, 6 = 3$

and multiple of 3 also = $6 = 1$ only

Number of possible outcomes = $\{ 6 \}$

n(A)= 1

Number of Total outcomes= $1, 2, 3, 4, 5, 6$

n(S)= 6

$\therefore\ P(A) = \dfrac{n(A)}{n(S)} = \dfrac{1}{6}$

23(A). Let a be the first term and d be the common difference of the AP.

Given, $a_3 = 12$ and $a_{50} = 106$, find a_{29}

we know,

$T_n = a + (n - 1)d$

$a = $ first term

$d = $ common difference

$T_n = n^{\text{th}}$ term

$\Rightarrow\ T_3 = a + (3 - 1)d = 12$

$\Rightarrow\qquad a + 2d = 12 \qquad \ldots \ldots (i)$

$\Rightarrow\ T_{50} = a + (50 - 1)d = 106$

$\Rightarrow\qquad a + 49d = 106 \qquad \ldots \ldots (ii)$

Subtracting (i) from (ii), we get

$47d = 94 \Rightarrow d = 2$

Putting $d = 2$ in (i), we get

$a + 2 \times 2 = 12 \Rightarrow a + 4 = 12 \Rightarrow a = 8$

$\therefore\ 29^{th}$ term of the $AP = a + (29 - 1)d = 8 + 28 \times 2 = 8 + 56 = 64$

24(A). Let a be the first term, d be the common difference and n be the total number of terms of the AP,

Given,

$a_{26} = 0, a_{11} = 3$ and $a_n = -\dfrac{1}{5}$

We know,

$T_n = a + (n - 1)d$

$a = $ first term

$d = $ common difference

$T_n = n^{\text{th}}$ term

So,

$a_{26} = 0 \Rightarrow a + 25d = 0 \qquad \ldots \ldots (i)$

$a_{11} = 3 \Rightarrow a + 10d = 3 \qquad \ldots \ldots (ii)$

$a_n = -\dfrac{1}{5}$

$\Rightarrow a + (n - 1)d = -\dfrac{1}{5} \qquad \ldots \ldots (iii)$

Subtracting (ii) from (i), we get

$15d = -3 \Rightarrow d = -\dfrac{1}{5}$.

Putting $d = -\dfrac{1}{5}$ in (i), we get

$a + 25\left(-\dfrac{1}{5}\right) = 0$

$\Rightarrow a - 5 = 0$

$\Rightarrow a = 5$.

Putting $a = 5$ and $d = -\dfrac{1}{5}$ in (iii), we get

$5 + (n - 1)\left(-\dfrac{1}{5}\right) = -\dfrac{1}{5}$

$\Rightarrow 25 + (n - 1)(-1) = -1$

$\Rightarrow 25 - n + 1 = -1$

$\Rightarrow n = 27$

So, the common difference is $-\dfrac{1}{5}$ and the number of terms is 27.

25(A). Given:

$ABCD$ is trapezium where $AB\|DC$ and diagonals intersect at O

$AB = 2CD$

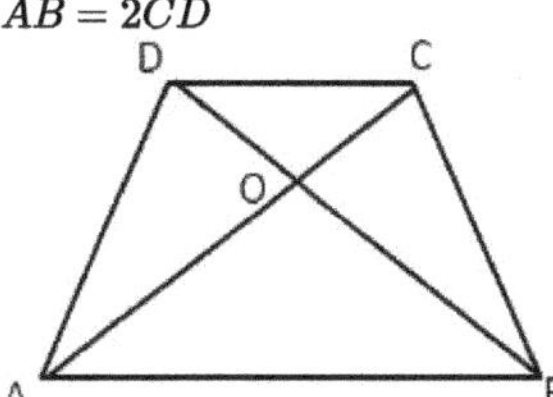

To find: $\dfrac{ar\triangle AOB}{ar\triangle COD}$

Since we need to find ratio of area of $\triangle AOB$ and $\triangle COD$.

Lets first prove $\triangle AOB$ and $\triangle COD$ are similar.

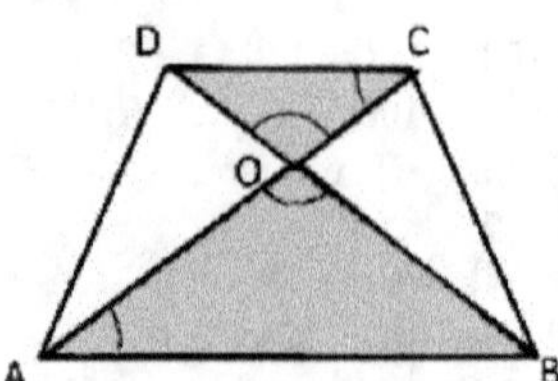

In $\triangle AOB$ and $\triangle COD$

$\angle AOB = \angle COD$ (Vertically opposite angles)

$\angle OAB = \angle OCD$ (since $AB \parallel CD$ with AC as traversal, alternate angle are equal)

So, $\triangle AOB \sim \triangle COD$ (AA similarity)

We know that if two triangle are similar,
Ratio of areas is equal to square of ratio of its corresponding sides.

So, $\dfrac{ar\triangle AOB}{ar\triangle COD} = \left(\dfrac{AB}{CD}\right)^2$

$\dfrac{ar\triangle AOB}{ar\triangle COD} = \left(\dfrac{2CD}{CD}\right)^2$ ($AB = 2CD$ given)

$\dfrac{ar\triangle AOB}{ar\triangle COD} = \left(\dfrac{2}{1}\right)^2$

$\dfrac{ar\triangle AOB}{ar\triangle COD} = \dfrac{4}{1}$

$\therefore ar\triangle AOB : ar\triangle COD = 4 : 1$

So, ratio of areas is $4 : 1$

26(B). Given:

$\triangle ABC$

and D, E, F mid-points of AB, BC and CA respectively

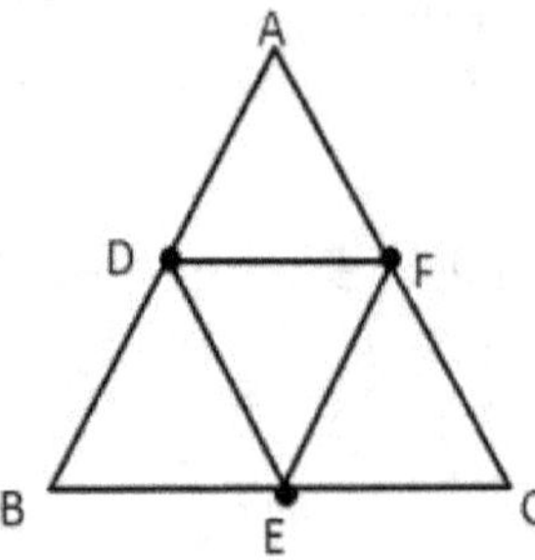

Note: Since we need to find ratio of area of $\triangle DEF$ and $\triangle ABC$. We first need to prove these triangles are similar.

We know that,
line joining mid-points of two sides of a triangle is parallel to the 3rd side.

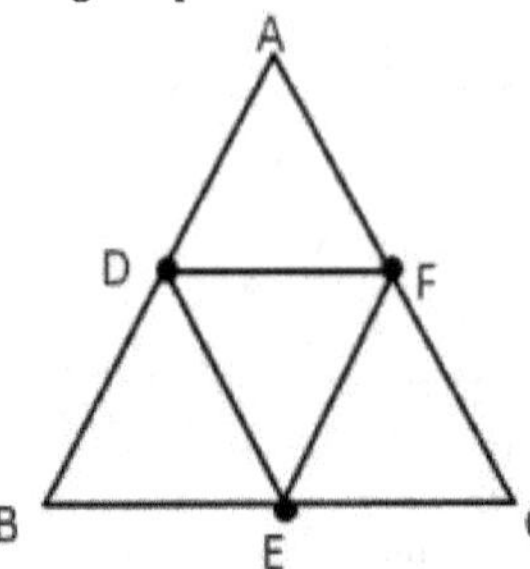

In $\triangle ABC$,

D and F are mid-points of AB and AC resp.,

$\therefore DF \parallel BC$

So, $DF \parallel BE$ also ......(1)

Similarly,

E and F are mid-points of BC and AC resp.

$EF \parallel AB$

So, $EF \parallel DB$ ......(2)

From (1) and (2),

$DF \parallel BE$ and $FE \parallel DB$

Therefore, opposite sides of quadrilateral is parallel.

$DBEF$ is a parallelogram,

$DBEF$ is a parallelogram

Now we know that,

in parallelogram, opposite angle are equal.

So, $\angle DFE = \angle ABC$ ......(3)

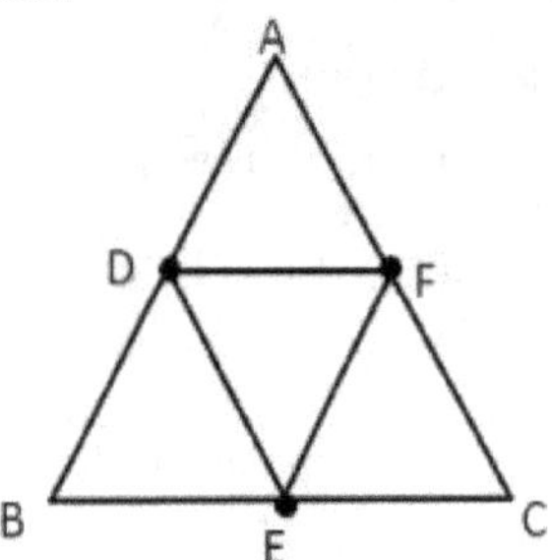

Similarity,

We can prove $DECF$ is a parallelogram,

In a parallelogram, opposite angles are equal

So, $\angle EDF = \angle ACB$ ......(4)

Now, in $\triangle EDF$ and $\triangle ABC$

$\angle DFE = \angle ABC$ and from 3,

$\angle EDF = \angle ACB$ and from 4,

By using AA similarity criterion,

$\triangle DEF \sim \triangle ABC$

We know that if two triangles are similar, the ratio of their area is always equal to the square of the ratio of their corresponding side.

$\therefore \dfrac{ar\triangle DEF}{ar\triangle ABC} = \dfrac{DE^2}{AC^2}$

$\dfrac{ar\triangle DEF}{ar\triangle ABC} = \dfrac{FC^2}{AC^2}$ (Since $DECF$ is a parallelogram, opposite sides are equal, i.e $DE = FC$.)

$\dfrac{\text{Area of } \triangle DEF}{\text{Area of } \triangle ABC} = \dfrac{\left(\frac{AC}{2}\right)^2}{(AC)^2}$ (As F is the mid-point of AC)

$\dfrac{\text{Area of } \triangle DEF}{\text{Area of } \triangle ABC} = \dfrac{\frac{(AC)^2}{4}}{(AC)^2}$

$\dfrac{\text{Area of } \triangle DEF}{\text{Area of } \triangle ABC} = \dfrac{\frac{1}{4}}{1}$

So, $\dfrac{\text{Area of } \triangle DEF}{\text{Arae of } \triangle ABC} = \dfrac{1}{4}$

27(C). If the angle of the base radius is the same then the corresponding length of sides will be the same.

AB = 4 cm

Therefore, BC = 4 cm

28(D). As we know that if the angle of the base radius is the same then the corresponding length of sides will be the same.

So, we see in the diagram that,

$\angle XYB = 90°$ and so $\angle XYA$ will also be equal to $90°$.

And according to the statement given above, we can say that $AY = BY$

29(C). Now, length of the diagonal $AB =$ Distance between the points $A(0, 3)$ and $B(5, 0)$.

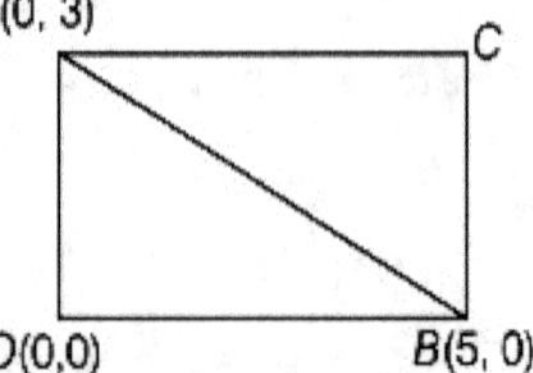

$\because$ Distance between the points (x_1, y_1) and (x_2, y_2)

$d = \sqrt{(x_2 - x_1)^2 + (y_2 - y_1)^2}$

Here, $x_1 = 0, y_1 = 3$ and $x_2 = 5, y_2 = 0$

$\therefore$ Distance between the points $A(0, 3)$ and $B(5, 0)$

$AB = \sqrt{(5 - 0)^2 + (0 - 3)^2}$

$= \sqrt{25 + 9} = \sqrt{34}$

So, the required length of its diagonal is $\sqrt{34}$ units.

30(B). We plot the vertices of a triangle i.e., $(0, 4)$, $(0, 0)$ and $(3, 0)$ on the paper shown as given below,

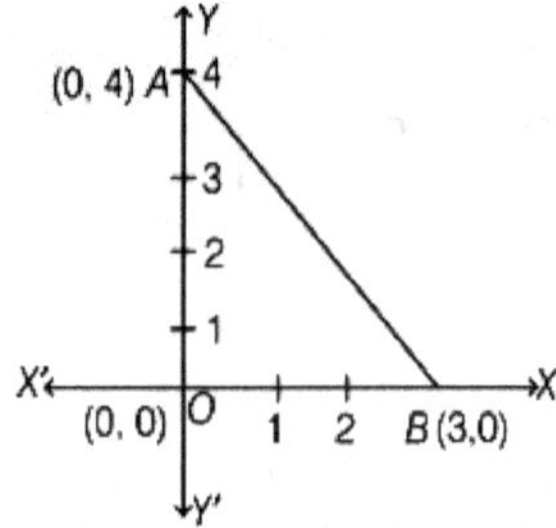

Now, perimeter of $\triangle AOB =$ Sum of the length of all its sides

$= d(AO) + d(OB) + d(AB)$

$\because$ Distance between the points (x_1, y_1) and (x_2, y_2) , is

$d = \sqrt{(x_2 - x_1)^2 + (y_2 - y_1)^2}$

$=$ Distance between $A(0, 4)$ and $O(0, 0)+$ Distance between $O(0, 0)$ and $B(3, 0)+$ Distance between $A(0, 4)$ and $B(3, 0)$

$= \sqrt{(0 - 0)^2 + (0 - 4)^2} + \sqrt{(3 - 0)^2 + (0 - 0)^2} + \sqrt{(3 - 0)^2 + (0 - 4)^2}$

$= \sqrt{0 + 16} + \sqrt{9 + 0} + \sqrt{(3)^2 + (4)^2}$

$= 4 + 3 + \sqrt{9 + 16}$

$= 7 + \sqrt{25} = 7 + 5 = 12$

So, the required perimeter of triangle is 12 units.

31(D). The trophic level of an organism is the place it has in a food chain. A food chain is mostly made up of three trophic levels. However, some trophic levels have 4 trophic levels which include:-

- Primary producers are plants that are autotrophs and belong to the first trophic level.
- Primary consumers are animals that belong to the second trophic level and feed on plants. They are called herbivores.
- Secondary consumers feed on herbivores and belong to the third trophic level. They are called primary carnivores.
- Tertiary consumers feed on primary carnivores and belong to the fourth trophic level. They are called secondary carnivores.

32(C). The autotrophs capture the energy present in sunlight and convert it into chemical energy. This energy supports all the activities of the living world. From the Autotrophs, the energy goes to the heterotrophs and then finally to the decomposers.

33(A). The size of non-metals is small as compared to metals due to which electrons are more tightly held in non-metals. Non-Metals are electronegative elements and tend to share or accept electrons in a chemical reaction. Due to the electrons accepting nature of non-metals, they gains more electrons to complete their octet.
So, non-metals have high ionization enthalpy due to their small size and high electronegativity as compared to metal.

34(A). Mg metal evolves hydrogen on reacting with cold dilute HNO_3. Only magnesium and manganese react with nitric acid to release hydrogen gas.
Hydrogen gas is not evolved when other metals react with nitric acid because it is a strong oxidising agent. It oxidises hydrogen produced to water and itself gets reduced to a nitrogen oxide.

35(D). Our sympathetic nervous system is best known for its role in responding to dangerous or stressful situations. In these situations, your sympathetic nervous system activates to speed up your heart rate, deliver more blood to areas of your body that need more oxygen or other responses to help your get out of danger.

36(A). Axon transmits impulse away from cell body and dendrites transmit impulse towards cell body.
Neurons are the structural and functional units of the nervous system.
A typical neuron has three components; cell body (cyton), dendrons (dendrites) and axon.
Cell body is the broader part which contains the nucleus and various cell organelles. Cell body bears short branched processes called dendrites. Dendrites

transmit impulses from synapses to the cell body. Axon is a long process which develops from a conical prolongation of cyton called axon hillock. Axon is branched distally. The branch ends are expanded to form synaptic knobs. These knobs possess neurotransmitters containing synaptic vesicles. Axon carries the impulse away from the cell body.

37(D). The chemical equation of the reaction between carbon monoxide gas and hydrogen gas can be written as:
$$CO + H_2 \rightarrow CH_3OH$$
The chemical formula of carbon monoxide is CO and its physical state is gas, the chemical formula of hydrogen is H_2 and its physical state is also gaseous. In the above reaction we can see that the number of carbon and oxygen atoms are balanced on both sides. But the number of H on the reactant side is 2 whereas the number of H on the product side is 4. And hence, multiplying 2 as the coefficient of H_2, we will get a balanced chemical equation. So, the balanced chemical equation is:
$$CO(g) + 2H_2(g) \xrightarrow{340\ atm} CH_3OH(l)$$

38(C). Exposure of silver chloride to sunlight for a long duration turns grey due to the formation of silver by decomposition of silver chloride.
We know that the decomposition reaction in reactants broken down to simpler substances by absorbing energy from photons is defined as a photolytic decomposition reaction.
Silver halides, especially silver chloride undergo decomposition in presence of sunlight to produce silver metal and a halogen gas (chlorine or bromine gas). White color of silver chloride changes to grey due to formation of silver metal. The reaction for the exposure of silver chloride to sunlight is:
$$2AgCl(s) \xrightarrow{Sunlight} 2Ag(s) + Cl_2(g)$$

39(C). Soap is sodium or potassium salt of a higher fatty acid. Soapy surfactants are used for washing, bathing, and housekeeping.In industrial settings, soaps are used as thickeners, components of some lubricants, and precursors to catalysts.

40(A). A homologous series is a family of hydrocarbons with similar chemical properties that share the same general formula.
The general formula of the compound in the question is C_nH_2n 2 with n = 3.
Only the compound in option A satisfies the given general formula with n = 4.
So, homologue of C_3H_4 is C_4H_6.

41(D). Starfish are known for their ability to regenerate amputated limbs and are characterized by flexible arms attached to a central disc. The central disc is essential for complete regeneration, however arms that

are partially damaged/lost are regenerated by the organism.

42(B). Puberty is the process due to which growing boys or girls undergo the process of sexual maturation. Puberty involves a series of physical stages or steps that lead to the achievement of fertility and the development of secondary sex characteristics. Some of the other secondary signs of puberty in girls are:
Breast tissue development
Initiation of menstrual periods
Increasing in sweat production
Presence of pubic hair

43(B). A monohybrid cross is a mating between individuals who have different alleles at one genetic locus of interest. In a monohybrid cross, the pure breed tall and dwarf homozygous plants were crossed.
Genotype: TT × tt
Gametes: T t
Offspring: Tt
Selfing of F_1: F_2: Tt × Tt
Gametes: T, t T, t
F_2 generation: TT, Tt, Tt. and tt
Genotypic ratio: 1 : 2 : 1

44(C). Mendel studied the common garden pea plant, Pisum sativum because it was easy to cultivate and had a relatively short life cycle of 3 months. The plant exhibited discontinuous characteristics such as flower color and pea texture. Owing to its anatomy, it was easy to control the self-pollination of the plant, and cross-fertilization between desired parents could be accomplished artificially. The presence of pure breeding varieties and easily visible contrasting characters and the presence of F_1 fertile hybrids were the additional advantageous characters for which Mendel chose garden pea as experimental material.

45(D). The following are the conditions for the interference to happen:
- The source should emit light waves continuously.
- Light waves emitted should have a single wavelength.
- Waves should either have a constant phase difference or be in phase.
- The light sources should be close to each other and narrow.
- Coherent source: The source of light have a constant phase difference is called a coherent source.

The interference will happen if the two light sources are coherent and they have single wave length light rays.
Therefore, both (A) and (B) are correct.

46(B). In the process of refraction, speed of light and wavelength of light changes.
In a medium, speed of light is given by $v = \frac{c}{\mu}$ where μ is refractive index of the medium. Hence, for medium with different refractive index, speed of light is different.
Frequency will not change because at the

boundary/interface of the medium, the number of waves you send is the number of waves you receive at the other side, almost instantly.

Since, for a travelling wave we have a relation $v = \frac{v}{\lambda}$. Hence wavelength also changes in the process of refraction.

47(D). An electric current will produce a magnetic field, which can be visualized as a series of circular field lines around a wire segment. So, given statement is true.

An electric current produces a magnetic field. This is possible when an electric charge is in motion. When the electric charge is at rest, there is no production of the magnetic field. When the atom spins and orbits the nucleus there is a production of the magnetic field. Also, the direction of the magnetic field is determined by the direction of spin and orbiting of the electric charge.

48(B). Overloading is caused by connecting too many appliances to a single socket.

Overloading takes place when the live wire comes into direct contact with the neutral wire (This occurs when the insulation of wires is damaged or there is a fault in the appliance). In such a situation, the current in the circuit abruptly increases. This is called Short-circuiting.

Overloading can be avoided by connecting many appliances at a time in the circuit. A person connects too many electrical applianes to a single socket in his house. When all these electrical appliances connected to the single socket are switched on at the same time, the electric fuse of circuit blows off.

49(C). Chief function of HCl is to maintain low pH to activate pepsinogen to form pepsin.

The gastric juice is made up of hydrochloric acid, pepsinogen and other digestive enzymes, intrinsic factor, gastrin, mucus, and bicarbonates. It has a pH ranging from 1 to 2 . Its low pH is essential in activating digestive enzyme pepsinogen and convert it into the pepsin fro protein digestion and in destroying various pathogens.

Hence, the correct option is (A).

50(C). Mammal excretes nitrogenous wastes in the form of urea.

The process of eliminating the metabolic and toxic substances such as nitrogenous wastes from the body of living organisms is called excretion.

Nitrogenous waste is produced during the degradation of proteins due to the chemical transformations of the amine group of amino acid molecules.

Nitrogenous wastes excreted by living organisms include ammonia, uric acid, and urea.

Mammals such as humans excrete urea, while birds, reptiles, and some terrestrial invertebrates produce uric acid as waste.

51(D). Tartaric acid is added to baking powder for neutralization of the bitter taste of base produced by baking powder. Baking powder is a mixture of baking soda i.e., sodium bicarbonate, $NaHCO_3$ and an edible acid i.e., tartaric acid. The reaction between baking soda and tartaric acid is:
$NaHCO_3 + H^+ \rightarrow Na^+ + CO_2 + H_2O$
So, to neutralize bitter taste because of Na_2CO_3 , tartaric acid is added in the baking powder. If tartaric acid is not added in baking powder, the sodium carbonate remains in the cake resulting in a bitter taste.

52(C). Vinegar is added while preparing beetroot soup to neutralise the basic nature of beetroot soup.

It's best to boil beets whole to keep their color from leeching out; simply place them in a pot of water seasoned with a bit of vinegar or lemon (a further deterrent to the juice staining everything it touches), and cook for about 1 hour. Rinse under cold water when cooked, and the skins should slip right off.

53(C). A person may suffer from both myopia and hypermetropia. Such people often require bi-focal lenses. The upper part of bifocal lens is made up of concave lens and the lower part of a small circular section is made up of convex lens. Thus, spectacles made of such a lens help to see nearby as well as distant objects clearly, a defect which is known as presbyopia.

54(C). Given:
Outer radii $= R = 4$
Inner radii $= r = 2$
$l = 3m$
$\rho = 2.2 \times 10^{-8} \, \Omega - m$
We know that,
$R = \frac{\rho \times l}{A}$
where,
$R =$Resistance
$\rho =$Resistivity
$l =$lenght
Now,
Area of hollow cylinder $= \pi \left(R^2 - r^2 \right)$
Area of hollow cylinder
$= \pi \left(2^2 - 1^2 \right) = 3.14 \times 3 \times 10^{-6} = 9.42 \times 10^{-6}$
$R = 2.2 \times 10^{-8} \left[\frac{3}{9.42 \times 10^{-6}} \right]$
$R = 0.7 \times 10^{-2} \, \Omega$
$R = 7 \times 10^{-3} \, \Omega$

55(D). Treating initially that there is no radiation and on applying a voltage to the heater, the temperature of the heater rises. As the temperature rises, the radiation also increases.

As the input power i^2r is constant, the output power should also be constant. Initially, the temperature will be increasing and radiation as well. When the heater reaches a certain temperature, the radiation power equals the input power and the temperature of the heater stops rising.

Thus temperature becomes constant after some time.

56(C). According to the hydrological cycle, by groundwater, we can obtain fresh water.
Freshwater sources include:
Groundwater: Water found in shallow aquifers beneath the earth's surface. This water is generally found at depths up to 2,000 feet deep.
Precipitation: It is nothing but rainwater which is an important source of freshwater. In fact, it is the purest natural source of fresh water.
Surface water: Water found in streams, rivers, lakes, and reservoirs.

57(D).
Under Endemic category of species the Andaman wild pig comes.
Wild pig of Andaman (Sus scrofa andamanensis) is a most endangered porcine species of Andaman and Nicobar islands. Jarawa tribes in Andaman Islands prefer this wild pig as a good protein source. It is black in colour, short legged, small to medium sized and a prolific breeder. Litter size varies from 4 to 7 numbers.

58(A). Cobalt is an example of Ferrous minerals.
Ferrous minerals are metallic minerals containing iron. While non-ferrous minerals are also metallic, but they do not contain iron.
Cobalt (Co) is a bluish-gray, shiny, brittle metallic element. It has magnetic properties similar to iron. There are no significant minerals of cobalt. It is rare and obtained mostly through refining of nickel ore. It is used in superalloys for jet engines, chemicals magnets, and cemented carbides for cutting tools.

59(B). The employment and non-employment figures taken from National Statistical Office (NSO) to study the data.
NSO consists of the Central Statistical Office (CSO), the Computer Center and the National Sample Survey Office (NSSO). CSO coordinates the statistical activities in the country and also evolves statistical standards the primary function of the National Statistics Office is to collect, compile and release official statistics that are produced "subject to the principles of reliability, objectivity, relevance, statistical confidentiality, transparency, specificity and proportionality"

60(D). Economic development do not depend on factors like profit-loss, sales and Import-Export.
Economic development of a country can be

measured by its per capita income, literacy rate, health status, infant mortality rate and life expectancy of persons living in that country. Economists and statisticians use several methods to track economic growth, the most well-known and frequently tracked is the gross domestic product (GDP). Illegal transactions, such as the black market, sales of stocks and bonds, things produced at home but not sold (cooking, pluming etc), sale of used goods, value of leisure, social well-being, and pollution and other negative externalities cannot be measured under GDP.

61(C). The new name of the Estates General is National Assembly.
The Estates-General had ceased to exist, having become the National Assembly (after 9 July 1789, renamed the National Constituent Assembly). On 13 June 1789, the Third Estate had arrived at a resolution to examine and settle the powers of the three orders. They invited the clergy and nobles to work with them on this endeavor. On 17 June, with the failure of efforts to reconcile the three estates, the Communes completed their own process of verification and almost immediately voted a measure far more radical: they declared themselves redefined as the National Assembly, an assembly not of the estates, but of the people.

62(C). AGMARK is a certification mark employed on agricultural products in India, assuring that they conform to a set of standards approved by the Directorate of Marketing and Inspection, an agency of the Government of India. AGMARK acts as a third-party guarantee for the agricultural products that are produced and consumed in India.

63(B). The Cooperative Societies are supposed to be the cheapest and most important source of rural credit.
A co-operative society is a voluntary association of individuals having common needs who join hands for the achievement of common economic interest . Its aim is to serve the interest of the poorer sections of society through the principle of self-help and mutual help. Cooperative Societies Act is a Central Act. A minimum of ten members are required to form a cooperative society. The Cooperative societies Act do not specify the maximum number of members for any co-operative society.

64(C). Commercial Bank Is not an informal source of credit.
Formal sources may be defined as those which are constituted in some regularized or legal manner in relation to the user , whereas informal sources have no such basis. Banks and cooperative societies constitute the formal sector of credit. Landlords, moneylenders, traders, relatives, friends and other sources of credit constitute the informal sector of credit. Borrowers choose formal credit for riskier (larger) loans while informal credit is preferred for (smaller) projects with low default risk.

65(B). Special Economic Zones (SEZs) are being set up to attract foreign investment.
A special economic zone (SEZ) is an area in which the business and trade laws are different from the rest of the country. SEZs are located within a country's national borders, and their aims include increasing trade balance, employment, increased investment, job creation and effective administration. The main objectives of the SEZ Scheme is generation of additional economic activity, promotion of exports of goods and services, promotion of investment from domestic and foreign sources, creation of employment opportunities along with the development of infrastructure facilities.
Special Economic Zones in India-
• Noida SEZ.
• Kandla SEZ.
• SEEPZ SEZ.
• Cochin SEZ.
• Madras EPZ SEZ.

66(C). Ford Motors set up its first plant in India at Chennai.
Ford entered India back in1995 and has since invested billions of US dollars to set up manufacturing facilities and a network of sales and service centres for new and existing customers across the country. Foreign investment is freely permitted in almost all sectors. Foreign Direct Investments (FDI) can be made under two routes(i) Automatic Route and(ii) Government Route. Under the Automatic Route, the foreign investor or the Indian company does not require any approval from RBI or Government of India for the investment. FDI increases job opportunities in many sectors and uplifts the lifestyle. FDI promotes investment in key areas such as infrastructure development; as a result, there will be more production of capital goods.

67(B). An individual citizen can seek information under the RTI Act, 2005.
The Right to Information (RTI) is an act of the Parliament of India which sets out the rules and procedures regarding citizens' right to information. Under the provisions of RTI Act, any citizen of India may request information from a "public authority" (a body of Government) which is required to reply expeditiously or within thirty days. In case of matter involving a petitioner's life and liberty, the information has to be provided within 48 hours. The basic object of the Right to Information Act is to empower the citizens, promote transparency and accountability in the working of the Government, contain corruption, and make our democracy work for the people in real sense.

68(C). Consumers International is a civil society organisation.
Consumers International is the membership organisation for consumer groups around the world. Founded on 1 April 1960, it has over 250 member organisations in 120 countries. Its head office is based in London, England, with regional offices in Latin America, Asia Pacific, Middle East and Africa. Its aim is to defend, promote, develop and pursue consumer rights as the international basis of consumer protection.

69(B). The imperial state in China was, for a very long time, the major producer of printed material.
The earliest kind of print technology was developed in China, Japan and Korea. This was a system of hand printing. From AD 594 on wards, books in China were printed by rubbing paper – also invented there-against the inked surface of woodblocks. As both sides of the thin, porous sheet could not be printed, the traditional Chinese 'accordion book' was folded and stitched at the side. Superbly skilled craftsmen could duplicate, with remarkable accuracy, the beauty of calligraphy.

70(A). The candidates prepare for this examination from studying textbooks printed for the preparation of this exam.
Textbooks for this examination were printed in vast numbers under the sponsorship of the imperial state. From the sixteenth century, the number of examination candidates went up and that increased the volume of print.

71(B). Linguistic diversity can be found in Belgium.
• Dutch and French are major communities in Belgium.
• 59% of Belgium population speaks Dutch.
• 1% of Belgium population speaks German.
• Rest of them speaks French.

72(B). Both linguistic and religious differences exist in SriLanka.
• Linguistic-Lankan Tamils and Sinhalese
• Religious-Buddhism, Muslim and Hinduism
Roughly three-quarters of SriLankans are Sinhalese; Tamils and Tamil-speaking Muslims make up the remaining quarter. But the population is relatively segregated, with most Tamils concentrated in the north and east. Unlike most officials in the provinces, police are recruited at national level and rotated around the country during their careers (doctors in government hospitals are another troublesome exception). The result is that police stations in Tamil areas are staffed mainly by

Sinhalese, who struggle to communicate with the people they are supposed to be protecting. This, in addition to the mistrust bred by the civil war, puts Tamils off joining the police, compounding the problem.

73(C). In Berlin where European powers meets in 1885 to divide Africa.

With the Berlin Conference, held around 1884-1885, the partition of Africa began. The conference took place in Berlin, the capital city of Germany. During this meeting, Africa was divided between distinct European nations.

74(D). If it is desired in India to switch over to a unitary system of government from the present federal structure such a change can be brought about by A special procedure in Parliament and ratification by a majority of states in the Indian Union.

In India, any changes in the federal features of the constitution, the amendment procedure requires a special majority in parliament and ratification by a majority of states(more than 50 % ratification of the states).

Article 368 of the Indian constitution mentions the procedure for amendments.

75(B). The existence of the three-tier system in India is the key feature of the existence of federalism.

The Central government, the State government, and the Local Self Governments i.e. the Municipalities and Panchayats at the local level makes the governance efficient.

76(B). London in fact came to be known as a Finishing Center before the cloth was sold in the international market.

As we all know, we, Indians were under British imperial rule during the pre-independent period. We are also familiar with the fact that all the Raw materials were exported from India to England in order to process them in the industries present in England and make them into finished goods. London is called a finishing center.

77(C). The method by which soil is formed is called weathering.

Weathering is the process of breaking down rocks by the action of heavy wind, water flow, and climate. Breaking down of rocks yields some small particles which mix with hummus. This mixture of small rocks and humus makes the soil fertile.

So, wind, water, and climate- all three help in soil-formation.

78(A). India has the highest support for democracy.

India's government is loosely modelled on the British Westminster system. It consists of a president as head of state; an executive headed by the prime minister; a legislature consisting of a parliament with an upper and lower house (the Rajya Sabha and Lok Sabha); and a judiciary with a supreme court at its head.

Indian democracy is considered the largest democracy in the world because, its the worlds second largest country in terms of population, people have direct representation in the legislative processes through regular elections and the right to adult suffrage.

79(D). Cooperation from other countries, size of the population, economic priorities adopted by the government these all factors play a role in the economic development of a country.

Some factors for economic development:

- There are two vital factors that influence the economic development of a country, those are; Natural resources and artificial resources.
- Natural resources are the prime factor affecting economic development.
- Natural resources include land area, the quality of soil, forest wealth, rivers, minerals, and oil.
- The secondary factor is also known as non-economic factors in economic development.
- These are mainly, human resources, technical know-how and general education, political freedom, corruption, social organization and desire to develop.

80(B). Gandhi first organised Satyagrah movement in South Africa. Later, he organised it at Champaran in Bihar, Kheda in Gujarat and Ahmedabad in Gujarat.

Mahatma Gandhi went to Champaran in the state of Bihar in the year 1916 and started Satyagraha along with the peasants as a struggle against the exploitative plantation system. Ahmedabad: Another Satyagraha movement was launched in the year 1918. This movement was organised among the workers of cotton mills.

81(B). Famous musician Shakoor Khan was associated with Sarangi.

Ustad Shakoor Khan (1905-1975) was one of the outstanding sarangi players of the twentieth century. He was firmly identified with the Kirana Gharana, being the nephew and student of Ustad Abdul Waheed Khan.

82(A). The Supreme Court and High Courts has/have the power to implement the Fundamental Right. The Fundamental Rights are enshrined in Part III of the Constitution (Articles 12-35). Part III of the Constitution is described as the Magna Carta of India.

83(A). India ranks first in milk production, accounting for 18.5 per cent of world production, achieving an annual output of 146.3 million tones during 2014-15 as compared to 137.69 million tonnes during 2013-14 recording a growth of 6.26 per cent. In terms of per capita consumption, in 2014-15, Punjab had the highest (1032 grams/day) consumption followed by Haryana (877 grams/day). The national capital has the lowest per capita consumption of milk per day at 36 grams.

84(B). Patna High Court exercised jurisdiction over the territories of the Province of Bihar & Orissa till 26 July 1948, when a separate High Court was constituted for Orissa.

85(C). The earthquake in Bhuj in Gujarat on 26 January 2001 was very devastating and devastating. Thousands of people died and millions were injured in this earthquake.

86(B). Linear momentum is defined as the product of a system's mass multiplied by its velocity. In symbols, linear momentum is expressed as p = mv. Momentum is directly proportional to the object's mass and also its velocity. Thus, the greater an object's mass or the greater its velocity, the greater its momentum.

87(D). Lakshadweep is India's smallest Union Territory. Our country, Indian consists of 28 states and 8 union territories. The union territory is not an independent unit but is run by the administrators appointed by the President of India.

- About Lakshadweep:
- The Kavaratti is the capital of the Union Territory Lakshadweep in India.
- India's smallest Union Territory Lakshadweep is an archipelago consisting of 36 islands with an area of 36 sq km.^{2} only Hence option 4 is correct.
- The population on this island is approximately 65,000.

Hence, the correct option is (C).

88(A). Kanada was associated with Vaisheshika School of Philosophy.

- The Sanskrit philosopher Kanada Kashyapa (2nd–3rd century) expounded its theories and is credited with founding the school.
- Vaisheshika, one of the six systems (darshans) of Indian philosophy, significant for its naturalism.
- The Vaisheshika school attempts to identify, inventory, and classify the entities and their relations that present themselves to human perceptions.

89(A). Narmada river ends in the Arabian Sea. Narmada River is also known as Rewa. It is also known as "Life Line of Madhya Pradesh and Gujarat". Narmada rises from Amarkantak Plateau near Anuppur district Madhya Pradesh.

90(C). After the end of the stone Age, man used copper and stone tools together for a long time. These were called the copper age or Chalcolithic age.

91(D). The Battle of Chanderi took place

in the aftermath of the Battle of Khanwa in which the Mughal Emperor Babur had defeated the Rajput Confederacy and firmly established Mughal rule. Babur decided to isolate the Rana by inflicting a military defeat on one of his vassals Medini Rai who was the ruler of Malwa.

92(A). Only A and C are correct.
- The Bengal Army, which in strength formed the bulk of India's three Presidency Armies, had been serving as the 'sword arm' of British Imperialism not only in India but also other countries.
- The recruits in Bengal Army primarily came from an area comprising the present territories of Uttar Pradesh, Western Bihar and Haryana.
- Another point about the Bengal Army was that it was recruited largely on a caste basis.
- The Brahmins and the Rajputs constituted a very large part of the army.
- The Brahmins were often literate, and were seen to be more prone to accept the discipline needed for modern warfare, than the usual 'martial' elements in traditional Indian armies.
- On the other hand, the Rajputs were recruited due to their physical strength and prior military experiences.

So, we can conclude that the Brahmins and the Rajputs were dominating group among the sepoys of Bengal Army around 1857.

93(A). Solar radiation heat-up land faster than the water bodies.

The land has compactly arranged molecules through which conduction takes place and as it is an insulator heat, the heat remains on the surface of the earth i.e. land whereas water has loosely packed molecule heat is transferred by convection and thus it takes a longer time to heat up. Also, water has a higher specific heat capacity, meaning that it requires more energy to heat water to the same temperature as a piece of land. Water also reflects more incoming radiation. The land is dark, rough, and solid, which all contribute to the absorption of the radiation. Unlike water, the land is unable to retain heat for as long as water.

94(C). The Ninth Schedule to the Indian Constitution was added by First Amendment.

The Ninth Schedule contains a list of central and state laws which cannot be challenged in courts. Currently, 284 such laws are shielded from judicial review.

The Schedule became a part of the Constitution in 1951, when the document was amended for the first time. It was created by the new Article 31B, which along with 31A was brought in by the government to protect laws related to agrarian reform and for abolishing the Zamindari system. While. 31A extends protection to 'classes' of laws. 31B shields specific laws or enactments.

95(C). India has won the Women's Doubles and Mixed Doubles Squash titles held in Glasgow in April 2022.

Dipika Pallikal won the women's doubles and mixed doubles titles with Joshna Chinappa and Saurav Ghosal, respectively at the World Doubles Squash Championships in Glasgow on 9 April 2022. Dipika Pallikal and Saurav Ghosal defeated England's Adrian Waller and Alison Waters 11-6, 11-8 in the final at the Scotstoun Leisure Centre.

96(A). On 30 December 1949, he became independent India's first recipient of the Mahavir Chakra.

On 21st October 1947, the Jammu & Kashmir State Forces were ordered to fight and push back thousands of Pakistani raiders all along its borders. The small troop with limited ammunitions sans any road communication, they fought the raiders tenaciously. Kohla-Domel garrison fell to the invaders the following day. Brigadier Singh, the Chief of Military Staff, lead a column to fight the invaders. Maharaja Hari Singh, meanwhile, ordered a further troop of 100 to assist Brigadier Singh. He had to hold off the raiders till help came after 4 days. He defended and saved the Uri-Rampur sector with the help of the Indian Army, but not without sacrificing his life in the process.

97(A). **Newton's First Law of Motion** :
- Everybody continues to be in its state of rest or of uniform motion in a straight line unless compelled by some external force to act otherwise. Therefore, statement 1 is correct.
- The state of rest or uniform linear motion both implies zero acceleration.
- The first law of motion can, therefore, be simply expressed as: If the net external force on a body is zero, its acceleration is zero.
- Acceleration can be non-zero only if there is a net external force on the body.
- The first law refers to the simple case when the net external force on a body is zero.

Newton's Second Law of Motion:
- The second law of motion refers to the general situation when there is a net external force acting on the body.
- The momentum of a body is defined to be the product of its mass m and velocity v and is denoted by p: [p = mv]
- Momentum is clearly a vector quantity.
- The same force for the same time causes the same change in momentum for different bodies.
- The rate of change of momentum of a body is directly proportional to the applied force and takes place in the direction in which the force acts. Therefore, statement 3 is incorrect.

Newton's Third Law of Motion:
- To every action, there is always an equal and opposite reaction. Therefore, statement 2 is incorrect.
- There is no cause-effect relation implied in the third law.
- Consider a pair of bodies A and B. According to the third law, $F_{AB} = -F_{BA}$ [(force on A by B) = − (force on B by A)]

98(C). The first FRB was discovered in 2007. Essentially, FRBs are bright bursts of radio waves.
- Therefore statement A is Correct.

Its durations lie in the millisecond-scale, because of which it is difficult to detect them and determine their position in the sky.
- Therefore statement B is Correct.

Initially, it was believed that the collision of black holes or neutron stars triggers them. But the discovery of repeating FRBs debunked the theory of colliding objects. The source of the FRB detected in April in the Milky Way is a very powerful magnetic neutron star, referred to as a magnetar.

99(D). **"The French Revolution was fought between 1775 and 1783 "** this statement is not correct about the French Revolution.

French Revolution (1789-1799) was a period of social and political upheaval in France resulting in the overthrow of the Monarchy and the establishment of the Republic. American Revolution was fought between 1775 and 1783. American colonies threw off British rule to establish the sovereign United States of America, founded with the Declaration of Independence in 1776 as a result of the American Revolution.

100(D). The United Arab Emirates (UAE) on 21 July 2022 granted Kamal Haasan, one of the Tamil film industry's top stars, its prestigious 'Golden Visa.'

The UAE Golden Visa is a long-term residence visa system, extending from 5 to 10 years. It is granted to achievers from various fields, professionals and those with promising abilities.

Mathematics

1. To construct a pair of tangents to a circle at an angle of $60°$ to each other, it is needed to draw tangents at endpoints of those two radii of the circle, the angle between them should be:

(a) $100°$ (b) $90°$
(c) $120°$ (d) $180°$

2. To divide a line segment PQ in the ratio $m : n$, where m and n are two positive integers, a ray has been draw PX so that $\angle PQX$ makes acute angle and then mark points on ray PX at equal distances such that the minimum number of these points is ______.

(a) $m + n$
(b) $m - n$
(c) $m + n - 1$
(d) Greater than m and n

3. A class teacher has the following absentee record of 40 students of a class for the whole term. Find the mean number of days a student was absent.

Number of days	$0-6$	$6-10$	$10-14$	$14-20$	$20-28$	$28-38$	$38-40$
Number of students	11	10	7	4	4	3	1

(a) 12.475 (b) 15.475
(c) 18.475 (d) 12.575

4. The radii of the two-cylinder are in the ratio of $2 : 3$ and their heights are in the ratio of $5 : 3$. Find the ratio of their volumes.

(a) $20 : 27$ (b) $21 : 28$
(c) $22 : 27$ (d) $23 : 29$

5. A solid piece of iron in the form of a cuboid of dimensions $49cm \times 33cm \times 24cm$ is moulded to form a solid sphere. The radius of the sphere is:

(a) $21cm$ (b) $23cm$
(c) $25cm$ (d) $19cm$

6. Find the smallest positive integer value of k for which quadratic equation $\sqrt{3}x^2 - \sqrt{2}kx + 2\sqrt{3} = 0$, will have distinct real roots?

(a) 3 (b) 4
(c) 1 (d) 2

7. If the roots of the quadratic equation $x^2 - 4x - \log_{10} N = 0$ are real, then what is the minimum value of N?

(a) 1 (b) $\frac{1}{10}$
(c) $\frac{1}{1000}$ (d) $\frac{1}{10000}$

8. The radii of two circles are 19 cm and 9 cm respectively. Find the radius of the circle which has circumference equal to the sum of the circumferences of the two circles.

(a) 28 (b) 38
(c) 48 (d) 58

9. The length of the minute hand of a clock is 14 cm. Find the area swept by the minute hand in 5 minutes. $(\pi = \frac{22}{7})$

(a) $\frac{134}{3}$ cm^2 (b) $\frac{144}{3}$ cm^2
(c) $\frac{154}{3}$ cm^2 (d) $\frac{164}{3}$ cm^2

10. In Figure, find $\tan P - \cot R$.

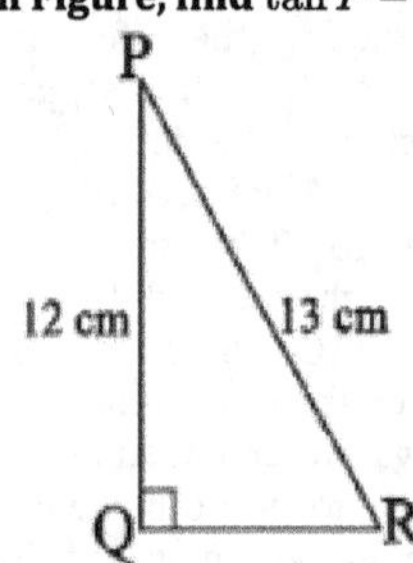

(a) 0 (b) 1
(c) -1 (d) $\frac{1}{2}$

11. Evaluate the following expression:
$\sin x + \sin(x - \pi) + \sin(x + \pi)$

(a) $-\sin x$ (b) $\sin x$
(c) $\sec x$ (d) $\cos x$

12. If $\sec^2 \theta + \tan^2 \theta = 3$ then find the value of $\cot \theta$.

(a) 0 (b) 1
(c) 2 (d) $\sqrt{3}$

13. The shadow of a tower standing on a level plane is found to be 50 m longer when Sun's elevation is $30°$ than when it is $60°$. Find the height of the tower.

(a) $20\sqrt{3}$ (b) $25\sqrt{3}$
(c) $10\sqrt{3}$ (d) $30\sqrt{3}$

14. A system of two linear equations in two variables is inconsistent, if their graphs:

(a) do not intersect at any point
(b) coincide
(c) cut the x-axis
(d) intersect only at a point

15. Solve the linear equations by using elimination method.
$3x - 5y - 4 = 0$ and $9x = 2y + 7$

(a) $x = \frac{2}{13}$ (b) $x = \frac{3}{12}$
(c) $x = \frac{4}{15}$ (d) $x = \frac{9}{13}$

16. If the HCF of 65 and 117 is expressible in the form $65m - 117$, then the value of m is:

(a) 4 (b) 2
(c) 1 (d) 3

17. The largest number which divides 70 and 125, leaving remainders 5 and 8, respectively, is:

(a) 13 (b) 65
(c) 875 (d) $1,750$

18. If a and b are two coprime numbers, then a^3 and b^3 are:

(a) Coprime   (b) Not coprime
(c) Even   (d) Odd

19. Find the HCF and LCM of 84 and 144 by prime factorisation method?

(a) 12 and 1008 (b) 24 and 1009
(c) 48 and 1010 (d) 68 and 1011

20. If $p(x)$ is a polynomial of degree one and $p(a) = 0$, then a is said to be:

(a) Zero of $p(x)$
(b) Value of $p(x)$
(c) Constant of $p(x)$
(d) None of the above

21. Zeroes of a polynomial can be expressed graphically. The number of zeroes of a polynomial is equal to the number of points where the graph of a polynomial:

(a) Intersects x-axis
(b) Intersects y-axis
(c) Intersects x-axis or y-axis
(d) None of the above

22. It is given that in a group of 3 students, the probability of 2 students not having the same birthday is 0.992. What is the probability that the 2 students have the same birthday?

(a) 0.08 (b) 0.008
(c) 0.009 (d) 0.006

23. A sum of $Rs.\,1000$ is invested at 8% simple interest per year. Calculate the interest at the end of each year. Do these interests form an AP? If so, find the interest at the end of 30

years making use of this fact:

(a) $Rs.\,2600$ (b) $Rs.\,2500$
(c) $Rs.\,2400$ (d) $Rs.\,2300$

24. **Find the nth term of the given sequence.**
$4, 6, 8, 10, \ldots$
(a) $2n+4$ (b) $2n-2$
(c) $2n+2$ (d) $2n-4$

25. ABC and BDE are two equilateral triangles such that D is the midpoint of BC. Ratio of the areas of triangles ABC and BDE is:
(a) $2:1$ (b) $1:2$
(c) $4:1$ (d) $1:4$

26. **A guy wire attached to a vertical pole of height 18 m is 24 m long and has a stake attached to the other end. How far from the base of the pole should the stake be driven so that the wire will be taut?**
(a) $6\sqrt{7}\,\text{m}$ (b) $6\sqrt{3}\,\text{m}$
(c) $9\sqrt{7}\,\text{m}$ (d) $9\sqrt{3}\,\text{m}$

27. **A ______ is a simple closed curve all of whose points are at the same distance from a fixed point.**
(a) diameter (b) radius
(c) triangle (d) circle

28. **In the given figure, O is the centre of the circle and L and M are the mid points of AB and CB respectively. If $\angle OAB = \angle OCB$, then:**

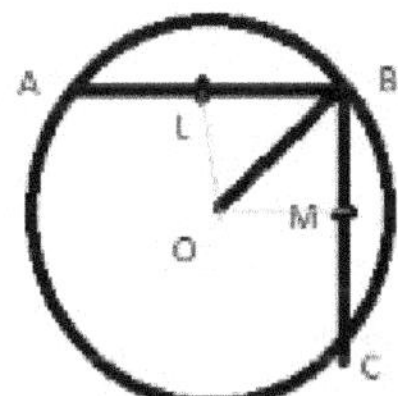

(a) $AM = OB$ (b) $OA = LB$
(c) $BL = BM$ (d) $LM = AB$

29. **If the point $P(x, y)$ is equidistant from the points $A(5, 1)$ and $B(1, 5)$, then:**
(a) $y = 3x$ (b) $x = y$
(c) $x = -8y$ (d) $-8x = y$

30. **The radius of the circle whose end points of diameter are $(24, 1)$ and $(2, 23)$ is:**
(a) $22\sqrt{2}$ units
(b) $23\sqrt{2}$ units
(c) $11\sqrt{2}$ units
(d) None of these

31. **We should reduce the use of plastic**

bags, bottles, etc. because:
(a) They react with the atmospheric gases
(b) They are not durable
(c) They are non-biodegradable
(d) They are made of toxic materials

32. **Among the following choose the correct option which contains only biodegradable items?**
(i) Wood, paper, leather
(ii) Polythene, detergent, PVC
(iii) Plastic, detergent, grass
(iv) Plastic, bakelite, DDT
(a) (i), (ii) and (iii)
(b) (i) and (iii)
(c) (ii), (iii) and (iv)
(d) (ii) and (iv)

33. **A student was given few metals Mg, K, Fe and Cu. Which of them will react only with steam and not with cold or hot water to give H_2 gas?**
(a) Mg (b) K
(c) Fe (d) Cu

34. **Argentite is a mineral of:**
(a) Au (b) Pt
(c) Ag (d) Cu

35. **Which of the following hormones inhibits growth in plants?**
(a) Abscisic acid (b) Cytokinin
(c) Gibberellin (d) Auxin

36. **Which of the following gland has both exocrine and endocrine parts?**
(a) Thyroid
(b) Pituitary
(c) Adrenal
(d) None of the above

37. **Which of the following represents the balanced chemical equation for the reaction of potassium metal with water to form metal hydroxide?**
(a) $2\,K + H_2O \longrightarrow KOH + H_2$
(b) $2\,K(s) + 2H_2O(I) \rightarrow 2KOH(q) + H_2 \uparrow (g)$
(c) $4\,K + 2H_2O \longrightarrow 2KOH + 2H_2$
(d) $K + 2H_2O \longrightarrow KOH + H_2$

38. **Which out of the following statements is true about the below given reaction?**
$4Na(s) + O_2(g) \rightarrow 2Na_2O(s)$
(a) It is an example of a redox reaction.
(b) It is an example of a displacement reaction.
(c) It is an example of reduction of sodium.
(d) It is an example of oxidation of sodium.

39. **The soap molecule has a:**
(a) hydrophilic head and a hydrophobic tail
(b) hydrophobic head and a hydrophilic tail
(c) hydrophobic head and a hydrophobic tail
(d) hydrophilic head and a hydrophilic tail

40. **Which of the following compounds cannot undergo addition reaction, but can undergo substitution reaction?**
(a) Methane (b) Ethene
(c) Acetylene (d) Benzene

41. **Which of the following characteristics does not appear in a girl during puberty?**
(a) Hair growth in armpits
(b) Deepening of voice
(c) Onset of menstruation
(d) Increase in breast size

42. **In humans, the development of embryo takes place in the**
(a) Seminal vesicles
(b) Uterus
(c) Oviduct
(d) Ovaries

43. **Which of the following is a heterozygous-dominant dihybrid condition?**
(a) TTRR (b) Ttrr
(c) TtRr (d) ttRr

44. **Which of the following are the methods of dating fossils?**
(i) Artificial selection
(ii) Relative method
(iii) Selecting isotopic ratio
(iv) Comparing DNA
(a) (i) and (ii) (b) (i) and (iii)
(c) (ii) and (iii) (d) (ii) and (iv)

45. **A plane mirror reflects a beam of light to form a real image. The incident beam is:**
(a) Parallel
(b) Convergent
(c) Divergent
(d) None of the above

46. **A light ray is traveling from air to glass. The angle of incidence on the boundary is $30°$. Find the sine of the angle of refraction.**
(a) $\frac{1}{3}$ (b) 2

(c) 3 (d) 1

47. Find the incorrect statement:
(a) A wire with a red insulation is usually the neutral wire of an electric supply
(b) Field lines emerge from the south pole and merge at north pole
(c) Magnetic field lines can intersect each other
(d) All of the above

48. The right-hand thumb rule is used to find:
(a) Force on a charged particle passing through the magnetic field
(b) Force on a current-carrying conductor placed in a magnetic field
(c) Direction of induced current
(d) Direction of the magnetic field around a current-carrying straight conductor

49. Alcohol is produced by which of the following processes?
(a) Aerobic respiration
(b) Photosynthesis
(c) Anaerobic respiration
(d) Photorespiration

50. Which pigment helps in the transportation of oxygen in humans?
(a) Leghaemoglobin
(b) Haemoerythrin
(c) Haemoglobin
(d) Haemolysin

51. What are the products formed when sodium reacts with acetic acid?
(a) Sodium hydroxide and hydrogen gas
(b) Sodium ethanoate and water
(c) Sodium hydroxide and water
(d) Sodium ethanoate and hydrogen gas

52. If a few drops of a concentrated acid accidentally spills over the hand of a student, what should be done?
(a) Wash the hand with saline solution
(b) Wash the hand immediately with plenty of water and apply a paste of sodium hydrogen carbonate
(c) After washing with plenty of water apply a solution of sodium hydroxide on the hand
(d) Neutralise the acid with a strong

alkali

53. The human eye forms the image of an object at its:
(a) Pupil (b) Retina
(c) Cornea (d) Iris

54. For a circuit shown in the figure, the total current in the circuit is:

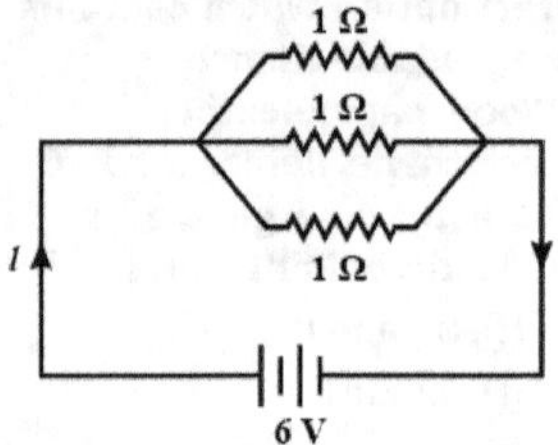

(a) 0.1 A (b) 0.2 A
(c) 18 A (d) 1 A

55. A wire of resistance R divided in 10 equal parts. These parts are connected in parallel. Then equivalent resistance is:
(a) 0.01 R (b) 0.1 R
(c) 10 R (d) 100 R

Social Science

56. Even when water is available in many cities in abundance why is there water scarcity?
(a) Using to utility
(b) Unequal distribution of water
(c) Default in technical areas
(d) Lack of infrastructure for proper distribution

57. Which one of these is a vulnerable species?
(a) Asiatic Buffalo
(b) Desert fox
(c) Gangetic dolphin
(d) Nicobar pigeon

58. Sandstone and Mica are examples of __________.
(a) Non-metallic minerals
(b) Energy minerals
(c) Non-ferrous minerals
(d) Ferrous minerals

59. Name one functioning activity of the Tertiary sector.
(a) Goods that are produced would need to be transported by trucks or trains and then sold in wholesale and retail shops
(b) This sector gradually became associated with the different kinds of industries
(c) Activities in which natural products are changed into other

forms through ways of manufacturing
(d) Produce a good by exploiting natural resources

60. The final price of goods and services produced within the boundary of country is called:
(a) Capital Income
(b) National Income
(c) Per capita income
(d) GDP

61. What actions were taken in the name of the nation?
(a) Army was formed
(b) Social work was done
(c) Hymns were composed, oaths taken and martyrs commemorated, custom duties were abolished
(d) Regular meetings were held

62. Over these years, cultivation methods have changed significantly depending upon the characteristics of:
(a) Type of crop
(b) Technological know-how
(c) Type of season
(d) Government intervention

63. A typical Self Help Group usually has:
(a) 100-200 members
(b) 50-100 members
(c) Less than 10 members
(d) 15-20 members

64. The act of stripping a currency unit of its status as legal tender:
(a) Digital banking
(b) Banking
(c) Demonetisation
(d) Monetization

65. Which of the following industries have been hard hit by foreign competition?
(a) Dairy products
(b) Leather industry
(c) Cloth industry
(d) Vehicle industry

66. In which year did the government decide to remove barriers on foreign trade and investment in India?
(a) 1993 (b) 1992
(c) 1991 (d) 1990

67. Name the court to which a consumer can approach, having a claim of Rs. 40 lakhs:

(a) National Consumer Court
(b) State Consumer Court
(c) District Consumer Court
(d) None of the above

68. The organisation which lays down standards of products at the international level is called:
(a) ISI
(b) ISRO
(c) ISO
(d) WCF

69. What changes occurred in the seventeenth century, as urban culture bloomed in China?
(i) Print was no longer used just by scholar officials
(ii) Merchants used print in their everyday life, as they collected trade information.
(iii) New readership preferred fictional narratives, poetry, autobiographies, anthologies of literary masterpieces, and romantic plays
(iv) women began publishing their poetry and plays. Wives of scholar-officials published their works and courtesans wrote about their lives.
(a) (i) only
(b) (i) and (ii)
(c) All of the above
(d) None of the above

70. What further advancement did this new reading culture bring about?
(a) Mechanical presses were made in China.
(b) Western printing techniques and mechanical presses were imported.
(c) More stress on the block printing method.
(d) Mechanical presses were exported to other countries.

71. What is the percentage of German speaking people in Belgium?
(a) 30
(b) 59
(c) 10
(d) 1

72. Sri Lanka is an island nation, just a few kilometers from the southern coast of:
(a) Goa
(b) Tamil Nadu
(c) Kerala
(d) Lakshadweep

73. Which one of the following countries has an effective right of veto over IMF and World Bank?
(a) India
(b) USA
(c) Srilanka
(d) Japan

74. If it is desired in India to switch over to unitary system of government from the present federal structure such a change can be brought about by ______________.
(a) a simple majority of the members of the Parliament
(b) a two-third majority of members present and voting, provided it is not less than the majority of the total members
(c) a two-third majority of the total membership of the Parliament
(d) a special procedure in Parliament and ratification by a majority of Sates in the Indian Union

75. India is a federal state because its Constitution provides for ______________.
(a) dual citizenship
(b) division of powers between the Union and the States
(c) a written constitution
(d) election of members of Parliament by the people

76. Who introduced the cotton mill?
(a) James Watt
(b) Mathew Boulton
(c) Henry Patullo
(d) Richard Arkwright

77. Land left without cultivation for one or less than one agricultural year is called:
(a) Culturable waste land
(b) Current fallow land
(c) Waste land
(d) None of the above

78. The rates of economic growth for different countries from 1950 to 2000 was highest among ______.
(a) All democratic regimes
(b) Poor countries under dictatorship
(c) Poor countries under democracy
(d) All dictatorial regimes

79. Which of the following statements are true?
(a) Non-democratic regimes often turn a blind eye to or suppress internal social differences.
(b) Ability to handle social differences, divisions and conflicts is thus a definite plus point of democratic regimes.
(c) Democracies usually develop a procedure to conduct their competition.
(d) All of the above.

80. When did Mahatma Gandhi return to India from South Africa?
(a) 1920
(b) 1915
(c) 1921
(d) 1914

General Awareness/ Knowledge

81. Born in Seoni district of Madhya Pradesh, who among the following freedom fighters later became famous Shankaracharya?
(a) Nischalanand Saraswati
(b) Bharati Theertha Mahaswami
(c) Brahmananda Saraswati
(d) Swaroopanand Saraswati

82. What is the maximum strength of the Lok Sabha as envisaged by the Constitution?
(a) 550
(b) 250
(c) 552
(d) 6000

83. The difference between Revenue deficit and grants for creation of Capital assets is:
(a) Revenue deficit
(b) Primary deficit
(c) Effective revenue deficit
(d) Fiscal deficit

84. Provides for physical examination of the victim of rape.
(a) Section 164 (a)
(b) Section 153
(c) Section 153 (6)
(d) Section 154

85. Which of the following statement is not true?
(a) Most of the earth is mantle
(b) Earth's crust is made of sial
(c) The ocean floor is made up of sima
(d) Sima floats over the sial

86. Which of the following term defined SONAR?
(a) Sound Nautical Ranging
(b) Sound Navigation and Ranging
(c) Super Nautical Range
(d) Sound Navigate Ray

87. The jurisdiction of which of the following high courts extends to the Union Territory of Lakshadweep?
(a) Kerala
(b) Tamil Nadu
(c) Bombay
(d) Delhi

88. To which state of India do the 'Khuded' folk songs belong?
(a) Chhattisgarh
(b) Odisha
(c) Jharkhand
(d) Uttarakhand

89. In which union territory of India, Bastille Day is celebrated?

(a) Pondicherry

(b) Daman & Diu

(c) Dadra and Nagar Haveli

(d) Lakshadweep

90. Which of the following is not common in Buddhism and Jainism?

(a) Nonviolence

(b) Indifference to Vedas

(c) S elf-restraint

(d) Rejection of customs and traditions

91. In which year was the first battle of Panipat fought?

(a) In 1226   (b) In 1530

(c) In 1526   (d) In 1556

92. Who implemented the Permanent Settlement?

(a) Wellesley

(b) Warren Hastings

(c) Lord cornwallis

(d) Lord dufferin

93. One of the following factors does not lead to soil formation in nature:

(a) The Sun

(b) Water

(c) Wind

(d) Polythene bags

94. Examine the following statements:
A. The subject prevention of food adulteration is in the 'central list' of Indian Constitution.
B. The Prevention of Food adulteration Act 1954 came into force on 28th September 1954 in India.
Chose the correct answer.

(a) Both A and B are incorrect

(b) Only A is correct

(c) Only B is correct

(d) Both A and B are correct

95. Which country has won the ICC Women's Cricket World Cup 2022 held on 03 April 2022?

(a) England   (b) Pakistan

(c) India   (d) Australia

96. Name the first woman who became a doctor in India?

(a) Kadambini Ganguli

(b) Cornelia Sorabji

(c) Ujwala Rai

(d) Anita Bose

97. Which one of the following statements is correct?
Wavelength of microwaves ranges between

(a) infrared waves and radio waves.

(b) visible waves and infrared light.

(c) γ-rays and X-rays.

(d) X-rays and visible waves.

98. Which one of the following, on adding to water, will not scatter a beam of light ?

(a) Copper sulphate

(b) Chalk powder

(c) Milk

(d) Ink

99. At which of the following was the American Declaration of Independence adopted on 4 July, 1776?

(a) Washington Conference

(b) San Francisco Conference

(c) Second Continental Congress

(d) First Continental Congress

100. Which Indian film bagged two Golden Globe Award nominations?

(a) The Kashmir Files

(b) RRR

(c) Bediya

(d) Avatar

// Hints and Solutions //

1(C). We have constructed a figure according to the ques:

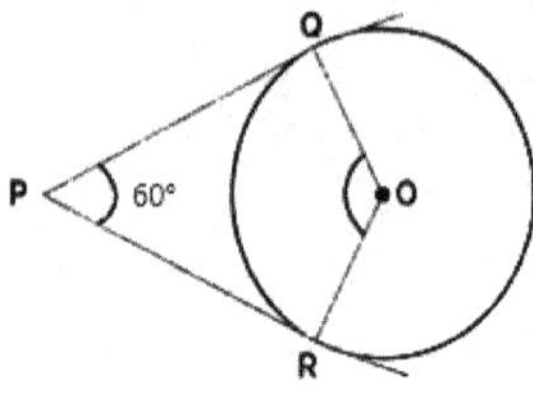

It is given that
O is the centre of a circle to which a pair of tangents PQ and PR from the point P touches the circle at Q and R
$\angle RPQ = 60°$
We know that
$\angle OQP = 90° = \angle ORP$
The angle between a tangent to a circle and the radius of the same circle passing through the point of contact is $90°$
Using the angle sum property of quadrilaterals
$\angle OQP + \angle RPQ + \angle ORP + \angle ROQ = 360°$
Substituting the values
$90° + 60° + 90° + \angle ROQ = 360°$
$\angle ROQ = 120°$
Therefore, the angle between them should be $120°$.

2(A). To divide a line segment PQ in the ratio $m : n$, where m and n are two positive integers, draw a ray PX so that $\angle PQX$ is an acute angle and then mark points on ray PX at equal distances such that the minimum number of these points is $m + n$.

3(A). Let the class size of the data be h. The mean can be found as given below:
$$\bar{X} = a + \left(\frac{\sum f_i u_i}{\sum f_i}\right)$$
Suppose the assured mean (a) of the data is 17.
Class mark (x_i) for each interval is calculated as follows:
$$x_i = \frac{(\text{Upper class limit} + \text{Lower class limit})}{2}$$
d_i, u_i, and $f_i u_i$ can be calculated as follows:

Number of Days	Number of St udents f_i	x_i	$d_i = x_i - 17$	$f_i d_i$
$0 - 6$	11	3	-14	$\overline{15}4$
$6 - 10$	10	8	-9	$\overline{90}$
$10 - 14$	7	$\frac{1}{2}$	-5	$\overline{35}$
$14 - 20$	4	$\frac{1}{7}$	0	0
$20 - 28$	4	$\frac{2}{4}$	7	28
$28 - 38$	3	$\frac{3}{3}$	16	48
$38 - 40$	1	$\frac{3}{9}$	22	22
Total	40			$\overline{18}1$

It can be observed that from the above table
$\sum f_i = 40$
$\sum f_i u_i = -181$
Substituting the value of u_i, and $f_i u_i$ in the formula of mean we get:
$$\bar{X} = a + \left(\frac{\sum f_i u_i}{\sum f_i}\right)$$
$$\overline{X} = 17 + \left(\frac{-181}{40}\right)$$
$$\overline{X} = 17 - 4.525$$
$$\overline{X} = 12.475$$
So, the mean number of days is 12.475 days for which a student was absent.

4(A). Given,
The radii of the two cylinders are in the ratio $2 : 3$.
Let the radius of the first cylinder be $2r$ and the radius of the second cylinder be $3r$.
As the heights are in the ratio of $5 : 3$.
So, the height of the first cylinder be $5h$ and the height of the second cylinder be $3h$.
As we know,
Volume of cylinder $= \pi r^2 h$
Ratio of their volumes $= \dfrac{\pi (r_1)^2 (h_1)}{\pi (r_2)^2 (h_2)}$
$= \dfrac{\pi (2r)^2 (5h)}{\pi (3r)^2 (3h)}$
$= \dfrac{20}{27}$
So, the ratio of their volume is $20 : 27$.

5(A). Given,
Length $(l) = 49 cm$
Breadth $(b) = 33 cm$
Height $(h) = 24 cm$
Let r be the radius of the sphere.
As we know,

Volume of sphere $= \frac{4}{3}\pi r^3$

Volume of cuboid $= l \times b \times h$

Volume of cuboid = Volume of sphere molded

$l \times b \times h = \frac{4}{3}\pi r^3$

$\Rightarrow 49 \times 33 \times 24 = \frac{4}{3} \times \frac{22}{7} r^3$

$\Rightarrow \frac{49 \times 33 \times 24 \times 3 \times 7}{4 \times 22} = r^3$

$\Rightarrow 9261 = r^3$

$\Rightarrow (21)^3 = r^3$

$\therefore r = 21 cm$

So, the radius of sphere is $21 cm$.

6(B). Given:

Quadratic equation $\sqrt{3}x^2 - \sqrt{2}kx + 2\sqrt{3} = 0$, has distinct real roots.

As we know that, if a quadratic equation $ax^2 + bx + c = 0$ has distinct real roots then $\Delta > 0$ where $\Delta = b^2 - 4ac$.

Here, $a = \sqrt{3}, b = -\sqrt{2}k$ and $c = 2\sqrt{3}$

$\Rightarrow (-\sqrt{2}k)^2 - 4 \times \sqrt{3} \times 2\sqrt{3} > 0$

$\Rightarrow 2k^2 - 24 > 0$

$\Rightarrow k^2 > 12$

$\because k$ is smallest positive integer. so $k = 4$

7(D). Given:

The quadratic equation $x^2 - 4x - \log_{10} N = 0$

As we know,

The quadratic equation $ax^2 + bx + c = 0$

For minimum value of $b^2 - 4ac \geq 0$

If $\log_a b = c$

Then $b = a^c$

Now,

The quadratic equation $x^2 - 4x - \log_{10} N = 0$

Compare the above equation $ax^2 + bx + c = 0$

Then $a = 1, b = -4$ and $c = -\log_{10} N$

Putting the value of $b^2 - 4ac \geq 0$

$\Rightarrow (-4)^2 - 4 \cdot 1 \cdot (-\log_{10} N) \geq 0$

$\Rightarrow 16 = -4 \cdot \log_{10} N$

$\Rightarrow \log_{10} N = -4$

$\Rightarrow N = (10)^{-4}$

$\Rightarrow N = \frac{1}{10000}$

8(A). Given,

Radius of 1st circle $= r_1 = 19$ cm

Radius of 2nd circle $= r_2 = 9$ cm

Circumference of 3rd circle = Circumference of 1st circle + Circumference of 2nd circle

Let the radius of $3rd$ circle be r cm

Now,

Circumference of $1st$ circle $= 2\pi r_1$

$= 2\pi(19)$

$= 38\pi$

Circumference of 2nd circle $= 2\pi r_2$

$= 2\pi(9)$

$= 18\pi$

Circumference of 3rd circle $= 2\pi r$

Using given condition,

$2\pi r = 38\pi + 18\pi$

$= 56\pi$

$\Rightarrow r = \frac{56\pi}{2\pi}$

$= 28$

Therefore, the radius of the circle which having circumference equal to the sum of the circumference of the given two circles is 28 cm.

9(C).

Given that,

Radius of clock or circle $= r = 14$ cm.

We know that, in 1 hour (i.e., 60 minutes), the minute hand rotates $360°$.

Thus, in 5 minutes, minute hand will rotate

$= \frac{360°}{60°} \times 5$

$= 30°$

Now,

the area swept by the minute hand in 5 minutes = the area of a sector of $30°$ in a circle of 14 cm radius.

Area of sector of angle $\theta = \frac{\theta}{360°} \times \pi r^2$

Thus, Area of sector of $30° = \frac{30°}{360°} \times \frac{22}{7} \times 14 \times 14$

$= \frac{11 \times 14}{3}$

$= \frac{154}{3}$ cm^2

Therefore, the area swept by the minute hand in 5 minutes is $\frac{154}{3}$ cm^2.

10(A). Given,

In $\triangle PQR$,

PQ=12 cm, PR=13 cm, $\angle Q = 90°$

Apply Pythagoras theorem in $\triangle PQR$

Hypotenuse^2= Perpendicular^2 + Base^2

$PR^2 = PQ^2 + QR^2$

$(13)^2 = (12)^2 + QR^2$

$169 = 144 + QR^2$

$25 = Q^2$

$QR = 5$

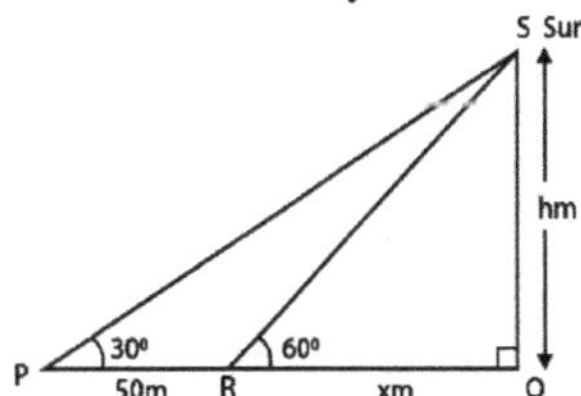

$\tan P = \frac{\text{Side opposite to } \angle P}{\text{Side adjacent to } \angle P} = \frac{QR}{PQ}$

$= \frac{5}{12}$

$\cot R = \frac{\text{Side adjacent to } \angle R}{\text{Side opposite to } \angle R} = \frac{QR}{PQ}$

$= \frac{5}{12}$

$\tan P - \cot R = \frac{5}{12} - \frac{5}{12} = 0$

11(A). Given,

$\sin x + \sin(x - \pi) + \sin(x + \pi)$

As we know that,

$\sin(\pi - x) = \sin x$

$\sin(\pi + x) = -\sin x$

$\sin(-x) = -\sin x$

Therefore,

$= \sin x - \sin(\pi - x) - \sin(\pi + x)$

$= \sin x - \sin(\pi - x) - \sin x$

$= -\sin(\pi - x)$

$= -\sin x$

12(B). Given,

$\sec^2 \theta + \tan^2 \theta = 3$ ...(i)

Subtracting 1 from both sides in equation (i) we get,

$\sec^2 \theta + \tan^2 \theta - 1 = 3 - 1$ $(\because$

$\sec^2 \theta - 1 = \tan^2 \theta)$

$\Rightarrow \tan^2 \theta + \tan^2 \theta = 2$

$\Rightarrow 2\tan^2 \theta = 2$

$\Rightarrow \tan^2 \theta = 1$

$\Rightarrow \tan \theta = 1$

Now,

$\cot \theta = \frac{1}{\tan \theta}$

$= 1$

13(B). Let $SQ = h$ be the height of tower. $\angle SPQ = 30°$ and $\angle SRQ = 60°$

According to the question, the length of shadow is $50m$ long hen angle of elevation of the sun is $30°$ than when it was $60°$. So, $PR = 50m$ and $RQ = xm$

In $\triangle SRQ$,

$\tan 60° = \frac{SQ}{RQ}$ $\left[\because \tan \theta = \frac{\text{Perpendicular}}{\text{Base}}\right]$

$\Rightarrow \sqrt{3} = \frac{h}{x}$ $[\because \tan 60° = \sqrt{3}]$

$\Rightarrow x = \frac{h}{\sqrt{3}}$

In $\triangle SPQ$,

$\tan 30° = \frac{SQ}{PQ} = \frac{SQ}{PR+RQ}$

$\Rightarrow \frac{1}{\sqrt{3}} = \frac{h}{50+x}$ $\left[\because \tan 30° = \frac{1}{\sqrt{3}}\right]$

$\Rightarrow 50 + x = \sqrt{3}h$

Substituting the value of x in the above equation, we get

$50 + \frac{h}{\sqrt{3}} = \sqrt{3}h$

$\Rightarrow \frac{50\sqrt{3}+h}{\sqrt{3}} = \sqrt{3}h$

$\Rightarrow 50\sqrt{3} + h = 3h$

$\Rightarrow 50\sqrt{3} = 3h - h$

$\Rightarrow 3h - h = 50\sqrt{3}$

$\Rightarrow 2h = 50\sqrt{3}$

$\Rightarrow h = \frac{50\sqrt{3}}{2}$

$\Rightarrow h = 25\sqrt{3}$

So, the height of the tower is $25\sqrt{3}\,m$.

14(A). A system of two linear equations in two variables is inconsistent, if their graphs do not intersect at any point.

If a consistent system has an infinite number of solutions, it is dependent. When you graph the equations, both equations represent the same line. If a system has no solution, it is said to be inconsistent. The graphs of the lines do not intersect, so the graphs are parallel and there is no solution.

15(D). $3x - 5y = 4 \ldots\ldots$ (i)

$9x - 2y = 7 \ldots\ldots$ (ii)

Multiplying eqn (i) by 3

$9x - 15y = 12 \ldots\ldots$ (iii)

subtract eqn (iii) from (ii)

$13y = -5$

$y = -\dfrac{5}{13}$

Put in eqn (i)

$3x - 5 \times \dfrac{-5}{13} = 4$

Multiplying by 13 on both side

$39x + 25 = 52$

$39x = 27$

$x = \dfrac{9}{13}$

16(B). Finding HCF of 65 and 117

$$\begin{array}{r|l} 5 & 65 \\ \hline 13 & 13 \\ \hline & 1 \end{array} \qquad \begin{array}{r|l} 3 & 117 \\ \hline 3 & 39 \\ \hline 13 & 13 \\ \hline & 1 \end{array}$$

$65 = 5 \qquad \times \boxed{13}$

$117 = 3 \times 3 \times \boxed{13}$

So, HCF of 65 and 117 = 13

Now,

As per question,

HCF $= 65m - 117$

$13 = 65m - 117$

$13 + 117 = 65m$

$130 = 65m$

$65m = 130$

$m = \dfrac{130}{65}$

$m = 2$

17(A). Let's subtract the remainders from the numbers:

$70 - 5 = 65$

$125 - 8 = 117$

So, we need to find largest number which divides 65 and 117, and leaves remainder 0

.

Thus, we need largest number which divides 65 and 117.

$\therefore$ We need to find HCF of 65 and 117.

$$\begin{array}{r|l} 5 & 65 \\ \hline 13 & 13 \\ \hline & 1 \end{array} \qquad \begin{array}{r|l} 3 & 117 \\ \hline 3 & 39 \\ \hline 13 & 13 \\ \hline & 1 \end{array}$$

$65 = 5 \qquad \times \boxed{13}$

$117 = 3 \times 3 \times \boxed{13}$

So, HCF of 65 and 117 = 13

18(A). Since a and b are coprime a^3 and b^3 will also be co-prime

Example:

2 and 3 are coprime

And, $2^3 = 8$, and $3^3 = 27$

$\therefore$ 8 and 27 are also coprime.

19(A). Prime factorisation of 84 and 144 are:

$84 = 2 \times 2 \times 3 \times 7 = 2^2 \times 3^1 \times 7^1$ and

$144 = 2 \times 2 \times 2 \times 2 \times 3 \times 3 = 2^4 \times 3^2$

$\therefore$ HCF $(84, 144) = 2^2 \times 3^1 = 4 \times 3 = 12$ and

LCM $(84, 144) = 2^4 \times 3^2 \times 7^1 = 16 \times 9 \times 7 = 1008$

20(A). Let $p(x) = mx + n$ (given in question that $p(x)$ is one degree polynomial)

Put $x = a$

$p(a) = ma + n = 0$

So, a is zero of $p(x)$.

21(A). When the graph of the polynomial does not intersect the x-axis then the number of zeroes of that polynomial is 0. Hence, the number of zeroes of a polynomial is equal to the number of times the graph of the polynomial intersects the x-axis.

Hence, the correct option is (B).

22(B). Given,

$P(E) = 0.992$

Let the event wherein 2 students having the same birthday be E.

As we know that,

$P(E) + P(\text{not } E) = 1$

Or, $P(\text{not } E) = 1 - 0.992 = 0.008$

$\therefore$ The probability that the 2 students have the same birthday is 0.008.

23(C). We know that the formula to calculate simple interest is given by

$\text{Simple Interest} = \dfrac{P \times R \times T}{100}$

So, the interest at the end of the 1st year

$= Rs. \dfrac{1000 \times 8 \times 1}{100} = Rs. 80$

The interest at the end of the 2nd year

$= Rs. \dfrac{1000 \times 8 \times 2}{100} = Rs. 160$

The interest at the end of the 3rd year

$= Rs. \dfrac{1000 \times 8 \times 3}{100} = Rs. 240$

Similarly, we can obtain the interest at the end of the 4th year, 5th year, and so on.

So, the interest (in $Rs.$) at the end of the $1^{st}, 2^{nd}, 3^{rd}, \ldots$ years, respectively are $80, 160, 240, \ldots$

It is an AP as the difference between the consecutive terms in the list is 80, i.e., $d = 80$.

Also, $a = 80$.

So, to find the interest at the end of 30 years, we shall find a_{30}.

Now,

$a_{30} = a + (30 - 1)d = 80 + 29 \times 80 = 2400$

So, the interest at the end of 30 years will be $Rs. 2400$.

24(C). The given sequence is $4, 6, 8, 10 \ldots n^{th}$

The general or n^{th} term of an AP is given as

$T_n = a + (n - 1)d$

Where

$a = $ first term

$d = $ common difference

In this given sequence, the value of d is 2.

$\therefore d = a_2 - a_1 = a_3 - a_2 \ldots$

Substitution the given values,

$T_n = 4 + (n - 1) \times 2$

$\Rightarrow T_n = 4 + 2n - 2$

$\Rightarrow T_n = 2n + 2$

25(C). Given:

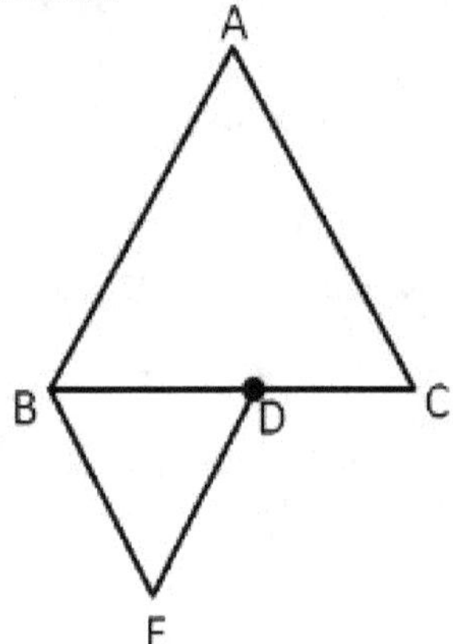

Given:

$\triangle ABC$ is equilateral

$\triangle BDE$ is equilateral

$BD = \dfrac{1}{2}BC$ as D is midpoint of BC

To find: $\dfrac{ar \triangle ABC}{ar \triangle BDE}$

Since, $\triangle ABC$ and $\triangle BDE$ are equilateral, Their sides would be in the same ratio

$\dfrac{AB}{BE} = \dfrac{AC}{ED} = \dfrac{BC}{BD}$

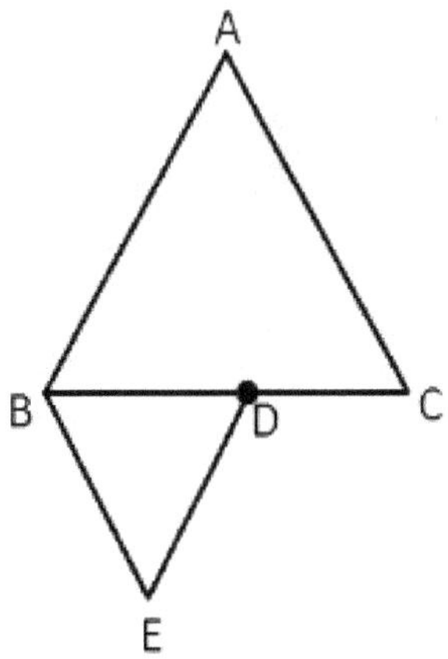

So, by SSS similarity
$\triangle ABC \sim \triangle BDE$
And, we know that ratio of area of triangle is equal To the ratio of square of corresponding sides.

So, $\dfrac{\text{area of } \triangle ABC}{\text{area of } \triangle BDE} = \dfrac{(BC)^2}{(BD)^2}$

$= \dfrac{(BC)^2}{\left(\frac{BC}{2}\right)^2}$ (Since $BD = \frac{1}{2}BC$)

$= \dfrac{BC^2}{\frac{BC^2}{4}}$

$= \dfrac{4BC^2}{BC^2}$

$= \dfrac{4}{1}$

So, $\dfrac{\text{area of } \triangle ABC}{\text{area of } \triangle BDE} = \dfrac{4}{1}$ i.e. $4:1$

26(A). Given:
Let Height of vertical pole $= AB = 18$ m
Let length of wire $= AC = 24$ m

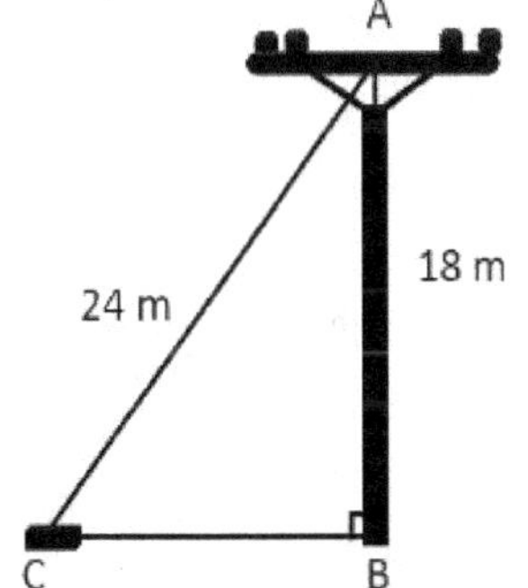

To Find: Distance from the base of the pole to the another end of the wire i.e., (BC).
Since the pole will be perpendicular (vertical) to ground.
$\angle ABC = 90°$
$\Rightarrow \triangle ABC$ is a right angle triangle.
So, in right angle triangle ABC
Using Pythagoras theorem,

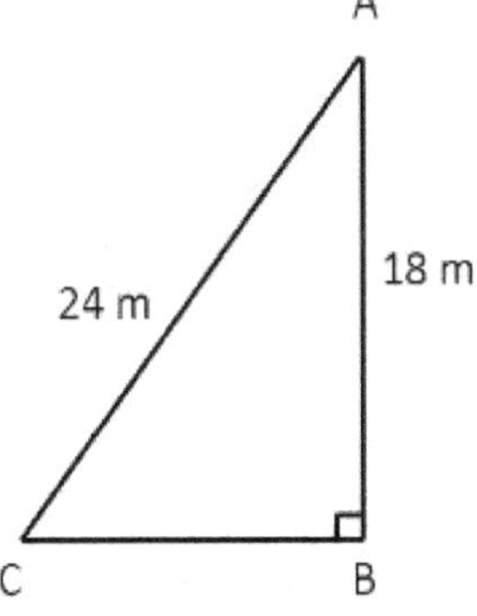

(Hypotenuse) $^2 =$ (Height) $^2+$ (Base) ^{2}
$(AC)^2 = (AB)^2 + (BC)^2$
$(24)^2 = (18)^2 + (BC)^2$
$576 = 324 + B^2$
$576 - 324 = B^2$
$252 = BC^2$
$BC = \sqrt{252}$
$BC = \sqrt{36 \times 7}$
$BC = \sqrt{6 \times 6 \times 7}$
$BC = 6\sqrt{7}$
So, the stake may be placed at distance $(BC) = 6\sqrt{7}$ m, from the base of the pole.

27(D). A circle is a simple closed curve all of whose points are at the same distance from a fixed point.
A circle is a figure consisting of all points in a plane that lie at a given point, a certain distance from the center; uniformly it is a curve formed by a point that moves in a plane so that its distance from a given point is constant. The distance between any point on the circle and the center is called the radius. Radius is a positive number.

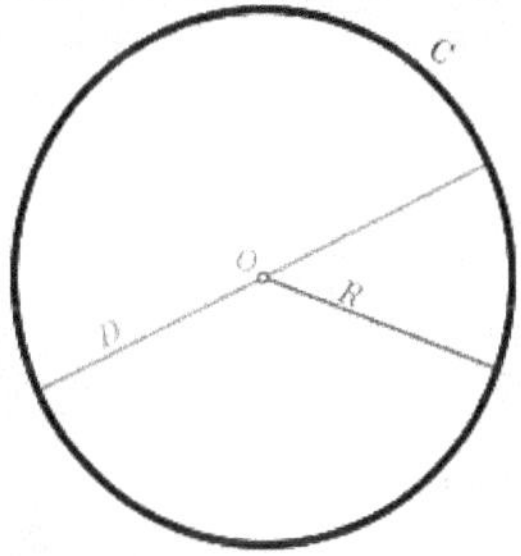

28(C). As we know that,

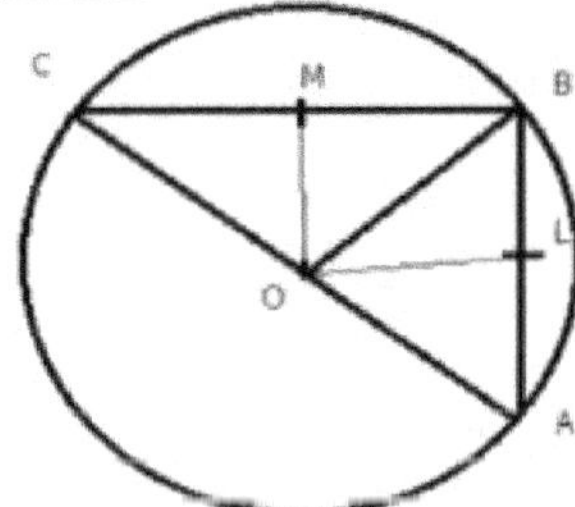

In $\triangle ALO$ and $\triangle OCM$,
$OA = OC$ [radius of the same circle]
$\angle OAL = \angle OCM$ [Given]
$\angle OLA = \angle OMC = 90°$ [length of bisector of chord is $\perp r$ to the chord]
$\triangle ALO \cong \triangle OCM$ [Angle-Angle-Side Postulate]

$\therefore AL = CM$ [by Corresponding parts of Congruent triangles]
$BL = BM$ [L and M are the midpoints of AB and BC respectively]

29(B). Given, point $P(x, y)$ is equidistant from the points $A(5, 1)$ and $B(1, 5)$.
So, $AP = BP$
$\Rightarrow AP^2 = BP^2$ [on squaring both sides]
$\Rightarrow (x - 5)^2 + (y - 1)^2 = (x - 1)^2 + (y - 5)^2$

$\because \text{distance} = \sqrt{(x_2 - x_1)^2 + (y_2 - y_1)^2}$

$\Rightarrow x^2 + 25 - 10x + y^2 + 1 - 2y = x^2 + 1 - 2x + y^2 + 25 - 10y$
$\Rightarrow \left[\because (a - b)^2 = a^2 + b^2 - 2ab\right]$
$\Rightarrow -10x + 2x = -10y + 2y$
$\Rightarrow -8x = -8y$
$\Rightarrow x = y$

30(C). The distance between ends points of the diameter gives the value of the diameter.
Here, the points are $(24, 1)$ and $(2, 23)$
$\therefore d = \sqrt{(2 - 24)^2 + (23 - 1)^2}$
$= \sqrt{(-22)^2 + (22)^2}$
$= \sqrt{(22)^2(1 + 1)}$
$= 22\sqrt{2}$ units

$\therefore$ Radius of a circle $r = \dfrac{d}{2} = \dfrac{22\sqrt{2}}{2}$

$= 11\sqrt{2}$ units.

31(C). Plastics bags and bottles come under the category of non-biodegradable products because they cannot be broken down by natural processes and tend to damage the safety of the environment.
Plastic bags and bottles start out as fossil fuels and end up as deadly waste in landfills and the ocean. Birds often mistake shredded plastic bags for food, filling their stomachs with toxic debris. For hungry sea turtles, it's nearly impossible to distinguish between jellyfish and floating plastic shopping bags.

32(D). Biodegradable items are those, which can be degraded by biological agencies like detrivores. These organisms feed on the dead and decaying matter and convert them into minerals and return those minerals back to the environment, thus completing the cycle of nutrients. Non-biodegradable items are those which cannot be acted upon by detrivores. Thus, such items cannot be degraded or decomposed. In a way, they are a permanent addition to the environment and cannot be done away with. For example, polythene, thermosetting plastics like bakelite, insecticides like DDT, detergent, PVC, etc. These items cannot be degraded biologically.

33(C). Iron (Fe) does not react with hot or cold water. It only reacts with steam to give hydrogen gas.
Magnesium (Mg) does not react with cold water but reacts with hot water to give

hydrogen gas.
Potassium (K) reacts violently with cold water to give hydrogen gas.
Copper (Cu) does not react with hot/cold water or steam.

34(C). Argentite is a mineral of Ag . Argentite is a silver sulfide mineral and is an important constituent of silver ore deposits. It contains around 87% silver.

35(A). Abscisic acid is the plant growth hormone which is responsible for inhibiting growth. The hormone causes inhibition in the growth of the roots and shoots. The hormone also causes abscission which is the falling of the leaves, fruits and flowers. The hormone suppresses all the processes in the plants during unfavourable conditions.

36(D). The endocrine system is composed of ductless glands. Endocrine glands secrete hormones. Glands that have ducts are called exocrine glands. The secretions of exocrine glands reach their target by travelling through a duct (tube). The mixed gland is a gland that produces endocrine and exocrine secretions. The pancreas is an example of a mixed gland because it secretes hormones in the circulation, like insulin and glucagon, but it also releases an exocrine secretion, the pancreatic juice. Whereas, thyroid, pituitary and adrenal glands are not having both endocrine and exocrine system.

37(B). Potassium K metal reacts with water H_2O to give potassium hydroxide (KOH) and hydrogen gas (H_2) . The reaction for this process is:
$$K + H_2O \rightarrow KOH + H_2 \uparrow \text{(gas)}$$
A balanced chemical equation represents a chemical equation in which the number of atoms of each element on both reactant and product sides are the same. The balanced chemical equation for the given reaction is:
$$2K(s) + 2H_2O(l) \rightarrow 2KOH(aq) + H_2 \uparrow (g)+$$
heat energy.

38(D). The substance that loses electrons is oxidized and is called reducing agent. The substance that gains electrons is reduced and is called oxidizing agent. In the given equation, the addition of sodium (Na) , oxygen (O_2) to sodium oxide (Na_2O) is getting oxidised.
$$4Na(s) + O_2(g) \rightarrow 2Na_2O(s)$$
Oxidized substance- Na
Reduced substance- O_2

39(A). The basic structure of all soaps is essentially the same, consisting of a long hydrophobic (water-fearing) hydrocarbon chain tail and a hydrophilic (water-loving) anionic head.

40(A). Addition reactions are limited to chemical compounds that have multiple bonds, such as compounds with carbon-carbon double bonds (alkenes), or with triple bonds (alkynes), and compounds that have rings, Methane does not undergo an addition reaction as it is a saturated compound but it can undergo substitution reaction as it has replaceable hydrogen atom.

41(B). Deepening of voice does not appear in a girl during puberty.
Girls' breasts begin to develop during puberty. The ovaries grow in girls, and eggs begin to develop. Ovaries also begin to release mature eggs (Menstruation starts). As a result of increased sweat and sebaceous gland activity, girls develop acne and pimples and hair growth in their body.

42(B). Once the fertilization takes place in the Fallopian tube, the zygote then moves to the uterus. In uterus, implantation occurs and then the further development of the embryo takes place in the uterus until birth. A special pouch like structure is formed in the uterus to provide nutrients and for the excretion of metabolites from the fetus.

43(C). A phenomenon in which two organisms with two pairs of traits or contrasting characters are crossed is called a dihybrid cross. In the genotype TtRr, T and R are gametes for dominant traits and t and r are gametes for recessive traits.

44(C). Relative dating is used to determine a fossils approximate age by comparing it to similar rocks and fossils of known ages. Absolute dating is used to determine a precise age of a fossil by using radiometric dating to measure the decay of isotopes, either within the fossil or more often the rocks associated with it. There are several common radioactive isotopes that are used for dating rocks, artifacts and fossils.

45(B). A plane mirror reflects a beam of light to form a real image. The incident beam is convergent.
You should be able to show this by drawing a "ray diagram" for the light beam. The reflected rays converge and that's what's needed to produce a real image.
A "real object" always produces a "virtual image" in a plane mirror. That's because the reflected rays diverge.
Interestingly, a plane mirror can form a real image of the object itself as virtual.

46(A). Given:
The angle of incidence is i $= 30°$
Refractive index of glass is $n_g = 1.5$
Refractive index of air is $n_a = 1$
The sine angle of refraction $\sin r = ?$
Using Snell's law we can write,
$$n_a \times \sin i = n_g \times \sin r$$
$$\therefore \sin r = \frac{n_a \times \sin i}{n_g}$$
$$= \frac{1 \times \sin 30°}{1.5}$$
$$= \frac{1}{3}$$

47(D). Magnetic field emerges from north pole to south pole and have only one direction, thus no two field lines overlap. A wire with a red insulation is usually the live wire of an electric supply. In old convention, the red wire is the live wire, the black wire is neutral and the earth wire is given green insulation. So, all sentence are incorrect.

48(D). The right-hand thumb rule is used to find the direction of the magnetic field around a current-carrying straight conductor.
Right-hand rules states that "If the current carrying conductor is held in the right hand by pointing thumb finger towards the direction of current flow and the other fingers curled around the conductor then the curled fingers indicate the direction of the magnetic field due to the current carrying conductor". This rule only gives the direction of the magnetic field of the current carrying conductor.

49(C). Alcohol is produced by anaerobic respiration processes. Anaerobic respiration is the type of respiration through which cells can break down sugars to generate energy in the absence of oxygen. Alcohol is produced in alcoholic fermentation. In this type of anaerobic respiration, glucose is split into ethanol or ethyl alcohol. This process also produces two ATP per sugar molecule. This occurs in yeast and even in some types of fish, such as goldfish.

50(C). Haemoglobin transports oxygen molecules to all the body cells for cellular respiration. The haemoglobin pigment present in the blood gets attached to O_2 molecules that are obtained from breathing and thus forms oxyhaemoglobin. This oxygenated blood is then distributed to all the body cells by the heart. After giving away O_2 to the body cells, blood takes away CO_2 which is the end product of cellular respiration and blood becomes de-oxygenated.

51(D). Sodium ethanoate and hydrogen gas are the products formed when sodium reacts with acetic acid. Organic acids react with acids to form strong alkali metals to form strong basic salts with the liberation of hydrogen gas.
As we know ethanoic acid is a weak organic acid and when it reacts with sodium metal it results in the formation of sodium ethanoate or commonly called sodium acetate and the liberation of hydrogen takes place.
$$2CH_3COOH + 2Na \longrightarrow 2CH_3COONa + H_2$$
The product formed from the reaction is enthanote or sodium acetate.

52(B). Washing affected hand with plenty

of water will reduce the concentration of the acid. Remaining traces of the acid can be neutralized by applying a paste of Hydrogen carbonate which is basic in nature. Though $NaOH$ is also a base but it is corrosive in nature hence it is not used to neutralize the acid.

53(B). The human eye forms the image of an object at its retina.
Retina works like a screen or camera film. Retina is full of light and colour sensitive cells. These cells, upon receiving image send electrical signals to the brain, which processes these information to make a mental image of what we see.

54(C). Given,
Resistance of each resistors, $R = 1\Omega$
$R_1 = R_2 = R_3 = R$
Voltage across the battery,
$V = 6\,V$
Equivalent resistances of 3 resistors connected in parallel
$$\frac{1}{R_{eq}} = \frac{1}{R_1} + \frac{1}{R_2} + \frac{1}{R_3}$$
$$\frac{1}{R_{eq}} = \frac{1}{R} + \frac{1}{R} + \frac{1}{R} = \frac{3}{R}$$
$$R_{eq} = \frac{1}{3}\Omega$$
We know that,
Current, $I = \dfrac{V}{R}$
$I = 6 \times 3$
$I = 18\,A$

55(A). Given:
Resistance of wire $= R$
Resistance of a wire is proportional to its length. The wire is cut into 10 equal parts.
So, resistance of each part $= \dfrac{R}{10}$. Then all 10 wires are connected in parallel.
the equivalent resistance is:
$$\frac{1}{R_{eq}} = \frac{1}{\frac{R}{10}} + \frac{1}{\frac{R}{10}} + \ldots\ldots\ldots (10 \text{ times })$$
$$\frac{1}{R_{eq}} = \frac{100}{R}$$
$$R_{eq} = \frac{R}{100}$$
$$R_{eq} = 0.01\,R$$

56(B). Due to unequal distribution of water there is scarcity in water:
- The availability of water resources varies over space and time, mainly due to the variations in seasonal and annual precipitation.
- Over-exploitation, excessive use and unequal access to water among different social groups may cause water scarcity.
- Water scarcity may also be an outcome of large and growing population and consequent greater demands for water. A large population means more water to produce more food. Hence, to facilitate higher food-grain production, water resources are being over exploited to expand irrigated areas for dry-season agriculture.
- Most farmers have their own wells and tubewells in their farms for irrigation to

increase their production. But it may lead to falling groundwater levels, adversely affecting water availability and food security of the people. Thus, in spite of abundant water there is water scarcity.

57(C). Gangetic dolphin is one of these vulnerable species.
Ganges River dolphins (Platanista gangetica gangetica) occur in the Ganges-Brahmaputra River system primarily in India and Bangladesh. It is listed as an endangered species in the International Union for Conservation of Nature (IUCN) Red Book and as a Flagship Species by WWF. It is placed in Schedule-I of the Wildlife (Protection) Act, 1972.

58(A). Sandstone and Mica are examples of Non-metallic minerals.
Rocks are combinations of homogeneous substances called minerals. Ranging from the hardest diamond to the softest talc, minerals are found in varied forms in nature. Minerals are usually found in "ores". An accumulation of any mineral mixed with other elements is known as ore. To make its extraction commercially viable, the mineral content of the ore must be in sufficient concentration. Minerals are classified into three types- Metallic, Non-Metallic, and Energy Minerals, out of which Metallic minerals are of three types- Ferrous, Non-Ferrous, and Precious metals.

59(A). One activity of the Tertiary sector is goods that are produced would need to be transported by trucks or trains and then sold in wholesale and retail shops.
The tertiary sector covers a wide range of activities from commerce to administration, transport, financial and real estate activities, business and personal services, education, health and social work. It is made of the non-market sector (public administration, education, human health, social work activities). The tertiary industry sector makes up the vast majority of employment opportunities and is solely focused on providing services, not goods, to consumers and other organizations. For this reason, it is also known as the service sector.

60(D). The final price of goods and services produced within the boundary of country is called GDP.
GDP can be calculated by adding up all of the money spent by consumers, businesses, and government in a given period. It may also be calculated by adding up all of the money received by all the participants in the economy. In either case, the number is an estimate of "nominal GDP. "Nominal GDP is an assessment of economic production in an economy but includes the current prices of goods and services in its calculation. GDP is typically measured as the monetary value of goods and services produced.

61(C). Actions were taken in the name of the nation are hymns were composed, oaths taken and martyrs commemorated, custom duties were abolished.
In the name of the nation, New hymns were composed, oaths taken and martyrs commemorated. They established a centralized administrative system, which formulated uniform laws for all citizens. They adopted a uniform system of weights and measures. All internal custom duties were abolished.

62(B). Over these years, cultivation methods have changed significantly depending upon the characteristics of physical environment, technological know-how and socio-cultural practices.
Farming varies from subsistence to commercial type. At present, in different parts of India, the following farming systems are practised.With progress of time, man has improved and modernised the methods of cultivation. Depending upon the climate, environment, needs of the people and the agricultural tools and equipments they possess, different cultivation methods prevail in different parts of India and the world. They range from subsistence to commercial types. They are as rudimentary as shifting cultivation to as sophisticated as plantations and horticulture.

63(D). A typical Self Help Group usually has 15-20 members.
Self-Help Groups (SHGs) are informal associations of people who choose to come together to find ways to improve their living conditions . It can be defined as self governed, peer controlled information group of people with similar socio-economic background and having a desire to collectively perform common purpose. It has three components i.e. microcredit, entrepreneurship and empowerment. It has three tier structure as neighborhood groups (SHG) , area development society (15-20 SHGs) and Community development society (federation of all groups).

64(C). The act of stripping a currency unit of its status as legal tender is called Demonetisation.
It occurs whenever there is a change in national currency. The current form or forms of money is pulled from circulation and retired, often to be replaced with new notes or coins. The following are the main features of Demonetisation:
(i) Elimination of Black Money: Black money is a household name in India. It refers to unaccounted money.
(ii) Eradication of Corruption: High-value currency notes are the commonly accepted medium or bribe. The government wants to strike at the root of corruption by banning these notes.
(iii) Elimination of Counterfeit Currency: A

note ban would have implied the elimination of counterfeit currency.

(iv) Money Laundering: Demonetisation is expected to check money laundering. It refers to the hidden transfer of funds across different regions of the country.

65(A). Dairy products have been hard hit by foreign competition.

India is the world's largest milk producer, with 22 percent of global production, followed by the United States of America, China, Pakistan and Brazil. Dairy products include fluid beverage milk, cheese, butter, ice cream, yogurt, dry milk products, condensed milk, and whey products . The dairy market has been taking hits in recent years, due to both a variety of economic upsets and consumers' increasing shift towards milk alternatives . In order to recover, the sector needs to be able to adapt and innovate.

66(C). The government decided to remove barriers on foreign trade and investment and introduce a new series of economic reforms in India in the year 1991. he government of India, after independence from British Rule, decided in favour of putting barriers to foreign trade and foreign investment in order to protect the domestic producers from foreign competition. The economy was weak at that stage and it was in the best interest of India to do so. However, after a long period of time, it was thought to be necessary to open up the Indian economy that was previously secured with barriers and regulations.

67(B). A consumer can approach State Consumer Court having a claim of Rs. 40 lakhs.

Consumer Court is a special purpose court in India that deals with cases regarding consumer disputes, conflicts and grievances. They are judiciary hearings set up by the government to protect the consumers' rights. Its main function is to maintain the fair practices and contracts by sellers. The Consumer Protection Act 2019 Act provides for a three tier Consumer Disputes Redressal Agencies. These are: District Consumer Disputes Redressal Commission in the District, State Consumer Disputes Redressal Commission at the state level and the National Consumer Disputes Redressal Commission at the national level.

68(C). The organisation which lays down standards of products at the international level is called ISO((International Organization for Standardization).

ISO is an independent, non-governmental international organization with a membership of 166 national standards bodies. Through its members, it brings together experts to share knowledge and develop voluntary, consensus-based, market relevant International Standards that support innovation and provide solutions to global challenges. ISO certification certifies that a management system, manufacturing process, service, or documentation procedure has all the requirements for standardization and quality assurance. ISO standards are in place to ensure consistency. Each certification has separate standards and criteria and is classified numerically.

69(C). Changes occurred in the seventeenth century, as urban culture bloomed in China are:

- Print was no longer used just by scholar officials
- Merchants used print in their everyday life, as they collected trade information.
- New readership preferred fictional narratives, poetry, autobiographies, anthologies of literary masterpieces, and romantic plays
- Women began publishing their poetry and plays. Wives of scholar-officials published their works and courtesans wrote about their lives.

Printing in the 17th century : By the seventeenth century, as urban culture bloomed in China, the uses of print diversified. Print was no longer used just by scholar officials. Merchants used print in their everyday life, as they collected trade information. Reading increasingly became a leisure activity. The new readership preferred fictional narratives, poetry, autobiographies, anthologies of literary masterpieces, and romantic plays. Rich women began to read, and many women began publishing their poetry and plays. Wives of scholar-officials published their works and courtesans wrote about their lives.

70(B). This new reading culture bring about w estern printing techniques and mechanical presses were imported in further advancements.

With the printing press, a new reading public emerged.

- Printing reduced the cost of books.
- The time and labours to produce each book came down. Multiple copies could be produced easily.
- Books flooded the market, reaching out to an ever growing readership.
- It created a new culture of reading.
- Common people could not read books earlier, only the elite could. Common people heard a story or saw a performance collectively.
- Instead of a hearing public now there was a reading public.
- The rate of literacy in European countries was also low till the 20th century. Publishers reached out to people by making them listen to books being read out.
- Printers published popular ballads and folktales, profusely illustrated. These were then sung and recited at village gatherings in taverns in towns. Oral culture thus entered print and printed material was orally transmitted, Hearing and reading public, thus became one.

71(D). Less than one percent of the German-speaking people live in Belgium.

German is one of the least common languages in Belgium, and only 1% of the population speaks German. It is confined only to the East cantons part of Belgium, where mainly german-speaking people reside. Of the country's total population, 59 per cent lives in the Flemish region and speaks Dutch language. Another 40 per cent people live in the Wallonia region and speak French. Remaining 1 per cent of the Belgians speak German.

72(B). Sri Lanka is an island nation in Southeast Asia that is surrounded by the Indian Ocean from all sides.Located just a few kilometres away from the southern coast of Tamil Nadu, Sri Lanka is separated from India by the Palk Strait.The Palk strait connects the Bay of Bengal of India located in the Southeast with Palk bay of Sri Lanka located in the Southwest.

73(B). USA has an effective right of veto over IMF and World Bank.

The veto power originates in Article 27 of the United Nations Charter, which states:

1. Each member of the Security Council shall have a vote.
2. Decisions of the Security Council on procedural matters shall be made by an affirmative vote of nine members.
3. Decisions of the Security Council on all other matters shall be made by an affirmative vote of nine members including the concurring votes of the permanent members; provided that, in decisions under Chapter VI, and under paragraph 3 of Article 52, a party to a dispute shall abstain from voting.
4. A negative vote from any of the permanent members will block the adoption of a draft resolution. However, a permanent member that abstains or is absent from the vote will not block a resolution from being passed.

Although the "power of veto" is not mentioned by name in the UN Charter, Article 27 requires concurring votes from the permanent members. For this reason, the "power of veto" is also referred to as the principle of "great power unanimity" and the veto itself is sometimes referred to as the "great power veto".

74(D). If it is desired in India to switch over to a unitary system of government from the present federal structure such a change can be brought about by A special procedure in Parliament and ratification by a majority of states in the Indian Union.

In India, any changes in the federal features of the constitution, the amendment procedure requires a special majority in parliament and ratification by a majority of states(more than 50 % ratification of the states).

Article 368 of the Indian constitution mentions the procedure for amendments.

75(B). India has borrowed the concept of federalism from Canada. In this system, there is a clear division of powers between the Union and States.

Federalism is a system of government in which the power is divided between a central authority and various constituent units of the country. Usually, a federation has two levels of government. One is the government for the entire country that is usually responsible for a few subjects of common national interest. The others are governments at the level of provinces or states that look after much of the day-to-day administering of their state. Both these levels of government enjoy their power independent of the other. In India, we have a three-tier government, i.e. government at the central level, state level, and local level.

76(D). Richard Arkwright introduced the cotton mill.

The First American Cotton Mill Began Operation. Samuel Slater built that first American mill in Pawtucket based on designs of English inventor Richard Arkwright. Though it was against British law to leave the country if you were a textile worker, Slater fled anyway in order to seek his fortune in America.

77(B). Land left without cultivation for one or less than one year is called as current fallow.

Fallow land – Fallow land is that land which is not fertile for harvesting i.e., land is left without sowing for more or more vegetative cycles. This type of land has lost its moisture and organic matters which in result the land is left without cultivated. This land is also known as uncultivated land.

This is a natural process where land is given rest to gain its lost fertility naturally.

78(D). The rates of economic growth for different countries from 1950 to 2000 was highest among all dictatorial regimes.

Democracy and economic growth have had a strong correlative relationship. The economic growth of dictatorship governments between 1950 - 2000 is 3.95 . A 3 -fold increase of the world population would have meant that on average everyone in the world would now be 3 -times poorer than in 1950 . The average income in the world would have fallen to $1,100$. Before economic growth the world was exactly this: a zero-sum game in which more people meant less for everyone else, and if one person is better off in a stagnating economy then that means that someone else needs to be worse off.

79(D). All statements are true.

Non-democratic regimes often turn a blind eye to or suppress internal social differences. It is one of the merits of democracy that it can handle social differences, divisions, and conflicts. Also, the conflicts among different groups can be resolved in democracy through negotiations.

Ability to handle social differences, divisions and conflicts is thus a definite plus point of democratic regimes By extending political and legal equality and freedom to all. which allows for participation of all groups in the political affairs. This ensures government is representative of majority of the population.

Democracies usually develop a procedure to conduct their competition among the social differences. This reduces the possibility of social tensions becoming explosive or violent.

80(B). Mahatma Gandhi return to India from South Africa in 1915.

Gandhi returned to India from South Africa in 1915 at the request of Gopal Krishna Gokhale. Gokhale insisted to Gandhiji that he has been far away from his nation. He wanted Gandhiji to come to India and know the situation in India under British Rule. After arriving in India, Mahatma Gandhi successfully organized Satyagraha Movements in various places.

81(D). The freedom fighter named Swaroopanand Saraswati later became the famous Shankaracharya.

- Shankaracharya Swami Swaroopananda Saraswati was also an Indian freedom fighter and religious leader.
- He was imprisoned for his active participation in the Quit India Movement and had served two prison terms in 1942.
- He was known as the "Revolutionary Sadhu".

82(C). Maximum strength of the Lok Sabha as envisaged by the Constitution is 552. The Lok Sabha is composed of representatives of people chosen by direct election on the basis of Universal Adult Suffrage.

83(C). The difference between Revenue deficit and grants for creation of Capital assets is Effective revenue deficit.

Effective Revenue Deficit is the difference between revenue deficit and grants for the creation of capital assets. Every year the Central Government gives grants to State Government and Union Territories and with the help of these grants both create capital assets however these capitals are not added to the capital expenditure of the central government. Therefore to measure such expenditure an effective revenue deficit has been introduced.

84(A). Under section (164-a) of the Criminal Procedure Code, there is a provision for physical examination of the victim of rape. Inspection of weights and measures in section 153 is related to information in section 154 contingent cases.

85(D). Statement, "Sima floats over the sial," is not true.

Based on the concept of Swaes, three layers have been mentioned under the upper layer of the Earth, which are Sial, Sima, and Nife respectively. The thickness of Sial ranges between 50 to 300 km. Beneath it the boundary whose thickness varies from 1000 km to 2000 km. Till then. At the bottom is the Nife which is called the central layer of the Earth.

86(B). SONAR is defined as (Sound Navigation and Ranging) it is a technique that uses Sound Propagation (usually underwater, as in submarine navigation)(Basically used by the Indian Navy) to Navigate, communicate or Detect objects on or under the surface of the water, such as other vessels, submarine, etc.

There are two types of technology using by "SONAR" they are as follows

- Passive Sonar is essential to help to listen for the sound made by Vessels.
- Active Sonar helps to detect the emitting pulses of sounds and listening for Echoes.

87(A). Kerala's High Court has jurisdiction over Lakshadweep. A Munsiff Court is located in Andrott, and it has jurisdiction over the islands of Kavaratti, Andrott, Minicoy, and Kalpeni.

88(D). "Khuded" is one of the famous folk songs of Uttarakhand. The song describes the misery and pain of a lady who has been living apart from her husband. This song is very painful and emotional. It echoes the suffering of the woman who is left alone after her husband leaves her and goes to another place in search of a job. This song depicts the life of a low-income family where the husband has to move out in search of a better job so that he can run his family. Each and every word of this folk song has a very deep meaning attached to it.

89(A). Bastille day is celebrated as the national day in France and it is also celebrated in various countries other than France, including India in Pondicherry on 14th July.

Pondicherry was under French dominance for a period of 300 years and thus the blend of west and east can be felt cherishing, which unites to form a new tradition.

90(C). S elf-restraint is not the same in Buddhism and Jainism. Both Buddhism and Jainism believe in non-violence. Both religions are against the Vedas and rituals.

91(C). The First Battle of Panipat (21 April 1526) fought near a small village of Panipat Haryana.

The battle was fought between the invading forces of Zahir-ud-din Babur and Lodi Empire during the rule of Ibrahim Lodi. The Mughal forces of Babur, the ruler of Kabulistan, defeated the ruling army of Ibrahim Lodi, Sultan of Delhi. Babur's tactics of Tulughma and Araba led him to victory.

92(C). The Permanent Settlement was implemented by Lord Cornwallis. In 1793, Cornwallis introduced a permanent settlement system of land revenue, also known as Istmari, Jagidari, Malgujari and Bisvedari.

93(D). Weathering is the name given to the process by which rocks are broken down to form soils. There are three main types of weathering, physical, chemical and biological. Polythene bags does not lead to soil formation in nature.

When they are thrown on land it makes soil less fertile. They slowly release toxic chemicals that certain animals use as a resource. These are a non-biodegradable waste.

94(A). Statement A and B: The adulteration of food is a subject in the Concurrent List of the Constitution. The Prevention of Food Adulteration Act, 1954 aims at making provisions for the prevention of adulteration of food. The Act extends to the whole of India and came into force on 1st June 1955.

Food Safety and Standards Authority of India is an autonomous body established under the Ministry of Health & Family Welfare, Government of India. The FSSAI has been established under the Food Safety and Standards Act, 2006, which is a consolidating statute related to food safety and regulation in India.

95(D). Australia was crowned the winner of the 2022 ICC Women's Cricket World Cup, on 3 April 2022. This was their seventh title. Australia defeated England in the final by 71 runs at Hagley Oval in Christchurch, New Zealand. Alyssa Healy became the first batter in the history of the game to hit a hundred in the semi-final and the final of the World Cup.

96(A). Kadambini Ganguli, the first woman became a doctor in India.

Kadambini Ganguly was one of the first Indian female doctors who practiced with a degree in modern medicine. She was the first Indian woman to practice medicine in India.

97(A). The wavelength of microwaves ranges between infrared waves and radio waves.

98(A). Copper sulphate, on adding to water, will not scatter a beam of light.

Copper sulfate, being a compound that dissociates completely into its constituent ions (Cu_2^+ and SO_4^{2-}) in water, does not form any colloidal particles that are large enough to scatter light.

99(C). At Second Continental Congress was the American Declaration of Independence adopted on 4 July, 1776.

- Continental Congress was the body of delegates who spoke and acted collectively for the people of the colony-states that later became the USA during the American Revolution.
- Second Continental Congress included Benjamin Franklin and Thomas Jefferson.
- John Hancock and John Jay were among those who served as president.
- Declaration of Independence was the document that was approved by the Continental Congress on July 4, 1776.
- It announced the separation of 13 North American British colonies from Great Britain.

100(B). SS Rajamouli's RRR has become the first Indian film to bag two nominations at Golden Globe awards and the Indian film industry is effusive in praise, saying that not just the visual effects but story and streaming of the film played a big role in increasing its global traction.

Mathematics

1. To construct a triangle similar to a $\triangle PQR$ with its sides, 9/5 of the corresponding sides of $\triangle PQR$ a ray QX has been drawn such that $\angle QRX$ makes an acute angle and X is on the opposite side of P with respect to QR. The minimum number of points to be located at equal distances on ray QX is ______.

(a) 5   (b) 9
(c) 10   (d) 14

2. To draw a pair of tangents to a circle which are inclined to each other at an angle of $45°$, it is required to draw tangents at the endpoints of those two radii of the circle, the angle between which is:

(a) $155°$ (b) $135°$
(c) $160°$ (d) $120°$

3. The following table shows the ages of the patients admitted in a hospital during a year:

Age (in years)	$\frac{5}{15}$	$\frac{15}{25}$	$\frac{25}{35}$	$\frac{35}{45}$	$\frac{45}{55}$	$\frac{55}{65}$
Number of patients	6	11	21	23	14	5

Find the mean of the data given above.

(a) 30.38   (b) 35.38
(c) 45.38   (d) 55.38

4. A toy is in the form of a cone mounted on a hemisphere of radius $3.5cm$. The total height of the toy is $15.5cm$, find the total surface area and volume of the toy.

(a) $214.5cm^2, 243.83cm^3$
(b) $214.3cm^2, 242.84cm^3$
(c) $214.8cm^2, 245.83cm^3$
(d) $214.5cm^2, 246.83cm^3$

5. An ice cream cone full of ice cream has radius $5cm$ and height $10cm$ as shown. Calculate the volume of ice cream (to the nearest integer, in cm^3), provided that its $\frac{1}{6}$ th part is left unfilled with ice cream. Insert answer in nearest integer.

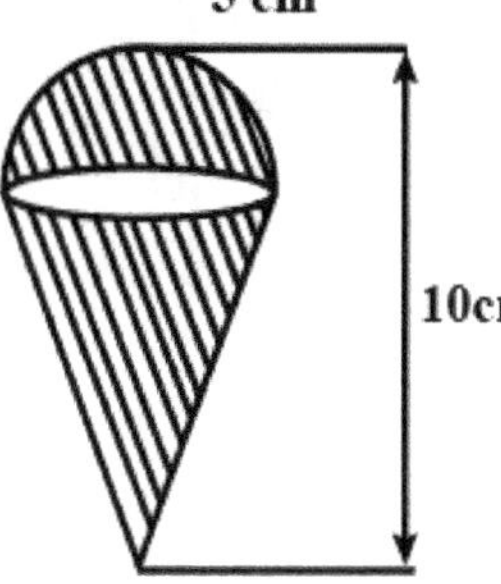

(a) 327   (b) 328
(c) 329   (d) 330

6. If $\left(a^2 + b^2\right)x^2 + 2(ab + bd)x + c^2 + d^2 = 0$ has no real roots then:

(a) $ad = bc$ (b) $ab = cd$
(c) $ac = bd$ (d) $ad \neq bc$

7. If $\log_{10}\left(x^2 - 6x + 45\right) = 2$, then the value of x are:

(a) $6, 9$ (b) $9, -5$
(c) $10, 5$ (d) $11, -5$

8. The area of a circle is 38.5 sq. cm. Its circumference is:

(a) $11\ cm$ (b) $44\ cm$
(c) $33\ cm$ (d) $22\ cm$

9. The circumference of a circle whose diameter is $4.2\ cm$ is:

(a) $22\ cm$ (b) $11\ cm$
(c) $4.2\ cm$ (d) $13.2\ cm$

10. In a right triangle PQR, right-angled at $Q, \sin P = \dfrac{6}{3\sqrt{5}}$ and $\cos P = \dfrac{3}{3\sqrt{5}}$. What is the value of $\sec P \cdot \csc P$?

(a) $\frac{2}{5}$ (b) $\frac{5}{2}$
(c) 5 (d) 2

11. What is the value of $\csc\theta \cdot \cot\theta$?

(a) $\frac{1}{\cos\theta}$ (b) $\frac{1}{\sin\theta}$
(c) $\frac{\cos\theta}{\sin^2\theta}$ (d) 1

12. In a right triangle PQR, right-angled at $Q, \sin P = \dfrac{6}{10}$. What is the value of $\cos^2 P$?

(a) $\frac{4}{5}$ (b) $\frac{16}{25}$
(c) $\frac{36}{100}$ (d) $\frac{13}{25}$

13. The angle of depression of a car, standing on the ground, from the top of a $75m$ tower, is $30°$. The distance of the car from the base of the tower (in metres) is:

(a) $25\sqrt{3}$ (b) $50\sqrt{3}$
(c) $75\sqrt{3}$ (d) 150

14. Solve $2x + 3y = 11$ and $2x - 4y = -24$ and hence find the value of 'm' for which $y = mx + 3$.

(a) $m = -1$ (b) $m = -3$
(c) $m = -5$ (d) $m = -9$

15. Solve the following pairs of linear equations.
$x + y = 5$ and $2x - 3y = 4$

(a) $x = \frac{12}{5}, y = \frac{18}{5}$
(b) $x = \frac{17}{5}, y = \frac{16}{5}$
(c) $x = \frac{29}{5}, y = \frac{6}{5}$
(d) $x = \frac{19}{5}, y = \frac{6}{5}$

16. If $M = 77 \times 144 \times 45$, which of the following groups gives the prime factors of M?

(a) $2, 3, 5, 7, 11, 13$
(b) $2, 3, 5, 19$
(c) $2, 3, 5, 7, 11, 13, 14$
(d) $2, 3, 5, 7, 11$

17. Consider the numbers 4^n, where n is a natural number. The value of n for which 4^n ends with the digit zero is:

(a) 1
(b) 3
(c) $\frac{1}{2}$
(d) There is no other primes in the factorisation of 4^n

18. Which of the following has a non-terminating non-repeating decimal expansion?

(a) $\frac{\sqrt{2} \times \sqrt{3}}{\sqrt{6}}$ (b) $\frac{1}{\sqrt{2}}$
(c) $\frac{\sqrt{15} \times \sqrt{5}}{\sqrt{3}}$ (d) $\frac{17}{5}$

19. Dudhnath has two vessels containing $720ml$ and $405ml$ of milk respectively. Milk from these containers is poured into glasses of equal capacity to their brim. Find the minimum number of glasses that can be filled:

(a) 20   (b) 25
(c) 30   (d) 40

20. The number of polynomials having zeroes as -2 and 5 is:

(a) 1   (b) 2
(c) 3   (d) More than 3

21. Zeroes of $p(x) = x^2 - 27$ are:

(a) $\pm 9\sqrt{3}$

(b) $\pm 3\sqrt{3}$

(c) $\pm 7\sqrt{3}$

(d) None of the above

22. One card is drawn from a well shuffled pack of 52 cards. The probability of getting an ace is:

(a) $\frac{2}{13}$

(b) $\frac{1}{52}$

(c) $\frac{1}{13}$

(d) $\frac{4}{13}$

23. Write the first term and the common difference of the given sequence.
$\frac{1}{3}, \frac{5}{3}, \frac{9}{3}, \frac{13}{3}$

(a) $\frac{4}{3}$

(b) $\frac{2}{8}$

(c) $\frac{7}{1}$

(d) $\frac{6}{5}$

24. 30th term of the AP: $10, 7, 4, \ldots$ is:

(a) 97

(b) 77

(c) -77

(d) -87

25. Two poles of heights 6 m and 11 m stand on a plane ground. If the distance between the feet of the poles is 12 m, find the distance between their tops.

(a) 20 meter

(b) 18 meter

(c) 15 meter

(d) 13 meter

26. If $\triangle ABC \sim \triangle PQR$, perimeter of $\triangle ABC = 32$ cm, perimeter of $\triangle PQR = 48$ cm and $PR = 6$ cm, then find the length of AC .

(a) 4 cm

(b) 6 cm

(c) 8 cm

(d) 10 cm

27. In the figure given below, if O is the centre of the circle, $\angle AOB = \angle EOF = \angle COD = 60°$ and $AB = 4$ units, then find $EF + CD$.

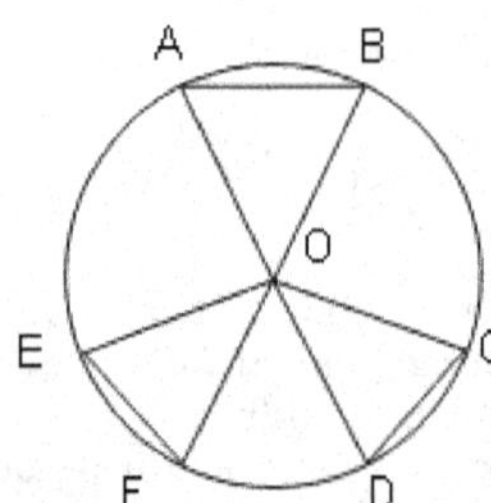

(a) 4 units

(b) 8 units

(c) 16 units

(d) 32 units

28. In the given figure, O is the centre of the circle, $\angle AOB = \angle POQ = 30°$ and $\angle XOY = \angle ZOW = 40°$. Also, $XY = 4$ units and $AB = 3.5$ units. The value of $(AB + ZW + PQ + XY)$ is:

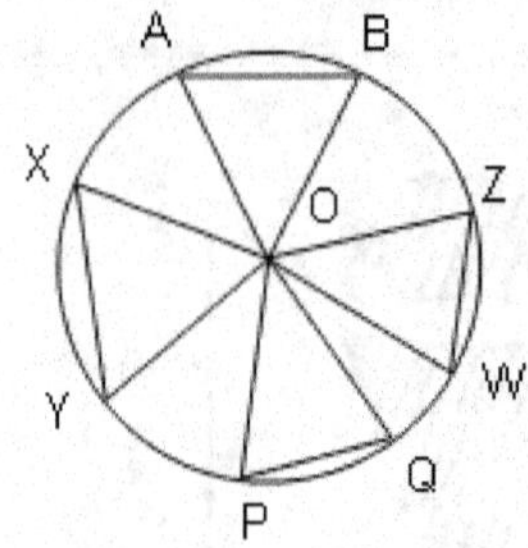

(a) 11.25 units

(b) 22.5 units

(c) 15 units

(d) 7.8 units

29. $(5, -2), (6, 4)$ and $(7, -2)$ are the vertices of an _______ triangle.

(a) equilateral

(b) right angle

(c) isosceles

(d) None of these

30. The value of y , if the distance between the points $(2, y)$ and $(-4, 3)$ is 10 is:

(a) 6

(b) -11

(c) 5

(d) 11

Science

31. A group of interbreeding individuals forms a:

(a) community

(b) species

(c) ecosystem

(d) population

32. _______ is the abiotic component of a pond ecosystem.

(a) Fish

(b) Frog

(c) Water

(d) Bacteria

33. The metal which does not displace hydrogen from dil. HCl is:

(a) Ag

(b) Mg

(c) Al

(d) Fe

34. Identify the non-metal which is a good conductor of electricity.

(a) Chlorine

(b) Sulphur

(c) Graphite

(d) Phosphorus

35. The growth of pollen tube towards an ovule is an example of:

(a) phototropism

(b) hydrotropism

(c) chemotropism

(d) geotropism

36. The movement of root away from light is:

(a) Positive hydrotropism

(b) Negative hydrotropism

(c) Positive phototropism

(d) Negative phototropism

37. Which of the following is getting

oxidised in the below given reaction?
$$CuO + H_2 \xrightarrow{\text{heat}} Cu + H_2O$$

(a) Copper

(b) Hydrogen

(c) Oxygen

(d) Copper di-oxide

38. Which one of the following is an example of combination reaction?

(a) $MgO(s) + H_2O(l) \rightarrow Mg(OH)_2(aq) +$ Heat

(b) $2FeSO_4(s) \rightarrow Fe_2O_3(s) + SO_2(g) + SO_3(g)$

(c) $Fe(s) + CuSO_4(aq) \rightarrow Cu(s) + FeSO_4(aq)$

(d) $Na_2SO_4(aq) + BaCl_2(aq) \rightarrow BaSO_4(s) \downarrow + 2NaCl$

39. The general formula of alkynes is:

(a) C_nH_{2n+2}

(b) C_nH_{2n}

(c) C_nH_{2n-2}

(d) C_nH_n

40. The number of oxygen molecules used in the combustion of 1 molecule of ethanol is?

(a) 1

(b) 2

(c) 3

(d) 4

41. The first sign of puberty in females is:

(a) Breast development

(b) Menstruation

(c) High pitch of voice

(d) Appearance of pubic hair

42. Regeneration occurs in which of the following organisms?

(a) Planaria

(b) Hydra

(c) Saccharomyces

(d) Both A and B

43. The transmission of characters from one generation to the next is termed as:

(a) variation

(b) heredity

(c) evolution

(d) diversity

44. The 'Mendelian factor' is now known as:

(a) gene

(b) chromosome

(c) DNA

(d) chromatid

45. It is desired to photograph the image of an object placed at a distance of 3 m from a plane mirror. The camera, which is at a distance of 4.5 m from the mirror should be focused for a distance of :

(a) 3 m

(b) 4.5 m

(c) 6 m   (d) 7.5 m

46. **The given figure shows a ray of light as it travels from medium A to medium B. Refractive index of the medium B relative to medium A is:**

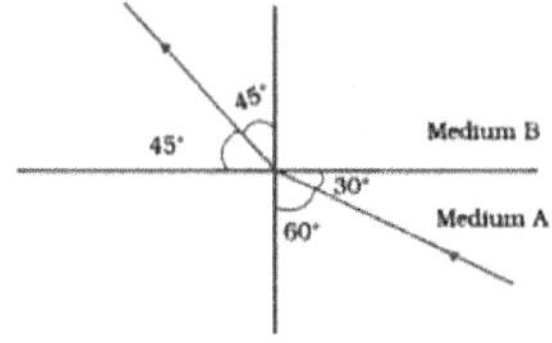

(a) $\dfrac{\sqrt{3}}{\sqrt{2}}$ (b) $\dfrac{\sqrt{2}}{\sqrt{3}}$

(c) $\dfrac{1}{\sqrt{2}}$ (d) $\sqrt{2}$

47. **What are the factors affecting the strength of the magnetic field at a point due to a straight conductor carrying current?**
    (a) Distance of the point from the wire only
    (b) Current, length and distance of the wire
    (c) Current only
    (d) Length of the wire only

48. **You have a coil and a bar magnet, you can produce an electric current by moving ______.**
    (a) The magnet, but not the coil
    (b) Neither the magnet nor the coil
    (c) The coil, but not the magnet
    (d) Either the magnet or the coil or both

49. **The longest part of the alimentary canal is ________.**
    (a) small intestine
    (b) large intestine
    (c) oesophagus
    (d) rectum

50. **Saprozoic organisms feed on ________.**
    (a) blood
    (b) dead decayed matter
    (c) fruits
    (d) members of its own species

51. **Which of the following is not true for sodium hydroxide?**
    (a) Bitter taste
    (b) Slippery to touch
    (c) Changes the colour of blue litmus solution
    (d) Changes the colour of red litmus solution

52. **Sodium zincate is produced when zinc is heated with:**
    (a) Baking soda
    (b) Caustic soda
    (c) Sulphuric acid
    (d) Nitric acid

53. **Which phenomenon does not play a role in the formation of rainbow?**
    (a) Reflection   (b) Refraction
    (c) Dispersion   (d) Absorption

54. **How much work is done in moving a charge of 2C across two points having a potential difference 12 V ?**
    (a) 28 J   (b) 29 J
    (c) 24 J   (d) 20 J

55. **Consider the given circuit diagram. A voltmeter connected between the points A and C would read:**

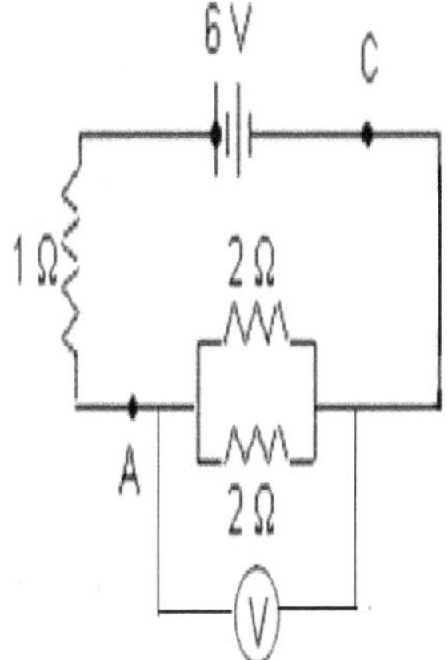

(a) 0 V   (b) 1.2 V
(c) 3.0 V   (d) 4.8 V

Social Science

56. **What is the largest consumer of water?**
    (a) City dwellers
    (b) Irrigated agriculture
    (c) Villages
    (d) Industry

57. **What are rare species?**
    (a) These are species whose population has declined to levels
    (b) Species with small population
    (c) Species which are only found in some particular areas usually isolated by natural or geographical barriers
    (d) Species with small population

58. **Coal and Natural Gas are examples of ________ minerals.**
    (a) Non-metallic (b) Energy
    (c) Ferrous   (d) Non-ferrous

59. **The sum of production in the primary, secondary and tertiary sectors of the Indian Economy gives the value of:**
    (a) Gross income
    (b) Gross Domestic Product
    (c) Net Domestic Product
    (d) Net income

60. **One common development goal among the people is:**
    (a) family   (b) freedom
    (c) income   (d) security

61. **What happened when the news of the events in France reached the different cities of Europe?**
    (a) There was tumult.
    (b) The people did not know how to react.
    (c) Students and other members of educated middle classes began setting up Jacobin clubs.
    (d) There was confusion and dissatisfaction in the air.

62. **Risk in agriculture is the least in which type of agriculture?**
    (a) Specialized agriculture
    (b) Miscellaneous agriculture
    (c) Mixed agriculture
    (d) Intensive agriculture

63. **In rural areas, most of the credit is demanded for:**
    (a) Industry
    (b) Crop production
    (c) Irrigation
    (d) Cultivation

64. **Banks in India these days hold about ________ of their deposits as cash. This is kept as a provision to pay the depositors who might come to withdraw money from the bank on any given day.**
    (a) 20%   (b) 25%
    (c) 30%   (d) 15%

65. **The most common route for investments by MNCs in countries around the world is to:**
    (a) Set up new factories
    (b) Buy existing local companies
    (c) Form partnerships with local companies
    (d) None of these

66. **Entry of MNCs in a domestic market may prove harmful for:**
    (a) All large scale producers
    (b) All domestic producers
    (c) All substandard domestic producers
    (d) All small scale producers

67. **MRP on a product represents:**

(a) minimum retail price

(b) maximum retail price

(c) micro retail price

(d) None of the above

68. Why did the consumer movement arise?

(a) High rates of products

(b) Total false claims

(c) The dissatisfaction of the consumers as many unfair practices were being indulged in by the sellers

(d) None of the above

69. _____ became the hub of the new print culture, catering to the Western-style schools.

(a) Beijing   (b) Hangzhou

(c) Shanghai   (d) Guangzhou

70. Who introduced hand-printing technology into Japan around AD 768-770?

(a) Chinese travelers

(b) Chinese Scholars

(c) Buddhist missionaries from China

(d) Chinese teachers

71. Which one of the following languages was recognized as the official language of Sri Lanka in 1956?

(a) English   (b) Tamil

(c) Urdu   (d) Sinhala

72. Belgium government is a good example of________.

(a) Monarchy

(b) Community government

(c) Unitary government

(d) Federal government

73. Which of the following was the most powerful weapon used by Spanish to conquer America?

(a) Atom Bomb

(b) Navy

(c) Germs

(d) Poisonous gas

74. The main objective of the federal system is to __________.

(a) accommodate regional diversity

(b) promote diversity

(c) make center more powerful

(d) distribute finances to different organs

75. One of the following is false.

(a) India is a federal country as the USA

(b) India has adopted the parliamentary form of government

(c) Residuary powers are vested in the Center

(d) India is a Union of States

76. What changes took place after the creation of the mill?

(a) Production was brought together under one roof and management.

(b) Cotton became costly

(c) Production became difficult

(d) Designs were limited

77. In India the percentage of wasteland due to water erosion is _____.

(a) 56%   (b) 28%

(c) 10%   (d) 6%

78. ________ stands much superior to any other form of Government in promoting dignity and freedom of the individual.

(a) Theocracy   (b) Oligarchy

(c) Dictatorship   (d) Democracy

79. Accountability to the citizens is the most basic outcome of _____.

(a) Theocracy   (b) Autocracy

(c) Democracy   (d) Socialism

80. Which areas did Gandhiji organise the satyagraha?

(a) Champaran in Bihar and Ahmedabad

(b) Champaran in Bihar, Kheda district of Gujarat, Ahmedabad

(c) Kheda district of Gujarat, Ahmedabad

(d) Champaran in Bihar, Kheda district of Gujarat

General Awareness/ Knowledge

81. Who is referred to as the 'Darwin of the 20 [th] Century'?

(a) Ernst Mayr

(b) Har Gobind Khorana

(c) Marshall Warren Nirenberg

(d) Katherine Esau

82. One of the important attributes of the Parliamentary form of government is:

(a) Fixed tenure for the executive

(b) Executive is answerable to the people

(c) Executive is separate from the legislature

(d) Cabinet is responsible before the legislature.

83. India's economic planning cannot be said to be:

(a) Imperative   (b) Indicative

(c) Limited   (d) Democratic

84. Consider the following two statements A and B on Judicial Review and choose the correct answer:
A: The judiciary can strike down particular laws passed by the Parliament if there is a violation of the basic structure of the Constitution.
B: A bill cannot become a law unless it is passed by the Judiciary.

(a) A is true and B is false.

(b) Both A and B are true.

(c) A is false and B is true.

(d) Both A and B are false.

85. Lines called isotherms are drawn to represent the locations on the map where:

(a) Temperature remains the same

(b) Pressure remains the same

(c) Have the same salinity

(d) Is the same height

86. Transpiration takes place from _____.

(a) All parts of the plant

(b) Only leaves

(c) Only the aerial parts

(d) Only stem

87. Which of the following is NOT possible by a law of Parliament under Article 3 of the Constitution?

(a) Formation of new States

(b) Alteration of areas of States

(c) Alternation of boundaries of States

(d) Admission of new States

88. "Thulo Dhuska" (Thulo Khela) in Uttarakhand culture is:

(a) Revolution

(b) Marriage

(c) Wrestling

(d) Pahadi Ramayana

89. On which river is the Chamera Dam built?

(a) Sutlej   (b) Ravi

(c) Beas   (d) Chenab

90. The Khajuraho temple architecture was supported by:

(a) Chandelas

(b) Gurjara-Pratihara

(c) Chahamana

(d) Parmar

91. Direction : Read the passage carefully and answer the following questions:

Mystics, who are called Sufis, had risen in Islam at a very early stage. Most of them were persons of deep devotion, who were disgusted by the vulgar display of wealth and degeneration of morals following the establishment of the Islamic empire. Some of the early sufi saints, such as the woman mystic Rabia (8th century) and Mansur bin Halla (10th century), laid great emphasis on love as the bond between God and the individual sole.

Sufis were organised into orders or silsilas. A silsila was generally led by a prominent mystic who lived in a khanqah or hospice along with his disciples. The link between the teacher or pir and his disciples or murids was a vital part of the sufi system. Each pir nominated a successor or wali to carry his work. The monastic organisation of the Sufis and some of their practices such as penanace, fasting and holding the breath are sometimes traced to Buddhist and Hindu yogic influences.

Most Sufis were persons of deep devotion who:

(a) believed that Islam is the only religion, which can solve their problems.

(b) were poor people and lived in forests

(c) were nomads and moved from village to village begging for food.

(d) were disgusted by the vulgar display of wealth and degeneration of morals following the establishment of the Islamic empire.

92. Hindustan Socialist Republic Association was founded by:

(a) Veer Savarkar

(b) Udham Singh

(c) Bhagat Singh

(d) Chandrashekhar Azad

93. Nitromonas bacteria convert:

(a) Nitrite to nitrate

(b) Ammonia into nitrate

(c) Ammonia into nitrite

(d) Nitrite into ammonia

94. Department-related Standing Committees were set up in ______ to scrutinise the functioning of the various Ministries/Departments of the Union Government assigned to them in order to further strengthen the accountability of the Government to Parliament.

(a) 1991   (b) 1993

(c) 1999   (d) 2000

95. Karim Benzema announced his retirement on 20 December 2022 . He is related to which of the following sports?

(a) Cricket   (b) Football

(c) Basketball   (d) Hockey

96. Who was India's first man in space?

(a) Rakesh Sharma

(b) Ravish Malhotra

(c) Kalpana Chawla

(d) None of the above

97. Anemophily defines as:

(a) It is the pollination by sunlight.

(b) It is the pollination by wind.

(c) It is the pollination by both wind and sunlight.

(d) None of the above

98. Nylon is made up of:

(a) Polyamide

(b) Polyester

(c) Polyethylene

(d) Polypropylene

99. Who of the following was not a leader of the French Revolution?

(a) Maximilien Robespierre

(b) Frederick William IV

(c) Georges-Jacques Danton

(d) Jean-Paul Marat

100. Kalidas Samman award is presented by which state government?

(a) Tamil Nadu

(b) Karnataka

(c) Andhra Pradesh

(d) Madhya Pradesh

// Hints and Solutions //

1(B). To draw a triangle similar to a given triangle with its sides m/n of the similar sides of a given triangle, the minimum number of points to be located at an equal distance is equal to m or n , whichever is greater.

Here, $\frac{m}{n} = \frac{9}{5}$

$9 > 5$, therefore the minimum number of points to be located is 9 .

2(B). We have constructed a figure according to the ques:

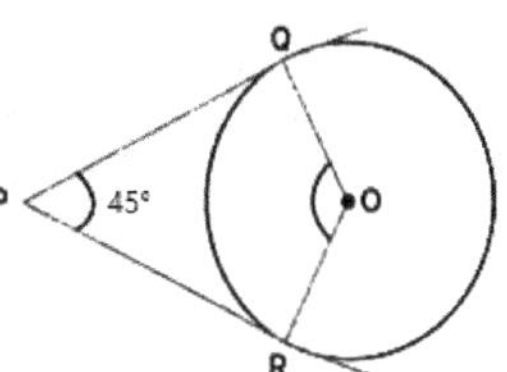

O is the centre of a circle to which a pair of tangents PQ and PR from the point P touches the circle at Q and R

$\angle RPQ = 45°$

We know that

$\angle OQP = 90° = \angle ORP$

The angle between a tangent to a circle and the radius of the same circle passing through the point of contact is $90°$

Using the angle sum property of quadrilaterals

$\angle OQP + \angle RPQ + \angle ORP + \angle ROQ = 360°$

Substituting the values

$90° + 45° + 90° + \angle ROQ = 360°$

$\angle ROQ = 135°$

Therefore, the angle between them should be $135°$.

3(B). The mean can be found as given below:

$$\overline{X} = a + \left(\frac{\sum f_i u_i}{\sum f_i} \right)$$

Suppose the assured mean (a) of the data is 30 . Class mark (x_i) for each interval is calculated as follows:

$$x_i = \frac{\text{Upper class limit} + \text{Lower class limit}}{2}$$

d_i, u_i , and $f_i u_i$ can be evaluated as follows:

Age (in years)	Number of patients f_i	Class mark x_i	$d_i = x_i - 30$	$f_i d_i$
5 − 15	6	10	−20	−120
15 − 25	11	20	−10	−110
25 − 35	21	30	0	0
35 − 45	23	40	10	230
45 − 55	14	50	20	280
55 − 65	5	60	30	150
Total	80			430

It can be observed that from the above table

$\sum f_i = 80$

$\sum f_i d_i = 430$

Substituting the value of u_i , and $f_i u_i$ in the formula of mean we get:

The required mean:

$$\overline{X} = a + \left(\frac{\sum f_i u_i}{\sum f_i} \right)$$

$$\overline{X} = 30 + \left(\frac{430}{80} \right)$$

$$\overline{X} = 30 + 5.375$$

$$\overline{X} = 35.38$$

So, the mean of this data is 35.38 . It demonstrates that the average age of a patient admitted to hospital was 35.38 years.

4(A).

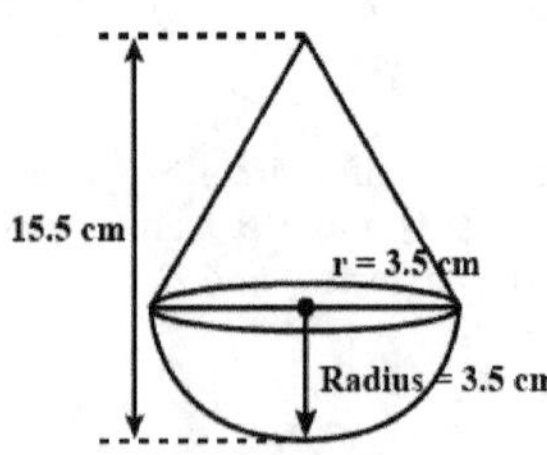

Given that the toy is in form of a cone mounted on a hemisphere.

The radius of hemisphere = Radius of the circular base of cone = $3.5cm$

Total height of toy = $15.5cm$

Height of cone = Total height of cone − Radius of hemisphere

$= (15.5 - 3.5)cm = 12cm$

Slant height of cone $(l) = \sqrt{h^2 + b^2}$

$= \sqrt{(12)^2 + (3.5)^2}$

$= \sqrt{144 + 12.25}$

$= \sqrt{156.25}$

$= 12.5cm$

As we know,

Curved surface area of cone $= \pi r l$ [Where r = radius and l = slant height of cone]

Curved surface area of hemisphere $= 2\pi r^2$ [Where r = radius of hemisphere]

Total surface area of toy = Curved surface area of cone + Curved surface area of hemisphere

Total surface area of toy $= \pi r l + 2\pi r^2$

$= \frac{22}{7} \times 3.5 \times 12.5 + 2 \times \frac{22}{7} \times (3.5)^2$

$= \frac{22}{7} \times 43.75 + \frac{22}{7} \times 24.5$

$= \frac{962.5}{7} + \frac{539}{7}$

$= 137.5cm^2 + 77cm^2$

$= 214.5cm^2$

Volume of toy = Volume of Cone + Volume of hemisphere

Volume of toy $= \frac{1}{3}\pi r^2 h + \frac{2}{3}\pi r^3$

$= \frac{1}{3}\pi r^2 [h + 2r]$

$= \frac{1}{3} \times \frac{22}{7} \times 3.5 \times 3.5 \times [12 + 2 \times 3.5]$

$= \frac{77}{6} \times [12 + 7]$

$= \frac{77 \times 19}{6}$

$= \frac{1463}{6}$

$= 243.83cm^3$

So, the total surface area and volume of the toy are $214.5cm^2$ and $243.83cm^3$.

5(A). Given,

Radius of hemisphere = Radius of cone $= 5cm$

Height of cone full of ice cream $= 10cm$

Height of hemisphere $= 5cm$

Height of cone $= (10 - 5)cm = 5cm$

As we know,

Volume of hemisphere $= \frac{2}{3}\pi r^3$

Volume of cone $= \frac{1}{3}\pi r^2 h$

Volume of ice cream = Volume of hemisphere + Volume of cone

$\therefore$ Volume of ice cream $= \frac{2}{3}\pi r^3 + \frac{1}{3}\pi r^2 h$

$= \frac{1}{3}\pi r^2(2r + h)$

$= \frac{1}{3} \times \frac{22}{7} \times (5)^2(2 \times 5 + 5)$

$= \frac{1}{3} \times \frac{22}{7} \times 25 \times 15$

$= \frac{2750}{7}$

$= 392.85cm^3$

As $\frac{1}{6}$ th part is left unfilled with ice cream

$= \frac{392.85}{6} = 65.475cm^3$

$\therefore$ Volume of required portion of ice cream $= (392.85 - 65.47)cm^3 = 327.375cm^3$

So, the volume of ice cream to the nearest integer is $327cm^3$.

6(D). Given,

Equation:

$(a^2 + b^2)x^2 + 2(ab + bd)x + c^2 + d^2 = 0$

We know, for no real roots,

$D = b^2 - 4ac < 0$

Here,

$a = (a^2 + b^2), b = 2(ab + bd), c = c^2 + d^2$

$[(ac + bd)^2] - 4(a^2 + b^2)(c^2 + d^2) < 0$

$\Rightarrow [4(a^2c^2 + b^2d^2 + 2abcd)] - 4(a^2 + b^2)(c^2 + d^2) < 0$

$\Rightarrow 4[(a^2c^2 + b^2d^2 + 2abcd) - (a^2c^2 + a^2d^2 + b^2c^2 + b^2)] < 0$

$\Rightarrow 4[a^2c^2 + b^2d^2 + 2abcd - a^2c^2 - a^2d^2 - b^2c^2 - b^2] < 0$

$\Rightarrow 4[2abcd - b^2c^2 - a^2d^2] < 0$

$\Rightarrow -4[a^2d^2 + b^2c^2 - 2abcd] < 0$

$\Rightarrow -4[ad - bc]^2 < 0$

Therefore.

$(ad - bc) < 0$

Or

$ad < bc$

$\therefore ad \neq bc$

7(D). Given,

$\log_{10}(x^2 - 6x + 45) = 2$

If $\log_{10}(x) = a$

then, $x = 10^a$

$\log_{10}(x^2 - 6x + 45) = 2$

$\Rightarrow (x^2 - 6x + 45) = 10^2$

$\Rightarrow x^2 - 6x + 45 - 100 = 0$

$\Rightarrow x^2 - 6x - 55 = 0$

$\Rightarrow x^2 - 11x + 5x - 55 = 0$

$\Rightarrow x(x - 11) + 5(x - 11) = 0$

$\Rightarrow (x + 5)(x - 11) = 0$

$\Rightarrow x = -5$ and $x = 11$

$\therefore$ The value of x are 11 and -5

8(D). Given,

The area of the circle = 38.5

As we know,

The area of the circle $= \pi r^2$

So,

$\pi r^2 = 38.5$

$r^2 = \frac{38.5}{\pi}$

$r = 3.5$

Circumference of circle $= 2\pi r$

$= 2 \times \pi \times 3.5$

$= 22$

Hence circumference of the circle is 22 cm .

9(D). Given,

diameter = 4.2

As we know,

Circumference $= \pi d$

$= \pi \times 4.2$

$= 13.2\ cm$

10(B). Given:

$\sin P = \frac{6}{3\sqrt{5}}$

$\cos P = \frac{3}{3\sqrt{5}}$

squaring both of them we get,

$\sin^2 P = \frac{36}{45}$

$\cos^2 P = \frac{9}{45}$

$\sin^2 P = \frac{(\text{Perpendicular})^2}{(\text{Hypotenuse})^2} = \frac{30}{45}$

$\cos^2 P = \frac{(\text{Base})^2}{(\text{Hypotenuse})^2} = \frac{9}{45}$

Now,

$\sec^2 P = \frac{(\text{Hypotenuse})^2}{(\text{Base})^2} = \frac{45}{9}$

$\csc^2 P = \frac{(\text{Hypotenuse})^2}{(\text{Perpendicular})^2} = \frac{45}{36}$

$\sec^2 P \cdot \csc^2 P = \frac{45}{9} \cdot \frac{45}{36} = \frac{25}{4}$

$\sec P \cdot \csc P = \sqrt{\frac{25}{4}} = \frac{5}{2}$

11(C). We know that,

$\csc \theta = \frac{1}{\sin \theta} \cdots\cdots (1)$

$\Rightarrow \cot \theta = \frac{1}{\tan \theta} \cdots\cdots (2)$

$\Rightarrow \tan \theta = \frac{\sin \theta}{\cos \theta}$

Now multiplying equation (1) and equation (2)

$\Rightarrow \csc \theta \cdot \cot \theta = \frac{1}{\sin \theta} \cdot \frac{1}{\tan \theta}$

$\Rightarrow \frac{1}{\sin \theta} \cdot \frac{1}{\frac{\sin \theta}{\cos \theta}}$

$\Rightarrow \frac{1}{\sin \theta} \cdot \frac{\cos \theta}{\sin \theta}$

$\Rightarrow \frac{\cos \theta}{\sin^2 \theta}$

12(B). Given:

$\Rightarrow \sin P = \frac{\text{Perpendicular}}{\text{Hypotenuse}} = \frac{6}{10}$

squaring it we get,

$\Rightarrow \sin^2 P = \frac{(\text{Perpendicular})^2}{(\text{Hypotenuse})^2}$

$\Rightarrow \frac{(6)^2}{(10)^2}$

$\Rightarrow \frac{36}{100}$

We know that,

$\Rightarrow (\text{Hypotenuse})^2 = (\text{Base})^2 + (\text{Perpendicular})^2$

$\Rightarrow (\text{Base})^2 = (\text{Hypotenuse})^2 - (\text{Perpendicular})^2$

$\Rightarrow (\text{Base})^2 = (10)^2 - (6)^2 = 64$

Now,

$\Rightarrow \cos^2 P = \frac{(\text{Base})^2}{(\text{Hypotenuse})^2}$

$\Rightarrow \cos^2 P = \frac{64}{100}$

$\Rightarrow \cos^2 P = \frac{16}{25}$

13(C). Let AB be a tower.
Given,
The length of tower (AB) = 75m
From A, the angle of depression of a car C on the ground is 30°.

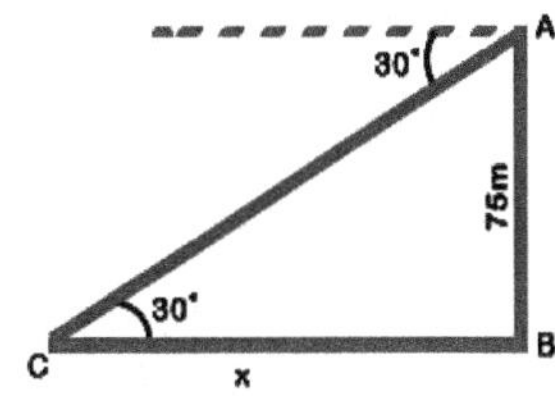

Let the distance of the car from the base of the tower BC be x.
In right angle $\triangle ACB$,
$\tan \theta = \frac{AB}{BC}$
$\Rightarrow \tan 30° = \frac{75}{x}$
$\Rightarrow \frac{1}{\sqrt{3}} = \frac{75}{x}$
$\Rightarrow x = 75\sqrt{3}m$
$\therefore BC = 75\sqrt{3}m$
So, the distance of the car from the base of the tower is $75\sqrt{3}m$.

14(A). Given,
$2x + 3y = 11$ ......(1)
$2x - 4y = -24$ ......(2)
From (1),
$2x + 3y = 11$
$2x = 11 - 3y$
$x = \frac{11-3y}{2}$
Substituting value of x in (2),
$2x - 4y = -24$
$2\left(\frac{11-3y}{2}\right) - 4y = -24$
$11 - 3y - 4y = -24$
$11 - 7y = -24$
$-7y = -24 - 11$
$-7y = -35$
$y = \frac{-35}{-7}$
$y = 5$
Putting $y = 5$ in (1),
$2x + 3y = 11$
$2x + 3(5) = 11$
$2x + 15 = 11$
$2x = 11 - 15$
$2x = -4$
$x = \frac{-4}{2}$
$x = -2$
So, $x = -2$ and $y = 5$ is the solution of the equation.
Now,
We have to find the value of m.
$y = mx + 3$
Putting $y = 5, x = -2$,
$5 = m(-2) + 3$
$5 = -2m + 3$
$5 - 3 = -2m$
$2 = -2m$

$m = \frac{2}{-2}$
$m = -1$
Thus, value of m is -1.

15(D). Given,
$x + y = 5$ ......(1)
$2x - 3y = 4$ ......(2)
Multiplying equation (1) by (2),
$2(x + y) = 2 \times 5$
$2x + 2y = 10$ ......(3)
Solving (3) and (2) by Elimination,
$2x - 3y = 4$
$2x + 2y = 10$
$(-) \quad (-) \quad (-)$
$\overline{\quad -5y = -6\quad}$
$-5y = -6$
$5y = 6$
$y = \frac{6}{5}$
Putting $y = \frac{6}{5}$ in (1),
$x + y = 5$
$x + \frac{6}{5} = 5$
$x = 5 - \frac{6}{5}$
$x = \frac{5 \times 5 - 6}{5}$
$x = \frac{25 - 6}{5}$
$x = \frac{19}{5}$
So, $x = \frac{19}{5}, y = \frac{6}{5}$

16(D). Given:
$M = 77 \times 144 \times 45$
After factorisation of each number we get:
$M = 7 \times 11 \times 12 \times 12 \times 9 \times 5$
$\Rightarrow M = 7 \times 11 \times 2 \times 2 \times 3 \times 2 \times 2 \times 3 \times 3 \times 3 \times 5$
Or
$M = 7 \times 11 \times 2 \times 2 \times 2 \times 2 \times 3 \times 3 \times 3 \times 3 \times 5$
We can see from the above expression,
The prime factor of M are $2, 3, 5, 7$ and 11.

17(D). If the number 4^n, for any n, were to end with the digit zero, then it would be divisible by 5. That is, the prime factorisation of 4^n would contain the prime 5. This is not possible because $4^n = (2)^{2n}$.
So the only prime in the factorisation of 4^n is 2. So, there are no other primes in the factorisation of 4^n.

18(B). A non-terminating non-repeating decimal is a decimal number that continues endlessly with no group of digit repeating endlessly.
(A) $\frac{\sqrt{2} \times \sqrt{3}}{\sqrt{6}}$
$= \frac{\sqrt{2} \times \sqrt{3}}{\sqrt{2} \times \sqrt{3}} = 1$
So, this is incorrect option.
(B) $\frac{1}{\sqrt{2}}$
This is non-terminating non-repeating decimal expansion.
So, this is the correct option.
(C) $\frac{\sqrt{15} \times \sqrt{5}}{\sqrt{3}}$

$= \frac{\sqrt{5} \times \sqrt{3} \times \sqrt{5}}{\sqrt{3}} = 5$
So, this is incorrect option.
(D) $\frac{17}{5} = 3.4$
So, this is incorrect option.
Non-terminating non-repeating decimal expansion $= \frac{1}{\sqrt{2}}$.

19(B). 1 st vessel $= 720ml$; 2nd vessel $= 405ml$
We find the HCF of 720 and 405 to find the maximum quantity of milk to be filled in one glass.
$405 = 3^4 \times 5$
$720 = 2^4 \times 3^2 \times 5$
HCF $= 3^2 \times 5 = 45ml =$ Capacity of glass
No. of glasses filled from 1 st vessel
$= \frac{720}{45} = 16$
No. of glasses filled from 2 nd vessel
$= \frac{405}{45} = 9$
Total number of glasses $= 25$

20(D). Let the zeroes of the polynomial be $\alpha = -2$ and $\beta = 5$.
The general form of polynomial with α and β as the zeroes is given by:
$k\left[x^2 - (a + \beta)x + a\beta\right], k$ is any real number
$= k\left[x^2 - (-2 + 5)x + (-2)(5)\right]$
$= k\left(x^2 - 3x - 10\right)$
Hence, more than 3 polynomials can have the zeroes -2 and 5.

21(B). The given polynomial is:
$p(x) = x^2 - 27$
Since the degree of the polynomial $= 2$
For Zeroes of the polynomial we have,
$p(x) = 0$
$x^2 - 27 = 0$
$x^2 = 27$
$x = \pm\sqrt{27}$
$x = \pm\sqrt{3^2 \times 3}$
$x = \pm 3\sqrt{3}$
Zeroes of $p(x) = x^2 - 27$ are $\pm 3\sqrt{3}$

22(C). Total number of cards in a deck $= 52$
Number of aces in a deck $= 4$
$\Rightarrow$ Probability $=$ Number of aces that can be drawn $\div$ Total number of cards in deck
$= \frac{4}{52} = \frac{1}{13}$

23(A). Given AP is $\frac{1}{3}, \frac{5}{3}, \frac{9}{3}, \frac{13}{3}, \dots$
Here, $a_1 = \frac{1}{3}, a_2 = \frac{5}{3}, a_3 = \frac{9}{3}, a_4 = \frac{13}{3}$
First term $= a_1 = \frac{1}{3}$
Common difference, $d = a_2 - a_1 = a_3 - a_2$
$d = a_2 - a_1 = \frac{5}{3} - \frac{1}{3} = \frac{5-1}{3} = \frac{4}{3}$
$= a_3 - a_2 = \frac{9}{3} - \frac{5}{3} = \frac{9-5}{3} = \frac{4}{3}$
$= a_4 - a_3 = \frac{13}{3} - \frac{9}{3} = \frac{13-9}{3} = \frac{4}{3}$

24(C). Given, AP is $10, 7, 4, \dots$
$a = 10$
$\because d = 7 - 10 = 4 - 7 = -3$

$a_n = a + (n-1)d$

Now,

$a_{30} = 10 + (30-1)(-3) = 10 - 87 = -77$

25(D). Given:

Height of first pole $= AB = 6$ m

Height of second pole $= CD = 11$ m

Distance between feet of poles $= AC = 12$ m

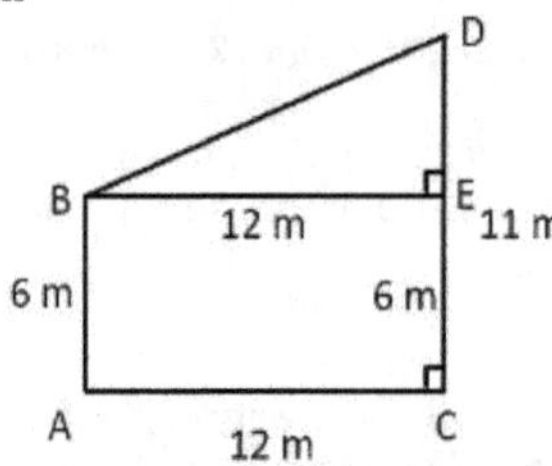

To Find: Distance between the tops of the pole ,i.e., BD

Let we draw a line BE perpendicular to DC i.e. $BE \perp DC$

Since AC is also perpendicular to DC as pole is vertical to ground,

So, $BE = AC = 12$ m

Similarly, $AB = EC = 6$ m

Now,

$DE = DC - EC$

$DE = 11 - 6$

$DE = 5$ m

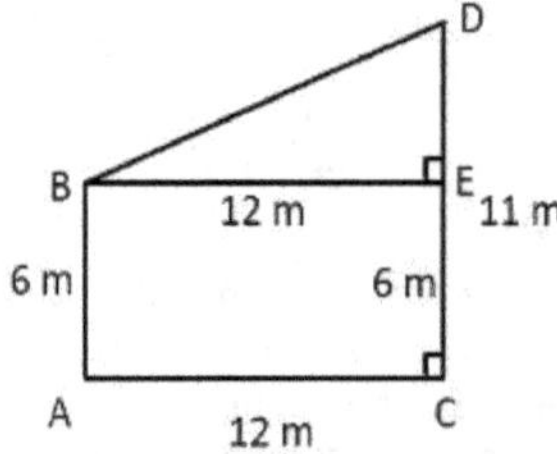

Since $\angle BED = 90°$ as $BE \perp DC$

$\triangle BED$ is right triangle

Using Pythagoras theorem in right angle triangle AEB.

$(\text{Hypotenuse})^2 = (\text{Height})^2 + (\text{Base})^2$

$(BD)^2 = (DE)^2 + (BE)^2$

$(BD)^2 = (5)^2 + (12)^2$

$(BD)^2 = 25 + 144$

$(BD)^2 = 169$

$BD = \sqrt{169}$

$BD = \sqrt{13 \times 13}$

$BD = \sqrt{(13)^2}$

$BD = 13$

So, the distance between tops of the pole $= 13$ meter.

26(A). $\triangle ABC \sim \triangle PQR \dots$

Given,

$\therefore \dfrac{\text{Perimeter of } \triangle ABC}{\text{Perimeter of } \triangle PQR} = \dfrac{AC}{PR}$

$\Rightarrow \dfrac{32}{48} = \dfrac{AC}{6}$

$\Rightarrow AC = 4$ cm

27(B). Given,

$\angle AOB = \angle EOF = \angle COD = 60°$, AB = 4 units

Since the central angle of all the triangles are same and they are formed from the common center with radius as their sides,

the length of the chord would also be the same. So, the chords will become equal as well $AB = 4$ units

Therefore, $AB = EF = CD = 4$ units

$EF + CD = 4 + 4 = 8$ units

28(C). Given, $\angle AOB = \angle POQ = 30°$

$\angle XOY = \angle ZOW = 40°$

$XY = 4$ units and $AB = 3.5$ units

As we know that, opposite side of equal angles of two different traingles are always same. Therefore, $AB = PQ = 3.5$ and $XY = ZW = 4$

$\therefore AB + ZW + PQ + XY = 3.5 + 4 + 3.5 + 4$

$\Rightarrow 15$ units

29(C). Let $P(5, -2), Q(6, 4)$ and $R(7, -2)$ are the given points.

Then, $PQ = \sqrt{(6-5)^2 + (4+2)^2}$

$\left[\because d = \sqrt{(x_2 - x_1)^2 + (y_2 - y_1)^2} \right]$

$= \sqrt{1 + 36} = \sqrt{37}$ units

$QR = \sqrt{(7-6)^2 + (-2-4)^2}$

$= \sqrt{1 + 36} = \sqrt{37}$ units

Since, $PQ = QR$

$\therefore \triangle PQR$ is an isosceles triangle.

30(D). Let points are $A(2, y)$ and $B(-4, 3)$.

Here, $(x_1, y_1) = (2, y)$ and $(x_2, y_2) = (-4, 3)$

$\therefore$ Distance between two points,

$AB = \sqrt{(x_1 - x_2)^2 + (y_1 - y_2)^2}$

[by distance formula]

$\Rightarrow AB = \sqrt{(2+4)^2 + (y-3)^2}$

$\Rightarrow 10 = \sqrt{(6)^2 + y^2 + 9 - 6y}$

$[\because AB = 10 \text{ and } (a-b)^2 = a^2 + b^2 - 2ab]$

On squaring both sides, we get

$\Rightarrow \quad (10)^2 = (6)^2 + y^2 + 9 - 6y$

$\Rightarrow \quad 100 = 36 + y^2 + 9 - 6y$

$\Rightarrow \quad 100 = 45 + y^2 - 6y$

$\Rightarrow \quad y^2 - 6y - 55 = 0$

$\Rightarrow \quad y^2 - 11y + 5y - 55 = 0$

[by factorisation]

$\Rightarrow \quad y(y - 11) + 5(y - 11) = 0$

$\Rightarrow \quad (y - 11)(y + 5) = 0$

$\Rightarrow \quad y - 11 = 0 \text{ or } y + 5 = 0$

So, the required values of y are 11 and -5.

31(B). According to the biological concept of species, a natural population of organisms who resemble each other in morphological and reproductive ways to be able to produce fertile offspring and interbreed freely is termed as a species.

32(C). Abiotic factor means the non-living chemical or physical parts of the ecosystem. So, considering that only water and temperature are the abiotic components out of all the given options. Since the pond is the ecosystem here, water is the most important abiotic factor, because the pond is essentially made of up water. If water isn't present no pond ecosystem will exist.

33(A). Ag does not displace hydrogen from dil. HCl .

Metals such as copper, silver, gold and platinum are less reactive than hydrogen. Hence, they cannot displace hydrogen from dil. HCl .

34(C). Non-metals, in general, are bad conductors of electricity. But graphite, an allotrope of carbon, and a non-metal is an exception. It is a good conductor of electricity.

35(C). Chemotropism is a type of tropic movement in which the growth or movement of a plant or plant part in response to a chemical stimulus. The growth of the pollen tube towards the ovule occurs in response to the presence of sugars in the style. Hence it is an example for chemotropism.

36(D). The directional growth movements in which the direction of growth is determined by the direction of stimulus are known as tropic movements. Tropic movement of plants/plant parts in response to moisture or water is called hydrotropism.

The growth movement of plants in response to light is known as phototropism. Growth movement of plants towards the stimulus is known as positive tropism while the movement of plant/plant parts away from the stimulus is known as negative tropism.The movement of root away from light is known as negative phototropism.

37(B). An oxidising agent is the one which oxidises other substances (by removal of hydrogen or addition of oxygen) and itself gets reduced(addition of hydrogen or removal of oxygen).

$CuO + H_2 \xrightarrow{\text{heat}} Cu + H_2O$

In above reaction, cupric oxide (CuO) acts as an oxidising agent as it oxidises hydrogen (H_2) to form water (H_2O) and copper (Cu) .

So, the hydrogen is getting oxidised in the given reaction.

38(A). A reaction in which two or more substances combine together to form a single product is known as a combination reaction.

The reaction between magnesium oxide and water is an example of combination reaction. The reaction is:

$MgO(s) + H_2O(l) \rightarrow Mg(OH)_2(aq) + \text{Heat}$

The reaction with magnesium oxide with water gives magnesium hydroxide and heat.

39(C). Alkynes are unsaturated hydrocarbons that contain at least one carbon-carbon triple bond without any functional groups.

The general structure of alkynes is as shown below:

$-C \equiv C-$

Some alkynes and their chemical formulas

are written below:
Ethyne $-C_2H_2$
Propyne $-C_3H_4$
Butyne $-C_4H_6$
Therefore, from here, we can deduce that the general formula of the alkynes is C_nH_{2n-2}

40(C). Balanced equation for combustion of ethanol can be written as:
$$C_2H_5OH + 3O_2 \rightarrow 2CO_2 + 3H_2O$$
Therefore, for combustion of 1 molecule of ethanol, 3 molecules of oxygen are required.

41(A). Breast development is the secondary sexual characteristic in females which occurs during puberty due to the hormones like estrogen and progesterone. Secretion of these hormones starts at puberty and thus contributes to the appearance of secondary sexual characteristics at this age.

42(D). If the individual is cut or broken up into many pieces accidentally, these pieces can regrow into separate individuals. This is called regeneration.
Some species, like Hydra and Planaria, undergo regeneration. Budding occurs in Saccharomyces (yeast).

43(B). Heredity can be defined as the passing of phenotypic traits from parents to their offspring, either through asexual reproduction or sexual reproduction. This is the process by which an offspring cell or organism acquires or becomes predisposed to the characteristics of its parent cell or organism. Through heredity, variations exhibited by individuals can accumulate and cause some species to evolve through the natural selection of specific phenotypic traits.

44(A). Mendel's factor is called a gene. Mendel believed that heredity is the result of discrete units of inheritance, and every single unit (or gene) was independent in its actions in an individual's genome.

45(D). The distance between the object and the mirror is 3 m, i.e., $d_1 = 3m$
Hence image distance also equals $d_1 = 3$ m
Also, the distance between the mirror and the camera is 4.5 m, i.e., $d_2 = 4.5$ m.
So, the focus of the camera,
$f = d_1 + d_2 = 3 + 4.5$
$= 7.5$ m

46(A). The Snell's law simply relates angles i and r to the refraction indices of the two media A and B. Therefore, refractive index of medium B relative to medium A is:
$$n = \frac{\sin i}{\sin r}$$
$$= \frac{\sin 60°}{\sin 45°}$$
$$= \frac{\sqrt{3}}{\sqrt{2}}$$

47(B). The factors affecting the strength of the magnetic field at a point due to a straight conductor carrying current are current, length, and distance of the wire.
The strength of the magnetic field depends upon:
- The amount of current flowing in the wire, more current will produce a stronger field.
- Length of wire, the longer wire will produce a stronger field.
- The distance of a point from the wire, the more the distance of point from the wire weaker the field.

48(D). You have a coil and a bar magnet, you can produce an electric current by moving either the magnet or the coil or both.
Moving a magnet around a coil of wire, or moving a coil of wire around a magnet, pushes the electrons in the wire and creates an electrical current.

49(A). The longest part of the digestive tract or the alimentary canal is the small intestine about 10 feet long (approximately 3 metres) in a person who is living and in a cadaver, it is twice as long as a result of loss of muscle tone.

50(B). Saprozoic organisms feed on dead decayed matter. These organism that feeds on nonliving organic matter known as detritus at a microscopic level. The etymology of the word saprotroph comes from the Greek saprós ("rotten, putrid") and trophē ("nourishment").

51(C). Changes the colour of blue litmus solution is not true for sodium hydroxide. Sodium hydroxide is a base. The base turns red litmus into the blue. Thus Sodium hydroxide turns red litmus into the blue.

52(B). Sodium zincate is produced when zinc is heated with caustic soda.
When zinc granules are heated with sodium hydroxide solution, then sodium zincate salt and hydrogen gas are formed.

$$\underset{\text{Sodium hydroxide (Base)}}{2NaOH(aq)} + \underset{\text{Zinc}}{Zn(s)} \xrightarrow{\text{Heat}} \underset{\text{Sodium zincate (salt)}}{Na_2ZnO_2(aq)} + \underset{\text{Hydrogen}}{H_2(g)}$$

53(D). Absorption does not play any role in the formation of rainbow. When light enters the water drop from atmosphere, refraction takes place. When light after refraction enters the drop at an angle greater than critical angle, total internal reflection takes place. The water droplets act like tiny prisms and disperse light into its constituent seven colours. So dispersion takes place.

54(C). The amount of charge Q, that flows between two points at potential difference $(V = 12$ V$)$ is $2C$.
Thus, the amount of work W, done in moving the charge is:
$W = VQ$
$= 12$ V $\times 2C$
$= 24$ J

55(C). Total resistanance in circuit when R_1 and R_2 are in Parallel connection with R_3 in series.
$R \Rightarrow \left(\frac{R_1 \times R_2}{R_1 + R_2}\right) + R_3$
$R \Rightarrow \left(\frac{2 \times 2}{2 + 2}\right) + 1$
$R = 2$ ohm
Curent in Circuit from ohm's law
$V = iR$
$R \Rightarrow \left(\frac{2 \times 2}{2 + 2}\right) + 1 \Rightarrow 6 = i \times 2$
$i = 3$ Amp
Voltage across A and C is
$V = iR$
$\Rightarrow 3 \times 1$
$V = 3$ volt

56(B). Irrigation agriculture is the largest consumer of water.
Irrigation is the agricultural process of applying controlled amounts of water to land to assist in the production of crops, as well as to grow landscape plants and lawns, where it may be known as watering. Agriculture that does not use irrigation but instead relies only on direct rainfall is referred to as rain-fed.

57(B).
Species with small population are rare species.
A rare species is a group of organisms that are very uncommon, scarce, or infrequently encountered. This designation may be applied to either a plant or animal taxon, and is distinct from the term endangered or threatened. Designation of a rare species may be made by an official body, such as a national government, state, or province. The term more commonly appears without reference to specific criteria. The IUCN does not normally make such designations, but may use the term in scientific discussion. Rarity rests on a specific species being represented by a small number of organisms worldwide, usually fewer than 10,000. However, a species having a very narrow endemic range or fragmented habitat also influences the concept. Almost 75% of known species can be classified as "rare".

58(B). Coal and Natural Gas are examples of energy minerals.
Coal and petroleum are categorized as fuel minerals. These are carbonaceous fuels. These are extracted from earth and are formed by fossil decomposition and are hence called fossil fuels. These fuels form a major source of energy. These are also non-renewable because these are the sources that cannot be renewed and are available in limited quantities. Coal, crude oil and natural gas are all considered fossil fuels because they were formed from the fossilized, buried remains of plants and animals that lived millions of years ago.

59(B). The sum of production in the primary, secondary, and tertiary sectors of the Indian Economy gives the value of Gross Dometic Product.

Gross domestic product (GDP) is defined as the total market value at current prices of all final goods and services produced within a year by the factors of production located within a country.

Functions of GDP:

- GDP is used to calculate the per annum percentage change in the growth rate of an economy.
- It is a quantitative aspect and its size gives an estimate of the internal strength of the economy.
- It is used by the IMF and World Bank to do a comparative analysis of its members.

60(C). One common development goal among the people is income.

Developmental goal common to all is high levels of income and better quality of life. High levels of income and better quality of life is a developmental goal common to all. HDI measures the average income, health and education.

61(C). When the news of the events in France reached the different cities of Europe, students and other members of educated middle classes began setting up Jacobin clubs.

Their activities and campaigns prepared the way for the French armies which moved into Holland, Belgium, Switzerland and much of Italy in the 1790s.

62(B). Miscellaneous agriculture is the system in which farming is done keeping in mind the land, area, and ecological diversity. Following are the major advantages of miscellaneous/multivariate agriculture -

- Protection of fertile land
- Low risk
- Proper use of resources
- Proper use of by-products
- Continuity of income
- Support more people
- Opportunity to gain more knowledge

63(B). In rural areas, most of the credit is demanded for crop production.

The crop production involves considerable costs on seeds, fertilisers, pesticides, water, electricity, repair of equipment etc. Farmers usually takes crop loans at the beginning of the season and repay the loan after harvest. The farmer gets a credit card called the Kisan Credit Card on availing this type of loan which they can use to withdraw money to make necessary purchases to meet their farming needs. Agricultural Term Loans (ATL) means, a term loan that farmers get extended repayment period of upto 15 years as an investment credit to specific agricultural activities.

64(D). Banks in India these days hold about 15% of their deposits as cash. This is kept as a provision to pay the depositors who might come to withdraw money from the bank on any given day.

Some banks are exempt from holding reserves, but all banks are paid a rate of interest on reserves. Banks keep a fraction of deposits as Cash Reserves because a prudent banker, by his experience, knows that all the depositors do not approach the banks for withdrawal of money at the same time and also they do not withdraw the entire amount in one go.

65(A). The most common route for investments by MNCs in countries around the world is to set up new factories.

An MNC is a company that owns or controls production in more than one nation . These companies set up offices and factories for production in regions where they can get cheap labour and other resources. LTI, TCS, Tech Mahindra, Deloitte, Capgemini are some of the examples of MNCs in India. A multinational corporation helps the technological growth of the country as well . They bring new innovations and technological advancements to the host country. They help modernize the industry in developing countries. MNCs also reduce the host countries dependence on imports.

66(D). Entry of MNCs in a domestic market may prove harmful for all small scale producers.

Disadvantages Of Multinational Corporations:

(1) Harmful for host country: The main objective of the MNCs is to earn maximum profit. They over exploit the natural resources of the host country.

(2) Harmful all small scale producers: Most of the small scale producers have failed to compete with the MNCs so, either they have sold their units to MNCs or have been wiped off.

(3) Harmful for Economic Equality: MNCs are interested in setting up industries in particular region and hence those regions develop very rapidly and other regions remain under developed. As MNC's pay more salaries and perks, it creates gap between the local employers and those of MNC's.

67(B). MRP on a product represents maximum retail price.

Maximum retail price (MRP) is a manufacturer calculated price that is the highest price that can be charged for a product sold in India and Bangladesh. However, retailers may choose to sell products for less than the MRPIt was meant to prevent tax evasion and protect consumers from profiteering by retailersNo retailer can charge a price higher than the MRP, and if anyone does so, the customer can take up the matter to the consumer court.

68(C). The consumer movement arose because of the dissatisfaction of the consumers as many unfair practices were being indulged in by the sellers.

Objective of consumer movement is to safeguard the interest for the consumer from the malpractices taken as one's own by the business community such as imposing high prices, supplying low quality goods, creating an artificial shortage. Rampant food shortages, hoarding, black marketing, adulteration of food, and edible oil gave birth to the consumer movement in India, an organized form in 1960s.

69(C). Shanghai became the hub of the new print culture, catering to the Western-style schools.

In the late 19th century, Western publication methods and mechanical presses were introduced in China as a result of the establishment of Western powers outposts in China. Thereon, Shanghai became the hub of the new print culture, provisioning to the western school.

70(C). Buddhist missionaries from China Introduced hand-printing technology into Japan around AD 768-770.

The Buddhist missionaries from China brought hand-printing innovation into Japan around 768 – 770 AD. The Buddhist Diamond Sutra which was imprinted in 868 AD was the most established Japanese book.

Libraries and book shops were pressed with hand-printed materials of different kinds. These remembered books for ladies, instruments, estimations, tea function, bloom courses of action, appropriate behavior, cooking, and celebrated spots.

The first sort of printing framework was the press-printing framework. The most punctual sort of print innovation was created in China, Japan, and Korea.

This was an arrangement of hand printing. In AD 594 in China printing was finished by scouring paper with wooden squares. It completely relied upon squeezing one against the other on which the issue must be printed.

71(D). Sinhala was recognized as the official language of Sri Lanka in 1956.

The Official Language Act No.33 of 1956, commonly referred to as the Sinhala Only Act, was an act passed in the Parliament of Ceylon in 1956. The act replaced English with Sinhala as the sole official language of Ceylon, with the exclusion of Tamil.

At the time, Sinhala (also known as Sinhalese) was the language of Ceylon's majority Sinhalese people, who accounted for around 70% of the country's population. Tamil was the first language of Ceylon's three largest minority ethnic groups, the Indian Tamils, Sri Lankan Tamils and Moors, who together accounted for around 29% of the country's population.

72(B). Belgium government is a good example of Community government.
- This 'community government' is elected by people belonging to one language community – Dutch, French and German-speaking – no matter where they live.
- This government has the power regarding cultural, educational and language-related issues.
- Dutch and French form the major communities and minor community group is German community.

73(C). The most powerful weapon used by the Spanish to conquer America is smallpox as a Germs.
Conventional weapons are those weapons that are used for mass destruction and these weapons include: combat helicopters, combat aircrafts, light weapons and war ships etc.
In the mid-16th century Spanish and Portuguese were the first European countries to conquer America and their conquest was not the result of any conventional military weapons or military power but they use germs of diseases i.e. smallpox because American inhabitant does not have any immunity against these smallpox and these smallpox have long isolation that came from Europe and as a result it turns out to be one of the deadliest weapon for mass killing in America.
Spread of smallpox has some historical highlights: In 6th century - smallpox was introduced in Japan so that trade can be Increased with China and Korea, 7th century - Arab expansion spreads smallpox into Spain, and Portugal and northern Africa, 11th century -Crusades spread smallpox in Europe, 15th century – Portuguese introduces smallpox in some parts of Western Africa, 16th century – Spanish uses smallpox as bio weapon against American natives and European colonization and the African slave trade import smallpox into the Caribbean and Central and South America, 17th century - European colonization imports smallpox into North America, 18th century - Great Britain introduces smallpox into Australia.

74(A). The federal system has dual objectives: to safeguard and promote unity of the country, while at the same time accommodate regional diversity.
Therefore, two aspects are crucial for the institutions and practice of federalism. Governments at different levels should agree to some rules of power sharing. They should also trust that each would abide by its part of the agreement.
An ideal federal system has both aspects : mutual trust and agreement to live together.

75(A). India is a federal country as the USA is false statement.
In India, the Central government is more powerful than the state government.
Federalism in India refers to relationship between the Central Government and the State governments of India. The Constitution of India establishes the structure of the Indian government. Part XI of the Indian constitution specifies the distribution of legislative, administrative and executive powers between the union government and the States of India. The legislative powers are categorized under a Union List, a State List and a Concurrent List, representing, respectively, the powers conferred upon the Union government, those conferred upon the State governments and powers shared among them.
In USA, all the constituent states have equal power and are strong vis-a-vis the federal government.

76(A). After the creation of the mill production was brought together under one roof and management. This allowed a more careful supervision over the production process, a watch over quality, and the regulation of labour.
Increased efficiency in production process which increased the output per worker. Production of stronger threads and yarn. Introduction of new and expensive machinery which thereby improved the quality of cloth. Improved management and supervision system because all activities took place under one roof.

77(A). In India the percentage of wasteland due to water erosion is 56%.
At present, there are about 130 million hectares of degraded land in India. Approximately, 28 per cent of it belongs to the category of forest degraded area,56 per cent of it is water eroded area and the rest is affected by saline and alkaline deposits. Some human activities such as deforestation, over grazing, mining and quarrying too have contributed significantly in land degradation.

78(D). Democracy stands much superior to any other form of Government in promoting dignity and freedom of the individual.
- Every individual wants to receive respect from fellow beings.
- The passion for respect and freedom are the basis of democracy.
- Democracy stands for respect and equal treatment of women.
- Democracy in India has strengthened the claims of the disadvantaged and discriminated groups for equal status and equal opportunities.
- It provides methods to resolve conflicts.

79(C). Accountability to the citizens is the most basic outcome of democracy.
The most basic outcome of democracy is that it produces a government that is accountable to the citizens, and responsive to the needs and expectations of the citizens. Transparency and accountability is one of the most essential feature of democracy. Whenever possible and necessary, citizens should be able to participate in decision making, that affects them all. Therefore, the most basic outcome of democracy should be that it produces a government that is accountable to the citizens, and responsive to the needs and expectations of the citizens.

80(B). Gandhiji organise the satyagraha in the areas of Champaran in Bihar, the Kheda district of Gujarat, and Ahmedabad.
After arriving in India, Mahatma Gandhi successfully organised satyagraha movements in various places. In 1917 he travelled to Champaran in Bihar to inspire the peasants to struggle against the oppressive plantation system. Then in 1917, he organised a satyagraha to support the peasants of the Kheda district of Gujarat. Affected by crop failure and a plague epidemic, the peasants of Kheda could not pay the revenue, and were demanding that revenue collection be relaxed. In 1918, Mahatma Gandhi went to Ahmedabad to organise a satyagraha movement amongst cotton mill workers.

81(A). Ernst Mayr established evolutionary biology as a separate field of research in the United States which earned him the name "Darwin of the 20th century." Ernst Mayr from Germany helped to define the modern synthesis of evolutionary theory.

82(D). Important attributes of the Parliamentary form of government:-
1. Legislature and executive are closely related and share powers with each other.
2. The cabinet is formed by the parliament and parliament is the superior organ.
3. There are two executives i.e. the elected president or king and the Prime Minister. President represents the state and Prime Minister represents the government.
4. The cabinet is responsible before the legislature.

83(A). India's economic planning cannot be said to be Imperative.
In imperative planning, on the other hand, all economic activities are controlled by the state. There is complete control of the government over the factors of production. Even the private sector needs to strictly abide by government policies and decisions, which are rigid.

84(A). Judicial Review:
- As the final interpreter of the Constitution, the judiciary also has the power to strike down particular laws passed by the Parliament if it believes that these are a violation of the basic

structure of the Constitution. This is called judicial review.

- It is a type of court proceeding in which a judge reviews the lawfulness of a decision or action made by a public body.
- In other words, judicial reviews are a challenge to the way in which a decision has been made, rather than the rights and wrongs of the conclusion reached.
- Judicial review has two important functions, legitimizing government action and the protection of the constitution against any undue encroachment by the government.

From the above, we can conclude that statement A is correct.

85(A). Lines called isotherms are drawn on the map to represent the locations where the uniform temperature resides.]

86(C). Transpiration is the evaporation of water from the aerial parts of plants, especially leaves but also stems, flowers and roots.

87(D). Article 3 of the Indian Constitution:

- It empowered the Parliament to make laws relating to the formation of new states and alteration of existing states.
- Parliament may by law:
1. Form a new State by separation of territory from a State or by uniting two or more States or parts of States
2. Increase the area of any State
3. Diminish the area of any State
4. Alter the boundaries of any State
5. Alter the name of any State

Hence, the correct option is (C).

88(D). "Thulo Dhuska" (Thulo Khela) in Uttarakhand culture is Pahadi Ramayana. Thulo Dhuska is folklore in the Eastern Kumaon, Uttarakhand. It means play of Rama. In this play, the story of Rama is depicted.

There are 2 different versions of Thulo Khela. It has divided version 1 into 15 episodes and version 2 into 11 episodes. These two versions are preserved in manuscripts by the families of principal singers called Bakhani.

The Thulo Khela is sung mainly in three tunes, the principal one is termed Dhuska. Dhuska is based on classical music. The other main tunes are termed Khela and Chalali. The accompanying musical instruments in the Thulo Khela are hudka and mijara (pair of cymbals).

89(B). Chamera Dam is built on Ravi River in Himachal Pradesh.

90(A). The temples of Khajuraho were built by the Chandelas. There are about 30 temples here, which are dedicated to Vishnu, Shiva and Jain Tirthankaras. Among these the temple of 'Kandariya Mahadev' is the most famous.

91(D). Most Sufis were persons of deep devotion who were disgusted by the vulgar display of wealth and degeneration of morals following the establishment of the Islamic empire.

- Sufis were Muslim mystics.
- In the early centuries of Islam a group of religious-minded people called sufis turned to asceticism and mysticism in protest against the growing materialism of the Caliphate as a religious and political institution.
- Most of them were persons of deep devotion, who were disgusted by the vulgar display of wealth and degeneration of morals following the establishment of the Islamic empire.
- They were critical of the dogmatic definitions and scholastic methods of interpreting the Qur'an and sunna (traditions of the Prophet) adopted by theologians.
- Instead, they laid emphasis on seeking salvation through intense devotion and love for God by following His commands, and by following the example of the Prophet Muhammad whom they regarded as a perfect human being.
- The sufis thus sought an interpretation of the Qur'an on the basis of their personal experience.
- They rejected outward religiosity and emphasised love and devotion to God and compassion towards all fellow human beings.

92(D). Hindustan Socialist Republican Association was founded on December 10, 1928 at Feroz Shah Kotla Ground in Delhi. Hindustan Socialist Republican Association was founded by Chandra Shekhar Azad. The purpose of the establishment of the Hindustan Socialist Republican Association was to establish a socialist republican state in India. In this, everyone was obliged to accept the decision of the majority. The first revolutionary act of the Hindustan Socialist Republican Association was to assassinate Saunders, assistant superintendent of police of Lahore.

93(C). Nitromonas are rod shaped bacteria that oxidize ammonia into nitrite. Nitrosomonas are useful in bioremediation. The nitrification process requires the mediation of two distinct groups: bacteria that convert ammonia to nitrites (Nitrosomonas, Nitrosospira, Nitrosococcus, and Nitrosolobus) and bacteria that convert nitrites (toxic to plants) to nitrates (Nitrobacter, Nitrospina, and Nitrococcus).

94(B). Department-related Standing Committees were set up in 1993 to scrutinise the functioning of the various Ministries/Departments of the Union Government assigned to them in order to further strengthen the accountability of the Government to Parliament.

95(B). French footballer Karim Benzema announced his retirement from International football on 20 December 2022.

Benzema made his debut for France against Austria in March 2007, he scored while playing as a substitute. He was included in the France team for Euro 2020, and he ended up being the third-highest scorer with four goals.

96(A). Rakesh Sharma was the first man in space.

Wing Commander Rakesh Sharma, AC (born 13 January 1949) is a former Indian Air Force pilot who flew aboard Soyuz T-11 on 3 April 1984 as part of the Soviet Interkosmos programme. He is the only Indian citizen to travel in space, although there have been other astronauts with an Indian background who were not Indian citizens.

Hence the correct option is (A).

97(B). Anemophily or wind pollination is a form of pollination whereby pollen is distributed by wind. Almost all gymnosperms are anemophilous, as are many plants in the order Poales, including grasses, sedges and rushes.

98(A). Nylon is a generic designation for a family of synthetic polymers, more specifically aliphatic or semi-aromatic polyamides. They can be melt-processed into fibers, films, or shapes.

99(B). Frederick William IV was not a leader of the French Revolution.

French Revolution (1789-1799) was a period of social and political upheaval in France resulting in the overthrow of the Monarchy and establishment of the Republic.

The three main leaders of the French Revolution for the rebels were Georges-Jacques Danton, Jean-Paul Marat, and Maximilien Robespierre.

100(D). The Kalidas Samman is a prestigious arts award presented annually by the government of Madhya Pradesh in India. The award is named after Kalidasa, a renowned Classical Sanskrit writer of ancient India. The Kalidas Samman was first awarded in 1980.

Mathematics

1. To construct a triangle similar to a $\triangle PQR$ with its sides, $\frac{9}{5}$ of the corresponding sides of $\triangle PQR$ a ray QX has been drawn such that $\angle QRX$ makes an acute angle and X is on the opposite side of P with respect to QR. The minimum number of points to be located at equal distances on ray QX is:

(a) 5   (b) 9

(c) 10   (d) 14

2. A pair of tangents can be constructed from a point P to a circle of radius 3.5 cm situated at a distance of from the centre.

(a) 3.5 cm   (b) 2.5 cm

(c) 5 cm   (d) 2 cm

3. The following data gives the information on the observed lifetimes (in hours) of 225 electrical components:

Lifetimes	0–20	20–40	40–60	60–80	80–100	100–120
Frequency	10	35	52	61	38	29

Determine the modal lifetimes of the components.

(a) 65.625   (b) 75.625

(c) 85.625   (d) 65.665

4. A well of diameter $3m$ is dug $14m$ deep. The earth taken out of it has been spread evenly all around it in the shape of a circular ring of width $4m$ to form an embankment. Find the height of the embankment.

(a) $2.125m$ (b) $3.125m$

(c) $1.125m$ (d) $4.125m$

5. A cylinder of radius $6cm$ and height hcm is filled with ice cream. The ice cream is then distributed among 10 children in identical cones having a hemispherical top. The radius of the base of the cone is $3cm$ and its height is $12cm$. Then the height h of the cylinder must be:

(a) $\frac{100}{7}cm$ (b) $18cm$

(c) $15cm$ (d) $\frac{200}{11}cm$

6. If the roots of the quadratic equation $x^2 + 2x + k = 0$ are real, then:

(a) $k < 0$ (b) $k \leq 0$

(c) $k < 1$ (d) $k \leq 1$

7. If α and β are the roots of the equation $4x^2 + 2x - 1 = 0$, then which one of the following is correct?

(a) $\beta = -2\alpha^2 - 2\alpha$

(b) $\beta = 4\alpha^2 - 3\alpha$

(c) $\beta = \alpha^2 - 3\alpha$

(d) $\beta = -2\alpha^2 + 2\alpha$

8. The length of the wire is $66\ cm$. The number of circles of circumference $13.2\ cm$ that can be made from the wire is:

(a) 8   (b) 6

(c) 5   (d) 3

9. The perimeter of a protractor is:

(a) $\pi r + 2r$ (b) πr

(c) $\pi + r$ (d) $\pi + 2r$

10. Solve the number of solution of the equation: $\sin(x) + \cos(x) = 1$ on the interval $0° \leq x < 360°$.

(a) 2   (b) 3

(c) 4   (d) 5

11. In a right angle triangle, ABC right angled at B, $\cos A = \frac{1}{\sqrt{5}}$. Find the value of $\sin A$.

(a) 1   (b) $\frac{2}{\sqrt{5}}$

(c) $\frac{1}{3}$ (d) $\frac{1}{4}$

12. What is the value of $\sec^3\theta \cdot \cot\theta$?

(a) $\sec^2\theta \cdot \text{cosec}\,\theta$

(b) $\sec^2\theta$

(c) $\text{cosec}\,\theta$

(d) $\sin^2\theta \cdot \cos\theta$

13. An observer 1.5 metres tall is 20.5 metres away from a tower 22 metres high. Determine the angle of elevation of the top of the tower from the eye of the observer.

(a) 30°   (b) 45°

(c) 60°   (d) 90°

14. Solve the following pairs of linear equations.
$3x + 4y = 10$ and $2x - 2y = 2$

(a) $x = 2, y = 1$ (b) $x = 3, y = 4$

(c) $x = 1, y = 2$ (d) $x = 5, y = 3$

15. If we add 1 to the numerator and subtract 1 from the denominator, a fraction reduces to 1. It becomes $\frac{1}{2}$ if we only add 1 to the denominator. What is the fraction?

(a) $\frac{2}{5}$ (b) $\frac{3}{5}$

(c) $\frac{9}{5}$ (d) $\frac{10}{5}$

16. Find the HCF and LCM of 96 and 404 by prime factorisation method.

(a) 10 and 8595   (b) 6 and 10520

(c) 4 and 9696   (d) 8 and 2653

17. For any positive integer ' a ' and 3 , there exist unique integers ' q ' and ' r ' such that $a = 3q + r$ where ' r ' must satisfy:

(a) $1 < r < 3$ (b) $0 < r < 3$

(c) $0 \leqslant r < 3$ (d) $0 < r \leqslant 3$

18. Find LCM of numbers whose prime factorisation are expressible as 3×5^2 and $3^2 \times 7^2$:

(a) 11023   (b) 11024

(c) 11025   (d) 11026

19. In a school, there are two Sections A and B of class X. There are 48 students in Section A and 60 students in Section B. Determine the least number of books required for the library of the school so that the books can be distributed equally among all students of each Section:

(a) 250   (b) 240

(c) 220   (d) 230

20. Given that two of the zeroes of the cubic polynomial $ax^3 + bx^2 + cx + d$ are 0, the third zero is:

(a) $\frac{-b}{a}$ (b) $\frac{b}{a}$

(c) $\frac{c}{a}$ (d) $\frac{-d}{a}$

21. If one zero of the quadratic polynomial $x^2 + 3x + k$ is 2 , then the value of k is:

(a) 10   (b) -10

(c) 5   (d) -5

22. A number is selected at random from the numbers $7, 3, 9, 7, 9, 5, 7, 9, 9, 5$. The probability that the selected number is their average is:

(a) $\frac{7}{10}$ (b) $\frac{5}{10}$

(c) $\frac{3}{10}$ (d) $\frac{1}{10}$

23. The sum of 4 th term and 8 th term of an AP is 24 and the sum of the 6 th and 10 th terms is 44 . Find the first three terms of the AP.

(a) $+13, -8, +3$

(b) $-13, -8, -3$

(c) $-18, -8, -13$

(d) $+13, +8, -18$

24. The eighth term of an AP is half of

its second term and 11 th term exceeds one third of fourth term by 1. Find the 15 th term.

(a) 3 (b) 4
(c) 5 (d) 6

25. $\triangle ABC \sim \triangle DEF$ If $AB = 4$ cm, $BC = 3.5$ cm, $CA = 2.5$ cm and $DF = 7.5$ cm, find the perimeter of $\triangle DEF$.

(a) 20 cm (b) 25 cm
(c) 30 cm (d) 35 cm

26. If $\triangle ABC \sim \triangle RPQ, AB = 3$ cm, $BC = 5$ cm, $AC = 6$ cm, $RP = 6$ cm and $PQ = 10$ cm, then find QR.

(a) 10 cm (b) 12 cm
(c) 14 cm (d) 16 cm

27. AB and CD are the diameters of a circle which intersects at P. Join AC, CB, BD and DA. If $\angle PAD = 60°$, then what is $\angle BPD$ equal to?

(a) 30° (b) 60°
(c) 90° (d) 120°

28. The distance between two parallel tangents of a circle of radius 4 cm is:

(a) 2 cm (b) 4 cm
(c) 8 cm (d) 16 cm

29. A line intersects the Y-axis and X-axis at the points P and Q, respectively. If $(2, -5)$ is the midpoint of PQ, then the coordinates of P and Q are, respectively:

(a) $(0, -5)$ and $(2, 0)$
(b) $(0, 10)$ and $(-4, 0)$
(c) $(0, 4)$ and $(-10, 0)$
(d) $(0, -10)$ and $(4, 0)$

30. The points $(2, 3), (3, 4), (5, 6)$ and $(4, 5)$ are the vertices of a _______.

(a) Parallelogram
(b) Triangle
(c) Square
(d) None of these

Science

31. Out of these, which group has biodegradable wastes?

(a) Plastic, polyethylene, DDT
(b) Leather, paper, cloth
(c) DDT, Mercury, lead
(d) Synthetic fibres, aluminium cans, wood

32. Ozone hole means:

(a) Hole in the stratosphere
(b) Same concentration of ozone
(c) Decrease in the concentration of ozone
(d) Increase in the concentration of ozone

33. The state in which NaCl is a bad conductor of electricity is _______ and the state in which NaCl is a good conductor of electricity is _______.

(a) solid, vapour
(b) vapour, molten
(c) molten, solid
(d) solid, molten

34. Generally, pure metals react with acids to give salt and hydrogen gas. Which of the following acids does not give hydrogen gas on reacting with metals (except Mn and Mg)?

(a) H_2SO_4
(b) HCl
(c) HNO_3
(d) All of the above

35. The positive response of the plants towards the gravitation is called _______.

(a) Phototropism
(b) Geotropism
(c) Hydrotropism
(d) Chemotropism

36. Which hormonal secretion in the body leads to the development mustache and beard in males during puberty?

(a) Progesteron (b) Estrogen
(c) Insulin (d) Testosterone

37. The reaction in which anions and cations of two different molecules exchange places, forming two completely different compounds, is called:

(a) Decomposition reaction
(b) Double displacement reaction
(c) Combination reaction
(d) Redox reaction

38. Which of the statements about the following reaction are incorrect?
$$2PbO(s) + C(s) \rightarrow 2\,Pb(s) + CO_2(g)$$

(a) Lead is getting reduced
(b) Lead oxide is getting reduced
(c) Carbon dioxide is getting oxidised
(d) Both (A) and (C)

39. Name the type of reaction when ethanol is warmed with ethanoic acid to form ethyl acetate in the presence of concentrated H_2SO_4.

(a) Esterification reaction
(b) Neutralisation reaction

(c) Decomposition reaction
(d) Double displacement reaction

40. Ethanol reacts with sodium and forms two products. These are:

(a) Sodium ethanoate and hydrogen
(b) Sodium ethanoate and oxygen
(c) Sodium ethoxide and hydrogen
(d) Sodium ethoxide and oxygen

41. Transfer of pollen to the stigma of another flower of the same plant is:

(a) Autogamy
(b) Allogamy
(c) Xenogamy
(d) Geitonogamy

42. What carries the egg from the ovary to the uterus?

(a) Vas deferens
(b) Epididymis
(c) Fallopian tube
(d) Vagina

43. The forelimbs of a man, a bat, a horse and a whale are the examples of;

(a) analogous organs
(b) vestigial organs
(c) homologous organs
(d) fossils

44. Which of the following options is not a reason for the development of a new species?

(a) Genetic drift
(b) Heredity
(c) Natural selection
(d) Geographic isolation

45. Concave lenses are also known as:

(a) Converging lenses
(b) Diverging lenses
(c) Plane lenses
(d) Circular lenses

46. An object is placed at a distance $2f$ from the pole of a convex mirror of focal length f. The linear magnification is:

(a) $\frac{1}{3}$ (b) $\frac{2}{3}$
(c) $\frac{3}{4}$ (d) 1

47. An electric motor _______.

(a) Measures electric current
(b) Converts electrical energy into mechanical energy
(c) Provides a constant potential difference
(d) Measures potential difference

48. What will happen when a magnet is taken towards a circular coil?

(a) No effect on the circular coil

(b) No effect of magnetic field

(c) Induced current will start flowing

(d) No current will flow in the circuit

49. The cup-shaped part of nephron which receives the glomerular filtrate is called:

(a) Bowman's capsule

(b) Vasa recta

(c) Collecting duct

(d) Vena cava

50. Which of the following options is not a mode of excretion in plants?

(a) Transpiration

(b) Translocation

(c) Secretion of resins and gums

(d) Through leaves

51. Which of the following indicators is not edible?

(a) Turmeric solution

(b) Vanilla essence

(c) Indicator prepared from red cabbage leaves

(d) Beetroot solution

52. Which of the following are the constituents of baking powder?

(a) Baking soda and washing soda

(b) Baking soda and carbon dioxide

(c) Baking soda and tartaric acid

(d) Caustic soda and tartaric acid

53. The process of re-emission of absorbed light in all directions with different intensities by the atom or molecule is called ________.

(a) Scattering of light

(b) Dispersion of light

(c) Reflection of light

(d) Refraction of light

54. Several electric bulbs designed to be used on a $220\,V$ electric supply line, are rated $10\,W$. How many bulbs can be connected in parallel with each other across the two wires of $220\,V$ line if the maximum allowable current is $5\,A$?

(a) 110　　　(b) 120

(c) 100　　　(d) 150

55. The SI unit of resistivity is:

(a) coulomb　　　(b) volt

(c) ohm　　　(d) ohm metre

Social Science

56. In hill and mountainous regions, people built diversion channels like ________.

(a) Gullies　　　(b) Ravines

(c) Tributaries　　(d) Guls or kuls

57. Which of the given below is a rare species?

(a) Blue sheep

(b) Andaman wild pig

(c) Asiatic buffalo

(d) Pink head duck

58. Coal mining in Jowai and Cherapunjee is done by family members in the form of a long narrow tunnel, known as ________ mining.

(a) Rathole

(b) Opencast mining

(c) Underground mining

(d) None of the above

59. Which of these can be considered as basic services?

(a) Growing of wheat

(b) Internet

(c) Storage

(d) Police station

60. Different persons could have ________ notions of a country's development.

(a) different as well as conflicting

(b) same

(c) indifferent

(d) No

61. What was the result of the activities and campaigns held at the Jacobin clubs?

(a) Prepared the way for the French armies to move to different countries.

(b) They brought about unrest in the society.

(c) They brought about crime and destruction.

(d) There was immediate peace.

62. Farming has varied from subsistence to ____ type.

(a) intensive　　　(b) extensive

(c) commercial　　(d) plantation

63. In situations with high risks, credit might create further problems for the borrower, what is it called?

(a) Absence of collateral

(b) Debt trap

(c) Debit

(d) Demand deposits

64. Grameen Bank of Bangladesh is one of the biggest success stories, in 2018 it had over______ million members in about 81,600 villages.

(a) 8　　　(b) 10

(c) 7　　　(d) 9

65. Which one of the following has benefited least because of Globalisation in India?

(a) Agriculture Sector

(b) Industrial Sector

(c) Service Sector

(d) Secondary Sector

66. Integration of markets means:

(a) Operating beyond the domestic markets

(b) Wider choice of goods

(c) Competitive price

(d) All the above

67. The basic rights of a consumer is/ are:

(a) Right to basic needs

(b) Right to safety

(c) Right to choose

(d) All of them

68. What is the function of the Bureau of Indian Standards?

(a) Certification of edible oil and cereals

(b) Develop standards for goods and services

(c) Global level institution of consumer welfare organisations

(d) Right to information

69. When did Chinese paper reach Europe?

(a) 8th century　　(b) 11th century

(c) 12th century　(d) 7th century

70. In 1295, Marco Polo, a great explorer, returned to Italy after many years of exploration in China, what knowledge did he carry back with him?

(a) How to make paper

(b) Art of calligraphy

(c) The technology of woodblock printing

(d) Visual printing

71. Which of the following country has the headquarter of the European Union?

(a) USA　　　(b) France

(c) Belgium　　(d) Australia

72. The political reason behind the conflicts in Sri Lanka is ________.

(a) Preferential policies of government

(b) Failure of non government organizations

(c) Unwillingness of parties to resolve conflict

(d) Absence of representation for weak

73. Most Indian indentured workers came from present regions of?
(a) Uttar Pradesh
(b) Bihar
(c) Dry districts of Tamil Nadu
(d) All the above

74. The first state in the Indian Union formed on the basis of linguistic differences is _______.
(a) Uttar Pradesh
(b) Andhra Pradesh
(c) Tamil Nadu
(d) Kerala

75. In which of the following lists of Indian constitution is the subject of 'population' control and family planning included?
(a) Union list
(b) Concurrent list
(c) State list
(d) Residuary list

76. What did the most dynamic industries in Britain produce?
(a) Polyester and Metals
(b) Jute and Cotton
(c) Cotton and Metals
(d) Furniture and Food processing

77. Resources which are surveyed and their quantity and quality have been determined for utilisation are known as:
(a) Potential resources
(b) Stock
(c) Developed resources
(d) Reserves

78. In a democracy, a citizen who wants to know if a decision was taken through the correct procedures can find this out, this is the hallmark of _____.
(a) Transparency
(b) Lack of transparency
(c) Opacity
(d) Ambiguity

79. Democracy is based on the idea of:
(a) Majority
(b) Minority
(c) Deliberation and negotiation
(d) None of these

80. When did the infamous Jallianwalla Bagh incident take place?
(a) 13 April 1919
(b) 10 April 1920
(c) 10 April 1919
(d) 13 April 1920

General Awareness/ Knowledge

81. ____is the founder of the Gulabi Gang an Uttar Pradesh and Madhya Pradesh based social organization that works for women welfare and empowerment.
(a) Sangeeta Pal Devi
(b) Sampat Pal Devi
(c) Sheila Pal Devi
(d) Mishi Choudhary

82. Who among the following is the current member of the International Law Commission from India?
(a) Nagender Singh
(b) P.S. Rao
(c) Aniruddha Rajput
(d) Dalbir Bhandari

83. The most important fishing industry sector in India is:
(a) deep sea
(b) in offshore
(c) cultural hinterland
(d) natural intraterrestrial

84. Which of the following Article talks about the establishment of the Supreme Court?
(a) Article 176   (b) Article 153
(c) Article 124   (d) Article 324

85. In the context of geomorphology, the term playas refer to:
(a) Shallow lakes in the depressions of plains found in desert regions.
(b) Unassorted coarse and fine debris dropped by melting glaciers.
(c) Large-sized angular blocks plucked from land by glaciers.
(d) Small round shallow depressions formed on limestone surfaces.

86. Which smartphone maker launched the first 5G-enabled smartphone of India?
(a) Xiaomi   (b) Realme
(c) Oppo   (d) Vivo

87. The constitution of India describes India as
(a) A Union of States
(b) Quasi-federal
(c) A federation of state and union territories
(d) A Unitary State

88. What do Madhubani paintings depict?
(a) Life of Bhagwan Buddha
(b) Western Culture
(c) Nature and Hindu religious figure
(d) Life of Birsa Munda

89. One of the distinct features of the peninsular plateau is the black soil area known as _____.
(a) Chotanagpur plateau
(b) Deccan trap
(c) Singur plateau
(d) Rohtas plateau

90. Which one of the following ancient towns is well-known for its elaborate system of water harvesting and management by building a series of dams and channelizing water into connected reservoirs?
(a) Dholavira   (b) Kalibangan
(c) Rakhigarhi   (d) Ropar

91. Which of the following statements about Saguna bhakti traditions is/ are correct?
1. Saguna bhakti traditions focus on the worship of specific deities such as Vishnu or his avatars.
2. In Saguna bhakti traditions, Gods and Goddesses are conceptualised in anthropomorphic forms.
Select the correct answer using the code given below:
(a) 1 only
(b) 2 only
(c) Both 1 and 2
(d) Neither 1 nor 2

92. Assertion (A): Indigo plantations came up in many parts of North and South America by the seventeenth century
Reasoning (R): The high demand and competition from Indian indigo led to European producers to pressurise their governments to ban the import of indigo and look for alternatives.
Choose the correct option.
(a) Both (A) and (R) are true and (R) is the correct explanation of (A)
(b) Both (A) and (R) are true and (R) is not the correct explanation of (A)
(c) (A) is true but (R) is false
(d) Both (A) and (R) are false

93. The only planet that contains living organisms is

(a) Mars   (b) Uranus
(c) The earth   (d) Mercury

94. Which among the following are guaranteed by the Constitution of India?
A. Freedom to move freely throughout the country.
B. Freedom to assemble peacefully without arms.
C. Freedom to own, acquire and dispose of a property anywhere in the country.
D. Freedom to practice any trade or profession.
(a) B & D only   (b) A, B & D only
(c) A, C & D only   (d) A, B & C only

95. ____________ state has won "Ranji Trophy 2022" Title.
(a) Bihar
(b) Madhya Pradesh
(c) Maharashtra
(d) Odisha

96. The first woman in the world to climb Mount Everest twice is __________.
(a) Sherpa Tenzing
(b) Edmund Hillary
(c) Premlata Agarwal
(d) Santosh Yadav

97. Ground Source Heat Pumps (GSHPs) or Geo-exchange Pumps work on the principle of:
(a) Dalton's law of partial pressure
(b) Refrigeration cycle
(c) Heat Doppler Effect
(d) Electromagnetic induction

98. Autotrophic Nutrition is mainly associated with:
(a) Fungi   (b) Protozoa
(c) Algae   (d) Virus

99. The international conflict known as the Vietnam War was fought between Vietnam and:
(a) U.S.A.   (b) Russia
(c) China   (d) North Korea

100. On 22 December 2022, writer M. Rajendran from Tamil Nadu has received Sahitya Akademi award for his novel:
(a) Kala Pani
(b) Handbook of Vegetables
(c) Service Uninterrupted
(d) None of these

___// Hints and Solutions //___

1(B). To draw a triangle similar to a given triangle with its sides m/n of the similar sides of a given triangle, the minimum number of points to be located at an equal distance is equal to m or n , whichever is greater.
Here, $\frac{m}{n} = \frac{9}{5}$
$9 > 5$, therefore the minimum number of points to be located is 9.

2(C). We know that the pair of tangents can be drawn from an external point only, so its distance from the centre must be greater than the radius. Since only 5 cm is greater than the radius of 3.5 cm . So the tangents can be drawn from the point situated at a distance of 5 cm from the centre.

3(A). Mode can be calculated as,
$$M = 1 + \left(\frac{f_1 - f_0}{2f_1 - f_0 - f_2}\right) \times h$$
Where
$I = $ Lower limit of modal class
$f_1 = $ Frequency of modal class
$f_0 = $ Frequency of class preceding the modal class
$f_2 = $ Frequency of class succeeding the modal class
$h = $ Class size
From the data given above, it can be noticed that the maximum class frequency is 61 belongs to class interval $60 - 80$.
Therefore, Modal class $= 60 - 80$
The values of unknowns are given as below as per given data:
$l = 60$
$f_1 = 61$
$h = 20$
$f_0 = 52$
$f_2 = 38$
Substituting these values in the formula of mode we get:
$$M = l + \left(\frac{f_1 - f_0}{2f_1 - f_0 - f_2}\right) \times h$$
$$M = 60 + \left(\frac{61 - 52}{2(61) - 52 - 38}\right) \times 20$$
$$M = 60 + \left[\frac{9}{122 - 90}\right] \times 20$$
$$M = 360 + \left(\frac{9 \times 20}{32}\right)$$
$$M = 60 + \frac{90}{16} = 60 + 5.625$$
$$M = 65.625$$
So, modal lifetime of electrical components is 65.625 hours.

4(C). The shape of the well will be cylindrical as shown in the figure below:

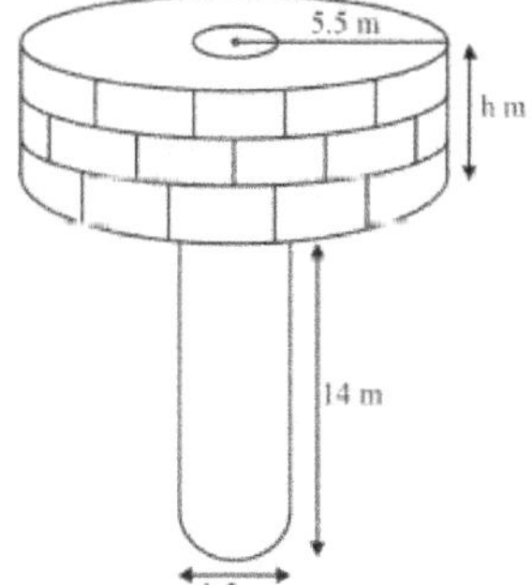

Given,
Depth of well $(h_1) = 14m$
Radius of the circular end of well $= \frac{3}{2}m$
Width of embankment $= 4m$
From the figure, it can be observed that our embankment will be in a cylindrical shape having outer radius $(r_2) = 4 + \frac{3}{2}$
$= \frac{11}{2}m$
Let the height of embankment be h_2 .
As we know,
Volume of cylinder $= \pi r^2 h$
Volume of soil dug from well = Volume of earth used to form the embankment
$\pi \times r_1^2 \times h_1 = \pi \times (r_2^2 - r_1^2) \times h_2$
$\Rightarrow \pi \times \left(\frac{3}{2}\right)^2 \times 14 = \pi \times \left[\left(\frac{11}{2}\right)^2 - \left(\frac{3}{2}\right)^2 \times h_2\right]$
$\Rightarrow \frac{9}{4} \times 14 = \left(\frac{121}{4} - \frac{9}{4}\right) \times h_2$
$\Rightarrow \frac{9}{4} \times 14 = \frac{121 - 9}{4} \times h_2$
$\Rightarrow \frac{9}{4} \times 14 = \frac{112}{4} \times h_2$
$\Rightarrow \frac{9 \times 14}{112} = h_2$
$\Rightarrow \frac{9}{8} = h_2$
$\therefore h_2 = 1.125m$
So, the height of the embankment is $1.125m$
.

5(C). Given,
Radius of cylindrical container $(r) = 6cm$
Height of cylindrical container $= h$
Volume of the cylinder $= \pi r^2 h$
$= \frac{22}{7} \times 6 \times 6 \times h$
For a conical part of ice cream
Radius of cone $(r) = 3cm$
Height of cone $(h) = 12cm$
Radius of hemisphere $(r_1) = 3cm$
As we know,
Volume of the cylinder $= \pi r^2 h$
Volume of cone $= \frac{1}{3}\pi r^2 h$
$\therefore$ Volume of ice cream in the cone with hemisphere over it = Volume of cone + volume of hemisphere
$= \frac{1}{3}\pi r^2 h + \frac{2}{3}\pi r_1^2$
$= \frac{1}{3}\pi r^2 [h + 2r] \quad [\because r = r_1]$
$= \frac{1}{3} \times \frac{22}{7} \times (3)^2 \times [12 + 2 \times 3]$
$= \frac{22}{7} \times 3 \times 18$
Let n be the number of such ice cream filled cones.
$\therefore n \times$ Volume of ice cream cones = Volume of cylindrical ice cream container
Given that 10 cones filled with the ice cream.
$n = 10$
$\Rightarrow 10 \times \frac{22}{7} \times 3 \times 18 = \frac{22}{7} \times 6 \times 6 \times h$
$\Rightarrow 10 \times 3 \times 18 = 36h$
$\Rightarrow \frac{10 \times 3 \times 18}{36} = h$
$\therefore h = 15cm$
So, the height of of the cylinder is $15cm$.

6(D). Given,
$x^2 + 2x + k = 0$

On comparing with general form:
$a = 1, b = 2, c = k$
According to the question roots are real,
$D \geq 0$
$\Rightarrow b^2 - 4ac \geq 0$
$\Rightarrow 2^2 - 4 \times 1 \times k \geq 0$
$\Rightarrow 4 - 4k \geq 0$
$\Rightarrow 4 \geq 4k$
$\Rightarrow 1 \geq k$
$\therefore k \leq 1$

7(B). Given,
$4x^2 + 2x - 1 = 0$
$x = \dfrac{b \pm \sqrt{b^2 - 4ac}}{2a}$
$\Rightarrow x = \dfrac{-2 \pm \sqrt{2^2 - 4(4)(-1)}}{2(4)}$
$\Rightarrow \alpha = \dfrac{-1 + \sqrt{5}}{4}$ and $\beta = \dfrac{-1 - \sqrt{5}}{4}$

As we know that $\sin 18° = \dfrac{-1 + \sqrt{5}}{4}$ and
$\sin 54° = \dfrac{1 + \sqrt{5}}{4}$
So, We can say that $\alpha = \sin 18°$ and
$\beta = -\sin 54°$ ... (i)
Now, From the given formula
$\sin 3\theta = 3 \sin \theta - 4 \sin^3 \theta$
On putting $\theta = 18°$ in the above
trigonometric formula, we get
$\Rightarrow \sin 54° = 3 \sin 18° - 4 \sin^3 18°$ ... (ii)
From (i) and (ii), we get
$\Rightarrow -\beta = 3\alpha - 4\alpha^3$
$\Rightarrow \beta = 4\alpha^2 - 3\alpha$
$\therefore$ The correct relation is $\beta = 4\alpha^2 - 3\alpha$.

8(C). Given,
The length of the wire is $66 \, cm$
let the no.of circles with 13.2 cm
circumference be ' x '
So,
$x \times$ circumference of each circle $= 66 \, cm$
$x \times 13.2 = 66$
$x = \dfrac{66}{13.2}$
$= 5$ circles

9(A). Let the radius of the protractor be r
$\therefore$ The perimeter of the protractor =
Perimeter of semicircle + Diameter of a
semicircle
So, Perimeter of protractor = πr + 2r

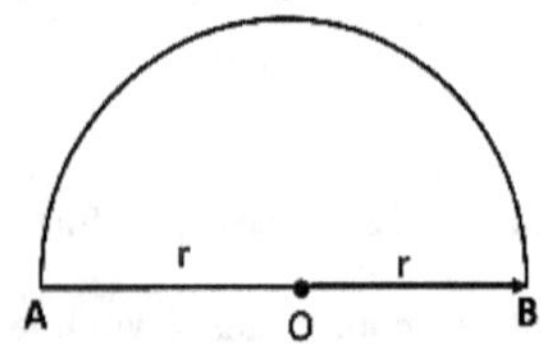

10(A). Let us take $45°$
on Squaring the equation,
$(\sin x + \cos x)^2 = (1)^2$
$= \sin^2(x) + \cos^2(x) + 2 \sin(x) \cos(x)$
$= \left(\dfrac{1}{\sqrt{2}}\right)^2 + \left(\dfrac{1}{\sqrt{2}}\right)^2 + 2 \times \left(\dfrac{1}{\sqrt{2}}\right) \times \left(\dfrac{1}{\sqrt{2}}\right)$
$= \dfrac{1}{2} + \dfrac{1}{2} + 2 \times \dfrac{1}{2}$
$= \dfrac{1 + 1 + 2}{2}$

$= \dfrac{4}{2}$
$= 2$

11(B). Given,
$\cos A = \dfrac{1}{\sqrt{5}} = \dfrac{\text{Base}}{\text{Hypotenuse}}$
As we know,
$(\text{Hypotenuse})^2 = (\text{Perpendicular})^2 + (\text{Base})^2$
$(\text{Perpendicular})^2 = (\text{Hypotenuse})^2 - (\text{Base})^2$
$= (\sqrt{5})^2 - (1)^2$
$= 5 - 1$
$= 4$
Perpendicular $= \sqrt{4} = 2$
$\sin A = \dfrac{\text{Perpendicular}}{\text{Hypotenuse}} = \dfrac{2}{\sqrt{5}}$

12(A). Given,
$\sec^3 \theta \times \cot \theta$
$\Rightarrow \dfrac{1}{\cos^3 \theta} \times \dfrac{1}{\tan \theta}$
Converting it into angle formula
$\Rightarrow \left(\dfrac{1}{\frac{\text{Base}}{\text{Hypotenuse}}}\right)^3 \times \left(\dfrac{1}{\frac{\text{Perpedicular}}{\text{Base}}}\right)$
$= \dfrac{(\text{Hypotenuse})^3}{(\text{Base})^2} \times \dfrac{1}{\text{Perpendicular}}$
$= \dfrac{(\text{Hypotenuse})^2}{(\text{Base})^2} \times \dfrac{\text{Hypotenuse}}{\text{Perpendicular}}$
$= \sec^2 \theta \times \operatorname{cosec} \theta$

13(B). Given:
AB = 22 m
PQ = 1.5 m = MB
QB = PM = 20.5 m
AM = AB−MB =22 − 1.5 = 20.5 m
Let the angle of elevation of the tower from
the eye of the observer be θ.
Now in triangle APM,

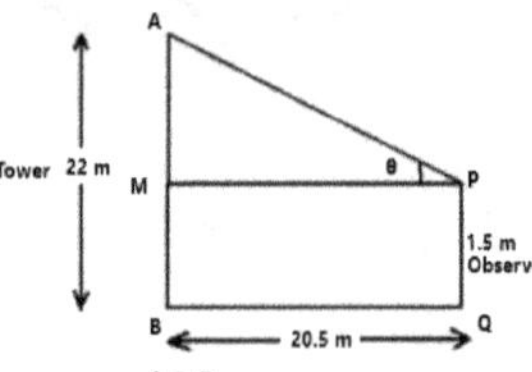

$\tan \theta = \dfrac{AM}{PM}$
$\Rightarrow \tan \theta = \dfrac{20.5}{20.5}$
$\Rightarrow \tan \theta = 1$
$\Rightarrow \tan \theta = \tan 45°$
$\theta = 45°$

14(A). Given,
$3x + 4y = 10$ ...... (1)
$2x - 2y = 2$ ...... (2)
From (1),
$3x + 4y = 10$
$3x = 10 - 4y$
$x = \left(\dfrac{10 - 4y}{3}\right)$
Putting value of x in (2),
$2x - 2y = 2$
$2\left(\dfrac{10 - 4y}{3}\right) - 2y = 2$
$\dfrac{2(10 - 4y)}{3} - 2y = 2$

$\dfrac{2(10 - 4y) - 2y \times 3}{3} = 2$
$2(10 - 4y) - 6y = 2 \times 3$
$20 - 8y - 6y = 6$
$-8y - 6y = 6 - 20$
$-14y = -14$
$y = \dfrac{-14}{-14}$
$y = 1$
Putting $y = 1$ in (2),
$2x - 2y = 2$
$2x - 2(1) = 2$
$2x - 2 = 2$
$2x = 2 + 2$
$2x = 4$
$x = \dfrac{4}{2}$
$x = 2$
Therefore, $x = 2, y = 1$ are the solution of
the given equations.

15(B). Let Numerator be x
and Denominator be y
So, Fraction is $\dfrac{x}{y}$
Given that,
If 1 is added to numerator and 1 is
subtracted from the denominator, fraction
becomes 1.
$\dfrac{\text{Nunerator} + 1}{\text{Denominator} - 1} = 1$
$\dfrac{x + 1}{y - 1} = 1$
$(x + 1) = (y - 1)$
$x - y = -1 - 1$
$x - y = -2$ ......(1)
Also,
If we add 1 to the denominator, fraction
becomes $\dfrac{1}{2}$.
$\dfrac{\text{Numerator}}{\text{Denominator} + 1} = \dfrac{1}{2}$
$\dfrac{x}{y + 1} = \dfrac{1}{2}$
$2x = y + 1$
$2x - y = 1$ ......(2)
So, our equations are
$x - y = -2$ ......(1)
$2x - y = 1$ ......(2)
We use elimination method with equation
(1) and (2)
$\quad x - y = -2$
$\quad 2x - y = 1$
$\quad (-) \quad (+) \quad (-)$
$\overline{\quad -x \quad = -3}$
$-x = -3$
$x = 3$
Putting $x = 3$ in equation (1)
$x - y = -2$
$3 - y = -2$
$-y = -2 - 3$
$-y = -5$
$y = 5$
So, $x = 3, y = 5$ is the solution of our
equation
$\therefore$ Numerator $= x = 3$
\& Denominator $= y = 5$
So, Original Fraction $= \dfrac{\text{Numerator}}{\text{Denominator}}$
$= \dfrac{x}{y} = \dfrac{3}{5}$

16(C). Prime factor of given numbers,
$96 = 2 \times 2 \times 2 \times 2 \times 2 \times 3 = 2^5 \times 3^1$ and
$404 = 2 \times 2 \times 101 = 2^2 \times (101)^1$
HCF $(96, 404) = 2^2 = 4$
We know that HCF $\times$ LCM = product of two natural numbers.
HCF $(96, 404) \times$ LCM $(96, 404) = 96 \times 404$
$\Rightarrow 4 \times$ LCM $(96, 404) = 96 \times 404$
$\Rightarrow$ LCM $(96, 404) = \frac{96 \times 404}{4} = 96 \times 101 = 9696$

17(C). Given,
$a = 3q + r$
By Euclid's division algorithm if a and b are positive integers then there exists a unique pair of integers q and r satisfying $a = bq + r$ and $0 \leq r < b$.
By comparing the given equation with euclid division algorithm.
We will have $a = 3q + r$ and $b = 3$
The value of r can take $0 \leqslant r < 3$

18(C). LCM of given number
3×5^2 and $3^2 \times 7^2$
$\Rightarrow 3^2 \times 5^2 \times 7^2$
$= 9 \times 25 \times 49$
$= 11025$

19(B). Since the books are to be distributed equally among the students of Section A and Section B. therefore, the number of books must be a multiple of 48 as well as 60.
So, required number of books is the LCM of 48 and 60.
$48 = 2^4 \times 3$
$60 = 2^2 \times 3 \times 5$
$LCM = 2^4 \times 3 \times 5 = 16 \times 15 = 240$

2	48
2	24
2	12
2	6
	3

2	60
2	30
3	15
	5

20(A). Let $p(x) = ax^3 + bx^2 + cx + d$
Given that two zeroes are 0
$\therefore \alpha = 0, \beta = 0$
and we need to find γ
We know that
Sum of zeroes $= \frac{-b}{a}$
$\alpha + \beta + \gamma = \frac{-b}{a}$
$0 + 0 + \gamma = \frac{-b}{a}$
$\gamma = \frac{-b}{a}$
Thus, the third zero is $\frac{-b}{a}$

21(B). Given, the quadratic polynomial is $x^2 + 3x + k$.
One zero of the polynomial is 2.
We have to find the value of k.

Let $f(x) = x^2 + 3x + k$
$f(2) = 0$
Put $x = 2$ in the polynomial
$(2)^2 + 3(2) + k = 0$
$4 + 6 + k = 0$
$10 + k = 0$
$k = -10$
Therefore, the value of k is -10

22(C). Average of given numbers $= \frac{7+3+9+7+9+5+7+9+9+5}{10} = \frac{70}{10} = 7$
(There are 3 times 7 in the given numbers)
Therefore Number of outcomes $n(A) = 3$
Number of total outcomes $n(S) = 10$
$\therefore$ Required Probability $= \frac{n(A)}{n(S)}$
$\Rightarrow \frac{3}{10}$

23(B). Let a be the first term and d be the common difference of the AP.
Given,
$a_4 + a_8 = 24$ and $a_6 + a_{10} = 44$
We know,
$T_n = a + (n-1)d$
$a =$ first term
$d =$ common difference
$T_n = n^{\text{th}}$ term
So,
$\Rightarrow (a + 3d) + (a + 7d) = 24$
$\Rightarrow 2a + 10d = 24$
$\Rightarrow a + 5d = 12 \qquad \ldots\ldots(i)$
$\Rightarrow (a + 5d) + (a + 9d) = 44$
$\Rightarrow 2a + 14d = 44$
$\Rightarrow a + 7d = 22 \qquad \ldots\ldots(ii)$
Subtracting (i) from (ii), we get
$2d = 10$
$\Rightarrow d = 5$.
Putting $d = 5$ in (i), we get
$a + 5 \times 5 = 12$
$\Rightarrow a + 25 = 12$
$\Rightarrow a = -13$
So, the first three terms of the AP are
$-13, (-13 + 5), (-13 + 2 \times 5)$ i.e.
$-13, -8, -3$.

24(A). Let a be the first term and d be the common difference of the AP.
Given,
$a_8 = \frac{1}{2}a_2$ and $a_{11} = \frac{1}{3}a_4 + 1$
We know,
$T_n = a + (n-1)d$
$a =$ first term
$d =$ common difference
$T_n = n^{\text{th}}$ term
So,
$\Rightarrow a + 7d = \frac{1}{2}(a + d) \Rightarrow 2a + 14d = a + d$
$\Rightarrow a = 13d \qquad \ldots\ldots(i)$
Also,
$a_{11} = \frac{1}{3}a_4 + 1 \Rightarrow a + 10d = \frac{1}{3}(a + 3d) + 1$
$\Rightarrow 3a + 30d = a + 3d + 3 \Rightarrow 2a + 27d = 3$
$\Rightarrow 2(-13d) + 27d = 3$ putting the value of a from (i)
$\Rightarrow -26d + 27d = 3 \Rightarrow d = 3$
From (i), $a = (-13) \times 3 \Rightarrow a = -39$

Now, 15 th term
$= a + 14d = -39 + 14 \times 3 = -39 + 42 =$
So, the 15 th term of the AP is 3.

25(C). Given,
$\triangle ABC \sim \triangle DEF$
$\therefore \frac{(\text{Perimeter of } \triangle ABC)}{(\text{Perimeter of } \triangle DEF)} = \frac{AC}{DF}$
$\frac{(AB + BC + CA)}{(\text{Perimeter of } \triangle DEF)} = \frac{AC}{DF}$

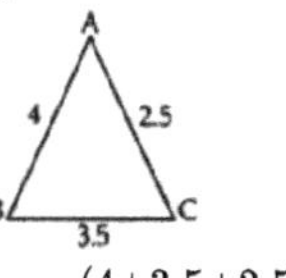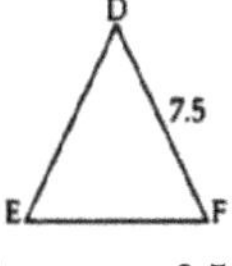

$\frac{(4 + 3.5 + 2.5)}{(\text{Perimeter of } \triangle DEF)} = \frac{2.5}{7.5}$
$\frac{(10)}{(\text{Perimeter of } \triangle DEF)} = \frac{1}{3}$
$\therefore$ perimeter of $(\triangle DEF) = 30$ cm

26(B). Given,
$AB = 3$ cm
$BC = 5$ cm
$AC = 6$ cm
$RP = 6$ cm
$PQ = 10$ cm
$\triangle ABC \sim \triangle RPQ \ldots.$

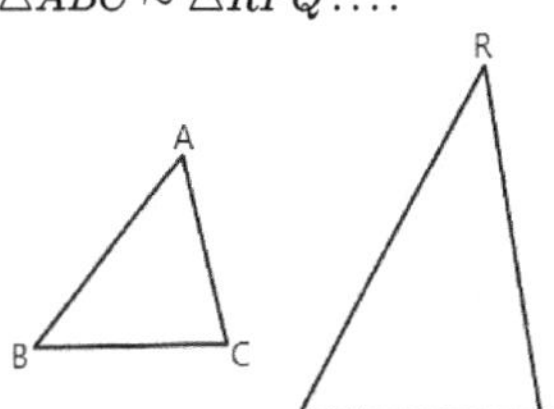

$\therefore \frac{AB}{RP} = \frac{BC}{PQ} = \frac{AC}{RQ}$ (In $\sim \triangle$ s corresponding sides are proportional)
$\Rightarrow \frac{3}{6} = \frac{5}{10} = \frac{6}{QR}$
$\Rightarrow \frac{1}{2} = \frac{6}{QR}$
$\therefore QR = 12$ cm

27(D). Given,
$\angle PAD = 60°$

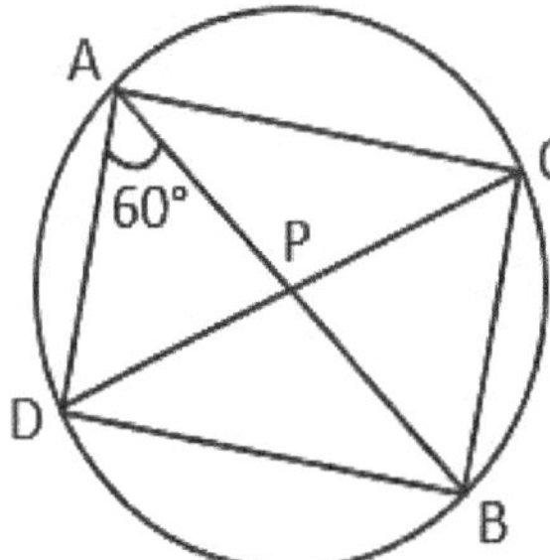

In $\triangle APD$, $AP = DP$ (Radii of circle)
In a triangle angles opposite to equal sides are equal.
$\angle PAD = \angle PDA = 60°$
$\angle PAD + \angle PDA + \angle APD = 180°$ (Angle sum property of $\triangle$)
$60° + 60° + \angle APD = 180°$
$\angle APD = 60°$
$\angle APD + \angle BPD = 180°$ (Linear pair)
$\angle BPD = 120°$

28(C). As we know that, the d istance between the two parallel tangent to a circle is equal to the diameter. As, according to the diagram given below,
$PQ = PO + OQ$
$= 2\times$ radius
$= 2 \times 4$ cm
$= 8$ cm

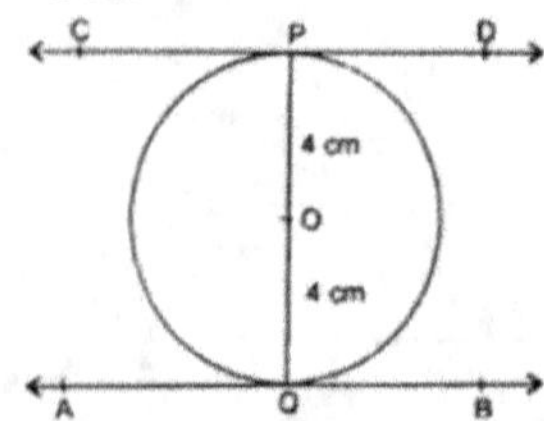

29(D). Let the coordinates of P and $Q(0, y)$ and $(x, 0)$, respectively.
So, the mid-point of $P(0, y)$ and $Q(x, 0)$ is
$M\left(\dfrac{0+x}{2}, \dfrac{y+0}{2}\right)$
$\because$ mid-point of a line segment having points (x_1, y_1) and $(x_2, y_2) = \left(\dfrac{x_1+x_2}{2}, \dfrac{y_1+y_2}{2}\right)$
But it is given that, mid-point of PQ is $(2, -5)$.

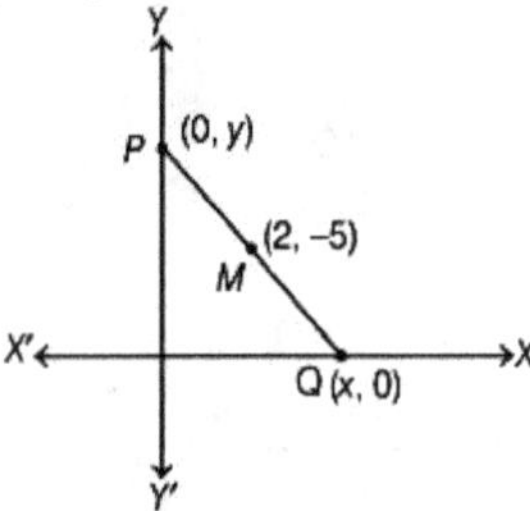

$\therefore 2 = \dfrac{x+0}{2}$ and $-5 = \dfrac{y+0}{2}$
$\Rightarrow 4 = x$ and $-10 = y$
$\Rightarrow x = 4$ and $y = -10$
So, the coordinates of P and Q are $(0, -10)$ and $(4, 0)$.

30(A). Let the points are $A(2, 3), B(3, 4), C(5, 6)$ and $D(4, 5)$.
Distance $= \sqrt{(x_2 - x_1)^2 + (y_2 - y_1)^2}$
Then, by distance formula
$AB = \sqrt{(3 - 2)^2 + (4 - 3)^2} = \sqrt{(1)^2 + (1)^2}$
$= \sqrt{2}$ units
$BC = \sqrt{(5 - 3)^2 + (6 - 4)^2}$
$= \sqrt{(2)^2 + (2)^2} = \sqrt{4 + 4}$
$= \sqrt{8} = 2\sqrt{2}$ units
$CD = \sqrt{(4 - 5)^2 + (5 - 6)^2}$
$= \sqrt{(-1)^2 + (-1)^2} = \sqrt{2}$ units
and
$AD = \sqrt{(4 - 2)^2 + (5 - 3)^2} = \sqrt{(2)^2 + (2)^2}$
$= \sqrt{4 + 4} = \sqrt{8} = 2\sqrt{2}$ units
Here, $AB = CD$ and $AD = BC$ i.e. the opposite sides are equal. So, given points are vertices of a parallelogram.

31(B). Biodegradable is the waste which can be degraded by the activity of microbes.

The leather is obtained from the skin of the animals which is degradable. Paper is made from wood and contains cellulose which can be degraded by the microbes producing cellulose. Cloth contains cellulosic fibres which can be broken down by the microbes.

32(C). Due to the depletion of stratospheric ozone, a seasonal hole in the ozone layer at polar regions is formed in the atmosphere. This is known as the ozone hole.
The depletion of ozone causes harmful UV rays to reach the earth. UV radiations are responsible for causing skin cancers and various diseases in humans.

33(D). The state in which NaCl is a bad conductor of electricity is solid and the state in which NaCl is a good conductor of electricity is molten.
NaCl is a bad conductor of electricity in the solid-state as there are no free ions. In the molten state, the ions are free to move around and therefore, can conduct electricity.

34(C). Some of the metals react with dilute acid, forming metal salt and hydrogen, while a few do not react with dilute acids.
Hydrogen gas is not evolved when a metal reacts with nitric acid. It is because HNO_3 is a strong oxidizing agent. It oxidises the H_2 produced to water and itself gets reduced to any of the nitrogen oxides (N_2O, NO, NO_2).

35(B). The positive response of the plants towards the gravitation is called geotropism.
Geotropism means response to gravity if the response is in the direction of the gravity then it is called positive geotropism since root is growing downwards (in the direction of gravity) so it is called positive geotropism.

36(D). Testosterone is the primary male sex hormone and an anabolic steroid. In male humans, during puberty, the growth of mustache and beard is seen as a sign of growth. It is a sex hormone that plays important roles in the body. In men, it's thought to regulate sex drive (libido), bone mass, fat distribution, muscle mass and strength, and the production of red blood cells and sperm. A small amount of circulating testosterone is converted to estradiol, a form of estrogen.

37(B). The reaction, in which anions and cations of two different molecules exchange places, forming two completely different compounds, is called double displacement reaction. The chemical bonds between the reactants may be either covalent or ionic. A double displacement reaction is also called a double replacement reaction, salt metathesis reaction, or double

decomposition. The reaction between silver nitrate and sodium chloride is a double displacement reaction. The silver gives its nitrite ion for the sodium's chloride ion, causing the sodium to pick up the nitrate anion.
$AgNO_3 + NaCl \rightarrow AgCl + NaNO_3$

38(D). Lead oxide reacts with carbon to form lead and carbon dioxide. The balanced chemical equation is:
$2PbO(s) + C(s) \rightarrow 2\,Pb(s) + CO_2(g)$
Gain of oxygen is oxidation and loss of oxygen is reduction. Lead oxide loses oxygen. Hence, it is reduced. So the statement, "Lead oxide is getting reduced" is correct statement.
Lead gains oxygen. Hence, it is oxidised. The statement, "Lead is getting reduced." is incorrect and carbon dioxide loses oxygen. Hence, it is reduced. So, the statement, "Carbon dioxide is getting oxidised." is incorrect.

39(A). Reaction of ethanol with warm ethanoic acid to form ethyl acetate (an ester) and water can be written as:
$C_2H_5OH + CH_3COOH \xrightarrow{H^+} CH_3COOC_2H_5 + H_2O$
(ethanol) (ethanoic acid) (ester)
The above reaction is an esterification reaction as alcohol and an acid are combined to form an ester.

40(A). The equation for the reaction between sodium and ethanol can be written as:
$2CH_3CH_2OH + 2Na \rightarrow 2CH_3CH_2ONa + H_2$
Therefore, the products formed are sodium ethoxide and hydrogen.

41(D). The transfer of pollen grain from the anther to the stigma of a pistil is called pollination. It is a mechanism by which non-motile male and female gametes are brought together for the fertilization.
Pollination in which pollen grains from the anther fuse with the stigma of the same flower or with the stigma of another flower but of the same plant is called self-pollination.
Self- Pollination is of two types: Autogamy and geitonogamy. The transfer of pollen grains from the anther of one flower to the stigma of another flower of the same plant is called geitonogamy. This transfer involves an agent of pollination. Genetically, it is similar to autogamy since the pollen grains come from the same plant.

42(C). Fallopian tube carries the egg from the ovary to the uterus.
The ovaries produce the egg cells, called the ova or oocytes. The oocytes are then transported to the fallopian tube where fertilization by a sperm may occur. The fertilized egg then moves to the uterus, where the uterine lining has thickened in response to the normal hormones of the

reproductive cycle.

43(C). The forelimbs of man, cat, bat and whale are homologous organs.
Organs, which have a common fundamental anatomical plan and similar embryonic origin whatever varied functions they may perform are regarded as homologous organs. For instances, the flippers of a whale, a bat's wing, forelimb of a horse, a bird's wing and forelimbs of human are structurally as well as functionally different. Whale's flippers help in swimming, wings of birds and bat are used in flying, horse's forelimb help in running and human's hand is meant for grasping. They have structurally modified accordingly. However, anatomically they have similar bones, humerus in the upper arm, radius ulna in the forearm, carpals and metacarpals in the wrist and hand. The presence of homologous organs in different groups of animals indicates their common origin or ancestry and degree of closeness to the difference among various groups.

44(B). A) A second process called genetic drift describes random fluctuations in allele frequencies in populations, which can eventually cause a population of organisms to be genetically distinct from its original population and result in the formation of a new species.
B) Heredity, also called inheritance or biological inheritance, is the passing on of traits from parents to their offspring; either through asexual reproduction or sexual reproduction, the offspring cells or organisms acquire the genetic information of their parents.
C) New species can also be created through hybridisation followed, if the hybrid is favoured by natural selection, by reproductive isolation.
D) The development of new species due to geographical separation is known as allopatric speciation. With the two groups of organisms no longer interbreeding, their gene pools become separate. Genes are no longer exchanged between the two groups, allowing them to diverge into two different species.

45(B). Concave lenses are also known as diverging lenses. Concave lenses are thinner in the middle. Rays of light that pass through the lens are spread out (they diverge).

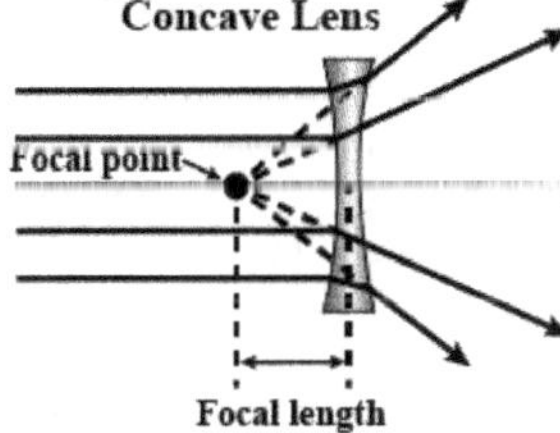

46(A). Given,
Object distance, $u = -2f$

Image distance, $v = ?$
From mirror formula,
$$\frac{1}{v} + \frac{1}{u} = \frac{1}{f}$$
$$\frac{1}{v} + \frac{1}{-2f} = \frac{1}{f}$$
$$\frac{1}{v} = \frac{3}{2f}$$
$$v = \frac{2f}{3}$$
Now,
Magnification, $M = \frac{-v}{u}$
$$= -\frac{\frac{2f}{3}}{(-2f)}$$
$$= \frac{1}{3}$$
(M is positive for convex mirror)

47(B). An electric motor is an electrical machine that converts electrical energy into mechanical energy. The reverse of this is the conversion of mechanical energy into electrical energy and is done by an electric generator, which has much in common with a motor.

48(C). According to Lenz's law, when a closed coil is linked with a varying magnetic flux, then some current is induced in the coil.
So, when a magnet is taken towards a circular coil, then a varying magnetic flux is linked with the coil so that current is induced in the coil. This phenomenon is said to be electromagnetic induction.

49(A). The cup-shaped part of nephron which receives the glomerular filtrate is called 'Bowman's capsule'.
The Bowman's capsule is a membranous, double-walled capsule-like structure. It lies below the glomerulus surrounding it from the ventral side. It is the initial portion of the renal corpuscle of the nephron. It is involved in blood plasma filtration. It continues with the proximal convoluted tubule.

50(B). Mode of excretion in plants are transpiration, secretion of resins and gums and through leaves.
All plants perform transpiration that is that the method by that plants transport water from the roots to the aerial components of the plant for elimination within the style of water droplets or water vapor.
Excess carbon dioxide and oxygen are excreted from the plant through the stomata in the leaves.
Liquid waste products are excess water, gums. These are excreted via stomata or hydathodes.

51(A). Turmeric solution indicator is not edible. Turmeric is an acid-base indicator. When it reacts with bases, it changes color to deep red. This red form of the indicator can change back to yellow when acids are added. Turmeric compound is a naturally occurring yellow colour compound. It is an acid-base indicator, turmeric compound remains yellow when acid or neutral

solutions are added to it.

52(C). Baking soda and tartaric acid are the constituents of baking powder.
Baking powder is a mixture of sodium hydrogen carbonate and edible acid-like tartaric acid. It is a raising agent that is commonly used in cake-making. It is made from an alkali, bicarbonate of soda, an acid, cream of tartar, and a filler like corn flour or rice flour, which absorbs moisture. The powder is activated when liquid is added, producing carbon dioxide and forming bubbles that cause the mixture to expand.

53(A). The process of absorbed light in all possible directions with different intensities and frequencies by an atom or a molecule is called the scattering of light. When a beam of light strikes such fine particles, the path of the beam becomes visible. The light reaches us, after being reflected diffusely by these particles.

54(A). The resistance of bulb can be calculated by the formula-
$$P = \frac{V^2}{R}$$
So,
$$R = \frac{V^2}{P}$$
$$= 220 \times \frac{220}{10}$$
$$= 4840\,\Omega$$
Now coming on to the circuit,
$V = 220\,V$
$I = 5\,A$
So by Ohm's law, we get
$$R = \frac{V}{I} = \frac{220}{5} = 44\,\Omega$$
Let there be n resistances of $4840\,\Omega$ in parallel and net resistance $= 44\,\Omega$
So,
$$\frac{1}{44} = \frac{1}{4840} + \frac{1}{4840} \ldots n \text{ times}$$
This implies that,
$$R = \frac{4840}{n}$$
$$\frac{4840}{n} = 44$$
Therefore $n = 110$
This tells us that 110 bulbs can be connected in parallel.

55(D). We all know,
$$R = \text{Resistivity} \times \frac{\text{length}}{\text{Area}}$$
and, R have unit Ω and length and area have units Meter and Meter^2
therefore,
from the above formula,
$$\text{Resistivity} = \Omega \frac{\text{Meter}^2}{\text{Meter}}$$
therefore,
$\text{Resistivity} = \Omega - \text{Meter i.e, ohm metre}$

56(D). In hill and mountainous regions, people built diversion channels like guls or kuls.
Kuls:
- People are developing channels like 'guls' or 'kuls' in the Western Himalayas.
- Agricultural fields have been converted to rain-fed storage systems in arid and

semi-arid areas.
- For the purpose of irrigation, they are made and used.
- There are channels of diversion.
- In the state of Himachal Pradesh, they are mostly used.
- They serve a very important role during construction and maintenance, and careful care should be taken.

57(C). Asiatic buffalo is a rare species.
These species are decreased to levels, to move into the endangered category in the near future.
Examples: Blue sheep, Asiatic elephant, Gangetic dolphin, etc.

58(A). Coal mining in *Jowai* and *Cherapunjee* is done by family members in the form of a long narrow tunnel, known as rathole mining.
Rat-hole mining refers to the mining of minerals like coal, limestone, iron ore, etc., by drilling long tunnels downwards from the surface is called Rat-hole mining. Generally, mining of minerals is done by the Government. Since the 1980 s, rat-hole mining is the primarily practiced mining technique in Meghalaya in which deep vertical shafts with narrow horizontal tunnels of 3 to 4 feet diameter are dug and miners are sent down to extract coal till 100 to 150 metre and in some case even more than that. This process mostly involves children because of their small body frame. Since the coal seams are very thin in Meghalaya, rat-hole mining is considered to be an economically viable method of coal extraction rather than removal of rocks from hilly terrains and putting up pillars inside the mine to prevent collapse like open cast mining.

59(D). Police station can be considered as basic services.
In any country, several services such as hospitals, educational institutions, post and telegraph services, police stations, courts, village administrative offices, municipal corporations, defence, transport, banks, insurance companies, etc., are required. These can be considered as basic services. the government of respected countries and the UN (United Nation Organisation) is responsible for providing basic services in developing countries like India

60(A). Different persons could have different as well as conflicting notions of a country's development.
Different persons have different notions of development because life scenario of persons are different. Some persons are poor and some are rich. They think about those things which are most important to them. Thus people have different notions of development and think according to their life situations. For some, development may mean the mushrooming of tall buildings, the rampant growth of shopping malls and a phenomenal rise in GDP. But for others, it should be a means to access education, health, decent housing and other amenities.

61(A). The result of the activities and campaigns held at the Jacobin clubs they prepared the way for the French armies to move to different countries.
Jacobin club belonged mainly to the less prosperous section of society. It was a political club formed to discuss government policies and plan their own forms of action. Jacobins planned an insurrection of a large number of Parsians who were angered by the short supplies and high prices of food.

62(C). Farming has varied from subsistence to commercial type.
Commercial Farming is a type of farming that uses higher doses of modern inputs to achieve higher productivity, like high-yielding variety seeds, chemical fertilisers, insecticides and pesticides. A plantation is a form of commercial farming where a single crop is cultivated in a wide area.

63(B). In situations with high risks, credit might create further problems for the borrower, it is called debt trap.
A debt trap is defined as "A situation in which a debt is difficult or impossible to repay, typically because high interest payments prevent repayment of the principal. Such a situation arises when you spend more than you earn. But life happens unexpected events, a decision to pursue an education or bad planning can push you into taking on debt that may take years to pay off.
Normally, debt trap will result in default of payments or bankruptcies.

64(D). Grameen Bank of Bangladesh is one of the biggest success stories, in 2018 it had over nine million members in about 81,600 villages.
Grameen Bank, Bangladeshi bank founded by economist Muhammad Yunus as a means of providing small loans to poor individuals (see microcredit). In 2006 Grameen and Yunus were awarded the Nobel Prize for Peace. More than 97 percent of Grameen's loan recipients have been women. The success of Grameen Bank as a bank for the poor is its creation of a market niche as well as outreach to women among the poor.
Similarly, although subsidized funds and grants were instrumental for institutional development, Grameen Bank has the potential capacity to operate with resources from market sources.

65(A). Agriculture sector has benefitted least because of Globalisation in India.
The impact of globalization on Indian agriculture has been felt since colonial times. Raw cotton and species were important export items from India. In 1917, Indian farmers revolted in Champaran against being forced to grow indigo instead of food grains, in order to supply dye to Britain's flourishing textile industry. Following are some positive consequences of globalization on Indian agriculture. 1) Availability of modern agro- technologies: There is availability of modern agro technologies in pesticides, herbicides, and fertilizers as well as new breeds of high yield crops were employed to increase food production. On the other hand negative Impacts on Agriculture are due to globalization, Indian farmers will try to grow more cash crops and there will be a shortage of food in our country. Multinational Companies [MNCs] of developed countries will exploit our farmers as Indian farmers are poor and illiterate.

66(D). Integration of market includes operating beyond the domestic markets, wider choice of goods and competitive price.
Market integration occurs when prices among different locations or related goods follow similar patterns over a long period of time . Groups of goods often move proportionally to each other and when this relation is very clear among different markets it is said that the markets are integrated. Market integration provides a number of social benefits , including broadening the range of financial services and investment opportunities available to consumers and increasing competition in the provision of those services.

67(D). All of the given options are the basic rights of a consumer.
The eight consumer rights are:
- Right to basic needs
- Right to safety
- Right to information
- Right to choose
- Right to representation
- Right to redress
- Right to consumer education
- Right to healthy environment

68(B). The function of the Bureau of Indian Standards is to Develop standards for goods and services
Bureau of Indian Standards (BIS) is the National Standard Body of India. BIS is responsible for the harmonious development of the activities of standardization, marking and quality certification of goods and for matters connected therewith or incidental thereto.

69(A).
In 8th Century Chinese paper reach Europe. During the 8th century, Chinese papermaking spread to the Islamic world, where pulp mills and paper mills were used for papermaking and money making. By the 11th century, papermaking was brought to Europe.

70(C).

In 1295, Marco Polo, a great explorer, returned to Italy after many years of exploration in China, the knowledge of the technology of woodblock printing he carry back with him back.

Marco Polo, the great Venetian explorer/merchant is said to have brought back with him from his fabled visits to China, noodles, which became the pasta that Italy is famed for today. To be more specific, the legend is that he brought back macaroni, which is today a generic term for all dried alimentary pastas made from hard wheat (which the Chinese did not cultivate or consume). Basically, the idea is that he brought back dried "filamentous" pasta or noodles.

71(C). Brussels (Belgium) is considered the de facto capital of the European Union, having a long history of hosting a number of principal EU institutions within its European Quarter.

The EU has no official capital, and no plans to declare one, but Brussels hosts the official seats of the European Commission, Council of the European Union, and European Council, as well as a seat (officially the second seat but de facto the most important one) of the European Parliament. In 2013, this presence generated about 250 million euros (8.3% of the regional GDP) and 121,000 jobs (16.7% of the regional employment).

72(A). The political reason behind the conflicts in Sri Lanka is Preferential policies of government.

The origins of the Sri Lankan Civil War lie in the continuous political rancor between the majority Sinhalese and the minority Tamils, and the preference given to Sinhalese by the government in the policies enacted especially Sinhala only act. The rest of the factors do not figure as the political reason.

73(D). Most Indian indentured workers came from the present-day regions of eastern Uttar Pradesh, Bihar and the dry districts of Tamil Nadu.

The main destinations of Indian indentured migrants were the Caribbean islands, Mauritius and Fiji. Nineteenth-century indenture has been described as a new system of slavery.

74(B). The first state in the Indian Union formed on the basis of linguistic differences is Andhra Pradesh.

Andhra Pradesh was initially a part of Tamil Nadu. The people in the Southern region of the combined state spoke Tamil and people in the northern part spoke Telugu. Hence the people who spoke Telugu demanded a separate state for better governance and separate statehood. Andhra Pradesh was created based on a Linguistic basis on 1st October 1953.

75(B). Concurrent List of Indian constitution is the subject of 'population' control and family planning included.

Both the Parliament and state legislatures can legislate on items mentioned in the Concurrent List. The Concurrent List has 47 numbered topics and population control and family planning are one of them. It is listed as item 20A under economic and social planning. The Concurrent list or List-III (Seventh Schedule) is a list of 52 items given in the Seventh Schedule to the Constitution of India.

76(C). The most dynamic industries in Britain were clearly cotton and metals.

Growing at a rapid pace, cotton was the leading sector in the first phase of industrialisation up to the 1840s. After that the iron and steel industry led the way. Among these two industries, cotton was the leading sector up to the 1840s.

77(C). Developed resources are the resources which are surveyed and their quality and quantity have been determined for utilisation.

The development of resources depends on technology and level of their feasibility. For estimating their quantity and quality. Those resources that exist in a special area and can be practiced in future are known as Potential Resources.

Developed Resources: Resources which are created and studied for use and are being utilized in the present time are known as developed resources. The advancement of these resources relies upon innovation and level of their attainability. For e.g., Petroleum and liquid gas in Bombay High in Maharashtra.

78(A). In a democracy, a citizen who wants to know if a decision was taken through the correct procedures can find this out – this is the hallmark of Transparency. Democracy ensures that decision making will be based on norms and procedures. So, a citizen who wants to know if a decision was taken through the correct procedures can find this out. She has the right and the means to examine the process of decision making. This is known as transparency.

79(C). Democracy is based on the idea of deliberation and negotiation.

The key to the success of a democracy is discussion an negotiation. It is through discussions only that the problems are discussed and various solutions are brought up. Negotiation help in deciding as to which option is best suited to a particular problem. Thus, democracy is based on the idea of deliberation and negotiation. With its emphasis on notions of social contract and the collective will of all the voters, democracy can also be characterised as a form of political collectivism because it is defined as a form of government in which all eligible citizens have an equal say in lawmaking.

Hence, the correct option is (D).

80(A). The infamous Jallianwalla Bagh incident take place on 13 April 1919.

Jallianwalla Bagh also called the Massacre of Amritsar, incident on April 13, 1919, in which British troops fired on a large crowd of unarmed Indians in an open space known as the Jallianwala Bagh in Amritsar in the Punjab region of India, killing several hundred people and wounding many hundreds more.

81(B). Sampat Pal Devi is the founder of the Gulabi Gang an Uttar Pradesh and Madhya Pradesh based social organization that works for women welfare and empowerment.

The Gulabi Gang is an exceptional women's movement began in 2006 by Sampat Pal Devi in the Banda District of Uttar Pradesh India. The Gulabi Gang was at first intended to punish repressive husbands, fathers and brothers, and battle domestic violence and desertion. The Gulabi Gang consists of women between the age of18 and 60 years.

83(B). India has the advantage of being a rich fishery area due to the wide continental shelf, active ocean currents and large rivers bringing continuous food material for fish.

84(C). Article 124 was debated on 24th May 1949. It established the Supreme Court of India and also laid out provisions relating to the appointment, impeachment, and conduct of its judges.

85(A). Plains are by far the most prominent landforms in the deserts. In basins with mountains and hills around and along, the drainage is towards the center of the basin, and due to the gradual deposition of sediment from basin margins, a nearly level plain forms at the center of the basin. Sometimes the water collected in the depression does not completely disappear by evaporation or seepage covering the depression or plain with a shallow water body. Such types of shallow lakes are called playas where water is retained only for a short duration due to evaporation and quite often the playas contain heavy deposition of salts. Thus these are landforms formed by the action of water in deserts. The playa plain covered up by salts is called alkali flats.

Small round shallow depressions formed on limestone surfaces through solution are called Swallow holes, a common erosional feature of karst topography. Unassorted coarse and fine debris dropped by melting glaciers is called Glacial till.

86(B). The Chinese smartphone manufacturer Realme introduced India's first 5G-enabled smartphone, which is named as 'Realme X50 Pro'.

The flagship smartphone was also

simultaneously launched in Spain. The phone can switch to 5G when is outside India via 'Smart 5G', as 5G is not completely available in India, yet. It can be still used in 4G mode, till it is introduced.

87(A). The constitution of India describes India as a Union of State.
- Article 1 describes India, i.e. Bharat, as a Union of States.
- According to Article 1, the Territory of India can be classified into three categories:
1. Territories of the States.
2. Union Territories.
3. Territories that may be acquired by the Government of India at any time.

88(C). Madhubani paintings depict nature and Hindu religious figure.
Madhubani painting is one of the many famous Indian art forms. As it is practised in the Mithila region of Bihar and Nepal, it is called Mithila or Madhubani art.
The colours used in Madhubani paintings are usually derived from plants and other natural sources. Women usually paint their homes to celebrate festivals and theme of the painting can be varied from nature to myths.

89(B). One of the distinct features of the peninsular plateau is the black soil area known as the Deccan trap.

90(A). Dholavira is well known for its elaborate system of water harvesting and management by building a series of dams and channelizing water into connected reservoirs.

91(C). At a different level, historians of religion classified bhakti traditions into two broad categories:
- Saguna (with attributes): The Saguna included traditions focused on the worship of specific deities such as Shiva, Vishnu, and his avatars (incarnations). So, statement 1 is correct.
- Forms of the goddess or Devi, all often conceptualized in anthropomorphic forms. So, statement 2 is correct.
- Nirguna (without attributes): Nirguna bhakti on the other hand was the worship of an abstract form of god.

92(A). India is a tropical country and indigo grows well in tropical regions. In the 13th century, Indian indigo was used by cloth manufacturers from France, Italy, and Britain.
- indigo was very expensive, so the European cloth manufacturers were dependent on another plant called woad.
- Due to fear of competition from indigo, woad producers demanded a ban on the import of indigo.
- the government looks for various alternatives for indigo and this increases the growth in plantation of indigo in various parts of north and south America.

So, Due to high competition and demand for Indian indigo, Europeans ban the import of indigo and it resulted in the growth of the indigo plantation in north and south America.

93(C). The only planet that contains living organisms is Earth.
The Earth was also seen from space by the more discerning eye of instruments, and it was this view that confirmed James Hutton's vision of a living planet. When seen in infrared light, the Earth is a strange and wonderful anomaly among the planets of the solar system.

94(B). Article 19 of the Indian constitution consists the freedom of Speech and Expression, Assembly, Association, Movement, Residence, Profession.
Freedom to own, acquire and dispose of property anywhere in the country is not guaranteed by the Constitution of India. The Indian Constitution does not recognize property rights as a fundamental right. In 1977, the 44th amendment removed the right to acquire, hold and dispose of the property as a fundamental right.

95(B). In the first semi-final, Madhya Pradesh beat Bengal by 174 runs to reach their first final in the tournament since the 1998–99 edition. The second semi-final, between Mumbai and Uttar Pradesh was drawn, with Mumbai advancing to the final on their first-innings lead. In the final, Madhya Pradesh beat Mumbai by six wickets to win their first Ranji Trophy title.

96(D). Famous Indian mountaineer Santosh Yadav achieved the feat to be the first woman in the world to climb Mount Everest twice.
She was born in 1969 and hails from the small village of Adygreg in Haryana.Her first time to scale Mt Everest was in May 1992 followed by another one in May 1993 she even saved the life of another mountaineer by sharing her oxygen.

97(B). The basic principle on which the GSHP works is the "refrigeration cycle". Ground Source Heat Pumps (GSHP's) use the earth's relatively constant temperature (instead of the outside air) between 16 - 240C at a depth of 20 feet to provide heating, cooling, and hot water for homes and commercial buildings. GSHP harvests heat absorbed at the Earth's surface from solar energy.

98(C). Autotrophic Nutrition is mainly associated with Algae.
Autotrophs manufacture their own food. The most known example is plants that fulfill their carbon and energy requirements by photosynthesis. Algae have photosynthetic machinery ultimately derived from cyanobacteria that produce oxygen as a by-product of photosynthesis. Fungi, Protozoa, and Virus do not manufacture food.

99(A). The international conflict known as the Vietnam War was fought between Vietnam and U.S.A.
The Vietnam War (also known by other names) was a conflict in Vietnam, Laos, and Cambodia from 1 November 1955 to the fall of Saigon on 30 April 1975. It was the second of the Indochina Wars and was officially fought between North Vietnam and South Vietnam. North Vietnam was supported by the Soviet Union, China, and other communist allies; South Vietnam was supported by the United States and other anti-communist allies. The war is widely considered to be a Cold War-era proxy war. It lasted almost 20 years, with direct U.S. involvement ending in 1973. The conflict also spilled over into neighbouring states, exacerbating the Laotian Civil War and the Cambodian Civil War, which ended with all three countries becoming communist states by 1975.

100(A). The Sahitya Akademi announced the winners of Sahitya Akademi Awards 2022 in 24 Indian languages(including English) on 22 December 2022. Novelist Anuradha Roy, Tamil author M. Rajendran has received Sahitya Akademi award for his novel Kala Pani. He was among 23 litterateurs awarded the Sahitya Akademi Awards for 2022.
The winners include 7 books of poetry, 6 novel, 2 short stories, 3 dramas/plays, 2 literary criticism and 1 each under autobiographical essays.

Practice Test   06

1. If the scale factor is $\frac{3}{5}$, then the new triangle constructed is __________ the given triangle.
   (a) smaller than (b) greater than
   (c) overlaps   (d) congruent to

2. By geometrical construction, which one of the following ratios is not possible to divide a line segment?
   (a) $1:10$
   (b) $\sqrt{9}:\sqrt{4}$
   (c) $10:1$
   (d) $4+\sqrt{3}:4-\sqrt{3}$

3. A student noted the number of cars passing through a spot on a road for 100 periods each of 3 minutes and summarized it in the table given below. Find the mode of the data:

Number of cars	$\frac{0}{10}$	$\frac{10}{20}$	$\frac{20}{30}$	$\frac{30}{40}$	$\frac{40}{50}$	$\frac{50}{60}$	$\frac{60}{70}$	$\frac{70}{80}$
Frequency	7	14	13	12	20	11	15	8

   (a) 35.7   (b) 40.7
   (c) 44.7   (d) 45.7

4. If the volume of a cylinder is $3080 cm^3$ and the base radius is $7cm$, find the height of the cylinder.
   (a) $24cm$ (b) $35cm$
   (c) $22cm$ (d) $20cm$

5. A solid wooden toy is in the shape of a right circular cone mounted on a hemisphere of radius $4.2cm$. The total height of the toy is $10.2cm$ find the volume of the toys.
   (a) $266.112cm^3$ (b) $267.113cm^3$
   (c) $286.114cm^3$ (d) $278.113cm^3$

6. If one root of $5x^2+26x+k=0$ is reciprocal of the other, then what is the value of k?
   (a) 2   (b) 3
   (c) 5   (d) 8

7. If k is one of the roots of the equation $x(x+1)+1=0$, then what is its other root?
   (a) 1   (b) $-k$
   (c) k^2 (d) $-k^2$

8. A chord of a circle of radius 10 cm subtends a right angle at the center. Find the area of the corresponding minor segment.
   (a) 29.5 cm^2 (b) 27.5 cm^2
   (c) 28.5 cm^2 (d) 29.5 cm^2

9. In a circle of radius 21 cm, an arc subtends an angle of $60°$ at the center. Find out the area of the sector formed by the arc.
   (a) 131 cm^2 (b) 121 cm^2
   (c) 221 cm^2 (d) 231 cm^2

10. If $\sin\theta=\frac{5}{13}$, where θ is an acute angle, then find the value of $\cos\theta$.
    (a) $\frac{13}{12}$ (b) $\frac{12}{5}$
    (c) $\frac{\sqrt{5}}{13}$ (d) $\frac{12}{13}$

11. If $\sin^4 x+2\cos^4 x=\frac{2}{3}$, then what is the value of $\sec^2 x$?
    (a) 2   (b) 3
    (c) 1   (d) 4

12. If $\sin\alpha+\cos\alpha=p$, then what is $\cos^2(2\alpha)$ equal to?
    (a) p^2 (b) p^2-1
    (c) $p^2(2-p^2)$ (d) p^2+1

13. The angle of elevation of the top of a vertical tower from a point on the ground is 60°. From another point, 10 m vertically above the first, its angle of elevation is 45°. Find the height of the tower.
    (a) $5(\sqrt{3}+3)m$ (b) $(\sqrt{3}+3)m$
    (c) $15(\sqrt{3}+3)$ (d) $5\sqrt{3}$

14. The sum of a two digit number and the number obtained by reversing the digits is 66 . If the digit of the number differ by 2 , find the number. How many such numbers are there?
    (a) 34 and 54   (b) 22 and 24
    (c) 42 and 24   (d) 14 and 34

15. The pair of linear equations $4x+6y=9$ and $2x+3y=6$ has:
    (a) No solution
    (b) Many solutions
    (c) Two solutions
    (d) One solution

16. If n is a natural number, then $2(5^n+6^n)$ always ends with:
    (a) 1   (b) 4
    (c) 3   (d) 2

17. Find the HCF and LCM of 6 , 72 and 120 by using prime factorisation method?
    (a) 3 and 330   (b) 4 and 340
    (c) 5 and 350   (d) 6 and 360

18. Find HCF of 96 and 404 by prime factorisation method. Hence, find their LCM?
    (a) 10 and 8595 (b) 6 and 10520
    (c) 4 and 9696   (d) 8 and 2653

19. The decimal expansion of the rational number $\frac{43}{2^4 5^3}$ will terminate after how many places of decimals?
    (a) After 2 decimal places.
    (b) After 3 decimal places.
    (c) After 4 decimal places.
    (d) After 5 decimal places.

20. A quadratic polynomial, whose zeroes are -3 and 4 , is:
    (a) x^2-x+12
    (b) x^2+x+12
    (c) $\frac{x^2}{2}-\frac{x}{2}-6$
    (d) $2x^2+2x-24$

21. The zeroes of the quadratic polynomial $x^2+7x+10$ are:
    (a) $-4,-3$ (b) $2,5$
    (c) $-2,-5$ (d) $-2,5$

22. A box contains 90 discs which are numbered from 1 to 90 . If one disc is drawn at random from the box, find the probability that it bears a two digit number.
    (a) 0.9   (b) 0.8
    (c) 0.7   (d) 0.5

23. If the 3 rd and the 9 th terms of an AP are 4 and -8 respectively, which term of this AP is zero?
    (a) 10   (b) 8
    (c) 6   (d) 5

24. Find a,b and c such that the following numbers $a,7,b,23,c$ are in AP.
    (a) $a=-1,b=15$ and $c=31$
    (b) $a=-2,b=10$ and $c=30$
    (c) $b=-1,a=15$ and $c=31$
    (d) $c=-1,a=15$ and $b=31$

25. In $\triangle DEW$, $AB \parallel EW$. If $AD = 4$ cm, $DE = 12$ cm and $DW = 24$ cm, then find the value of DB.
(a) 64 cm
(b) 32 cm
(c) 16 cm
(d) 8 cm

26. In $\triangle ABC$, $DE \parallel BC$, find the value of x.

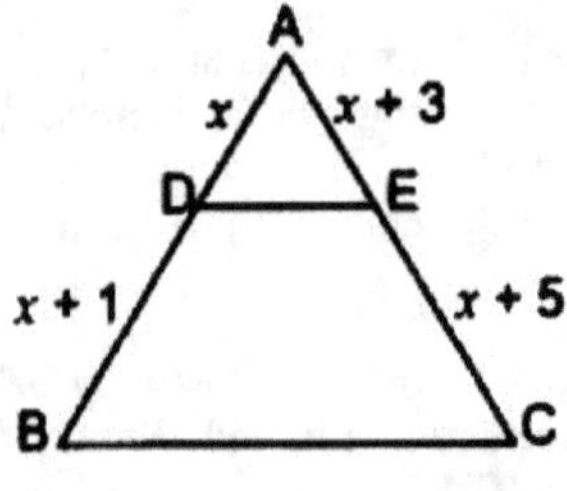

(a) 3 cm
(b) 6 cm
(c) 9 cm
(d) 12 cm

27. In the given figure, A is the centre of the circle. If diameters XY and MN bisect each other perpendicularly at A and $XM = 5$ cm, NY is equal to:

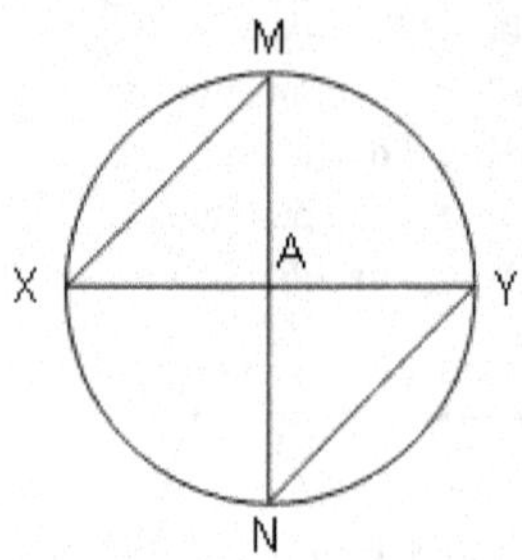

(a) 2.5 cm
(b) 5 cm
(c) 10 cm
(d) 15 cm

28. In the given circle, AB is a chord and OL is the perpendicular drawn to it from centre O . If $AL = 3.2$ units, find the length of AB.

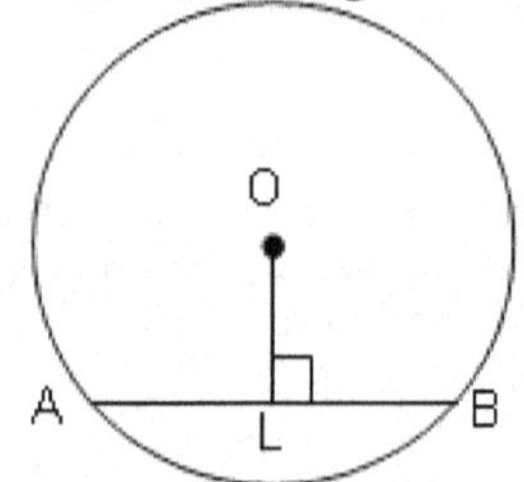

(a) 64 units
(b) 6.4 units
(c) 1.6 units
(d) 3.2 units

29. The points $(3, 2)$, $(-2, -3)$ and $(2, 3)$ form a triangle name the type of triangle formed:
(a) equilateral
(b) isosceles
(c) right angle
(d) None of these

30. A point on X -axis which is equidistant from the points $(1, 3)$ and $(-1, 2)$:

(a) $\left(\frac{5}{2}, 0\right)$
(b) $(5, 0)$
(c) $(4, 0)$
(d) $\left(\frac{5}{4}, 0\right)$

31. Which of the following components is not recycled in nature?
(a) Nitrogen
(b) Water
(c) Energy
(d) Carbon

32. ____ is a biodegradable substance.
(a) Paper
(b) Polythene
(c) Glass
(d) None of the above

33. The gas given off when a metal reacts with an acid is:
(a) hydrogen
(b) oxygen
(c) carbon dioxide
(d) water vapour

34. Elements and compounds that occur naturally in the earth's crust are called:
(a) materials
(b) metals
(c) gases
(d) minerals

35. __________ are the chemical messengers that are used by multicellular organisms for control and coordination.
(a) Vitamins
(b) Minerals
(c) Antibiotics
(d) Hormones

36. Movement of a plant part in response to water is called________.
(a) phototropism
(b) geotropism
(c) chemotropism
(d) hydrotropism

37. $Fe(s) + CuSO_4(aq) \rightarrow FeSO_4(aq) + Cu(s)$
The above reaction is an example of a:
(a) Combination reaction
(b) Double displacement reaction
(c) Displacement reaction
(d) Decomposition reaction

38. What happens when dilute hydrochloric acid is added to iron filings?
(a) Hydrogen gas and iron chloride are produced
(b) Chlorine gas and iron hydroxide are produced
(c) No reaction takes place
(d) Iron salt and water are produced

39. In which of the following compounds maximum heat is liberated on combustion of one mole of the compound?
(a) Hydrogen
(b) Methane
(c) Ethane
(d) Butane

40. All homologues have similar but graded:
(a) Solubility
(b) Melting point
(c) Boiling point
(d) All of the above

41. Which of the following methods of preventing pregnancy, act by changing hormonal balance of the body so that eggs are not released and fertilization cannot occur?
(a) Creating a mechanical barrier
(b) Taking oral pills
(c) Sterilization method
(d) Using Copper-T

42. What is the purpose of combining variations from two or more individuals by sexual reproduction?
(a) To create new combinations of variants
(b) To make DNA copying mechanism accurate
(c) To decrease the chances of survival
(d) To ensure no variants are created

43. What do we call the differences in the traits among the individuals of a species?
(a) Evolution
(b) Inheritance
(c) Heredity
(d) Variation

44. What is the name given to the plants produced from cross-pollination of parent plants?
(a) F3 plants
(b) F1 plants
(c) F2 plants
(d) F4 plants

45. A convex mirror used for rear-view on an automobile has a radius of curvature of 3.00 m . If a bus is located at 5.00 m from this mirror, find the magnification of the image.
(a) 0.25
(b) 0.35
(c) 0.23
(d) 0.26

46. A 2.0 cm tall object is placed perpendicular to the principal axis of a convex lens of focal length 10 cm . The distance of the object from the lens is 15 cm . Find the position of the image.
(a) 10 cm
(b) 20 cm
(c) 15 cm
(d) 30 cm

47. Who said that current can cause magnetic field?
    (a) Oersted
    (b) Fleming
    (c) Maxwell
    (d) Michael Faraday

48. An electron beam is moving vertically upwards if it passes through a magnetic field which is directed from south to north in a horizontal plane then in which direction will the beam be deflected?
    (a) Towards south
    (b) Towards east
    (c) Towards west
    (d) Towards north

49. Muscle Fatigue is caused by the accumulation of
    (a) lactic acid
    (b) acetic acid
    (c) citric acid
    (d) hydrochloric acid

50. Which is the respiratory organ of fishes?
    (a) Gills　　　　(b) Lungs
    (c) Liver　　　　(d) Skin

51. Which of the following substances is not an acid?
    (a) HCl
    (b) HNO_3
    (c) CH_3COOH
    (d) $(CH_3COO)_2Zn$

52. Which of the following gases is produced when baking soda is heated?
    (a) Hydrogen
    (b) Carbon monoxide
    (c) Carbon dioxide
    (d) Hydrogen sulphide

53. When sunlight enters into an atmosphere, it gets refracted, which is called atmospheric refraction. Due to this atmospheric refraction, the day __________.
    (a) becomes four minutes longer than the actual one.
    (b) becomes four minutes shorter than the actual one.
    (c) becomes longer in summer and shorter in winter.
    (d) length of the day can not be said anything.

54. $1\,kWh$ is equal to:
    (a) $3.6 \times 10^6\,MJ$
    (b) $3.6 \times 10^5\,MJ$
    (c) $3.6 \times 10^2\,MJ$
    (d) $3.6\,MJ$

55. A circular conductor is made of a uniform wire of resistance 2×10^{-3} ohm/metre and the diameter of this circular conductor is 2 metres. Then the resistance measured between the ends of the diameter is (in ohms):
    (a) $\pi \times 10^{-3}$　　(b) $2\pi \times 10^{-3}$
    (c) $4\pi \times 10^{-3}$　　(d) 4×10^{-3}

Social Science

56. How did the increasing number of industries affect the water condition?
    (a) No effect on water
    (b) Pressure on existing freshwater resources
    (c) Balance between use of water and industry
    (d) Unequal distribution of water

57. Which movement in the Himalayas has successfully resisted deforestation?
    (a) The Himalayan movement
    (b) Chipko movement
    (c) Save Forests movement
    (d) Save trees Movement

58. Which of the following is the main area for producing 'Tidal Energy'?
    (a) Gulf of Bengal
    (b) Gulf of Mannar
    (c) Gulf of Khambhat (Cambay)
    (d) Gulf of Kutch

59. Which of the following examples does not fall under unorganized sector?
    (a) A farmer irrigating his field
    (b) A daily wage labourer working for a contractor
    (c) A doctor in a hospital treating a patient
    (d) A handloom weaver working on a loom in her house

60. What brings about stable income?
    (a) Better wages
    (b) Work opportunities
    (c) Regular work
    (d) Decent price for their crops or other products

61. What did Napoleon do in the territory that was under his control?
    (a) Set about introducing many reforms
    (b) Set about war strategies
    (c) Worked for peace
    (d) Worked towards democratic ideas

62. What is the most important component of farm management?
    (a) Heavy farm equipment
    (b) Livestock
    (c) Agricultural budget
    (d) Labour cost

63. Banks do not give loans:
    (a) To small farmers
    (b) To marginal farmers
    (c) To industries
    (d) Without proper collateral and documents

64. Which of the following households constitutes the largest segment of borrowers in the formal sector of credit?
    (a) Poor households
    (b) Rich households
    (c) Well-off households
    (d) Households with few assets

65. Which Indian companies have invested abroad?
    (a) Coca Cola　　(b) Ranbaxy
    (c) Nike　　　　(d) Pepsi

66. Give examples of industries in India where the small manufacturers have been hit hard due to competition:
    (a) Toys
    (b) Tyres
    (c) Weaving
    (d) Both (A) & (B)

67. Which is a high safety required product?
    (a) Medicines
    (b) LPG Cylinder
    (c) Pressure cooker
    (d) All of the above

68. Consumer Complaint forum is called ?
    (a) Consumer forum
    (b) RTI
    (c) High court
    (d) Police Station

69. What is Vellum?
    (a) Base made from synthetic
    (b) A parchment made from the skin of animals
    (c) Base made from cloth to write on
    (d) Paper made from bark

70. What was the reason behind the popularity of woodblock printing in 15th century Europe to print textiles, playing cards, and religious pictures with simple, brief texts.
(i) demand for books increased, booksellers all over Europe began exporting books to many different countries.
(ii) Production of handwritten manuscripts was also organised in new ways to meet the expanded demand.
(iii) Production of handwritten manuscripts could not satisfy the ever-increasing demand for books.
(iv) Copying was an expensive, laborious and time-consuming business.
(a) (i) only
(b) (i) and (ii)
(c) (i), (ii) and (iii)
(d) (i), (ii), (iii) and (iv)

71. A belief that the majority community should be able to rule a country in whichever way it wants, by disregarding the wishes and needs of the minority is:
(a) Power Sharing
(b) Central Government
(c) Majoritarianism
(d) Community Government

72. Prudential reasons of power sharing are __________.
(a) The stability of political order
(b) To reduce the possibility of conflict between social groups
(c) A fair share to minority
(d) All of these

73. Who among the following discovered the continent of America?
(a) Vasco da Gama
(b) Ferdinand Magellan
(c) Christopher Columbus
(d) Copernicus

74. India is a federal state because its Constitution provides for __________.
(a) Dual citizenship
(b) Division of powers between the Union and the States
(c) A written constitution
(d) Election of members of Parliament by the people

75. The distinguishing feature of a federal government is _____.
(a) National government gives some powers to the provincial government
(b) Power is distributed among the legislature, executive and judiciary
(c) Governing or ruling power is divided between different levels of government
(d) Elected officials exercise supreme power in the government

76. Were the new industries easily able to displace traditional industries?
(a) Yes, the new industry took over easily
(b) No, a large portion of the output was produced not within factories, but outside, within domestic units
(c) The new industry dominated most sectors
(d) The new industry partially managed to make place for itself

77. Which one of the following statements is correct as regards to international resources?
(a) Resources which are regulated by international institutions.
(b) Resources which lie beyond the territorial waters.
(c) Resources which are found along the international frontier.
(d) Resources which are not yet developed.

78. "Democracy is a government of the people, by the people and for the people." is said by:
(a) Abraham Lincoln
(b) Gittel
(c) Mahatma Gandhi
(d) Jawahar Lal Nehru

79. Regular, free and fair elections are the identity of_____.
(a) Military rule
(b) Dictatorship
(c) Democracy
(d) None of the above

80. What was the Rowlatt Act of 1919?
(a) Detention after trial for 3 years
(b) No hearing of cases
(c) Detention of prisoners for 3 years without trial
(d) Allowed detention of political prisoners without trial for two years

81. What is the full form of the "APJ" in Dr. Kalam's name?
(a) Ahmed Panthwawala Jain
(b) Avul Pakir Jainulabdeen
(c) Ali Ponnuswamy Jampiru
(d) Akbar Panneer Jalant

82. What ensures economic justice to Indian citizens?
(a) Fundamental Rights
(b) Fundamental Duties
(c) Directive Principles of State Policy
(d) None of these

83. In India, the term 'hot money' is used to refer to:
(a) Currency + Reserves with the RBI
(b) Net GDR
(c) Net Foreign Direct Investment
(d) Foreign Portfolio Investment

84. The Supreme Court of India decriminalised adultery, striking down Section 497 of the Indian Penal Code, 1860 , in the case of __________.
(a) Nitin Walia v. Union of India
(b) Nandini Sundar v. State of Chhattisgarh (Chosen option)
(c) Joseph Shine v. Union of India
(d) Fazal Rab Choudhary v. State of Bihar

85. What is the source of the most important information regarding the internal structure of the Earth?
(a) Unnatural means
(b) Seismology
(c) Volcanic action
(d) Plate tectonics

86. Typhoid fever is caused by :-
(a) Bacterium (b) Protozoa
(c) Fungi (d) Virus

87. Under which Article of the Indian Constitution, the Parliament can make laws on State list subject for giving effect to international agreements?
(a) Article 249 (b) Article 250
(c) Article 252 (d) Article 253

88. 'Matki' is a popular folk dance of which of the following?
(a) Assam
(b) Madhya Pradesh
(c) Bihar
(d) Rajasthan

89. Which of the following tribes is NOT residing in the Nilgiri Hills?
(a) Toda (b) Kota

(c) Kurumba   (d) Mogh

90. Who built the Brihadishwara temple in Thanjavur, Tamil Nadu?
(a) Rajaraja Chola I
(b) Vijayalaya
(c) Sundara Chola
(d) Rajendra Chola I

91. The Mosque of Moth was constructed during whose reign?
(a) Sikandar Lodhi
(b) Muhammad Tughlaq
(c) Alauddin Khilji
(d) Qutbuddin Aibak

92. Hindustan Socialist Republican Association was formed-
(a) By Subhash Chandra Bose
(b) By Rash Behari Bose
(c) By Chandrashekhar Azad
(d) By Sardar Bhagat Singh

93. If there were no atmosphere around the Earth, the temperature of the Earth will:
(a) Increase
(b) Go on decreasing
(c) Increase during day and decrease during night
(d) Be unaffected

94. Which one of the following public sector undertakings is established by passing a special law under Parliament?
(a) Departmental Undertaking
(b) Statutory Corporation
(c) Sole Proprietorship
(d) None of these

95. Which Indian player won the first Olympic Medal in badminton?
(a) Kidambi Srikanth
(b) Saina Nehwal
(c) Prakash Padukone
(d) P. Gopichand

96. The first woman who received a Sena Medal in India?
(a) Dicky Dolma
(b) Santosh Yadav
(c) Bimla Devi
(d) Kiran Devi

97. The acceleration due to gravity on any planet does not depend on which of the following?
(a) Radius of the planet
(b) Mass of the planet
(c) Density of the planet
(d) Mass of the object

98. When the water is heated from 0°C to 10°C, its volume __________.
(a) will increase
(b) will decrease
(c) first decreases, then increases
(d) will remain constant

99. Which of the following was the first to develop the art of agriculture?
(a) Indus Valley Civilization
(b) Nile Valley Civilization
(c) Chinese Civilization
(d) Mesopotamian Civilization

100. The Jamnalal Bajaj Foundation has announced the winners of the Jamnalal Bajaj award 2022. The Foundation gives how many awards in different categories?
(a) 2   (b) 3
(c) 4   (d) 5

// Hints and Solutions //

1(A). The scale factor determines the ratio of the triangle sides to be constructed with the corresponding sides of the given triangle. If the scale factor is $\frac{3}{5}$, then the new triangle constructed is smaller than the given triangle, because in $\frac{3}{5}$, the numerator is less than the denominator.

2(D). The ratio $\sqrt{9} : \sqrt{4}$ can be simplified to the ratio $3 : 2$. So the $1 : 10$, $10 : 1$ and $3 : 2$ all are in the form of integers. So it is possible to divide a line segment with these options but the ratio $4 + \sqrt{3} : 4 - \sqrt{3}$ can not be simplified in the form of integers like other given ratios. So, by geometrical construction from the ratio $4 + \sqrt{3} : 4 - \sqrt{3}$, it is not possible to divide a line segment.

3(C). Mode can be calculated as
$$M = l + \left(\frac{f_1 - f_0}{2f_1 - f_0 - f_2} \right) \times h$$
Where
l = Lower limit of modal class
f_1 = Frequency of modal class
f_0 = Frequency of class preceding the modal class
f_2 = Frequency of class succeeding the modal class
h = Class size
From the given data, it can be observed that the maximum class frequency is 20,
Belonging to $40 - 50$ class intervals.
Therefore, modal class $- 40 - 50$
$I = 40$
$f_1 = 20$
$f_0 = 12$
$f_2 = 11$
$h = 10$
Substituting these values in the formula of mode we get:
$$M = 1 + \left(\frac{f_1 - f_0}{2f_1 - f_0 - f_2} \right) \times h$$

$$M = 40 + \left(\frac{20 - 12}{2(20) - 12 - 11} \right) \times 10$$
$$M = 40 + \left(\frac{80}{40 - 23} \right)$$
$$M = 44.7$$
So, mode of this data is 44.7 cars.

4(D). Given,
Volume of a cylinder $= 3080 cm^3$
Radius of a cylinder $(r) = 7 cm$
Let the height of the cylinder be $h cm$.
As we know,
Volume of the cylinder $= \pi r^2 h$
$\Rightarrow \frac{22}{7} \times 7 \times 7 \times h = 3080$
$\Rightarrow 154 \times h = 3080$
$\Rightarrow h = \frac{3080}{154}$
$\therefore h = 20 cm$
So, the height of the cylinder is $20 cm$.

5(A).

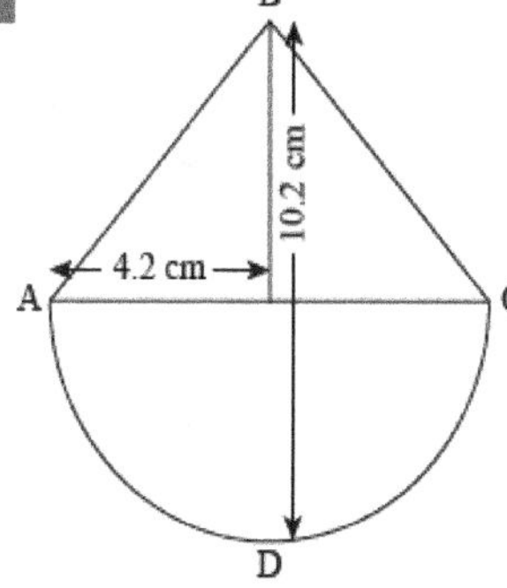

Given,
The radius of hemisphere $= 4.2 cm$
Height of toy $= 10.2 cm$
Height of the cone $= 10.2 - 4.2 = 6 cm$
The radius of the cone $= 4.2 cm$
Volume of the toy $=$ Volume of the hemisphere $+$ Volume of the cone
Volume of the toy $= \frac{2}{3} \pi r^3 + \frac{1}{3} \pi r^2 h$
$= \frac{1}{3} \pi r^2 (2r + h)$
$= \frac{1}{3} \times \frac{22}{7} \times (4.2)^2 \times (2 \times 4.2 + 6)$
$= \frac{1}{3} \times \frac{22}{7} \times 17.64 \times (8.4 + 6)$
$= \frac{1}{3} \times \frac{22}{7} \times 17.64 \times 14.4$
$= 266.112 cm^3$

6(C). Let the roots of $5x^2 + 26x + k = 0$ are α and β
Given,
$\alpha = \frac{1}{\beta}$
$\Rightarrow \alpha \cdot \beta = 1 \quad \dots \text{(i)}$
Compare with general equation
$ax^2 + bx + c = 0$ $a = 5, b = 26, c = k$
According to the concept used
$\Rightarrow a \cdot \beta = \frac{k}{5} \quad ..\text{(ii)}$
From (i) and (ii), we get
$\frac{k}{5} = 1$
$\therefore$ The value of k is 5.

7(C). Given,
Equation: $x(x + 1) + 1 = 0$
Let the other root be β
$\Rightarrow x^2 + x + 1 = 0$
$a = 1, b = 1$ and $c = 1$

As k is the root of the equation
$$\Rightarrow k^2 + k + 1 = 0$$
$$\Rightarrow k^2 = -1 - k \quad \ldots(i)$$
The sum of the roots $= -\frac{1}{1} = -1$
$$\Rightarrow \beta + k = -1$$
$$\Rightarrow \beta = -1 - k \quad \ldots(ii)$$
From equation (i) and (ii), we get
$$\Rightarrow \beta = k^2$$
$\therefore$ The other root $= k^2$

8(C). Given,
$OA = OB = $ radius $= 10$ cm
$\theta = 90°$

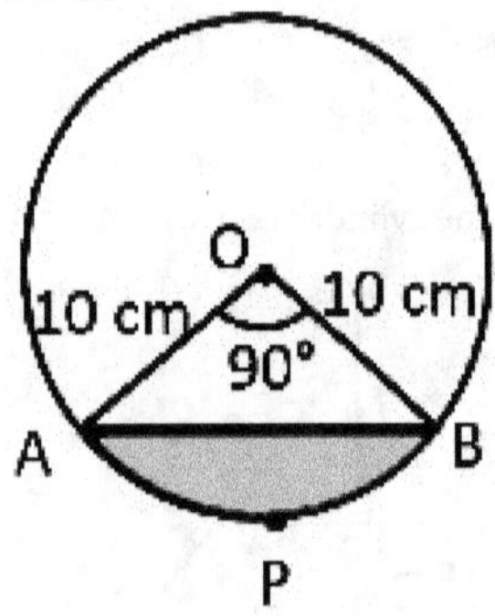

Area of segment $APB = $ Area of sector $OAPB - $ Area of $\triangle AOB$

Area of sector $OAPB = \frac{\theta}{360°} \times \pi r^2$
$$= \frac{90}{360} \times 3.14 \times (10)^2$$
$$= \frac{1}{4} \times 3.14 \times 100$$
$$= \frac{1}{4} \times 314$$
$$= 78.5 \text{ cm}^2$$
Area of $\triangle AOB$
Now, $\triangle AOB$ is a right triangle
where, $\angle O = 90°$ having Base $= OA$ Height $= OB$

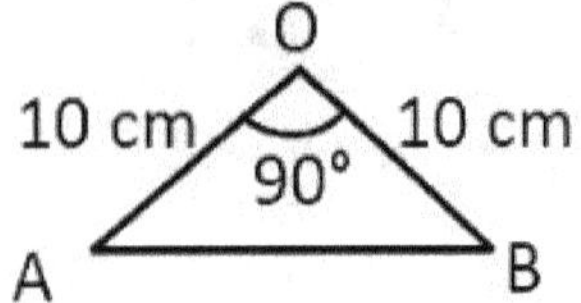

Area of $\triangle AOB = \frac{1}{2} \times$ Base $\times$ Height
$$= \frac{1}{2} \times OA \times OB$$
$$= \frac{1}{2} \times 10 \times 10$$
$$= 50 \text{ cm}^2$$
Now,
Area of segment $APB = $ Area of quadrant $OAPB - $ Area of $\triangle AOB$
$$= 78.5 - 50$$
$$= 28.5 \text{ cm}^2$$

9(D). Given,
$r = 21$ cm, angle $\theta = 60°$

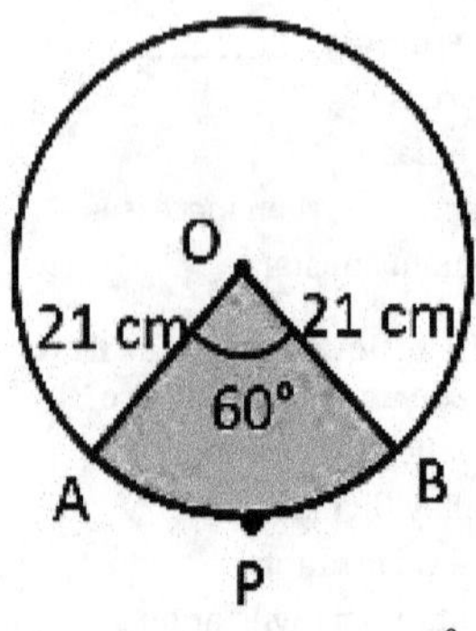

Area of sector $OAPB = \frac{\theta}{360} \times \pi r^2$
$$= \frac{60}{360} \times \frac{22}{7} \times 21 \times 21$$
$$= \frac{1}{6} \times \frac{22}{7} \times 21 \times 21$$
$$= \frac{1}{6} \times 22 \times 3 \times 21$$
$$= 231 \text{ cm}^2$$

10(D).

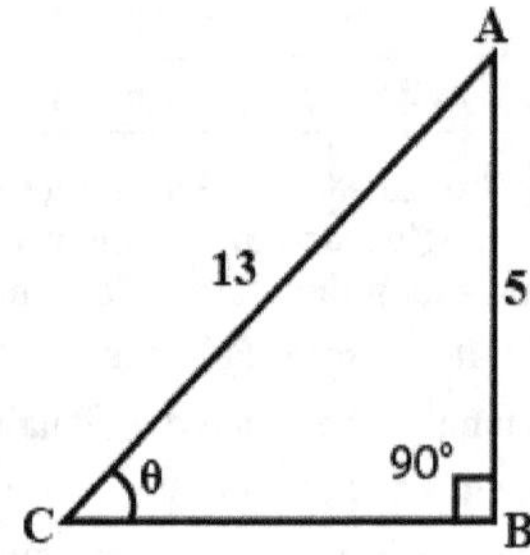

Given,
$\sin\theta = \frac{5}{13}$
To find: $\cos\theta = ?$
We know that,
$$\sin\theta = \frac{Perpendicular}{Hypotnuse} = \frac{AB}{AC} = \frac{5}{13}$$
According to Pythagoras theorem, we get
$$Perpendicular^2 + Base^2 = Hypotnuse^2$$
$$\Rightarrow (5)^2 + Base^2 = (13)^2$$
$$\Rightarrow Base^2 = 169 - 25$$
$$\Rightarrow Base^2 = 144$$
$$\Rightarrow Base = 12 = BC$$
Now,
$$\cos\theta = \frac{Base}{Hypotnuse} = \frac{BC}{AC} = \frac{12}{13}$$
$$\Rightarrow \cos\theta = \frac{12}{13}$$

11(B). Given:
$\sin^4 x + 2\cos^4 x = \frac{2}{3}$
$$\Rightarrow \sin^4 x + \cos^4 x + \cos^4 x = \frac{2}{3}$$
$$\Rightarrow 1 - 2\sin^2 x \cos^2 x + \cos^4 x = \frac{2}{3}$$
$$\Rightarrow 1 - 2\left(1 - \cos^2 x\right)\cos^2 x + \cos^4 x = \frac{2}{3}$$
$$\left[\because 1 - \sin^2 x = \cos^2 x\right]$$
$$\Rightarrow 1 - 2\cos^2 x + 2\cos^4 x + \cos^4 x = \frac{2}{3}$$
$$\Rightarrow 9\cos^4 x - 6\cos^2 x + 1 = 0$$
$$\Rightarrow \left(3\cos^2 x - 1\right)^2 = 0$$
$$\Rightarrow \cos^2 x = \frac{1}{3}$$
$$\Rightarrow \sec^2 x = 3$$

12(C). Given,
$\sin\alpha + \cos\alpha = p$

By squaring both the sides, we get
$$\Rightarrow \sin^2 a + \cos^2 a + 2\sin a \cos a = p^2 \quad [$$
$$\because (a+b)^2 = a^2 + b^2 + 2ab\,]$$
As we know that,
$\sin^2 x + \cos^2 x = 1$ and $\sin 2x = 2\sin x \cos x$
$$\Rightarrow 1 + \sin 2a = p^2$$
$$\Rightarrow \sin 2a = p^2 - 1$$
By squaring both sides, we get
$$\Rightarrow \sin^2 2a = \left(p^2 - 1\right)^2$$
$$\Rightarrow 1 - \cos^2 2a = \left(p^2 - 1\right)^2$$
$$= p^2\left(2 - p^2\right)$$

13(A). According to the question,

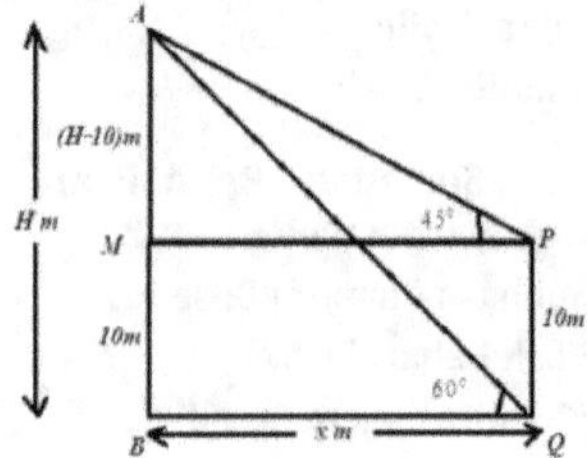

Let the height of the tower be Hm.
In $\triangle ABQ$
$$\tan 60° = \frac{AB}{QB}$$
$$\Rightarrow \sqrt{3} = \frac{H}{x} \quad [\because \tan 60° = \sqrt{3}]$$
$$\Rightarrow x = \frac{H}{\sqrt{3}}$$
Now, In $\triangle AMP$
$$\tan 45° = \frac{AM}{MP}$$
$$\Rightarrow 1 = \frac{H-10}{x} \quad [\because \tan 45° = 1]$$
$$\Rightarrow x = H - 10$$
Substituting value of x in above equation, we get
$$\frac{H}{\sqrt{3}} = H - 10$$
$$\Rightarrow H - \frac{H}{\sqrt{3}} = 10$$
$$\Rightarrow \frac{\sqrt{3}H - H}{\sqrt{3}} = 10$$
$$\Rightarrow \frac{H(\sqrt{3}-1)}{\sqrt{3}} = 10$$
$$\Rightarrow H = \frac{10\sqrt{3}}{\sqrt{3}-1}$$
$$\Rightarrow H = \frac{10\sqrt{3}}{\sqrt{3}-1} \times \frac{\sqrt{3}-1}{\sqrt{3}-1}$$
$$\Rightarrow H = 5(\sqrt{3} + 3)m$$
So, the height of the tower is $5(\sqrt{3} + 3)m$.

14(C). Let the two digit be x and y
$\therefore$ Number (2-digit) $= 10 \times x + y$
Sum of 2-digit and reverse of it
$$\Rightarrow 10x + y + 10y + x = 66 \text{ (given)}$$
$\therefore x + y = 6$ (equation 1)
Digits differ by 2
$\therefore x - y = 2$ (equation 2)
On adding,
$2x = 8$
$$\Rightarrow x = 4$$
$\therefore y = 2$
or, $x + y = 6$ From 1 equation
and $y - x = 2$ From 2 equation
On adding:
$2y = 8$

$y = 4$
$x = 2$
$\therefore$ Two digit numbers are: 42 and 24
There are two such numbers.

15(A). Given system of linear equations
$4x + 6y - 9 = 0 \Rightarrow a_1 = 4, b_1 = 6, c_1 = -9$
$2x + 3y - 6 = 0 \Rightarrow a_2 = 2, b_2 = 3, c_2 = -6$
As we know a pair of linear equations is inconsistent (no solution) if
$\frac{a_1}{a_2} = \frac{b_1}{b_2} = \frac{c_1}{c_2}$
We have $\frac{4}{2} = \frac{6}{3} = \frac{-9}{-6}$
Hence, no solution.

16(D). As we know,
5^n always ends with 5
6^n always ends with 6
Thus, $(5^n + 6^n)$ always ends with $5 + 6 = 11$
Thus,
$2 \times (5^n + 6^n)$ always ends with $2 \times 11 = 22$
i.e. it always ends with 2 .

Prime factorisation of given numbers are,
17(D). $6 = 2 \times 3 = 2^1 \times 3^1$
$72 = 2 \times 2 \times 2 \times 3 \times 3 = 2^3 \times 3^2$
$120 = 2 \times 2 \times 2 \times 3 \times 5 = 2^3 \times 3^1 \times 5^1$
Here, 2^1 and 3^1 are the smallest powers of the common prime factors 2 and 3 in the given numbers.
$\therefore$ HCF $(6, 72, 120) = 2^1 \times 3^1$
$= 2 \times 3$
$= 6$
We note that $2^3, 3^2, 5^1$ are the greatest powers of the prime factors 2 , 3 and 5 involved in the given numbers.
$\therefore$ LCM $(6, 72, 120) = 2^3 \times 3^2 \times 5^1$
$= 8 \times 9 \times 5$
$= 360$.

18(C). Prime factor of given numbers,
$96 = 2 \times 2 \times 2 \times 2 \times 2 \times 3 = 2^5 \times 3^1$ and
$404 = 2 \times 2 \times 101 = 2^2 \times (101)^1$
HCF $(96, 404) = 2^2 = 4$
We know that HCF $\times$ LCM $=$ product of two natural numbers
HCF $(96, 404) \times$ LCM $(96, 404) = 96 \times 404$
$\Rightarrow 4 \times$ LCM $(96, 404) = 96 \times 404$
$\Rightarrow$ LCM
$(96, 404) = \frac{96 \times 404}{4} = 96 \times 101 = 9696$.

19(C). $\frac{43}{2^4 \times 5^3}$
$= \frac{43}{2^4 \times 5^3} \times \frac{5^1}{5^1}$
$= \frac{43 \times 5}{2^4 \times 5^4}$
$= \frac{215}{10^4}$
After 4 decimal places.

20(C). Quadratic equation with α and β as roots can be written as
$x^2 - (\alpha + \beta) + \alpha\beta = 0$
Here, $\alpha = -3$ and $\beta = 4$
$\therefore \alpha + \beta = -3 + 4 = 1$
and $\alpha - \beta = -3 \times 4 = -12$
$\therefore$ The quadratic equation is
$x^2 - (\alpha + \beta)x + \alpha\beta = 0$

$x^2 - 1x - 12 = 0$
$\frac{x^2}{2} - \frac{x}{2} - \frac{12}{2} = 0$
$\frac{x^2}{2} - \frac{x}{2} - 6 = 0$
So, the quadratic polynomial is $\frac{x^2}{2} - \frac{x}{2} - 6$
.

21(C). Let us split the middle term to find the factors of the equation $x^2 + 7x + 10$
$x^2 + 7x + 10 = x^2 + 2x + 5x + 10$
Taking out the common terms, we get
$x(x + 2) + 5(x + 2)$
$(x + 2)(x + 5)$
Put both the factors equal to zero.
$x + 2 = 0$ and $x + 5 = 0$
$x = -2$ and $x = -5$
The zeroes of the polynomial $x^2 + 7x + 10$ are -2 and -5 .

Q.22 The total numbers of discs $= 90$
$P(E) = \frac{\text{(Number of favourable outcomes)}}{\text{(Total number of outcomes}}$

22(A). Total number of discs having two digit numbers $= 81$
(Since 1 to 9 are single digit numbers and so, total 2 digit numbers are $90 - 9 = 81$)
P (bearing a two-digit number)
$= \frac{81}{90} = \frac{9}{10} = 0.9$

23(D). Let a be the first term and d be the common difference of AP ,
Given, $a_3 = 4$ and $a_9 = -8$
We know,
$T_n = a + (n - 1)d$
$a = $ first term
$d = $ common difference
$T_n = n^{\text{th}}$ term
$\Rightarrow T_3 = a + (3 - 1)d = 4$
$\Rightarrow a + 2d = 4$ $\quad \ldots \ldots (i)$
$\Rightarrow T_9 = a + (9 - 1)d = -8$
$\Rightarrow a + 8d = -8$ $\quad \ldots \ldots (ii)$
Subtracting (i) from (ii) , we get
$6d = -12$
$\Rightarrow d = -2$
Putting $d = -2$ in (i) , we get
$a + 2 \times (-2) = 4$
$\Rightarrow a - 4 = 4$
$\Rightarrow a = 8$.
Let n th term of this AP be zero i.e. $a_n = 0$
$\Rightarrow a + (n - 1)d = 0$
$\Rightarrow 8 + (n - 1)(-2) = 0$
$\Rightarrow 8 - 2n + 2 = 0$
$\Rightarrow 2n = 10$
$\Rightarrow n = 5$.
So, the 5 th term of the AP is zero.

24(A). Let d be the common difference of the AP ,
Given,
$a_2 = 7$ and $a_4 = 23$
$T_n = a + (n - 1)d$
$a = $ first term
$d = $ common difference
$T_n = n^{\text{th}}$ term
$\Rightarrow a + d = 7$ $\quad \ldots \ldots (i)$ and
$a + 3d = 23$ $\quad \ldots \ldots (ii)$

Subtracting (i) from (ii) , we get
$2d = 16 \Rightarrow d = 8$
Putting $d = 8$ in (i) , we get
$a + 8 = 7 \Rightarrow a = -1$
Now,
$b = a_3 = a + 2d = -1 + 2 \times 8 = 15$ and
$c = a_5 = a + 4d = -1 + 4 \times 8 = 31$
So, $a = -1, b = 15$ and $c = 31$

25(D). Given,
In $\triangle DEW, AB \| EW$,
$AD = 4$ cm, $DE = 12$ cm and $DW = 24$ cm
Let $BD = x$ cm
then $BW = (24 - x)$ cm
$AE = 12 - 4 = 8$ cm
In $\triangle DEW, AB \| EW$
$\frac{AD}{AE} = \frac{BD}{BW}$
(Thales' Theorem)

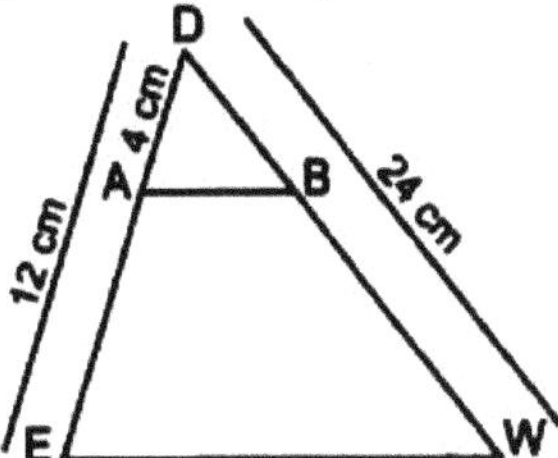

$\frac{4}{8} = \frac{x}{24 - x}$
$8x = 96 - 4x$
$\Rightarrow 12x = 96$
$\Rightarrow x = \frac{96}{12} = 8$ cm
$\therefore DB = 8$ cm

26(A). Given,
In $\triangle ABC, DE \| BC$
$\frac{AD}{BD} = \frac{AE}{EC}$
(Thales' theorem)
$\frac{x}{x + 1} = \frac{x + 3}{x + 5}$
$x(x + 5) = (x + 3)(x + 1)$
$x^2 + 5x = x^2 + 3x + x + 3$
$x^2 + 5x - x^2 - 3x - x = 3$
$\therefore x = 3$ cm

27(B). Given, XM $= 5$ cm
XY and MN bisect each other therefore
NA $=$ MA, YA $=$ XA
In $\triangle YNA$ and $\triangle XMA$
$\angle YNA = \angle XMA$
NA $=$ MA
YA $=$ XA
by RHS congruence rule
$\triangle YNA$ and $\triangle XMA$ are congruent
$\therefore \triangle AMX$ and $\triangle ANY$ are also congruent
and hence XM $=$ NY
XM $=$ NY $= 5$ cm

28(B). Given, $AL = 3.2$ units
Since the angular bisector divides the chord into equal parts.
$\therefore AL = LB$
$LB = 3.2$ units
$AB = AL + LB$
$\Rightarrow 3.2 + 3.2$
$= 6.4$ units

29(C). Let the points are

$A(3,2), B(-2,-3)$ and $C(2,3)$.
Then, $AB = \sqrt{(-2-3)^2 + (-3-2)^2}$
$\left[\because \text{distance} = \sqrt{(x_2-x_1)^2 + (y_2-y_1)^2}\right]$
$= \sqrt{(-5)^2 + (-5)^2} = \sqrt{25+25} = \sqrt{50}$
$= 7.07$ units (approx)
$BC = \sqrt{(2+2)^2 + (3+3)^2} = \sqrt{(4)^2 + (6)^2}$
$= \sqrt{16+36} = \sqrt{52} = 7.21$ units (approx)
and $CA = \sqrt{(3-2)^2 + (2-3)^2}$
$= \sqrt{(1)^2 + (-1)^2} = \sqrt{1+1}$
$= \sqrt{2} = 1.41$ (approx)
Also, $(\sqrt{52})^2 = (\sqrt{50})^2 + (\sqrt{2})^2$
$\Rightarrow \quad BC^2 = AB^2 + CA^2$
So, by converse of Pythagoras theorem,
$\angle A = 90°$
Therefore, $\triangle BAC$ is a right angled triangle.

30(D). Let $A(x, 0)$ be any point on X-axis, which is equidistant from points $B(1,3)$ and $(-1,2)$.
$AB = AC$
$\Rightarrow \quad AB^2 = AC^2$
[squaring both sides]
$\Rightarrow (1-x)^2 + (3-0)^2 = (-1-x)^2 + (2-0)^2$
$\left[\because \text{distance} = \sqrt{(x_2-x_1)^2 + (y_2-y_1)^2}\right]$
$\Rightarrow 1 + x^2 - 2x + 9 = 1 + x^2 + 2x + 4$
$\Rightarrow \quad 9 - 4 = 2x + 2x$
$\Rightarrow \quad 5 = 4x \Rightarrow x = \frac{5}{4}$
So, point on X-axis is $\left(\frac{5}{4}, 0\right)$.

31(C). Nitrogen, oxygen, carbon, phosphorous, sulfur are essential elements which are recycled in the ecosystem by biogeochemical cycles. They pass from producer to consumer to decomposer to back to the environment. Similarly, water is also recycled in the ecosystem by the water cycle. However, energy is not recycled in the ecosystem. From one trophic level to another trophic level, only 10% of the energy is transferred. The rest, that is 90% of energy is lost or utilized during this process.

32(A). Paper is biodegradable because is made from plant materials and most plant materials are biodegradable. Paper is easily recycled and can be recycled up to 6 or 7 times before the paper fibres become too short to be used for paper production.

33(A). Hydrogen gas is produced when a metal reacts with an acid. For example, when zinc reacts with hydrochloric acid, it produces zinc chloride and hydrogen gas.
Metal + Acid → Salt + Hydrogen.

34(D). The elements or compounds of the metals which occur in nature in the earth crust are called minerals. Minerals are substances that are formed naturally in the Earth. They are usually solid, inorganic, have a crystal structure, and form naturally by geological processes. A mineral can be made of a single chemical element or more usually a compound. They can be metals as well as non-metals.

35(D). Hormones are the chemical messengers that are produced by the endocrine system (composed of glands) but are transported to different parts of the body through the bloodstream.
Hormones play an important role in the control and coordination of the body. For example, the growth of an individual is regulated by growth hormones secreted by the pituitary gland.

36(D). The movement of plants in response to water is called hydrotropism.
The movement or direction of growth depends upon the concentration or gradient of water. Auxin plays an important role in bending of roots towards water. It causes on side of the roots to grow faster and the other side grows slowly. This leads to bending of roots towards water.

37(C).
$Fe(s) + CuSO_4(aq) \rightarrow FeSO_4(aq) + Cu(s)$
The above reaction is an example of a displacement reaction. In the above reaction, iron has displaced or removed another element, copper, from copper sulphate solution.
The reaction in which one atom or a group of atoms of a compound is replaced by another atom, is called a displacement reaction. Generally, a more reactive metal displaces a less reactive metal from its salt solution in displacement reaction.

38(A). When dilute hydrochloric acid is added to iron filings, hydrogen gas and iron chloride are produced.
We know that, addition of acid with metal gives salt and hydrogen gas. When dilute Hydrochloric acid is added to iron filings, iron chloride and hydrogen gas is produced. In this reaction iron displaces hydrogen from hydrochloric acid to form iron chloride \& hydrogen gas this reaction is a single displacement reaction. The chemical reaction is given below:
$Fe_{(s)} + 2HCl \longrightarrow FeCl_2(aq) + H_2(g) \uparrow$

39(D). The heat liberated on combustion for a hydrocarbon depends on the number of carbon atoms. As the number of carbon atoms increases, the heat liberated during combustion also increases.
Butane has the highest number of carbon atoms and is the biggest alkane among the given options. Therefore maximum heat is liberated on its combustion.

40(D). Organic compounds that are part of the same homologous series generally have similar chemical properties as each other, due to the presence of the same functional group in the molecules of all compounds in the series.
But they graded in physical properties, like solubility, melting, and boiling point of homologous series register a gradual changes. They increases as one move from lower to the higher series of member. Thus all homologues have similar but graded physical properties.

41(B). Oral contraceptives are commonly known as 'the pill', or 'birth control pill'.
Most birth control pills contain a combination of the hormones estrogen and progestin, which is why they are also called 'combined pills' or 'combination pills'.
The pill works mainly by changing the body's hormone balance so that the woman does not ovulate.
It is more effective if taken correctly and consistently.

42(A). Combining variations from two or more individuals would create new combinations of variants. Each combination would be novel since it would involve two different individuals.

43(D). Variation is any difference between cells, individual organisms, or groups of organisms of any species caused either by genetic differences (genotypic variation) or by the effect of environmental factors on the expression of the genetic potentials (phenotypic variation). Speciation is the evolutionary formation of new biological species, usually by the division of a single species into two or more genetically distinct ones. The formation of new biological species by the development or branching of one species into two or more genetically distinct ones.

44(B). cross-pollination, also called heterogamy, type of pollination in which sperm-laden pollen grains are transferred from the cones or flowers of one plant to egg-bearing cones or flowers of another.Cross-pollination is found in both angiosperms (flowering plants) and gymnosperms (cone-bearing plants) and facilitates cross-fertilization and outbreeding. This movement of pollen may occur by wind, as in conifers, or via symbiotic relationships with various animals (e.g., bees and certain birds and bats) that carry pollen from plant to plant while feeding on nectar.

45(C). Given,
Radius of curvature, $R = +3.00$ m;
Object-distance, $u = -5.00$ m;
Image-distance, $v = ?$
Height of the image, $h' = ?$
Focal length, $f = \frac{R}{2}$
$= +\frac{3.00 \text{ m}}{2}$
$= +1.50$ m (as the principal focus of a convex mirror is behind the mirror)
Since $\frac{1}{v} + \frac{1}{u} = \frac{1}{f}$
Or, $\frac{1}{v} = \frac{1}{f} - \frac{1}{u}$

$= +\frac{1}{1.50} - \frac{1}{(-5.00)}$

$= \frac{1}{1.50} + \frac{1}{5.00}$

$= \frac{5.00+1.50}{7.50}$

$v = \frac{+7.50}{6.50}$

$= +1.15\ m$

The image is $1.15\ m$ at the back of the mirror.

Magnification, $m = \frac{h'}{h}$

$= -\frac{v}{u}$

$= -\frac{1.15\ m}{-5.00\ m}$

$= +0.23$

46(D). Height of the object $h = +2.0\ cm$
Focal length $f = +10\ cm$
object-distance $u = -15\ cm$
Image-distance $v = ?$
Since $\frac{1}{v} - \frac{1}{u} = \frac{1}{f}$

Or, $\frac{1}{v} = \frac{1}{u} + \frac{1}{f}$

$\frac{1}{v} = \frac{1}{(-15)} + \frac{1}{10}$

$= -\frac{1}{15} + \frac{1}{10}$

$\frac{1}{v} = \frac{-2+3}{30}$

$= \frac{1}{30}$

Or, $v = +30\ cm$

47(A). Hans Christian Oersted was a Danish Physicist who discovered that electric current can create magnetic fields which was the first connection between electricity and magnetism. The wire will carry a current that creates a magnetic field around itself. Bringing the compass near the wire or in the loop will cause the compass needle to move. The current had produced a magnetic field strong enough to cause the compass needle to turn.

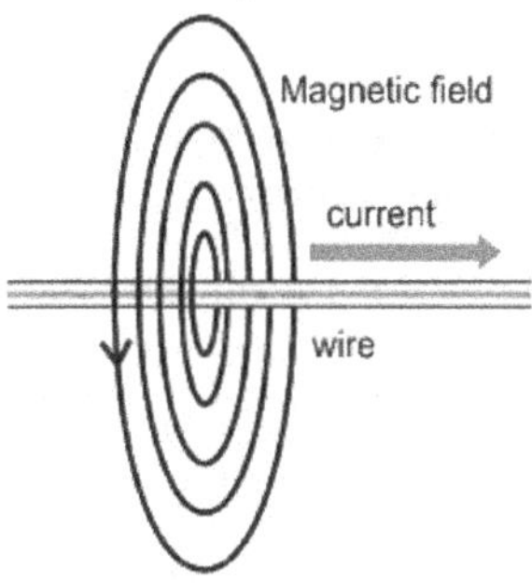

48(C). When a current-carrying conductor is exposed to an external magnetic field, it is subjected to a force that is perpendicular to both the field and the current flow direction. John Ambrose Fleming was the one who came up with the idea. In this rule a left hand may be held in such a way that the thumb, forefinger, and middle finger serve three mutually orthogonal axes.
When the thumb, centre finger, and forefinger of the left hand are arranged at right angles to one another, the thumb points in the direction of magnetic power, the centre finger points in the direction of current, and the forefinger points in the direction of a magnetic field.
So, the magnetic field is from south to north, and electrons are travelling upwards, but we can consider the conventional direction, which is downwards, so we can deflate the beam to the west using the left hand thumb law.

49(A). Muscle Fatigue is caused by the accumulation of lactic acid. Lactic acid is a byproduct of anaerobic metabolism, in which the body produces energy without using oxygen. Since the discovery of lactic acid, the popular notion has been that it is responsible for muscle fatigue and also tissue damage induced by the lactic acid following an intense workout.

50(A). The respiratory organs of fish are gills. Aquatic respiration is the process whereby an aquatic animal obtains oxygen from water. Most fish exchange gases using gills on either side of the pharynx (throat). Gills are tissues that consist of threadlike structures called filaments. These filaments have many functions and "are involved in ion and water transfer as well as oxygen, carbon dioxide, acid, and ammonia exchange.

51(D). ($CH_3COO)_2Zn$ is not an acid.
Salts, basic, such as Zinc acetate, are generally soluble in water. The resulting solutions contain moderate concentrations of hydroxide ions and have pH's greater than 7.0. They react as bases to neutralize acids. These neutralizations generate heat, but less or far less than is generated by neutralization of the bases in reactivity group 10 (Bases) and the neutralization of amines. They usually do not react as either oxidizing agents or reducing agents but such behavior is not impossible.

52(C). Carbon dioxide is produced when baking soda is heated.
The reaction which takes place when baking soda is heated for cooking is:
$2NaHCO_3 + H^+ \rightarrow CO_2 + H_2O +$ Sodium salt of acid

53(A). When sunlight enters into an atmosphere, it gets refracted. Due to this fact, the position of Sun appears to be slightly above the actual position during sunrise and sunset. Due to this atmospheric refraction, the day becomes 4 minutes longer than the actual one.

54(D). We know that,
1 kilowatt hour is the energy produced by 1 kilowatt power source in 1 hour.
Now,
$1\ kWh = 1\ kW \times 1\ hour = 1000 \times 3600\ W.sec$
$\Rightarrow 1\ kWh = 3.6 \times 10^6\ J$
$\Rightarrow 1\ kWh = 3.6\ MJ$

55(A). The resistance per unit length is given to be $R' = 2 \times 10^{-3}$
The length can be calculated as $L = \pi \times D$, where D is given diameter of $2\ m$.
Hence,
$L = 2\pi$
Therefore,
Resistance $= 2 \times 10^{-3} \times 2\pi = 4\pi \times 10^{-3}$ Ohms.
Now, when the resistance is measured between ends of any diameter, it can be seen as parallel connection of two resistances $\frac{R}{2}$ each (R being the total resistance of the entire loop).
So the resistance between two end points of a diameter will be $\frac{R}{4}$ i.e.

$= \frac{4\pi \times 10^{-3}}{4}$ Ohms

$= \pi \times 10^{-3}$ Ohms.

56(B). Increasing number of industries exert pressure on water resources in the following manner:
- Excessive use of ground water leading to ground water depletion.
- Pollution by industries which may be toxic is excreted in water leading to deterioration in the quality of water.
- Extensive usage of water in the industries to generate electricity.

57(B).
The famous Chipko movement in the Himalayas has not only successfully resisted deforestation in several areas but has also shown that community afforestation with indigenous species can be enormously successful.
The movement originated in 1973 at the Himalayan region of Uttarakhand (then part of Uttar Pradesh) and went on to become a rallying point for many future environmental movements all over the world. It created a precedent for starting nonviolent protest in India. However, it was Sunderlal Bahuguna, a Gandhian activist, who gave the movement a proper direction and its success meant that the world immediately took notice of this non-violent movement, which was to inspire in time many similar eco-groups by helping to slow down the rapid deforestation, expose vested interests, increase social awareness and the need to save trees, increase ecological awareness, and demonstrate the viability of people power. He used the slogan "Ecology is the permanent economy".

58(C). The main area for producing 'Tidal Energy' is the Gulf of Khambhat (Cambay). According to the estimates of the Indian government, the country has a potential of 8,000 MW of tidal energy. This includes about 7,000 MW in the Gulf of Cambay in Gujarat, 1,200 MW in the Gulf of Kutch, and 100 MW in the Gangetic delta in the Sunderbans region of West Bengal.

59(C). A doctor in a hospital treating a

patient does not fall under unorganized sector.

Unorganised Sector : It means an undertaking owned by individuals or self-employed employees engaged in manufacturing or selling products or some form of service and employing less than 10 staff in the business.

Example : plantation labour, handloom workers, fishermen, weavers, toddy tappers, beedi workers

60(C). Regular work brings about stable income.

A stable income will only be possible if a person earns continuously. On some days, the person might earn more and other days he might earn less. But working regularly will show consistency and will be a source of stable income. In order to develop their quality of life, individuals need to have more money. More money also helps I n future investments. In the modern economy, money is the primary exchange medium. In order to purchase or sell any item required for our existence, money is mandatory.

61(A). Napolean set about introducing many reforms in the territory that was under his control.

Napoleon introduced the following changes to make the administrative system more efficient in the areas ruled by him. He established civil code in 1804 also known as the Napoleonic Code. It did away with all privileges based on birth. It established equality before the law and secured the right to property.

62(C). The agricultural budget is the most important component of farm management. The agricultural budget considers aspects of the crop, livestock, production methods, and marketing in an integrated manner and estimates the overall farm costs and returns.

63(D). Banks do not give loans without proper collateral and documents.

Collateral is an item of value used to secure a loan . Collateral minimizes the risk for lenders. If a borrower defaults on the loan, the lender can seize the collateral and sell it to recoup its losses. Collateral can make a lender more comfortable extending the loan since it protects their financial stake if the borrower ultimately fails to repay the loan in full.

64(B). Rich households constitutes the largest segment of borrowers in the formal sector of credit.

Rich households take 90 percent of their loans from formal sector. Banks and cooperative societies constitute the formal sector of credit. Landlords, moneylenders, traders, relatives, friends and other sources of credit constitute the informal sector of credit. The formal sector provides only marginally more credit than the informal sector currently.

65(B). Ranbaxy has invested abroad.

An Indian company can make overseas investment in any activity (except those that are specifically prohibited) in which it has experience and expertise.

66(D). Toys and tyres industries have been hit in India due to competition.

Industries manufacturing batteries, capacitors, plastics, toys, tyres, dairy products and vegetable oil have been hit hard due to competition. Several units have been shut down rendering many workers jobless. The small industries in India employ largest number of workers in the country after agriculture.

67(D). All of the given products is a high safety required product.

Product safety is the ability of a product to be safe for intended use, as determined when evaluated against a set of established rulesner. Product safety needs to be ensured in every stage of the product manufacturing process, as unsafe causes can occur at any phase. Potential causes of a product being unsafe include- Manufacturers are required to include a warning if the product has potential danger or could cause a hazard to the consumer.

68(A). Consumer Complaint forum is called Consumer forum.

Consumer forum is a forum where a consumer may file a case against a seller in the case where the consumer feels that he has been cheated or exploited by the seller. The point of having a separate forum for consumer disputes is to ensure that such disputes are speedily resolved and make is less expensive. There are three tier Consumer Disputes Redressal Agencies. These are: District Consumer Disputes Redressal Forum in the District, State Consumer Disputes Redressal Commission at the state level and the National Consumer Disputes Redressal Commission at the national level.

69(B). Vellum is a parchment made from the skin of animals.

Vellum is prepared animal skin or "membrane", typically used as a material for writing on. Parchment is another term for this material, and if vellum is distinguished from this, it is by its being made from calfskin, as opposed to that from other animals, or otherwise being of higher quality.

70(D).

The reason behind the popularity of woodblock printing in 15th century Europe to print textiles, playing cards, and religious pictures with simple, brief texts are:

- Demand for books increased, booksellers all over Europe began exporting books to many different countries
- Production of handwritten manuscripts was also organised in new ways to meet the expanded demand
- Production of handwritten manuscripts could not satisfy the ever-increasing demand for books
- Copying was an expensive, laborious and time-consuming business.

The production of handwritten manuscripts could not satisfy the ever-increasing demand for books. It was because copying a manuscript was an expensive, laborious and time-consuming business. Their circulation therefore remained limited. Against this, the woodblock printing was not difficult. It was also not as fragile as the manuscripts. Thus, woodblock printing began to be widely used in Europe to print textiles, playing cards, and religious pictures with simple, brief texts.

71(C). A belief that the majority community should be able to rule a country in whichever way it wants, by disregarding the wishes and needs of the minority.

Majoritarianism is a traditional political philosophy or agenda that asserts that a majority (sometimes categorized by religion, language, social class, or some other identifying factor) of the population is entitled to a certain degree of primacy in society, and has the right to make decisions that affect the society. This traditional view has come under growing criticism, and democracies have increasingly included constraints on what the parliamentary majority can do, in order to protect citizens' fundamental rights.

72(D). The prudential reasons for power sharing include the desired stability of political order and the reduction of the possibility of conflict or violence between social groups. This is done to maintain civility and possibly harmony between different social groups otherwise it results in the tyranny of the majority over the minority.

Power-sharing as a concept describes a system of governance in which all major segments of society are provided with a share of power mainly to engender consensus and compromise in deeply divided societies, unlike strict government vs. opposition systems.

There are also moral reasons for power-sharing which embody the spirit of democracy. A democratic government is supposed to function for the people and is elected by the people, therefore, the concept of power-sharing legitimises citizens consent to be governed as everyone has a stake in the system. In modern democracies, there are different forms of power-sharing such as among different organs of the government (legislature, executive and judiciary); among governments at different levels (federal, state and local); among different social groups; and among non-statutory bodies (political parties, pressure groups, movements, etc).

73(C). Christopher Columbus discovered the continent of America.
Americans get a day off work on October 10 to celebrate Columbus Day. It's an annual holiday that commemorates the day on October 12, 1492, when the Italian explorer Christopher Columbus officially set foot in the Americas, and claimed the land for Spain. It has been a national holiday in the United States since 1937.

74(B). India has borrowed the concept of federalism from Canada. In this system, there is a clear division of powers between the Union and States.
Federalism is a system of government in which the power is divided between a central authority and various constituent units of the country. Usually, a federation has two levels of government. One is the government for the entire country that is usually responsible for a few subjects of common national interest. The others are governments at the level of provinces or states that look after much of the day-to-day administering of their state. Both these levels of government enjoy their power independent of the other. In India, we have a three-tier government, i.e. government at the central level, state level, and local level.

75(C). Federalism is a system of government in which the power is divided between a central authority and various constituent units of the country.
Usually, a federation has two levels of government. One is the government for the entire country that is usually responsible for a few subjects of common national interest. The others are governments at the level of provinces or states that look after much of the day-to-day administering of their state. Both these levels of governments enjoy their power independent of the other.

76(B). No, a large portion of the output was produced not within factories, but outside, within domestic units this is why the new industries did not easily able to displace traditional industries.
The new industries could not easily displace traditional industries. At the end of 19th century itself, less than 20% of total workforce was employed in advanced technological industrial centres. Their growth was slow as new technology was expensive and often broke down; and repairs are costly. The Industrial Revolution transformed economies that had been based on agriculture and handicrafts into economies based on large-scale industry, mechanized manufacturing, and the factory system. New machines, new power sources, and new ways of organizing work made existing industries more productive and efficient.

77(A). There are international institutions which regulate such resources.
The oceanic resources beyond 200 nautical miles of the Exclusive Economic Zone belong to the open ocean and no individual country can utilize these without the concurrence of international institutions.The international resources are those that lie beyond the nation's borders and they are defined in terms of the land, water and other resources like those of the human and the natural resources.

78(A). Abraham Lincoln said, "Democracy is a rule of the people, for the people and by the people".
Democracy as defined by Abraham Lincoln, the sixteenth president of the USA, is government of the people, for the people and by the people. It means that democracy is a form of government in which the rulers are elected by the people. The citizens of the country elect the Government to rule the country and the elected government work for the welfare of the people.

79(C). Regular, free and fair elections are the identity of democracy.
Free and fair elections play a critical role in political transitions by advancing democratization and encouraging political liberalization – helping to promote peaceful, democratic political transformation that lead to increased stability and prosperity. A country cannot be truly democratic until its citizens have the opportunity to choose their representatives through elections that are free and fair.

80(D). The Rowlatt Act of 1919 was Allowed detention of political prisoners without trial for two years.
The British colonial government passed the Rowlatt Act which gave powers to the police to arrest any person without any reason whatsoever. The purpose of the Act was to curb the growing nationalist upsurge in the country.
Rowlatt Acts, (February 1919), legislation passed by the Imperial Legislative Council, the legislature of British India. The acts allowed certain political cases to be tried without juries and permitted internment of suspects without trial.The British colonial government passed the Rowlatt Act which gave powers to the police to arrest any person without any reason whatsoever. The purpose of the Act was to curb the growing nationalist upsurge in the country.

81(B). Avul Pakir Jainulabdeen is the full form of the "APJ" in Dr. Kalam's name.
A.P.J. Abdul Kalam, in full Avul Pakir Jainulabdeen Abdul Kalam, (born October 15, 1931, Rameswaram, India, Died July 27, 2015, Shillong), Indian scientist and politician who played a leading role in the development of India's missile and nuclear weapons programs. He was president of India from 2002 to 2007.

82(C). Directive Principles of State Policy ensures economic justice to Indian citizens.
Directive Principle of State Policy down that the State shall strive to promote the welfare of people by securing and protecting as effectively as it may, a social order, in which justice-social, economic and political-shall form in all institutions of national life.

83(D). Hot money is the flow of funds from one country to another in order to earn a short-term profit on interest rate differences.
A global depositary receipt (GDR) is a bank certificate issued in more than one country for shares in a foreign company.
Foreign direct investment is an investment in the form of a controlling ownership in a business in one country by an entity based in another country.
Foreign portfolio investment is the entry of funds into a country where foreigners deposit money in a country's bank or make purchases in the country's stock and bond markets. In FPI, the investor does not have direct control over the securities or businesses.
Hot money is generally referred to as FPI.

84(C). The Supreme Court of India decriminalized adultery while striking down section 497 of the Indian Penal Code, 1860, in the case 'Joseph Shine v Union of India' (2018 SC).
According to the decision of the Supreme Court:
- Section 497 of the Indian Penal Code violates the right to dignity of a woman. Hence it is a violation of Article 21 of the Constitution.
- Section 497 is clearly arbitrary because the legal sovereignty of a man over a woman is wrong. Therefore the wife is not the property of the husband.
- Adultery does not fit the concept of crime. If this is treated as a crime, there will be excessive intrusion into the excessive privacy of the matrimonial sphere.
- Section 497 violates Articles 14 and 15 (right to equality) as it discriminates on the basis of gender and punishes only men under it.
- Treating adultery as a crime is an 'archaic idea' in which the man is considered the perpetrator and the woman the victim, but this is not the case in the present scenario.
- Section 497 was replete with institutional discrimination and anomalies and inconsistencies.
- Section 497 is based on the principle according to which, with marriage, a

woman loses her identity and legal rights. It violates their fundamental rights. This principle is not recognized by the Constitution. Adultery may be immoral but not illegal.

85(B). The source of the most important information regarding the internal structure of the Earth is seismology. Seismology is a major branch of physical geography, which includes scientific study and factual analysis of earthquakes.

86(A). Typhoid fever is an acute illness associated with fever that is most often caused by the Salmonella typhi bacteria. It can also be caused by Salmonella paratyphi, a related bacterium that usually leads to a less severe illness.

87(D). Article 253 of the Indian constitution empowers the Parliament to make laws on the State list subject.
The article gives power to Parliament to form any law for the whole or any part of the territory of India.
Such power is given for the implementation of any international treaty, agreement, and convention.

88(B). 'Matki' is a popular folk dance of Madhya Pradesh.
- Matki dance form has been developed by nomadic tribes in Madhya Pradesh.
- Performed using a small pitcher is a folk dance originating from central India known as the "Matki Dance".
- This "pitcher dance" belongs to the state of Madhya Pradesh, and is mainly performed in the Malwa region.

89(D). The Toda, Kota, and Kurumba tribes live in the Nilgiri Hills, while the Mogha tribes are found in the state of Tripura.

90(A). Rajaraja Chola I built the Brihadishwara temple in Thanjavur, Tamil Nadu.
He was one of the greatest emperors of the Chola empire. In his reign, the Cholas expanded beyond South India stretching from Kalinga in the north to Sri Lanka in the south. He fought many battles with the Chalukyas in the north and the Pandyas in the south. He built the Brihadishwara temple in Thanjavur dedicated to Lord Shiva.

91(A). The Mosque of Moth was constructed during the reign of Sikandar Lodi.
Moth Ki Masjid was built in 1505 by Wazir Miya Bhoiya who was a Prime Minister at the Royal Courts of Sultan Sikandar Lodhi. Sikandar Lodhi (1489 AD-1517 AD) was the son of Bahlol Lodhi who conquered Bihar and western Bengal. Noblest of the three Lodhi rulers, real name was Nizam Khan

(son of Bahalul Lodhi). He conquered Bihar and Bengal in 1504 AD. He built a new city named Agra and made it his capital. He shifted his capital from Delhi to Agra, a city founded by him. He broke the sacred images of the Jwalamukhi Temple at Nagarkot and ordered the temples of Mathura to be destroyed. He introduced the Gaz-i-Sikandari (Sikandar's yard) of 32 digits for measuring cultivated fields. He was a poet and wrote verses in Persian under the pet name Gularukh. He repaired Qutub Minar.

92(C). Hindustan Socialist Republican Association was formed in Kanpur in October 1924 by the revolutionary Ramprasad Bismil, Yogesh Chandra Chatterjee, Chandrashekhar Azad and Shachindranath Sanyal etc. of Indian freedom struggle.

93(C). The atmosphere around the Earth prevents the heat radiation to escape into the outer space. Thus, in the absence of the atmosphere, the temperature of Earth will decrease up to freezing point during night and increase during day because atmosphere is no longer there to absorb radiations.
The earth is surrounded by a layer of a gas called atmosphere. The atmosphere contains different layers, with variable density and temperature. Density is highest when it is near the surface of the earth and it decreases with increasing altitude.
Atmosphere is divided into five concentric layers of air or regions, depending upon the temperature conditions. These layers are:
1. Troposphere – It is the lowest region of atmosphere in which the human beings along with their organisms lives are called the troposphere. It extended up to the height of 8 to 18 km from sea level. It contains more than 90% of gas.
2. Stratosphere - It extends 50km above the sea level and lies in the stratosphere. It contains dinitrogen, dioxygen, ozone and little water vapor. At the height of 15-30 km, a thin layer of ozone is present in the stratosphere.
3. Mesosphere - It extended up to an altitude of 50 -85km that shows a decrease of temperature with the height. Minimum temperature of it is 92°C.
4. Ionosphere - It extends up to 85-500 km. In this region gases are ionized due to high temperature (up to 1200°C). The Ionosphere protects from the cosmic rays and site of wireless communication.
5. Exosphere - It is outer space.
As per the above description of atmosphere and its layer, we can easily understand that the atmosphere has an average temperature for day and night. If there were no atmosphere around the earth, the temperature would get affected. In the

absence of atmosphere, there would be no life, no rains, no winds, no fires and also no ozone layer that would be used as a protection layer against harmful radiations. The earth was becoming like a moon that had temperatures ranging from 190°C to 110°C.

94(B). A statutory corporation is formed by passing a special act of parliament or state legislature. Example: Airports Authority of India.

95(B). Saina Nehwal is the first Indian player who the first Olympic medal in Badminton in 2012. She is a professional badminton player from India. Saina Nehwal has achieved several milestones in the field of badminton for India. As one of India's most successful badminton players, Nehwal is also credited for increasing the popularity of badminton in India in recent years.

96(C). Bimla Devi, the first woman received a Sena Medal in India.
The Sena Medal is awarded to members of the Indian army, of all ranks, "for such individual acts of exceptional devotion to duty or courage as having special significance for the Army." Awards may be made posthumously and a bar is authorized for subsequent awards of the Sena Medal.

97(D). The value of acceleration due to gravity on any planet depends upon the mass, radius and density of the planet and it is independent of the mass, shape and density of the object placed on the surface of the planet.

98(C). When the water is heated from 0°C to 10°C, its volume first decreases, then increases. Mostly on heating the liquids there is an increase in their volume and a decrease in density, but the behavior of water is exactly the opposite between 0°C to 4°C. If heated in a vessel with water, the volume decreases from 0°C to 4°C and the density increases.

99(B). Nile Valley Civilization was the first to develop the art of agriculture. The people of Nile Valley Civilization were skilled agriculturists. They knew the art of irrigation and were quick to take advantage of the annual summer floods of the Nile.

100(C). The Jamnalal Bajaj Foundation has announced the winners of the Jamnalal Bajaj award 2022. The Foundation gives 4 awards in different categories.
Three are given to Indians and one award, for promoting Gandhian values outside is given to a foreigner.
The Jamnalal Bajaj Foundation was established in 1977. Jamnalal Bajaj was among the stalwarts of India's freedom movement.

Mathematics

1. To divide a line segment AB in the ratio $5 : 6$, draw a ray AX such that $\angle BAX$ is an acute angle, then draw a ray BY parallel to AX and the points $A_1, A_2, A_3 \ldots$ and $B_1, B_2, B_3 \ldots$ are located at equal distances on ray AX and BY, respectively. Then the points joined are:
   (a) A_4 and B_5
   (b) A_6 and B_5
   (c) A_5 and B_6
   (d) A_5 and B_4

2. To construct a triangle similar to a given $\triangle PQR$ with its sides $\frac{3}{7}$ of the similar sides of $\triangle PQR$, draw a ray QX such that $\angle QRX$ is an acute angle and X lies on the opposite side of P with respect to QR. Then locate points $Q_1, Q_2, Q_3, \ldots$ on QX at equal distances, and the next step is to join:
   (a) Q_{10} to C
   (b) Q_3 to C
   (c) Q_7 to R
   (d) Q_4 to C

3. If the median of the distribution is given below is 28.5, find the values of x and y.

Class interval	Frequency
$0 - 10$	5
$10 - 20$	X
$20 - 30$	20
$30 - 40$	15
$40 - 50$	Y
$50 - 60$	5
Total	60

   (a) $x = 8, y = 7$
   (b) $x = 7, y = 8$
   (c) $x = 9, y = 8$
   (d) $x = 8, y = 9$

4. The external and internal diameters of a hollow cylinder are $42cm$ and $28cm$ respectively. Find the cost of painting the cylinder completely at the cost of Rs $0.5/cm^2$ if the height of the cylinder is $5cm$.
   (a) Rs. 2640
   (b) Rs. 550
   (c) Rs. 1925
   (d) Rs. 1320

5. A toy is in the form of a cone mounted on a hemisphere of diameter $7cm$. The total height of the toy is $14.5cm$. Find the volume of the toy. (Take $\pi = \frac{22}{7}$)

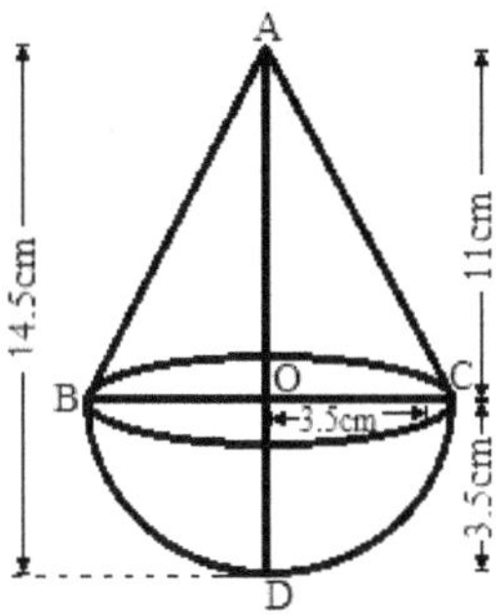

   (a) $231cm^3$
   (b) $232cm^3$
   (c) $233cm^3$
   (d) $234cm^3$

6. If $\sin\theta - \cos\theta = 0$, then the value of $(\sin^4\theta + \cos^4\theta)$ is:
   (a) 1
   (b) $\frac{3}{4}$
   (c) $\frac{1}{2}$
   (d) $\frac{1}{4}$

7. The roots of the equation $x^2 + \frac{x}{\sqrt{3}} + 1 = 0$ are:
   (a) Imaginary
   (b) Real and equal
   (c) Real and distinct
   (d) Imaginary and distinct

8. For which value(s) of k will the roots of $3x^2 + 3 = 2kx$ be real and equal?
   (a) ± 2
   (b) ± 4
   (c) ± 3
   (d) ± 5

9. In a circle of radius 21 cm, an arc subtends an angle of $60°$ at the center. Find out the length of the arc?
   (a) 22 cm
   (b) 24 cm
   (c) 26 cm
   (d) 28 cm

10. A chord of a circle of radius 15 cm subtends an angle of $60°$ at the center. Find the areas of the corresponding minor and major segments of the circle. $\pi = 3.14$ and $\sqrt{3} = 1.73$
    (a) 20.4375 cm^2 and 686.0625 cm^2
    (b) 30.4375 cm^2 and 786.0625 cm^2
    (c) 50.4375 cm^2 and 886.0625 cm^2
    (d) 60.4375 cm^2 and 986.0625 cm^2

11. In $\triangle ABC$, right-angled at $B, AB = 24$ cm, $BC = 7$ cm. Determine: $\sin A, \cos A$
    (a) $\frac{7}{25}, \frac{24}{25}$
    (b) $\frac{7}{24}, \frac{20}{25}$
    (c) $\frac{8}{24}, \frac{24}{26}$
    (d) $\frac{7}{26}, \frac{23}{25}$

12. In $\triangle ABC$, right-angled at $B, AB = 24$ cm, $BC = 7$ cm. Determine: $\sin C, \cos C$
    (a) $\frac{23}{24}, \frac{7}{25}$
    (b) $\frac{24}{25}, \frac{7}{24}$
    (c) $\frac{24}{25}, \frac{7}{25}$
    (d) $\frac{24}{25}, \frac{7}{26}$

13. Direction: Evaluate the following.
    $\sin 60° \cos 30° + \sin 30° \cos 60°$
    (a) -1
    (b) 1
    (c) 0
    (d) $\sqrt{3}$

14. The values of x and y satisfying the two equations $32x + 33y = 31, 33x + 32y = 34$ respectively will be:
    (a) $-1, 2$
    (b) $2, -1$
    (c) $0, 0$
    (d) $2, 3$

15. From Delhi station, if we buy 2 tickets for station A and 3 tickets for station B, the total cost is Rs. 77. But if we buy 3 tickets for station A and 5 tickets for station B, the total cost is Rs. 124. What are the fares from Delhi to station A and to station B?
    (a) $A =$ Rs. 12 ; $B =$ Rs. 17
    (b) $A =$ Rs. 13 ; $B =$ Rs. 17
    (c) $A =$ Rs. 18 ; $B =$ Rs. 17
    (d) $A =$ Rs. 19 ; $B =$ Rs. 17

16. If two positive integers a and b are written as $a = x^3 y^2$ and $b = xy^3; x, y$ are prime numbers, then HCF a, b is:
    (a) xy
    (b) xy^2
    (c) $x^3 y^3$
    (d) $x^2 y^2$

17. Find the largest number that will divide 398 , 436 and 542 leaving remainders 7 , 11 , and 15 respectively:
    (a) 25
    (b) 21
    (c) 19
    (d) 17

18. If the HCF of 408 and 1032 is expressible in the form $1032 \times 2 + 408 \times p$, then find the value of p:
    (a) $p = -5$
    (b) $p = -3$
    (c) $p = -4$
    (d) $p = -2$

19. HCF and LCM of two numbers is 9 and 459 respectively. If one of the numbers is 27 , find the other number:
    (a) 155
    (b) 154
    (c) 153
    (d) 152

20. Determine the discriminant of the quadratic equation $5x^2 + 3x + 2 = 0$.
    (a) -21
    (b) 21
    (c) 31
    (d) -31

21. If on division of a polynomial $p(x)$ by a polynomial $g(x)$, the quotient

is zero, then the relation between the degrees of $p(x)$ and $g(x)$ is:

(a) Degree of $p(x)$ < degree of $g(x)$

(b) Degree of $p(x)$ = degree of $g(x)$

(c) Degree of $p(x)$ > degree of $g(x)$

(d) Nothing can be said about degrees of $p(x)$ and $g(x)$

22. A box contains 90 discs which are numbered from 1 to 90. If one disc is drawn at random from the box, find the probability that it bears a perfect square number.

(a) 1 (b) 0.1

(c) 0.6 (d) 0.4

23. Two APs have the same common difference. The first term of one of these is -1 and that of the other is -8. The difference between their 4th terms is:

(a) -1 (b) -8

(c) 7 (d) -9

24. Find the 9th term of the sequence given below $9, 18, 27, \ldots$

(a) 54 (b) 52

(c) 65 (d) 81

25. In the given figure, $XY \| QR$, $\dfrac{PQ}{XQ} = \dfrac{7}{3}$ and $PR = 6.3$ cm, find YR.

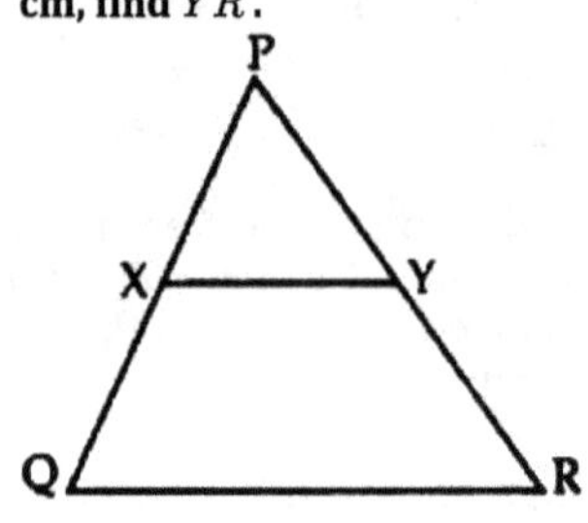

(a) 2.1 cm   (b) 2.5 cm

(c) 2.7 cm   (d) 3.7 cm

26. In the given figure, if $DE \| BC$, $AE = 8$ cm, $EC = 2$ cm and $BC = 6$ cm, then find DE.

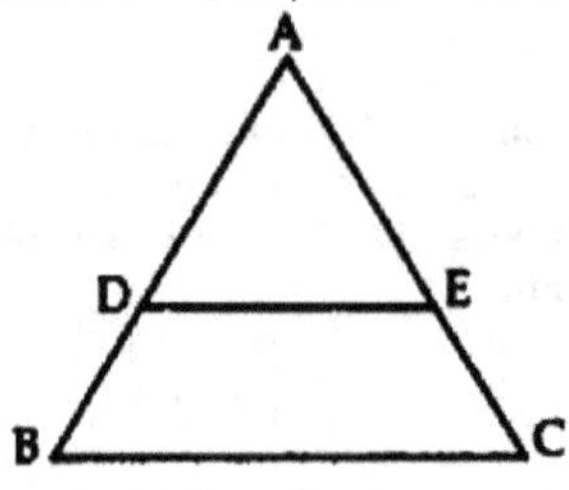

(a) 5.8 cm   (b) 4.8 cm

(c) 6.8 cm   (d) 7.8 cm

27. O is the centre of the circle passing through the points A, B and C such that $\angle BAO = 30°$, $\angle BCO = 40°$ and $\angle AOC = x°$. What is the value of x?

(a) $70°$ (b) $140°$

(c) $210°$ (d) $280°$

28. In the given figure if $OA = 5$ cm, $AB = 8$ cm and OD is perpendicular to AB, then CD is equal to:

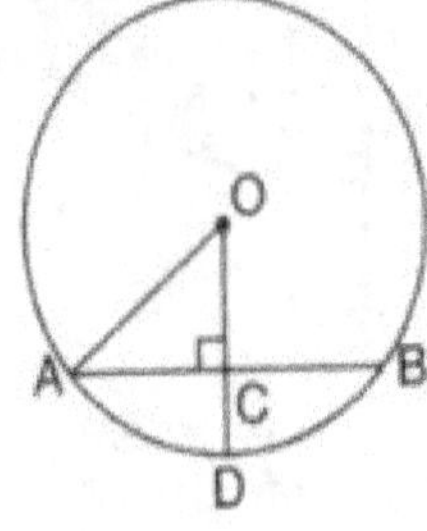

(a) 5 cm   (b) 4 cm

(c) 2 cm   (d) 3 cm

29. The point which divides the line segment joining the points $(7, -6)$ and $(3, 4)$ in ratio $1 : 2$ internally lies in the ________.

(a) I quadrant

(b) II quadrant

(c) III quadrant

(d) IV quadrant

30. The point $(-4, 6)$ divides the line segment joining the points $A(-6, 10)$ and $B(3, -8)$. The ratio is:

(a) $1 : 2$ (b) $7 : 2$

(c) $2 : 7$ (d) $4 : 1$

Science

31. Producers in an ecosystem are:

(a) Green organisms which fix solar energy by photosynthesis

(b) Animals which cause an increase in biomass by rapid multiplication

(c) Animals in the food chain which produce more energy than they consume

(d) Organisms that can be used as manures

32. In a food chain the second trophic level is occupied by:

(a) Autotrophs   (b) Producers

(c) Carnivores   (d) Herbivores

33. Carbon cannot reduce the oxides of sodium to sodium because:

(a) Na has less affinity for oxygen

(b) Na has more affinity for carbon than oxygen

(c) Na is non-reactive

(d) Na has more affinity for oxygen than carbon

34. Fill in the blanks by selecting the option with the correct words.

The process of removing impurities from the impure metal to obtain pure metal is known as ________ of metal. The most widely used method for refining is ________ .In this method, the impure metal is taken as ________ and the pure metal is taken as ________ .

(a) refining, electrolytic refining, anode, cathode

(b) calcination, electrolysis, cathode, anode

(c) refining, smelting, cathode, anode

(d) smelting, calcination, anode, cathode

35. Junctions of two neurons are called ________.

(a) synapse   (b) synapsis

(c) joint   (d) junction

36. Which of the following is a plant hormone?

(a) Insulin   (b) Thyroxin

(c) Oestrogen   (d) Cytokinin

37. Which of these is a combination reaction?

(a) $2CO_{(g)} + O_2(g) \rightarrow 2CO_2(g)$

(b) $Mg(s) + CuSO4(aq) \rightarrow Cu(s) + MgSO_4(aq)$

(c) $2AgNO_3(aq) + Cu(s) \rightarrow 2Ag(s) + Cu(NO_3)2(aq)$

(d) $2HgO(s) \rightarrow 2Hg(l) + O_{2(g)}$

38. During decomposition of an activated complex:

(a) Energy is always released

(b) Energy is always absorbed

(c) Energy does not chnage

(d) None of these

39. Carbon is used as abrasive as well as a ________.

(a) drying agent

(b) lubricant

(c) explosive

(d) None of these

40. Which of the following is used as lubricant?

(a) Graphite   (b) Charcoal

(c) Diamond   (d) Coke

41. The production of offspring by the sexual or asexual process is known as:

(a) Division

(b) Growth

(c) Reproduction

(d) All of the above

42. On reaching puberty, a woman's ovaries usually release ___________ egg each month.
(a) One   (b) Two
(c) Three   (d) Many

43. Which of the following options best describes homologous organs?
(a) Organs which are similar in structure, origin and function
(b) Organs which are similar in structure and origin, but different in function
(c) Organs which are similar in function, but different in structure and origin
(d) Organs which are similar in function and structure, but different in origin

44. The intentional reproduction of individuals to generate desirable traits is known as;
(a) natural selection
(b) artificial selection
(c) altered selection
(d) favoured selection

45. Which one of the following materials can not be used to make a lens?
(a) Water   (b) Glass
(c) Plastic   (d) Clay

46. No matter how far you stand from a mirror, your image appears erect. The mirror is likely to be ________.
(a) only plane
(b) only concave
(c) only convex
(d) either plane or convex

47. The fuse wire should have ________.
(a) Low resistance, Low melting point
(b) High resistance, Low melting point
(c) High resistance, High melting point
(d) Low resistance, High melting point

48. Transformer works on the principle of ________.
(a) Electricity
(b) Electric field
(c) Electro magnetic Induction
(d) Magnetic field

49. The fluid present between the blood capillaries and the cell membrane, through which gasses, nutrients, and metabolic wastes are exchanged between the blood and the cells are called as:
(a) Lymph
(b) Plasma
(c) Serum
(d) Normal saline

50. Which of the following substances is/are transported by blood plasma?
(a) Food   (b) Potassium
(c) Alcohol   (d) All of these

51. A student was provided a few samples of edible substances for tasting and asked to record the tastes. Which of the following samples would have tasted bitter?
(a) Baking soda (b) Orange juice
(c) Tamarind   (d) Vinegar

52. Direction: Match acids given in the first column with their natural sources listed in the second column:

(A) Acetic acid	(i) Grape
(B) Citric acid	(ii) Curd
(C) Lactic acid	(iii) Vinegar
(D) Tartaric acid	(iv) Orange

(a) (A) - (ii), (B) - (i), (C) - (iv), (D) - (iii)
(b) (A) - (iv), (B) - (i), (C) - (ii), (D) - (iii)
(c) (A) - (iii), (B) - (iv), (C) - (ii), (D) - (i)
(d) (A) - (i), (B) - (iii), (C) - (ii), (D) - (iv)

53. A person who can see the nearer objects clearly but not distant objects is suffering from:
(a) Emnetropia
(b) Blindness
(c) Myopia
(d) None of these

54. An electric motor takes 5 A from a 220 V line. What will be the energy consumed by it in 2 hours?
(a) 7920000 J   (b) 790000 J
(c) 11000 J   (d) 80000 J

55. The effective resistance of the given network is:

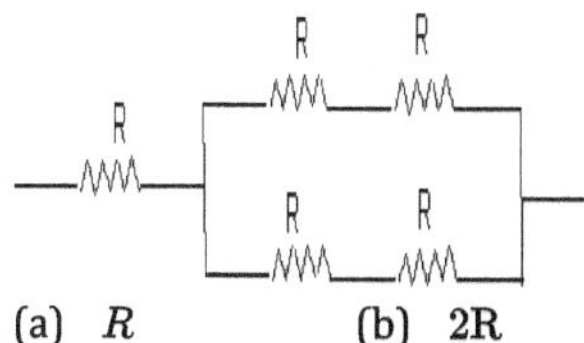

(a) R (b) 2R
(c) 54R (d) 32R

Social Science

56. In India hydroelectric power contributes approximately ________ percent of the total electricity produced.
(a) 22   (b) 25
(c) 20   (d) 26

57. What are Endemic species?
(a) Species with small population
(b) Species which are only found in some particular areas usually isolated by natural or geographical barriers
(c) These are species whose population has declined to levels
(d) These are species which are not found after searches

58. Magnetite is the finest iron ore with a very high content of iron up to _____.
(a) 70 percent   (b) 50 percent
(c) 40 percent   (d) 30 percent

59. When income levels rise, certain sections of people start demanding many more services like _____.
(a) more food   (b) Hospitals
(c) defense   (d) tourism

60. Which of the following is not an income?
(a) Wages
(b) Salary
(c) Freelance payments
(d) Donations

61. Napoleon had destroyed ______ in France.
(a) monarchy   (b) democracy
(c) federal rule (d) sovereignty

62. Agriculture is practised on small patches of land with the help of primitive tools like hoe, dao and digging sticks, and family/community labour. What type of agriculture is this?
(a) Intensive
(b) Primitive subsistence
(c) Extensive
(d) Plantation

63. What kind of loans do members of

SHG take?

(a) Individual loans
(b) Group loans
(c) Society loans
(d) None of the above

64. Which of the following statements is false?

(a) Demand deposits are not legal tender
(b) Currency notes issued are not legal
(c) Term deposits are not legal tender
(d) Wheat is legal tender

65. _______ in the labour laws can attract foreign investment.

(a) Stagnancy
(b) Flexibility
(c) Stringency
(d) None of the above

66. Which of the following is an example of Trade Barrier?

(a) Tax on Imports
(b) Custom Duty
(c) Transit Permits
(d) All of the above

67. World Consumer Rights Day is celebrated on:

(a) 5 March   (b) 10 March
(c) 15 March   (d) 20 March

68. Adulteration is:

(a) Selling defective items
(b) Overpricing
(c) Underweight measurement
(d) Mixing cheap materials

69. When did Johann Gutenberg developed the first-known printing press at Strasbourg, Germany?

(a) 1430s   (b) 1420s
(c) 1520s   (d) 1450s

70. Which was the first publication that Gutenberg printed?

(a) Political articles
(b) Bible
(c) Newspapers
(d) Travel stories

71. Consider the following statements about the ethnic composition of Sri Lanka:

A. Major social groups are the Sinhala- speaking (74%) and Tamil-speaking (18%).
B. Among the Tamils, there are two sub-groups, Sri Lankan Tamils and Indian Tamils.
C. There are about 7% Christians, who are both Tamil and Sinhala.
D. Most of the Sinhala-speaking are Hindus or Muslims and most of the Tamil-speaking are Buddhists.
Which of the above statements are correct?

(a) A, B, C   (b) A, B, D
(c) B, C, D   (d) A, B, C, D

72. Social division takes place when some social differences________ with other differences.

(a) Get mixed   (b) Undergo
(c) Overlaps   (d) Criss-cross

73. Why did the wheat price in India fall down by 50 percent between 1928 and 1934?

(a) Due to less production
(b) Due to floods
(c) Due to Great Depression
(d) Due to droughts

74. The main objective of the federal system is to __________.

(a) Accomodate regional diversity
(b) Promote diversity
(c) Make center more powerful
(d) Distribute finances to different organs

75. Besides Hindi, there are __________ other languages recognised as scheduled languages by the Constitution.

(a) 11   (b) 21
(c) 22   (d) 20

76. Which were the non mechanical sectors that were coming up?

(a) Building, pottery
(b) Food processing
(c) Food processing, building, pottery, glass work, tanning, furniture making
(d) Hand made goods such as embroidery

77. The first International Earth Summit was held in:

(a) Geneva
(b) New York
(c) Japan
(d) Rio de Janeiro

78. The two Greek words demos and kratia stand for:

(a) People/Government
(b) Government/ People
(c) Ruler/Government
(d) Ruler/People

79. Which one of these is not the feature of Democracy?

(a) Rule of people

(b) Monopoly over power
(c) Equality and freedom
(d) Guaranteed rights

80. What actions were taken during the Non-Cooperation Movement?

(a) The surrender of titles that the government awarded, and a boycott of civil services, army, police, courts and legislative councils, schools, and foreign goods
(b) Boycott of foreign goods and services
(c) Surrender of titles that the government awarded
(d) Boycott of civil services, army, police, courts and legislative councils, schools, and foreign goods

General Awareness/ Knowledge

81. 'Medha Patekar' is associated with which movement?

(a) Chipko movement
(b) Maitri Movement
(c) Save The Narmada Movement
(d) Save the Western Ghats Movement

82. The president of India can be removed from his office by the __________.

(a) Prime Minister
(b) Parliament
(c) Chief Justice of India
(d) Lok Sabha

83. Which is the tax that is imposed by the Central Government, but the income received from it is divided between the Center and the States?

(a) Central duty
(b) Central excise duty
(c) Corporation tax
(d) None of these

84. Who can remove the Judge of the Supreme Court?

(a) Chief Justice of the Supreme Court
(b) Only President
(c) Only Parliament
(d) Both Parliament and President

85. With reference to the earth's gravity(g), consider the following statements:

1. It is influenced by the distribution of mass of material within the earth.
2. It is greater near the poles than

at the equator.
Which of the statements given above is/are correct?
(a) 1 only
(b) 2 only
(c) Both 1 and 2
(d) Neither 1 nor 2

86. **In which among the following disorders is "memory loss" the main symptom?**
(a) Alzheimer disease
(b) Multiple sclerosis
(c) Parkinson's disease
(d) None

87. **When Telangana formed, Telangana became the ____ state of India.**
(a) 29th
(b) 25th
(c) 27th
(d) 30th

88. **Which one of the following is a major tribal group of Uttarakhand?**
(a) Jaunsari tribe
(b) Tharu tribe
(c) Raji tribe
(d) All of the above

89. **The second most important source after fossil fuels contributing to Indian energy need is:**
(a) Hydropower energy
(b) Wind energy
(c) Nuclear energy
(d) Solar energy

90. **Which of the following kings founded Pataliputra?**
(a) Shishunaga
(b) Bimbisara
(c) Ajatshatru
(d) Udayin

91. **Which of the following land revenue arrangement is called 'Todarmal System'?**
(a) Zabti System
(b) GallaBakshi System
(c) Kankut System
(d) Nasaq System

92. **Direction** : Read the passage carefully and answer the following questions.
The sepoys in the East India Company's army had a number of grievances, which led to the Revolt of 1857. The sepoys of the Bengal army, were mostly Brahmins and Rajputs having grievances of their own. Among them were unsatisfactory conditions of service, encroachment upon their religious customs and offences against their dignity and self-respect. They had a strong sense of resentment, as their salary scale was very low compared to their English counterparts. There was discrimination in matters of promotion and pension also.
In the guise of enforcing discipline, the British authorities prohibited the Hindus and the Muslim sepoys displaying their religious marks. These restrictions harmed the religious sentiments of the sepoys. The sepoys realised that their service conditions, at times impinged upon their religious beliefs. For example at Vellore, there was a mutiny by the sepoys due to the replacement of the turban they wore, by a leather cockade.
The Indian soldiers also had grievances against the British as they were forced to go for the military expeditions to abroad. In order to prevent any kind of resistance from the sepoys against their deployment abroad, Lord Canning's government passed an act in 1856.
Which among the following in not true regarding the grievances of the sepoys in East India Company's Army?
(a) Unsatisfactory service conditions
(b) Encroachment on religious matters
(c) Offences against their dignity and self-respect
(d) Equality with their English counterparts

93. **Percentage of total water found as fresh water is:**
(a) 46%
(b) 32%
(c) 16%
(d) 2.5%

94. **Which of the following is incorrectly matched?**
(a) Satyasodhak Samaj - Jyotiba Phule
(b) S. N. D. P. Yogam - Periyar Ramaswamy Naikar
(c) Bahishkrit Bharat - B. R. Ambedkar
(d) Sadharana Brahmosamaj - Pandit Shivanata Shastry

95. **Which Formula One racing driver won the 2022 the United States Formula1 Grand Prix in October 2022?**
(a) Max Verstappen
(b) Sergio Perez
(c) Charles Leclerc
(d) George Russell

96. **Who was the first man to fly into the space?**
(a) Richard Nixon
(b) Alexei Leonov
(c) James cook
(d) Yuri Gagarin

97. **Consider the following balanced equation:**
$$CO(g) + 2H_2(g) \longrightarrow CH_3OH(l)$$
How many moles of $CH_3OH(l)$ can be obtained by reacting 2.0 mole of $CO(g)$ with 2.0 mole of H_2 (g)?
(a) 1
(b) 2
(c) 3
(d) 4

98. **Which of the following pairs is/are correct?**
1. When a satellite is at its closest point from the earth, it is at the apogee of the orbit.
2. When a satellite is at its farthest point to the earth, it is at the perigee of the orbit.
(a) 1 only
(b) 2 only
(c) Both 1 and 2
(d) Neither 1 nor 2

99. **What are U-boats?**
(a) German military submarines used during the two world wars.
(b) These were Russian submarines, which were used against Japan.
(c) American ships used in World War II that were capable of flying fighter jets.
(d) These were French ships that were used against Britain during World War I.

100. **Which of the following award is given to the best goalkeeper of FIFA football?**
(a) Golden Boot
(b) Golden Ball
(c) Golden Goalpost
(d) Golden Gloves

// Hints and Solutions //

1(C).

Given ratio is $5:6$. That means, we have to locate 5 points such as A_1, A_2, A_3, A_4, A_5 on the ray AX and 6 points such as $B_1, B_2, B_3 B_4, B_5, B_6$, on ray BY. Also, we need to join A_5 and B_6.

2(C). To construct the similar triangle with sides $\frac{3}{7}$ of the similar sides of $\triangle PQR$ we should divide QR in the ratio $3:7$.
We should locate points $Q_1, Q_2, Q_3, Q_4, Q_5, Q_6$ and Q_7 and QX at equal distances and in next step join the last point Q_7 to R.
$\therefore QX$ need to have 7 equidistant points on it.

3(A). We can calculate the median as given below:
$$m = 1 + \left(\frac{\frac{n}{2}-cf}{f}\right) \times h$$
Where
$1 = $ Lower limit of median class
$h = $ Class size
$f = $ Frequency of median class
$\(\ cf = \)$ cumulative frequency of class preceding median class
The cumulative frequency for the given data is calculated as follows.

Class interval	Frequency	Cumulative frequency
$0-10$	5	5
$10-20$	X	$5+x$
$20-30$	20	$25+x$
$30-40$	15	$40+x$
$40-50$	Y	$40+x+y$
$50-60$	5	$45+x+y$
Total (n)	60	

It is given that the value of n is 60
From the table, it can be noticed that the cumulative frequency of last entry is $45+x+y$
Equating $45+x+y$ and n, we get:
$45+x+y = 60$
$x+y = 15$
It is given that.
Median of the data is given 28.5 which lies in interval $20-30$.
Therefore, median class $= 20-30$.
$l = 20$
$cf = 5+x$
$f = 20$
$h = 10$
Substituting these values in the formula of median we get:
$$m = 1 + \left(\frac{\frac{n}{2}-cf}{f}\right) \times h$$
$$28.5 = 20 + \left(\frac{\frac{60}{2}-(5+x)}{20}\right) \times 10$$
$$8.5 = \left(\frac{25-x}{2}\right)$$
$17 = 25 - x$
$x = 8$
Substituting $x=8$ in equation (1), we get:
$+y = 15$
$y = 7$
So, the values of x and y are 8 and 7 respectively.

4(D). Given,
External diameter of a hollow cylinder $= 42cm$
External radius of a hollow cylinder $(R) = \frac{42}{2} = 21cm$
Internal diameter of a hollow cylinder $= 28cm$
Internal radius of a hollow cylinder $(r) = \frac{28}{2} = 14cm$
Cost of painting $= $ Rs. $0.5/cm^2$
Height of cylinder $= 5cm$
As we know,
Total surface area of a hollow cylinder $= 2\pi h(R+r) + 2\pi\left(R^2 - r^2\right)$
Where $R = $ external radius, $r = $ internal radius.
Total surface area of a hollow cylinder
$$= 2 \times \frac{22}{7} \times 5 \times (21+14) + 2 \times \frac{22}{7}\left[(21)^2 - (14)^2\right]$$
$$= \frac{44}{7} \times 5 \times 35 + \frac{44}{7} \times (441-196)$$
$$= \frac{44}{7} \times 175 + \frac{44}{7} \times 245$$
$$= 1100 + 1540$$
$$= 2640cm^2$$
$\therefore$ Total cost of painting the cylinder $= 2640 \times 0.5 = $ Rs. 1320

5(A). Given,
Diameter of a hemisphere $= 7cm$
So, radius of a hemisphere $(r) = \frac{7}{2} = 3.5cm$
Height of the cone $(h) = (14.5 - 3.5)cm = 11cm$
Volume of a toy $= $ Volume of cone $+$ Volume of a hemisphere
$\therefore$ Volume of a toy $= \frac{1}{3}\pi r^2 h + \frac{2}{3}\pi r^3$
$$= \frac{1}{3}\pi r^2 (h + 2r)$$
$$= \frac{1}{3} \times \frac{22}{7} \times 3.5 \times 3.5(11 + 2 \times 3.5)$$
$$= \frac{1}{3} \times 22 \times 0.5 \times 3.5 \times 18$$
$$= 231cm^3$$
So, the volume of the toy is $231cm^3$.

6(C). Given,
$\sin\theta - \cos\theta = 0$
$\Rightarrow \sin\theta = \cos\theta \;...(i)$
So,
$\theta = 45°$
As we know,
$\sin 45° = \cos 45° = \frac{1}{\sqrt{2}}$
Now,
$\sin^4\theta + \cos^4\theta = \sin^4 45° + \cos^4 45°$
$= \sin^4 45° + \sin^4 45°$ [From equation (i)]
$= 2\sin^4 45°$
$= 2 \times \left(\frac{1}{\sqrt{2}}\right)^4$
$= 2 \times \frac{1}{4}$
$= \frac{1}{2}$

7(A). Let us consider the standard form of a quadratic equation, $ax^2 + bx + c = 0$
Discriminant $= D = b^2 - 4ac$
If the Discriminant > 0 then the roots are real and distinct.
If the Discriminant $= 0$ then the roots are real and equal.
If the Discriminant < 0 then the roots are Imaginary.

$$x^2 + \frac{x}{\sqrt{3}} + 1 = 0$$
$$\Rightarrow \sqrt{3}x^2 + x + \sqrt{3} = 0$$
Comparing this with the standard form $ax^2 + bx + c = 0$, we get $a = \sqrt{3}, b = 1$ and $c = \sqrt{3}$.
$\therefore D = b^2 - 4ac$
$= 1^2 - 4 \times \sqrt{3} \times \sqrt{3}$
$= 1 - 12 = -11$
$\therefore D < 0$
Thus, the roots are imaginary.

8(C). Given,
$3x^2 + 3 = 2kx$
Quadratic equation is $ax^2 + bx + c$
Discriminant $D = b^2 - 4ac$
$D = 0$ means two real and both are identical roots.
$3x^2 - 2kx + 3 = 0$
Compare with standard form $ax^2 + bx + c$
$a = 3, b = -2k, c = 3$
Discriminant $D = b^2 - 4ac$
$D = (-2k)^2 - 4(3)(3) = 4k^2 - 36$
For real and equal roots, $D = 0$.
$\therefore 4k^2 - 36 = 0$
$\Rightarrow 4\left(k^2 - 9\right) = 0$
$\Rightarrow k^2 - 9 = 0$
$k = \pm 3$

9(A). Given:
Radius of circle, $r = 21$ cm
Angle of sector, $\theta = 60°$

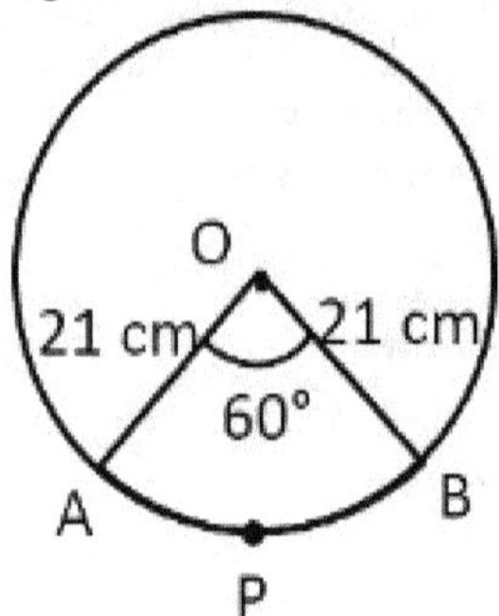

Length of the arc $APB = \frac{\theta}{360°} \times 2\pi r$
$$= \frac{60°}{360°} \times 2 \times \frac{22}{7} \times 21 = \frac{1}{6} \times 2 \times 22 \times 3$$
$$= 22 \text{ cm}$$

10(A). Given that,
Radius of circle $= r = 15$ cm
Angle subtended by chord $= \theta = 60°$

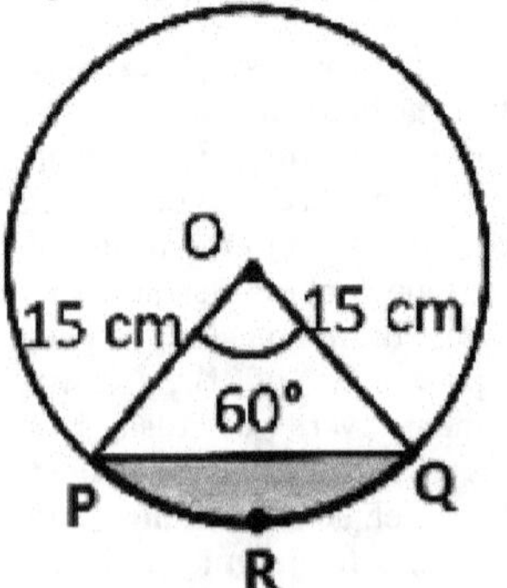

Area of circle $= \pi r^2 = 3.14(15)^2$
$= 706.5$ cm^2

Area of sector $= \dfrac{\theta}{360^\circ} \times \pi r^2$

Area of sector $OPRQ = \dfrac{60^\circ}{360^\circ} \times \pi r^2$

$= \dfrac{1}{6} \times 3.14(15)^2 = 117.75 \text{ cm}^2$

Now, for the area of major and minor segments,

In $\triangle OPQ$,

Since, $OP = OQ$

$\Rightarrow \angle OPQ = \angle OQP$

$\angle OPQ = 60^\circ$

Thus, $\triangle OPQ$ is an equilateral triangle.

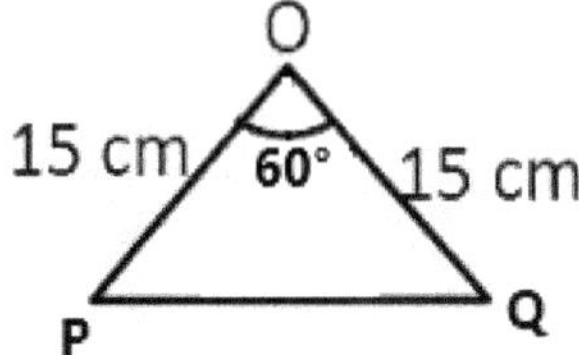

Area of $\triangle OPQ = \dfrac{\sqrt{3}}{4} \times (\text{side})^2$

$= \dfrac{\sqrt{3}}{4} \times (r)^2$

$= \dfrac{\sqrt{3}}{4} \times (15)^2$

$= \dfrac{225\sqrt{3}}{4} = 97.3125 \text{ cm}^2$

Now,

Area of minor segment $PRQP = $ Area of sector $OPRQ - $ Area of $\triangle OPQ$

$= 117.75 - 97.3125$

$= 20.4375 \text{ cm}^2$

Area of major segment $PSQP = $ Area of circle $- $ Area of minor segment $PRQP$

$= 706.5 - 20.4375$

$= 686.0625 \text{ cm}^2$

Therefore, the areas of the corresponding minor and major segments of the circle are 20.4375 cm^2 and 686.0625 cm^2 respectively.

11(A). Given,

In $\triangle ABC$,

$AB = 24 \text{ cm}, BC = 7 \text{ cm}, \angle B = 90^\circ$

In $\triangle ABC$, apply Pythagoras theorem

$\text{Hypotenuse}^2 = \text{Base}^2 + \text{Perpendicular}^2$

$AC^2 = AB^2 + BC^2 = (24)^2 + (7)^2 = 625$

$AC = \sqrt{625} = 25 \text{ cm}$

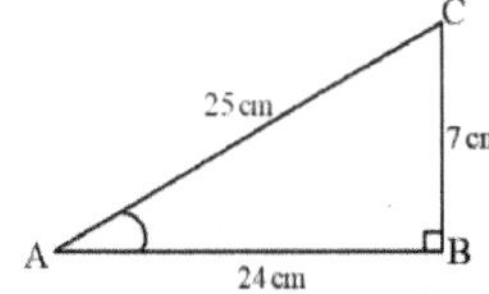

$\sin A = \dfrac{\text{Perpendicular}}{\text{Hypotenuse}} = \dfrac{\text{Side opposite to } \angle A}{\text{Hypotenuse}} = \dfrac{BC}{AC}$

$= \dfrac{7}{25}$

$\cos A = \dfrac{\text{Base}}{\text{Hypotenuse}} = \dfrac{\text{Side adjacent to } \angle A}{\text{Hypotenuse}} = \dfrac{AB}{AC}$

$= \dfrac{24}{25}$

12(C). Given,

In $\triangle ABC$,

$AB = 24 \text{ cm}, BC = 7 \text{ cm}, \angle B = 90^\circ$

In $\triangle ABC$, apply Pythagoras theorem

$\text{Hypotenuse}^2 = \text{Base}^2 + \text{Perpendicular}^2$

$AC^2 = AB^2 + BC^2 = (24)^2 + (7)^2 = 625$

$AC = \sqrt{625} = 25 \text{ cm}$

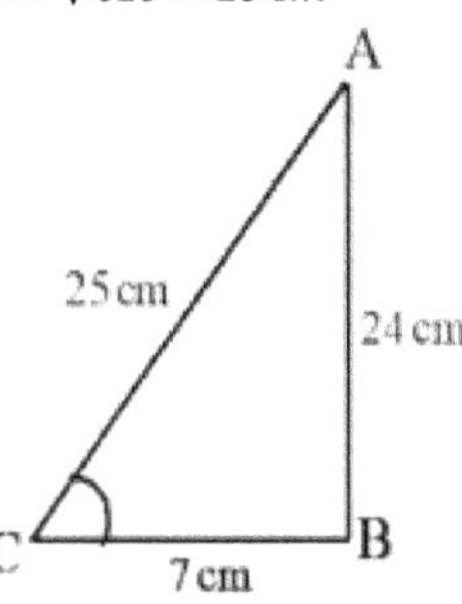

$\sin C = \dfrac{\text{Perpendicular}}{\text{Hypotenuse}} = \dfrac{\text{Side opposite to } \angle C}{\text{Hypotenuse}} = \dfrac{AB}{AC}$

$= \dfrac{24}{25}$

$\cos C = \dfrac{\text{Base}}{\text{Hypotenuse}} = \dfrac{\text{Side adjacent to } \angle C}{\text{Hypotenuse}} = \dfrac{BC}{AC}$

$= \dfrac{7}{25}$

13(B). Given,

$\sin 60^\circ \cos 30^\circ + \sin 30^\circ \cos 60^\circ$

As we know that:

$\sin 60^\circ = \dfrac{\sqrt{3}}{2}, \cos 30^\circ = \dfrac{\sqrt{3}}{2}, \sin 30^\circ = \dfrac{1}{2},$

$\cos 60^\circ = \dfrac{1}{2}$

$= \left(\dfrac{\sqrt{3}}{2}\right)\left(\dfrac{\sqrt{3}}{2}\right) + \left(\dfrac{1}{2}\right)\left(\dfrac{1}{2}\right)$

$= \dfrac{3}{4} + \dfrac{1}{4} = \dfrac{4}{4} = 1$

14(B). Given

$32x + 33y = 31,$

$33x + 32y = 34$

Multiplying $32x + 33y = 31$ with 33, we get

$1056x + 1089y = 1023 \cdots (1)$

Multiplying $33x + 32y = 34$ with 32, we get

$1056x + 1024y = 1088 \cdots (2)$

Subtracting (2) from (1),

$1056x + 1089y - 1056x - 1024y = 1023 - 1088$

$65y = -65$

$y = -1$

Substituting $y = -1$ in $32x + 33y = 31$,

We get $32x - 33 = 31$

$32x = 64$

$\Rightarrow x = 2$

The values of $x = 2$ and $y = -1$

15(B). Step -1: Writing mathematical equations according to conditions given in question

Let the price of ticket for station A be Rs. x and for station B be Rs. y,

According to question,

$2x + 3y = 77 \rightarrow$ Equation 1

$3x + 5y = 124 \rightarrow$ Equation 2

Step -2: Calculating fares for station A and station B.

Solving Equation 1 and Equation 2,

Multiplying Equation 1 by 3,

$6x + 9y = 231 \rightarrow$ Equation 3

Multiplying Equation 2 by 2,

$6x + 10y = 248 \rightarrow$ Equation 4

Subtracting Equation 3 from Equation 4,

$\Rightarrow y = 248 - 231$

$\Rightarrow y = 17$

Substituting value of y in Equation 1,

$\Rightarrow 2x + 3(17) = 77$

$\Rightarrow 2x + 51 = 77$

$\Rightarrow 2x = 26$

$\Rightarrow x = 13$

Thus, the fare to station A is Rs. 13 and to station B is Rs. 17.

16(B). Since:

$a = x^3 y^2 = \boxed{x} \, x \cdot x \cdot \boxed{y}\boxed{y}$

$b = xy^3 = \boxed{x} \, y \cdot \boxed{y}\boxed{y}$

Thus, HCF $= x \cdot y \cdot y$

$= xy^2$

17(D). Subtract the remainders from the numbers

$398 - 7 = 391$

$436 - 11 = 425$

$542 - 15 = 527$

So, we need to find largest number which divides 391, 425 and 527

and leaves remainder 0

Thus, we need largest number which divides 391, 425, and 527

HCF of 391, 425, 527

$391 = 23 \times 17$

$425 = 5^2 \times 17$

$527 = 31 \times 17$

HCF $= 17$

18(A). HCF of 408 and 1032

$\Rightarrow 408 = 17 \times 3 \times 2^3$

$\Rightarrow 1032 = 43 \times 3 \times 2^3$

so HCF $= 3 \times 2^3$

$\Rightarrow 24$

As per question,

$1032 \times 2 + 408 \times (p) = 24$

$408p = 24 - 2064$

$p = -5$

19(C). Given,

HCF and LCM of two numbers is 9 and 459

We know,

1st number $\times$ 2nd number $= $ HCF $\times$ LCM

$\Rightarrow 27 \times$ 2nd number $= 9 \times 459$

$\Rightarrow$ 2nd number $= \dfrac{9 \times 459}{27}$

$= 153$

20(D). The given quadratic equation is $5x^2 + 3x + 2 = 0$

Comparing this with $ax^2 + bx + c = 0$, we get $a = 5, b = 3,$ and $c = 2$.

Using discriminant formula,

$D = b^2 - 4ac$

$= 3^2 - 4(5)(2)$

$= 9 - 40$

$= -31$

21(A). We know that,

$p(x) = g(x) \times q(x) + r(x)$

Given that, $q(x) = 0$

When $q(x) = 0$, then $r(x) = 0$

So, now when we divide $p(x)$ by $g(x)$,
Then $p(x)$ should be equal to zero.
If $r(x) = 0$, then the degree of $p(x) <$ degree of $g(x)$.

Q.22 The total numbers of discs $= 90$

$$P(E) = \frac{\text{(Number of favourable outcomes)}}{\text{(Total number of outcomes)}}$$

22(B). Total number of perfect square numbers $= 9(1, 4, 9, 16, 25, 36, 49, 64$ and $81)$

P (getting a perfect square number)
$= \frac{9}{90} = \frac{1}{10} = 0.1$

23(C). Let the common difference of two APs be d.
The first term of first AP,
$a_1 = -1$
The first term of second AP,
$b_1 = -8$
We know that, the nth term of an AP,
$T_n = a + (n-1)d$
$\therefore 4^{th}$ term of first AP,
$= a_1 + (4-1)d = -1 + 3d$
4th term of second AP,
$= b_1 + (4-1)d$
$= -8 + (4-1)d$
$= -8 + 3d$
Now, the difference between their 4th terms is i.e.,
$= (-1 + 3d) - (-8 + 3d)$
$= -1 + 3d + 8 - 3d = 7$
So, the required difference is 7.

24(D). The general or n^{th} term of an AP is given as:
$T_n = a + (n-1)d$
Where,
$a = $ first term
$d = $ common difference
$n = 9^{th}$ (given)
Substitution the given values
$\Rightarrow T_9 = 9 + (9-1) \times 9$
$\Rightarrow T_9 = 9 + 8 \times 9$
$\Rightarrow T_9 = 9 + 72 = 81$

25(C). Let $YR = x$
$$\frac{PQ}{XQ} = \frac{PR}{YR} \cdots$$
(Thales' theorem)

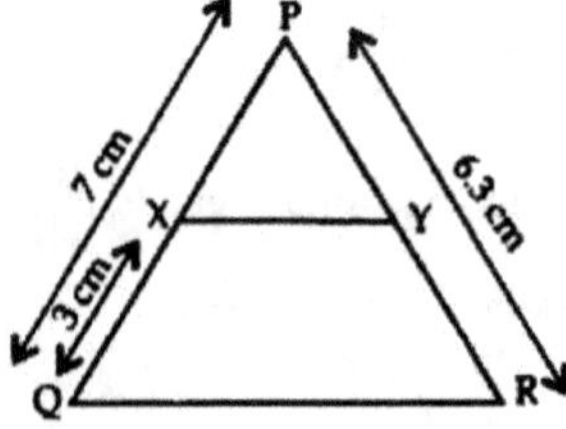

$\frac{7}{3} = \frac{6.3}{x}$
$\Rightarrow x = \frac{6.3 \times 3}{7} = 2.7$
$\therefore YR = 2.7$ cm

26(B). In $\triangle ADE$ and $\triangle ABC$,
$\angle DAE = \angle BAC$ ...Common
$\angle ADE = \angle ABC$ ... Corresponding angles
$\triangle ADE \sim \triangle ABC$ ..... AA corollary

$\therefore \frac{AE}{AC} = \frac{DE}{BC}$ ... (In $\sim \triangle$ s corresponding sides are proportional)
$\frac{8}{8+2} = \frac{DE}{6}$
$10DE = 48$
$\Rightarrow DE = 4.8$ cm

27(B). According to the information given in the question we get the diagram as:

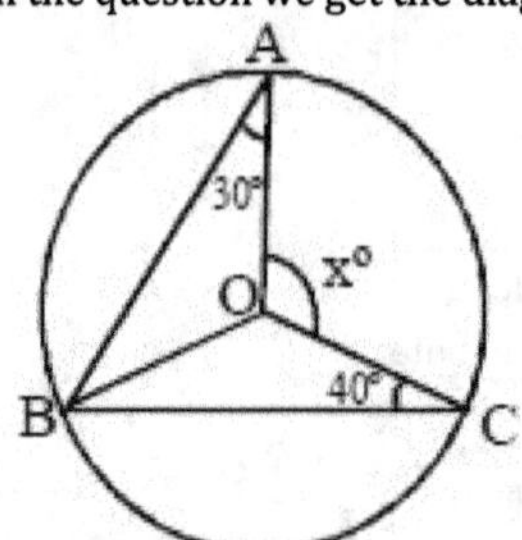

Now, in $\triangle AOB$,
$AO = BO$ (radii of circles)
$\angle ABO = \angle BAO = 30°$
Also, in $\triangle BOC$,
$BO = CO$ (radii of circles)
$\angle BCO = \angle OBC = 40°$
So,
$\angle ABC = \angle ABO + \angle OBC$
$\angle ABC = 30° + 40°$
$\angle ABC = 70°$
Therefore, $2 \times \angle ABC = \angle AOC$
$x = 140°$

28(C).

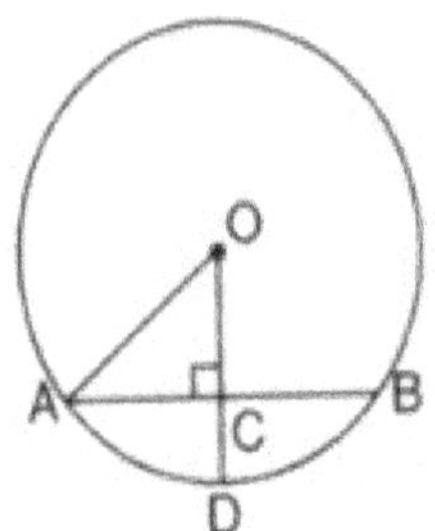

OC is perpendicular on chord AB.
$\therefore$ OC bisects the chord AB
$\Rightarrow AC = CB$
Now,
$AC + CB = AB$
$\Rightarrow AC + CB = 8$
$\Rightarrow AC + AC = 8$
$\Rightarrow 2AC = 8$
$\Rightarrow AC = \frac{8}{2}$
$\Rightarrow 4$cm
$\triangle OCA$ is a right angled triangle.
$\therefore AO^2 = AC^2 + OC^2$
$\Rightarrow 5^2 = 4^2 + OC^2$
$\Rightarrow 5^2 - 4^2 = OC^2$
$\Rightarrow OC^2 = 9$
$\Rightarrow OC = 3$
Since, OD is the radius of the circle.
$\Rightarrow OA = OD = 5$ cm
$\Rightarrow CD = OD - OC$
$\therefore 5 - 3 = 2$ cm

29(D). If $P(x, y)$ divides the line segment joining $A(x_1, y_1)$ and $B(x_2, y_2)$ internally in the ratio

$m : n$, then $x = \frac{mx_2 + nx_1}{m+n}$ and
$y = \frac{my_2 + ny_1}{m+n}$
Given that,
$x_1 = 7, y_1 = -6, x_2 = 3, y_2 = 4$, $m = 1$ and $n = 2$
$\therefore x = \frac{1(3) + 2(7)}{1+2}, y = \frac{1(4) + 2(-6)}{1+2}$
$\Rightarrow x = \frac{3+14}{3}, y = \frac{4-12}{3}$
$\Rightarrow x = \frac{17}{3}, y = -\frac{8}{3}$
So, $(x, y) = \left(\frac{17}{3}, -\frac{8}{3}\right)$ lies in IV quadrant.
[since, in IV quadrant, x-coordinate is positive and y-coordinate is negative]

30(C). Let point $P(-4, 6)$ divides the line segment joining the points $A(-6, 10)$ and $B(3, -8)$ in the ratio $m_1 : m_2$.

$$P = \left(\frac{m_1 x_2 + m_2 x_1}{m_1 + m_2}, \frac{m_1 y_2 + m_2 y_1}{m_1 + m_2}\right)$$

By using section formula, we get
$(-4, 6) = \left(\frac{3m_1 - 6m_2}{m_1 + m_2}, \frac{-8m_1 + 10m_2}{m_1 + m_2}\right) \cdots$ (i)

On equating x-coordinate from both sides of Eq. (i), we get
$-4 = \frac{3m_1 - 6m_2}{m_1 + m_2}$
$\Rightarrow -4(m_1 + m_2) = 3m_1 - 6m_2$
$\Rightarrow -4m_1 - 4m_2 = 3m_1 - 6m_2$
$\Rightarrow -4m_1 - 3m_1 = -6m_2 + 4m_2$
$\Rightarrow -7m_1 = -2m_2$
$\Rightarrow \frac{m_1}{m_2} = \frac{2}{7}$
$m_1 : m_2 = 2 : 7$

31(A). Producers, consumers, and decomposers are all interrelated in food chains and food webs and dependent on one another for survival. Producers make their own food. They do not have to obtain energy from other organisms. They obtain their energy from the sun and make food with that energy through the process of photosynthesis. They are also called autotrophs and are at the beginning of any simple food chain.

32(D). Herbivores are always at the second trophic level of food chains. A herbivore is an animal anatomically and physiologically adapted to eating plant material, for example foliage or marine algae, for the main component of its diet. As a result of their plant diet, herbivorous animals typically have mouthparts adapted to rasping or grinding. Horses and other herbivores have wide flat teeth that are adapted to grinding grass, tree bark, and other tough plant material.

33(D). The metals high up in the activity series are very reactive. They cannot obtain by reduction of their oxides by carbon. Since, sodium Na is high up in the acitivity series, carbon cannot reduce the oxides of sodium because it has more affinity for oxygen than carbon.

34(A). The process of removing impurities from impure metal is called refining.

Electrolytic refining is a widely used method of refining as it is a cost-effective and efficient method.

During the process, the impure metals are taken as anode and, pure metals are taken as the cathode. As electrolysis proceeds, the pure metal keeps depositing on the cathode and, the impurities settle at the bottom.

35(A). Synapse is the junction between two neurons, a neuron and a muscle cell or a neuron and a glandular cell. Synapses help to regulate the speed and direction of nerve impulses.

36(D). Cytokinin is the plant hormone which has a major role in growth and development of the plants. It helps in embryogenesis, cell division, chloroplast differentiation and many other important roles in plants. Therefore, it is clear from above the options that cytokinin is the plant hormone.

37(A). $2CO_{(g)} + O_2(g) \rightarrow 2CO_2(g)$ is a combination reaction as two reactants are combining to give one product.

Options (B) and (C) are displacement reactions as one element is replacing another element in the reactants to give new products.

Option (D) is a decomposition reaction as one substance is breaking down into simpler products.

38(A). During decomposition of an activated complex energy is always released.

Some energy is released when the complex decomposes to form a product. The entire concentration of an activated complex does not convert into product, but some of the concentration can convert into reactant as well.

39(B). Carbon is used as an abrasive as well as a lubricant

A drying agent is a chemical that is used to remove water from a substance. But carbon is not used as a drying agent or as an explosive. Due to different allotropic forms of carbon, it is used as an abrasive as well as lubricant. Graphite is the allotrophic form of carbon that is used as a lubricant. Diamond is another allotropic form of carbon that is very hard and, so makes an excellent abrasive.

40(A). Graphite is used as a lubricant. Graphite is a mineral made of loosely bonded sheets of carbon atoms, giving it a slippery texture that makes it a very effective lubricant. This slippery quality also makes graphite a good material for pencil lead because it easily sloughs off onto paper.

41(C). Reproduction is the process by which organisms produce offspring that are similar to themselves.

Reproduction can be either sexual or asexual. Asexual reproduction involves only a single organism while sexual reproduction involves gamete formation from two different sexes and the fusion of gametes.

42(A). When a girl is born, the ovaries already contain thousands of immature eggs that remain inactive.

When the girl reaches puberty, the FSH is released which stimulates the ovary to mature one egg every month.

This egg is released from the ovary every month which enters the fallopian tube and waits for fertilization.

43(B). Homologous organs are those that develop from the same structure along different directions due to adaptations to different needs and shows common ancestry. For example whales, bats, cheetah and human share similarities in the pattern of bone and forelimbs.

44(B). Artificial Selection. is the intentional reproduction of individuals in a population that have desirable traits. In organisms that reproduce sexually, two adults that possess a desired trait — such as two parent plants that are tall — are bred together.

45(D). Clay can not be used to make a lens.

Glass and water are transparent materials. There is a certain amount of plastic that is transparent so that the plastic can be used to make a lens, but the clay is an opaque substance so that the light can not be transmitted into it and the clay can not be used to create the lens.

Lens: A lens is a transmissive optical device which focuses or disperses a light beam by means of refraction . A simple lens consists of a single piece of transparent material, while a compound lens consists of several simple lenses (elements), usually arranged along a common axis.

46(C). No matter how far you stand from a mirror, your image appears erect. The mirror is likely to be only convex.

In a plane mirror, the image formed is always erect. In a convex, the image formed is always virtual and erect, irrespective of where the object is placed. Thus, the mirror in this case, is likely to be either plane or convex in nature.

47(B). Fuse wire should have high resistance and low melting point. So that it prevents current higher than the prescribed value to pass . Low melting point will let it to break when high current passes through it because of the heat generated.

48(C). Transformer works on the principle of electro magnetic Induction.

The transformer does this by linking together two or more electrical circuits using a common oscillating magnetic circuit which is produced by the transformer itself. A transformer operates on the principals of "electromagnetic induction", in the form of Mutual Induction.

Mutual induction is the process by which a coil of wire magnetically induces a voltage into another coil located in close proximity to it. Then we can say that transformers work in the "magnetic domain", and transformers get their name from the fact that they "transform" one voltage or current level into another.

49(A). The fluid present between the blood capillaries and the cell membrane, through which gasses, nutrients, and metabolic wastes are exchanged between the blood and the cells are called as Lymph. The lymphatic system is responsible for returning excess interstitial fluid to the blood. Of the fluid that leaves the capillary, about 90 per cent is returned. The 10 per cent that does not return becomes part of the interstitial fluid that surrounds the tissue cells. It helps in the exchange of gases, nutrients and removes metabolic waste.

50(A). Food, is transported by blood plasma.

- After the digestion of the food the essential nutrients needed by the body is carried to the whole body with the help of blood plasma
- Bloodstream acts like a river and carries these elements to the different parts of the body cells as per requirement
- These nutrients include glucose, amino acids, fats, vitamins, minerals, etc.
- All the nutrients required by the organs of our body are delivered through the blood plasma.
- The waste product resulting from the metabolic reaction is transmitted to the kidney, and liver through this blood plasma.
- The blood plasma transmits the nutrients obtained in the body from the food.
- The blood plasma is in charge of passing amino acids, nutrients, vitamins, minerals, fats, cholesterol, glucose, etc.

51(A). When a student is given some samples of edible substances to taste and asked to record the taste, he or she will find the taste of baking soda to be bitter.

Baking soda is a basic substance as it contains a base called sodium bicarbonate. It is a base as it produces negative hydroxide ions when dissolved in water. It is a base with the chemical formula $NaHCO_3$. It taste bitter due to the OH^- ion. Bases produce pH more than 7 . Our tongue corresponds to a sour taste if its taste buds register a drop in pH below 7 and bitter taste if pH is above 7 .

52(C).

(A) Acetic acid	(iii) Vinegar
(B) Citric acid	(iv) Orange
(C) Lactic acid	(ii) Curd
(D) Tartaric acid	(i) Grape

Acetic acid: Acetic acid is used in making of vinegar. Vinegar is basically a diluted solution of acetic acid in water.
Citric acid: Citric acid is present in orange juice. Some other fruits high in citric acid include lemons and limes.
Lactic acid: Lactic acid is present in curd. Lactic acid bacteria produces lactic acids by converting the milk sugars that coagulate and partially digest the milk protein, giving rise to curd.
Tartaric acid: Tartaric acid is present in grapes. Grape berries accumulate tartaric acid in their pulp, which strongly impacts the taste of the juice and the final product.

53(C). A person who can see the nearer objects clearly but not distant objects is suffering from myopia.
Myopia or near-sightedness is the condition in which the eye lens can focus images of nearby objects on the retina effectively but cannot form images of faraway objects (image is formed in the front of retina). A nearsighted person cannot see clear images of distant objects.

54(A). Power (P) is given by the expression, $P = Vi$
Where, Voltage, V = 220 V
Current, i = 5 A
$P = 220 \times 5 = 1100$ W
Energy consumed by the motor = Pt
Where,
Time, t = 2 h = $2 \times 60 \times 60 = 7200$ s
Energy consumed
= $1100 \times 7200 = 7.92 \times 10^6 = 7920000$ J

55(B).

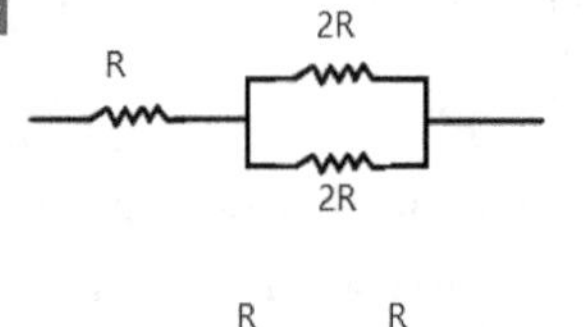

When Resistance is Connected in Parallel, then Resultant Resistance R_x is
$$\frac{1}{R_x} = \frac{1}{2R} + \frac{1}{2R}$$
$$\frac{1}{R_x} = \frac{2}{2R}$$
$$\frac{1}{R_x} = \frac{1}{R}$$
$$R_x = R$$
When R_x and R are connected in series

then,
$R_y = R_x + R$
$R_y = R + R \qquad \because (R_x = R)$
$R_y = 2R$

56(A). In India hydroelectric power contributes approximately 22 percent of the total electricity produced.
From the total electricity consumption of India, About 65% comes from thermal power plants, 22% from hydroelectric power plants, 3%from nuclear power plants and rest 10% from alternative sources of energy such as solar, biomass etc.

57(B).
Endemic species are plant and animal species that are found in a particular geographical region and nowhere else in the world.
Some species are endemic to a continent while the others can be endemic to an island. E.g., Lemurs of Madagascar and Tortoises of Galapagos.
Some endemic species of India.
Asiatic Lion in Gir Forest, Lion-tailed Macaque in Western Ghats of India, Nilgiri Tahr, Malabar large spotted civet, Nilgiri Blue Robin, Jerdon's Corser, Nilgai, Nicobar megapode are some of the species of animals endemic to India.

58(A). Magnetite is the finest iron ore with a very high content of iron up to 70 per cent.
It has excellent magnetic qualities, especially valuable in the electrical industry. Hematite ore is the most important industrial iron ore in terms of the quantity used, but has a slightly lower iron content than magnetite. (50 - 60 per cent). Haematite, Magnetite, Siderite, Iron pyrites are the ores of the metal Iron. Among all the ores of Ferrous (Iron) magnetite is the finest quality of iron ore. Magnetite is the finest iron ore with a very high content of iron, up to 70% . It has excellent magnetic qualities. Fe_3O_4 is the chemical formula of magnetite ore.

59(D). When income levels rise, certain sections of people start demanding many more services like tourism.
The income effect may have positive or negative consequences on a small business, depending on many factors. The income effect relates to how a consumer spends money based on an increase or decrease in their income. An increase in income (the ability to spend more money) results in a demand for more services and goods. A decrease in income results in the exact opposite. In general, when incomes are lower, less spending occurs, and businesses are hurt by the effect. But this is not always the case.

60(D). Donation is not an income.
To donate means to give something — money, goods, or time — to some cause, such as a charity. The word has a more altruistic meaning than does simply "giving"; it suggests that you don't expect anything in return for the contribution. donations are considered income and only taxable income if donors receive something in exchange for their donation, such as a service or product. If not, they're nontaxable gifts—at least if you're a private individual and not a business.

61(B). Napoleon had destroyed Democracy in France.
Napoleon had destroyed democracy in France but in administrative field he had incorporated revolutionary principles in order to make the whole system more rational and efficient. All priviledges based on birth were removed.

62(B). Primitive Subsistence Farming is a type of farming that is still practiced in a few areas of India. It is practiced on small patches of land using primitive tools like hoe, dao, and digging sticks and the labor is usually a family or the community.

63(B). Members of SHG take group loans. Self Help Group (SHG) is a group of about 15-20 members who pool their savings together. Members can take loans from the group's savings themselves on a decided rate of interest. SHG borrowers overcome the problem of non-availability of collateral documents. They creates tremendous opportunities for self-employment of the members. They are the building blocks of the rural organisation.

64(B). Currency and notes are legal tender.
Legal tender is anything recognized by law as a means to settle a public or private debt or meet a financial obligation , including tax payments, contracts, and legal fines or damages. A creditor is legally obligated to accept legal tender toward repayment of a debt. A coin or a banknote is legal tender in India used for discharge of debt or obligation.

65(B). Flexibility in the labour laws can attract foreign investment.
FDI provides several job opportunities for skilled manpower in the service sector than manufacturing sector and primary sector. FDI also helps to increase output and production in the service sector in India. Thus FDI inflows, employment generation and economic growth are correlated and directly related to each other. In the recent years the Indian Government has taken special steps to attract foreign companies to invest in India. The government has set up industrial zones called special Economic Zones SEZs. SEZs provide world class facilities electricity water roads transport storage recreational and educational facilities.

66(D). Tax on imports, custom duty and

transit permits all are example of Trade barrier.

Trade barriers refer to the obstacles that are put in place by governments to limit free trade between national economies. Trade barriers are thus essentially interventions in markets that happen to operate internationally. The four different types of trade barriers are Tariffs, Non-Tariffs, Import Quotas and Voluntary Export Restraints. Countries put up barriers to trade for a number of reasons. Sometimes it is to protect their own companies from foreign competition. Or it may be to protect consumers from dangerous or undesirable products. Or it may even be unintended, as can happen with complicated customs procedures.

67(C). World consumer rights day is celebrated on 15th March.

World Consumer Rights Day is observed every year to protect the rights of consumers and to ensure that the consumer' are not subjected to market abuse or social injustice that may undermine their rights. World Consumer Rights Day was inspired by President John F Kennedy, who sent a special message to the US Congress on 15th March 1962, in which he formally addressed the issue of consumer rights. He was the first world leader to do so.

68(D). Adulteration is Mixing cheap materials.

Adulteration is an illegal practice of adding raw and other cheaper ingredients to excellent quality products to increase the quantity.

Generally, if a food contains a poisonous or deleterious substance that may render it injurious to health, it is considered to be adulterated. Adding certain chemicals for faster ripening of fruits. Mixing of decomposed fruits and vegetables with the good ones, Cheaper and inferior substances are added wholly or partially with the good ones to increase the weight or nature of the product are some of the adulteration method.

69(A). In 1430s Johann Gutenberg developed the first-known printing press at Strasbourg, Germany.

Goldsmith and inventor Johannes Gutenberg was a political exile from Mainz, Germany when he began experimenting with printing in Strasbourg, France in 1440. He returned to Mainz several years later and by 1450, had a printing machine perfected and ready to use commercially; The Gutenberg press

70(B).

The Gutenberg Bible was printed in Mainz in 1455 by Johann Gutenberg and his associates, Johann Fust and Peter Schoeffer. Johann Gutenberg's Bible is probably the most famous Bible in the world. It is the earliest full-scale work printed in Europe using moveable type. Printing with moveable type had been developed earlier in East Asia. The earliest type of this kind is documented in Chinese sources in the 11th century. Metal moveable type was developed in Korea in the 13th century with a number of officially commissioned fonts being created from the early 15th century.

71(A). Sri Lanka has a multi-culture population. Sri Lanka has two major social groups, Sinhalese and Sri Lankan Tamils. People who speak Sinhala are known as the Sinhalese. People who speak Tamil are the Sri Lankan Tamils. The Sinhalese comprise 74 percent of the total population in Sri Lanka while Tamils make up 18 percent of the total population in Sri Lanka.

Composition of Sri lanka:
- The bulk of the population of the Sinhalese group of around 74 per cent
- Tamils around 18 per cent, who are mainly concentrated in the north and east of the island, making the largest ethnic minority.
- Muslims are representative of other communities.
- Two sub-groups exist among Tamils. Among Tamils, two sub-groups exist.
- The Tamil natives of the country are called Sri Lankan Tamils of around 13 per cent.
- The Indian Origin Tamils are the Tamils who were brought from India by British colonists to serve on estate plantations as indentured workers of around 5 per cent.
- Buddhists are predominantly Sinhala-speaking people, while the majority of Tamils are Hindus or Muslims.
- Around 7% of Christians are both Tamil & Sinhalese.
- The Sri Lankan Tamils launched parties and struggles for the recognition of Tamil as an official language, for regional autonomy and equality of opportunity in securing education and jobs.
- But their demand for more autonomy to provinces populated by the Tamils was repeatedly denied.
- Protecting and fostering Buddhism was stipulated by the new constitution.

72(C). Social division takes place when some social differences overlaps with other differences.
- The difference between the Blacks and Whites became a social division in the United States because the Blacks end to be poor, homeless and discriminated against.
- One kind of social difference becomes more important when other people start feeling that they belong to different communities.

73(C). Due to Great Depression the wheat price in India fall down by 50 percent between 1928 and 1934.

The Great Depression in 1929 had a major effect on prices, income, and production of goods in many countries. India also faced many such negative effects in the rural segments. One such effect was the decline in the wheat prices. It fell to almost 50% during 1928-1934. This in turn worsened the plight of the farmers. There was a large amount of unused crop and nobody to purchase it.

74(A). The federal system has dual objectives: to safeguard and promote unity of the country, while at the same time accommodate regional diversity.

Therefore, two aspects are crucial for the institutions and practice of federalism. Governments at different levels should agree to some rules of power sharing. They should also trust that each would abide by its part of the agreement.

An ideal federal system has both aspects : mutual trust and agreement to live together.

75(C). Besides Hindi, there are 22other languages recognised as scheduled languages by the Constitution.

The Eighth Schedule to the Constitution of India records the official dialects of the Republic of India. When the Constitution was established, consideration in this rundown implied that the language was qualified for portrayal on the Official Languages Commission, and that the language would be one of the bases that would be attracted upon to improve Hindi, the official language of the Union. The rundown has since, be that as it may, obtained further importance. Per Articles 344(1) and 351 of the Indian Constitution, the eighth timetable incorporates the acknowledgment of the accompanying 22 dialects:

1) Assamese
2) Bengali
3) Bodo
4) Dogri
5) Gujarati
6) Hindi
7) Kannada
8) Kashmiri
9) Konkani
10) Maithili
11) Malayalam
12) Meitei (Manipuri)
13) Marathi
14) Nepali
15) Odia
16) Punjabi
17) Sanskrit
18) Santhali
19) Sindhi
20) Tamil
21) Telugu
22) Urdu

As indicated by the Census of India of 2001, India has 122 significant dialects and 1599 different dialects. In any case, figures from different sources change, principally because of contrasts in meaning of the expressions "language" and "tongue". The 2001 Census recorded 30 dialects which were spoken by in excess of 1,000,000 local speakers and 122 which were spoken by more than 10,000 people. Two contact dialects have assumed a significant part throughout the entire existence of India: Persian and English. Persian was the court language during the Mughal time frame in India. It ruled as an authoritative language for a few centuries until the period of British colonisation. English keeps on being a significant language in India. It is utilized in advanced education and in certain regions of the Indian government. Hindi, the most usually communicated in language in India today, fills in as the most widely used language across quite a bit of North and Central India. Bengali is the second generally communicated in and comprehended language in the nation with a lot of speakers in Eastern and North-eastern districts. Marathi is the third generally communicated in and comprehended language in the nation with a lot of speakers in South-Western regions.

76(C). The non mechanised sector of industries which were grown with small innovation were food processing, building, pottery , glass work, tanning, furniture making and production of implements.
The Industrial Revolution was the transition to new manufacturing processes in Britain, continental Europe and the United States, in the period from between 1760 to 1820 and 1840. This transition included going from hand production methods to machines, new chemical manufacturing and iron production processes, the increasing use of steam power and water power, the development of machine tools and the rise of the mechanized factory system. The Industrial Revolution also led to an unprecedented rise in the rate of population growth.

77(D). The first International Earth Summit was held in Rio de Janeiro.
23-27 June 1997, New York, in 1992, more than 100 heads of state met in Rio de Janeiro, Brazil for the first international Earth Summit convened to address urgent problems of environmental protection and socio-economic development.
The assembled leaders signed the Convention on Climate Change and the Convention on Biological Diversity, endorsed the Rio Declaration on Environment and Development and the Forest Principles, and adopted Agenda 21, a 300 page plan for achieving sustainable development in the 21st century.

78(A). The term 'democracy' is derived from two Greek words 'demos' and 'Kratia'. 'demos' means 'people' and 'kratia' means

'to rule'. So democracy literally means rule of the people.
Democracy is a form of government in which the people have the authority to choose who they are governed by. In short, we use the term "of the people, by the people, for the people" to represent democracy. So the government is made of the people, chosen by the people, for the welfare of the people is the principle. Government is formed by the elected representatives who are chosen by the people directly by voting. The elected representatives then chose a head of the government from among themselves who runs the government.

79(B). Monopoly over power is not the feature of Democracy. Democracy is a form of government in which the supreme power is vested in the people and exercised directly by them or by their elected agents under a free electoral system. Monopoly over people is not a feature of democracy.
The features of democracy are:
- Elected representatives of the people rule and these representatives have power of making final decisions;
- Elections are conducted in free and fair atmosphere;
- Adult franchise is provided and every vote has equal value;
- Fundamental Rights and freedom of the people are protected.

80(A). The surrender of titles that the government awarded, and a boycott of civil services, army, police, courts and legislative councils, schools, and foreign goods these actions were taken during the Non-Cooperation Movement.
Gandhiji proposed that the movement should unfold in stages:
1st Stage- Surrender of titles that the government awarded.
2nd Stage- Boycott of civil services army police courts and legislative councils schools and foreign goods.
3rd Stage- Then in case the government used repression a full civil disobedience campaign would be launched.

81(C). Medha Patekar is a social worker and social reformer. She is associated with 'Narmada Bachao Andolan'. He has been honored with awards like Prabha Puraskar, Mahatma Phule Award, Janaseva Puraskar, Deenanath Mangeshkar Award etc.

82(B). Parliament of India can remove the president from office prior to completing the tenure for impeachment or violating the Constitution of India.
- This process may be started by the two houses of parliament against the charges.
- The Parliament of India is the supreme body of the Legislature of India.
- The Rajya Sabha is the council of the states and Lok Sabha is the house of the

people.
- The Indian Parliament has three parts: the President, the Rajya Sabha, and the Lok Sabha.

83(B). Central excise duty is a tax that is levied by the central government, but the income received from it is divided between the center and the states.

84(D). The proposal for the removal of the judge should be passed with a special majority in both the Houses of Parliament, while the decision to remove from the post is taken by the President.
Article 124(4) of the Constitution:
- The article says that a Judge of the Supreme Court can not be removed from his office except by an order of the President.
- The order should be passed by each House of Parliament supported by a majority of the total membership of that House.
- The majority should not less than two-thirds of the members of that House.

85(C). The gravitation force (g) is not the same at different latitudes on the surface. The reading of the gravity at different places is influenced by many other factors including the uneven distribution of mass of material within the earth influences this value. The gravity values also differ according to the mass of the material. It is greater near the poles and less at the equator. This is because of the distance from the centre at the equator being greater than that at the poles. These readings differ from the expected values. Such a difference is called a gravity anomaly. Gravity anomalies give us information about the distribution of mass of the material in the crust of the earth.

86(A). Alzheimer's is a neural disorder that has "memory loss" as the main symptom.
It is a brain disorder that damages the brain cells and slowly destroys mental and thinking ability.

87(A). Telangana became the 29th state of India. Telangana was separated from the state of Andhra Pradesh.
- On November 1, 1956, Telangana merged with the State of Andhra Pradesh after the separation from Madras.
- The States Reorganisation act of 1956 merged the Telugu speaking areas of Hyderabad state with Andhra Pradesh.
- The capital of Telangana is Hyderabad.

88(D). Tribes of Uttarakhand mainly comprise five major groups namely Jaunsari tribe, Tharu tribe, Raji tribe, Buksa tribe, and Bhotiyas.
- In terms of population, the Jaunsari tribe is the largest tribal group in the state.
- Tribes of Uttarakhand represent the

ethnic groups residing in the state.
- Every district of Uttarakhand has more or less a moderate percentage of the tribal population.
- In the state of Uttarakhand, the main concentration of the tribal population is in rural areas.
- As per records, around 94.50 per cent of the total tribal population resides in rural areas and the remaining percentage of the tribal population lives in urban centres.
- These tribes of Uttarakhand have been scheduled in the Constitution of India.

89(D). Solar energy has become the second most important source after fossil fuels contributing to India's energy needs for several reasons:
- India is blessed with abundant solar energy resources.
- The cost of solar energy has been decreasing in recent years, making it more cost-effective compared to other sources of energy.
- The Indian government has been promoting the use of solar energy through various initiatives, such as the Jawaharlal Nehru National Solar Mission and the National Solar Energy Fund.
- As the world becomes more aware of the environmental impact of fossil fuels, there has been a growing demand for alternative, clean energy sources.
- Solar energy is a domestic energy source, reducing India's dependence on imported fossil fuels.

90(D). The city of Pataliputra was founded by Haryankavanshi King Udayin/ Udyabhadra (460-444 BC) of Magadha and shifted his capital from Rajagriha to here.

91(A). 'Todarmal system' is also known as Zabti or Dahsala system. This system of land revenue became very popular and continued for a very long time.

92(D). The sepoys in the East India Company's army had a number of grievances, which led to the Revolt of 1857. Some of the grievances of the sepoys in East India Company's Army were:
- Unsatisfactory service conditions
- Encroachment on religious matters
- Offences against their dignity and self-respect
- Low salary scale compared to their English counterparts
- Discrimination in matters of promotion and pension

- In the guise of enforcing discipline, the British authorities prohibited the Hindus and the Muslim sepoys displaying their religious marks.
- The Indian soldiers were also forced to go for the military expeditions to other countries like Burma and Afghanistan.

So, we can conclude that 'Equality with their English counterparts' is not true regarding the grievances of the sepoys in East India Company's Army.

93(D). Only 2.5 percent of total water is found as fresh water which occurs in lakes and rivers.
The total volume of water on Earth is estimated at 1.386 billion km^3 (333 million cubic miles), with 97.5% being salt water and 2.5% being fresh water. Of the fresh water, only 0.3% is in liquid form on the surface.

94(B). Satya Shodhak Samaj was founded by Jyotiba Phule in 1873 in Maharashtra. S.N.D.P. Yogam stands for Sree Narayana Dharma Paripalana Yogam (SNDP) which is Indian charitable society. S.N.D.P. was founded in 1903 by Dr. Padmanabhan Palpu with the guidance and blessings of Sree Narayana Guru. B.R. Ambedkar established the Bahishkrit Hitakarini Sabha to promote education and socio-economic improvements among the Dalits. He started magazines like Mooknayak, Equality Janta, and Bahishkrit Bharat for the same cause. The Sadharan Brahmo Samaj was started with three distinguished men as its leaders on 15th May 1870. Shivnath Shastri was one of the principal members of the fraction that formed this Samaj.

95(A). Red Bull's Max Verstappen on 24th Oct 2022 won the United States Formula1 Grand Prix.
Mercedes' Lewis Hamilton and Ferrari's Charles Leclerc came at the second and third positions respectively. It was Verstappen's 75th podium finish & 33rd race win of his career. Verstappen ha s won 13 races in the 2022 season. He also won the Japanese Grand Prix on 9th Oct 2022.

96(D). Yuri Gagarin was the first man to fly into the space.
Yuri Alekseyevich Gagarin (9 March 1934 – 27 March 1968) was a Soviet pilot and cosmonaut who became the first human to journey into outer space, achieving a major milestone in the Space Race; his capsule, Vostok 1, completed one orbit of Earth on 12 April 1961. Gagarin became an

international celebrity and was awarded many medals and titles, including Hero of the Soviet Union, his nation's highest honour.
Hence the correct option is (D).

97(A). In the chemical equation:
$$CO(g) + 2H_2(g) \longrightarrow CH_3OH(l)$$
For one mole of CO, 2 mole of H_2 is needed
$\therefore$ for 2 mole of CO, 4 mole of H_2 will be needed
But in case of only 2 mole of H_2 is given, H_2 will act as limiting agent and only one mole of CH_3OH will be produced.

98(D). Earth satellites are objects which revolve around the earth.
- Their motion is very similar to the motion of planets around the Sun and Therefore Kepler's laws of planetary motion are equally applicable to them.
- In particular, their orbits around the earth are circular or elliptic.

When a satellite is at its farthest point from the earth, it is at the apogee of the orbit. Therefore, statement 2 is incorrect.
When a satellite is at its closest point to the earth, it is at the perigee of the orbit. Therefore, statement 1 is incorrect.
In accordance with Kepler's second law, the satellites are fastest at the perigee and slowest at the apogee.
There are two important forces acting on the satellite:
- the gravitational force which will pull the satellite towards earth and
- the centrifugal force (due to revolution) which counters the gravitational pull.

99(A). U-boats were German military submarines used during the two world wars.
U-Boat is the English version of 'U-Boot' in the German language. U-boot is a German abbreviation for Unterseeboot, which in English means boat under the sea. These were submarines used by the German Navy Friksmarine in the First and Second World Wars.

100(D). The 'Golden Glove Award' is presented to the most outstanding goalkeeper at each FIFA World Cup finals. The award is given to the best goalkeeper since the first World Cup in 1930. Golden Glove Award previously known as the "Lev Yashin Award" from 1994 to 2006 for best goalkeeper, first awarded in 1994. The award winner is decided by the FIFA Technical Study Group.

Mathematics

1. In geometrical constructions, the scale factor is used to construct _____ triangles.
(a) right angled (b) equilateral
(c) similar (d) congruent

2. A point P is at a distance of 8 cm from the centre of a circle of radius 5 cm. How many tangents can be drawn from point P to the circle?
(a) 0 (b) 2
(c) 1 (d) Infinite

3. 100 surnames were randomly picked up from a local telephone directory and the frequency distribution of the number of letters in the English alphabets in the surnames was obtained as follows:

Number of letters	$\frac{1}{4}$	$\frac{4}{7}$	$\frac{7}{10}$	$\frac{10}{13}$	$\frac{13}{16}$	$\frac{16}{19}$
Number of Surnames	6	30	40	16	4	4

Determine the mean of number of letters in the surnames.
(a) 8.32 (b) 9.32
(c) 32.9 (d) 32.8

4. The cost of painting a cubical box of side $3\,m$ at the rate of Rs. 2 per $sq.\,m$ is:
(a) Rs. 125 (b) Rs. 108
(c) Rs. 120 (d) Rs. 112

5. If two identical solid cubes of side 'x' are joined end to end, then the Total surface area of the resulting cuboid is:
(a) $12x^2$ (b) $10x^2$
(c) $15x^2$ (d) x^2

6. If $\cos A + \cos^2 A = 1$, then the value of $\sin^2 A + \sin^4 A$ is:
(a) -1 (b) 0
(c) 1 (d) 2

7. A quadratic equation whose one root is 3 is:
(a) $x^2 - 5x + 6 = 0$
(b) $x^2 + 6x - 5 = 0$
(c) $x^2 - 5x - 6 = 0$
(d) $x^2 - 6x - 5 = 0$

8. One of the roots of the quadratic equation $a^2x^2 - 3abx + 2b^2 = 0$ is:
(a) $\frac{-2a}{b}$ (b) $\frac{2b}{a}$
(c) $\frac{2a}{b}$ (d) $\frac{-2b}{a}$

9. A chord of a circle of radius 12 cm subtends an angle of $120°$ at the center. Find the area of the corresponding segment of the circle. $\pi = 3.14$ and $\sqrt{3} = 1.73$
(a) 88.44 cm^2 (b) 98.44 cm^2
(c) 78.44 cm^2 (d) 68.44 cm^2

10. A horse is tied to a peg at one corner of a square shaped grass field of side 15 m by means of a 5 m long rope (see the given figure). Find out the area of that part of the field in which the horse can graze.

(a) 19.625 m^2 (b) 18.625 m^2
(c) 17.625 m^2 (d) 16.625 m^2

11. If $\sec^2\theta + \tan^2\theta = 7$ then, find the value of $\sec\theta$.
(a) 4 (b) 2
(c) 1 (d) 0

12. If $\sin\theta + \cos\theta = \sqrt{2}\cos\theta$, then what is $(\cos\theta - \sin\theta)$ equal to?
(a) $-\sqrt{2}\cos\theta$ (b) $-\sqrt{2}\sin\theta$
(c) $\sqrt{2}\sin\theta$ (d) $-2\sin\theta$

13. If $\tan\frac{\alpha}{3} = \frac{1}{2}$, then the value of $\tan\alpha + \cot\alpha$ is:
(a) $\frac{11}{23}$ (b) $\frac{12}{23}$
(c) $\frac{121}{46}$ (d) $\frac{125}{22}$

14. The sum of the digits of a two-digit number is 9. Also, nine times this number is twice the number obtained by reversing the order of the digits. Find the number.
(a) 16 (b) 18
(c) 20 (d) 25

15. Meena went to a bank to withdraw Rs. 2000. She asked the cashier to give her Rs. 50 and Rs. 100 notes only. Meena got 25 notes in all. Find how many notes of Rs. 50 and Rs. 100 she received.
(a) Rs. 100 notes = 50 , Rs. 50 notes = 10
(b) Rs. 50 notes = 10 , Rs. 100 notes = 15
(c) Rs. 150 notes = 20 , Rs. 200 notes = 15
(d) Rs. 100 notes = 30 , Rs. 50 notes = 15

16. Which of the following fractions will have a terminating decimal expansion?
(a) $\frac{25}{3^2 \times 2^3}$ (b) $\frac{41}{2^2 \times 7^3}$
(c) $\frac{69}{3^2 \times 2^2 \times 5^2}$ (d) $\frac{343}{2^2 \times 5^2 \times 7^3}$

17. Find the HCF and LCM of $6, 72$ and 120 by using prime factorization method?
(a) 3 and 330 (b) 4 and 340
(c) 5 and 350 (d) 6 and 360

18. When three persons step off together, their steps measure 15 cm, 25 cm and 40 cm. What is the minimum distance that each person should walk in order to cover the same distance in integral number of steps?
(a) 5 cm (b) 250 cm
(c) 1500 cm (d) 600 cm

19. There are 104 students in class X and 96 students in class IX in a school. In a house examination, the students are to be evenly seated in parallel rows such that no two adjacent rows are of the same class. Fine out the total number of rows.
(a) 25 (b) 28
(c) 35 (d) 38

20. The zeroes of the quadratic polynomial $x^2 + 99x + 127$ are:
(a) Both positive
(b) Both negative
(c) One positive and one negative
(d) Both equal

21. By division algorithm of polynomials, find the value of $p(x)$.
(a) $g(x) \times q(x) + r(x)$
(b) $g(x) \times q(x) - r(x)$
(c) $g(x) \times q(x) \times r(x)$
(d) $g(x) + q(x) + r(x)$

22. A box contains 90 discs which are numbered from 1 to 90. If one disc is drawn at random from the box, find the probability that it bears a number divisible by 5.
(a) 0.4 (b) 0.3
(c) 0.5 (d) 0.2

23. The sum of three numbers in AP is 24 and the sum of their squares is 194 . Find the numbers.
(a) $5, 8, 9$ (b) $9, 8, 6$
(c) $6, 8, 7$ (d) $7, 8, 9$

24. If the sum of the first 14 terms of an AP is 1050 and its first term is 10 , find the 20 th term.
(a) 100 (b) 150
(c) 200 (d) 300

25. The lengths of the diagonals of a rhombus are 24 cm and 32 cm. Calculate the length of the altitude of the rhombus.
(a) 16.2 cm   (b) 17.2 cm
(c) 18.2 cm   (d) 19.2 cm

26. In the figure, $EF \| AC, BC = 10$ cm , $AB = 13$ cm and $EC = 2$ cm, find AF .

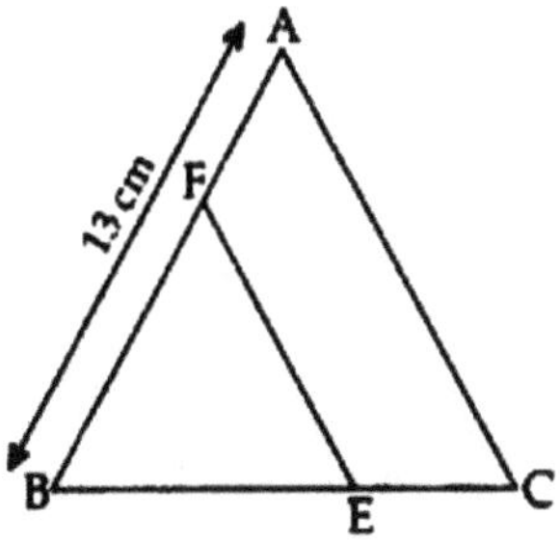

(a) 2.6 cm   (b) 3.6 cm
(c) 4.6 cm   (d) 5.6 cm

27. In the given figure, O is the centre of the circle of radius 5 cm . If $OM = 4$ cm , find the length of PN :

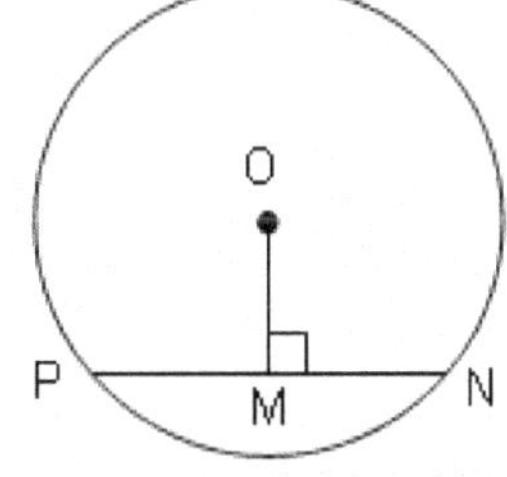

(a) 8 cm   (b) 3 cm
(c) 6 cm   (d) 2 cm

28. In the given circle, O is the centre, $AB = BC$ and $OM = 5$ **units. The** length of ON is equal to________

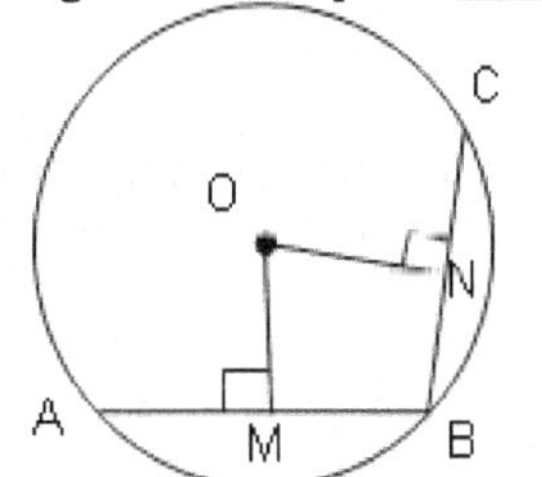

(a) 5 units   (b) 2.5 units
(c) 10 units   (d) 15 units

29. Point on the x -axis which is equidistant from $(2, -5)$ and $(-2, 9)$ is:
(a) $(-7, 0)$ (b) (-14.0)
(c) $(7, 0)$ (d) $(14, 0)$

30. If the distance between the points $(a, 2)$ and $(3, 4)$ be 8 then a =
(a) $2 + 3\sqrt{15}$ (b) $2 - 3\sqrt{15}$
(c) $2 \pm 3\sqrt{15}$ (d) $3 \pm 2\sqrt{15}$

Science

31. The organisms which consume both plants as well as animal products are known as:
(a) herbivores   (b) carnivores
(c) piscivores   (d) omnivores

32. Ecosystem may be defined as:
(a) A species along with environment
(b) Plants found in water
(c) Plants found on land
(d) All plants and animal species along with environment

33. Which one of the following metal do not react with cold or hot water?
(a) Sodium (Na)
(b) Calcium (Ca)
(c) Magnesium (Mg)
(d) Iron (Fe)

34. Which one of the following four metals would be displaced from the solution of its salts by other three metals?
(a) Mg   (b) Ag
(c) Zn   (d) Cu

35. Brain depends on blood for the supply of:
(a) Oxygen and ATP
(b) Oxygen and Carbon dioxide
(c) Oxygen and Glucose
(d) ATP and Glucose

36. Internal activities are controlled by:
(a) CNS
(b) ANS
(c) PNS
(d) None of these

37. Identify the substances that is oxidized and the substances that is reduced in the following reaction:
$4Na(s) + O_2(g) \longrightarrow 2Na_2O(s)$
(a) Na_2, O_2 (b) Na, Na
(c) O_2, Na (d) O_2, O_2

38. The oxidation of oils or fats in a food is known as:

(a) Corrosion   (b) Rust
(c) Reduction   (d) Rancidity

39. C_5H_{10} is the formula of which hydrocarbon?
(a) Pentane   (b) Pentene
(c) Pentyne   (d) Pentadiene

40. Methane, ethane and propane are said to form a homologous series because all are:
(a) Hydrocarbons
(b) Saturated compounds
(c) Aliphatic compounds
(d) Differ from each other by a CH_2 group

41. Which of the given organisms reproduce sexually?
(a) Amoeba   (b) Paramecium
(c) Anura   (d) Hydra

42. In which process is the number of chromosomes is reduced to half?
(a) Mitosis
(b) Meiosis
(c) Budding
(d) Fragmentation

43. Which of the following traits always appears in two opposite forms?
(a) contrasting   (b) recessive
(c) dominant   (d) homoallelic

44. The plants produced from self-pollination of first generation plants constitute the.
(a) parent plants
(b) F1 plants
(c) F2 plants
(d) F3 plants

45. An object, 4.0 cm in size, is placed at 25.0 cm in front of a concave mirror of focal length 15.0 cm . At what distance from the mirror should a screen be placed in order to obtain a sharp image?
(a) -37.5 (b) 31.5
(c) 35.5 (d) 37

46. A concave lens has focal length of 15 cm . At what distance should the object from the lens be placed so that it forms an image at 10 cm from the lens?
(a) -55 cm   (b) -30 cm
(c) -45 cm   (d) -20 cm

47. For a current in a long straight solenoid N-pole and S-pole are created at the two ends. Among the following statements, the incorrect statement is:
(a) The field lines inside the

solenoid are in the form of straight lines which indicates that the magnetic field is the same at all points inside the solenoid.

(b) The strong magnetic field produced inside the solenoid can be used to magnetise a piece of magnetic material like soft iron, when placed inside the coil.

(c) The pattern of the magnetic field associated with the solenoid is different from the pattern of the magnetic field around a bar magnet.

(d) The N-pole and S-pole exchange position when the direction of current through the solenoid is reversed.

48. **The main advantage of A.C power transmission over D.C power transmission over' long distance is:**
(a) AC transmit without much loss of energy
(b) Less insulation problem
(c) Less problem of instability
(d) Easy transformation.

49. **Which of the following is responsible for bringing about the emulsification of fats?**
(a) Amylase   (b) Pepsin
(c) Mucus   (d) Bile

50. **The energy trapped by chlorophyll molecule is used for ________.**
(a) the generation of ATP
(b) the generation of NADPH
(c) the splitting of water molecule
(d) All of the above

51. **Match the chemical substances given in Column (A) with their appropriate application given in Column (B)**

Column (A)	Column (B)
(A) Bleaching powder	(i) Preparation of glass
(B) Baking soda	(ii) Production of H_2 and Cl_2
(C) Washing soda	(iii) Decolourisation
(D) Sodium chloride	(iv) Antacid

(a) A—(ii), B—(i), C—(iv), D—(iii)
(b) A—(iii), B—(ii), C—(iv), D—(i)
(c) A—(iii), B—(iv), C—(i), D—(ii)
(d) A—(ii), B—(iv), C—(i), D—(iii)

52. **What is the chemical nature of soap?**

(a) Neutral   (b) Highly acidic
(c) Mildly acidic   (d) Basic

53. **A rainbow is formed when the air is:**
(a) Full of moisture
(b) Completely Dry
(c) Hot
(d) Cold

54. **Work done in moving a charge through an electric circuit connected to a $5V$ battery which produces $3A$ current in the circuit is $15J$. What is the duration of the current?**
(a) $0.5\ sec$ (b) $1.0\ sec$
(c) $2.0\ sec$ (d) $2.5\ sec$

55. **Resistance is the property of a circuit, which limits the magnitude of _____.**
(a) voltage
(b) electric current
(c) resistivity
(d) all of these

Social Science

56. **In which other places is Rooftop rainwater harvesting common other than Rajasthan?**
(a) Shillong   (b) Gujarat
(c) West Bengal   (d) Sikkim

57. **What type of species is the mithun in Arunachal Pradesh?**
(a) Rare   (b) Endemic
(c) Vulnerable   (d) Extinct

58. **Very high grade haematite ores are found in the Durg-Bastar-Chandrapur belt that lies in _____ and _____.**
(a) Rajasthan and Uttar Pradesh
(b) Chhattisgarh and Maharashtra
(c) Gujarat and Madhya Pradesh
(d) Madhya Pradesh and Odisha

59. **Over the past decade or so, certain new services such as ________ have become important and essential.**
(a) private hospitals
(b) professional training
(c) information and communication technology
(d) Insurance

60. **What will be the aspiration of an educated urban unemployed youth?**
(a) An educated urban unemployed youth will aspire for better

opportunities in agriculture.
(b) Support from government at every step in life for his upward movement.
(c) An urban educated unemployed will aspire for good job opportunities where his education can be made use.
(d) Better facilities of recreation for his leisure time.

61. **The Civil Code of 1804, also known as the Napoleonic Code, established:**
(a) Equality before the law
(b) Secured the right to property
(c) Did away with all the privileges based on birth
(d) All of the above

62. **What does the mean of "Operation Holding"?**
(a) Total land area owned by a farmer
(b) Cultivation done by a farmer in total cropped area
(c) Net land area cultivated by a farmer
(d) Total land taken by a farmer

63. **________is the main source of money supply in an economy.**
(a) Central Bank
(b) Commercial banks
(c) Both (A) and (B)
(d) Government

64. **Which state accounts for maximum percentage of SHGs (self-help groups) in bank credit?**
(a) Andhra Pradesh
(b) Tamil Nadu
(c) Kerala
(d) Karnataka

65. **T he main channel that connected the countries in past was _____.**
(a) Labour   (b) Religion
(c) Technology   (d) Trade

66. **Which of the following factors has not facilitated globalisation?**
(a) Technology
(b) Liberlisation of trade
(c) WTO
(d) Nationalisation of banks

67. **Which mark should you look for while buying honey?**
(a) ISI
(b) ISO
(c) Agmark
(d) None of these

68. **Factors which cause the exploitation of the consumer:**
    (a) Limited and wrong information
    (b) Illiteracy and ignorance of the consumer
    (c) Few sellers and limited competition
    (d) All the above

69. **What were the main characteristics of printed books?**
    (i) The metal letters imitated the ornamental handwritten styles
    (ii) Borders were illuminated by hand with foliage and other patterns, and illustrations were painted
    (iii) In the books printed for the rich, space for decoration was kept blank on the printed page
    (iv) Each purchaser could choose the design and decide on the painting school that would do the illustrations
    (a) (i) only
    (b) (i) and (ii)
    (c) (i), (ii) and (iii)
    (d) (i), (ii), (iii) ans (iv)

70. **How did the print media affect the religious systems?**
    (a) There was no affect
    (b) No questioning and debates came up
    (c) Those who disagreed with established authorities could now print and circulate their ideas. Through the printed message, they could persuade people to think differently
    (d) Print media and religion stayed away from each other

71. **A government in which different social groups are given the power to handle the affairs related to their communities is called __________.**
    (a) Community government
    (b) Coalition government
    (c) Democratic
    (d) Monarchy

72. **Which of the following ethnic groups in Belgium has the largest population?**
    (a) Walloon
    (b) Flemish
    (c) German
    (d) None of the above

73. **From which century China is said to have restricted overseas contacts and retreated into isolation?**
    (a) 14th Century
    (b) 15th Century
    (c) 16th Century
    (d) 17th Century

74. **Which of the following federal principles are found in the Indian Federation?**
    A. Equal representation of states in the Second House of Parliament.
    B. Bicameral Legislature at federal level.
    C. Double citizenship.
    D. Independent and Impartial judiciary.
    (a) A, B and C
    (b) B, C and D
    (c) B and D
    (d) A and C

75. **The Constitution of India was amended in 1992 to make the third-tier of democracy more effective. As a result, at least one-third of all positions in the local bodies are reserved for women. This is because __________.**
    (a) Women are good at managing resources
    (b) Women had inadequate representation in decision-making bodies
    (c) We have many powerful women leaders
    (d) Women are obedient and would follow the constitutional provisions well

76. **What was the rate of technological changes occurring in England at the time?**
    (a) Rapid
    (b) Moderate
    (c) Slow
    (d) No change

77. **The most widespread relief feature of India is:**
    (a) Mountains
    (b) Forests
    (c) Plains
    (d) Plateaus

78. **Which one of these is the feature of dictatorship?**
    (a) Monopoly over power
    (b) No constitution
    (c) No value of public opinion
    (d) All of the above

79. **On which factor economic development of country depends?**
    (a) Cooperation with other countries
    (b) Population size
    (c) Global situation
    (d) All of the above

80. **When and where was the Khilafat Committee formed?**
    (a) February 1920 Bombay
    (b) March 1918, Gujarat
    (c) January 1919, Bombay
    (d) March 1919 Bombay

81. __________ famous personality founded the Marathi newspaper 'Kesari'.
    (a) Lokmanya Tilak
    (b) Vallabhbhai Patel
    (c) Lala Lajpat Rai
    (d) Mahatma Gandhi

82. **Who among the following was not a member of the Constituent Assembly of India?**
    (a) Lakshmi Sehgal
    (b) Rajkumari Amrit Kaur
    (c) Hansa Mehta
    (d) Sarojini Naidu

83. **Interest payment is an item of:**
    (a) Revenue expenditure
    (b) Capital expenditure
    (c) Plan expenditure
    (d) None of the above

84. **In which of the following disputes is the jurisdiction of the Supreme Court of India Original and Exclusive?**
    (a) Violation of Fundamental Rights
    (b) Election Disputes of Member of Parliament
    (c) Election Disputes of Members of Legislative Assembly
    (d) Any dispute between the Government of India and one or more States

85. **Which of the following rocks is the oldest in terms of construction?**
    (a) Igneous
    (b) Metamorphosed
    (c) Sedentary
    (d) Adrenaline

86. **What is the best way to conserve our water resources?**
    (a) Rainwater harvesting
    (b) Sustainable water utilization
    (c) Encouragement of natural regeneration of vegetation
    (d) All of the above

87. **Which Article of the Constitution of India vests the power to form new States in the Parliament?**
    (a) Article 2
    (b) Article 1
    (c) Article 4
    (d) Article 3

88. **Bhand Pather theatre is a tradition**

primarily of which of the following States/UTs of India?

(a) Dadra and Nagar Heveli
(b) Goa
(c) Jammu and Kashmir
(d) Kerala

89. Indian Standard Time is ahead of the Greenwich Mean Time by ________.

(a) 4 Hours and 30 Minutes
(b) 5 Hours
(c) 4 Hours and 45 Minutes
(d) 5 Hours and 30 Minutes

90. Why was Indus Valley Civilization named Harappan Civilization?

(a) Because the name of the archaeologist who discovered the site Harappa
(b) Because the first site of the civilization excavated was Harappa
(c) Because Mohanjodaro old name was Harappa
(d) The dock of Indus Valley Civilization was known as Harappa

91. Who among the following Rajput rulers defeated Muhammad Ghori in the First Battle of Tarain in 1191 AD?

(a) Maldeo Rathore
(b) Rana Kumbha
(c) Prithviraj Chauhan
(d) Bappa Rawal

92. Ishwar Chandra Vidyasagar used the ancient texts to suggest:

(a) End of sati
(b) Girls could study
(c) Widows could remarry
(d) Equality of all castes

93. Living organisms do not have any effect on the abiotic components around them in an ecosystem.

(a) True
(b) False
(c) Ambiguous
(d) Data insufficient

94. Arrange the names of the following Speakers of Lok Sabha in chronological order of the office they held:
a. K. S Hegde
b. Rabi Ray
c. Balram Jakhar
d. Shivraj Patil
e. P.A. Sangma

(a) c, a, d, b & e   (b) c, b, a, d & e
(c) a, c, b, d & e   (d) a, d, e, c, & b

95. The 2023 Men's Boxing World Championships will be held in which country?

(a) Turkmenistan
(b) Uzbekistan
(c) Kazakhstan
(d) Tajikistan

96. Who was the first recipient of the Gyanpith award?

(a) Shri Shankar Kurup
(b) Dr. Radhakrishnan
(c) S. Mukharji
(d) None of the above

97. Which of the following mosquito causes Malaria?

(a) Female Culex mosquito
(b) Female Anopheles mosquito
(c) Male Culex mosquito
(d) Male Anopheles mosquito

98. Which among the following is Quick Silver?

(a) Aluminium   (b) Mercury
(c) Lead   (d) Zinc

99. Pearl Harbour is a US naval base near Honolulu, Hawaii, that was the scene of a devastating surprise attack on 7 December 1941. Name the country that attacked Pearl Harbour.

(a) China   (b) Japan
(c) Israel   (d) Russia

100. Grammy Award is given in the field of:

(a) Acting   (b) Music
(c) Singing   (d) Boxing tivate

// Hints and Solutions //

1(C). In geometrical constructions, the scale factor is used to construct similiar triangles.

Scale factor is the ratio of the sides of the triangle to be constructed with the corresponding sides of the given triangle. This construction involves two different situations:

- The triangle to be constructed is smaller than the given triangle, here scale factor is less than 1.
- The triangle to be constructed is bigger than the given triangle, here scale factor is greater than 1.

When two triangles are similar, the reduced ratio of any two corresponding sides is called the scale factor of the similar triangles.

2(B).

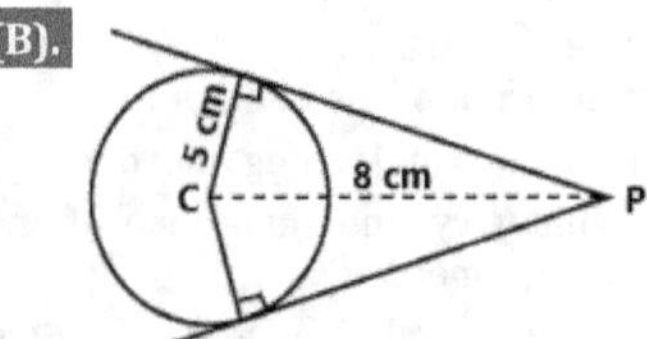

It is given that the distance of a point P from the radius is 8 cm and the radius of the circle is 5 cm. It means the distance of the point from the centre of the circle is greater than the radius of the circle. So, the point lies outside the circle. Hence, we can draw 2 tangents to the circle from the point P.

3(A). The mean can be found as given below:

$$\overline{X} = a + \left(\frac{\sum f_i u_i}{\sum f_i}\right)h$$

Suppose the assured mean (a) of the data is 11.5.

Class mark (x_i) for each interval is calculated as follows:

$$\text{Class mark } (x_i) = \frac{(\text{Upper class limit} + \text{Lower class limit})}{2}$$

Class size (h) of this data is:

$h = 4 - 1$

$h = 3$

d_i, u_i, and $f_i u_i$ can be calculated according to step deviation method as follows:

Number of letters	Number of surnames f_i	x_i	$d_i = x_i - 11.5$	$u_i = \dfrac{d_i}{2{.}0}$	$f_i u_i$
1 – 4	6	2.5	−9	−3	−18
4 – 7	30	5.5	−6	−2	−60
7 – 10	40	8.5	−3	−1	−40
10 – 13	16	11.5	0	0	0
13 – 16	4	14.5	3	1	4
16 – 19	4	17.5	6	2	8
Total	100				−106

It can be observed from the above table

$\sum f_i u_i = -106$

$\sum f_i = 100$

Substituting u_i, and $f_i u_i$ in the formula of mean

The required mean:

$$\overline{X} = a + \left(\frac{\sum f_i u_i}{\sum f_i}\right) \times h$$

$$\overline{X} = 11.5 + \left(\frac{-106}{100}\right) \times 3$$

$$\overline{X} = 11.5 - 3.18$$

$$\overline{X} = 8.32$$

So, the mean of number of letters in the surnames is 8.32.

4(B). Given:

Side of the cube $(a) = 3\,m$

$\therefore$ Surface Area of Cube $= 6a^2 = 6 \times 3 \times 3 = 54\ sq.\ cm$

Now:

Cost of painting the cubical box of $1\ sq.\ m =$ Rs. 2

$\therefore$ Cost of painting the cubical box of $54\ sq.\ m = 54 \times 2 =$ Rs. 108

5(B). Given :

Two identical solid cubes of side ' x '. If two cubes are joined end to end, then

Length of resulting cuboid $l = x + x = 2x$

Breadth of resulting cuboid $b = x$

And Height of the resulting cuboid $h = x$

$\therefore$ Total surface area of cuboid

$= 2(lb + bh + hl)$

$= 2(2x \times x + x \times x + x \times 2x)$

$= 2\left(5x^2\right) = 10x^2$

6(C). Given,

$\cos A + \cos^2 A = 1$

$\Rightarrow \cos A = 1 - \cos^2 A$

$\Rightarrow \cos A = \sin^2 A \ ...(1)$

Now,

$\sin^2 A + \sin^4 A = \sin^2 A + \left(\sin^2 A\right)^2$

From equation (1),we have

$\sin^2 A + \sin^4 A = \sin^2 A + \cos^2 A$ $[\because \sin^2 A + \cos^2 A = 1]$

$\therefore \sin^2 A + \sin^4 A = 1$

7(A). A quadratic equation has always two roots. Standard form of a quadratic equation.

$ax^2 + bx + c = 0$ (where a can't be zero)

Given one root is 3 .

Let first check the equation $x^2 - 5x + 6 = 0$

By putting $x = 3$ in the equaion

$x^2 - 5x + 6 = 0$

$(3)^2 - 5(3) + 6 = 0$

$9 - 15 + 6 = 0$

$\therefore 0 = 0$

It means LHS $=$ RHS

So, $x^2 - 5x + 6 = 0$ is a required equation which has root $x = 3$

8(B). Given equation is:

$a^2 x^2 - 3abx + 2b^2 = 0$

$\Rightarrow a^2 x^2 - 2abx - abx + 2b^2 = 0$

$\Rightarrow ax(ax - 2b) - b(ax - 2b) = 0$

$\Rightarrow (ax - b)(ax - 2b) = 0$

If $ax - b = 0$

$\therefore x = \dfrac{b}{a}$

If $ax - 2b = 0$

$\therefore x = \dfrac{2b}{a}$

So the roots are $\dfrac{b}{a}$ and $\dfrac{2b}{a}$.

9(A).

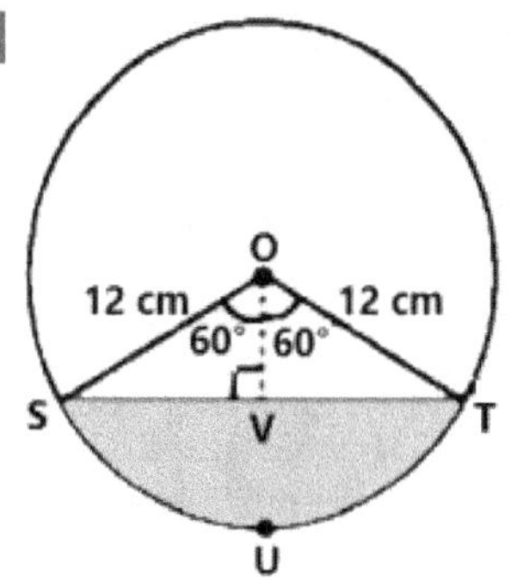

Drawing a perpendicular OV on chord ST bisecting the chord ST such that $SV = VT$

Now, values of OV and ST are to be found.

Therefore,

In $\triangle OVS$,

$\cos 60° = \dfrac{OV}{OS}$

$\Rightarrow \dfrac{OV}{12} = \dfrac{1}{2}$

$\Rightarrow OV = 6$ cm

Also, $\dfrac{SV}{SO} = \sin 60°$

$\Rightarrow \dfrac{SV}{12} = \dfrac{\sqrt{3}}{2}$

$\Rightarrow SV = 6\sqrt{3}$

Now, $ST = 2SV = 2 \times 6\sqrt{3} = 12\sqrt{3}$ cm

Area of $\triangle OST = \dfrac{1}{2} \times ST \times OV$

$= \dfrac{1}{2} \times 12\sqrt{3} \times 6$

$= 62.28$ cm^2

Area of sector $= \dfrac{\theta}{360°} \times \pi r^2$

Area of sector $OSUT = \dfrac{120°}{360°} \times \pi(12)^2$

$= 150.42$ cm^2

Area of segment $SUTS =$ Area of sector $OSUT -$ Area of $\triangle OVS$

$= 150.72 - 62.28$

$= 88.44$ cm^2

So, the area of the corresponding segment of the circle is 88.44 cm^2 .

10(A).

15 m

B

C

90°

O

5 m

A

It is evident from the figure,

Area that can be grazed by horse $=$ Area of sector $OACB$

$-\dfrac{\theta}{360°} \times \pi r^2$

Length of rope $=$ radius of sector $= 5$ m

$= \dfrac{90°}{360°} \times \pi r^2$

$= \dfrac{1}{4} \times 3.14 \times (5)^2 = 19.625$ m^2

11(B). Given,

$\sec^2 \theta + \tan^2 \theta = 7 \ ...(i)$

Adding 1 both sides in eqaution (i) we get,

$\sec^2 \theta + \tan^2 \theta + 1 = 7 + 1$

$\Rightarrow \sec^2 \theta + \sec^2 \theta = 8$

$(\because 1 + \tan^2 \theta = \sec^2 \theta)$

$\Rightarrow 2\sec^2 \theta = 8$

$\Rightarrow \sec^2 \theta = 4$

$\Rightarrow \sec \theta = 2$

12(C). Given,

$\sin \theta + \cos \theta = \sqrt{2} \cos \theta$

$\Rightarrow \sin \theta = \sqrt{2} \cos \theta - \cos \theta$

$\Rightarrow \sin \theta = (\sqrt{2} - 1) \cos \theta$

Multiple by $\sqrt{2} + 1$ both sides;

$\Rightarrow (\sqrt{2} + 1) \sin \theta = (\sqrt{2} + 1)(\sqrt{2} - 1) \cos \theta$

$\Rightarrow \sqrt{2} \sin \theta + \sin \theta = (2 - 1) \cos \theta$

$\Rightarrow \sqrt{2} \sin \theta = \cos \theta - \sin \theta$

$\therefore \cos \theta - \sin \theta = \sqrt{2} \sin \theta$

13(D). Given:

$\tan \dfrac{\alpha}{3} = \dfrac{1}{2}$

As we know that:

$\tan 3A = \dfrac{3\tan A - \tan^3 A}{1 - 3\tan^2 A}$

Here $\alpha = 3A, A = \dfrac{\alpha}{3}$

$\tan \alpha = \dfrac{3\tan \frac{\alpha}{3} - \tan^3 \frac{\alpha}{3}}{1 - 3\tan^2 \frac{\alpha}{3}}$

$= \dfrac{3 \times \left(\frac{1}{2}\right) - \left(\frac{1}{2}\right)^3}{1 - 3\left(\frac{1}{2}\right)^2}$

$= \dfrac{\frac{3}{2} - \frac{1}{8}}{\frac{1}{4}}$

$= \dfrac{11}{2}$

To find $\cot \alpha$,

We use $\cot \alpha = \dfrac{1}{\tan \alpha}$

$= \dfrac{1}{\frac{11}{2}}$

$= \dfrac{2}{11}$

$\tan \alpha + \cot \alpha$

$= \dfrac{11}{2} + \dfrac{2}{11}$

$= \dfrac{121 + 4}{4}$

$= \dfrac{125}{22}$

14(B). Number is of the form,

$$\underset{\underset{\text{Tens placee}}{\uparrow}}{x} \quad \underset{\underset{\text{Units placee}}{\uparrow}}{y}$$

Let Digit at Units place $= y$

and Digit at Tens place $= x$

Given that

Sum of digits of two digit number is 9

$\therefore$ Digit at tens place $+$ Digit at units place $= 9$

$x + y = 9$ $\quad ......(1)$

Also,

9 times the number is twice the number obtained by reversing digits

$9 \times ($ Number $) = 2 \times ($ Reversed number $)$

$9(10x + y) = 2(10y + x)$

$90x + 9y - 20y + 2x$

$90x - 2x + 9y - 20y = 0$

$88x - 11y = 0$

$11(8x - y) = 0$

$(8x - y) = \dfrac{0}{11}$

$8x - y = 0$ $\quad ......(2)$

So, our equations are,

$x + y = 9 \quad \ldots\ldots(1)$

$8x - y = 0 \quad \ldots\ldots(2)$

Using elimination method with equations (1) and (2),

$x + y = 9$

$\underline{8x - y = 0}$

$\quad 9x = 9$

$9x = 9$

$x = \dfrac{9}{9}$

$x = 1$

Putting $x = 1$ in (1),

$x + y = 9$

$1 + y = 9$

$y = 9 - 1$

$y = 8$

So, $x = 1, y = 8$ is the solution of our equation

Therefore,

Number

$= 10x + y = 10(1) + 8 = 10 + 8 = 18$

So, Required number is 18.

15(B). Let Number of Rs. 50 notes $= x$ \& Number of Rs. 100 notes $= y$

Given that

Total notes is 25

(Number of Rs. 50 notes) + (Number of Rs. 100 notes) = 25

$x + y = 25 \quad \ldots\ldots(1)$

Also given,

Total amount withdrawn $= 2000$

Rs. 50 notes	Rs. 100 notes	Total Amount
1	1	$50 \times 1 + 100 \times 1 = 50 + 100 = 150$
1	3	$50 \times 2 + 100 \times 3 = 100 + 300 = 400$
x	y	$50 \times x + 100 \times y = 50x + 100y$

Thus,

$50x + 100y = 2000$

$50(x + 2y) = 2000$

$x + 2y = \dfrac{2000}{50}$

$x + 2y = 40 \quad \ldots\ldots(2)$

So, our equations are

$x + y = 25 \quad \ldots\ldots(1)$

$x + 2y = 40 \quad \ldots\ldots(2)$

Using elimination method,

$x + y = 25$

$x + 2y = 40$

$\underline{(-)(-) \quad (-)}$

$\quad -y = -15$

$-y = -15$

$y = 15$

Putting $y = 15$ in equation (1),

$x + y = 25$

$x + 15 = 25$

$x = 25 - 15$

$x = 10$

So, $x = 10 \& y = 15$ are the solution of our equations,

Therefore,

Number of Rs. 50 notes $= x = 10$

Number of Rs. 100 notes $= y = 15$

16(D). We know that, if the denominator of rational number contains no prime factors other then 2 or 5 or both, then this rational number can be expressed as terminating decimal.

In option (A), we can clearly see that, along with 2 there is prime factors of 3 , so this will not have terminating decimal expansion.

In option (B), we can clearly see that, along with 2 there is prime factors of 7 , so this will also not have terminating decimal expansion.

In option (C), we can clearly see that, along with 2 and 5 there is prime factors of 3 , so this will also not have terminating decimal expansion.

In option (D), expansion of $\dfrac{343}{2^2 \times 5^2 \times 7^3}$ is

$\dfrac{7^3}{2^2 \times 5^2 \times 7^3} = \dfrac{1}{2^2 \times 5^2}$

We can see that have only factors of 2 and 5 in their denominator. So $\dfrac{343}{2^2 \times 5^2 \times 7^3}$ have a terminating decimal expansion.

17(D). Prime factorization of given numbers are,

$6 = 2 \times 3 = 2^1 \times 3^1$

$72 = 2 \times 2 \times 2 \times 3 \times 3 = 2^3 \times 3^2$

$120 = 2 \times 2 \times 2 \times 3 \times 5 = 2^3 \times 3^1 \times 5^1$

Here, 2^1 and 3^1 are the smallest powers of the common prime factors 2 and 3 in the given numbers.

$\therefore$ HCF $(6, 72, 120) = 2^1 \times 3^1$

$= 2 \times 3$

$= 6$

We note that $2^3, 3^2, 5^1$ are the greatest powers of the prime factors $2, 3$ and 5 involved in the given numbers.

$\therefore$ LCM $(6, 72, 120) = 2^3 \times 3^2 \times 5^7$

$= 8 \times 9 \times 5$

$= 360$

18(D). The minimum distance covered by each of them in complete steps $=$ LCM of the measures of their steps

LCM of $15, 25, 40$ is:

$15 = 3 \times 5$

$25 = 5 \times 5$

$40 = 2 \times 2 \times 2 \times 5 = 2^3 \times 5$

LCM of $(15, 25, 40) = 2^3 \times 3 \times 5^2 = 600$

So the minimum distance that each person should walk in order to cover the same distance in integral number of steps 600 cm.

19(A). Given,

Number of students in class $X = 104$

Number of students in class $IX = 96$

The students are to be evenly seated in parallel rows.

So, we have to find out the HCF of 104 and 96

$104 = 2^3 \times 13$

$96 = 2^5 \times 3$

HCF $= 2^3 = 8$

Number of rows of students of class

$X = \dfrac{104}{8} = 13$

Number of rows of students of class

$IX = \dfrac{96}{8} = 12$

Total number of rows $= 13 + 12 = 25$

20(B). Given quadratic polynomial is

$x^2 + 99x + 127$

By comparing with the standard form, we get;

$a = 1, b = 99$ and $c = 127$

$a > 0, b > 0$ and $c > 0$

We know that in any quadratic polynomial, if all the coefficients have the same sign, then the zeroes of that polynomial will be negative.

Therefore, the zeroes of the given quadratic polynomial are negative.

21(A). The division algorithm states that given any polynomial $p(x)$ and any non-zero polynomial $g(x)$, there are polynomials $q(x)$ and $r(x)$ such that

$p(x) = g(x) \times q(x) + r(x)$,

where $r(x) = 0$ or degree $r(x) <$ degree $g(x)$

Q.22 The total numbers of discs $= 90$

$P(E) = \dfrac{\text{(Number of favourable outcomes)}}{\text{(Total number of outcomes}}$

22(D). Total numbers which are divisible by

$5 = 18(5, 10, 15, 20, 25, 30, 35, 40, 45, 50, 55, 60, 65$

$, 70, 75, 80, 85$ and $90)$

P (getting a number divisible by 5)

$= \dfrac{18}{90} = \dfrac{1}{5} = 0.2$

23(D). Given,

The sum of three numbers in AP is 24 and the sum of their squares is 194 ..

Let the three numbers in AP be $(a - d), a, (a + d)$

According to question,

$(a - d) + a + (a + d) = 24$

$\Rightarrow 3a = 24$

$\Rightarrow a = 8$

and $(a - d)^2 + a^2 + (a + d)^2 = 194$

$\Rightarrow a^2 + d^2 - 2ad + a^2 + a^2 + d^2 + 2ad = 194$

$\Rightarrow 3a^2 + 2d^2 = 194$

Putting the value of a from above,

$\Rightarrow 3 \times 64 + 2d^2 = 194$

$\Rightarrow 192 + 2d^2 = 194$

$\Rightarrow 2d^2 = 2$

$\Rightarrow d^2 = 1$

$\Rightarrow d = 1$

So, number are,

$\Rightarrow (a - d), a, (a + d)$

$\Rightarrow (8 - 1), 8, (8 + 1)$

$7, 8, 9$

24(C). Given,

$S_{14} = 1050, n = 14$ and $a = 10$

$S_n = \dfrac{n}{2}[2a + (n - 1)d]$

$a =$ first term

$d =$ common difference

$S_n =$ Sum of nth term

So,

$1050 = \dfrac{14}{2}[2 \times 10 + (14 - 1)d]$

$\Rightarrow 1050 = 7(20 + 13d)$

$\Rightarrow 150 = 20 + 13d$

$\Rightarrow 13d = 130$
$\Rightarrow d = 10$
$T_n = a + (n-1)d$
$a = $ first term
$d = $ common difference
$T_n = n^{\text{th}}$ term
$\therefore$ 20 th term
$= a + (20-1)d = 10 + 19 \times 10 = 200$

25(D). Diagonals of a rhombus are $\perp$ bisectors of each other.
$\therefore AC \perp BD$,
$OA = OC = \dfrac{AC}{2}$
$\Rightarrow \dfrac{24}{2} = 12$ cm
$OB = OD = \dfrac{BD}{2}$
$\Rightarrow \dfrac{32}{2} = 16$ cm
In rt. $\triangle BOC$,

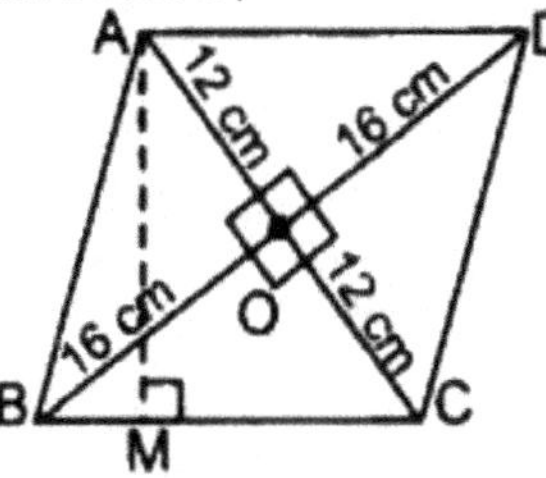

$(BC) = \sqrt{(OC)^2 + (OB)^2}$
$= \sqrt{12^2 + 16^2}$
$= \sqrt{144 + 256}$
$\therefore$ Side of rhombus, BC
$= \sqrt{400} = 20$ cm
ar. $(\triangle ABC)$
$= $ ar. $(\triangle ABC)$
(Taking BC as base)
(Taking AC as base)
$\dfrac{1}{2} \times BC \times AM$
$= \dfrac{1}{2} \times AC \times OB$
$\because$ area of $\Delta = \dfrac{1}{2} \times$ base $\times$ altitude
$20 \times AM = 24 \times 16$
$\therefore AM = \dfrac{24 \times 16}{20} = \dfrac{96}{5}$
$= 19.2$ cm

26(A). Given,
$BE = BC - EC = 10 - 2 = 8$ cm
Let $AF = x$ cm,
then $BF = (13 - x)$ cm
In $\triangle ABC, EF \| AC$
Given,
$\dfrac{BF}{FA} = \dfrac{BE}{EC}$
(Thales' theorem)
$\dfrac{13-x}{x} = \dfrac{8}{2}$
$\Rightarrow 4x = 13 - x$
$4x + x = 13$
$\rightarrow 5x = 13$
$x = \dfrac{13}{5} = 2.6$ cm
$\therefore AF = 2.6$ cm

27(C). Given radius $= 5$ cm and $OM = 4$ cm
Now by Pythagoras Theorem,
$r^2 = OM^2 + PM^2$
$5^2 = 4^2 + PM^2$

$25 = 16 + PM^2$
$PM^2 = 25 - 16 = 9$
$PM = \sqrt{9} = 3$
Now length of chord $PN = 3 + 3 = 6$ cm
(Since the angular bisector divides the chord into equal parts.)

28(A). Given, $AB = BC$, $OM = 5$ units
OM and ON are perpendicular to AB and BC chords
Since, equal chords of a circle are equidistant from the centre.
Therefore, $OM = ON = 5$ units

29(A). Since the point is on the x-axis, then the coordinate of the point will be $(x, 0)$.
As we know,
Distance between the points (x_1, y_1) and (x_2, y_2) is $\sqrt{(x_1 - x_2)^2 + (y_1 - y_2)^2}$
According to the question,
This point $(x, 0)$ is equidistant from the points $(2, -5)$ and $(-2, 9)$.
So, distance from $(x, 0)$ and $(2, -5)$ is equal to distance from $(x, 0)$ and $(-2, 9)$.
$\therefore \sqrt{(2-x)^2 + (-5-0)^2} = \sqrt{(-2-x)^2 + (9-0)^2}$
$\Rightarrow (2-x)^2 + (-5)^2 = (-2-x)^2 + (9)^2$
$\Rightarrow 4 - 4x + x^2 + 25 = 4 + 4x + x^2 + 81$
$\Rightarrow 8x = 25 - 81$
$\Rightarrow 8x = -56$
$\Rightarrow x = -7$
So, the point is $(-7, 0)$.

30(D). Given,
Distance between $(a, 2)$ and $(3, 4) = 8$
As we know,
Distance between two points (x_1, y_1) and (x_2, y_2) is $\sqrt{(x_2 - x_1)^2 + (y_2 - y_1)^2}$.
$\therefore \sqrt{(3-a)^2 + (4-2)^2} = 8$
$\Rightarrow \sqrt{9 + a^2 - 6a + 4} = 8$
$\Rightarrow \sqrt{a^2 - 6a + 13} = 8$
$\Rightarrow a^2 - 6a + 13 = 64$
$\Rightarrow a^2 - 6a - 51 = 0$
Using Sridharacharya Formula,
$x = \dfrac{-b \pm \sqrt{b^2 - 4ac}}{2a}$
$\Rightarrow a = \dfrac{-(-6) \pm \sqrt{(-6^2) - 4(1)(-51)}}{2(1)}$
$\Rightarrow a = \dfrac{6 \pm \sqrt{36 + 204}}{2}$
$\Rightarrow a = 3 \pm 2\sqrt{15}$

31(D). Plants prepare their own food using solar energy. They are the primary producers. The food prepared by plants is used by other organisms in an ecosystem either directly or indirectly. There are three groups of consumers, namely herbivores, carnivores, and omnivores. Primary consumers are herbivores. They feed on only plants. Carnivores are those animals that feed on other animals. Animals and human that eat both animals and plants are called omnivores. Decomposers are the last organisms in a food chain. They feed on

decaying matter and releases minerals back into the food chain.

32(D). Ecosystem is a biological community that lives in conjugation with the nonbiological community. It can also be defined as all plants and animal species along with environment. It includes all living things like plants, animals and non-living things like air, water, land, etc.
So, the correct answer is 'All plants and animal species along with environment.'

33(D). Reaction of metals with cold or hot water depends on the reactivity of the metals. Reactive metals like sodium, potassium, calcium, etc. react with cold or hot water. Moderately reactive metals like magnesium react with hot water. Less reactive metals do not react with cold or hot water but react with steam. Least reactive metals like gold, silver, etc. do not react at all. Less reactive metals like iron react with steam to form an oxide and release hydrogen gas. The reaction is as follows:
$3\text{Fe}(s) + 4\text{H}_2\text{O}(g) \rightarrow \text{Fe}_3\text{O}_4(s) + 4\text{H}_2(g)$

34(B). In a displacement reaction, a more reactive metal of the activity series can displace a less reactive one in its salt solution.
Reactivity order is: $\text{Mg} > \text{Zn} > \text{Cu} > \text{Ag}$
Thus, we see that Ag is least reactive and of the given four metals, Ag would be displaced from the solution of its salts by the other three metals.

35(C). The movement of blood through a network of cerebral veins and arteries is called cerebral circulation. The brain is a very sensitive organ and it will suffer damage in the case of stoppage of blood flow from the network of cerebral arteries and veins.
Approximately 750 milliliters of blood is circulated through the network of veins and arteries of the brain in a minute. This is the rate of cerebral blood flow in a healthy human adult. The rate of cerebral circulation is approximately 15% of the cardiac output of the body in a healthy adult.
The cerebral circulatory network has an internal adaptive mechanism in the form of autoregulation of the blood vessels which provides the brain with sufficient amounts of blood for it to function with minimal damage.
The cerebral arteries circulate oxygenated blood, glucose and various nutrients to the brain. The cerebral veins carry the blood consumed by the brain back to the heart where the deposited carbon dioxide, lactic acid and various metabolic products are removed.
Therefore the brain depends on blood for the supply of oxygen and glucose.

36(A). The internal activities are controlled by CNS.

The central nervous system CNS is responsible for integrating sensory information and responding accordingly. The central nervous system is the body's processing centre. The nervous system transmits signals between the brain and the rest of the body, including internal organs. The brain controls most of the functions of the body, including awareness, movement, thinking, speech, and the 5 senses of seeing, hearing, feeling, tasting and smelling. Central nervous system (CNS) controls the activities of internal organs such as hormone release, movement of food through the stomach and intestines, and the sensations from and muscular control to all internal organs.

37(A). $4Na(s) + O_2(g) \longrightarrow 2Na_2O(s)$
The substance that gains oxygen is being oxidised and is called as oxidised substance. The substance that loses oxygen is being reduced and is called as the reduced substance. In the above reaction, sodium Na is gaining oxygen to form Na_2O. So, sodium (Na) is being oxidized so it is oxidising substance and oxygen is getting reduced, so it is a reduced substance.

38(D). The oxidation of oils or fats in a food is known as rancidity.
When fats and oils are oxidised, they become rancid and their smell and taste change. This phenomenon is called rancidity. Usually substances which prevent oxidation (antioxidants) are added to foods containing fats and oil. They are often used as preservatives in fat-containing foods to delay the onset or slow the development of rancidity due to oxidation. An example of rancidity is when a chips pack is exposed to atmospheric air which results in a change in taste and odour.

39(B). C_5H_{10} is the formula of Pentene hydrocarbon. Pentene is a colorless liquid with a strong gasoline-like odor. It is an unsaturated hydrocarbon due to the presence of a carbon double bond in its carbon chain. The structure of pentene:

$$H-\overset{\overset{\displaystyle H}{|}}{\underset{\underset{\displaystyle H}{|}}{C}}-\overset{\overset{\displaystyle H}{|}}{\underset{\underset{\displaystyle H}{|}}{C}}=\overset{\displaystyle H}{\underset{}{C}}-\overset{\overset{\displaystyle H}{|}}{\underset{\underset{\displaystyle H}{|}}{C}}-\overset{\overset{\displaystyle H}{|}}{\underset{\underset{\displaystyle H}{|}}{C}}-H$$

40(D). Methane, ethane and propane are said to form a homologous series because all are differ from each other by a CH_2 group. Methane, ethane and propane are all alkanes with the general formula C_nH_{2n+2}.

41(C). Frog (Anura) reproduces sexually by the process of external fertilization, where male and female gametes fuse outside the body of the female. Here, both the gametes are released into water bodies like ponds, where they fertilize.
In Amoeba, Paramoeium, and Hydra undergo asexual reproduction.

42(B). Meiosis is the process in which a cell divides in a reduced manner so that only half of the genetic material is left in each new cell.
Meiosis is a type of cell division that reduces the number of chromosomes in the parent cell by half and produces four gamete cells. This process is required to produce egg and sperm cells for sexual reproduction.

43(A). The law of dominance states that in a cross of parents that are pure for contrasting traits, only one form of the trait will appear in the next generation.

44(C). The F2 generation results from self-pollination of F1 plants, and contained 75 % purple flowers and 25 % white flowers. This type of experiment is known as a monohybrid cross.

45(A). Object-size, h = +4.0 cm
Object-distance, u = −25.0 cm
Focal length, f = −15.0 cm
Image-distance, v =?
$$\frac{1}{v} + \frac{1}{u} = \frac{1}{f}$$
Or, $\frac{1}{v} = \frac{1}{f} - \frac{1}{u}$
$$= \frac{1}{-15.0} - \frac{1}{-25.0}$$
$$= -\frac{1}{15.0} + \frac{1}{25.0}$$
Or, $\frac{1}{v} = \frac{-5.0+3.0}{75.0}$
$$= \frac{-2.0}{75.0}$$
Or, v = −37.5 cm

46(B). A concave lens always forms a virtual, erect image on the same side of the object.
Image-distance v = −10 cm
Focal length f = −15 cm
Object-distance u =?
Since $\frac{1}{v} - \frac{1}{u} = \frac{1}{f}$
Or, $\frac{1}{u} = \frac{1}{v} - \frac{1}{f}$
$$\frac{1}{u} = \frac{1}{-10} - \frac{1}{(-15)}$$
$$= -\frac{1}{10} + \frac{1}{15}$$
$$= \frac{-3+2}{30}$$
$$= \frac{1}{-30}$$
Or, u = −30 cm

47(C). A solenoid behaves like a bar magnet. Hence the pattern of magnetic field associated with solenoid and around the bar magnet is same.The pattern of the magnetic field associated with the solenoid is exactly same as the pattern of the magnetic field around a bar magnet. It also has two poles on the two extreme end and the field lines are also looks same (figure).

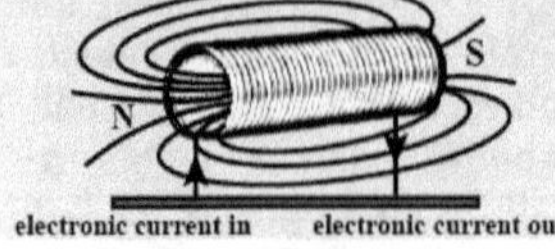

48(A). The main advantage of A.C power transmission over D.C power transmission over' long distance is AC transmit over a long distance without much loss of energy as compare to DC.
Higher voltage is more efficient for transmitting power over long distances (it minimizes the current, and thus the size of the conductors). With AC distribution, high voltage can easily be produced from lower voltages by a transformer, and transformers can be very efficient

49(D). Bile is responsible for bringing about the emulsification of fats. The bile released into the duodenum contains bile pigments (bilirubin and biliverdin), bile salts, cholesterol and phospholipids but no enzymes. Bile salts helps in emulsification of fats, i.e., breaking down of the large fat droplets into very small micelles. Bile also activates lipase enzymes, which digests fats.

50(D). The energy trapped by chlorophyll molecule is used for the generation of ATP, the generation of NADPH and the splitting of water molecule. Chlorophyll is what absorbs the sun's energy and turns it into chemical energy. ATP is also formed from the process of cellular respiration in the mitochondria of a cell. NADP is created in anabolic reactions, or reaction that build large molecules from small molecules. NADPH donates the hydrogen (H) and associated electrons, oxidizing the molecule to create NADP.

51(B).
The answer is (c) A—(iii), B—(iv), C—(i), D—(ii)

Column (A)	Column (B)
(A) Bleaching powder	(iii) Decolourisation
(B) Baking soda	(iv) Antacid
(C) Washing soda	(i) Preparation of glass
(D) Sodium chloride	(ii) Production of H_2 and Cl_2

Hence, the correct option is (C).

52(D). The chemical nature of soap is basic.
Soaps are fatty acid sodium or potassium salts that are water soluble. The process is known as saponification, and it involves heating a strong base with a fatty acid or fat (or oils) to produce a salt and an alkanol (usually glycerin). Soap with water has a pH above 7 , has a basic behavior, and tastes sour, implying that the base has a sour taste as well.

53(A). A rainbow is a meteorological phenomenon that is caused by reflection, refraction and dispersion of light in water droplets resulting in a spectrum of light appearing in the sky. These water droplets are due to moisture present in air during or after raining. It is caused by reflection, refraction and dispersion of light in water droplets resulting in a spectrum of light appearing in the sky.

54(B). Given, $H = 15J, V = 5V, i = 3A$
From ohm's law
$V = iR \Rightarrow 5 = 3 \times R$
$R = \frac{5}{3}$
from Joule's law
$H = i^2 Rt$
$15 = 9 \times \frac{5}{3} \times t$
$t = \frac{15}{15} \Rightarrow 1.0\,\text{sec}$

55(B). Ohm's law states that the current through a conductor between two points is directly proportional to the voltage across the two points. Introducing the constant of proportionality, the resistance, one arrives at the usual mathematical equation that describes this relationship.
$I = \frac{V}{R}$

56(A). Rooftop water harvesting is the most widely recognized practice in Shillong, Meghalaya.
It is intriguing on the grounds that Cherapunjee and Mawsynram arranged a way off of 55 km. from Shillong to get the most noteworthy precipitation on the planet, yet the state capital Shillong faces intense lack of water.

57(B).
Mithun is Endemic species in Arunachal Pradesh.
India at large and specifically the North-East India is the hotspot of floral and faunal biodiversity and the habitat of a number endemic species. Of these species, Mithun (Bos frontalis) is an important one which needs support for healthy propagation.
A bovine species mithun (Bos frontalis) is intricately related to the mythology of Arunachal Pradesh. This bovine is found in Arunachal Pradesh and other North East states like Nagaland, Manipur and Mizoram besides Bhutan (Heli 1994).

58(B). Very high grade haematite ores are found in the Durg-Bastar-Chandrapur belt that lies in Chhattisgarh and Maharashtra.
Very high grade haematite ores are found in the famous Bailadila ranges of hills in the Bastar district. The range of hills comprises of 14 deposits of super high grade haematite iron ore. The iron-ore extracted from these mines have the best physical properties needed for steel making. It lies in Chattisgarh and Maharashtra.

59(C). Over the past decade or so, certain new services such as information and communication technology have become important and essential.

The ICT sector combines manufacturing and services industries whose products primarily fulfil or enable the function of information processing and communication by electronic means, including transmission and display. The ICT sector contributes to technological progress, output and productivity growth.

60(C). An urban educated unemployed will aspire for good job opportunities where his education can be made use.
An urban unemployed youth aspires to get an acceptable job where he can extend his level of skills and abilities, gain a decent salary, and provide his family with great economic backing. Get an enrolment in the career-oriented program. Urban unemployment problem became acute:
• Increase in the size of urban population.
• Increasing migration of rural people to urban industrial areas in search of employment.
• Educational facilities have increased very fast during the Five Year Plans.

61(D). The Civil Code of 1804, also known as the Napoleonic Code, established by all of them.
The Napoleonic Code (French: Code Napoleon; officially Code civil des Franais, referred to as (le) Code civil) is the French civil code established under Napoleon I in 1804.
It was drafted by a commission of four eminent jurists and entered into force on 21 March 1804. The Code, with its stress on clearly written and accessible law, was a major step in replacing the previous patchwork of feudal laws. Historian Robert Holtman regards it as one of the few documents that have influenced the whole world.
The Napoleonic Code was not the first legal code to be established in a European country with a civil legal system; it was preceded by the Codex Maximilianeus bavaricus civilis (Bavaria, 1756), the Allgemeines Landrecht (Prussia, 1794), and the West Galician Code (Galicia, then part of Austria, 1797). It was, however, the first modern legal code to be adopted with a pan-European scope, and it strongly influenced the law of many of the countries formed during and after the Napoleonic Wars. The Napoleonic Code influenced developing countries outside Europe, especially in the Middle East, attempting to modernize their countries through legal reforms.

62(A). "Operation Holding" refers to the land area that is used wholly or partially for agricultural production and it is operated as a technical entity by one person, either alone or with others, without regard to title, legal form, size, or location. "Operation Holding" refers to the total land area owned by a farmer.

63(A). Central bank is the main source of money supply in an economy.
A central bank is a public institution that manages the currency of a country or group of countries and controls the money supply – literally, the amount of money in circulation. The main objective of many central banks is price stability. The Reserve Bank of India is the central bank of the country.
Functions of the Central Bank are:
• Currency regulator or bank of issue.
• Bank to the government.
• Custodian of Cash reserves.
• Custodian of International currency.
• Lender of last resort.
• Clearing house for transfer and settlement.
• Controller of credit.
• Protecting depositors interests.

64(A).
Andhra Pradesh accounts for maximum percentage of SHGs (self-help groups) in bank credit.
The average amount of loan per SHG is highest in Andhra Pradesh with Rs. 215,875. The origin of self-help group can be traced is from Grameen bank of Bangladesh, which was founded by Mohamed Yunus. SGHs were started and formed in 1975. In India NABARD initiated in 1986-1987. The absence of institutional credits available in the rural area has led to the establishment of SHGs.

65(D). The main channel that connected the countries in past was trade.
The winds and waters of commerce carry opportunities that help nations grow and bring citizens of the world closer together. Put simply, increased trade spells more jobs, higher earnings, better products, less inflation, and cooperation over confrontation. The Silk Road may be the most famous ancient trade route. This route connected China and the ancient Roman Empire, and people traded silk along this pathway. Not only was the Silk Road used for transportation of goods, it was also the way that people shared ideas, knowledge, religion, and technology with each other.

66(D). Nationalisation of banks has not facilitated globalisation.
Nationalisation of banks in India initiated in 1969 because of socialistic principles of government. Capitalists say that new ideas – innovations – come from competition and the search for profits. They claim that socialism would end innovation . However, socialists want a system that is far more innovative than capitalism. They mean the destructive competition between businesses for profit creates imbalance in economic world.

67(C). Agmark should be looked while buying honey.
Agmark, or Agriculture Mark, is the

certification mark to assure the quality of agricultural products in India. Agmark acts as a third party guarantee for the agricultural products that are produced and consumed in India. The certification is voluntary. For Blended Edible Vegetable Oils and Fat Spread certification under Agmark is necessary as per terms in the Food Safety and Standards Act and regulations, 2006.

68(D). All the above statements cause the exploitation of the consumer.

Consumer exploitation refers to taking undue advantage of consumers or a group of consumers by the sellers for their own benefit or purpose. The other reasons for consumer exploitation are ignorance, superstitions, social factors, shortage of goods and service to prevent the exploitation faced by the consumers in the market, the Consumers Protection Act was enacted in 1986. The act was enacted to protect the interests of the consumers give them the right to be protected against various exploitations faced by them.

69(D).

The characteristic features of printed books were:

- The metal letters imitated the ornamental handwritten styles.
- Borders were illuminated by hand with foliage and other patterns, and illustrations were painted
- In the books printed for the rich, space for decoration was kept blank on the printed page
- Each purchaser could choose the design and decide on the painting school that would do the illustrations.

70(C).

Those who disagreed with established authorities could now print and circulate their ideas. through the printed message, they could persuade people to think differently can affect the religious systems. With an increase in literacy, the more opportunities to own personal religious texts and growth of individual reading, the printing press ultimately undermined the Catholic Church and disrupted the European religious culture by spreading religious knowledge and shifting the power to the people.

71(A). A government in which different social groups are given the power to handle the affairs related to their communities is called Community government.

They are expected to work jointly for the benefit of the common masses without undermining any one community. Community government is an elected body by people belonging to one language, one culture or any common property no matter where they live. This government has the power regarding cultural, educational and language related issues.

72(B). Flemish ethnic groups in Belgium has the largest population.

In terms of ethnicity, the Flemish community is a majority in the country. More than 6 million inhabitants of Belgium are Flemish, while the French speaking Walloon are a minority but make up the next biggest population group with around 3.5 million inhabitants.

73(B). However, from the fifteenth century, China is said to have restricted overseas contacts and retreated into isolation.

After Zheng He's voyages in the 15th century, the foreign policy of the Ming dynasty in China became increasingly isolationist. The Hongwu Emperor was not the first to propose the policy to ban all maritime shipping in 1390. The Qing dynasty that came after the Ming dynasty often continued the Ming dynasty's isolationist policies. Wokou, which literally translates to "Japanese pirates" or "dwarf pirates", were pirates who raided the coastlines of China, Japan, and Korea, and were one of the key primary concerns, although the maritime ban was not without some control.

Since the division of the territory following the Chinese Civil War in 1949, China is divided into two regimes with the People's Republic of China solidified control on mainland China while the existing Republic of China was confined to the island of Taiwan as both governments lay claim to each other's sovereignty. While the PRC is recognized by the United Nations, European Union, and the majority of the world's states, the ROC remains diplomatically isolated although 15 states recognize it as "China" with some countries maintain unofficial diplomatic relations through trade offices.

74(C). B and D follows federal principles are found in the Indian Federation.

Federal features of the Indian Constitution are:

- Bicameralism at Federal level
- Independent and Impartial Judiciary
- Division of powers
- Written Constitution
- Rigid feature
- Supremacy of the Constitution.

75(B). The Constitution of India was amended in 1992 to make the third-tier of democracy more effective. As a result, at least one-third of all positions in the local bodies are reserved for women. This is because Women had inadequate representation in decision-making bodies. The 73rd and 74th Constitutional Amendment Acts added the third -tier to the Indian federalism, and also gives one-third reservation to women at the local level political institutions, but the reservation is lesser than the percentage of women's population in India.

76(C). Slow rate of technological changes occurring in England at the time.

There were two technological innovations that profoundly changed daily life in the 19th century: steam power and electricity. The railroad helped expand the U.S. the telegraph, the telephone, and the typewriter brought people together that were far away. America began producing more steel than England.

77(C). The most widespread relief feature of India is Plains.

India's most prevalent relief feature is plains, i.e., 42.2 percent of the landscape.

The Indian peninsula consists mainly of plains and occupies a total area of 700,000 sq km.

It is referred to as the wide plains of the Indo Gangetic and has main rivers such as the Ganga, Yamuna, Brahmaputra & total boundary of 15. 200 km.

This 43% of the land area is appropriate for irrigation and is for industrial use, covering states such as UP (Uttar Pradesh), Bihar, Rajasthan Haryana & Punjab that together occupies the north Indian plains.

78(D). Monopoly over power, no constitution, no value of public opinion all are the feature of dictatorship. Dictators usually resort to force or fraud to gain despotic political power, which they maintain through the use of intimidation, terror, and the suppression of basic civil liberties. They may also employ techniques of mass propaganda in order to sustain their public support.

6 most important features of Dictatorship:

- One Party, One Leader and One Programme
- Absence of Individual Liberty
- National Glorification
- Glorification of War
- Totalitarian State
- Racialism

79(D). A country's economic development depends on the all factors;

- Cooperation with other countries
- Global situation
- Population size

In matters of economic development, not all the democracies get developed because of various factors like population, lack of basic infrastructure, etc. If you consider all democracies and all dictatorships for the fifty years between 1950 and 2000 , dictatorships have slightly higher rate of economic growth. The inability of democracy to achieve higher economic development worries us. However, the difference in the rates of economic development between less developed countries with dictatorships and democracies is negligible. Overall, we cannot say that democracy is a guarantee of economic development.

Democracy does not appear to be successful in reducing economic inequalities. A small number of ultra rich enjoy a highly disproportionate share of wealth and income. Their share in total income is increasing. People at the bottom of society have very little to depend on.

80(D). In March 1919, Bombay the Khilafat Committee was formed.
Objective of Khilafat Committee:
(i) To defend the temporal powers of the Khalifa of Turkey, the spiritual head of Islamic world.
(ii) To avert a harsh peace treaty (which was in apprenhension to be imposed on the Ottoman empire.

81(A). Lokmanya Tilak founded the Marathi newspaper 'Kesari'. The Kesari newspaper is a Marathi-language Indian newspaper.
- The newspaper was initially founded in 1881 by a prominent personality of the Indian Independence Movement, Lokmanya Bal Gangadhar Tilak.
- The Kesari newspaper was originally started as a co-operative effort by Agarkar (the paper's first editor), Chiplunkar, and Tilak, and was published along with Tilak's English newspaper, the Mahratta, to encourage people to rise against the oppressive regime of the time, instead of being submissive.
- the Kesari is still published from the original offices in Pune. Reporting local, national, and international news, the paper today is still one of the leading dailies of Maharashtra.

83(A). The interest payment is an item of Revenue expenditure .

84(D). In dispute between the Government of India and one or more States are is the jurisdiction of the Supreme Court of India Original and Exclusive.
The original jurisdiction of the Supreme Court has been described in Article 131 of the Constitution. According to which the Supreme Court has original jurisdiction in the following matters-
- A dispute between the Government of India and one or more States,
- A dispute between the Government of India and any State or States on the one hand and one or more other States on the other,
- Disputes between two or more states.

85(A) The igneous rock is the oldest in terms of construction. The rocks formed by fire, ie the rocks which are formed when the lava, magma and dust particles emanate from the volcano are called igneous rocks.

86(D). The best way to conserve our water resources is to encourage rainwater harvesting, sustainable water use, and natural regeneration of vegetation. All these are used to conserve our water resources.

87(D). Article 3 of the Constitution of India vests the power to form new States in the Parliament.

88(C). Bhand Pather theatre is a tradition primarily of Jammu and Kashmir.
- Bhand pather, folk theatre of Kashmir. The bhand pather is a popular form of folk theatre and the word bhand stands for 'jester' while pather means 'drama'.
- It is exclusively associated with the community of bhands or folk theatre actors.
- The bhands enact around twelve types of bhand pather and across the valley, the bhands form a well-organized folk theatre community

89(D). Indian Standard Time is 5 hours and 30 minutes ahead of Greenwich Mean Time. Indian Standard Time was adopted on 1 September 1947. Indian Standard Time passes through Naini of Allahabad (Prayagraj).

90(B). The Indus Valley Civilization is also known as the Harappan Civilization. After Harappa, the first of its sites to be excavated in the 1920s, in what was then the Punjab province of British India, and now in Pakistan.
- The Indus Valley was home to the largest of the four ancient urban civilizations of Egypt, Mesopotamia, India, and China.
- The drainage system of Mohenjodaro was very impressive.
- In almost all cities, every big or small house had its own courtyard and bathroom.
- The people of the Indus valley civilization worshipped the mother Goddess.
- It is said that the Harappan people worshipped a Mother goddess as it symbolizes fertility.
- The Indus Valley Civilization script is not alphabetical but is pictographic.
- The script has not been deciphered yet, but overlaps of letters show that it was written from right to left in the first line and left to right in the second line.
- This style is called 'Boustrophe

91(C). The Rajput ruler Prithviraj Chauhan defeated Muhammad Ghori in the First Battle of Tarain in 1191 AD .
- Near Tarain, in 1191, the invading Ghurid army led by Muhammad of Ghor and the Rajput confederacy led by Prithviraj Chauhan fought the First Battle of Tarain, also known as the First Battle of Taroari (modern Taraori in Haryana, India).
- The Rajputs won the battle decisively, but Shihabuddin managed to flee and return to Ghor.
- After the Ghorid armies were routed, they retreated to the Ghazni, leaving a garrison of 2,000 soldiers under Zia ud-Din Tulaki to secure the fort of Tabarhind and delay the Rajput army for thirteen months, during this time Shahabuddin raised a stronger army of 120,000 men and invaded again, leading to the Second Battle of Tarain .
- Prithviraj III, also known as Prithviraj Chauhan, was a monarch of the Chauhan (Chahamana) dynasty who controlled the Sapadalaksha region, with his capital in Ajmer, Rajasthan.
- He inherited an empire that stretched from Thanesar in the north to Jahazpur (Mewar) in the south, which he sought to expand through military campaigns against neighbouring kingdoms, particularly the Chandelas.
- Muhammad Ghori's initial raids were against Multan and the citadel of Uch in 1175, with the goal of reuniting the Muslim nations of India.

92(C). Ishwar Chandra Vidyasagar was an Indian educator and social reformer of the nineteenth century. He is also considered the "father of Bengali prose".
- Ishwar Chandra Vidyasagar used the ancient texts to suggest that widows could remarry.
- He was the most prominent campaigner for Hindu widow remarriage. he petitioned the legislative council for the same.
- Despite severe opposition in 1856, the Hindu widows remarriage act was passed by the government.
So, Ishwar Chandra Vidyasagar used the ancient text to suggest that widows could remarry.

93(B). Living organisms constantly take in or give out various abiotic factors. Thus, each biotic factor affects the quality of the abiotic factor around itself and thus affects the lives of the other biotic factors with which it share the ecosystem.

94(C). The chronological order of the given Lok Sabha speakers are:
a. K S Hegde: 1977-1980
c. Balram Jakhar: 1980-1984
b. Rabi Ray: 1989-1991
d. Shivraj Patil: 1991-1996
e. P.A. Sangma: 1996-1998

95(B). The 2023 Men's Boxing World Championships will be held in Uzbekistan capital Tashkent.
International Boxing Association (AIBA) President Umar Kremlev has confirmed Tashkent as the host city. The 22nd edition of the competition will be the first time when Uzbekistan will be hosting it. The central Asian nation won 3 gold medals in boxing at the Rio 2016 Olympic Games.

96(A). Shri Shankar Kurup was the first man recipient of the Gyanpith award.

The first recipient of the award was the Malayalam writer G. Sankara Kurup who received the award in 1965 for his collection of poems, Odakkuzhal (The Bamboo Flute), published in 1950.

97(B). Female Anopheles mosquito causes Malaria. Malaria is a mosquito-borne infectious disease of humans and other animals caused by parasitic protozoa. Anopheles is a mosquito genus that was first described and named by J. W. Meigen, in 1818. There are about 430 Anopheles mosquito species but only between 30 and 40 of those mosquito species are actual malaria vectors. Sir Ronald Ross, proved the transmission of malaria by the Anopheles mosquito.

98(B). Mercury is a chemical element with the symbol Hg and atomic number 80. The element is also known as Quick Silver for its mobility. Mercury is one of the oldest and deadliest poisons, a highly toxic metal mined from a brilliant red ore.

99(B). Japan attacked Pearl Harbour. Pearl Harbor, Hawaii, is located near the centre of the Pacific Ocean, roughly 2,000 miles from the U.S. mainland and about 4,000 miles from Japan. Pearl Harbor is a U.S. naval base near Honolulu, Hawaii. Japanese planes attacked the United States Naval Base at Pearl Harbor on December 7, 1941.

100(B). The Grammy Award is given in the field of music.

Mathematics

1. If the line segment is divided in the ratio $3:7$, then how many parts does it contain while constructing the point of division?
(a) 3
(b) 7
(c) 4
(d) 10

2. To divide a line segment AB in the ratio $5:6$, draw a ray AX such that $\angle BAX$ is an acute angle, then draw a ray BY parallel to AX and the points $A_1, A_2, A_3.....$ and $B_1, B_2, B_3.....$ are located at equal distances on ray AX and BY, respectively. Then the points joined are:
(a) A_4 and B_5
(b) A_6 and B_5
(c) A_5 and B_6
(d) A_5 and B_4

3. The distribution below gives the weights of 30 students of a class. Find the median weight of the students.

Weight (in kg)	40 – 45	45 – 50	50 – 55	55 – 60	60 – 65	65 – 70	70 – 75
Number of students	2	3	8	6	6	3	2

(a) 86.67 kg
(b) 76.67 kg
(c) 66.67 kg
(d) 56.67 kg

4. A solid cylinder of radius 'r' and height 'h' is placed over other cylinder of same height and radius. The total surface area of the shape so formed is:
(a) $4\pi rh + 2\pi r^2$
(b) $2\pi rh + 2\pi r^2$
(c) $2\pi rh + 4\pi r^2$
(d) $4\pi rh + 4\pi r^2$

5. If two solid hemispheres of same base radius 'x' cm are joined together along their bases, then the curved surface area of the new solid formed is:
(a) $8\pi x^2 cm^2$
(b) $6\pi x^2 cm^2$
(c) $5\pi x^2 cm^2$
(d) $4\pi x^2 cm^2$

6. If $\tan\theta = \dfrac{4}{3}$, then the value of $\dfrac{3\sin\theta + 2\cos\theta}{3\sin\theta - 2\cos\theta}$ is:
(a) 0.5
(b) -0.5
(c) 3.0
(d) -3.0

7. Every quadratic equation $ax^2 + bx + c = 0$ where $a, b, c \in R, a \neq 0$ has:
(a) Exactly one real root
(b) At least one real root
(c) At least two real roots
(d) At most two real roots

8. The roots of $100x^2 - 20x + 1 = 0$ is:
(a) $\dfrac{1}{20}$ and $\dfrac{1}{20}$
(b) $\dfrac{1}{10}$ and $\dfrac{1}{20}$
(c) $\dfrac{1}{10}$ and $\dfrac{1}{10}$
(d) None of the above

9. The circumference of a circle exceeds its diameter by $120\,cm$, then its radius is:
(a) $14\,cm$
(b) $42\,cm$
(c) $56\,cm$
(d) $28\,cm$

10. The area of a square inscribed in a circle of diameter d is:
(a) $\dfrac{d}{2}$
(b) d^2
(c) $\dfrac{d^2}{2}$
(d) $\dfrac{d^2}{4}$

11. What is the value of $\sin 60° \cdot \sin 30° + \cos 60° \cdot \cos 30° - \dfrac{\sqrt{3}}{2}$?
(a) 2
(b) 1
(c) $\dfrac{\sqrt{3}}{2}$
(d) 0

12. If $\cos(A + B) = \cos A \cos B - \sin A \sin B$, what is the value of $\cos 120°$?
(a) $\dfrac{\sqrt{3}}{2}$
(b) $\dfrac{-1}{2}$
(c) $\dfrac{2}{\sqrt{3}}$
(d) $\dfrac{1}{2}$

13. For what value of θ is $\sin\theta = \dfrac{1}{\sec\theta}$?
(a) $0°$
(b) $90°$
(c) $45°$
(d) $60°$

14. A lending library has a fixed charge for the first three days and an additional charge for each day thereafter. Saritha paid Rs. 27 for a book kept for seven days, while Susy paid Rs. 21 for the book she kept for five days. Find the fixed charge and the charge for each extra day.
(a) Fixed charge Rs. 15, Additional charges Rs. 3 per day
(b) Fixed charge Rs. 50, Additional charges Rs. 5 per day
(c) Fixed charge Rs. 35, Additional charges Rs. 3 per day
(d) Fixed charge Rs. 65, Additional charges Rs. 3 per day

15. A fraction becomes $\dfrac{1}{3}$ when 1 is subtracted from the numerator it becomes $\dfrac{1}{4}$ when 8 is added to its denominator. Find the fraction.
(a) $\dfrac{25}{12}$
(b) $\dfrac{15}{12}$
(c) $\dfrac{10}{12}$
(d) $\dfrac{5}{12}$

16. The LCM of two numbers $7^2 \times 3^2 \times 5 \times 2$ and $2^3 \times 5 \times 7$ is of form $2^a \times 3^b \times 5^c \times 7^d$. What are the respective value of $a, b, c,$ and d?
(a) $1, 0, 1$ and 0
(b) $3, 2, 0$ and 2
(c) $3, 2, 1$ and 2
(d) $3, 2, 2$ and 1

17. A wholesale dealer has stocks of three different varieties of tea weighing 408 kg, 468 kg and 516 kg. He wants to pack all of these into boxes of equal size, without mixing. What is the capacity of the largest possible box such that all the boxes are completely filled?
(a) 12 kg
(b) 24 kg
(c) 36 kg
(d) 50 kg

18. Find the greatest number that will divide 90 and 107 and leave remainders 2 and 3, respectively.
(a) 8
(b) 10
(c) 40
(d) 16

19. Which of following is true for Euclid's division algorithm between two numbers 'a' and 'b'?
(a) $a = bq + r; 0 < r < a$
(b) $a = b + rg; 0 \leq r < b$
(c) $a + bq = r; 0 < q < b$
(d) $a = bq + r; 0 \leq r < b$

20. Which of the following numbers represents the sum of zeroes of the polynomial $x^2 - 9$?
(a) -6
(b) 6
(c) 0
(d) 9

21. If sum of squares of zeroes of the polynomial $x^2 + 9x + 3k$ is 21, then find the value of k:
(a) -17
(b) 10
(c) 30
(d) 20

22. Harpreet tosses two different coins simultaneously (say, one is of ₹ 1 and other of ₹ 2). What is the probability that she gets at least once head?
(a) 1
(b) $\dfrac{1}{3}$
(c) $\dfrac{3}{4}$
(d) $\dfrac{1}{2}$

23. In an AP, the p th term is $\dfrac{1}{q}$ and the q th term is $\dfrac{1}{p}$. Find its (pq) th term.
(a) 1
(b) 2

(c) 3   (d) 4

24. The first term of an AP is -5 and the last term is 45. If the sum of the terms of the AP is 120, then find the number of terms and the common difference.
(a) 6, 10   (b) 6, 20
(c) 6, 30   (d) 6, 40

25. In triangles ABC and PQR, $AB = AC, \angle C = \angle P$ and $\angle B = \angle Q$. Then the two triangles are:

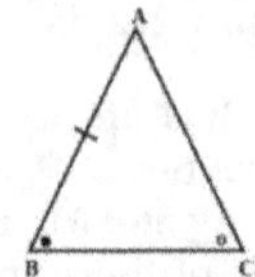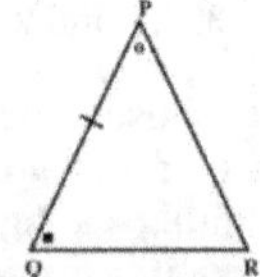

(a) Isosceles but not congruent
(b) Isosceles and congruent
(c) Congruent but not isosceles
(d) Neither congruent nor isosceles

26. If in a triangle, square of one side is equal to the sum of the squares of the other two sides. What is the angle opposite to the longest side?
(a) $60°$ (b) $30°$
(c) $90°$ (d) $120°$

27. In the given figure, X is the centre of the circle, $XM \perp AB, XM = 3$ units and $MB = 3$ units. What is the length of AM?

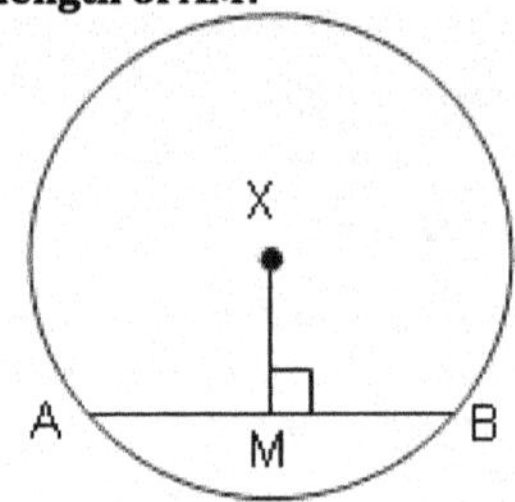

(a) 3 units   (b) 6 units
(c) 1.5 units   (d) 9 units

28. How many tangents can a circle have?
(a) Zero
(b) One
(c) Infinite
(d) None of these

29. The coordinates of the point P dividing the line segment joining the points A(1,3) and B(4,6) in the ratio 2:1 are:
(a) $(2, 4)$ (b) $(3, 5)$
(c) $(4, 2)$ (d) $(5, 3)$

30. If the distance between the points A(2, -2) and B(-1, x) is equal to 5, then the value of x is:
(a) 2   (b) -2
(c) 1   (d) -1

Science

31. Green plants utilize _______ percent of the sun's energy to prepare their food by the process of photosynthesis.
(a) 10 percent   (b) 1 percent
(c) 99 percent   (d) 20 percent

32. The process of accumulation of harmful chemical substances like pesticides in the body of organisms living at each trophic level in the food chain is as follows:
(a) Chemical magnification
(b) Chemical accumulation
(c) Biological accumulation
(d) Biological magnification

33. A metal M does not liberate hydrogen from dilute hydrochloric acid but reacts with oxygen to give a black coloured product. Identify the black coloured product:
(a) MgO (b) CuO
(c) FeO (d) ZnO

34. Which of the following gases is produced during calcination?
(a) CO_2 (b) CO
(c) SO_2 (d) SO_3

35. Junctions of two neurons in called:
(a) Synapse   (b) Synapsis
(c) Joint   (d) Junction

36. Leaves of which of the following plants are sensitive to touch?
(a) Mimosa   (b) Mangifera
(c) Ipomoea   (d) Hibiscus

37. In the reaction given below, hydrogen is getting:
$CuO + H_2 \rightarrow Cu + H_2O$.
(a) Reduced
(b) Oxidized
(c) No change
(d) None of these

38. When diluted HCl reacts with zinc metal what is required to identify the gas evolved?
(a) Red litmus solution
(b) Lime water
(c) Blue litmus solution
(d) A burning splinter

39. Which of the following is a primary suffix?
(a) -ane
(b) -ene

(c) -yne
(d) All of the above

40. The fuel used in a steam engine is:
(a) Water
(b) Carbon dioxide
(c) Carbon monoxide
(d) Coal

41. In human female, immature eggs are seen for the first time in the ovary during which stage?
(a) At puberty
(b) Before birth, at the foetus stage
(c) During menstrual cycle
(d) After the first year of birth

42. The connecting link between a mother's blood and fetal blood is termed as:
(a) Uterus
(b) Placenta
(c) Fallopian tube
(d) Ovary

43. Which of the following statement can be related to Mendel's experiments?
(a) Habits are inherited
(b) Characters are inherited
(c) Characters cannot be inherited
(d) None of the above

44. In evolutionary terms, we have more in common with
(a) A Chinese school-boy
(b) A chimpanzee
(c) A bacterium
(d) A spider

45. A convex mirror used for rear-view on an automobile has a radius of curvature of $3.00\,m$. If a bus is located at $5.00\,m$ from this mirror, find the position of the image.
(a) 0.15 m   (b) 2.15 m
(c) 1.15 m   (d) 1.5 m

46. Virtual, erect and diminished image are the characteristic features of a _______.
(a) Concave mirror
(b) Biconcave mirror
(c) Convex mirror
(d) Plane mirror

47. A D.C generator works on the principle of:
(a) Ohnis law
(b) Joule's law of heating
(c) Faraday's law of electromagnetic induction
(d) None of the above

48. **A.C generator works on the principle of:**
    (a) Force experience by a conductor in magnetic field
    (b) Electromagnetic induction
    (c) Electrostatic
    (d) Force experience by a charge particle in electric field

49. **What is the principle used for purification of blood in kidneys?**
    (a) Filtration
    (b) Diffusion
    (c) Osmosis
    (d) Reabsorption

50. **Which part of nephron pours urine into the ureter?**
    (a) Tubular part
    (b) Glomerulus
    (c) Collecting duct
    (d) Bowman's capsule

51. **Direction: In the table given below, match the bases in the first column with their applications mentioned in the second column.**

(A) Calcium hydroxide	(i) Antacid
(B) Ammonium hydroxide	(ii) Soap
(C) Sodium hydroxide	(iii) Whitewash
(D) Magnesium hydroxide	(iv) Window cleaner

    (a) (A) - (ii), (B) - (i), (C) - (iv), (D) - (iii)
    (b) (A) - (iii), (B) - (ii), (C) - (iv), (D) - (i)
    (c) (A) - (ii), (B) - (iv), (C) - (iii), (D) - (i)
    (d) (A) - (iii), (B) - (iv), (C) - (ii), (D) - (i)

52. **Indicators are used to determine the nature of a substance (acidic or basic). How do indicators determine the nature of substance?**
    (a) By showing a change in the colour
    (b) By showing a change in the physical state
    (c) By showing a change in density
    (d) By showing a change in chemical properties

53. **The muscles of the iris control the:**
    (a) Shape of the crystalline lens
    (b) Optic nerve
    (c) Opening of the pupil
    (d) Focal length of the eye-lens

54. **The equivalent resistance of eight** equal resistances in series is 48 ohms. What would be the equivalent resistance if they are connected in parallel?
    (a) $\frac{3}{4}\,\Omega$ (b) $\frac{4}{3}\,\Omega$
    (c) $4\,\Omega$ (d) $3\,\Omega$

55. **The resistance of one conducting wire is 10 . How much electric current will flow by connecting it with a battery of $1.5\ V$?**
    (a) $0.15\ mA$ (b) $1.5\ mA$
    (c) $15\ mA$ (d) $150\ mA$

Social Science

56. **How are most of the housing societies or colonies in the cities resourcing their water needs?**
    (a) City waterworks
    (b) Own groundwater pumping devices
    (c) Community water pumps
    (d) Individual motors

57. **What resources can be found from the forest and wildlife resources?**
    (a) Wood, barks, leaves, rubber, medicines
    (b) Minerals
    (c) Rocks and minerals
    (d) Metals

58. **Ballari-Chitradurga-Chikkamagaluru-Tumakuru belt in Karnataka has large reserves of _____.**
    (a) Iron ore   (b) Copper
    (c) Uranium   (d) Granite

59. **Greater the development of the primary and secondary sectors, _____ would be the demand for such services.**
    (a) Equal   (b) More
    (c) Less   (d) Uneven

60. **What is the full form of UNDP?**
    (a) United Nations Development Project
    (b) United Nations Development Plan
    (c) United Nations Development Programme
    (d) United Nations Development Process

61. **What was the Civil Code of 1804 also known as?**
    (a) The Administrative Code
    (b) Code of Justice
    (c) The Napoleonic Code
    (d) The National Code

62. **What has been the main dependency of primitive farming?**
    (a) Monsoon
    (b) Labour
    (c) Suitability of other environment
    (d) Technical

63. **What are the modern forms of money?**
    (a) Currency
    (b) Plastic money
    (c) Demand deposits
    (d) All the above

64. **Everyone prefers to receive payments in:**
    (a) Goods   (b) Cheque
    (c) Draft   (d) Money

65. **What is the amalgamation and rapid unification between countries identified as?**
    (a) Globalisation
    (b) Liberalisation
    (c) Socialisation
    (d) Privatisation

66. **Which of the following is/are services?**
    (a) Teaching
    (b) Accounting
    (c) Toys
    (d) Both (i) and (ii)

67. **COPRA does not propose formation of:**
    (a) National Consumer Court
    (b) State Consumer Court
    (c) District Consumer Court
    (d) High Court

68. **Which is not a function of PDS?**
    (a) Control Hoarding
    (b) Control Prices
    (c) Control over charging
    (d) Consumer redressal

69. **In 1517, the religious reformer Martin Luther wrote Ninety Five Theses criticising many of the practices and rituals of the Roman Catholic Church, what was its outcome?**
    (i) They were ignored by the church
    (ii) A printed copy of this was posted on a church door in Wittenberg. It challenged the Church to debate his ideas
    (iii) Luther's writings were immediately reproduced in vast numbers and read widely
    (iv) This lead to a division within the Church and to the beginning of the Protestant Reformation. Luther's translation of the New

Testament sold 5,000 copies within a few weeks

(a) (i) only

(b) (i) and (ii)

(c) (ii), (iii) and (iv)

(d) All of the above

70. What is Heretical?

(a) Beliefs which do not follow the accepted teachings of the Church

(b) Self made religious beliefs

(c) Foreign accepted religious beliefs

(d) Accepted teachings of the Church

71. Which of the following features are common to Indian and Belgian form of power sharing arrangments:

(a) Power is shared among governments at different levels

(b) Power is shared among different organs of the government

(c) Power is shared among different social groups

(d) Power is shared among different parties and takes the form of competition

72. Consider the following two statements on power sharing and select the answer using the codes given below:
A. Power sharing is good for democracy.
B. It helps to reduce the possibility of conflict between social groups.
Which of these statements are true and false?

(a) A is true but B is false

(b) Both A and B are true

(c) Both A and B are false

(d) A is false but B is true

73. In _____ the big European powers met in Berlin to complete the carving up of Africa between them.

(a) 1880

(b) 1885

(c) 1890

(d) 1895

74. Which of the following is not the key feature of federalism?

(a) There are two or more levels (or tiers) of government

(b) The jurisdictions of the respective levels or tiers of government are specified in the constitution

(c) The central government can pass on orders to the provincial or the local government

(d) The fundamental provisions of the constitution cannot be unilaterally changed by one level of government. Such changes require the consent of both levels of government

75. Examine the following pairs that give the level of government in India and the powers of the government at that level to make laws on the subjects mentioned against each.
Which of the following pairs is not correctly matched?

(a) State government-State List

(b) Central government-Union List

(c) Central and State governments-Concurrent List

(d) Local governments-Residuary powers

76. Why didn't the technological changes spread dramatically across the industrial landscape?

(a) Merchants were not interested

(b) It was difficult to learn and train staff for new technology

(c) New technology was expensive and merchants and industrialists were cautious about using it.

(d) There were little resources for damage control

77. Resources which are found in a region, but have not been utilised:

(a) Renewable

(b) Developed

(c) National

(d) Potential

78. Which type of government exists in the world?

(a) Dictatorship

(b) Monarchy

(c) Democracy

(d) All of the above

79. What is regarded as a definite plus point of democratic regimes?

(a) Participative decision making

(b) Rule of majority

(c) Ability to handle Social differences, divisions, and conflicts

(d) None of the above

80. When did the Non-Cooperation-Khilafat Movement begin?

(a) August 1920

(b) August 1921

(c) August 1922

(d) August 1923

General Awareness/ Knowledge

81. The date on which Bachendri Pal stepped onto the peak of Mount Everest and pitched the Indian National Flag (Tiranga/Tricolour) is:

(a) 23rd May, 1984

(b) 23rd May, 1989

(c) 25th May, 1984

(d) 25th May, 1989

82. In India, The National Human Rights Commission is under which of the following ministry?

(a) Ministry of Home Affairs

(b) Defense Ministry

(c) Finance Ministry

(d) None of these

83. The largest sources of tax revenue to the Central Government of India are:

(a) Union excise duties and corporate tax

(b) Custom duty and corporate tax

(c) Union excise duty and custom duty

(d) Custom duty and income tax

84. The tenure of a Member of Rajya Sabha is-

(a) 6

(b) 5

(c) 4

(d) 8

85. In which of the following plate boundaries, new crust formation takes place?
1. Convergent Boundaries
2. Divergent Boundaries
3. Transform Boundaries
Select the correct answer using the code given below.

(a) 1 and 2 only

(b) 2 only

(c) 1 and 3 only

(d) 1, 2 and 3

86. The first official Telegraph Line was opened between which two cities?

(a) Kolkata and London

(b) Bombay and Thane

(c) Kanpur and Delhi

(d) Kolkata and Diamond harbor

87. The states of Maharashtra and Gujarat were created in _____.

(a) 1962

(b) 1959

(c) 1961

(d) 1960

88. The famous Brihadeshwara Temple is located in _____.

(a) Madurai

(b) Thanjavur

(c) Kanchipuram

(d) Rameshwaram

89. The first four planets nearest from the Sun are known as:

(a) Terrestrial Planets

(b) Jovian Planets

(c) Gaseous Planets

(d) Gas-Giant Planets

90. Who used the caves of Barabar as hermitage?

(a) the livelihoods

(b) the Tharus

(c) the Jains

(d) the magicians

91. Tansen, one of the well-known musicians of medieval India, was in the court of which of the following Mughal emperors?

(a) Akbar   (b) Babur

(c) Aurangzeb   (d) Humayun

92. Who were the first among the Europeans to come for trade?

(a) Dutch   (b) British

(c) French   (d) Portuguese

93. Which one of the following is not a fossil fuel?

(a) Petrol   (b) Natural gas

(c) Uranium   (d) Coal

94. Match the following:

List-1	List-2
A. National Commis sion for Backward C lasses	1. Justice K uldip Singh
B. Delimitation Co mmission	2. Justice V. Eswaraiah
C. National Commis sion for Scheduled Tribes	3. Dr. Rame shwar Orao n
D. National Commis sion for Women	4. Lalitha K umaraman galam

(a) A - 1, B - 4, C - 3, D - 2

(b) A - 1, B - 2, C - 3, D - 4

(c) A - 4, B - 3, C - 1, D - 2

(d) A - 2, B - 1, C - 3, D - 4

95. ___________ has lifted the ban imposed on the All India Football Federation (AIFF) in August 2022.

(a) International Federation of Association Football (FIFA)

(b) Asian Football Confederation (AFC)

(c) Confederation of African Football (CAF)

(d) Union of European Football Associations (UEFA)

96. _____ was the world's first female astronaut.

(a) Svetlana Savitskaya

(b) Valentina Tereshkova

(c) Sally Ride

(d) Judith Resnik

97. At which point of the Earth is there no gravity?

(a) At North and South Pole

(b) At equator

(c) On the ocean surface

(d) At centre of the Earth

98. A passenger in a moving bus is thrown forward when the bus suddenly stops. This is explained

(a) by Newton's first law

(b) by Newton's second law

(c) by Newton's third law

(d) by the principle of conservation of momentum

99. With respect to Industrial Revolution First, which among the following is also known as "Black Gold".

(a) Iron   (b) Coal

(c) Brass   (d) Crude oil

100. Which mathematician was awarded the Abel Prize for the year 2023?

(a) Luis Caffarelli

(b) Avi Wigderson

(c) Hillel Furstenberg

(d) Dennis Sullivan

// Hints and Solutions //

1(D). We know that to divide a line segment in the ratio $m : n$, first we draw a ray AX which makes an acute angle BAX, then we are required to mark $m + n$ points at equal distances from each other.

The line segment is divided in the ratio $3 : 7$ means, it contains 3 parts on one side and 7 parts on the other side of the point of division. Hence, there will be a total of $(3 + 7)$ parts, i.e. 10 parts.

So, the minimum number of these points $= 10$.

2(C). Given ratio is $5 : 6$. That means, we have to locate 5 points such as A_1, A_2, A_3, A_4, A_5 on the ray AX and 6 points such as $B_1, B_2, B_3 B_4, B_5, B_6$, on ray BY. Also, we need to join A_5 and B_6.

3(D). We can calculate the median as given below:

$$m = 1 + \left(\frac{\frac{n}{2} - cf}{f} \right) \times h$$

Where

$1 =$ Lower limit of median class

$h =$ Class size

$f =$ Frequency of median class

$cf =$ cumulative frequency of class preceding median class

The cumulative frequencies with their respective class intervals are as follows:

Weight (in kg)	Number of s tudents	Cumulative fr equency
40 − 45	2	2
45 − 50	3	2 + 3 = 5
50 − 55	8	5 + 8 = 13
55 − 60	6	13 + 6 = 19
60 − 65	6	19 + 6 = 25
65 − 70	3	25 + 3 = 28
70 − 75	2	28 + 2 = 30
Total (n)	30	

It can be observed from the given table

$n = 30$

$\frac{n}{2} = 15$

Cumulative frequency just greater than $\frac{n}{2}$ is 19 , Belongs to class interval $55 - 60$

Median class $= 55 - 60$

$l = 55$

$f = 6$

$cf = 13$

$h = 5$

Substituting these values in the formula of median we get:

$$m = 1 + \left(\frac{\frac{n}{2} - cf}{f} \right) \times h$$

$$m = 55 + \left(\frac{15 - 13}{6} \right) \times 5$$

$$m = 55 + \left(\frac{10}{6} \right)$$

$$m = 56.67$$

So, median weight is 56.67 kg.

4(A). Given, a solid cylinder of radius r and height h is placed over another cylinder of same height and radius.

We have to determine if the total surface area of the shape so formed is $4\pi rh + 4\pi r^2$.

Total surface area = curved surface area + area of the bases.

Curved surface area is defined as the area of only curved surface leaving the top and bottom bases.

Curved surface area of cylinder $= 2\pi rh$

Area of bases $= 2\pi r^2$

So, the total surface area of the cylinder $= 2\pi rh + 2\pi r^2$

Given, two cylinders of same dimensions are placed one over another.

Total surface area of cylinder $= 2$ (Total surface of single cylinder) -2 (Area of base of cylinder)

$= 2 \left(2\pi rh + 2\pi r^2 \right) - 2 \left(\pi r^2 \right)$

$= 4\pi rh + 2\pi r^2$

5(D). We know that,

Curved surface area of a hemisphere $= 2\pi r^2$

If two solid hemispheres of same base radius ' x ' cm are joined together along their bases, then the Curved surface area of the new solid formed is $4\pi r^2 = 4\pi x^2 cm^2$

6(C). Given,

$\tan \theta = \frac{4}{3}$

As we know,

$\frac{\sin \theta}{\cos \theta} = \tan \theta$

Now,

$\frac{3 \sin \theta + 2 \cos \theta}{3 \sin \theta - 2 \cos \theta}$

Divide numerator & denominator by $\cos \theta$, we get

$$= \frac{\frac{3\sin\theta}{\cos\theta} + \frac{2\cos\theta}{\cos\theta}}{\frac{3\sin\theta}{\cos\theta} - \frac{2\cos\theta}{\cos\theta}}$$

$$= \frac{3\tan\theta + 2}{3\tan\theta - 2}$$

Putting value of $\tan\theta$, we get

$$= \frac{3 \times \frac{4}{3} + 2}{3 \times \frac{4}{3} - 2}$$

$$= \frac{6}{2}$$

$$= 3$$

7(D). Consider the given quadratic equation $ax^2 + bx + c = 0$ where $a \neq 0$ and b and c are real numbers.

From the nature of roots we can say that, when $\Delta \geq 0$ the roots are real. Therefore, if it's less than zero the roots can not be real. So, in that case, there will be 0 real roots.

Similarly, for $\Delta = 0$ the roots are real numbers and equal which mean there is only one real root.

For $\Delta > 0$ the roots are real and unequal that means in that case there are two real roots.

Therefore, the given quadratic equation can have 0, 1, or 2 real roots depending on the nature of the discriminant.

Thus, the given quadratic equation has at most two real roots.

8(C). Given, $100x^2 - 20x + 1 = 0$
$\Rightarrow 100x^2 - 10x - 10x + 1 = 0$
$\Rightarrow 10x(10x - 1) - 1(10x - 1) = 0$
$\Rightarrow (10x - 1)^2 = 0$
$\therefore (10x - 1) = 0$ or $(10x - 1) = 0$
$\Rightarrow x = \frac{1}{10}$ or $x = \frac{1}{10}$

9(D). Let the radius be r, then according to the question,
$2\pi r = 2r + 120$
$2r(\pi - 1) = 120$
$r = 28\ cm$

10(C).

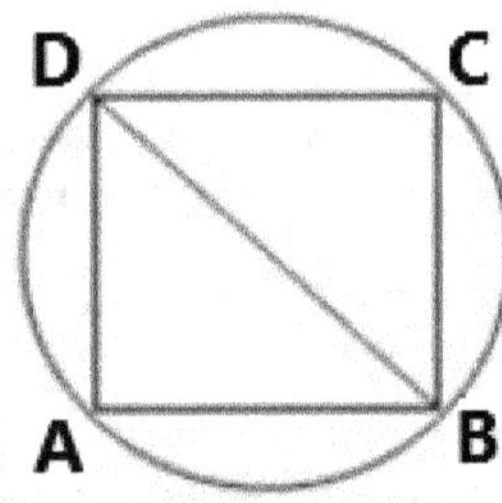

Area of square $= \dfrac{(\text{BD}^2)}{2}$

$= \dfrac{d^2}{2}$ $\quad (\because BD = d)$

So, the area is square $\dfrac{d^2}{2}$

11(D). Given:

$\sin 60° \cdot \sin 30° + \cos 60° \cdot \cos 30° - \dfrac{\sqrt{3}}{2}$

Putting the values we get:

$\Rightarrow \dfrac{\sqrt{3}}{2} \cdot \dfrac{1}{2} + \dfrac{1}{2} \cdot \dfrac{\sqrt{3}}{2} - \dfrac{\sqrt{3}}{2}$

$\Rightarrow \dfrac{\sqrt{3}}{4} + \dfrac{\sqrt{3}}{4} - \dfrac{\sqrt{3}}{2}$

$\Rightarrow \dfrac{\sqrt{3} + \sqrt{3} - 2\sqrt{3}}{4} = \dfrac{2\sqrt{3} - 2\sqrt{3}}{4}$

$\Rightarrow \dfrac{0}{4} = 0$

12(B). Given:
$\cos(A + B) = \cos A \cos B - \sin A \sin B$
Now,
$\cos 120° = \cos(90° + 30°)$
$\cos(90° + 30°) = \cos 90° \cos 30° - \sin 90° \sin 30°$
Putting values we get,

$\Rightarrow 0 \times \dfrac{\sqrt{3}}{2} - 1 \times \dfrac{1}{2}$

$\Rightarrow 0 - \dfrac{1}{2}$

$\Rightarrow \dfrac{-1}{2}$

13(C). Given:
$\sin\theta = \dfrac{1}{\sec\theta}$
Now,
$\sec\theta = \dfrac{1}{\cos\theta}$

$\therefore \sin\theta = \dfrac{1}{\frac{1}{\cos\theta}}$

$\sin\theta = \cos\theta$

and as we know that the value of $\sin\theta$ and $\cos\theta$ is equal at $45°$.

i.e., $\dfrac{1}{\sqrt{2}}$

So, $\sin\theta = \dfrac{1}{\sec\theta} = 45°$

14(A). Let Fixed charge for first 3 days = Rs. x
Additional charge after 3 days = Rs. y per day
Given,
Saritha paid Rs. 27 for a book kept for seven days
Fixed charge for first three days + (Number of additional days kept) × (Additional charges per day) = Rs. 27
$x + (7 - 3)y = 27$
$x + 4y = 27$ $\quad\ldots\ldots(1)$
Also,
Susy paid Rs. 21 for a book kept for five days
Fixed charge for first three days + (Number of additional days kept) × (Additional charges per day) = Rs. 21
$x + (5 - 3)y = 21$
$x + 2y = 21$ $\quad\ldots\ldots(2)$
We use elimination method with equation (1) and (2),

$\begin{array}{r} x + 4y = 27 \\ x + 2y = 21 \\ (-)(-)(-) \\ \hline 2y = 6 \end{array}$

$2y = 6$
$y = \dfrac{6}{2}$
$y = 3$
Putting $y = 3$ in equation (2),
$x + 2y = 21$
$x + 2(3) = 21$
$x + 6 = 21$
$x = 21 - 6$
$x = 15$
So, $x = 15, y = 3$ is the solution of the equations,
Therefore,
Fixed charge for the first 3 days $= x =$ Rs.

15
Additional charges after 3 days $= y =$ Rs. 3 per day

15(D). Let Numerator be x
Denominator be y
So, Fraction is $\dfrac{x}{y}$
Given that,
If 1 is subtracted from numerator fraction becomes $\dfrac{1}{3}$.

$\dfrac{\text{Numerator} - 1}{\text{Denominator}} = \dfrac{1}{3}$

$\dfrac{x - 1}{y} = \dfrac{1}{3}$

$3(x - 1) = y$
$3x - 3 = y$
$3x - y = 3$ $\quad\ldots\ldots(1)$
Also,
If 8 is added to the denominator, fraction becomes $\dfrac{1}{4}$.

$\dfrac{\text{Numerator}}{\text{Denominator} + 8} = \dfrac{1}{4}$

$\dfrac{x}{y + 8} = \dfrac{1}{4}$

$4x = y + 8$
$4x - y = 8$ $\quad\ldots\ldots(2)$
From (1),
$3x - y = 3$
$3x = y + 3$
$x = \left(\dfrac{y + 3}{3}\right)$
Putting value of x in (2),
$4x - y - 8 = 0$
$4\left(\dfrac{y + 3}{3}\right) - y - 8 = 0$
Multiplying both sides by 3
$3 \times 4\left(\dfrac{y + 3}{3}\right) - 3 \times y - 3 \times 8 = 3 \times 0$
$4(y + 3) - 3y - 24 = 0$
$4y + 12 - 3y - 24 = 0$
$y - 12 = 0$
$y = 12$
Putting $y = 12$ in equation (1),
$3x - y = 3$
$3x - 12 = 3$
$3x = 12 + 3$
$3x = 15$
$x = \dfrac{15}{3}$
$x = 5$
Therefore $x = 5, y = 12$ is the solution.
So,
Numerator $= x = 5$
Denominator $= y = 12$
$\therefore$ Original fraction
$= \dfrac{\text{Numerator}}{\text{Denominator}} = \dfrac{x}{y} = \dfrac{5}{12}$

16(C). It is given that, LCM of two numbers $7^2 \times 3^2 \times 5 \times 2$ and $2^3 \times 5 \times 7$ is of form $2^a \times 3^b \times 5^c \times 7^d$.
We know that, the highest power of each number is their respective values.
Highest power of value is:
$2^a = 2^3$
$3^b = 3^2$
$5^c = 5^1$
$7^d = 7^2$
By comparing the base, the value of a, b, c

and d is $3, 2, 1$ and 2 respectively.

17(A). To find the capacity of the largest possible box in which all the boxes are completely filled, we find the HCF of the weight of the tea pack 408 kg, 468 kg and 516 kg.

HCF of 408 , 468 and 516

$408 = 2 \times 2 \times 2 \times 3 \times 17$

$468 = 2 \times 2 \times 3 \times 3 \times 13$

$516 = 2 \times 2 \times 3 \times 43$

The common factors of the given numbers are 2^2 and 3

So, HCF of 408 , 468 and 516 = 12

So, the capacity of the largest possible box such that all the boxes are completely filled is 12 kg.

18(A). It is given that the number that will divide 90 leaving a reminder 2 and 107 leaving a remainder 3 , the number should divide numbers $(90 - 2) = 88$ and $(107 - 3) = 104$ i.e., it is the HCF of 88 and 104 .

$88 = 2 \times 2 \times 2 \times 11$

$104 = 2 \times 2 \times 2 \times 13$

$HCF = 2^3 = 8$

The greatest number which divides 90 and 107 leaving remainders 2 and 3 respectively is 8 .

19(D). According to Euclid's Division, if we have two positive integers a and b, then there would be whole numbers q and r that satisfy the equation: $a = bq + r$, where $0 \le r < b$. a is the dividend. b is the divisor. q is the quotient and r is the remainder. By using this, we can find the HCF of two numbers.

20(C). Polynomial $p(x) = x^2 - 9 = 0$

$\Rightarrow x^2 - 3^2 = 0$

According the formula

$a^2 - b^2 = (a + b)(a - b)$

$\Rightarrow (x + 3)(x - 3) = 0$

So,

$\Rightarrow (x + 3) = 0$ or $(x - 3) = 0$

$x = -3$ or $x = 3$

Zeroes are $(3, -3)$

Sum of zeroes are: $3 - 3 = 0$

21(B). Given:

$f(x) = x^2 + 9x + 3k$

sum of squares of zero = 21

Sum of zero $(a + \beta) = \dfrac{-b}{a}$

Product of zero $(\alpha \times \beta) = \dfrac{c}{a}$

Let α and β are the zeroes of polynomial $f(x)$

Sum of zero $= \dfrac{-b}{a} = \left(\dfrac{-9}{1}\right) = -9 \ldots (i)$

Product of zero $= \dfrac{c}{a} = \left(\dfrac{3k}{1}\right) = 3k \ldots (ii)$

Now, from equation (i)

$\alpha + \beta = -9$

Squaring both sides, we get

$(\alpha + \beta)^2 = (-9)^2$

$\Rightarrow \alpha^2 + \beta^2 + 2\alpha\beta = 81 \ldots (iii)$

Now, sum of squares of zero = 21

$\alpha^2 + \beta^2 = 21$

Putting the value of equation (i) and (ii) in (iii) , we get

$\Rightarrow 21 + 2 \times 3k = 81$

$\Rightarrow 6k = (81 - 21)$

$\Rightarrow 6k = 60$

$\Rightarrow k = 10$

$\therefore$ The value of k is 10 .

22(C). We write H for 'head' and T for 'tail'. When two coins are tossed simultaneously, the possible outcomes are $(H, H), (H, T), (T, H), (T, T)$, which are all equally likely. Here (H, H) means head up on the first coin (say on ₹ 1) and head up on the second coin (₹ 2) . Similarly (H, T) means head up on the first coin and tail up on the second coin and so on.

The outcomes favourable to the event E , 'at least one head' are $(H, H), (H, T)$ and (T, H) .

So, the number of outcomes favourable to E is 3 .

Therefore, $P(E) = \dfrac{3}{4}$

i.e., the probability that Harpreet gets at least one head is $\dfrac{3}{4}$.

You can also find $P(E)$ as follows:

$P(E) = 1 - P(\bar{E}) = 1 - \dfrac{1}{4} = \dfrac{3}{4}$

$\left(\text{Since } P(\bar{E}) = P(\text{ no head }) = \dfrac{1}{4} \right)$

23(A). Given,

In an AP , the p th term is $\dfrac{1}{q}$ and the q th term is $\dfrac{1}{p}$.

Let a be the first term and d be the common difference of the AP , then

$a_p = \dfrac{1}{q}$ and $a_q = \dfrac{1}{p}$

We know,

$T_n = a + (n - 1)d$

a = first term

d = common difference

$T_n = n^{\text{th}}$ term

$\Rightarrow a + (p - 1)d = \dfrac{1}{q} \qquad \ldots\ldots (i)$

and, $a + (q - 1)d = \dfrac{1}{p} \qquad \ldots\ldots (ii)$

Subtracting (ii) from (i) , we get

$(p - 1 - q + 1)d = \dfrac{1}{q} - \dfrac{1}{p}$

$\Rightarrow (p - q)d = \dfrac{p - q}{pq} \Rightarrow d = \dfrac{1}{pq}$

Substituting this value of d in (i) , we get

$a + (p - 1) \times \dfrac{1}{pq} = \dfrac{1}{q}$

$\Rightarrow a + \dfrac{1}{q} - \dfrac{1}{pq} = \dfrac{1}{q}$

$\Rightarrow a - \dfrac{1}{pq} = 0$

$\Rightarrow a = \dfrac{1}{pq}$

Now, (pq) th term

$= a + (pq - 1)d = \dfrac{1}{pq} + (pq - 1)\dfrac{1}{pq}$

$= \dfrac{1}{pq} + 1 - \dfrac{1}{pq} = 1$

So, (pq) th term = 1

24(A). Given,

a (first term) $= -5, l$ (last term) $= 45$ and sum of the terms = 120

Let the number of terms be n and the

common difference be d .

Using $S_n = \dfrac{n}{2}(a + l)$, we get

$120 = \dfrac{n}{2}(-5 + 45)$

$\Rightarrow 120 = \dfrac{n}{2} \times 40$

$\Rightarrow 20n = 120$

$\Rightarrow n = 6$

Using $l = a + (n - 1)d$, we get

$45 = -5 + (6 - 1)d$

$\Rightarrow 50 = 5d$

$\Rightarrow d = 10$

25(A). In $\triangle ABC$ and $\triangle PQR$

$\angle C = \angle P$ (Given)

$\angle B = \angle Q$ (Given)

$\angle A = \angle R$ (Third angle of the triangle)

Thus, $\triangle ABC \sim \triangle PQR$

Also , given, $AB = AC$

Thus, $\angle B = \angle C$ (Isosceles triangle Property)

But, $\angle B = \angle Q$ and $\angle C = \angle P$

Hence, $\angle Q = \angle P$

or $PR = QR$

Thus, both the triangles are Isosceles but not congruent.

26(C). Let the sides of triangle be h, p and b .

As per the given question

$h^2 = p^2 + b^2$ ....(Pythagoras Theorem)

So, the longest side is the hypotenuse.

In a right-angled triangle, angle opposite to hypotenuse is $90°$.

27(A). Given, $XM = 3$ units, $MB = 3$ units and $XM \perp AB$

As we know that, perpendicular line on a chord from the centre bisect it.

Therefore, $AM = MB = 3$ units

28(C). There can be infinite tangents to a circle. A circle is made up of infinite points which are at an equal distance from a point. Since there are infinite points on the circumference of a circle, infinite tangents can be drawn from them.

29(B). As we know,

if a point (x, y) divides the line joining the points (x_1, y_1) and (x_2, y_2) in the ratio $m : n$, then

$(x, y) = \left(\dfrac{mx_2 + nx_1}{m + n}, \dfrac{my_2 + ny_1}{m + n} \right)$ (by section formula)

Given,

$A(1, 3) = (x_1, y_1)$ and $B(4, 6) = (x_2, y_2)$

$m_1 = 2$ and $m_2 = 1$

Let the co-ordinates of P be (x, y) .

$\therefore x = \dfrac{2 \times 4 + 1 \times 1}{2 + 1}$

$\Rightarrow x = \dfrac{8 + 1}{3}$

$\Rightarrow x = \dfrac{9}{3}$

$\Rightarrow x = 3$

Similarly,

$y = \dfrac{2 \times 6 + 1 \times 3}{1 + 2}$

$\Rightarrow y = \dfrac{12 + 3}{3}$

$\Rightarrow y = \dfrac{15}{3}$

$\Rightarrow y = 5$

$\therefore$ The coordinates of the point P is $(3, 5)$.

30(A). As we know,

The distance between two points

$= \sqrt{(x_2 - x_1)^2 + (y_2 - y_1)^2}$

Given,

The distance between the points $A(2, -2)$ and $B(-1, x) = 5$

$\therefore \sqrt{(-1 - 2)^2 + (x + 2)^2} = 5$

$\Rightarrow \sqrt{(-3)^2 + (x + 2)^2} = 5$

$\Rightarrow \sqrt{9 + (x + 2)^2} = 5$

$\Rightarrow 9 + (x + 2)^2 = 25$

$\Rightarrow (x + 2)^2 = 25 - 9$

$\Rightarrow (x + 2)^2 = 16$

Take square root on both the sides, we get

$x + 2 = 4$

$\Rightarrow x = 4 - 2$

$\Rightarrow x = 2$

So, the value of x is 2.

31(B). The study of flow of energy between various ecosystems state that the autotrophs in a terrestrial ecosystem capture about 1 percent of the energy of sunlight that falls on their leaves and convert it into feed. An autotroph is an organism that can produce its own food using light, water, carbon dioxide, or other chemicals. Because autotrophs produce their own food, they are sometimes called producers.

32(D). Biomagnification, also known as bioamplification or biological magnification, is the increasing concentration of a substance, such as a toxic chemical, in the tissues of organisms at successively higher levels in a food chain. Biomagnification is the accumulation of a chemical by an organism from water and food exposure that results in a concentration that is greater than would have resulted from water exposure only and thus greater than expected from equilibrium.

33(B). The metal M is copper (Cu) which reacts with oxygen when heated in the air to form black coloured copper(ll) oxide. The reaction can be written as:

$2Cu + O_2 \rightarrow 2CuO$

Copper is present below hydrogen in the reactivity series of metals. So, it does not react with dilute acids like hydrochloric acid or sulfuric acid.

34(A). CO_2 is produced during calcination. It involves heating when the volatile matter escapes leaving behind the metal oxide.

$ZnCO_3(s) \xrightarrow{\Delta} ZnO(s) + CO_2(g)$

$CaCO_3 \cdot MgCO_3(s) \xrightarrow{\Delta} CaO(s) + MgO(s) + 2CO_2(g)$

35(A). Synapse is the junction between two neurons, a neuron and a muscle cell or a neuron and a glandular cell. Synapses help to regulate the speed and direction of nerve impulses.

Synapse, also called neuronal junction, the site of transmission of electric nerve impulses between two nerve cells (neurons) or between a neuron and a gland or muscle cell (effector). A synaptic connection between a neuron and a muscle cell is called a neuromuscular junction.

36(A). The leaves of Mimosa pudica (sensitive plant) are sensitive to touch.

Sensitive plant, (Mimosa pudica), also called humble plant, plant in the pea family (Fabaceae) that responds to touch and other stimulation by rapidly closing its leaves and drooping. Native to South and Central America, the plant is a widespread weed in tropical regions and has naturalized elsewhere in warm areas. The Mimosa plant folds the leaflets on stimulus with touch. The stimulus is passed on to the entire branch and then the whole plant with all the leaflets close. There is a loss of water from the cells at the base of the leaf. This is due to the passing of the impulse which causes a change in the turgor pressure in the cells causing the leaflets to be closed.

37(B). In this reaction, copper is losing oxygen and hydrogen is gaining oxygen. If a substance gains oxygen during a reaction, it is said to be oxidised. If a substance loses oxygen during a reaction, it is said to be reduced. So, in this reaction, hydrogen is getting oxidised while hydrogen is getting is reduced.

38(D). Zinc is a reactive metal that in reaction with HCl produces hydrogen gas.

$Zn + 2HCl \rightarrow ZnCl_2 + H_2 \uparrow$

If we introduce a Burning Splinter above the reaction the gas will burn with a pop sound which is a commonly used test for the presence of Hydrogen.

39(D). A primary suffix indicates the degree of saturation or unsaturation in carbon compounds. Example: For carbon atoms linked by a single covalent bond, suffix: ane, for carbon atoms linked by a double bond, suffix: ene, for carbon atoms linked by a triple bond, suffix: yne is used.

40(D). Steam engine as the name suggests it is the engine that works on steam.

The force produced by steam is used in the working of the steam engine.

Steam is produced by burning coal.

Coal is used to generate steam because as it has a high calorific value and easy to use.

41(A). During the birth of a girl child, there are many follicles that are present in the ovary. When the girl reaches puberty, many of the follicles die. During puberty, the viable follicles develop inside the ovary and can be observed as immature eggs. From these immature eggs, every month one egg matures and is released from one of the ovaries.

42(B). The connecting link between a mother's blood and fetal blood is termed as Placenta.

The fetus is connected by the umbilical cord to the placenta, the organ that develops and implants in the mother's uterus during pregnancy. Through the blood vessels in the umbilical cord, the fetus receives all the necessary nutrition, oxygen, and life support from the mother through the placenta.

43(B). The process by which the characters are transferred from one generation to the other is known as inheritance. Mendel gave law of inheritance on the basis of his experiments on pea plant. According to him, characters are inherited as distinct units. Two copies of the genetic material that determines characters are inherited over generations in which one copy comes from each the male and female parent.

44(A). In terms of evolution, organisms belonging to the same species have more in common than organisms belonging to different species of the same genus or different genus. We have more in common with a Chinese school-boy because both belongs to the same species of Homo sapiens, and thus, share a common ancestor.

45(C). Radius of curvature, $R = +3.00\,\text{m}$; Object-distance, $u = -5.00\,\text{m}$;

Focal length, $f = \dfrac{R}{2} = +\dfrac{3.00\,\text{m}}{2} = +1.50\,\text{m}$ (as the principal focus of a convex mirror is behind the mirror)

Since $\dfrac{1}{v} + \dfrac{1}{u} = \dfrac{1}{f}$

or,

$\dfrac{1}{v} = \dfrac{1}{f} - \dfrac{1}{u} = +\dfrac{1}{1.50} - \dfrac{1}{(-5.00)} = \dfrac{1}{1.50} + \dfrac{1}{5.00}$

$= \dfrac{5.00 + 1.50}{7.50}$

$v = \dfrac{+7.50}{6.50} = +1.15\,\text{m}$

The image is $1.15\,\text{m}$ at the back of the mirror.

46(C). Virtual, erect and diminished image are the characteristic features of a convex mirror. A convex mirror always forms an erect, and a virtual and diminished image, for any position of the object. Convex mirrors, or curved mirrors, always form a virtual image because the focus and centre of curvature are imaginary points inside the mirror and cannot be reached.

47(C). A D.C generator works on the principle of faraday's law of electromagnetic induction. faraday's law of electromagnetic induction.

A DC generator works on the principle of

Electro Magnetic Induction. When a DC current passes through a long straight conductor a magnetizing force and a static magnetic field are developed around it. If the wire is then wound into a coil, the magnetic field is greatly intensified producing a static magnetic field around itself and forming the shape of a bar magnet giving a distinct North and South pole. Then by either moving the wire or changing the magnetic field a voltage and current can be induced within the coil and this process is known as Electromagnetic Induction, which is the basic principle of operation of DC generators.

48(A). A.C generator works on the principle of force experience by a conductor in magnetic field. AC generators work on the principle of Faraday's law of electromagnetic induction, which states that electromotive force – EMF or voltage – is generated in a current-carrying conductor that cuts a uniform magnetic field.

49(A). Filtration is the principle used for purification of blood in kidneys.
Blood flows into your kidney through the renal artery. This large blood vessel branches into smaller and smaller blood vessels until the blood reaches the nephrons. In the nephron, your blood is filtered by the tiny blood vessels of the glomeruli and then flows out of your kidney through the renal vein.

50(C). Collecting duct is the part of nephron pours urine into the ureter.
The last part of a long, twisting tube that collects urine from the nephrons (cellular structures in the kidney that filter blood and form urine) and moves it into the renal pelvis and ureters. Also called renal collecting tubule.

51(D).

(A) Calcium hydroxide	(iii) Whitewash
(B) Ammonium hydroxide	(iv) Window cleaner
(C) Sodium hydroxide	(ii) Soap
(D) Magnesium hydroxide	(i) Antacid

Calcium hydroxide: The solution of the substance used for whitewashing is calcium oxide also called quicklime with the chemical formula CaO. Quicklime is used for whitewashing as it produces calcium hydroxide (CaOH) when it reacts with water (H_2O) and absorbs carbon dioxide (CO_2) from the environment, as a result, it produces calcium carbonate ($CaCO_3$) which creates a hard coating on the walls.
Ammonium hydroxide: Ammonium hydroxide is used for window cleaning. Ammonia evaporates quickly, it's most often used as a component in glass cleaning solutions to prevent the appearance of streaks.
Sodium hydroxide: Soap making requires sodium hydroxide, which is more commonly known as caustic soda or lye. That means every soap found in the market has been made using lye. As long as the other ingredients are natural, the soap will stay natural during the soap-making process because lye is not present in the final product.
Magnesium hydroxide: Magnesium hydroxide is used as an Antacid. Magnesium hydroxide reduces stomach acid and increases water in the intestines.

52(A). A substance which detects the acidic or basic nature of another substance by change in colour is called acid-base indicator. Indicators are substances whose solutions change color due to changes in pH. They are usually weak acids or bases, but their conjugate base or acid forms have different colors due to differences in their absorption spectra. So, acid-base indicators are used to check if a given substance is acid or base.

53(C). The pupil of an eye provide a variable aperture, whose size is controlled by iris.
a) When the light is bright: Iris contracts the pupil, so that less light enters the eye.
b) When the light is dim: Iris expand the pupil, so that more light enters the eye. Pupil open completely, when iris is relaxed.

54(A). Let the resistance of each resistor is R.
In series , equivalent resistance is
$R_S = nR$
According to question, Number of resistances is 8.
$\Rightarrow 48 = 8R\,\Omega$
$\Rightarrow R = 6\,\Omega$
In parallel, equivalent resistance is
$R_p = \dfrac{R}{n}$
$\Rightarrow R_p = \dfrac{6}{8}$
$\Rightarrow \dfrac{3}{4}\,\Omega$

55(D). As we know,
R=10 Ω
Voltage Rating $= 1.5V$
From Ohm's law,
$V = IR$
$\Rightarrow I = \dfrac{V}{R}$
$\Rightarrow \dfrac{1.5}{10}$
$\Rightarrow 0.15\,A$
$\rightarrow 150\,mA$

56(B). Own groundwater pumping devices are most of the housing societies or colonies in the cities resourcing their water needs.
You would find that most of these have their own groundwater pumping devices to meet their water needs. Not surprisingly, we find that fragile water resources are being over-exploited and have caused their depletion in several of these cities.

57(A).
They obtain different products directly and indirectly from the forests and wildlife such as wood, barks, leaves, rubber, medicines, dyes, food, fuel, fodder, manure, etc.

58(A). Ballari-Chitradurga-Chikkamagaluru-Tumakuru belt in Karnataka has large reserves of Iron ore.
The Kudermukh mines located in the Western Ghats of Karnataka are a 100 per cent export unit. Kudremukh deposits are known to be one of the largest in the world. The southernmost iron ore belt of India is Bellary-Chitradurga-Chikmaglur-Tumkur belt in Karnataka. Three characteristics of this belt are: It has large reserves of iron ore in India. The Kundermukh mines are located in the Western Ghats of Karnataka. Its deposits are one of the largest in the world and the ore is transported as slurry through a pipeline to a port near Mangalore.

59(B). Greater the development of the primary and secondary sector more would be the demand for such services.
The sectors all work together to create an economic chain of production. The primary sector gathers the raw materials, the secondary sector puts the raw materials to use, and the tertiary sector sells and supports the activities of the other two. Together these sectors make up the backbone of the modern economy. Share of primary (comprising agriculture, forestry, fishing, and mining & quarrying), secondary (comprising manufacturing, electricity, gas, water supply & other utility services, and construction), and tertiary (services) sectors have been estimated as 21.82 percent, 24.29 percent, and 53.89 percent.

60(C). The full form of UNDP is United Nations Development Programme.
The United Nations Development Programme (UNDP) is the United Nations' global development network. Headquartered in New York City, UNDP advocates for change and connects countries to knowledge, experience and resources to help people build a better life. It provides expert advice, training, and grants support to developing countries, with increasing emphasis on assistance to the least developed countries.

61(C). The Civil Code of 1004 also known as The Napoleonic Code.
The civil code is the napoleonic code established by napoleon in 1804. The code did not allow privileges based on birth (such as nobility). It allowed freedom of religion. It also set up a system of Civil service where government jobs would go

to the most qualified.The Civil code was exported to the regions under French control in the Dutch Republic, Switzerland, Italy and Germany.

62(A). Monsoon is the main dependency of primitive farming. Primitive farming is also called 'slash and burn' agriculture.
The following are the disadvantages of primitive subsistence farming:
- Such type of farming is dependent on monsoon.
- It results in natural fertility of soil.

63(D). Modern forms of money include currency, paper notes, coins, Plastic money, Demand deposits. Unlike the things that were used as money earlier, modern currency is not made of precious metals such as gold, silver, and copper. And unlike grain and cattle, they are neither of everyday use.

64(D). Everyone prefers to receive payments in money.
Goods and services can be bought and sold with the use of money. For example, someone who wants shoes can buy it with money and if someone wants to sell shoes, that also can be done by receiving money. Money is used as a medium of exchange because it's the intermediary in the exchange process .

65(A). Globalization is the amalgamation and rapid unification between countries.
Globalization is the word used to describe the growing interdependence of the world's economies, cultures, and populations, brought about by cross-border trade in goods and services, technology, and flows of investment, people, and information. Globalization also have its side effects to the developed nations. These include some factors which are jobs insecurity, fluctuation in prices, terrorism, fluctuation in currency, capital flows and so on. In developed countries people have jobs insecurity.

66(D). Teaching and accounting are services.
A service is a transaction in which no physical goods are transferred from the seller to the buyer. The service economy in developing countries is mostly concentrated in financial services, hospitality, retail, health, human services, information technology and education.

67(D). COPRA does not propose formation of High Court.
COPRA is the popular name of the Consumer Protection Act which was introduced by the Government of India in 1986 in order to protect the rights of the consumers. Under the Consumer Protection Act, a three-tier machinery comprising the District Forum, State Commission and National Commission has been formed with the basic objective of consumer redressal.

68(D). Consumer redressal is not the function of PDS.
The Public Distribution System contributes significantly to the provision of food security. Public Distribution System in the country enables the supply of food grains to the poor at a subsidized price. It also helps to control open - market prices for commodities that are distributed through the system. PDA (Public Distribution System) is a programme that provides food grains and other essential commodities at subsidised prices in rural and urban areas. It helps to control the open market program as for the commodities distributed through the system. It plays an important role in the national food security of the country. It coordinates along with FCI and ensures the proper distribution of the grains. It distributes essentials like wheat, rice, kerosene, sugar, etc.

69(D).
These are the outcomes for which Martine Luther are criticises:
- They were ignored by the church
- A printed copy of this was posted on a church door in Wittenberg. It challenged the Church to debate his ideas.
- Luther's writings were immediately reproduced in vast numbers and read widely.
- This lead to a division within the Church and to the beginning of the Protestant Reformation. Luther's translation of the New Testament sold 5,000 copies within a few weeks

70(D). Heretical is beliefs which do not follow the accepted teachings of Church.
Heresy is any belief or theory that is strongly at variance with established beliefs or customs, in particular the accepted beliefs of a church or religious organization.

71(B). In India and as well as Belgium, power is shared among different organs of a government.
In India it is shared between the three organs and in Belgium between their main and cultural government.
In the basis of power sharing arrangements, India and Belgium both countries are similar to a certain extent. Central government is the highest in both India and Belgium and then other governments are under Central government as well as the State governments. And both countries have 'Holding together federations'.

72(B). Both A and B are true.
Power-sharing in democracy describes a system of governance in which different segments of society are provided a share of power. Power-sharing is good for democracy. Power-sharing helps to reduce the possibility of conflicts between social groups. Power-sharing makes people dependent and responsible.

73(B). In 1885 the big European powers met in Berlin to complete the carving up of Africa between them.
Britain and France made vast additions to their overseas territories in the late nineteenth century. Belgium and Germany became new colonial powers. The US also became a colonial power in the late 1890s by taking over some colonies earlier held by Spain.

74(C). The central government can pass on orders to the provincial or the local government is not key feature of federalism.
Federations are contrasted with unitary governments. Under the unitary system, either there is only one level of government or the sub-units are subordinate to the central government. The central government can pass on orders to the provincial or the local government. But in a federal system, the central government cannot order the state government to do something. The state government has powers of its own for which it is not answerable to the central government. Both these governments are separately answerable to the people.

75(D). Local governments-Residuary powers pair is not correctly matched.
Schedule 7 of the Indian Constitution categorizes the legislative powers into Union List, State List and Concurrent List representing the powers conferred upon the Union, states and shared powers, respectively. The subjects not mentioned in any of the three lists are residuary powers. Parliament shall legislate upon the subjects in residuary list.

76(C). New technology was expensive and merchants and industrialists were cautious about using it this is why the technological didn't changes spread dramatically across the industrial landscape.
Technological changes occurred slowly because:
- New technology was expensive and merchants and industrialists were cautious about using it.
- They did not spread dramatically a cross the industrial landscap.
- The machines often broke down and repair was costly.
- They were not as effective as their inventors and manufacturers claimed.

77(D). Resources which are found in a region, but have not been utilised "Potential Resources.
These resources can be used in the future. For example, mineral oils exist in many parts of India but still, they are not put into use because of the need for the future.
- Developed resources- These are the resources that are surveyed and developed for utilization and are being used currently.

- It is also known as actual resources.
- For example liquid gas and petroleum in Bombay High of Maharashtra.
- Stock-These are resources that we know are present but we don't have any technology to extract them. For example, water is made up of hydrogen and oxygen which is inflammable but we do not know how to extract energy from these two elements.
- International resources- These are resources that belong to all the countries of the world. For example, oceanic resources after 200 km of the international border are controlled by international institutions.

78(D). Democracy is a form of government in which the rulers are elected by the people. This is a form of government that is found in most of the countries of the world. Some countries are still trying to get a democratic form of government. Democracy improves the quality of decision making. Democracy enhances the dignity of citizens. A democratic government is a better government because it is a more accountable form of government.
There are numerous political philosophies and systems, there are five specific types of government that are most common around the world. Most forms of government are some variation of one of the following:
- Authoritarian
- Democracy
- Monarchy
- Oligarchy
- Totalitarian

79(C). Ability to handle Social differences, divisions, and conflicts is regarded as a definite plus point of democratic regimes.
Ability to handle social differences, divisions, and conflicts is regarded as a 'definite plus point' of democratic regimes. The system of separation of powers divides the tasks of the state into three branches: legislative, executive and judicial. These tasks are assigned to different institutions in such a way that each of them can check the others. Due to separation of powers in democracy, it becomes easy for the government to handle social differences, divisions, and conflicts.

80(A). The non-Cooperation-Khilafat Movement begin in August 1920.
Gandhiji supported the Khilafat movement so as to bring unity between the Hindus and Muslims. Mahatma Gandhi was elected as President of the All - India Khilafat Committee in November 1919. He advised the Khilafat committee to adopt a policy of Non- Cooperation with the Government from August 1920 which is marked as the start of the Non-cooperation movement.

81(A). The date on which Bachendri Pal stepped onto the peak of Mount Everest and pitched the Indian National Flag (Tiranga/ Tricolour) is 23rd May, 1984.

82(A). The National Human Rights Commission (NHRC) is an independent statutory body in India and is not under any ministry. The NHRC was established in 1993 by the Protection of Human Rights Act, 1993, and it is responsible for promoting and protecting human rights in India.

83(B). Corporate tax is the single largest source of income to the government of India. It is a levy which the government imposes on the income of a company. The money collected from corporate taxes is used as the source of revenue for a country. Operating earnings of a company are determined by deducting costs from the cost of the product sold (COGS) and income depreciation.

84(A). Rajya Sabha is a permanent House and is not subject to dissolution. However, one-third of Members of the Rajya Sabha retire after every second year. A member who is elected for a full term serves for a period of six years.

85(B). Divergent Boundaries: Where a new crust is generated as the plates pull away from each other. The sites where the plates move away from each other are called spreading sites. The best-known example of divergent boundaries is the Mid-Atlantic Ridge. At this, the American Plate(s) is/are separated from the Eurasian and African Plates.

86(D). The first official Telegraph Line was opened between Kolkata and Diamond harbour. The first experimental electric telegraph line was started between Calcutta (now Kolkata) and Diamond Harbour in November 1850. It was completed and opened for the East India Company's traffic in the year 1851.

87(D). The states of Maharashtra and Gujarat were created in 1960.
Bombay State was finally dissolved with the formation of Maharashtra and Gujarat states on 1 May 1960. Following protests of Samyukta Maharashtra Movement, in which 107 people were killed by police, Bombay State was reorganised on linguistic lines.

88(B). The famous Brihadeshwara Temple is located in thanjavur.
Brihadeshwara Temple is a Hindu temple dedicated to Shiva. It is located in Thanjavur in Tamil Nadu. It was built by Tamil King Raja Raja Chola I. It is also known as Periya Kovil, RajaRajeswara Temple and Rajarajeswaram. It is one of the largest temples in India.

89(A). The four planets closest to the sun - Mercury, Venus, Earth, and Mars are called terrestrial planets.

These planets are solid and rocky like Earth. The Jovian Planets or Outer Planets are Jupiter, Saturn, Uranus, and Neptune because they are all gigantic compared to Earth, and they have gaseous nature.

90(A). During the time of Ashoka and his grandson Dasaratha, the hills of Barabar and Nagarjuni were cut to make houses for the livelihoods.

91(A). Tansen, one of the well-known musicians of medieval India, was in the court of Akbar Mughal emperors.
Emperor Akbar was a great lover of music. Abul Fazl, who was a historian during the reign of the Mughal emperor Akbar, mentioned in his work that Akbar patronised 36 musicians. The most famous among them was Tansen.

92(D). Portuguese were among the first Europeans to come for trade. After them, Dutch Englishmen came to Danish and French. The new sea route to India was discovered by Portuguese merchant Vasco da Gama on 17 May 1948, reaching Calicut, a port on the west coast of India.

93(C). Uranium is an element that consists of atoms of only uranium. Therefore, we can conclude that out of the given options uranium is not a fossil fuel.
Fossil Fuels:
- Fossil fuels are formed by natural processes such as anaerobic decomposition of buried organisms under heat and pressure.
- Fossil fuels like coal, petroleum, natural gas contain high percentages of carbon.
- Fossil fuels are non-renewable resources and must be burned to release their energy.
- It releases sulphur, nitrogen, carbon, etc. gases in the atmosphere which causes the greenhouse effect and pollution.

94(D). The right matching of list-1 and list-2 is A - 2, B - 1, C - 3, D - 4.
Vangala Eshwaraiah, also spelt as V. Eswaraiah was the former chairperson of, National commission for backward classes from 19.09.2013 to September 2016.
The delimitation commission was set up on 12 July 2002 after the 2001 census with Justice Kuldip Singh, a retired Judge of the Supreme Court as its Chairperson.
The first National Commission for Scheduled Tribes (NCST) was constituted in March 2004 and comprised Shri Kunwar Singh, Chairperson but Dr. Rameshwar Oraon assumed office of Chairperson on 28.10.2010.
Lalitha Kumaramangalam (born 1958) is an Indian politician who is a member of the Bharatiya Janata Party (BJP) and former chairperson of the National Commission for Women.

95(A). FIFA has lifted the ban imposed on the All India Football Federation (AIFF) after the Supreme Court terminated the mandate of the Committee of Administrators.

- This decision has cleared the decks for India to host the Women's U-17 World Cup scheduled to take place on 11-30 October 2022.
- FIFA had suspended the All India Football Federation on August 15 due to third-party interference.

96(B). On 16 June 1963, Soviet Cosmonaut Valentina Tereshkova became the first woman to travel into space.

By convention, an astronaut employed by the Russian Federal Space Agency (or its Soviet predecessor) is called a cosmonaut in English texts. Valentina Tereshkova was the first female cosmonaut and the first and youngest woman to have flown in space with a solo mission on the Vostok 6 in 1963. On July 20, 1969, Neil Armstrong became the first human to step on the moon. He and Aldrin walked around for three hours.

97(D). The centre of the Earth is such that if we are at that place, the mass around us can be considered to be condensed at the surface of the Earth itself, i.e considering the Earth as a spherical shell.

Inside a spherical shell, there is no change in potential as one moves inside, and since only a change in potential implies a force there is no force.

Hence the acceleration due to gravity is zero at the centre of the Earth.

98(A). Newton's first law states that, if a body is at rest or moving at a constant speed in a straight line, it will remain at rest or keep moving in a straight line at constant speed unless it is acted upon by force.

99(B). With respect to Industrial Revolution First, coal is also known as "Black Gold".

Coal became very useful at the time of the Industrial Revolution. It is used in Steam engines, the production of electricity, used in the manufacturing of Iron, etc. Because of all these uses, it is commonly known as "Black Gold".

100(A). Luis Caffarelli has won the 2023 Abel Prize for his contributions to regularity theory for nonlinear partial differential equations, including free-boundary problems and the Monge-Ampère equation.

Mathematics

1. To construct a triangle similar to a given $\triangle ABC$ with its sides $\frac{8}{5}$ of the corresponding sides of $\triangle ABC$ draw a ray BX such that $\angle CBX$ is an acute angle and X is on the opposite side of A with respect to BC. The minimum number of points to be located at equal distances on ray BX is:
   (a) 5
   (b) 8
   (c) 13
   (d) 3

2. To construct a triangle similar to given $\triangle ABC$ with its sides $\frac{2}{3}$ of that of $\triangle ABC$, locate points on ray BX at equal distances as $B_1, B_2, B_3, \ldots$. such that $\angle CBX$ is acute. The points to be joined in the next step are:
   (a) B_4, C
   (b) B_3, C
   (c) B_1, C
   (d) B_2, C

3. If $x_1, x_2, x_3, \ldots, x_n$ are the observations of a given data. Then the mean of the observations will be:
   (a) $\dfrac{\text{Sum of observations}}{\text{Total number of observations}}$
   (b) $\dfrac{\text{Total number of observations}}{\text{Sum of observations}}$
   (c) Sum of observations + Total number of observations
   (d) None of these

4. A hemispherical depression is cut out from one face of a cubical wooden block such that the diameter l cm of the hemisphere is equal to the edge of the cube. Determine the surface area of the remaining solid.
   (a) $\frac{1}{2}l^2(12+\pi)cm^2$
   (b) $\frac{1}{4}l^2(24+\pi)cm^2$
   (c) $\frac{1}{3}l^2(18+\pi)cm^2$
   (d) $\frac{1}{4}l^2(18+\pi)cm^2$

5. If two hemispheres of curved surface area $8\pi cm^2$ each are joined together to form a sphere. What is the total surface area of the sphere?
   (a) $4\pi cm^2$
   (b) $32\pi cm^2$
   (c) $8\pi cm^2$
   (d) $16\pi cm^2$

6. If $\tan\theta = \frac{3}{4}$, find the value of $\dfrac{4\sin\theta - 2\cos\theta}{4\sin\theta + 3\cos\theta}$.
   (a) $\frac{2}{3}$
   (b) $\frac{4}{3}$
   (c) $\frac{1}{6}$
   (d) $\frac{5}{6}$

7. The sum of two numbers is 27 and product is 182. The numbers are:
   (a) 12 and 13
   (b) 13 and 14
   (c) 12 and 15
   (d) 13 and 24

8. If $\frac{1}{2}$ is a root of the quadratic equation $x^2 - mx - \frac{5}{4} = 0$, then value of m is:
   (a) 2
   (b) -2
   (c) -3
   (d) 3

9. To warn ships for underwater rocks, a lighthouse spreads a red colored light over a sector of angle $80°$ to a distance of 16.5 km. Find the area of the sea over which the ships warned. $(\pi = 3.14)$
   (a) 189.97 km^2
   (b) 199.97 km^2
   (c) 179.97 km^2
   (d) 188.97 km^2

10. Find the area of the shaded region in the given figure, if $PQ = 24$ cm, $PR = 7$ cm and O is the center of the circle.

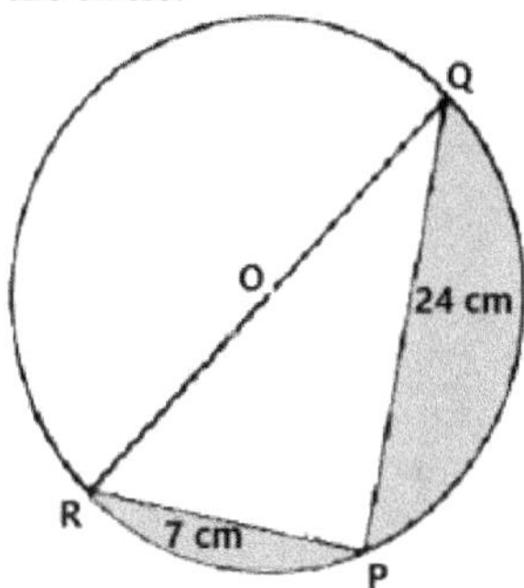

   (a) $\frac{2532}{28}$ cm^2
   (b) $\frac{3532}{28}$ cm^2
   (c) $\frac{4523}{28}$ cm^2
   (d) $\frac{5532}{28}$ cm^2

11. What is the value of $\sin 45° \cdot \cos 90° \cdot \tan 60° \cdot \cos 75° \cdot \cot 30°$?
    (a) 0
    (b) Not defined
    (c) 1
    (d) -1

12. If $\dfrac{\sec 45°}{\cot 60°} = \sqrt{\dfrac{3x}{2}}$, then what is the value of x?
    (a) 4
    (b) 2
    (c) 1
    (d) $\sqrt{2}$

13. If $x + y = \operatorname{cosec} 45°$ and $2x = \sin 30°$, what is the value of y?
    (a) $4\sqrt{2}$
    (b) $\sqrt{2} - \frac{1}{4}$
    (c) $\sqrt{8}$
    (d) $\sqrt{2} + \frac{1}{4}$

14. A part of monthly hostel charges is fixed and the remaining depends on the number of days one has taken food in the mess. When a student A takes food for 20 days she has to pay Rs. 1000 as hostel charges whereas a student B, who takes food for 26 days, pays Rs. 1180 as hostel charges. Find the fixed charges and the cost of food per day.
    (a) Fixed charges Rs. 500, cost of food per day Rs. 60
    (b) Fixed charges Rs. 400, cost of food per day Rs. 30
    (c) Fixed charges Rs. 700, cost of food per day Rs. 90
    (d) Fixed charges Rs. 300, cost of food per day Rs. 30

15. Yash scored 40 marks in a test, getting 3 marks for each right answer and losing 1 mark for each wrong answer. Had 4 marks been awarded for each correct answer and 2 marks been deducted for each incorrect answer, then Yash would have scored 50 marks. How many questions were there in the test?
    (a) 10
    (b) 20
    (c) 30
    (d) 40

16. Find the largest number which divides 70 and 125 leaving remainder 5 and 8 respectively:
    (a) 12
    (b) 13
    (c) 14
    (d) 115

17. Which of the following will be the HCF and LCM of 6, 72 and 120, using the prime factorisation method.
    (a) 5, 225
    (b) 6, 144
    (c) 6, 360
    (d) 4, 241

18. Two tankers contain 850 liters and 680 liters of petrol. Find the maximum capacity of a container which can measure the petrol of each tanker in the exact number of times:
    (a) 150 liters
    (b) 170 liters
    (c) 160 liters
    (d) 180 liters

19. For every positive integer 'n', $n^2 - n$ is divisible by:
    (a) 4
    (b) 8
    (c) 6
    (d) 2

20. What is the number of zeroes of the polynomial $y = p(x)$ in the given graph?

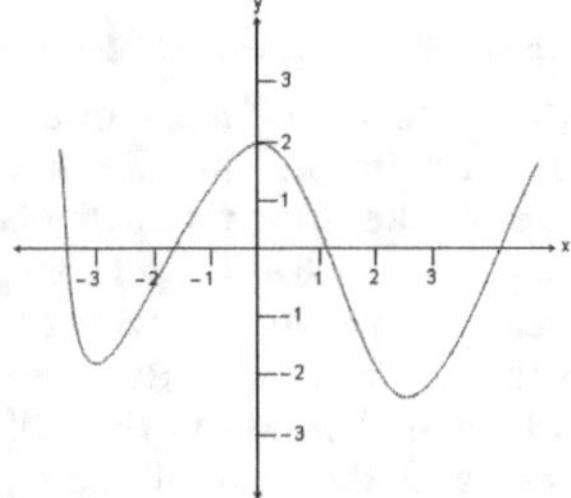

(a) 2   (b) 3
(c) 4   (d) 5

21. On dividing $x^3 + 2x^2 - 4x + 7$ by $x + 2$, the quotient and the remainder are $x^2 - a$ and 15 , respectively. What is the value of a ?
(a) -4 (b) 4
(c) 2   (d) -2

22. A bag contains 5 red balls and some blue balls. If the probability of drawing a blue ball is double that of a red ball, determine the number of blue balls in the bag.
(a) 8   (b) 12
(c) 11   (d) 10

23. Find the nth term of the given sequence.
$-9, -13, -17, -21, -25, \ldots$
(a) $-4n + 5$ (b) $-4n - 5$
(c) $-4n - 2$ (d) $-4n + 2$

24. Find the sum of the first 15 natural numbers:
(a) 155   (b) 125
(c) 120   (d) 132

25. A 6.5 m long ladder is placed against a wall such that its foot is at a distance of 2.5 m from the wall. Find the height of the wall where the top of the ladder touches it.
(a) 3 m   (b) 4 m
(c) 6 m   (d) 10 m

26. In the given figure, $QA \perp AB$ and $PB \perp AB$. If $AO = 20$ cm , $BO = 12$ cm , $PB = 18$ cm, find A .

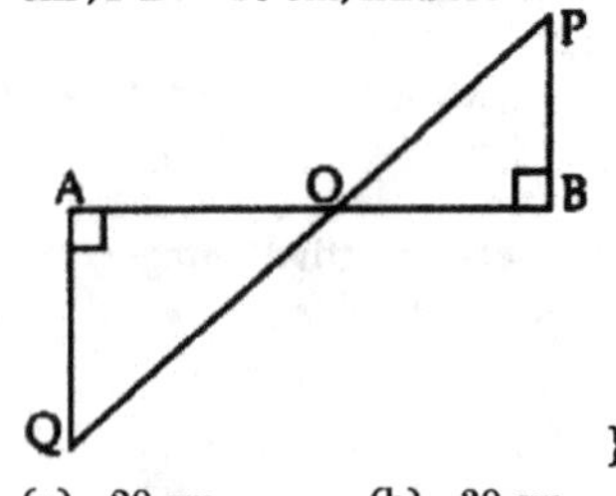

(a) 20 cm   (b) 30 cm
(c) 40 cm   (d) 50 cm

27. The length of tangents drawn from an external point to the circle:
(a) Are equal
(b) Are not equal
(c) Some time equal
(d) None of these

28. In the given figure ' O ' is the centre of the circle and AB, CD are equal chords. If $\angle AOB = 70°$. Find the $\angle OCD = ?$

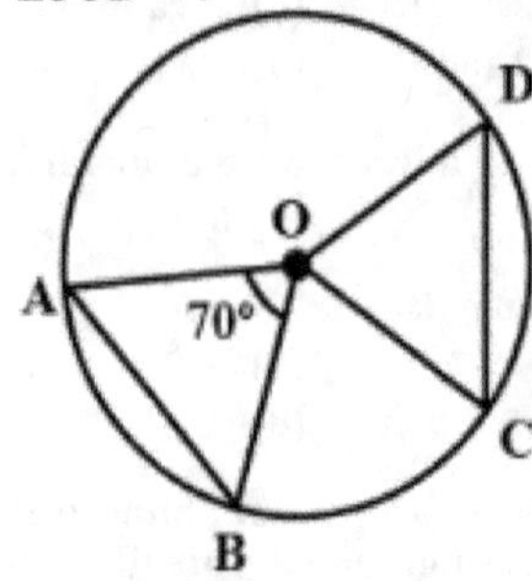

(a) $30°$ (b) $55°$
(c) $75°$ (d) $60°$

29. Find the distance between the points (2,3) and (0,6).
(a) $\sqrt{3}$ (b) $\sqrt{13}$
(c) $\sqrt{14}$ (d) $\sqrt{5}$

30. The perimeter of a triangle with vertices (0,4), (0,0) and (3,0) is:
(a) 8   (b) 10
(c) 12   (d) 15

Science

31. In which of the following trophic levels can the herbivores be found?
(a) First   (b) Second
(c) Third   (d) Fourth

32. _________ is an artificial ecosystem.
(a) Crop field (b) Pond
(c) Lake   (d) Forest

33. Which of the folloMark the correct statements:
(i) mercury can be refined by the process of distillation.
(ii) In poling, the molten impure metal is stirred with green poles of wood.
(iii) In electrolyte refining of metals, impure metal is made as cathode and a thin strip of pure metal is made as anode.wing non-metals exists as a solid at normal temperature and pressure?
(a) (i) and (ii)
(b) (i) and (iii)
(c) (ii) and (iii)
(d) (i), (ii) and (iii)

34. Generally metals reacts with acids to give salt and hydrogen gas. Which of the following acids does not give hydrogen gas on reacting with metals (except Mn and Mg) ?
(a) H_2SO_4 (b) HCl
(c) HNO_3 (d) All of these

35. When a person is suffering from severe cold, he or she cannot _________ .
(a) Differentiate the taste of an apple from that of an ice cream
(b) Differentiate the smell of a perfume from that of an agarbatti
(c) Differentiate red light from green light
(d) Differentiate a hot object from a cold object

36. The brain is lodged inside the cavity of the skull known as:
(a) Piamater (b) Duramater
(c) Cranium (d) Meninges

37. Which of the following statements is true about the precipitation reactions?
(a) In these reactions, all the reactants and products are in their solid states.
(b) In these reactions, only the reactants are in their solid state.
(c) In these reactions, one of the products formed is in the solid state.
(d) In these reactions, all the products formed are in their solid states.

38. Which two gases are released on heating lead nitrate?
(a) NO, O_2 (b) NO_2, O_2
(c) N_2O, O_2 (d) SO_2, O_2

39. The I.U.P.A.C name of $CH_3 CH_2 CH{=}CH_2$ is:
(a) 3-Butene (b) Prop-1-ene
(c) But-1-ene (d) Butyne

40. Which of the following compounds of carbon does not consist of ions?
(a) $CHCl_3$ (b) $CaCO_3$
(c) $NaHCO_3$ (d) $Ca_2 C$

41. Fusion of male and female gametes is called:
(a) Pollination (b) Fertilization
(c) Budding (d) Spore

42. The female reproductive hormone is:
(a) Testosterone (b) Osteocalcin
(c) Adrenaline (d) Estrogen

43. The human traits are influenced by the DNA of .
(a) mother

(b) father

(c) siblings

(d) Both (1) and (2)

44. **How many pairs of contrasting traits were considered by Mendel in the pea plant?**

(a) 6   (b) 7

(c) 8   (d) 9

45. **How does the frequency of a beam of ultra-violet light change when it goes from air into glass?**

(a) Frequency increases

(b) Frequency decreases

(c) Remains the same

(d) None of these

46. **Where will the image be formed if the object is at the focus of the concave mirror?**

(a) Infinity

(b) Beyond C

(c) Between C and F

(d) At C

47. **Which of the following components of electric motor, acts as a commutator?**

(a) Axle   (b) Magnets

(c) Brushes   (d) Split Rings

48. **The instrument that use to defect electric current in the circuit is known as:**

(a) Electric motor

(b) A.C generator

(c) Galvanometer

(d) None of the above

49. **Glottis opens at the surface of :**

(a) diaphragm

(b) bucco pharyngeal cavity

(c) trachea

(d) None of these

50. **Where does aerobic respiration take place in the cell?**

(a) Mitochondria

(b) Cytoplasm

(c) Nucleus

(d) Chloroplast

51. **Which of the following substances is not a visual indicator?**

(a) Litmus paper

(b) Vanilla essence

(c) Methyl orange

(d) Turmeric

52. **Equal volumes of hydrochloric acid and sodium hydroxide solutions of same concentration are mixed and the pH of the resulting solution is**

checked with a pH paper. What would be the colour obtained?

(a) Red

(b) Yellow

(c) Yellowish green

(d) Blue

53. **At what rate the event should be projected to have the clear image?**

(a) 25 frames per second

(b) 20 frames per second

(c) 22 frames per second

(d) 24 frames per second

54. **A current of** 0.5 **A is drawn by a filament of an electric bulb for** 10 **minutes. Find the amount of electric charge that flows through the circuit.**

(a) 200 C   (b) 250 C

(c) 400 C   (d) 300 C

55. **A current of** 2 A **passing through a conductor produces** 80 J **of heat in** 10 **seconds. The resistance of the conductor is:**

(a) 0.5Ω (b) 2Ω

(c) 4Ω (d) 20Ω

Social Science

56. **Even if there is ample amount of water in certain places there is hazardous water pollution, what are the causes?**

(a) Domestic and industrial wastes

(b) Wastage of water

(c) Over storage

(d) Community water pumps

57. **The greatest damage inflicted on Indian forests was during the colonial period due to_____.**

(a) Expansion of the railways, agriculture

(b) Trade

(c) Industry

(d) Taking complete control over the Indian forests

58. **______ is the largest producer of manganese ores in India.**

(a) Jharkhand

(b) Odisha

(c) Madhya Pradesh

(d) West Bengal

59. **Identify the natural product from the list of items given below:**

(a) Textile

(b) Wheat flour

(c) Cotton

(d) Tomato sauce

60. **Cause of high infant mortality rate is:**

(a) inadequate facilities of health

(b) lack of infrastructural facilities

(c) lack of awareness

(d) both (A) and (B)

61. **In mid-eighteenth-century Europe what was the status of Germany, Italy and Switzerland?**

(a) They were divided into kingdoms, duchies and cantons whose rulers had their autonomous territories.

(b) They were sovereign states.

(c) They were democracies.

(d) They were republics.

62. **What type of seed does the golden yellow tag represent?**

(a) Breeder seed

(b) Certified seed

(c) Foundation seed

(d) Registered seed

63. **No individual in India can:**

(a) Legally refuse a payment made in rupees

(b) Legally refuse a payment made by cheque

(c) Legally refuse a payment made by draft

(d) All the above

64. **Which of the following methods can reduce the dependence on informal sector?**

(a) Banks and cooperatives increase their lending particularly in the rural areas,

(b) Interest rates are decreased on credit

(c) Formal sector loans expands, and everyone receives loans

(d) All the above

65. **Which Indian Company has emerged as an MNC?**

(a) Mahindra & Mahindra

(b) Tata Motors

(c) Renault

(d) Maruti Suzuki

66. **______ has helped most in the spread of production of services?**

(a) Email   (b) Telegraph

(c) Call centres   (d) Fax

67. **Hallmark is the certification maintained for standardisation for which one of the following?**

(a) Jewellery

(b) Electrical goods

(c) Edible oil

(d) Refrigeration

68. **A shopkeeper insists that you buy a guide along with your NCERT textbook. Which right of the consumer is being violated?**
(a) Right to be informed
(b) Right to choose
(c) Right to information
(d) Right to safety

69. **Why did the Roman Church begin to maintain an Index of Prohibited Books from 1558?**
(i) Interference of foreign writers
(ii) Giving too many independent beliefs to people through books
(iii) Troubled by such effects of popular readings and questionings of faith
(iv) Writing and printing of heretical beliefs
(a) (i) only
(b) (i) and (ii)
(c) (ii), (iii) and (iv)
(d) (iii) and (iv)

70. **In the seventeenth and eighteenth centuries how did literacy rates grow?**
(a) Churches of different denominations set up schools in villages, carrying literacy to peasants and artisans
(b) The government took strong initiative to open schools
(c) Individual teacher to student teaching took on a major growth
(d) Self learning became the passion among people

71. **In which one of the following year Sri Lanka emerged as an independent country?**
(a) 1947   (b) 1948
(c) 1949   (d) 1950

72. **How many times was Belgium constitution amended between 1970 to 1993?**
(a) Three times (b) Four times
(c) Five times   (d) Six times

73. **People's livelihoods and local economy of which one of the following was badly affected by the disease named Rinderpest?**
(a) Asia
(b) Europe
(c) Africa
(d) South America

74. **In 'holding together federation' which government tends to be more powerful?**

(a) Central
(b) State
(c) Some times central and some time state
(d) Both have equal power

75. **Mark the correct example of 'coming together' federations.**
(a) India   (b) Spain
(c) USA   (d) China

76. **Who improved the steam engine produced by Newcomen and patented the new engine in 1781?**
(a) James Watt
(b) Mathew Boulton
(c) Richard Arkwright
(d) Henry Patullo

77. **Which one of the following statements is true about the term resources?**
(a) Resources are free gifts of nature.
(b) They are the functions of human activities.
(c) All those things which are found in nature.
(d) Things which cannot be used to fulfill our needs.

78. **Which of the following countries has the most stable democracy?**
(a) U.S.A   (b) Pakistan
(c) Norway   (d) Sri Lanka

79. **A government that takes decision by following norms and a proper procedure is:**
(a) An accountable government
(b) A responsible government
(c) A transparent government
(d) A stable government

80. **Which British officer open- fired at the Jallianwala Bagh congregation?**
(a) Sir John Simon
(b) General Dyer
(c) Montgomery
(d) Mountbatten

General Awareness/ Knowledge

81. **Kamala Narayan is known for which classical dance form?**
(a) Bharatanatyam
(b) Kathakali
(c) Odissi
(d) Kathak

82. **Which one of the following is not included in the state list in the**

Constitution of India?
(a) Police
(b) Law and Order
(c) Prison
(d) Criminal Procedure Code

83. **Examine the following statements:**
A. Dr. V.K.R.V Rao was the first person to estimate national income in India before independence.
B. Soon after independence, the central government appointed the 'National Income Committee' to estimate national income in India.
C. Dr. V. K. R. V. Rao was appointed as the chairman of the committee.
Choose the correct answer:
(a) A & C only   (b) B only
(c) C only   (d) A & B only

84. **Who was the Chief Justice of India when public interest litigation was introduced to the Indian Judicial System?**
(a) A. M. Ahmadi
(b) M. Hidayatullah
(c) A. S. Anand
(d) P. N. Bhagwati

85. **Which one of the following is not related to the function of a river?**
(a) River visarp (b) Natural dam
(c) Sandur   (d) Yazoo

86. **The world's first railway steam engine was invented by ______.**
(a) Otto Hahn
(b) James Watt
(c) Henri Becquerel
(d) Ernest Rutherford

87. **Which of the following is the capital of the Union Territory Daman and Diu?**
(a) Daman   (b) Diu
(c) Dabhel   (d) Bhimpore

88. **The paintings of Ajanta belongs to which religion?**
(a) Jain   (b) Sanatan
(c) Buddhism   (d) Christian

89. **Which is the longest mountain range in the lesser Himalayas?**
(a) Dhauladhar range
(b) Mahabharat range
(c) Pir Panjal range
(d) Shivalik range

90. **Therigatha is a part of________.**
(a) sutta pitaka
(b) vinay pitaka
(c) abhidhamma pitaka
(d) dirghanikaya

91. Mehrunnisa married Emperor Jahangir in ___.
(a) 1620   (b) 1602
(c) 1611   (d) 1603

92. When was the Lahore session of the Indian National Congress held?
(a) 1931   (b) 1929
(c) 1921   (d) 1930

93. 3/4th of our earth contains:
(a) Land   (b) Water
(c) Metals   (d) Non-metals

94. Which of the following is not the powers of Rajya Sabha?
(a) It makes laws on matters included in the Union List and the Concurrent List.
(b) It approves proposals for taxation, budgets and annual financial statements.
(c) It considers and approves non-money bills and suggests amendments to money bills.
(d) It approves the proclamation of emergency.

95. Mumtaz Khan, who was named the Emerging Player of the Year 2022 by the International Hockey Federation (FIH), belongs to which district?
(a) Azamgarh   (b) Lucknow
(c) Banda   (d) Chitrakoot

96. Who has become the first Indian woman to scale Mt Annapurna?
(a) Premlata Agrawal
(b) Shivangi Pathak
(c) Priyanka Mohite
(d) Santosh Yadav

97. Chemically silk fibers are predominantly___.
(a) Protein
(b) Carbohydrate
(c) Complex lipid
(d) Mixture of polysaccharide and fat

98. The casual organism of Polio is:
(a) A fungi   (b) A virus
(c) A worm   (d) A bacteria

99. When did the First World War start?
(a) 1845   (b) 1914
(c) 1714   (d) 1945

100. Who has been selected for the John F. Kennedy award 2022 in Courage Award for acting to protect democracy?
(a) Sahle-Work Zewde
(b) Narendra Modi
(c) Volodymyr Zelensky
(d) Boris Johnson

// Hints and Solutions //

1(B). To construct a triangle similar to a given triangle with its sides $\frac{m}{n}$ of the corresponding sides of given triangle, the minimum number of points to be located at equal distance is equal to the greater of m and n in $\frac{m}{n}$.

Here, $\frac{m}{n} = \frac{8}{5}$

So, m is greater then n,
∴ The minimum number of points to be located at equal distances on ray BX is 8.

2(B).

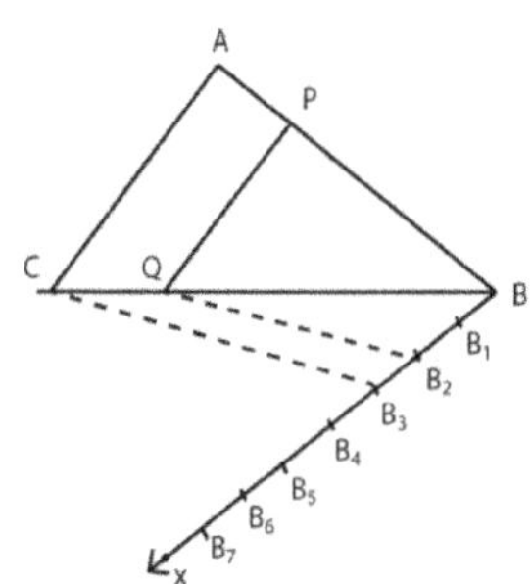

$\triangle PQB$ is the required triangle.
Since side BQ is $\frac{2}{3}$ times side BC.

$BQ = \frac{2}{3} \times (BQ + CQ)$
$\Rightarrow 3BQ = 2BQ + 2CQ$
$\Rightarrow BQ = 2CQ$
$\Rightarrow \frac{CQ}{BQ} = \frac{1}{2}$

Therefore, Q divides BC in ratio 2 : 1.
So, point B_3 should be connected to C, and B_2Q should be drawn parallel to B_3C.

3(A). The mean or average of observations will be equal to the ratio of sum of observations and total number of observations.

$$x_{\text{mean}} = \frac{x_1 + x_2 + x_3 + \ldots + x_n}{n}$$

4(B). As we know,
Surface area of cube $= 6(\text{side})^2$
Curved surface area of hemisphere $= 2\pi r^2$
Base area of hemisphere $= \pi r^2$
Given,
Diameter of hemisphere $= l\,cm$
Radius of hemisphere $(r) = \frac{l}{2}\,cm$
Curved surface area of hemisphere
$= 2\pi\left(\frac{l}{2}\right)^2 = \frac{2\pi l^2}{4} = \frac{\pi l^2}{2}$

Base area of hemisphere $= \pi\left(\frac{l}{2}\right)^2 = \frac{\pi l^2}{4}$

Surface area of the remaining solid = Surface area of cube + Curved surface area of hemisphere - Base area of hemisphere
∴ Surface area of the remaining solid
$= 6l^2 + \frac{\pi l^2}{2} - \frac{\pi l^2}{4}$
$= \frac{24l^2 + 2\pi l^2 - \pi l^2}{4}$
$= \frac{l^2(24 + 2\pi - \pi)}{4}$
$= \frac{l^2}{4} \times (24 + \pi)\,cm^2$

5(D). Given,
The curved surface area of each sphere $= 8\pi cm^2$
As we know,
Total surface area of the sphere = Curved surface area of first hemisphere + Curved surface area of the second hemisphere
∴ Total surface area of the sphere $= (8\pi + 8\pi)cm^2 = 16\pi cm^2$

6(C). Given,
$\tan \theta = \frac{3}{4}$
Now,
$\frac{4\sin\theta - 2\cos\theta}{4\sin\theta + 3\cos\theta}$
Dividing both numerator and denominator by $\cos\theta$ we get,
$= \frac{\frac{4\sin\theta}{\cos\theta} - 2\frac{\cos\theta}{\cos\theta}}{\frac{4\sin\theta}{\cos\theta} + 3\frac{\cos\theta}{\cos\theta}}$
$= \frac{4\tan\theta - 2}{4\tan\theta + 3}$
$= \frac{4 \times \frac{3}{4} - 2}{4 \times \frac{3}{4} + 3} \quad \left[\because \tan\theta = \frac{3}{4}\right]$
$= \frac{3-2}{3+3}$
$= \frac{1}{6}$
$\therefore \frac{4\sin\theta - 2\cos\theta}{4\sin\theta + 3\cos\theta} = \frac{1}{6}$

7(B). Let x is one number.
Another number $= 27 - x$
Product of two numbers $= 182$
$x(27 - x) = 182$
$\Rightarrow x^2 - 27x + 182 = 0$
$\Rightarrow x^2 - 13x - 14x + 182 = 0$
$\Rightarrow x(x - 13) - 14(x - 13) = 0$
$\Rightarrow (x - 13)(x - 14) = 0$
$\Rightarrow x = 13 \text{ or } x = 14$

8(B). Given,
$x = \frac{1}{2}$ as root of equation
$x^2 - mx - \frac{5}{4} = 0$.
$\left(\frac{1}{2}\right)^2 - m\left(\frac{1}{2}\right) - \frac{5}{4} = 0$
$\frac{1}{4} - \frac{m}{2} - \frac{5}{4} = 0$
$m = -2$

9(A).

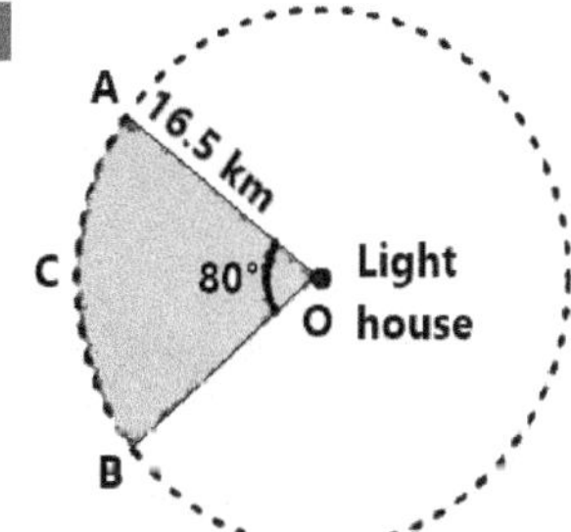

Given,
The lighthouse spreads light across a sector (represented by shaded part in the figure) of 80° in a circle of 16.5 km radius.
Area of sector $OACB = \frac{\theta}{360°} \times \pi r^2$

Area of sector $OACB = \frac{80°}{360°} \times \pi r^2$

$= \frac{2}{9} \times 3.14 \times (16.5)^2$

$= 189.97 \text{ km}^2$

So, the area of the sea over which the ships are warned is 189.97 km^2.

10(C). Given,

$PQ = 24$ cm , $PR = 7$ cm and O is the center of the circle

From the given figure,

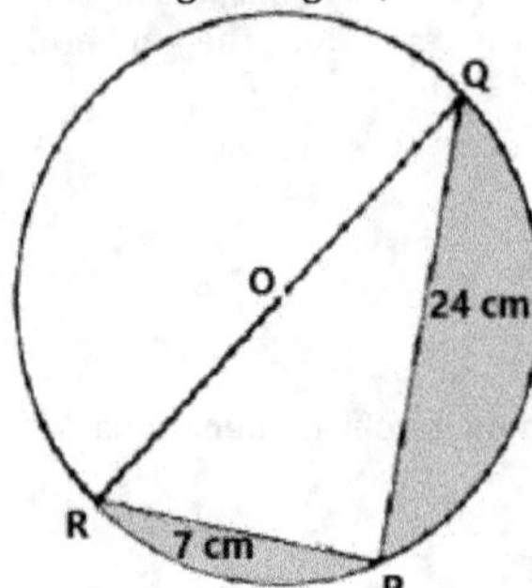

As we know,

The angle in a semicircle is right angle

RQ is the diameter of the circle which implies that $\angle RPQ = 90°$

Thus,

By applying Pythagoras theorem in $\triangle PQR$,

$(\text{Hypotenuse})^2 = (\text{Height})^2 + (\text{Base})^2$

$\Rightarrow RP^2 + PQ^2 = RQ^2$

$\Rightarrow (7)^2 + (24)^2 = RQ^2$

$RQ = \sqrt{625}$

$\Rightarrow RQ = 25$

Thus, Radius of circle, $OR = \frac{RQ}{2} = \frac{25}{2}$

We know that, RQ is the diameter of the circle, it divides the circle in two equal parts.

So,

Area of shaded region = Area of semi circle $RPQOR$ − Area of $\triangle PQR$

Area of semicircle $= \frac{1}{2}\pi r^2$

$= \frac{1}{2}\pi\left(\frac{25}{2}\right)^2$

$= \frac{1}{2} \times \frac{22}{7} \times \frac{625}{4}$

$= \frac{6875}{28} \text{ cm}^2$

Area of $\triangle PQR = \frac{1}{2} \times PQ \times PR$

$= \frac{1}{2} \times 24 \times 7$

$= 84 \text{ cm}^2$

Area of shaded region = Area of semi circle $RPQOR$ − Area of $\triangle PQR$

$= \frac{6875}{28} - 84 = \frac{4523}{28} \text{ cm}^2$

Therefore, the area of the shaded region in the given figure is $\frac{4523}{28} \text{ cm}^2$.

11(A). From the basic formula we can get the value of the following:

$\sin 45° = \frac{1}{\sqrt{2}}$

$\cos 90° = 0$

$\tan 60° = \sqrt{3}$

$\cos 75° = \frac{(\sqrt{6} - \sqrt{2})}{4}$

$\cos 75° = \cos(30° + 45°)$

$= \cos 30° \cos 45 - \sin 30° \sin 45°$

$= \frac{\sqrt{3}}{2} \times \frac{1}{\sqrt{2}} - \frac{1}{2} \times \frac{1}{\sqrt{2}}$

$\cos 75 = \frac{\sqrt{3}-1}{2\sqrt{2}}$

$\cot 30° = \sqrt{3}$

$\therefore \sin 45° \cdot \cos 90° \cdot \tan 60° \cdot \cos 75° \cdot \cot 30°$

$= \frac{1}{\sqrt{2}} \times 0 \times \sqrt{3} \times \frac{\sqrt{3}-1}{2\sqrt{2}} \times \sqrt{3}$

$= 0$

12(A). Given,

$\frac{\sec 45°}{\cot 60°} = \sqrt{\frac{3x}{2}}$

On Squaring we get,

$\frac{\sec^2 45°}{\cot^2 60°} = \left(\sqrt{\frac{3x}{2}}\right)^2$

$\left(\frac{\sqrt{2}}{\frac{1}{\sqrt{3}}}\right)^2 = \left(\sqrt{\frac{3x}{2}}\right)^2$

$\Rightarrow \frac{2}{\frac{1}{3}} = \frac{3x}{2}$

$\Rightarrow \frac{2}{1} \times \frac{3}{1} = \frac{3x}{2}$

$\Rightarrow x = \frac{2 \times 2 \times 3}{3}$

$= 4$

13(B). Given,

$2x = \sin 30°$

As we know,

$\sin 30° = \frac{1}{2}$

$\Rightarrow 2x = \frac{1}{2}$

$\Rightarrow x = \frac{1}{4}$

Put the value of x in $x + y = \text{cosec } 45°$

$\frac{1}{4} + y = \sqrt{2}$

$y = \sqrt{2} - \frac{1}{4}$

14(B). Let Fixed charge Rs. $= x$

Charge per day taken for food $=$ Rs. y per day

Given,

Charge paid by student A for 20 days is Rs. 1000

Fixed charge $+ 20 \times ($ Charge per day $) = 1000$

$x + 20y = 1000 \qquad \ldots\ldots (1)$

Also, Charge paid by student B for 26 days is Rs. 1180

Fixed charge $+ 26 \times ($ Charge per day $) =$ Rs. 1180

$x + 26y = 1180 \qquad \ldots\ldots (2)$

So, our equations are

$x + 20y = 1000 \qquad \ldots\ldots (1)$

$x + 26y = 1180 \qquad \ldots\ldots (2)$

From (1),

$x + 20y = 1000$

$x = 1000 - 20y$

Putting value of x in (2),

$x + 26y = 1180$

$(1000 - 20y) + 26y = 1180$

$-20y + 26y = 1180 - 1000$

$6y = 180$

$y = \frac{180}{6}$

$y = 30$

Putting $y = 30$ in equation (1),

$x + 20y = 1000$

$x + 20(30) = 1000$

$x + 600 = 1000$

$x = 1000 - 600$

$x = 400$

So, $x = 400, y = 30$ is the solution of the equations.

So, Fixed charges, $x =$ Rs. 400

Charge per day, $y =$ Rs. 30 per day

15(B). Let Number of right answers be x

Number of wrong answers be y

Given that,

Yash scored 40 marks if he get 3 marks for right answer and lose 1 mark for wrong answer,

		Marks	Total
Right answer	x	3	$3x - y$
Wrong answer	y	−1	

$3x - y = 40 \qquad \ldots\ldots (1)$

Also,

Yash scored 50 marks if he gets 4 marks for correct answer and loses 2 mark for wrong answer.

		Marks	Total
Right answer	x	4	$4x - 2y$
Wrong answer	y	−2	

$4x - 2y = 50$

$2(2x - y) = 50$

$(2x - y) = \frac{50}{2}$

$2x - y = 25 \qquad \ldots\ldots (2)$

So, our equations are

$3x - y = 40$

$2x - y = 25$

From (1),

$3x - y = 40$

$3x - 40 = y$

$y = 3x - 40$

Putting value of y in (2),

$2x - y = 25$

$2x - (3x - 40) = 25$

$2x - 3x + 40 = 25$

$2x - 3x = 25 - 40$

$-x = -15$

$x = 15$

Putting x in (1),

$3x - y = 40$

$3(15) - y = 40$

$3(15) - y = 40$

$45 - y = 40$

$45 - 40 = y$

$5 = y$

$y = 5$

Therefore $x = 15, y = 5$ is the solution

So, Number of right answers $= x = 15$

Number of wrong answers $= y = 5$

Total questions in the test $= x + y$

$= 15 + 5$

$= 20$

16(B). It is given that on dividing 70 and

125 leaving remainder 5 and 8 respectively. This means that $70 - 5 = 65$ is exactly divisible by the required number. Similarly, $125 - 8 = 117$ is also exactly divisible by the required number. We have to find out the HCF of 65 and 117.
$65 = 5 \times 13$
$117 = 3^2 \times 13$
HCF $= 13$
Required number $= 13$

17(C). Given:
The numbers are 6, 72 and 120.
Factorisation of these numbers;
$6 = 2 \times 3$,
$72 = 2^3 \times 3^2$,
$120 = 2^3 \times 3 \times 5$
Here, 2^1 and 3^1 are the smallest powers of the common factors 2 and 3, respectively.
So,   HCF   of
$(6, 72, 120) = 2^1 \times 3^1 = 2 \times 3 = 6$
$2^3, 3^2$ and 5^1 are the greatest powers of the prime factors 2, 3 and 5 respectively involved in the three numbers.
So, LCM of $(6, 72, 120) = 2^3 \times 3^2 \times 5^1 = 360$

18(B). To find the maximum capacity of a container which can measure the petrol of each tanker in the exact number of times, we find the HCF of 850 and 680.
$850 = 2 \times 5^2 \times 17$
$680 = 2^3 \times 5 \times 17$
HCF $= 2 \times 5 \times 17 = 170$
Maximum capacity of the container $= 170$ liters.

2	850
5	425
5	85
	17

2	680
2	340
2	170
5	85
	17

19(D). Case I : Let n be an even positive integer. When $n = 2q$
In   this   case,   we   have
$n^2 - n = (2q)^2 - 2q = 4q^2 - 2q = 2q(2q - 1)$
$n^2 - n = 2r$, where $r = q(2q - 1)$
$n^2 - n$ is divisible by 2.
Case II: Let n be an odd positive integer.
When $n = 2q + 1$
In this case
$n^2 - n = (2q + 1)^2 - (2q + 1) = (2q + 1)(2q + 1 - 1) = 2q(2q + 1)$
$n^2 - n = 2r$, where $r = q(2q + 1)$
$n^2 - n$ is divisible by 2.
$\therefore n^2 - n$ is divisible by 2 for every integer n.

20(C). The number of zeroes of $p(x)$ is the number of times the curve intersects the $x-$ axis, i.e; attains the value 0.
Here, the polynomial $p(x)$ meets the $x-$ axis at 4 points.
So, the number of zeroes $= 4$

21(B). We know that,
Dividend   =   Divisor   ×   Quotient   +   Remainder
Here Dividend $= x^3 + 2x^2 - 4x + 7$
Divisor $= x + 2$
Quotient $= x^2 - a$
Remainder $= 15$
$x^3 + 2x^2 - 4x + 7 = (x + 2) \times (x^2 - a) + 15$
$\Rightarrow x^3 + 2x^2 - 4x + 7 = x^3 - xa + 2x^2 - 2a + 15$
$\Rightarrow 7 - 4x = 15 - xa - 2a$
$\Rightarrow xa + 2a - 4x = 8$
$\Rightarrow xa + 2a = 8 + 4x$
$\Rightarrow a(x + 2) = 4(2 + x)$
$\therefore a = 4$

22(D). Let us consider, the number of blue balls be, x blue balls.
The total number of balls, $5 + x$ balls.
Now, it is also said, the probability of drawing a blue ball is double that of a red ball.
2 (probability of getting a blue ball) = probability of getting a red ball
$\Rightarrow 2\left(\dfrac{\text{number of blue balls}}{\text{total balls}}\right) = \dfrac{\text{number of red balls}}{\text{total balls}}$
Putting the values,
$2\left(\dfrac{5}{5+x}\right) = \dfrac{x}{5+x}$
$\Rightarrow x = 10$
Thus, the number of blue balls is, $x = 10$.

23(B). The general or n^{th} term of an AP is given as;
$T_n = a + (n - 1)d$
Where,
$a =$ first term
$d =$ common difference
Substitution the given values
$\Rightarrow T_n = (-9) + (n - 1) \times -4$
$\Rightarrow T_n = (-9) - 4n + 4$
$\Rightarrow T_n = -4n - 5$

24(C). Here, we need to find the sum of the first 15 natural numbers. We will calculate by using the following formula:
$s = \dfrac{n}{2}[2a + (n - 1)d]$
AP
$= 1, 2, 3, 4, 5, 6, 7, 8, 9, 10, 11, 12, 13, 14, 15$
Given, $a = 1, d = 2 - 1 = 1$ and $a_n = 15$
Now, by the formula, we know,
$\Rightarrow s = \dfrac{n}{2}[2a + (n - 1) \times d] = \dfrac{15}{2}$
$[2 \times 1 + (15 - 1) \times 1]$
$\Rightarrow s = \dfrac{15}{2}[2 + 14] = \dfrac{15}{2}[16] = 15 \times 8$
$\rightarrow s - 120$
So, the sum of the first 15 natural numbers is 120.

25(C). Let AC be the ladder and AB be the wall.
Given,
$AC = 6.5 \text{ m} = \dfrac{13}{2}$ m
$BC = 2.5 \text{ m} = \dfrac{5}{2}$ m

Since the pole is vertical to the ground, it will make a right angle to the ground.
In right angle $\triangle ABC$,
$AB^2 + BC^2 = AC^2$

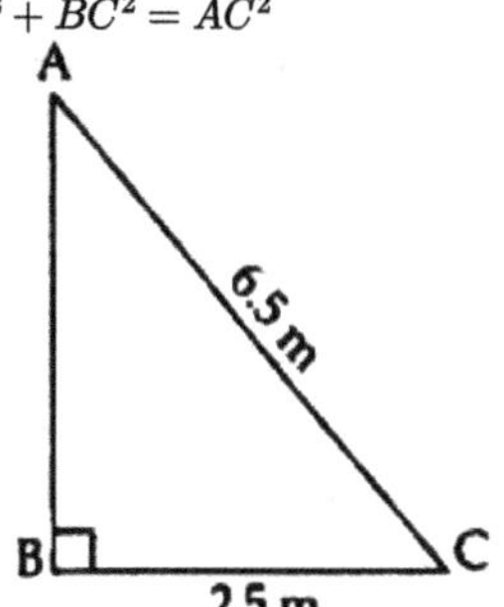

(Using Pythagoras theorem),
$AB^2 + \left(\dfrac{5}{2}\right)^2 = \left(\dfrac{13}{2}\right)^2$
$AB^2 = \dfrac{169}{4} - \dfrac{25}{4}$
$= \dfrac{169-25}{4} = \dfrac{144}{4}$
$= 36$
$AB = 6$ m
$\therefore$ Required height, $AB = 6$ m

26(B).

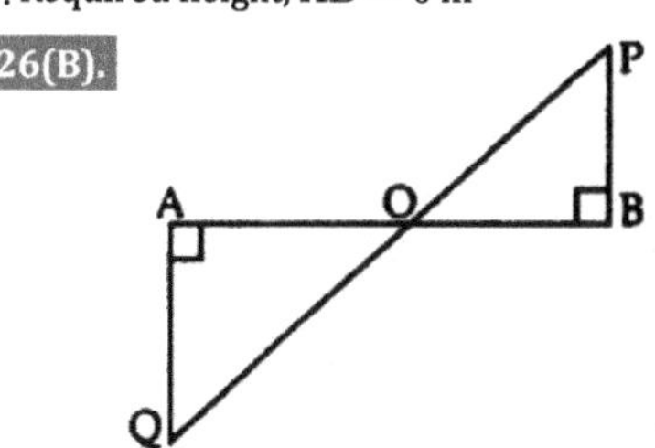

In $\triangle OAQ$ and $\triangle OBP$,
$\angle OAQ = \angle OBP \ldots$ [Each 90°
$\angle AOQ = \angle BOP \ldots ..$ [vertically opposite angles
$\therefore \triangle OAQ \sim \triangle OBP$
[By AA corollary
$\dfrac{AO}{BO} = \dfrac{AQ}{PB}$
$\because$ sides are proportional.
$\dfrac{20}{12} = \dfrac{AQ}{18}$
$\Rightarrow \quad AQ = \dfrac{18 \times 20}{12}$
$AQ = 30$ cm

27(A). As we known that, a tangent at any point of a circle is perpendicular to the radius through the point of contact.
Draw a circle with centre O; PA and PB are two tangents to the circle drawn from an external point P. Join $OA, OB,$ and OP.

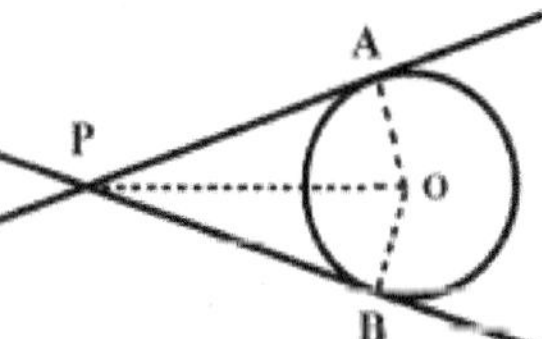

$OA \perp PA$
$OB \perp PB$
In $\triangle OPA$ and $\triangle OPB$
$\angle OPA = \angle OPB$ (Using (1))
$OA = OB$ (Radii of the same circle)
$OP = OP$ (Common side)
Therefore $\triangle OPA \cong \triangle OPB$ (RHS

congruency criterion)

$PA = PB$ (Corresponding parts of congruent triangles are equal)

Thus, it is proved that the lengths of the two tangents drawn from an external point to a circle are equal.

28(B). From the given figure in the question,

In $\triangle AOB$ and $\triangle COD$

$OA = OD$ [both are radius]

$OB = OC$ [both are radius]

$AB = DC$ [Chord are equal]

$\therefore \triangle AOB \cong \triangle COD$ (by s-s-s congruent)

$\therefore \angle AOB = \angle COD = 70°$

Now,

In $\triangle OCD$

$OC = OD$ (both are radius)

Then, $\angle ODC = \angle OCD = x$ (Let)

$\therefore$ Sum of angle of $\triangle = 180°$

$\therefore x + x + 70° = 180°$

$\Rightarrow 2x = 180° - 70°$

$\Rightarrow x = \dfrac{110°}{2}$

$\therefore x = 55°$

So, $\angle ODC = 55°$

29(B). The given two points are $(x_1, y_1) = (2, 3)$ and $(x_2, y_2) = (0, 6)$

As we know,

Distance between two points is given by,

$d = \sqrt{(x_2 - x_1)^2 + (y_2 - y_1)^2}$

$\Rightarrow d = \sqrt{(0 - 2)^2 + (6 - 3)^2}$

$\Rightarrow d = \sqrt{(-2)^2 + (3)^2}$

$\Rightarrow d = \sqrt{4 + 9}$

$\Rightarrow d = \sqrt{13}$

30(C).

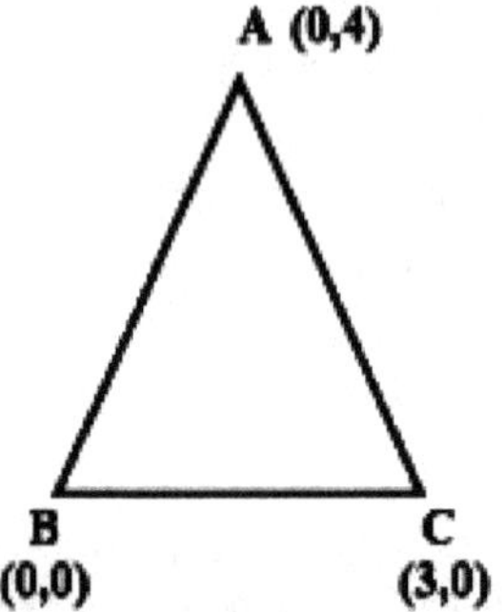

Let ABC be a triangle having $A(0, 4), B(0, 0), C(3, 0)$.

Using distance formula, we get

$AB = \sqrt{(0 - 0)^2 + (0 - 4)^2} = \sqrt{16} = 4$

$BC = \sqrt{(3 - 0)^2 + (0 - 0)^2} = \sqrt{9} = 3$

$CA = \sqrt{(0 - 3)^2 + (4 - 0)^2} = \sqrt{25} = 5$

Perimeter of $\triangle ABC = AB + BC + CA = 4 + 3 + 5 = 12$

31(B). The ecosystem is made up of living and nonliving things. An ecological pyramid is composed of producers, herbivores, carnivores. Producers occupy the first trophic level. They use solar energy to synthesize their food by the process of photosynthesis. Herbivores occupy the second trophic level. They are also called primary consumers. They feed on producers. The third trophic level is occupied by the carnivores which feed eat herbivores. They are also called secondary consumers.

32(A). The ecosystem is a segment of nature or biosphere consisting of a community of living beings and the abiotic or physical environment both interacting and exchanging materials between them. The ecosystem can be temporary (e.g. rainwater pond) or permanent (e.g. lake). The ecosystem is called anthropogenic or man-made if it is created and maintained by human beings (artificial ecosystem) e.g. gardens, piggery, poultry farms, apiary, crop fields, aquaria, etc.

33(A). Low boiling point metals like Mercury are purified with distillation.

The heat of copper makes the pole emit wood gas that reduces the cuprous oxide to copper. In poling, the molten impure metal is stirred with green poles of wood.

In electrolyte refining of metals, impure metal is made as Anode and a thin strip of pure metal is made as cathode.

34(C). Step 1:

Generally metals reacts with acids to give salt and hydrogen gas. For example:

$K(s) + H_2SO_4(aq) \rightarrow K_2SO_4(aq) + H_2(g)$

$2K(s) + 2HCl(aq) \rightarrow 2KCl(aq) + H_2(g)$

Step 2:

The end product of the reaction nitric acid with metals depends on the reactivity of the metal since nitric acid is a strong oxidizing agent that can oxidise hydrogen gas produced to water along with the production of oxides of nitrogen.

For example:

$Mg(s) + 2HNO_3(aq) \rightarrow Mg(NO_3)_2(aq)H_2(g)$

$8K(s) + 10HNO_3(aq) \rightarrow 8KNO_3(aq) + N_2O(g) + 5H_2O(l)$

Step 3:

In the second reaction of metal with nitric acid, no hydrogen gas is produced because the hydrogen gas produced by displacement is oxidised to water.

35(B). The clogging of the nose with phlegm is a common problem associated with common cold. It results in the blockage of the perception of smell. The olfactory nerves will fail to send the olfactory signals and thus won't be able to differentiate between the smell of agarbatti and perfume.

So, 'Differentiate the smell of a perfume from that of an agarbatti'.

36(C). The brain is lodged inside the cavity of the skull known as cranium. The cranial cavity, also known as intracranial space, is the space within the skull that accommodates the brain. The skull minus the mandible is called the cranium.

37(C). 'In precipitation reactions, one of the products formed is in the solid state'. is the true statement.

The term 'precipitation reaction' can be defined as " a chemical reaction occurring in an aqueous solution where two ionic bonds combine, resulting in the formation of an insoluble salt".

Precipitation reactions are usually double displacement reactions involving the production of a solid form residue called the precipitate. These reactions also occur when two or more solutions with different salts are combined, resulting in the formation of insoluble salts that precipitate out of the solution.

Hence, option (C) is correct.

38(B). Lead (II) nitrate is an inorganic compound having molecular formula $Pb(NO_3)_2$. It is also known as plumbous nitrate. It exists mainly in colourless crystalline forms and soluble in water. It is toxic in nature and hence, to be handled with care to prevent ingestion, inhalation and skin contact. The heating of lead (II) nitrate gives lead (II) oxide, nitrogen dioxide and oxygen. The balanced chemical reaction for the decomposition of lead (II) nitrate can be shown as below:

$2\,Pb(NO)_3(s) \rightarrow 2PbO(s) + 4NO_2(g) + O_2(g)$

From the above decomposition reaction of lead nitrate, we find that two gases are released in the reaction. The names of the gases are nitrogen dioxide and oxygen gas.

39(C). The I.U.P.A.C name of $CH_3CH_2CH=CH_2$ is But-1-ene.

Butene (or 1-Butylene) is the organic compound with the formula $CH_3CH_2CH=CH_2$. It is a colorless gas that is easily condensed to give a colorless liquid. It is classified as a linear alpha-olefin. It is one of the isomers of butene (butylene). It is a precursor to diverse products.

40(A). $CHCl_3$ compounds of carbon do not consist of ions.

Carbon always forms covalent compounds by sharing its electrons with other atoms. Now, in covalent bonding, the two electrons shared by the atoms are attracted to the nucleus of both atoms and neither atom completely loses or gains electrons as in ionic bonding. So the compounds in which all the atoms are directly attached to C-atom, contain covalent bonding and no ionic bond.

In $CHCl_3$, all the three chlorine atoms are bonded covalently to the carbon atom, not to the hydrogen atom. So, $CHCl_3$ is a covalent compound and does not consist of ions.

41(B). Fusion of male gamete (sperm) and female gamete (egg) takes place in the oviduct or fallopian tube and the process is called fertilization.

Fertilization is a complex multi-step

process that is complete in 24 hours. The sperm from a male meets an ovum from a female and forms a zygote; this is the point in which pregnancy begins and leads to a 280-day journey for a female. There are two ways to track this process, and they differ by the day counting begins.

42(D). In females, the ovary secretes two hormones, called female reproductive hormones. These are:
(a) Estrogen
(b) Progesterone
Estrogen is secreted before ovulation and progesterone is secreted to prepare the uterus for receiving the embryo.

43(D). A trait of an organism is influenced by both maternal and paternal DNA. It is passed down from one generation to another through genes found on the chromosomes. During sexual reproduction, both mother and father pass their genes to their offspring through gametes thus, determining their traits or characteristic features.

44(B). Mendel selected 7 pairs of characters. The plant which he choose was Pisum sativum. He selected characters such as flower colour, flower position, stem length, seed shape, seed colour, pod shape, and pod colour.

45(C). The frequency of light depends on the source of light and remains the same during refraction. The speed of the light changes when a ray of light passes from one medium to another. The speed of light is higher in a rarer medium than a denser medium. A ray of light travelling from a rarer medium to a denser medium slows down, due to which there is a change in the wave-length.

46(A). If the object is placed at the focus of the concave mirror, the image will be formed at infinity. The image will be highly enlarged, and will be real and inverted. As the parallel rays coming from the object converge at the principal focus, F of a concave mirror; after reflection through it. Therefore, when the object is at infinity the image will form at F.

47(D). Split Rings of electric motor, acts as a commutator.
A commutator is a rotary electrical switch in certain types of electric motors and electrical generators that periodically reverses the current direction between the rotor and the external circuit. It consists of a cylinder composed of multiple metal contact segments on the rotating armature of the machine.
The split ring in the electric motor also known as a commutator reverses the direction of current flowing through the coil after every half rotation of the coil. Due to this the coil continues to rotate in the same direction.

48(C). The instrument that use to defect electric current in the circuit is known as galvanometer.
It is connected in series with the circuit. When no current is flowing through a galvanometer, it's pointer is at the zero mark in the centre of semicircular scale. When an electric current passes through the galvanometer, then it's pointer deflects or move either to the left side of zero mark or to the right side of the zero mark, depending on the direction of current.

49(B). Glottis opens at the surface of bucco pharyngeal cavity. The glottis, a slit-like opening on the floor of the pharynx, is a valve that controls airflow in and out of the respiratory passages. The glottis opens directly into a boxlike larynx. The buccopharyngeal membranes serve as a respiratory surface in a wide variety of amphibians and reptiles. In this

50(A). In the cell, Aerobic respiration occurs within the mitochondria of a cell. While most aerobic respiration (with oxygen) takes place in the cell's mitochondria, and anaerobic respiration (without oxygen) takes place within the cell's cytoplasm.
Aerobic respiration is the process of cellular respiration that uses oxygen to produce energy from food. This type of respiration is common in most plants and animals, including humans, birds, and other mammals.

51(B). Vanilla essence is not a visual indicator.
An acid base indicator shows a colour change from red to blue or blue to red which is not recognisable by a visually impaired student. To detect this change, an olfactory indicator is required which gives a particular odour during this colour change. So vanilla essence is used because of its fruity smell.

52(C). Equal volumes of hydrochloric acid and sodium hydroxide solutions of same concentration are mixed and the pH of the resulting solution is checked with a pH paper. Yellowish green be the colour that obtained. Here neutralization takes place between HCL and $NaOH$ solution hence pH will remain neutral which will be in the yellowish-green zone in pH paper.

53(D). Frame rate (expressed in frames per second or fps) is the frequency (rate) at which consecutive images called frames are displayed in an animated display.The human eye is capable of differentiating between 10 and 12 still images per second before it starts just seeing it as motion. That is, at an FPS of 12 or less, our brain can tell that its just a bunch of still images in rapid succession, not a seamless animation. Once the frame rate gets up to around 18 to 26 FPS, the motion effect actually takes effect and our brain is fooled into thinking that these individual images are actually a moving scene. The current industry standard is 24 FPS.

54(D). We are given,
$I = 0.5$ A, $t = 10$ min $= 600$ s
As we know,
$Q = It$
$= 0.5$ A $\times 600$ s
$= 300$ C

55(B). Given,
$i = 2\ A$
$H = 80\ J$
$t = 10\ sec$
As we Know,
$H = i^2 Rt$
$R = \dfrac{H}{i^2 t}$
$R = \dfrac{80}{4 \times 10}$
$R = \dfrac{80}{40}$
$R = 2\Omega$
The resistance of the conductor is $R = 2\Omega$

56(A). There is ample amount of water in certain places there is hazardous water pollution, due to Domestic and industrial wastes.
- There is a situation when water is sufficiently available to meet the needs of the people but the area still suffers from water scarcity. This scarcity may be due to bad quality of water.
- Water gets polluted by domestic and industrial wastes, chemicals, pesticides and fertilizers used in agriculture, thus, making it hazardous for human use.
- India's rivers have turned into toxic streams.

57(A).
The greatest damage inflicted on Indian forests was during the colonial period due to expansion of the railways, agriculture.
- Forests provide us with food, wood, barks, leaves, rubber, medicines, dyes, wood fuel, manure, etc. So we ourselves (human beings) have depleted our forests and wildlife by overusing them.
- The greatest damage inflicted on Indian forests was during the colonial period due to the expansion of railways, agriculture, and commercial and scientific forestry and mining activities. Even after independence, agricultural expansion continues to be one of the major causes of depletion of forest resources.
- Major parts of the tribal belts, especially in north eastern and central India have been deforested or degraded by shifting cultivation, a type of slash and burn agriculture.
- Since 1951, lots of forests were cleared for river valley projects like the 'Narmada Valley Project' in Madhya Pradesh which has cleared 40,000 hectares of forests.

- Mining is another important factor behind deforestation. The Buxa Tiger Reserve in West Bengal is seriously threatened by the ongoing dolomite mining.
- Many environmentalists feel that the greatest degrading factors behind the depletion of forest resources are grazing and fuel wood collection.
- Large-scale developmental projects have also contributed to the loss of forests.

58(C). Madhya Pradesh is the largest producer of manganese ores in India.
Madhya Pradesh produces about 27.59 percent of India's manganese ore. Next in the order of production were Maharashtra and Odisha (25% each). The main belt extends in Balaghat and Chhindwara districts. Maharashtra produces about 27.66 percent of Indian manganese.The main belt is in Nagpur and Bhandara districts.Odisha accounts for 24 percent of production. It is 1*st* in reserves but 3*rd* in production.The deposits occur in the Sundargarh district and Kodurite and Khondolite deposits in Kalahandi and Koraput Districts.

59(C). Cotton is the natural product from the list.
The broadest definition of natural product is anything that is produced by life, and includes the likes of biotic materials (e.g. wood, silk), bio-based materials (e.g. bioplastics, cornstarch), bodily fluids (e.g. milk, plant exudates), and other natural materials (e.g. soil, coal).

60(D). Cause of high infant mortality rate is inadequate facilities of health and lack of infrastructure facilities.
There are a number of causes of infant mortality, including poor sanitation, poor water quality, malnourishment of the mother and infant, inadequate prenatal and medical care, and use of infant formula as a breast milk substitute. Women's status and disparities of wealth are also reflected in infant mortality rates.

61(A). In mid-eighteenth-century Europe the status of Germany, Italy and Switzerland were divided into kingdoms, duchies and cantons whose rulers had their autonomous territories.
Germany, Italy and Switzerland were ruled by different rulers with autonomous territories. Autocratic monarchies were there in eastern and central part of Europe. These areas were occupied by different peoples. They did not see themselves as sharing a collective identity or common culture.

62(A). Breeder seeds have a golden yellow tag, foundation seeds have a white tag, registered seeds have an opal blue tag and certified seeds have a green tag.

Breeder seed is prepared from the central seed under the supervision of the breeder (scientist) himself. It is the progeny of the central seed. This seed is 100% pure physically and genetically. The sack of breeder seed has a golden yellow colour tag.

63(A). No individual in India can legally refuse a payment made n rupees.
By law, the Reserve Bank of India (RBI) issues currency notes on behalf of the central government. The law legalizes the use of rupee as a medium of payment which cannot be refused in settling transactions in India. All banknotes issued by RBI are backed by assets such as gold, Government Securities and Foreign Currency Assets , as defined in Section 33 of RBI Act, 1934.

64(D). The dependence on the informal sector can be reduced by:
(i) Banks and cooperatives increase their lending particularly in the rural areas
(ii) Interest rates are decreased on credit
(iii) Formal sector loans expands, and everyone receives loans.
Some of the criticisms of informal sector include viewing the informal economy as a fraudulent activity that results in a loss of revenue from taxes, weakens unions, creates unfair competition, leads to a loss of regulatory control on the government's part, reduces observance of health and safety standards.

65(B). Tata Motors Limited is an Indian multinational automotive manufacturing company, headquartered in the city of Mumbai, India which is part of Tata Group. The company produces passenger cars, trucks, vans, coaches, buses, luxury cars, sports cars, construction equipment.

66(C). Call centres has helped most in the spread of production of services.
Multilingual call centers play a major role in the development of our world economy. By connecting people regardless of their language and geographical location, multilingual call centers are at the forefront of globalization and business expansion of companies all over the world. Due to all these benefits Indian BPOs are preferred more by companies across the world over the BPOs of other countries. All of this has happened due to globalization. The Indian BPO Services industry started booming and working on its facilities more to get ahead of the BPOs of other countries.

67(A). Hallmark is the certification maintained for standardisation for Jewellery.
The hallmark, a mark stamped on jewellery to certify the purity of gold, silver, platinum or palladium, is applied to jewellery after being thoroughly tested through the assaying process. The main reason for this is to provide consumer protection.The

government has said mandatory hallmarking of gold jewellery.

68(B). In above case, Right to choose is being violated.
A consumer has the right to choose from different options. A seller cannot just offer to sell only one brand to the consumer. The seller has to offer various options to the consumer. This right is usually enforced through laws against monopoly trade. The definition of Right to Choose as per the Consumer Protection Act 1986 is 'the right to be assured, wherever possible, to have access to a variety of goods and services at competitive prices'.

69(A). The Roman Church begin to maintain an Index of Prohibited Books from 1558 because of:
- Troubled by such effects of popular readings and questionings of faith
- Writing and printing of heretical beliefs
In the sixteenth century, The Roman Catholic Church had to face many dissents. People had written many books that interpreted the God and the creation in their own ways or as they liked. Menocchio, a miller In Italy, read a few books and interpreted the message of the bible and created a view of god and its creation. It infuriated the Roman Catholic Church. Menocchio was hauled up twice and ultimately executed. Then Erasmus, a Latin scholar and a Catholic reformer also criticized the extremes of Catholicism. The Roman church, in order to control these developments, imposed severe controls over publishers and booksellers. The church banned such books and started maintaining an index of prohibited books from 1558.

70(A). In the seventeenth century and eighteenth centuries the literacy rates grow by Churches of different denominations set up schools in villages, carrying literacy to peasants and artisans.
The number of books published in the period of the Enlightenment increased dramatically due to the increase in demand for books, which resulted from the increased literacy rates and the declining cost and easier availability of books made possible by the printing press.
Universal education was once considered a privilege for only the upper class. However, during the 17th and the 18th century, education was provided to all classes. The literacy rate in Europe from the 17th century to the 18th century grew significantly. The definition of the term literacy used to describe the 17th and 18th century is different from our definition of literacy now. Historians measure the literacy rate during 17th and 18th century by people's ability to sign their names. However, this method did not reflect people's ability to read and this affected the

women's literacy rate most of all because most women during this period could not write but could read to a certain extent. In general, the literacy rate in Europe during 18th century has almost doubled compare to the 17th century.

71(B). Sri Lanka emerged as an independent country in 1948.
- Majoritarianism was adopted by the democratically elected govt with Sinhala supremacy.
- Act of 1956, recognized Sinhala as the official language by disregarding Tamil.
- Govt. followed preferential policies –favouring Sinhala applicants for University positions and govt. jobs.
- Constitution stipulated Buddhism as the official religion of the State.
- All these increased a feeling of alienation among the Sri Lankan Tamils.
- Constitution and govt. policies denied equal political rights to the Tamilians.

72(B). Belgium constitution was amended four times between 1970 to 1993. First amendment took place in 1970. The second amendment took place in 1980. The third amendment took place in 1988-89. The fourth amendment took place in 1993.

73(C). Rinderpest refers to the cattle plague in Africa in 1890s.
This disease show that how during this era of conquest even a disease affecting cattle reshaped the lives and fortunes of thousands of people. The infected cattle was imported from British Asia into Africa to feed Italian soldiers. The following were the impact of Rinderpest on people's livelihoods and the local economy in Africa:
- It destroyed nearly 90% of the livestock.
- It destroyed the livelihood of the Natives.

Mine owners and colonial powers benefited by it as they monopolized what scarce cattle resources remained and Africa ceased to be a free continent.

74(A). Central government is more powerful in Holding together federation.
Holding together federation is nothing but the division of powers between the states of the country and central government of that country. India is an example of this kind of federation. In a holding together federation, the central government has more power than state governments. One of the most significant aspects of this is in India, which is a holding together federation, there is one Constitution, the final interpreter of which is the Supreme Court at the center.

75(C). USA is called a coming together federation.
Because in it various states have signed deal and are now united. In this way, the states have formed a bigger unit and also increased their security, power and also could avail better opportunities and facilities.

76(A). James Watt improved the steam engine produced by Newcomen and patented the new engine in 1781.
His industrialist friend Mathew Boulton manufactured the new model.
While repairing a model Newcomen steam engine in 1764, Watt was impressed by its waste of steam. In May 1765, after wrestling with the problem of improving it, he suddenly came upon a solution—the separate condenser, his first and greatest invention. Watt had realized that the loss of latent heat (the heat involved in changing the state of a substance—e.g., solid or liquid) was the worst defect of the Newcomen engine and that therefore condensation must be effected in a chamber distinct from the cylinder but connected to it. Shortly afterward he met British physician, chemist, and inventor John Roebuck, the founder of the Carron Works, who urged him to make an engine. He entered into partnership with him in 1768, after having made a small test engine with the help of loans from Joseph Black. The following year Watt took out the famous patent for "A New Invented Method of Lessening the Consumption of Steam and Fuel in Fire Engines."

77(B). Resources are the human activities function:
- Human themselves are vital elements of resources
- They (humans) transform material available (that is, apply processes to make a resource so as to utilise it to satisfy human needs) in our environment into resources and use them. For instance water is a natural resource however water become a resource when it used for solar energy or irrigation etc
- Resources are finite (limited) and must be utilised judiciously.

78(A). The United States has the oldest working written Constitution on Earth. The Constitution is not just a piece of parchment that is consulted only when convenient or expedient, but a living document that has helped produce the most stable government in the world. No constitutional system today has endured so long. And no system has evoked so much admiration and bafflement. Many nations have sought, in varying degrees, to emulate American representative democracy.

79(C). A government that takes decision by following norms and a proper procedure is a transparent government. Democracy is accountable and responsive to the needs and expectations of the citizens because:
- In a democracy, people have the right to choose their representatives and the people will have control over them.
- Citizens have the right to participate in decision-making that affects them all. This ensures that the working of the government is transparent.
- Everybody expects the government to be attentive to the needs and expectations of the people.
- It is expected that the democratic government develops mechanisms for citizens to hold the government accountable.
- The opposition parties can also question and criticize the government policies. They keep a check on the ruling party and make sure that it does not misuse the power.

80(B). General Dyer was the British officer who open- fired at the Jallianwala Bagh congregation.
However, none of them talked of apology by British government but the Mayor of London Sadiq Khan dared to call on British government to tender a full and formal apology for the Jallianwala Bagh pogrom killed hundreds of peaceful freedom fighter in cold blood after British army colonel Reginald Dyer ordered his troops to open fire on unarmed people on April 13, 1919- the day of Baiskahi festival.

81(A). Kamala Lakshmi Narayanan is recognized the world over as the foremost proponent of Bharatanatyam which is a southern Indian classical dance which combined artistic expression with rhythmic footwork.

82(D). Criminal Procedure Code is not included in the state list in the Constitution of India. Criminal law and criminal procedure fall under the Concurrent List while matters relating to Police and Prisons fall under the State List.

83(B). Statement B: The Central Government of India appointed "The National Income Committee" in 1949 after independence in India. In 1949 the Government of India, realizing the need for reliable estimates of national income for policy purposes.
Statement A: Dadabhai Naoroji was the first Indian to estimate the national income of the country.
Statement C: Professor Mahalanobis was appointed as the chairman of the committee. The Committee had two members:
1. Professor Gadgil of the Gokhale
2. Professor V.K.R.V. Rao

84(D). P. N. Bhagwati was the Chief Justice of India when public interest litigation was introduced to the Indian Judicial System.
P. N. Bhagwati, the 17th Chief Justice of India introduced the concepts of Public interest Litigation and absolute liability in India.
Public interest Litigation (PIL) is litigation filed in a court of law, for the protection

of "Public Interest", such as Pollution, Terrorism, Road safety, Constructional hazards, etc.

85(C). Sandur is not related to the function of a river.
There are mainly three functions of a river- Erosion, transportation and deposition. It is through deposits that the river forms various types of topographies.
- When the river does not move straight but moves along a zigzag path, then these bends are called river visarp.
- The long dams formed by the deposition of soil on both sides of the river, which are like ridges of low height, are called natural dam.

Yazoo - A type of tributary which is not able to meet due to the formation of a high natural dam on the bank of the main river and flows parallel to the main river and after walking for a sufficient distance, it is found somewhere in the lower part of the main river. The Yazoo River, a tributary of the Mississippi River in America, is a classic example of which it is named.

86(B). James Watt was the inventor of the first steam engine. He developed the first design of the steam engine in 1763.
The steam engines he developed were used to pump water out of mills. This design was later put into locomotives.

87(A). Daman is the capital of the Union Territory Daman and Diu.
- With an area of 112 km ^{2}, it was India's smallest federal division on the mainland.
- The territories consisted of two distinct regions - Daman and Diu - which are physically divided by the Gulf of Khambhat.
- The state of Gujarat and the Arab Sea bordered the territory.
- The territory of the Portuguese colony after the 1500s was occupied by India in 1961.
- Daman and Diu were administered as part of the union territory of Goa, Daman and Diu from 1961 to 1987 when they became a separate union territory.

88(C). The paintings of Ajanta belongs to buddhism religion.

It is located in Aurangabad, Maharashtra. It is an ancient rock-cut cave built in the 2nd century BC to the 5th century AD. There is a total of 29 caves in Ajanta related to Buddhist which were decorated with sculptures and paintings.

89(C). Pir Panjal range is the longest mountain range in the lesser Himalayas. It is the longest and most important of all the ranges in the Lesser Himalayas.

90(A). Therigatha is a part of Sutta Pitaka.
- Tripitaka or Three Baskets is a traditional term used for various Buddhist scriptures.
- The three pitakas are Sutta Pitaka, Vinaya Pitaka and Abhidhamma Pitaka.
- The Vinaya Pitaka consists of rules of conduct and discipline applicable to the monastic life of the monks and nuns.

The Sutta Pitaka consists of the main teaching or Dhamma of Buddha. It is divided into five Nikayas or collections:
- Digha Nikaya
- Majjhima Nikaya
- Samyutta Nikaya
- Anguttara Nikaya
- Khuddaka Nikaya

91(C). Mehrunnisa married Emperor Jahangir in 1611.
Mehrunnisa was born in 1577 in Qandahar. She was the twentieth and last wife of the Jahangir. After Mehrunnisa got married to Emperor Jahangir, in 1611 she received the title of Nur Jahan.

92(B). The Lahore session of the Indian National Congress was held in 1929 AD. It was presided over by 'Jawaharlal Nehru'. In this session. In this session, the resolution of 'Purna Swaraj' was passed.

93(B). Nearly three-fourths of the earth's surface is covered with water. 97% of the water on the Earth is salt water and only 3% percent is freshwater.

94(B). It approves proposals for taxation, budgets and annual financial statements is not the powers of Rajya Sabha.

95(B). Mumtaz Khan, who was named the Emerging Player of the Year by the International Hockey Federation (FIH),

hails from the Lucknow district of Uttar Pradesh. India's young hockey player Mumtaz Khan has been awarded the 'FIH Rising Women's Star of the Year 2021-22' award.

96(C). Priyanka Mohite has become the first Indian woman to climb the Annapurna mountain.
On April 16, 2021, mountaineer Priyanka Mohite became the first woman from India to climb Mt Annapurna, the world's tenth highest peak. She is also the first Indian woman to climb Mt Makalu, the world's fifth tallest mountain range at 8,485 meters. Mount Annapurna is a Himalayan massif. It lies in Nepal and has one summit over 8,000 meters, making it one of the most difficult mountains to climb.

97(A). Silk is a natural protein fiber, some forms of which can be woven into textiles.
The protein fiber of silk is composed mainly of fibroin and is produced by certain insect larvae to form cocoons.

98(B). Polio is a highly infectious disease caused by a virus.
Its causative agent, poliovirus, was identified in 1908 by Karl Landsteiner. The polio virus invades the nervous system. And can cause total paralysis in a matter of hours.

99(B). World War I was a global war that lasted from 1914 to 1918. The conflict began after the assassination of Archduke Franz Ferdinand of Austria-Hungary on 28 July 1914, and quickly escalated into a full-scale war involving many. The war was fought between the Central Powers, led by Germany Austria-Hungary and the Ottoman Empire, and the Allied Powers, led by France, the British Empire, and Russia.

100(C). Ukrainian President Volodymyr Zelensky has selected the John F. Kennedy Profile in Courage Award for acting to protect democracy. Zelensky was selected because he marshaled the spirit, patriotism and untiring sacrifice of the Ukrainian people in a life-or-death fight for their country.

Mathematics

1. If the mean of frequency distribution is 7.5 and $\sum f_i x_i = 120 + 3k, \sum f_i = 30$, then k is equal to:
   (a) 40   (b) 35
   (c) 50   (d) 45

2. The mode and mean is given by 7 and 8, respectively. Then the median is:
   (a) $\frac{1}{13}$ (b) $\frac{13}{3}$
   (c) $\frac{23}{3}$ (d) 33

3. If the surface area of the sphere is same as the Curved surface area of a right circular cylinder whose height and diameter are $12 cm$ each, then the radius of the sphere is:
   (a) $12 cm$ (b) $8 cm$
   (c) $6 cm$ (d) $3 cm$

4. A rectangular piece of paper is $44\ cm$ long and $18\ cm$ wide. If a cylinder is formed by rolling the paper along its length, then the radius of the base of the cylinder is:
   (a) $7\ cm$ (b) $22\ cm$
   (c) $21\ cm$ (d) $14\ cm$

5. Find the roots of the equation $5x^2 - 6x - 2 = 0$ by the method of completing the square.
   (a) $\frac{1+\sqrt{15}}{5}$ and $\frac{4-\sqrt{19}}{5}$
   (b) $\frac{5+\sqrt{18}}{3}$ and $\frac{3-\sqrt{18}}{5}$
   (c) $\frac{2+\sqrt{20}}{5}$ and $\frac{2-\sqrt{19}}{5}$
   (d) $\frac{3+\sqrt{19}}{5}$ and $\frac{3-\sqrt{19}}{5}$

6. Find two consecutive odd positive integers, sum of whose squares is 290.
   (a) 20 and 13   (b) 12 and 11
   (c) 11 and 13   (d) 18 and 13

7. If the equation $6x^2 + 4x - a = 0$ has equal roots, then choose the correct option.
   (a) $2a - 3 = 0$ (b) $3a + 2 > 0$
   (c) $3a + 2 < 0$ (d) $3a + 2 = 0$

8. Find the area of the shaded region in the given figure, where a circular arc of radius 6 cm has been drawn with vertex O of an equilateral triangle OAB of side 12 cm as centre.

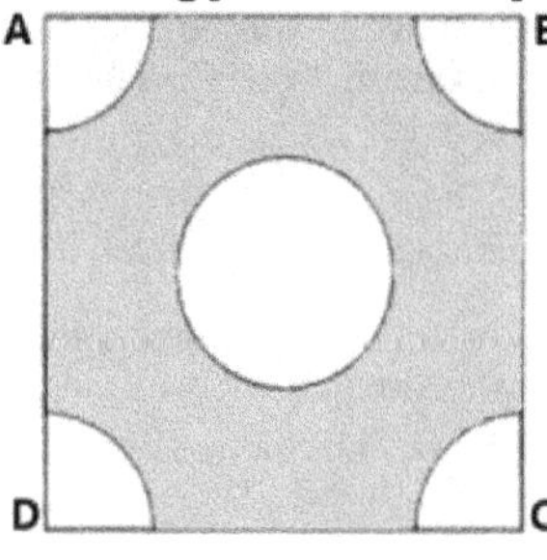

   (a) $\left(30\sqrt{2} + \frac{760}{7}\right)$ cm^2
   (b) $\left(36\sqrt{3} + \frac{660}{7}\right)$ cm^2
   (c) $\left(35\sqrt{2} + \frac{760}{7}\right)$ cm^2
   (d) $\left(46\sqrt{3} + \frac{660}{7}\right)$ cm^2

9. From each corner of a square of side 4 cm a quadrant of a circle of radius 1 cm is cut and also a circle of diameter 2 cm is cut as shown in the given figure. Find the area of the remaining portion of the square.

   (a) $\frac{68}{7}$ cm^2 (b) $\frac{78}{7}$ cm^2
   (c) $\frac{88}{7}$ cm^2 (d) $\frac{98}{7}$ cm^2

10. Direction: Evaluate the following.
    $2\tan^2 45° + \cos^2 30° - \sin^2 60°$
    (a) $\sqrt{2}$ (b) 2
    (c) $\sqrt{1}$ (d) 0

11. Direction: Evaluate the following.
    $\frac{5\cos^2 60° + 4\sec^2 30° - \tan^2 45°}{\sin^2 30° + \cos^2 30°}$
    (a) $\sqrt{2}$ (b) $\frac{87}{12}$
    (c) $\sqrt{1}$ (d) $\frac{67}{12}$

12. The value of $\sin 25° \cos 65° + \cos 25° \sin 65°$ is:
    (a) 1   (b) 2
    (c) $\frac{1}{2}$ (d) 0

13. $2x + 3y + 5 = 0$ and $px + 6y + 8 = 0$
    The pair of equations given above have a unique solution for all values of p except _______.
    (a) 4   (b) 6
    (c) 2   (d) 5

14. For what value of k the following system of equations has a unique solution $2x + 3y - 5 = 0, kx - 6y - 8 = 0$?
    (a) $k = -2$ (b) $k = -4$
    (c) $k = 4$ (d) $k = 2$

15. Three alarm clocks ring at intervals of 4, 12 and 20 minutes respectively. If they start ringing together, after how much time will they next ring together?
    (a) 60 minutes   (b) 40 minutes
    (c) 30 minutes   (d) 50 minutes

16. Three boys A, B and C started running around a circular stadium at the same time and in the same direction. 'A' completes one round of the stadium in 6 minutes, 'B' in 5 minutes and 'C' in 20 minutes (all started running from the same point). After what time will they meet again at the starting point for the first time?
    (a) 1 hour
    (b) 2 hours
    (c) 1 hour and 6 minutes
    (d) 2 hours and 6 minutes

17. If the HCF of 408 and 1032 is expressible in the form $1032 \times 2 + 408 \times p$, then find the value of p:
    (a) -5 (b) -3
    (c) -4 (d) -2

18. What is the greatest number that divides the numbers 38, 45 and 52 and leaves remainders 2, 3 and 4, respectively?
    (a) 6   (b) 8
    (c) 10   (d) 4

19. If α, β, γ are the roots of equation $x^3 + px^2 + qx + r = 0$, then $\sum \alpha^2(\beta + \gamma)$ is:
    (a) $3r + pq$ (b) $3r - pq$
    (c) $pq - 3r$ (d) $pq + r$

20. If α, β, γ are the roots of the equation $2x^3 - 3x^2 + 6x + 1 = 0$, then $\alpha^2 + \beta^2 + \gamma^2$ is equal to:
    (a) $-\frac{15}{4}$ (b) $\frac{15}{4}$
    (c) $\frac{9}{4}$ (d) 4

21. If 'p' is the probability of an event, then p satisfies:
    (a) $0 < p \le 1$ (b) $0 < p < 1$

(c) $0 \leq p \leq 1$ (d) $0 \leq p < 1$

22. **An unbiased die is thrown once. The probability of getting a prime or composite number is:**
(a) 1   (b) $\frac{5}{6}$
(c) $\frac{1}{2}$ (d) $\frac{1}{6}$

23. **How many terms of the** $AP\, 9, 17, 25,$ **... must be taken to give a sum of** 636 **?**
(a) 12   (b) 14
(c) 16   (d) 18

24. **Find the sum of first** 40 **positive integers divisible by** 6.
(a) 4520   (b) 4920
(c) 5920   (d) 6920

25. **Number of tangents drawn at a point of the circle is/are:**
(a) 1   (b) 2
(c) 3   (d) Infinite

26. **The tangents drawn at the extremities of the diameter of a circle are:**
(a) Perpendicular
(b) Parallel
(c) Equal
(d) None of these

27. **In the given figure, O is the centre of the circle and $AB = CD$. If $\angle AOB = 60°$, find $\angle COD$:**

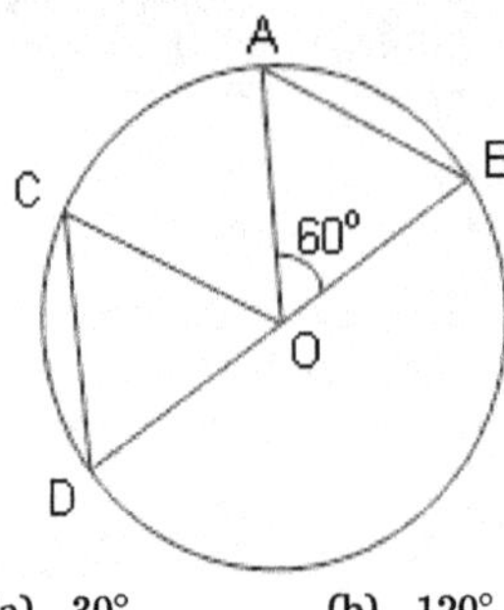

(a) $30°$ (b) $120°$
(c) $60°$ (d) $85°$

28. **In $\triangle ABC \sim \triangle DEF, BC = 4\,cm, EF = 5\,cm$ and $\text{area}(\triangle ABC) = 80\,cm^2$, the area($\triangle DEF$) is:**
(a) $100\,cm^2$ (b) $125\,cm^2$
(c) $150\,cm^2$ (d) $200\,cm^2$

29. **If in $\triangle ABC$ and $\triangle DEF, \frac{AB}{DE} = \frac{BC}{FD}$, then they will be similar if :**
(a) $\angle B = \angle E$ (b) $\angle A = \angle D$
(c) $\angle B = \angle D$ (d) $\angle A = \angle F$

30. **In triangle $ABC, BC^2 + AB^2 = AC^2$,**

then _________ is a right angle.
(a) $\angle A$
(b) $\angle B$
(c) $\angle C$
(d) None of the above

Science

31. **Which of the following may be a conclusion of the excessive exposure of humans to the sun's ultraviolet rays?**
(i) Damage to the immune system
(ii) Damage to lungs
(iii) Skin cancer
(iv) Peptic ulcers
(a) (i) and (iii)   (b) (i) and (ii)
(c) (ii) and (iv)   (d) (i) and (ii)

32. **The first link in any food chain is always a green plant, because**
(a) They are widely distributed.
(b) They are firmly fixed to the soil.
(c) They alone have a capacity to fix atmospheric CO_2 in the presence of sunlight.
(d) All of the above.

33. **The elements or compounds which occur naturally in the earth's crust are known as _______.**
(a) metals   (b) non–metals
(c) minerals   (d) metalloids

34. **All of the following compounds are non-ionic, except:**
(a) Calcium chloride
(b) Sodium chloride
(c) Potassium chloride
(d) Water

35. **The disease caused by hyposecretion of thyroxine is known as:**
(a) Goitre
(b) Cushing's syndrome
(c) Acromegaly
(d) Addison's disease

36. **Skeletal muscles are controlled by:**
(a) Sympathetic nervous system
(b) Parasympathetic nervous system
(c) Somatic nervous system
(d) Both sympathetic and parasympathetic

37. **The reaction between carbon and oxygen can be represented as:**
$C(s) + O_2(\,g) \rightarrow C_2(\,g) + \textbf{Heat}$
In which of the following type(s) the above reaction can be classified?

(a) Combustion reaction
(b) Combination reaction
(c) Both (A) and (B)
(d) Displacement reaction

38. $3MnO_2 + 4Al \longrightarrow 3Mn + 2Al_2O_3$
The reducing agent in the above equation is:
(a) Al   (b) Mn
(c) C_2 (d) Mn, O_2

39. **Which allotrope of carbon is a good conductor of electricity?**
(a) Diamond   (b) Graphite
(c) Fullerene   (d) Coke

40. **Which of the following belongs to a homologous series of alkynes?**
$C_6H_6, C_2H_6, C_2H_4, C_3H_4$
(a) C_6H_6 (b) C_2H_6
(c) C_2H_4 (d) C_3H_4

41. **Transfer of pollen from anthers of one flower to the stigma of another flower of the same plant is called:**
(a) No pollination
(b) Cross–pollination
(c) Self–pollination
(d) Geitonogamy

42. **The uterus opens into the vagina through:**
(a) Urethra   (b) Ureter
(c) Cervix   (d) Placenta

43. **Which of the following options best defines `Fossils`?**
(a) Dead remains of plants, preserved by humans
(b) Decayed remains of animals, caught under hard rocks
(c) Preserved remains of plants and animals, which existed in the past
(d) Non-living things under the ground

44. **The wings of a bat and a bird are examples of :**
(a) analogous organs
(b) speciation
(c) homologous organs
(d) fossils

45. **The image formed by a concave mirror is observed to be virtual, erect and larger than the object. Where should be the position of the object?**
(a) Between the principal focus and the centre of curvature
(b) At the centre of curvature
(c) Beyond the centre of curvature
(d) Between the pole of the mirror

and its principal focus

46. Where should an object be placed in front of a convex lens to get a real image of the size of the object?
(a) At the principal focus of the lens
(b) At twice the focal length
(c) At infinity
(d) Between the optical centre of the lens and its principal focus.

47. In electric motor, to make the coil rotating continuously in the same direction, current is reversed in the coil after every half rotation by a device called:
(a) Carbon brush
(b) Commutator
(c) Slip ring
(d) Armature

48. When current is parallel to magnetic field, then force experience by the current carrying conductor placed in uniform magnetic field is:
(a) Twice to that when angle is $60°$
(b) Thrice to that when angle is $60°$
(c) Zero
(d) Infinite

49. Which of the following pairs is incorrectly matched?
(a) Parasite : Cuscuta
(b) Parasite : Yeast
(c) Saprophyte : Mushroom
(d) Holozoic : Amoeba

50. Organisms from whose body the parasite derives the benefit are called _______.
(a) carrier
(b) host
(c) vector
(d) None of these

51. Which of the following types of medicine is used for the treatment of indigestion?
(a) Antiseptic
(b) Antacid
(c) Analgesic
(d) None of these

52. Which of the following acids is never stored in metal containers?
(a) HCl
(b) HNO_3
(c) H_2SO_4
(d) All of the above

53. What is the least distance of distinct vision for a normal human being?
(a) About 1 to 2 m
(b) About 2 to 3 m
(c) About 50 cm
(d) About 25 cm

54. It requires 6.4×10^{-4} Joule of work to move $2C$ of charge from point A to point B in an electric field. The potential difference between A and B (approximately) is:
(a) $1.6 \times 10^{-19}V$ (b) $4.0 \times 10^{-3}V$
(c) $3.2 \times 10^{-4}V$ (d) $1.0 \times 10^{-14}V$

55. What length of copper wire of resistivity 1.7×10^{-8} Ωm and radius $1\,mm$ is required so that its resistance is $1\,\Omega$?
(a) $184.7\,m$ (b) $200\,m$
(c) $190.5\,m$ (d) $150\,m$

Social Science

56. What are the causes of the Indian rivers becoming toxic?
(a) Fossils
(b) Agricultural
(c) Conservation of water
(d) Industrialisation

57. What are the main reasons for depletion of forests?
(a) Large-scale development projects
(b) Agriculture
(c) Trade
(d) Colonial rule

58. Which one of the following features is not true about copper?
(a) India is deficient in the reserve and production of copper
(b) It is reliable, ductile and a good conductor
(c) It is a ferrous ore
(d) It is mainly used in electrical cables and electronic goods

59. Which sector has emerged as the largest producing sector in India. Select one from the following alternatives:
(a) Secondary sector
(b) Tertiary sector
(c) Primary sector
(d) Science and Technology sector

60. The idea of development involves questions like:
(a) What are the essentials things that we require?
(b) What are the essential things that our ancestors required 100 year back?
(c) What are the essential things that nobody requires?
(d) None of the Above

61. When did Napoleon invade Italy?
(a) 1776 (b) 1796
(c) 1787 (d) 1766

62. Which type of agriculture is called 'slash and burn' agriculture?
(a) Plantation
(b) Intensive
(c) Primitive subsistence
(d) Extensive

63. Give an example of digital banking:
(a) Cheque
(b) Demand draft
(c) Deposit form
(d) ATM card

64. Rate of interest charged by moneylenders as compared to that charged by banks is:
(a) Lower
(b) Same
(c) Slightly higher
(d) Much higher

65. Large MNCs in the _______ industry in Europe and America order their products from Indian exporters?
(a) Automobile (b) Soft Drink
(c) Garment (d) Mineral

66. Governments use _______ to increase or decrease (regulate) foreign trade and to decide what kinds of goods and how much of each, should come into the country.
(a) Tax levies
(b) Increased taxes
(c) Relaxation of taxes
(d) Trade barrier

67. The Consumer Protection Act, 1986 ensures:
(a) Right to see movie
(b) Right to consumer education
(c) Right to having a computer
(d) Right to a facebook account

68. Which of the following is not a function of Consumer Protection Councils?
(a) To create awareness of consumer rights among consumers.
(b) To guide consumers on how to file cases in consumer courts.
(c) To provide compensation to consumers when they are cheated by shopkeepers.
(d) To represent consumers in

Consumer Courts at times.

69. What is a Chapbook?
(a) A literature book
(b) Coffee table book of arts and designs
(c) Pocket sized books that were sold by travelling pedlars called chapmen
(d) A religious book

70. What was the common conviction by the mid-eighteenth century, about printing and reading?
(a) That books were a means of spreading progress and enlightenment
(b) That people only read what the writer wanted them to read
(c) Books created discourses
(d) That book knowledge was uneven in the society

71. The horizontal distribution of power sharing takes place between the ___________.
(a) Legislature and executive
(b) Executive and judiciary
(c) Legislature, executive and judiciary
(d) Legislature, executive, judiciary and press

72. Consider the following statements about the power-sharing arrangement in Belgium and Sri Lanka and choose the correct code.
A. In Belgium, the Dutch-speaking majority people tried to impose their domination on the minority French-speaking community.
B. In Sri Lanka, the policies of government sought to ensure the dominance of Sinhala -speaking majority.
C. The Tamils in Sri Lanka demanded a federal arrangement of power -sharing to protect their culture, language and equal opportunity in education and jobs.
D. The transformation of Belgium from the unitary government to a federal one prevented a possible division of the country on linguistic lines.
(a) A, B, C and D
(b) A, B and D
(c) C and D
(d) B, C and D

73. From which one of the following countries did Britian borrow large sums of money during first World War?
(a) United States of America
(b) Russia
(c) Japan
(d) Germany

74. The Eighth Schedule of the Indian Constitution contains ___________.
(a) Scheduled Caste.
(b) Scheduled Languages
(c) Scheduled Tribes
(d) Scheduled Culture

75. In India, the relationship between the Centre and the States were deteriorated because of ___________.
(a) Formation of different party government at both levels
(b) Insurgency
(c) Indo-Pak and Indo-China War
(d) End of Congress era

76. What was the status of human labour in Victorian Britain? Was there a shortage?
(a) Yes, there were limited number of workers
(b) There was no shortage of human labour. Poor peasants and vagrants moved to the cities in large numbers in search of jobs
(c) Labour had to be imported
(d) There was uneven distribution of labour

77. The red soil is red in colour because:
(a) It is rich in humus.
(b) It is rich in iron compounds.
(c) It is derived from volcanic origin.
(d) It is rich in potash.

78. Why is the cost of time that democracy pays for arriving at a decision worthwhile?
(a) Decisions are taken following due procedures
(b) Decisions are always in favour of people
(c) Decisions are more likely to be acceptable to the people and more effective
(d) None of these

79. Democracy is considered to be better than other forms of government. Which of the following statements support this claim?
A. It is a more accountable form of government
B. It improves the quality of decision-making
C. It ensures rapid economic development of citizens
D. It enhances the dignity of citizens
(a) A,B and D
(b) A and C

(c) A, B and C
(d) B, C and D

80. Which two muslim brothers supported the movement along with Gandhi?
(a) Arbaaz Ali and Shujaat Ali
(b) Muhammad Ali and Shaukat Ali
(c) Arbaaz Ali and Shaukat Ali
(d) Shujaat Ali and Muhammad Ali

81. Who among the following was popularly known as "Surma Bhopali"?
(a) Manik Verma
(b) Rahat Indori
(c) Jagdeep
(d) Radheshyam Sharma

82. Basic structure of Constitution can be amended:
(a) By simple majority
(b) By 2/3rd of majority
(c) By special majority and ratification by half of states
(d) None of these

83. "Bad money (if not limited in quantity) drives good money out of circulation". Which law in economics says this?
(a) Keynes' law
(b) Wagner's law
(c) Gresham's law
(d) Grimm's law

84. Which qualification is wrong for being a judge in the Supreme Court?
(a) It is compulsory to be a citizen of India
(b) He should be a respected jurist in the eyes of Parliament
(c) Must be a judge in the High Court for at least 5 years
(d) He should be a lawyer in the High Court for at least 10 years

85. The word cole is related to:
(a) From glaciers
(b) from rivers
(c) From underground water
(d) From the waves of the sea

86. Recently seen in the news, DART mission is launched by _____.
(a) CNSA
(b) ISRO
(c) NASA
(d) ESA

87. By which Constitutional amendment, Sikkim became a new state in the Indian Union?

(a) 32nd, 1974 (b) 35 th, 1975
(c) 36th, 1975 (d) 37 th, 1978

88. Charkula is famous folk dance of:
(a) Bundelkhand
(b) Brij bhumi
(c) Avadh
(d) None of the above

89. Godawari river rises from the slopes of the Western Ghats in the ____ district of Maharashtra.
(a) Satara (b) Aurangabad
(c) Jalgaon (d) Nasik

90. Where did Mahavira Swami established Chaturvidha Sangh?
(a) In Pataliputra
(b) In Pava
(c) In Vallabhi
(d) In Vaishali

91. Name the author of the book 'Ain-i-Akbari'?
(a) Todar Mal
(b) Dara Shikoh
(c) Abu'l Fazl
(d) Abdul Rahim Khan-I-Khana

92. The first Satyagraha launched in India by Mahatma Gandhi was-
(a) Champaran Satyagraha
(b) Kheda Satyagraha
(c) Rowlatt Satyagraha
(d) None of these

93. Select the mismatched pair in the following.
(a) **Biomagnification - Accumulation of chemicals at the successive trophic levels of a food chain.**
(b) **Ecosystem - Biotic components of the environment.**
(c) **Aquarium - A man-made ecosystem.**
(d) **Parasites - Organisms that obtain food from other living organisms.**
(a) (a) and (b)
(b) Only (b)
(c) (a), (b) and (c)
(d) Only (d)

94. Who has the authority to proclaim emergency in the State?
(a) Governor
(b) Prime Minister
(c) President
(d) Parliament

95. Asian Games i.e. ASIAD 2022 was held in which city?
(a) Incheon, South Korea
(b) Colombo, Sri Lanka
(c) Hangzhou, China
(d) Seoul South Korea

96. Who is the first Indian woman President of the UN General Assembly?
(a) Kiran Bedi
(b) Indira Gandhi
(c) Vijaya Lakshmi Pandit
(d) Leila Seth

97. Plants receive nutrients from ________.
(a) atmosphere (b) chlorophyll
(c) soil (d) light

98. An alloy is an example of:
(a) Colloidal solution
(b) Emulsion
(c) Solid solution
(d) Heterogeneous mixture

99. The World's largest island is-
(a) Greenland (b) Iceland
(c) New Guinea (d) Madagascar

100. Arjuna Award is related to which field?
(a) Dance
(b) Cinema
(c) Doordarshan
(d) Sports

// Hints and Solutions //

1(B). As per the given question,
$$X_{\text{mean}} = \frac{\sum f_i x_i}{\sum f_i}$$
$$7.5 = \frac{(120+3k)}{30}$$
$$225 = 120 + 3k$$
$$3k = 225 - 120$$
$$3k = 105$$
$$k = 35$$

2(C). Using Empirical formula,
Mode $= 3$ Median -2 Mean
3 Median $=$ Mode $+2$ Mean
$$\text{Median} = \frac{(\text{Mode}+2\text{Mean})}{3}$$
$$\text{Median} = \frac{[7+2(8)]}{3} = \frac{(7+16)}{3} = \frac{23}{3}$$

3(C). Let, R is the radius of the sphere, r is the radius of the cylinder and h is the height of the cylinder.
Since, surface area of sphere is same as the curved surface area of cylinder.
Therefore,
$$4\pi r^2 = 2\pi Rh$$
$$2r^2 = 6 \times 12$$
$$r^2 = 36$$
$$r = 6 cm$$

4(A). 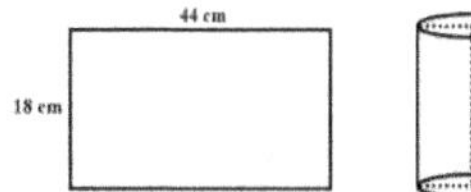

Let r be the radius of the cylinder.
Given: Circumference of cylinder $= 44\ cm$
$$\Rightarrow 2\pi r = 44$$
$$\Rightarrow 2 \times \frac{22}{7} \times r = 44$$
$$\Rightarrow r = 7\ cm$$

5(D). Multiplying the equation throughout by 5, we get
$$25x^2 - 30x - 10 = 0$$
This is the same as,
$$(5x)^2 - 2 \times (5x) \times 3 + 3^2 - 3^2 - 10 = 0$$
$$\Rightarrow (5x - 3)^2 - 9 - 10 = 0$$
$$\Rightarrow (5x - 3)^2 - 19 = 0$$
$$\Rightarrow (5x - 3)^2 = 19$$
$$\Rightarrow 5x - 3 = \pm\sqrt{19}$$
$$\Rightarrow 5x = 3 \pm \sqrt{19}$$
So, $x = \frac{3\pm\sqrt{19}}{5}$

Therefore, the roots are $\frac{3+\sqrt{19}}{5}$ and $\frac{3-\sqrt{19}}{5}$.

6(C). Let the smaller of the two consecutive odd positive integers be x. Then, the second integer will be $x+2$.
According to the question,
$$x^2 + (x + 2)^2 = 290$$
$$\Rightarrow x^2 + x^2 + 4x + 4 = 290$$
$$\Rightarrow 2x^2 + 4x - 286 = 0$$
$$\Rightarrow x^2 + 2x - 143 = 0$$
Which is a quadratic equation in x.
Using the quadratic formula, we get
$$x = \frac{-2\pm\sqrt{4+572}}{2} = \frac{-2\pm\sqrt{576}}{2} = \frac{-2\pm24}{2}$$
$$\Rightarrow x = 11 \text{ or } x = -13$$
But x is given to be an odd positive integer.
Therefore, $x \neq -13, x = 11$.
Thus, the two consecutive odd integers are 11 and 13.

7(D). Given:
$$6x^2 + 4x - a = 0$$
The roots of the given quadratic equation are real and equal.
So, the discriminant will be 0.
$$b^2 - 4ac = 0$$
$$(4)^2 - 4 \times 6 \times (-a) = 0$$
$$16 + 24a = 0$$
$$2 + 3a = 0$$
$$3a + 2 = 0$$

8(B).

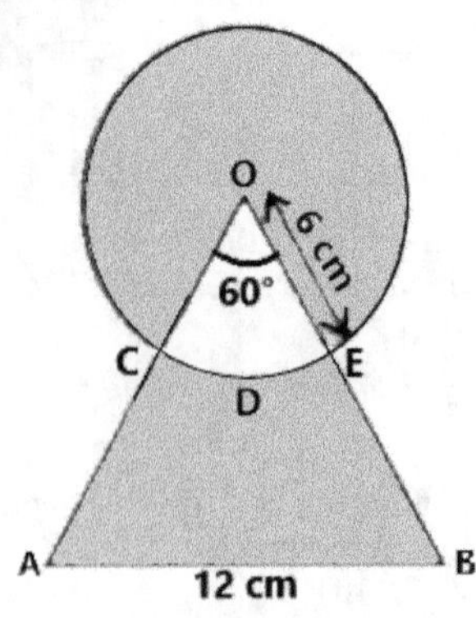

Given,
Radius of the circle is 6 cm We know that each interior angle of an equilateral triangle is of measure $60°$. For area of shaded region,

Area of sector $OCDE = \frac{\theta}{360°} \times \pi r^2$

Area of sector $OCDE = \frac{60°}{360°} \pi r^2$

$= \frac{1}{6} \times \frac{22}{7} \times (6)^2$

$= \frac{132}{7}$ cm^2

Area of $\Delta OAB = \frac{\sqrt{3}}{4}(12)^2$

Area of equilateral triangle $= \frac{\sqrt{3}}{4} \times (\text{side})^2$

$= 36\sqrt{3}$ cm^2

Area of circle $= \pi r^2$

$= \frac{22}{7} \times (6)^2$

$= \frac{792}{7}$ cm^2

Area of shaded region $=$ Area of $\Delta OAB +$ Area of circle $-$ Area of sector $OCDE$

$= 36\sqrt{3} + \frac{792}{7} - \frac{132}{7}$

$= \left(36\sqrt{3} + \frac{660}{7}\right)$ cm^2

So, the area of the shaded region in the given figure $\left(36\sqrt{3} + \frac{660}{7}\right)$ cm^2.

9(A).

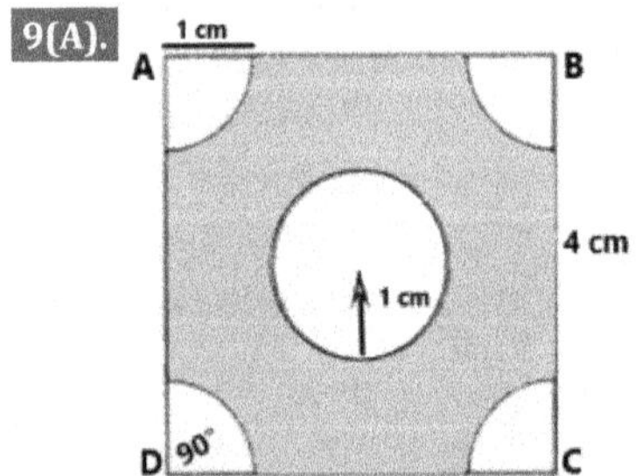

It is evident from the above figure that each quadrant is a sector of $90°$ in a circle of 1 cm radius.
For area of shaded region,

Area of sector $= \frac{\theta}{360°} \times \pi r^2$

Area of each quadrant $= \frac{90°}{360°} \pi r^2$

$= \frac{1}{4} \times \frac{22}{7} \times (1)^2$

$= \frac{22}{28}$ cm^2

Area of square $= (\text{side})^2$

$= (4)^2$

$= 16$ cm^2

Area of circle $= \pi r^2$

$= \pi(1)^2 = \frac{22}{7}$ cm^2

Area of the shaded region = Area of square $-$ Area of circle $-(4 \times$ Area of quadrant $)$

$= 16 - \frac{22}{7} - \left(4 \times \frac{22}{28}\right)$

$= 16 - \frac{44}{7}$

$= \frac{68}{7}$ cm^2

Therefore, the area of the remaining portion of the square is $\frac{68}{7}$ cm^2.

10(B). Given,
$2\tan^2 45° + \cos^2 30° - \sin^2 60°$
As we know that:

$\tan 45° = 1, \cos 30° = \frac{\sqrt{3}}{2}, \sin 60° = \frac{\sqrt{3}}{2}$

$= 2(1)^2 + \left(\frac{\sqrt{3}}{2}\right)^2 - \left(\frac{\sqrt{3}}{2}\right)^2$

$= 2 + \frac{3}{4} - \frac{3}{4} = 2$

11(D). Given,
$\frac{5\cos^2 60° + 4\sec^2 30° - \tan^2 45°}{\sin^2 30° + \cos^2 30°}$

As we know that:
$\cos 60° = \frac{1}{2}, \sec 30° = \frac{2}{\sqrt{3}}, \tan 45° = 1, \sin$

$30° = \frac{1}{2}, \cos 30° = \frac{\sqrt{3}}{2}$

$= \frac{5\left(\frac{1}{2}\right)^2 + 4\left(\frac{2}{\sqrt{3}}\right)^2 - (1)^2}{\left(\frac{1}{2}\right)^2 + \left(\frac{\sqrt{3}}{2}\right)^2}$

$= \frac{5\left(\frac{1}{4}\right) + \left(\frac{16}{3}\right) - 1}{\frac{1}{4} + \frac{3}{4}}$

$= \frac{\frac{15 + 64 - 12}{12}}{\frac{4}{4}}$

$= \frac{67}{12}$

12(A). Given,
$\sin 25° \cos 65° + \cos 25° \sin 65° \dots$ (i)
As we know that,
$\sin(A + B) = (\sin A \times \cos B + \cos A \times \sin B) \dots$
. (ii)
Comparing equation (i) with euation (ii) we get,
$A = 25°$
$B = 65°$
$\sin(25° + 65°)$
$\Rightarrow \sin 90° = 1$

13(A). The pair of equations has a unique solution if:
$\frac{a_1}{a_2} = \frac{b_1}{b_2}$

For the given pair of equations:
$2x + 3y + 5 = 0$ and $px + 6y + 8 = 0$;
$a_1 = 2; a_2 = p; b_1 = 3; b_2 = 6$
For $\frac{2}{p} = \frac{3}{6} \rightarrow p = 4$

Hence, the given pair of equations has a unique solution for all values of p except 4.

14(B). Given, equations are
$2x + 3y - 5 = 0, kx - 6y - 8 = 0$
Here, $a_1 = 2, b_1 = 3, c_1 = -5$ and
$a_2 = k, b_2 = -6, c_2 = -8$
For unique solutions, we know

$\frac{a_1}{a_2} = \frac{b_1}{b_2}$

$\Rightarrow \frac{2}{k} = \frac{3}{-6}$

$\Rightarrow 3k = -12$

$\Rightarrow k = -4$

15(A). To find the time when the clocks will next ring together,
We have to find LCM of $4, 12$ and 20 minutes.
$4 = 2^2$
$12 = 2^2 \times 3$
$20 = 2^2 \times 5$

$\begin{array}{c|c} 2 & 12 \\ \hline 2 & 6 \\ \hline & 3 \end{array}$

$\begin{array}{c|c} 2 & 20 \\ \hline 2 & 10 \\ \hline & 5 \end{array}$

LCM of $4, 12$ and $20 = 2^2 \times 3 \times 5 = 60$ minutes.
So, the clocks will ring together again after 60 minutes or one hour.

16(A). A complete his round in $6 \times 60 = 360$ seconds
B completes his round in $5 \times 60 = 300$ seconds
C completes his round in $20 \times 60 = 1200$ seconds.
We have to find the minimum time when they meet again at the starting point. So, for calculating minimum time we will find LCM of $360, 300$ and 1200.
LCM of $360, 300$ and 1200
$360 = 2 \times 2 \times 2 \times 3 \times 3 \times 5$
$300 = 2 \times 2 \times 3 \times 5 \times 5$
$1200 = 2 \times 2 \times 2 \times 2 \times 3 \times 5 \times 5$
Required   LCM
$= 2 \times 2 \times 2 \times 2 \times 3 \times 3 \times 5 \times 5 = 3600$
seconds $= 60$ minutes $= 1$ hour.
So they will meet again at the starting point for the first time after 1 hour.

17(A). HCF of 408 and 1032
$\Rightarrow 408 = 17 \times 3 \times 2^3$
$\Rightarrow 1032 = 43 \times 3 \times 2^3$
So HCF $= 3 \times 2^3$
$= 24$
As per question,
$1032 \times 2 + 408 \times (p) = 24$
$408p = 24 - 2064$
$p = -5$

18(A). Given:
Number $38, 45$ and 52 leaves $2, 3$ and 4 as remainder respectively.
By subtracting the remainders from the numbers, we get:
$38 - 2 = 36$
$45 - 3 = 42$
$52 - 4 = 48$
So, we need to find greatest number which divides $36, 42$ and 48.
HCF of $(36, 42, 48)$:
Factors of $36 = 2 \times 2 \times 3 \times 3$

Factors of $42 = 2 \times 3 \times 7$
Factors of $48 = 2 \times 2 \times 2 \times 2 \times 3$
So the HCF of $(36, 42, 48) = 2 \times 3 = 6$
Thus, 6 is the greatest number that will divide $38, 45$ and 52 leaving $2, 3$ and 4 as remainder respectively.

19(B). Given:
α, β, γ are the roots of equation $x^3 + px^2 + qx + r = 0$
We have
$\alpha + \beta + \gamma = -p$
$\alpha\beta + \beta\gamma + \gamma\alpha = q$
$\alpha\beta\gamma = -1$
Now,
$\sum \alpha^2(\beta + \gamma) = (\alpha^2\beta + \alpha^2\gamma) + (\beta^2\gamma + \beta^2\alpha)$
$+ (\gamma^2\alpha + \gamma^2\beta)$
$= (\alpha + \beta + \gamma)(\alpha\beta + \beta\gamma + \gamma\alpha) - 3\alpha\beta\gamma$
$= -pq + 3r$
$= 3r - pq$

20(A). Given equation
$2x^3 - 3x^2 + 6x + 1 = 0$,
Sum of roots:
$\alpha + \beta + \gamma = \frac{-b}{a}$
So, $\alpha + \beta + \gamma = \frac{3}{2}$,
Product of roots:
$\alpha\beta\gamma = \frac{-d}{a}$
$\alpha\beta\gamma = \frac{-1}{2}$
Sum of products taken 2 at a time:
$\Sigma\alpha\beta = \alpha\beta + \beta\gamma + \alpha\gamma = \frac{c}{a}$
$\alpha\beta + \beta\gamma + \alpha\gamma = \frac{6}{2} = 3$
Now, we know that
$(\alpha + \beta + \gamma)^2 = \alpha^2 + \beta^2 + \gamma^2 + 2(\alpha\beta + \beta\gamma + \gamma\alpha)$
Re-arranging, we get
$\alpha^2 + \beta^2 + \gamma^2 = (\alpha + \beta + \gamma)^2 - 2(\Sigma\alpha\beta)$
$\alpha^2 + \beta^2 + \gamma^2 = \left(\frac{3}{2}\right)^2 - 2 \times 3$
$= \frac{9}{4} - 6$
$= -\frac{15}{4}$

21(C). Probability is a value between (and including) zero and one.
Therefore, we can say that $0 \leq p \leq 1$

22(B). Prime numbers on a die are $2, 3, 5$
composite numbers on a die are $4, 6$
Prime and Composite numbers on a die $= 2, 3, 4, 5, 6$
Number of possible outcomes $n(A) = 5$
Number of Total outcomes $n(S) = 6$
Required Probability $= \frac{n(A)}{n(S)} = \frac{5}{6}$

23(A). Here, $a = 9$ and $d = 17 - 9 = 8$.
We are required to find n.
Using $S_n = \frac{n}{2}[2a + (n-1)d]$
$a = $ first term
$d = $ common difference
$S_n = $ Sum of nth term we get,
$\frac{n}{2}(2 \times 9 + (n-1) \times 8) = 636$
$\Rightarrow n(9 + (n-1)4) = 636$
$\Rightarrow n(4n + 5) = 636$
$\Rightarrow 4n^2 + 5n - 636 = 0$

$x = \frac{-b \pm \sqrt{b^2 - 4ac}}{2a}$
$\Rightarrow a = 4, b = 5$ and $c = -636$
$\Rightarrow n = \frac{-5 \pm \sqrt{5^2 - 4 \times 4(-636)}}{2 \times 4} =$
$\frac{-5 \pm \sqrt{10201}}{8}$
$= \frac{-5 \pm 101}{8} = \frac{96}{8}, -\frac{106}{8} = 12, -\frac{53}{4}$
But n being the number of terms, $n \neq -\frac{53}{4}$
so, $n = 12$
So, we take 12 term of the given AP to give the sum 636.

24(B). First 40 positive integers divisible by 6 are $6, 12, 18, 24, \ldots, 240$.
This list of numbers forms an AP with
$a = 6, l = 240$ and $n = 40$
$S_n = \frac{n}{2}(a + l)$
$a = $ first term
$l = $ last term
$S_n = $ Sum of nth term
Sum of these numbers $= \frac{40}{2}(6 + 240)$
$= 20 \times 246 = 4920$

25(A). Let P be any point on the circle with center O.
$OP = $ radius
Take a line L through P and Q as shown if L is perpendicular to OP.
$OQ \perp OP$ because the perpendicular distance is shortest.
Every point except P lies outside the circle and line 1 must be a tangent. At any given point one and only one tangent can be drawn.

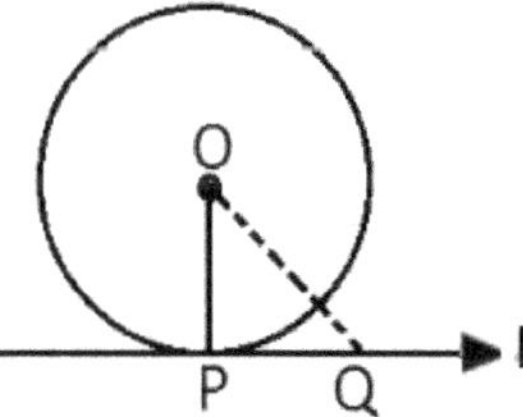

Thus, there is only one tangent at a point of the circle.

26(B). According to the given information the diagram is as:

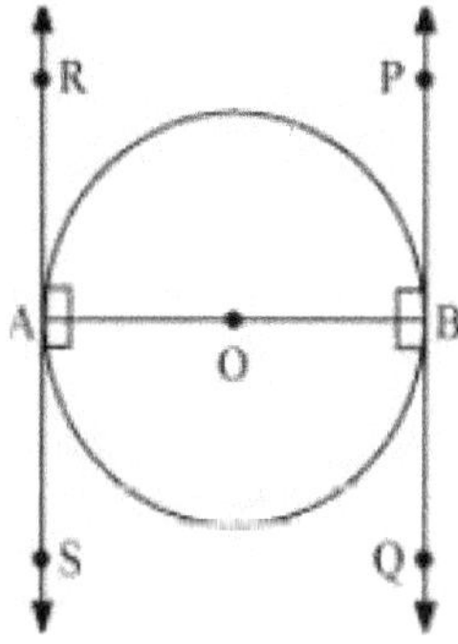

Now, as we know that,
AB is a diameter of the circle with centre O, two tangents PQ and RS drawn at points A and B respectively. Radius will be perpendicular to these tangents.

Thus, $OA \perp RS$ and $OB \perp PQ$
$\angle OAR = \angle OBP = \angle OBQ = 90°$
Therefore, $\angle OAR = \angle OBQ$ (Alternate interior angles)
$\angle OAS = \angle OBP$ (Alternate interior angles)
Since, alternate interior angles are equal, lines PQ and RS will be parallel.

27(C). As we know that,
In a circle, the equal chord of a circle subtends equal angle at the centre. So, it is given that,
$\angle AOB = 60°$
Where, AB is a chord.
We have to find the $\angle COD$. Here, the given chord is CD.
$\therefore \angle AOB = \angle COD = 60°$

28(B). Given $\triangle ABC \sim \triangle DEF$
In two similar triangles, the ratio of their areas is the square of the ratio of their sides
$\Rightarrow \frac{ar(ABC)}{ar(DEF)} = \left(\frac{BC}{EF}\right)^2$
$\Rightarrow \frac{80}{ar(DEF)} = \left(\frac{4}{5}\right)^2$
$\Rightarrow \frac{80}{ar(DEF)} = \frac{16}{25}$
$\Rightarrow ar(DEF) = 125 \text{ cm}^2$

29(C). In $\triangle ABC$ and $\triangle DEF$
Given $\frac{AB}{DE} = \frac{BC}{FD}$
Now included angle between side AB and BC of $\triangle ABC$ is $\angle B$.
Included angle between side DE and FD of $\triangle DEF$ is $\angle D$
So for triangles to be similar $\angle B = \angle D$

30(B). In $\triangle ABC$,
$\Rightarrow (AC)^2 = (BC)^2 + (AB)^2$ [Given $]\cdots(1)$
Pythagoras theorem,
$\Rightarrow (\text{Hypotenuse})^2 = (\text{one side})^2 + (\text{other side})^2 \cdots(2)$
Comparing (1) and (2) we get, AC is a hypotenuse of a triangle.
$\Rightarrow$ Hypotenuse is the longest side of a right-angled triangle, opposite the right angle.
$\Rightarrow$ Opposite angle of AC is $\angle B$.
$\therefore \angle B$ is a right angle of $\triangle ABC$.

31(A). According to the World health organization, prolonged human exposure to solar UV radiation may result in acute and chronic health effects on the skin, eye, and immune system.
Sunburn (erythema) is the best-known acute effect of excessive UV radiation exposure. Over the longer term, UV radiation induces degenerative changes in cells of the skin, fibrous tissue, and blood vessels leading to premature skin aging, photodermatoses, and actinic keratoses.
Another long-term effect is an inflammatory reaction of the eye. In the most serious cases, skin cancer and cataracts can occur.
Furthermore, a growing body of evidence suggests that environmental levels of UV

radiation may suppress cell-mediated immunity and thereby enhance the risk of infectious diseases and limit the efficacy of vaccinations. Both of these actions against the health of poor and vulnerable groups, especially children of the developing world. Many developing countries are located close to the equator and hence, people are exposed to the very high levels of UV radiation that occur in these regions.

32(C). The first link in any food chain is always a green plant, because they alone have a capacity to fix atmospheric CO_2 in the presence of sunlight.

In all the ecosystems, the sun is the ultimate source of energy. Green plants trap solar energy and convert it into a usable form, which can be used by other organisms at successive trophic levels.

33(C). The elements or compounds which occur naturally in the earth's crust are known as minerals.

Minerals are those elements on the earth and in foods that our bodies need to develop and function normally. Those essential for health include calcium, phosphorus, potassium, sodium, chloride, magnesium, iron, zinc, iodine, chromium, copper, fluoride, molybdenum, manganese, and selenium.

34(D). Water is a covalent compound. A single water molecule consists of an oxygen atom attached to two hydrogen atoms. Each of the hydrogen atoms is bound to the oxygen atom through a covalent bond.

Water has a covalent bond because of the nature of oxygen and hydrogen, they share electrons to attain stability, and their electronegativities are close enough for their bond to be considered covalent.

Covalent bond: The bond form between two atoms by mutual sharing of their electrons is known as a covalent bond and the compound is known as a covalent compound.

35(A). Goitre is the enlargement of thyroid gland which occurs due to deficiency of iodine in the body. Iodine is needed for the synthesis of thyroid hormone. When the iodine levels are low, thyroid gland becomes hyper active and enlarged to compensate for the deficiency of thyroid hormone in the body. The enlarged thyroid gland is visible as a swelling in the throat known as goitre.

So, cretinism and goitre are caused by hyper or hyposecretion of thyroxine.

36(C). Skeletal muscles are controlled by somatic nervous system.

Skeletal muscle, also called voluntary muscle, in vertebrates, most common of the three types of muscle in the body. Skeletal muscles are attached to bones by tendons, and they produce all the movements of body parts in relation to each other.

We order the skeletal muscles to function deliberately under the action of hypothalamus present below the brain. Thus, Skeletal muscles are controlled by the somatic nervous system part of the peripheral nervous system.

37(C). The given reaction can be classified as combustion reaction and combination reaction.

$$C(s) + O_2(g) \rightarrow C_2(g) + \text{Heat}$$

A combustion reaction is the reaction in which a substance reacts with the presence of oxygen gas and which releases the amount of energy in the form of gas or light and heat is produced during the reaction. On the reactants side, we can see that solid carbon is burnt in presence of air oxygen. And on the product side we have received the energy as the gas carbon dioxide and the amount of heat is produced. Thus, here we can see the combustion reaction.

In the above reaction, we can also observe that the carbon atom is with the oxygen to form the carbon dioxide. So, the combination reaction takes place.

So, we can see that combustion reaction and the combination reaction takes place in this reaction.

38(A). The reducing agent in the above equation is Al.

An oxidizing agent, or oxidant, absorbs electrons and is decreased in the event of a chemical reaction. A reducing agent, or a resistant agent, destroys electrons and is oxidized in a chemical reaction. A reducing agent is usually present in one of its lowest potential oxidation states and is known as an electron donor. Al is the reducing agent in the reaction. According to the reactivity series, aluminum remains in the Low Reactivity category compared to Manganese.

39(B). Graphite is a good conductor of electricity.

Graphite is an allotrope of carbon which conducts electricity due to de-localisation of the electrons above and below the planes of the carbon atoms.

Graphite is a good conductor of heat and electricity. This is because, like metals, graphite contains delocalised (free) electrons. These electrons are free to move through the structure of the graphite.

40(D). Homologous series is a series of compounds with similar chemical properties and some functional groups differing from the successive member by CH_2. Carbon chains of varying lengths have been observed in organic compounds having the same general formula. C_3H_4 belongs to a homologous series of alkynes.

41(D). The transfer of pollen grain from the anther to the stigma of a pistil is called pollination. It is a mechanism by which non-motile male and female gametes are

brought together for the fertilization. Self-Pollination is of two types: Autogamy and geitonogamy.

The transfer of pollen grains from the anther of one flower to the stigma of another flower of the same plant is called geitonogamy. This transfer involves a pollinating agent. Genetically, it is similar to autogamy since the pollen grains come from the same plant.

42(C). The uterus opens into the vagina through cervix.

The uterus is a bag like muscular secondary sex organ. The development of the fetus takes place in the uterus or the womb. The posterior end of the uterus is the cervix which opens into the vagina.

43(C). A fossil is any preserved remains, impression, or trace of any once-living thing from a past geological age. Examples include bones, shells, exoskeletons, stone imprints of animals or microbes, objects preserved in amber, hair, petrified wood, oil, coal, and DNA remnants. The totality of fossils is known as the fossil record.

44(A). Analogous organs are the organs that are different anatomically in structure but perform the same function. They are involved in convergent evolution. Convergent evolution is a form of evolution where other species evolve independently to develop to achieve a similar type of function. Examples of analogous organs are as follows :

Wind of bat and wing of bird are the example of the analogous organs. Bat wings consist of flaps of skin stretched between the bones of the fingers and arm. Bird wings consist of feathers extending all along the arm.

45(D). The image formed by a concave mirror is observed to be virtual, erect and larger than the object. Between the pole of the mirror and its principal focus of the object.

A concave mirror has a reflective surface that is curved inward and away from the light source. Concave mirrors reflect light inward to one focal point. Unlike convex mirrors, the image formed by a concave mirror shows different image types depending on the distance between the object and the mirror.

46(B). At twice the focal length an object be placed in front of a convex lens to get a real image of the size of the object.

When an object is placed at the centre of curvature in front of a convex lens, its image is formed at the centre of curvature on the other side of the lens. The image formed is real, inverted, and of the same size as the object.

47(B). In electric motor, to make the coil rotating continuously in the same direction, current is reversed in the coil after every half rotation by a device called commutation.

Commutation is a mechanism that reverses the direction of current in the arms of an armature through a circuit.

48(A). When current is parallel to magnetic field, then force experience by the current carrying conductor placed in uniform magnetic field is twice to that when angle is $60°$. The current carrying conductor placed in a magnetic field experiences zero force when placed parallel to the magnetic field and experiences maximum force when held perpendicular to the magnetic field.

49(B). Species of cuscuta are plant parasites. They lack chlorophyll hence cannot manufacture their own food through photosynthesis. They thrive on other plants, consuming their nutrients to grow, hence weakening its host.

Mushrooms are the advanced members of a fungi group belonging to the class Basidiomycetes. They grow on dead and decaying matters like dung, old rotten logs which are rich in organic matter. Therefore, they are saprophytic fungi

The mode of nutrition in amoeba is known as holozoic nutrition. It involves the ingestion, digestion and egestion of food material. Amoeba does not have any specialized organ for nutrition.

50(B). Organisms from whose body the parasite derives the benefit are called host. The host which harbors the adult parasites or where the parasite replicates sexually is called the definitive host. The definitive host can be a mammalian host or other living hosts.

51(B). Indigestion is a term generally used for stomach pain and heartburn, indigestion is mainly due to the increased acidity in the stomach. To treat indigestion we use a special kind of drug category which is named 'Antacids'.

Antacids actually are base-containing drugs who neutralizes the nyper acidic condition. Eg, milk of magnesia $(Mg(OH)_2)$.

52(D). Acids cannot be stored in metal containers as they will react with the metal, forming metal salt and liberating Hydrogen gas. Containers made of glass are ideal for storage of acid due to its chemical inertness.

In the given options HCl, HNO_3, and H_2SO_4 all are very strong acids who are also very corrosive in nature so cannot be stored in the metal containers.

53(D). The least distance of distinct vision for a normal human being is 25cm. For young people, the least distance of distant vision will be within 25cm which however it varies with age. For infants, the least distance of distinct vision is about 5 to 8

cm. As the person grows old, their culinary muscles responsible for adjusting the eye lens get weakened.

54(C). Given, work done 'w'= $6.4 \times 10^{-4} J$
$q = 2C$
find $V_A - V_B =$?
We know
$w = q(V_A - V_B)$
$(V_A - V_B) = \dfrac{6.4 \times 10^{-4} J}{2C}$
$(V_A - V_B) = 3.2 \times 10^{-4} V$

55(A). Step 1: The resistance of wire is expressed as
$R = \dfrac{\rho L}{A} \cdots (1)$
Given, $R = 1\,\Omega$,
$r = 1\,mm = 0.001\,m$
The area of cross section,
$A = \pi r^2 = 3.14 \times 0.001^2 = 3.14 \times 10^{-6}$
Resistivity $\rho = 1.7 \times 10^{-8}$ ohm-meter
Step 2: Putting above values in equation (1)
We get
$1 = \dfrac{1.7 \times 10^{-8} \times L}{3.14 \times 10^{-6}}$
$\Rightarrow L = \dfrac{1 \times 3.14 \times 10^{-6}}{1.7 \times 10^{-8}} = \dfrac{3.14 \times 10^{-6}}{1.7 \times 10^{-8}} = 1.847 \times 10^2\,m$
Therefore, the length of the wire is $184.7\,m$
.

56(D). Due to the Industrialisation of the Indian rivers becoming toxic.

The largest source of water pollution in India is untreated sewage. Other sources of pollution include agricultural runoff and unregulated small-scale industry. Most rivers, lakes and surface water in India are polluted due to industries, untreated sewage and solid wastes.

57(A).
The main causes of forest depletion are large scale development projects.

Farming, cutting of timber, mining and often indiscriminate dam building for hydro electric power projects are the foremost causes of deforestation in India. Another factor is the burgeoning population and its resultant growing urbanisation.

58(C). It is a ferrous ore is not true about features of copper.

Ferrous minerals like iron ore, manganese and chromites contain iron. A non-ferrous mineral does not contain iron but may contain some other metal such as gold, silver, copper or lead.

Ferrous Ore is a sandy yellow color ore that can be smelted to make ferrous ingots. It can be found in lower layers roughly when $y = 10$ in the co-ordinates. When put into a Pulverizer will produce 2 Pulverized Ferrous Metals and 10% chance of Pulverized Shiny Metal. Ferrous ore can not be macerated.

59(B). Tertiary sector has emerged as the largest producing sector in India.

The tertiary sector covers a wide range of

activities from commerce to administration, transport, financial and real estate activities, business and personal services, education, health and social work. It is made of the non-market sector (public administration, education, human health, social work activities).

60(A). The idea of development involves questions like "What are the essentials things that we require?".

Development means to progress in order to achieve a certain goal. These goals are different for different people or groups of people. Development can involve any area of specialization such as health, finance or education. Development means a gradual growth of a thing or a person.

61(B). In 1796 italy was invaded by Napolean.

Napoleon was appointed to command the French Army of Italy in March 1796. His orders were to invade northern Italy and occupy Lombardy, a move that the French Directory believed would force the Austrians to move troops south from the Rhine front. The army Napoleon inherited was in a terrible condition.

62(C). Primitive subsistence is the type of agriculture called 'slash and burn' agriculture.

- Slash and burn agriculture is a type of primitive subsistence agriculture.
- It is also called Jhum agriculture.
- It is a shifting cultivation practice.
- It is also known as fire-fallow cultivation.

63(D). ATM card is an example of the digital banking.

Digital banking enables a bank's customers to access banking products and services via an electronic/online platform. Digital banking means to digitize all of the banking operations and substitute the bank's physical presence with an everlasting online presence, eliminating a consumer's need to visit a branch.

64(D). Rate of interest charged by moneylenders as compared to that charged by banks is much higher.

Moneylender is a person or organization whose business is to lend money at interest . He lends small amounts of money at a higher rate of interest . The reason for charging higher rates of interest is that the money lender faces a higher risk of default than normal banks due to various reasons. He is an informal form of creditor.

65(C). Large MNCs in the garment industry in Europe and America order their products from Indian exporters.

Large MNCs in the garment industry in Europe and America order their products from Indian exporters. These large MNCs with worldwide network look for the cheapest goods in order to maximise their profits. To get these large orders, Indian garment exporters try hard to cut their own costs. As cost of raw materials cannot be reduced, exporters try to cut labour costs. Where earlier a factory used to employ workers on a permanent basis, now they employ workers only on a temporary basis so that they do not have to pay workers for the whole year. Workers also have to put in very long working hours and work night shifts on a regular basis during the peak season. Wages are low and workers are forced to work overtime to make both ends meet.

66(D). Governments use trade barriers to increase or decrease (regulate) foreign trade and to decide what kinds of goods and how much of each, should come into the country.

Tariffs are taxes on imports. They effectively raise the prices of those imports, providing an edge to domestic companies in the same markets. Governments usually impose tariffs to help domestic companies, or sometimes to punish foreign competitors for unfair trading practices.

67(B). The Consumer Protection Act, 1986 ensures Right to consumer education. The right to consumer education: It refers to a right that protects the consumer from various large companies of the products and services they sell. It is basically about informing people and giving them the required knowledge for living in a consumer society. Consumer education opens the eyes of buyers of goods and services to seek redress when they are cheated or purchased defective products.

68(C). Consumer Protection Councils do not provide compensation to consumers when they are cheated by shopkeepers. consumer protection council is a non-government organisation, spreading awareness among common people and help them to file cases in the court and get justice for the consumers. They represent individuals in the consumer courts. Consumer protection council has not any legal right and is a voluntary organization. Consumer courts are three tier quasi-judicial machinery set up for redressed of consumer disputes.

69(C). Chapbook is a Pocket sized books that were sold by travelling pedlars called chapmen.

A chapbook is a small publication of up to about 40 pages, sometimes bound with a saddle stitch. In early modern Europe a chapbook was a type of printed street literature. Produced cheaply, chapbooks were commonly small, paper-covered booklets, usually printed on a single sheet folded into books of 8, 12, 16 and 24 pages. They were often illustrated with crude woodcuts, which sometimes bore no relation to the text (much like today's stock

photos), and were often read aloud to an audience. When illustrations were included in chapbooks, they were considered popular prints.

70(A). In the mid-eighteenth century, there was a common conviction that books were a means of spreading progress and enlightenment.

Many believed that books could change the world, liberate society from despotism and tyranny, and herald a time when reason and intellect would rule. Louise-sebastian Mercier, a novelist in Prance declared. "The printing press is most powerful engine of progress and public- opinion is the force that will sweep despotism away."

71(C). Under Horizontal power sharing power is shared among different organs of the government namely Legislature, Executive and Judiciary.

These organs works differently but at same footing. This kind of distribution of powers creates the system of checks and balances over the function of one organ by the other organ while entitling them to work in their own spheres.

72(D). Among the given option, B, C and D are true.

Situation in Sri Lanka:
- The Sri Lankan Tamils launched parties and struggles for the recognition of Tamil as an official language, for regional autonomy and equality of opportunity in securing education and jobs. But their demand for more autonomy to provinces populated by the Tamils was repeatedly denied.
- Protecting and fostering Buddhism was stipulated by the new constitution.
- A series of MAJORITARIAN measures were adopted by the democratically elected Government, to establish Sinhala supremacy.
- By virtue of the majority of Sinhala community, the leaders of this community wanted to have dominance over the Government.
- To favour Sinhala applicants for government jobs and university positions, preferential policies favouring one community was followed by the governments.
- Disregarding Tamil, in 1956, an Act was passed to recognise Sinhala as the only official language.
- The feeling of alienation among the Sri Lankan Tamils increased gradually as all these government measures were implemented one after another.
- Sri Lankan Tamils felt that sensitivity was not shown towards their culture and language by the major political parties which were led by the Buddhist Sinhala leaders.
- They felt that the government policies and constitution ignored their interests,

discriminated against them in getting jobs and other opportunities and denied them equal political rights.
- It soon turned into a CIVIL WAR. As a result thousands of people of both the communities have been killed. Many families were forced to leave the country as refugees and many more lost their livelihoods.

Situation in Belgium:
- The Belgian leaders took a different path.
- The existence of cultural diversities and regional differences was recognised by the Belgian leaders.
- Belgian leaders worked out a very innovative and different arrangement when compared to any other country.
- To enable everyone to live together within the same country, to work out an arrangement, the constitution was amended four times, between 1970 and 1993.
- There will be an equal number of French speaking and Dutch speaking ministers, as per constitution.
- To make sure that unilateral decisions are not made by one single community, the support of a majority of members from each linguistic group is needed as per some special laws.
- The state governments are not subordinate to the Central Government.
- Many powers of the central government have been given to state governments of the two regions of the country.
- As the Dutch-speaking community has accepted equal representation in the Central Government, the French speaking people accepted equal representation in Brussels
- Brussels has a separate government in which both the communities have equal representation.

73(D). United States of America did Britian borrow large sums of money during first World War.

By 1916, Britain was funding most of the Empire's war expenditures, all of Italy's and two thirds of the war costs of France and Russia, plus smaller nations as well. The gold reserves, overseas investments and private credit then ran out forcing Britain to borrow $4 billion from the U.S. Treasury in 1917–18.

74(B). The Eighth Schedule to the Constitution of India lists the official scheduled languages of the Republic of India.

At the time when the Constitution was enacted, inclusion in this list meant that the language was entitled to representation on the Official Languages Commission, and that the language would be one of the bases that would be drawn upon to enrich Hindi, the official language of the Union. The list has since, however, acquired further significance. Per Articles 344(1) and 351 of the Indian Constitution, the eighth schedule includes the recognition of 22 languages.

75(A). In India, the relationship between the Centre and the States were deteriorated because of Formation of different party government at both levels.

For a long time, the same party ruled both at the Centre and in most of the States. This meant that the State governments did not exercise their rights as autonomous federal units.As and when the ruling party at the State level was different, the parties that ruled at the Centre tried to undermine the power of the States. All this changed significantly after 1990. This period saw the rise of regional political parties in many States of the country. Since no single party got a clear majority in the Lok Sabha, the major national parties had to enter into an alliance with many parties including several regional parties to form a government at the Centre. This led to a new culture of power sharing and respect for the autonomy of State Governments.

76(B). There was no shortage of human labor in victorian britain in the mid 19th century because the British used to take poor labourers and peasants from India. Indians were willing to work and migrate as well.

A range of products could be produced only with hand labour. Machines were oriented to producing uniforms, standardised goods for a mass market. But the demand in the market was often for goods with intricate designs and specific shapes. In mid-nineteenth-century Britain, for instance, 500 varieties of hammers were produced and 45 kinds of axes. These required human skills, not mechanical technology.

77(B). The red soil is red in colour because it is rich in iron compounds.

The color of red soil may vary from a variety of colors namely from red to brown, yellow, gray, or even black in some cases. Red soil contains a fairly high percentage of iron content, which is the reason for its color since iron oxide is reddish-brown in color. Red soil is deficient in common nutrients like nitrogen, humus, phosphoric acid, lime, magnesium, etc. but it is fairly rich in potash, and the pH of the soil ranges from neutral to acidic. Its formation occurs due to the weathering of ancient crystalline and metamorphic rocks generally acid granites, quartz rocks, gneiss, and feldspathic rocks.

78(C). The cost of time that democracy pays for arriving at a decision worthwhile because decisions are more likely to be acceptable to the people and more effective. Well a democratic government is supposed to be responsive towards the need of the people and fulfill their expectations . This is why in democracy, a decision which is acceptable and compatible to the people are considered only. Such decision need the time and cause the short delay in the procedure of decision making. But , in the result , only effective and acceptable decision are taken. This is why the cost of time is important in the democracy and worthwhile.

79(D). Democracy is considered to be better than other forms of government-It improves the quality of decision-making, it ensures rapid economic development of citizens, it enhances the dignity of citizens.

A democratic government is a better government because it is an accountable form of government. Democracy improves the quality of decision making. Democracy provides a method to deal with differences and conflicts. Democracy enhances the dignity of citizens.

80(B). Muhammad Ali and Shaukat Ali these two muslim brothers supported the movement along with Gandhi.

Ansari, Maulana Azad and Hakim Ajmal Khan remained strong supporters of Gandhi and the Congress. The Ali brothers joined Muslim League. They would play a major role in the growth of the League's popular appeal and the subsequent Pakistan movement.The Khilafat movement (1919-1924) was an agitation by Indian Muslims allied with Indian nationalism in the years following World War I. Its purpose was to pressure the British government to preserve the authority of the Ottoman Sultan as Caliph of Islam following the breakup of the Ottoman Empire at the end of the war.

81(C). Famous actor Jagdeep was popularly known as "Surma Bhopali".
- Jagdeep was passed away on 8 th July 2020 .
- He was born on 29 th March 1939 at Datiya district Madhya Pradesh.
- His original name was Saiyyad Ishtiyaq Ahmad Jafri .
- He played his famous role of Surma Bhopali in Sholay movie.

83(C). Gresham's law states that "Bad money (if not limited in quantity) drives good money out of circulation".

Gresham's law is a monetary principle stating that "bad money drives out good." It is primarily used for consideration and application in currency markets. Gresham's law was originally based on the composition of minted coins and the value of the precious metals used in them.

For example, If there are two forms of commodity money in circulation, which are accepted by law as having similar face value, the more valuable commodity will gradually disappear from circulation.

84(B). He should be a respected jurist in the eyes of Parliament is not the required qualification for being a judge in the Supreme Court.

The Supreme Court of India comprises the Chief Justice and not more than 30 other Judges appointed by the President of India. Supreme Court Judges retire upon attaining the age of 65 years. In order to be appointed as a Judge of the Supreme Court, a person must be a citizen of India and must have been, for at least five years, a Judge of a High Court or of two or more such Courts in succession, or an Advocate of a High Court or of two or more such Courts in succession for at least 10 years or he must be, in the opinion of the President, a distinguished jurist. Provisions exist for the appointment of a Judge of a High Court as an Ad-hoc Judge of the Supreme Court and for retired Judges of the Supreme Court or High Courts to sit and act as Judges of that Court.

85(A). In geology, the lowest point of the ridge between two mountains is called a call. It is a topography formed by glaciers cut over millions of years. When the two sides of a hill develop a cirque and meet, a crater is formed. Such a route is called a call or pass. There are many calls made by glaciers in the Alps Mountains.

86(C). DART mission is launched by NASA. The main aim of the mission is to test the newly developed technology that would allow a spacecraft to crash into an asteroid and change its course. DART is a low-cost spacecraft, weighing around 610 kg at launch and 550 kg at impact.

87(C). The Thirty-Sixth Amendment, 1975 of the Indian Constitution made two important changes. They are as follows: Sikkim was made a full-fledged State of the Indian Union. The tenth Schedule was omitted.

88(B). Charkula is a dance performed in the Braj region of Uttar Pradesh. In this dance, veiled women balancing large multi-tiered circular wooden pyramids on their heads dance to songs about Krishna.

89(D). Godawari river rises from the slopes of the Western Ghats in the Nasik district of Maharashtra. The Godavari River is the second longest river in India after the Ganges and the longest river in South India, with a length of 1465 km.

90(B). Mahavira Swami established Chaturvidha Sangh in Pava.
- Jainism is one of the world's oldest living religions.
- Jainism gained prominence under the aegis of Mahavira, during the sixth century BCE.
- In order to spread Jainism, Mahavira Swami established Chaturvidha Sangh at Pava in Uttar Pradesh.
- Lord Mahavira divided his followers into four parts - Muni, Aryika, Shravaka and Shravika to confirm the path of Kaivalya knowledge.

- The first two classes are for the householders and the last two for the people who left their house to become Jain monks.
- This was called his Chaturvidha-Sangha.

91(C). Abu'l Fazl is the author of the book 'Ain-i-Akbari'.
- Abu'l Fazl is written in the Persian Language in the 16th century.
- The book includes the administration of Mughal Emperor Akbar.
- It also includes revenue, geography, culture, etc during that time.
- Please note that Akbar Nama is divided into three books and Ain-i-Akbari is the third book.
- Henry Beveridge translated whole Akbar Nama into English.

92(A). A Satyagraha took place in Champaran district of Bihar in 1917 under the leadership of Gandhiji. It is known as Champaran Satyagraha. This was the first Satyagraha done in India under the leadership of Gandhiji.

93(B). Biomagnification: It is also known as bioamplification or biological magnification, occurs when the concentration of a substance, such as DDT or mercury, in an organism, exceeds the background concentration of the substance in its die and accumulation of chemicals at the successive trophic levels of a food chain. Ecosystem: An ecosystem is a community of living organisms in conjunction with the non-living components of their environment (things like air, water and mineral soil), interacting as a system. Aquarium: It is a transparent tank of water in which live fish and other water creatures and aquatic plants are kept and a man-made ecosystem. Parasite: A parasite is an organism that lives in or on another organism (its host) and benefits by deriving nutrients at the other's expense. Since, only the definition of ecology is wrong,

94(C). President has the authority to proclaim emergency in the State. A state of emergency India refers to a period of governance under an altered constitutional setup that can be proclaimed by the President of India, when the consultant group perceives and warns against grave threats to the nation from internal and external sources or from financial situations of crisis. Under the advice of the cabinet of ministers and using the Constitution of India, the President can overrule many provisions of the constitution, which guarantee fundamental rights to the citizens of India and acts governing devolution of powers to the states which form the federation. In the history of independent India, a state of emergency has been declared thrice. The first instance was between 26 October 1962 to 10 January 1968 during the India-China war, when "the security of India" was declared as being "threatened by external aggression". The second instance was between 3 and 17 December 1971, which was originally proclaimed during the Indo-Pakistan war. It was later extended along with the third proclamation between 25 June 1975 to 21 March 1977 under controversial circumstances of political instability under Indira Gandhi's premiership, when emergency was declared on the basis of "internal disturbance", In fact it is not due to internal disturbance, but the emergency was declared by then Prime Minister Indira Gandhi was to overrule the Allahabad High Court order against her that her election result became null and void and she was prohibited from contesting election for next 6 years. But this term was too vague and had a wider connotation and hence in 1978 the Forty-fourth Amendment of the Constitution of India substituted the words "internal disturbance" for "armed rebellion". The phrase Emergency period used loosely, when referring to the political history of India, often refers to the third and the most controversial of the three occasions. The President can declare three types of emergencies: national, state and financial emergency in a state.

95(C). The Chinese city of Hangzhou was the host of the 2022 Asian Games by the Olympic Council of Asia.
- China has hosted the Asian Games twice before, at Beijing in 1990 and Guangzhou in 2010, and has already been awarded the Winter Olympics in 2022.
- The first Asian Games were held from 4 March to 11 March 1951 in New Delhi.

96(C). Vijaya Lakshmi Pandit was the first Indian woman President of the UN General Assembly. Vijaya Lakshmi Pandit (18 August 1900 – 1 December 1990) was an Indian diplomat and politician who was the first female elected to 6th Governor of Maharashtra and 8th President of the United Nations General Assembly.

97(C). The plants mainly receive their nutrients from the soil. Soil is the main source of nutrients for plants because soil contains all minerals, water, humus and some useful microbes which are responsible for the proper growth of the plants. The pH is an important factor that influences the availability of essential nutrients to the plants. The soil of slightly acidic that is of 6 and slightly alkaline that is of 7.5 is satisfactory for the growth of most crops.

98(C). Alloy is an example of a solid solution. Alloy is the fusion or mixing of two or more metals and metals with non-metals. Example of an alloy is Brass that is a mixture of copper and zinc. The property of the resulting mixture differs from pure metals. For example, increasing hardness. An alloy retains all the property of metal-like electrical conductivity, ductility, lustre, etc. Alloys are used in applications like building, automobiles, surgical tools and aerospace industry etc.

99(A). With an area of 836,109 sq mi (2,166,086 sq km), Greenland is the largest island on Earth. It is geographically a lot closer to North America but unfortunately associates more with Europe.

100(D). The Arjuna Award is related to the sports field. The government has recently revised the scheme for arjuna award.

Practice Test 12

1. Construction of a cumulative frequency table is useful in determining the ______.
   (a) mean
   (b) median
   (c) mode
   (d) All of the above

2. The abscissa of the point of intersection of the less than type and of the more than type cumulative frequency curves of a grouped data gives its:
   (a) mean
   (b) median
   (c) mode
   (d) All of the above

3. A cone, a hemisphere and a cylinder stand on the same base and have equal height. Find the ratio of their volumes.
   (a) $1:3:2$
   (b) $1:2:3$
   (c) $1:4:3$
   (d) $3:2:3$

4. A sphere, a cylinder and a cone have the same radius and same height. Find the ratio of their volumes. [Diameter of the sphere is equal to the height of the cylinder and the cone]
   (a) $2:3:1$
   (b) $2:4:1$
   (c) $1:3:2$
   (d) $3:3:2$

5. The quadratic equation whose roots are $7+\sqrt{3}$ and $7-\sqrt{3}$ is:
   (a) $x^2 - 14x + 46 = 0$
   (b) $x^2 + 14x - 46 = 0$
   (c) $x^2 - 14x - 46 = 0$
   (d) $x^2 + 14x + 46 = 0$

6. If $x = 2$ is a root of the quadratic equation $3x^2 - px - 2 = 0$, then the value of 'p' is:
   (a) 0
   (b) 5
   (c) 3
   (d) 1

7. $5x^2 + 8x + 4 = 2x^2 + 4x + 6$ is a:
   (a) Cubic equation
   (b) Constant
   (c) Quadratic equation
   (d) Linear equation

8. The distance covered by a circular wheel of diameter d in 100 revolutions is:
   (a) 100π
   (b) πd
   (c) $100d$
   (d) $100\pi d$

9. The radius of the circle whose area is equal to the sum of the areas of the two circles of radii $24\,cm$ and $7\,cm$ is:
   (a) $24\,cm$
   (b) $25\,cm$
   (c) $7\,cm$
   (d) $31\,cm$

10. The value of $\sin 60° \cos 30° + \sin 30° \cos 60°$ is:
    (a) 0
    (b) 1
    (c) 2
    (d) 4

11. The Value of $\frac{\sin\theta - \cos\theta + 1}{\sin\theta + \cos\theta - 1}$ is:
    (a) $(\sec\theta + \tan\theta)$
    (b) $(\cos\theta + \operatorname{cosec}\theta)$
    (c) $(\sec\theta + \cos\theta)$
    (d) $(\sin\theta + \tan\theta)$

12. If $\tan\theta = \frac{a}{b}$, then $\frac{\cos\theta + \sin\theta}{\cos\theta - \sin\theta} = ?$
    (a) $\frac{b-a}{b+a}$
    (b) $\frac{b+a}{b-a}$
    (c) $\frac{a-b}{a+b}$
    (d) None of these

13. Solve the following pairs of equations by reducing them to a pair of linear equations:
    $$\frac{5}{x-1} + \frac{1}{y-2} = 2$$
    $$\frac{6}{x-1} - \frac{3}{y-2} = 1$$
    (a) $x = 6, y = 8$
    (b) $x = 2, y = 5$
    (c) $x = 4, y = 5$
    (d) $x = 3, y = 6$

14. Solve the following pairs of equations by reducing them to a pair of linear equations:
    $$\frac{10}{x+y} + \frac{2}{x-y} = 4$$
    $$\frac{15}{x+y} - \frac{5}{x-y} = -2$$
    (a) $x = 3, y = 2$
    (b) $x = 6, y = 2$
    (c) $x = 2, y = 3$
    (d) $x = 5, y = 3$

15. Three persons start walking from the same point in a circular track with the difference of $9, 12, 15$ minutes. After what time will they will meet together at the same point from where they had start walking?
    (a) 2 hours
    (b) 3 hours
    (c) 5 hours
    (d) 4 hours

16. Three bells toll at intervals of $9, 12, 15$ minutes respectively. If they start tolling together, after what time will they next toll together?
    (a) 2 hours
    (b) 3 hours
    (c) 5 hours
    (d) 4 hours

17. In Euclid's Division Lemma, when $a = bq + r$ where a and b are positive integers then what values r can take?
    (a) $r = 1$
    (b) $r \geq 0$
    (c) $r = b$
    (d) $r = a$

18. Every even integer is of the form ______ for some integer m.
    (a) m
    (b) $m + 1$
    (c) $2m$
    (d) $2m + 1$

19. If the graph of a polynomial intersects the $x-$ axis at three points, then the number of zeroes:
    (a) at most three
    (b) at least three
    (c) 3
    (d) 0

20. The zeroes of the polynomial $x^2 - 3x - m(m+3)$ are:
    (a) $m, m+3$
    (b) $-m, m+3$
    (c) $m, -(m+3)$
    (d) $-m, -(m+3)$

21. Find the probability of getting 4 when a die is thrown once.
    (a) $\frac{1}{4}$
    (b) $\frac{1}{6}$
    (c) $\frac{2}{8}$
    (d) $\frac{1}{3}$

22. Two die are thrown. Find the probability that the number on the upper face of the first dice is less than the number on the upper face of the second dice:
    (a) $\frac{1}{2}$
    (b) $\frac{7}{12}$
    (c) $\frac{1}{3}$
    (d) $\frac{5}{12}$

23. Find the number of given terms:
    $7, 13, 19, \ldots, 205$
    (a) 35
    (b) 30
    (c) 32
    (d) 34

24. An AP consists of 50 terms of which 3rd term is 12 and the last term is 106. Find the 29th term:
    (a) 68
    (b) 80
    (c) 64
    (d) 62

25. A tangent PQ at a point P of a circle of radius 5 cm meets a line through the centre O at a point Q so that OQ = 12 cm. Length PQ is:
    (a) 12 cm
    (b) 13 cm
    (c) 8.5 cm
    (d) None of these

26. A tangent to a circle intersects it in

__________ point(s).

(a) one   (b) infinite

(c) zero   (d) two

27. In figure given below, if TP and TQ are the two tangents to a circle with centre O so that $\angle POQ = 110°$, then $\angle PTQ$ is equal to:

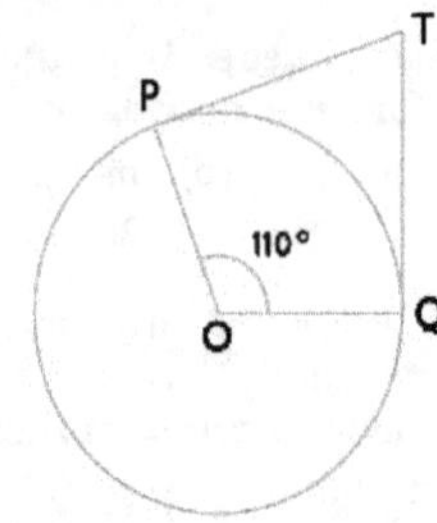

(a) 60°   (b) 70°

(c) 80°   (d) 90°

28. If the perimeters of two similar triangles ABC and DEF are 50 cm and 70 cm respectively and one side of $\triangle ABC$ is 20 cm, then find the corresponding side of $\triangle DEF$.

(a) 20 cm   (b) 25 cm

(c) 28 cm   (d) 38 cm

29. A vertical pole of length 8 m casts a shadow 6 cm long on the ground and at the same time a tower casts a shadow 30 m long. Find the height of tower.

(a) 10 m   (b) 20 m

(c) 30 m   (d) 40 m

30. In the given figure, the line segment XY is parallel to the side AC of $\triangle ABC$ and it divides the triangle into two parts of equal areas. Find the ratio $\dfrac{AX}{AB}$.

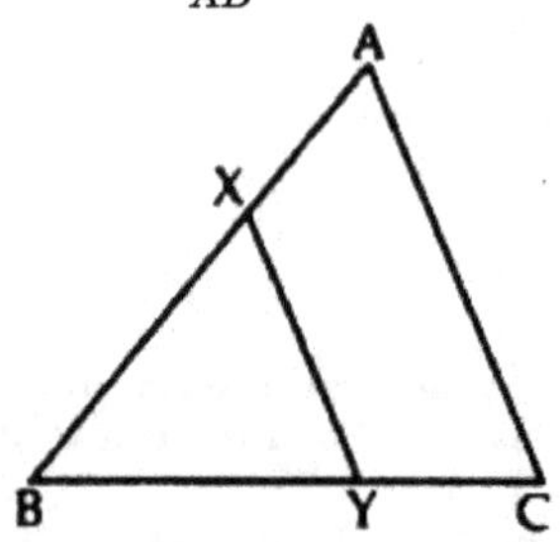

(a) $\dfrac{3-\sqrt{2}}{2}$ (b) $\dfrac{5-\sqrt{2}}{5}$

(c) $\dfrac{2-\sqrt{2}}{2}$ (d) $\dfrac{6-\sqrt{2}}{3}$

Science

31. Concentration of DDT is highest in:

(a) Primary consumer

(b) Producers

(c) Top consumer

(d) Decomposers

32. What do the interacting organisms in an area together with the non-living constituents of the environment form?

(a) Ecosystem   (b) Biome

(c) Trophic level   (d) Biotic factor

33. Which of the following oxide(s) of iron would be obtained on prolonged reaction of iron with steam?

(a) FeO

(b) Fe_2O_3

(c) Fe_3O_4

(d) Fe_2O_3 and Fe_3O_4

34. Metals are refined by using different methods. Which of the following metals are refined by electrolytic refining?

(i) Au

(ii) Cu

(iii) Na

(iv) K

(a) (i) and (ii)   (b) (i) and (iii)

(c) (ii) and (iii)   (d) (iii)and (iv)

35. The electrical impulse travels in a neuron from _________.

(a) Dendrite → Axon → Axonal end → Cell body

(b) Cell body → Dendrite → Axon → Axonal end

(c) Dendrite → Cell body → Axon → Axonal end

(d) Axonal end → Axon → Cell body → Dendrite

36. Which hormone brings about the development of the mammary gland?

(a) Estrogen

(b) Progesterone

(c) Relaxin

(d) Oxytocin

37. The bleaching action of chlorine is _________ reaction.

(a) decomposition

(b) hydrolysis

(c) reduction

(d) oxidation

38. Can we store $CuSO_4$ in iron container and why?

(a) Yes, but only in winter

(b) No

(c) Yes

(d) Yes, But only in summer

39. Give the IUPAC name for $CH_3 - CH_2 - CHO$.

(a) Propanal

(b) Propanol

(c) Propionic acid

(d) None of these

40. The ratio of the difference between number of hydrogens present in 'propane and propyne' and 'propane and propene' is:

(a) 1 : 2   (b) 2 : 1

(c) 3 : 2   (d) 2 : 3

41. The part of the flower that develops into a fruit after fertilization, is:

(a) Sepal   (b) Petal

(c) Ovary   (d) Stamen

42. The part of the flower that gives rise to the seed is:

(a) Ovary   (b) Petal

(c) Ovule   (d) Pollen grain

43. The theory of evolution of species by natural selection was given by ;

(a) Mendel   (b) Darwin

(c) Lamarck   (d) Weismann

44. If tall (TT) is cross-bred with short (tt), then what will be the characteristic(s) of the F_1 plants?

(a) All tall

(b) All short

(c) In between tall and short

(d) Both tall and short

45. The magnification of the plane mirror is:

(a) Infinite   (b) 2.0

(c) 1.0   (d) 3.0

46. Virtual, erect, and diminished images are the characteristic features of a:

(a) Concave mirror

(b) Biconcave mirror

(c) Convex mirror

(d) Plane mirror

47. The factors on which one magnetic field strength produced by current carrying solenoids depends are:

(a) Magnitude of current

(b) Number of turns

(c) Nature of core material

(d) All of the above

48. The strength of each of magnet reduces to half when it cut along its length into the equal parts magnetic field strength of a solenoid. Polarity of solenoid can be determined by:

(a) Use of compass needle

(b) Right hand thumb rule

(c) Fleming left hand rule

(d) Either (A) or (B)

49. How many chambers are present in the human heart?

(a) One   (b) Two

(c) Three   (d) Four

50. In humans, right atrium receives _____ blood from _____.

(a) oxygenated, aorta

(b) deoxygenated, vena cava

(c) oxygenated, vena cava

(d) deoxygenated, aorta

51. When hydrogen chloride gas is prepared on a humid day, the gas is usually passed through the guard tube containing calcium chloride. The role of calcium chloride taken in the guard tube is to:

(a) Absorb the evolved gas

(b) Moisture the gas

(c) Absorb moisture from the gas

(d) None of the above

52. A student has dipped blue litmus paper into a beaker containing a liquid. Its colour turned red. Which of the following is responsible for this change?

(a) Basic nature of the liquid

(b) Presence of a red pigment in the liquid

(c) Acidic nature of the litmus paper

(d) Acidic nature of the liquid in the beaker

53. The values of f and u for a concave lens are always:

(a) Positive

(b) Negative

(c) Positive and Negative both

(d) None of these

54. If the five equal pieces of a resistance wire having 5 resistance each is connected in parallel, then their equivalent resistance will be:

(a) $\frac{1}{5}\,\Omega$ (b) $1\,\Omega$

(c) $5\,\Omega$ (d) $25\,\Omega$

55. The amperage of the fuse wire used in a circuit that works on $230\,V$ is $2.2\,A$. If so, the power of the device is:

(a) less than $300\,W$

(b) $300\,W$ to $500\,W$

(c) Between $500\,W$ and $510\,W$

(d) more than $510\,W$

Social Science

56. What are the important things to do to prevent degradation of our natural ecosystems?

(a) Urbanization

(b) Industrialization

(c) Conserve and manage our water resources, to safeguard ourselves from health hazards

(d) Modern agriculture

57. A chemical compound called 'taxol' is extracted from _____ which is the drug that is now the biggest selling anti-cancer drug.

(a) Bark of the Himalayan yew

(b) Trees of the Nilgiri hills

(c) Plants from the Brahmaputra area

(d) Leaves of the Himalayan Yew

58. Kundremukh is an important Iron ore mine of:

(a) Kerala

(b) Madhya Pradesh

(c) Karnataka

(d) Andhra Pradesh

59. Identify the correct answer from the alternatives provided.
Tisco and Reliance Industries are owned by:

(a) The government

(b) Private company

(c) A cooperative society

(d) Jointly by private companies and the govt.

60. GDP is the total value of _____ produced.

(a) all goods and services

(b) all final goods and services

(c) all intermediate goods and services

(d) all of the above

61. Which territories were included under the Habsburg Empire?

(a) Alpine regions – the Tyrol, Austria-Hungry and the Sudetenland , Bohemia, Lombardy and Venetia

(b) Tyrol, Austria and the Sudetenland

(c) Bohemia, Lombardy and Venetia

(d) Sudetenland , Bohemia, Lombardy

62. Rearing of silkworms for the production of silk fibre is known as _____.

(a) Sericulture

(b) Apiculture

(c) Floriculture

(d) None of these

63. National Sample Survey Organisation is a:

(a) An institution responsible to collect data on formal sector credit

(b) Commercial bank organisation

(c) An organisation of World Bank

(d) An organisation associated with Indian Standard Institute

64. The exchange of goods for goods is:

(a) Barter

(b) Banker of option

(c) Bills of exchange

(d) Currency

65. Which of the following contributes to Globalisation?

(a) Internal trade

(b) External trade

(c) large scale trade

(d) Small scale trade

66. Cheaper imports, inadequate investment in infrastructure lead to:

(a) Slowdown in agricultural sector

(b) Replace the demand for domestic production

(c) Slowdown in industrial sector

(d) All the above

67. Which of the following is not a right of consumers?

(a) Right to safety

(b) Right to be informed

(c) Right to choose

(d) Right to constitutional remedies

68. Which one of the following is not true regarding the Right to Safety?

(a) Right to be protected against unsafe appliances.

(b) Right to protected against unsafe working conditions.

(c) Right to seek information about functioning of government departments.

(d) Right to be protected against services which are hazardous to life.

69. What impact did print have regarding the French Revolution?
(i) Print popularised the ideas of the Enlightenment thinkers, their writings provided a critical commentary on tradition, superstition and despotism and reasoning
(ii) Print created a new culture of dialogue and debate
(iii) By the 1780's there was literature that mocked the royalty and monarchy and criticised their

morality, along with cartoons and caricatures
(iv) People were not affected directly but they did pay attention
(a) (i) only
(b) (i) and (ii)
(c) (ii) and (iii)
(d) (i), (ii), (iii) and (iv)

70. **When was the children's press, devoted to literature for children alone, set up in France?**
(a) 1857   (b) 1855
(c) 1860   (d) 1854

71. **Which of the following languages is not spoken in Belgium?**
(a) Dutch   (b) French
(c) Spanish   (d) German

72. **Who elects the community government in Belgium?**
(a) The community leaders of Belgium
(b) The citizens of the whole country
(c) By the leaders of Belgium
(d) None of the above

73. **What is the name of the routes linking Asia with Europe and northern Africa?**
(a) Asian routes (b) Silk routes
(c) Trade routes (d) Africa routes

74. **Identify the personality who said, "it is the formation of linguistic states that has allowed India to escape what might have been a worse fate still".**
(a) Pt. Jawaharlal Nehru
(b) Bipin Chandra Pal
(c) Ramachandra Guha
(d) Dr. Rajendra Prasad

75. **Which of the following will come under concurrent list?**
(a) Police
(b) Trade and commerce
(c) Education
(d) Banking

76. **Why were handmade goods popular in England?**
(a) Cheaper rates
(b) Fast production
(c) Demand in the market was often for goods with intricate designs and specific shapes specially by the aristocrats and the bourgeoisie class
(d) Made at order was easier

77. **Soil formed by intense leaching is:**
(a) Alluvial soil (b) Red soil
(c) Laterite soil (d) Desert

78. **How many countries of the world today claim and practice some kind of democratic politics? Choose the correct option from the following ones:**
(a) Over eighty countries
(b) Over a hundred countries
(c) Over two hundred countries
(d) None of the above

79. **On which of the following pair of factors, economic development does not depend?**
(a) Country's population size and global situation
(b) Cooperation from other countries and country's economic priorities
(c) Global situation and resources available in the country
(d) Both (A) and (B)

80. **What were the effects of the Non-Cooperation movement On the economic front?**
(a) Foreign goods were boycotted, liquor shops picketed, and foreign cloth burnt in huge bonfires started wearing Indian clothes.
(b) Economy fell
(c) People did not take united action
(d) Financing foreign goods continued

General Awareness/ Knowledge

81. **Who is known as the 'Grand Old Man of India'?**
(a) Mahatma Gandhi
(b) Dadabhai Naoroji
(c) Rajendra Prasad
(d) Lala Lajpat Rai

82. **Which Schedule of the Constitution of India, 1950 prescribes the forms of oaths or affirmations for constitutional functionaries?**
(a) Sixth Schedule
(b) Second Schedule
(c) Fifth Schedule
(d) Third Schedule

83. **Fiscal deficit means:**
(a) Govt. expenditure minus Revenue receipts
(b) Public capital expenditure minus Surplus of revenue account
(c) Public expenditure minus Tax and non tax revenue receipts
(d) Public expenditure minus Debts from sources other than RBI

84. **Which level of judiciary cannot send a person to jail?**
(a) Supreme Court
(b) Nyaya Panchayat
(c) High Court
(d) Subordinate Court

85. **The word filament is used:**
(a) In the planetary hypothesis
(b) In the tidal hypothesis
(c) In the supernova hypothesis
(d) In the interstellar dust hypothesis

86. **GSAT is which kind of Satellite?**
(a) Student Satellite
(b) Communication Satellite
(c) Earth Observation Satellite
(d) Military Satellite

87. **Which of the following is the correct chronological order of the formation of the following states in India?**
1. Sikkim
2. Ngaland
3. Haryana
4. Arunachal Pradesh
(a) 3, 1, 2, 4   (b) 1, 2, 3, 4
(c) 2, 3, 1, 4   (d) 1, 4, 2, 3

88. **Which of the painting is mixture of Rajasthani and Mughal?**
(a) Kangra painting
(b) Pahari painting
(c) Madhubani painting
(d) Basohli painting

89. **The Salal hydro-electric project is located across the river:**
(a) Jhelum   (b) Ravi
(c) Chenab   (d) Beas

90. **Peshawar and Mathura were the two major centres of power during the rule of _________.**
(a) Gupta   (b) Mauryan
(c) Kushans   (d) Chalukya

91. **The Name of Shershah in childhood was:**
(a) Hasan
(b) Farid
(c) Sher Khan
(d) None of these

92. **When did the Jallianwala Bagh massacre take place?**
(a) April 13, 1918
(b) April 13, 1919

(c)　April 29, 1921
(d)　April 13, 1920

93. Sardar Sarovar Dam is constructed on which river?
(a)　Ganga　(b)　Sutlej
(c)　Narmada　(d)　Kaveri

94. Who is the appointing authority of the Governor of a State in India?
(a)　Prime Minister of India
(b)　Chief Minister of the concerned state
(c)　President of India
(d)　Union Cabinet headed by the Prime Minister of India

95. In which country did the International Shooting Sport Federation (ISSF) Junior World Cup begin in May 2022?
(a)　Italy　(b)　France
(c)　Germany　(d)　Spain

96. Who was the first chairman of ISRO?
(a)　Udupi Ramachandra Rao
(b)　Satish Dhawan
(c)　Vikram Sarabhai
(d)　M.G.K. Menon

97. The unit of electric power is:
(a)　Ampere　(b)　Volt
(c)　Coulomb　(d)　Watt

98. Dioptre is unit of ______.
(a)　Power of a lens
(b)　The focal length of a lens
(c)　Intensity of light
(d)　Intensity of sound

99. Who among the following is known as 'Fuehrer'?
(a)　Stalin　(b)　Lenin
(c)　Hitler　(d)　Bismarck

100. Who has won the Emmy Award for his narration in the Netflix documentary "Our Great National Parks"?
(a)　Barack Obama
(b)　Shah Rukh Khan
(c)　Bill Gates
(d)　Ratan Tata

❘❘ Hints and Solutions ❘❘

1(B). Construction of a cumulative frequency table is useful in determining the median.

2(B). The abscissa of the point of intersection of the less than type and of the more than type cumulative frequency curves of a grouped data gives its median.

3(B). Given that cone, hemisphere and cylinder have the same base and an equal height.
i.e., $r = h$
As we know,
Volume of cone $= \frac{1}{3}\pi r^2 h$
Volume of hemisphere $= \frac{2}{3}\pi r^3$
Volume of cylinder $= \pi r^2 h$
Ratio of volume of cone, hemisphere and cylinder $= \frac{1}{3}\pi r^2 h : \frac{2}{3}\pi r^3 : \pi r^2 h$
$= \frac{1}{3}\pi (h)^2 h : \frac{2}{3}\pi (h)^3 : \pi (h)^2 h$
$= \frac{1}{3}h^3 : \frac{2}{3}h^3 : h^3$
$= \frac{1}{3} : \frac{2}{3} : 1$
$= 1 : 2 : 3$
So, the ratio of their volumes is $1 : 2 : 3$.

4(A). 

Given that sphere, cylinder and cone have the same radius and same height.
As we know,
Volume of the sphere $= V_1 = \frac{4}{3}\pi r^3$
Volume of the cylinder $= V_2 = \pi r^2 h$
Volume of the cone $= V_3 = \frac{1}{3}\pi r^2 h$
Ratio of their volumes $= V_1 : V_2 : V_3$
$= \frac{4}{3}\pi r^3 : \pi r^2 h : \frac{1}{3}\pi r^2 h$
$= \frac{4}{3}\pi r^3 : \pi r^2 2r : \frac{1}{3}\pi r^2 2r \quad [\because h = 2r]$
$= 4\pi r^3 : 3 \times 2\pi r^3 : 2\pi r^3 \text{ (Multiply by 3)}$
$= 4r^3 : 6r^3 : 2r^3$
$= 4 : 6 : 2$
$= 2 : 3 : 1$
So, the ratio of their volumes is $2 : 3 : 1$.

5(A). We know that, the general form of a quadratic equation is
$x^2 - (M + N)x - MN = 0$
Here, M and N are the roots of the equation.
Let 1st root $M = 7 + \sqrt{3}$
And 2nd is $N = 7 - \sqrt{3}$
By puting the value of M and N and solving them, we get,
$x^2 - (7 + \sqrt{3} + 7 - \sqrt{3})x + [(7 + \sqrt{3}) \times (7 - \sqrt{3})] = 0$
We know that,
$[(a + b)(a - b) = (a^2 - b^2)]$
Then, $x^2 - 14x + (49 - 3) = 0$
So the quadratic equation is
$x^2 - 14x + 46 = 0$

6(B). The standard form of a quadratic equation is:
$ax^2 + bx + c = 0$
We know the value of a, x and c then put the all value in the equation and we get the value of b.
Given quadratic equation is
$3x^2 - px - 2 = 0$ and $x = 2$
Putting $x = 2$ in the equation,
$\Rightarrow 3x^2 - px - 2 = 0$

$\Rightarrow 3(2)^2 - 2p - 2 = 0$
$\Rightarrow 12 - 2p - 2 = 0$
$\Rightarrow 10 = 2p$
$\Rightarrow p = \frac{10}{2}$
$\therefore p = 5$

7(C). We know that degree of a quadratic equation is 2 and two roots.
General form of a quadratic equation is:
$ax^2 + bx + c = 0$
Given equation is
$5x^2 + 8x + 4 = 2x^2 + 4x + 6$
It is an equation where the degree of x is 2.
Now,
$5x^2 - 2x^2 + 8x - 4x + 4 - 6 = 0$
$\Rightarrow 3x^2 + 4x - 2 = 0$
This equation represents the quadratic equation because the degree is two 2.

8(D). Given,
Number of revolutions $= 100$
As we know,
$$\text{Number of revolutions} = \frac{\text{Total distance}}{\text{circumference of wheel}}$$
So,
$$100 = \frac{\text{Total distance}}{\pi d}$$
So, Total distance $= 100\pi d$

9(B). Given,
$r_1 = 24$
$r_2 = 7$
Let required radius be R.
Then according to the questions.
$\pi R^2 = \pi r_1^2 + \pi r_2^2$
$R^2 = 24^2 + 7^2$
$R^2 = 576 + 49$
$R^2 = 625$
$R = 25$ cm
Hence, the correct option is (B)

10(B). As we know that:
$\sin 60° = \frac{\sqrt{3}}{2}, \sin 30° = \frac{1}{2}, \cos 60° = \frac{1}{2}$
and $\cos 30° = \frac{\sqrt{3}}{2}$ Therefore,
$\left(\frac{\sqrt{3}}{2}\right) \times \left(\frac{\sqrt{3}}{2}\right) + \left(\frac{1}{2}\right) \times \left(\frac{1}{2}\right)$
$= \left(\frac{3}{4}\right) + \left(\frac{1}{4}\right)$
$= \frac{4}{4}$
$= 1$

11(A). Given,
$\frac{\sin\theta - \cos\theta + 1}{\sin\theta + \cos\theta - 1}$
[on dividing numerator and denominator by $\cos\theta$]
$= \frac{\frac{\sin\theta}{\cos\theta} - 1 + \frac{1}{\cos\theta}}{\frac{\sin\theta}{\cos\theta} + 1 - \frac{1}{\cos\theta}}$
$= \frac{\tan\theta - 1 + \sec\theta}{\tan\theta + 1 - \sec\theta}$
$= \frac{(\sec\theta + \tan\theta - 1)}{(\tan\theta - \sec\theta + 1)}$
$= \frac{(\sec\theta + \tan\theta) - (\sec^2\theta - \tan^2\theta)}{(\tan\theta - \sec\theta + 1)}$
$[\because 1 = \sec^2\theta - \tan^2\theta]$
$= \frac{(\sec\theta + \tan\theta)[1 - (\sec\theta - \tan\theta)]}{(\tan\theta - \sec\theta + 1)}$

$$= \frac{(\sec\theta+\tan\theta)(\tan\theta-\sec\theta+1)}{(\tan\theta-\sec\theta+1)}$$
$$= (\sec\theta + \tan\theta)$$

12(B). Given,
$$\tan\theta = \frac{a}{b}$$

Dividing all terms of $\frac{\cos\theta+\sin\theta}{\cos\theta-\sin\theta}$ by $\cos\theta$,

$$= \frac{1+\tan\theta}{1-\tan\theta}$$
$$= \frac{1+\frac{a}{b}}{1-\frac{a}{b}}$$
$$= \frac{b+a}{b-a}$$

13(C). Given,
$$\frac{5}{x-1} + \frac{1}{y-2} = 2 \quad \dots(1) \quad \text{Let } \frac{1}{x-1} = u$$
$$\frac{6}{x-1} - \frac{3}{y-2} = 1 \quad \dots(2) \quad \text{and } \frac{1}{y-2} = v$$

So, our equations become
$$5u + v = 2 \quad \dots\dots(3)$$
$$6u - 3v = 1 \quad \dots\dots(4)$$
Our equations are,
$$5u + v = 2$$
$$6u - 3v = 1$$
From (3),
$$5u + v = 2$$
$$v = 2 - 5u$$
Putting value of v in (4),
$$6u - 3v = 1$$
$$6u - 3(2 - 5u) = 1$$
$$6u - 6 + 15u = 1$$
$$6u + 15u = 1 + 6$$
$$21u = 7$$
$$u = \frac{7}{21}$$
$$u = \frac{1}{3}$$
Putting $u = \frac{1}{3}$ in (3),
$$5u + v = 2$$
$$5\left(\frac{1}{3}\right) + v = 2$$
$$\frac{5}{3} + v = 2$$
$$v = 2 - \frac{5}{3}$$
$$v = \frac{2(3)-5}{3}$$
$$v = \frac{1}{3}$$
So, $u = \frac{1}{3}$ and $v = \frac{1}{3}$
We need to find x and y
We know that,
$$u = \frac{1}{x-1}$$
$$\frac{1}{3} = \frac{1}{x-1}$$
$$x - 1 = 3$$
$$x = 3 + 1$$
$$x = 4$$
$$v = \frac{1}{y-2}$$
$$\frac{1}{3} = \frac{1}{y-2}$$
$$y - 2 = 3$$
$$y = 3 + 2$$
$$y = 5$$
So, $x = 4, y = 5$ is the solution of our equations.

14(A). $\frac{10}{x+y} + \frac{2}{x-y} = 4 \quad \dots\dots(1)$

Let $\frac{1}{x+y} = u$
$$\frac{15}{x+y} - \frac{5}{x-y} = -2 \quad \dots\dots(2) \quad \text{and}$$
$$\frac{1}{x-y} = v$$
So, our equations become
$$10u + 2v = 4 \quad \dots\dots(3)$$
$$15u - 5v = -2 \quad \dots\dots(4)$$
Now, we solve
$$10u + 2v = 4 \quad \dots\dots(3)$$
$$15u - 5v = -2 \quad \dots\dots(4)$$
From (3),
$$10u + 2v = 4$$
$$10u = 4 - 2v$$
$$u = \frac{4-2v}{10}$$
Putting value of u in (4),
$$15u - 5v = -2$$
$$15\left(\frac{4-2v}{10}\right) - 5v = -2$$
$$3\left(\frac{4-2v}{2}\right) - 5v = -2$$
Multiplying both sides by 2,
$$2 \times 3\left(\frac{4-2v}{2}\right) - 2 \times 5v = 2 \times -2$$
$$3(4 - 2v) - 10v = -4$$
$$12 - 6v - 10v = -4$$
$$-6v - 10v = -4 - 12$$
$$-16v = -16$$
$$v = \frac{-16}{-16}$$
$$v = 1$$
Putting $v = 1$ in (3),
$$10u + 2v = 4$$
$$10u + 2(1) = 4$$
$$10u + 2 = 4$$
$$10u = 4 - 2$$
$$10u = 2$$
$$u = \frac{2}{10}$$
$$u = \frac{1}{5}$$
So, $u = \frac{1}{5}$ and $v = 1$
But, we need to find x and y
$$u = \frac{1}{x+y}$$
$$\frac{1}{5} = \frac{1}{x+y}$$
$$x + y = 5 \quad \dots\dots(5)$$
$$v = \frac{1}{x-y}$$
$$1 = \frac{1}{x-y}$$
$$x - y = 1 \quad \dots\dots(6)$$
So, our equations become
$$x + y = 5 \quad \dots\dots(5)$$
$$x - y = 1 \quad \dots\dots(6)$$
Adding (5) and (6),
$$(x + y) + (x - y) = 5 + 1$$
$$2x = 6$$
$$x = \frac{6}{2}$$
$$x = 3$$
Putting value of x in (5),
$$x + y = 5$$
$$3 + y = 5$$
$$y = 5 - 3$$
$$y = 2$$
Therefore, $x = 3, y = 2$ is the solution of our equation.

15(B). Three persons will they will meet together at LCM of their time-intervals.
So LCM of 9, 12, 15
$$9 = 3^2$$
$$12 = 2^2 \times 3$$
$$15 = 3 \times 5$$
$$\text{LCM} = 2^2 \times 3^2 \times 5$$
$$= 4 \times 9 \times 5$$
$$= 180 \text{ minutes or 3 hours.}$$
They will meet together after 3 hours.

16(B). Three bells will toll together at LCM of toll intervals
so LCM of 9, 12, 15
$$9 = 3^2$$
$$12 = 2^2 \times 3$$
$$15 = 3 \times 5$$
$$\text{LCM} = 2^2 \times 3^2 \times 5$$
$$= 4 \times 9 \times 5$$
$$= 180 \text{ minutes or 3 hours.}$$
They will next toll together after 3 hours.

17(B). Euclid's division lemma:
It tells us about the divisibility of integers. It states that any positive integer 'a' can be divided by any other positive integer 'b' in such a way that it leaves a remainder 'r'. Euclid's Division Lemma states that for any two positive integers 'a' and 'b' there exist two unique whole numbers 'q' and 'r' such that, $a = bq + r$, where $0 \leq r < b$.
Here, $a =$ Dividend, $b =$ Divisor, $q =$ quotient and $r =$ Remainder.
Thus, the values 'r' can take $0 \leq r < b$.

18(C). Every even integer is a multiple of 2.
$\therefore 2m$ is an even integer.

19(C). If the graph of a polynomial intersects the x-axis at three points, then the number of zeroes are 3 because the x-axis is intersect three times by the three coordinates so,
Number of zeroes of the polynomial = number of the coordinates of the points (where its graph intersects the $x-$ axis).

20(B). Let $p(x) = x^2 - 3x - m(m + 3)$
$$\Rightarrow p(x) = x^2 - (m + 3)x + mx - m(m+3)$$
$$= x[x - (m + 3)] + m[x - (m + 3)]$$
For zeros of $p(x)$
$$\Rightarrow p(x) = (x + m)[(x - (m + 3)] = 0$$
$$\Rightarrow x = -m, m + 3$$
$\therefore$ Its zeros are $-m, m + 3$

21(B). Find the probability of getting 4.
Possible outcomes on rolling the dice are 1, 2, 3, 4, 5 and 6.
Total number of outcomes $= 6$
Number of favorable outcome $= 1$
Probability
$$= \frac{\text{Number of favorable outcome}}{\text{Total number of outcomes}} = \frac{1}{6}$$
So, the required probability is $\frac{1}{6}$.

22(D). Sample space of nos obtained is $= 6 \times 6 = 36$ (As two dices are independent)

No. obtained on first dice is less than second $= 15$
(if no on first dice is 1 then possibility on second dice are $5(2-6)$ and similarly for $2 = 4$, for $3 = 3$, for $4 = 2$, for $5 = 1$ total $5 + 4 + 3 + 2 + 1 = 15$)
$$P = \frac{\text{Number of favorable outcomes}}{\text{Total number of outcomes}}$$
probability of event $P = \frac{15}{36} = \frac{5}{12}$

23(D). We can use the general formula for the nth term,
$a_n = a + (n-1)d$
Given, AP is $7, 13, 19, \ldots, 205$
$a = 7$
$d = 13 - 7 = 6, a_n = 205$
Using formula, $a_n = a + (n-1)d$
$\Rightarrow 205 = 7 + (n-1)6$
$\Rightarrow (n-1)6 = 205 - 7$
$\Rightarrow (n-1) = \frac{198}{6} = 33$
$\Rightarrow n = 33 + 1 = 34$
So, 34th term of the AP is 205.

24(C). Let a and d be the first term and common difference of the given AP.
Given that, $a_3 = 12$
$\Rightarrow a + (3-1)d = 12 [\because a_n = a + (n-1)d]$
$\Rightarrow a + 2d = 12 \ldots$(i)
Last term $= T_{50} = 106$
$\Rightarrow a + (50-1)d = 106$
$\Rightarrow a + 49d = 106 \ldots$(ii)
Subtracting (i) from (ii), we have
$\Rightarrow 47d = 94$
$\Rightarrow d = \frac{94}{47} = 2$
Putting the value of d in (i), we have
$a + 2(2) = 12$
$\Rightarrow a + 4 = 12$
$\Rightarrow a = 8$
Now, $a_{29} = a + (29-1)d$
$= 8 + 28(2) = 8 + 56 = 64$

25(D).

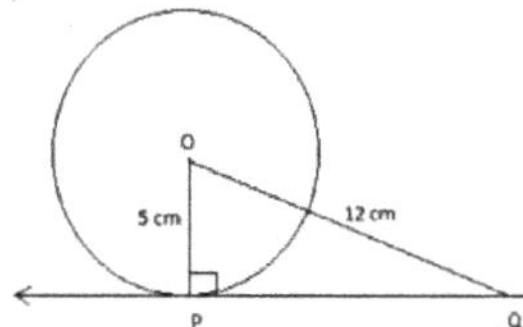

In the above figure, the line that is drawn from the centre of the given circle to the tangent PQ is perpendicular to PQ.
And so, $OP \perp PQ$
Using Pythagoras theorem in triangle $\triangle OPQ$ we get,
$OQ^2 = OP^2 + PQ^2$
$(12)^2 = 5^2 + PQ^2$
$PQ^2 = 144 - 25$
$PQ^2 = 119$
$PQ = \sqrt{119}$ cm

26(A). The tangent to a circle is a special case of the secant, when the two end points of its corresponding chord coincide. A tangent to a circle is a line that intersects the circle at only one point.

27(B). From the question, it is clear that

OP is the radius of the circle to the tangent PT and OQ is the radius to the tangents TQ.
So, $OP \perp PT$ and $TQ \perp OQ$
$\therefore \angle OPT = \angle OQT = 90°$
Now, in the quadrilateral POQT, we know that the sum of the interior angles is $360°$
So,
$\angle PTQ + \angle POQ + \angle OPT + \angle OQT = 360°$
Now, by putting the respective values we get,
$\angle PTQ + 90° + 110° + 90° = 360°$
$\angle PTQ = 70°$
So, $\angle PTQ$ is $70°$

28(C).

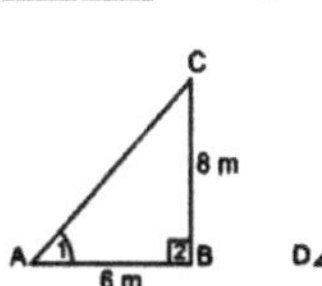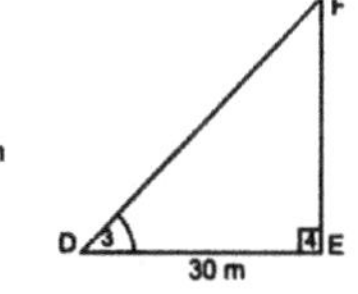

Given,
$\triangle ABC \sim \triangle DEF$,
Perimeter $(\triangle ABC) = 50$ cm
Perimeter $(\triangle DEF) = 70$ cm
One side of $\triangle ABC = 20$ cm
$\triangle ABC \sim \triangle DEF$
To find corresponding side DE of $\triangle DEF$
Given,
$$\frac{\text{Perimeter}(\triangle ABC)}{\text{Perimeter}(\triangle DEF)} = \frac{AB}{DE}$$
$\frac{50}{70} = \frac{20}{DE}$
$\Rightarrow 5DE = 140$
$DE = 28$ cm
$\therefore$ The corresponding side of $\triangle DEF = 28$ cm

29(D). Given,

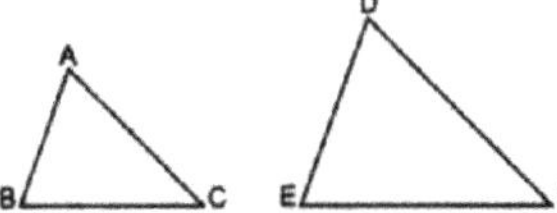

Let BC be the pole and EF be the tower and shadow $AB = 6$ m and $DE = 30$ m.
In $\triangle ABC$ and $\triangle DEF$,
$\angle 2 = \angle 4 \ldots$ [Each $90°$]
$\angle 1 = \angle 3 \ldots$ [Sun's angle of elevation at the same time].
$\triangle ABC \sim \triangle DEF \ldots [AA$ similarity]
$\frac{AB}{DE} = \frac{BC}{EF} \ldots$ [In-As corresponding sides are proportional]
$\Rightarrow \frac{6}{30} = \frac{8}{EF}$
$\therefore EF = 40$ m

30(C). We have $XY \parallel AC$
Given,
So, $\angle BXY = \angle A$ and $\angle BYX = \angle C$
...[Corresponding angles
$\therefore \triangle ABC \sim \triangle XBY \ldots [AA$ similarity criterion.
So, $\frac{ar(\triangle ABC)}{ar(\triangle XBY)} = \left(\frac{AB}{XB}\right)^2 \qquad \ldots\ldots$ (i)
Also, $ar(\triangle ABC) = 2ar(\triangle XBY)$
Given,
$\Rightarrow \frac{ar(\triangle ABC)}{ar(\triangle XBY)} = \frac{2}{1} \qquad \ldots\ldots$ (ii)

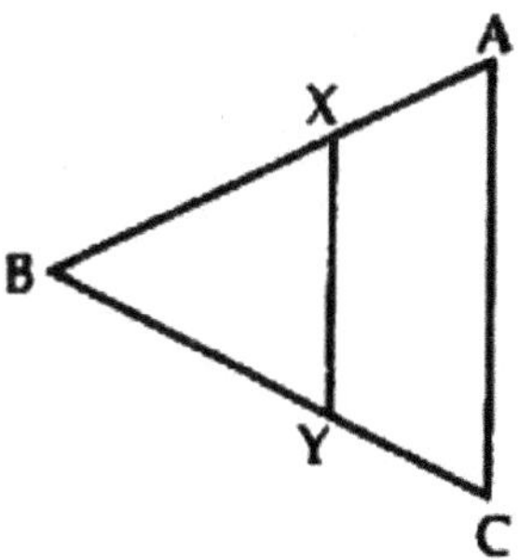

From (i) and (ii),
$\left(\frac{AB}{XB}\right)^2 = \frac{2}{1}$
i.e., $\frac{AB}{XB} = \frac{\sqrt{2}}{1}$
or,
$\frac{XB}{AB} = \frac{1}{\sqrt{2}}$
or, $\frac{XB}{AB} = \frac{1}{\sqrt{2}}$
or, $1 - \frac{XB}{AB} = 1 - \frac{1}{\sqrt{2}}$
or $\frac{AB - XB}{AB} = \frac{\sqrt{2}-1}{\sqrt{2}}$
i.e., $\frac{AX}{AB} = \frac{\sqrt{2}-1}{\sqrt{2}} = \frac{2-\sqrt{2}}{2}$

31(C). The concentration of DDT is highest in top consumers due to a phenomenon known as Biomagnification. Biomagnification refers to an increase in the concentration of toxic chemicals at successive trophic levels. This happens because a toxic substance accumulated by an organism cannot be metabolised or excreted, and is thus passed on to the next higher trophic level. This phenomenon is well known for mercury and DDT.

32(A). All the interacting organisms in an area together with the non-living constituents of the environment form an ecosystem. Thus, an ecosystem consists of biotic components comprising living organisms and abiotic components comprising physical factors like temperature, rainfall, wind, soil and minerals.

33(C). Step 1:
Reactive metals like sodium, potassium, calcium, etc. react with cold or hot water to form hydroxides and release hydrogen gas. Moderately reactive metals like magnesium react with hot water to form less soluble hydroxide and release hydrogen gas. Less reactive metals do not react with cold or hot water but react with steam to form metallic oxides.
Least reactive metals like gold, silver, etc. do not react at all.
Step 2:
Iron does not react with cold or hot water because it is a less reactive metal, but it reacts with steam to form mixed iron oxide and hydrogen gas. The reaction of iron with the steam is as follows:
$3Fe(s) + 4H_2O(g) \rightarrow Fe_3O_4(s) + 4H_2(g)$

Note: Fe_3O_4 is a mixed oxide of FeO and Fe_2O_3.

34(A). Electrolytic refining is used for metals like Cu, Zn, Ag, Au etc. The method to be used for refining an impure metal depends on the nature of the metals well as on the nature of impurities present in it. So, metals Au (gold) and Cu (copper) are refined by electrolytic refining.

35(C). The electrical impulse travels in a neuron from Dendrite → Cell body → Axon → Axonal end.
The electrical impulse travels in a neuron from Dendrite to cell body to axon end to axonal end. Dendrites are tree-like extensions at the beginning of a neuron that help increase the surface area of the cell body.

36(A). The ovarian hormone, estrogen, is another critical regulator of pubertal mammary development and is responsible for the tremendous surge in growth occurring during this period that generates a functional mammary gland.
Estrogen, a membrane-soluble ligand, is released from the ovary and activates gene expression through intracellular receptors. For a long time, it was unclear whether hormones such as estrogen had direct effects on mammary gland development or whether, instead, they functioned indirectly to stimulate the release of hormones such as prolactin from the pituitary.

37(D). The bleaching action of chlorine is an oxidation reaction.
It requires moisture for its bleaching action. Chlorine reacts with water to form hydrochloric and hypochlorous acids.
$Cl_2 + H_2O \longrightarrow HCl + HClO$
Hypochlorous acid (HClO) is unstable, and it easily separates to form nascent oxygen.
$HClO \longrightarrow HCl + [O]$
Nascent oxygen is the most powerful oxidizing agent. Its formation is responsible for the bleaching nature of chlorine in the presence of moisture.

38(B). The reaction will take place between Fe and $CuSO_4$ and Fe will displace Cu from $CuSO_4$.
Copper Sulphate cannot be stored in Iron Container as we know that Iron is more reactive than Copper, and it will immediately react and there will be a displacement reaction where Iron will displace Copper. This will corrode the container and Copper sulphate too.
The reaction will be:
$Fe + CuSO_4 = FeSO_4 + Cu$

39(A). As it contains three carbon atoms, so the word root will be "prop". Because of the presence of functional group aldehyde, we will use "al" as a secondary suffix. As the "al" begins with the vowel "a", we will drop down the "e" from "Propane" and replace with "al". Therefore, the naming for $CH_3 - CH_2 - CHO$ is "Propanal".

40(B). No. of hydrogen atoms in propane $(CH_3 - CH_2 - CH_3) = 8$
No. of hydrogen atoms in propene $(CH_3 - CH = CH_2) = 6$
No. of hydrogen atoms in propyne $(CH_3 - C \equiv CH) = 4$
The difference in no. of hydrogen atoms between propane and propyne $= 8 - 4 = 4$
The difference in no. of hydrogen atoms between propane and propene $= 8 - 6 = 2$
Therefore, the ratio $= 4 : 2 = 2 : 1$.

41(C). After fertilization, the ovary develops into fruit and the ovules develop into seeds. Sepals and petals fall off after fertilization. Stamen is the male reproductive part of the flower that does not develop into a fruit.

42(C). After fertilization in a flower, the parts of the flowers like sepals and petals fall off. The ovary becomes the fruit and the ovules develop into seeds.
The ovule is the organ that forms the seeds of flowering plants. It is borne in the ovary of the flower and consists of nucellus protected by integuments, precursors of embryo/endosperm, and seed coat, respectively.

43(B). The theory of evolution is a shortened form of the term "theory of evolution by natural selection," which was proposed by Charles Darwin and Alfred Russel Wallace in the nineteenth century.

44(A). According to the mechanism of inheritance, when a pure tall plant and short plant crossed together, the resulting offsprings of F_1 generation are all tall . Breeding of the offspring from F_1 generation results in the growth of both " tall and short plants ".

45(C). The magnification of the plane mirror is 1.0 since the size of the image is the same as the size of the object. The distance of the image from the mirror is the same as the distance of the object from the mirror.
Magnification
$$(m) = \frac{\text{Height of the image}}{\text{Height of the object}} = \frac{\text{Image distance}}{\text{Object distance}}$$

46(C). Convex Mirror is a curved mirror where the reflective surface bulges out towards the light source. This bulging-out surface reflects light outwards and is not used to focus light.
A convex mirror is also known as a diverging mirror as this mirror diverges light when they strike its reflecting surface. Virtual, erect, and diminished images are always formed with convex mirrors, irrespective of the distance between the object and the mirror.

47(D). The factors on which one magnetic field strength produced by current carrying solenoids depends on magnitude of current, number of turns, nature of core material. The strength of current in the solenoid that is larger the current passed through solenoid, stronger will be the magnetic field produced. The number of turns in the solenoid that is larger the number of turns in the solenoid, greater will be the magnetic field produced.

48(D). The strength of each of magnet reduces to half when it cut along its length into the equal parts magnetic field strength of a solenoid. Polarity of solenoid can be determined by use of compass needle and right hand thumb rule. A solenoid behaves like a bar magnet when a current is passed through it. The north and south poles of a current–carrying solenoid can be determined with the help of a bar magnet. We can bring the North of a Bar Magnet towards one end of the solenoid. If the magnet is repelled, the end is north end of the solenoid.

49(D). The heart consists of four chambers in which blood flows. Blood enters the right atrium and passes through the right ventricle. The right ventricle pumps the blood to the lungs where it becomes oxygenated. The oxygenated blood is brought back to the heart by the pulmonary veins which enter the left atrium. From the left atrium blood flows into the left ventricle. The left ventricle pumps the blood to the aorta which will distribute the oxygenated blood to all parts of the body.

50(B). In humans, the right auricle receives deoxygenated blood from the vena cava.
- In mammals, Double circulation is present i.e. two cycles of circulation - one is pulmonary circulation and another is systematic blood circulation.
- In humans, the heart is four-chambered.
- Right side of the heart receives deoxygenated blood whereas oxygenated blood flows from the left side of the heart.
- The right auricle receives deoxygenated blood from all parts of the body and the left ventricle pumps blood through the pulmonary artery to the lungs for oxygenation.
- The left auricle receives oxygenated blood from the lungs through the pulmonary vein and the left ventricle pumps blood to all parts of the body through the aorta.

51(C). Calcium chloride is used as an absorbent in the guard tube while hydrogen chloride is being formed on a humid day as it can absorb the moisture from the gas.

H ydrochloric acid corrosively reacts with water leading to the formation of hydrochloric acid as it is strongly acidic in nature. It gives out white fumes on reacting with moisture.

52(D). A student has dipped blue litmus paper in a beaker containing a liquid. Its color turned red. The acidic nature of the liquid in the beaker is responsible for this change.

Blue litmus paper turns red under acidic conditions and red litmus paper turns blue under basic or alkaline conditions, with the color change occurring over the pH range $4.5 - 8.3$ at $25°C$.

53(B). For a concave lens, the focal length is also always negative. In this case of a concave lens, u and f have negative non-zero values. Thus, under any conditions, v i.e. image distance is always negative. By convention, the focal length (f) of concave lens is always taken as negative. The object distance (u) from optical centre is always taken as negative.

54(B). Given:
Number of resistance $n = 5$
Resistance of each resistor $R = 5\Omega$
Now,
All resistors are connected in parallel
$$\frac{1}{R_{eq}} = \frac{1}{R_1} + \frac{1}{R_2} + \frac{1}{R_3} + \frac{1}{R_4} + \frac{1}{R_5}$$
$$\frac{1}{R_{eq}} = \frac{1}{5} + \frac{1}{5} + \frac{1}{5} + \frac{1}{5} + \frac{1}{5}$$
$$\frac{1}{R_{eq}} = \frac{5}{5}$$
$$\frac{1}{R_{eq}} = 1\,\Omega$$
$$R_{eq} = 1\,\Omega$$

55(C). Given:
$i = 2.2\,A$
$V = 230\,V$
Where,
i is current
V is voltage Rating
Now,
Power, $P = Vi$
$P = 230 \times 2.2$
$P = 506\,W$
Thus, the power of the device is between $500\,W$ and $510W$

56(C). Conserving and managing our water resources, to safeguard ourselves from health hazards are the important things to do to prevent the degradation of our natural ecosystems.
Solutions to Environmental Degradation are:
• Stop Deforestation
• Government Regulations.
• Fines and Punishment For Illegal dumping.
• Reduce Consumption Levels.
• Reuse and Reduce Waste Generation.
• Avoid Plastic.
• Education.
• Convince Others.

57(A).
A chemical compound called 'taxol' is extracted from Bark of the Himalayan yew which is the drug that is now the biggest selling anti-cancer drug.
At present Taxol is obtained mainly from the bark of the Yew tree but scientists have found that the substance can be extracted from the needles of the tree. However, the drug is only one-eighth as concentrated compared to the bark and this process leaves room for impurities within it.

58(C). Kundremukh is an important Iron ore mine of Karnataka.
Kudremukh Iron Ore Project is located in Karnataka. It is a Government of India enterprise with its head office and administrative activities in Bangalore. It has a pelletisation plant in Mangalore and had an iron ore mine in Kudremukh (Chikkamagaluru district). The Kudremukh mine, one of the largest iron ore mines in the world, was closed in 2006 . The captive mining took place at Kudremukh on the Western Ghats range.

59(B). Tisco and Reliance Industries are owned by p rivate company.
A private company is a firm held under private ownership. Private companies may issue stock and have shareholders, but their shares do not trade on public exchanges and are not issued through an initial public offering (IPO).
Tisco: Tata Steel Limited is an Indian multinational steel-making company based in Jamshedpur, Jharkhand, and is headquartered in Mumbai, Maharashtra, India. It is a subsidiary of the Tata Group.
Reliance : Reliance Group has five listed companies. Reliance Power, Reliance Infrastructure, Reliance Capital, Reliance Home Finance and Reliance Health. The group provides financial services, construction, entertainment, power, health care, manufacturing, defence, aviation, and transportation services.

60(B). GDP is the total value of all final goods and services produced.
GDP is the total value of all final goods and services produced during a particular year. The full form of GDP is a gross domestic product which mentions the flow of goods and services in an economy during a financial year.

61(A). Alpine regions-the Tyrol, Austria-Hungry and the Sudetenland, Bohemia, Lombardy and Venetia territories were included under the Habsburg Empire.
The Habsburg Empire ruled over Austria-Hungary. It included the Alpine regions-the Tyrol, Austria and the Sudetenland – as well as Bohemia, where the aristocracy was predominantly German-speaking.

62(A). Rearing of silkworms for the production of silk fibre is known as Sericulture.
Sericulture or silk farming is the cultivation of silkworms to produce silk. Although there are several commercial species of silkworms, Bombyx mori (the caterpillar of the domestic silkmoth) is the most widely used and intensively studied silkworm.

63(A). National Sample Survey Organisation is an institution responsible to collect data on formal credit.
The National Sample Survey Office (NSSO) in India is a unique setup to carry out surveys on socio-economic, demographic, agricultural and industrial subjects for collecting data from house holds and from enterprises located in villages and in the towns. It is a focal agency of the Govt.
The functions of NSSO are:
(A) To conduct mass-scale surveys across the country .
(B) To procure information on employment, health, income, expenditure areas of the country in the form of data.
(C) To organize annual surveys on the industrial sector.

64(A). The exchange of goods for goods is called Barter.
A barter system is known as an old method of exchange . This system has been practised for centuries and long before money was introduced. People started exchanging services and goods for other services and goods in return. The value of bartering items is negotiable with the other party. In a barter economy, an exchange between two people requires a double coincidence of wants, which means that what one person wants to buy is exactly what the other person wants to sell.

65(B). External trade contributes to Globalisation.
When buying and selling of goods take place across the national boundaries of different countries it is called External trade. It is also known as Foreign trade or International trade . Globalisation of trade offers immediate benefits: faster growth, higher living standards and new economic opportunities . On the downside, not all countries have benefited equally from the Globalisation phenomena.

66(D). Cheaper imports, inadequate investment in infrastructure leads to slowdown in agriculture sector, replace the demand for domestic production and slowdown in industrial sector.
Cheaper imports will lead to the fall in the demand of domestic goods because the imports are cheaper and people won't be willing to buy the domestic goods at a higher price. Inadequate investment in infrastructure means that the industries won't be able to compete with the imports of other countries and they won't be able to survive in the market. That would lead to the decrease in the demand produced in the

industrial sector. So, that would slowdown the capacity of the industrial sector.

67(D). Right to constitutional remedies is not a right of consumer.

There is a right in India which states that a person can move to Supreme court if he/she wants to get their fundamental rights protected. This right comes under article 32 for Supreme court an article 226 for the high court. It is known as the right to constitutional remedies. Consumers are protected by the Consumer Bill of Rights. The bill states that consumers have the right to be informed, the right to choose, the right to safety, the right to be heard, the right to have problems corrected, the right to consumer education, and the right to service.

68(C). Right to safety do not include the right to seek information about functioning of government departments.

Under the Consumer Protection Act, 1986, the government of India gives us six basic rights. Right to Safety is referred as 'right to be protected against the marketing of goods and services which are hazardous to life and property'.

69(D). Role of print revolution in French Revolution are:

- Print popularised the ideas of Enlightenment thinkers. Collectively, their writing provided a critical commentary on tradition, superstition and disposition. They argued for the rule of reason than custom.
- They attacked the sacred authority of the Church and despotic power of the state. This eroded the authority of a social order based on tradition. The writings of Voltaire and Rousseau made readers see the world through new eyes, eyes that questioned and were rational and critical.
- Secondly, print created a new culture of dialogue and debate. Now all values, norms and institutions were re-evaluated and discussed by the public, now aware of their power to question existing beliefs and ideas. It led to new ideas of social revolution. Thirdly, by the 1780s there was an output of literature that mocked reoyalty and questioned their morality. Cartoons and caricatures presented monarchy interested only in their own pleasures, while the ordinary people suffered immense hardships. Literature spread hostile sentiments against the monarchy, though it was circulated underground. But we must remember that to combat the above ideas was the influence of the Church. If people read Voltaire and Rousseau, they were also exposed to monarchical and Church propoganda. So print did not directly shape their minds, but it made it possible for people to think differently.

70(A).

In 1857, the children's press, devoted to literature for children alone, set up in France.

The nineteenth century saw vast leaps in mass literacy in Europe, bringing in large numbers of new readers among children, women and workers. As primary education became compulsory from the late nineteenth century, children became an important category of readers. Production of school textbooks became critical for the publishing industry. A children's press, devoted to literature for children alone, was set up in France in 1857. This press published new works as well as old fairy tales and folk tales. The Grimm Brothers in Germany spent years compiling traditional folk tales gathered from peasants. What they collected was edited before the stories were published in a collection in 1812. Anything that was considered unsuitable for children or would appear vulgar to the elites, was not included in the published version. Rural folk tales thus acquired a new form. In this way, print recorded old tales but also changed them.

71(C). Spanish languages is not spoken in Belgium.

The Kingdom of Belgium has three official languages: Dutch, French, and German. A number of non-official, minority languages and dialects are spoken as well. These languages are not spoken everywhere, because Belgium is subdivided into federated states. Each federated state has its own official language. Only the Brussels-Capital Region is bilingual.

72(B). The Belgium citizens elect the community government in Belgium.

Belgium is a federal state which is made up of three communities and three regions. The three regions are the Walloon region, the Flemish region and the Brussels region. Brussels is the capital region. The three communities are German, Dutch and French speaking people. This is the reason why the state structure of Belgium is so complex. A community government is the one in which different social categories are given the power to control the affairs related to their community. In Belgium, the community government is elected by the electors who belong to one linguistic community for example French, German and Dutch. The community Government has the power related to educational, cultural and linguistic issues of the people of their people. Community governments are expected to work closely for the benefit of the society without ignoring any community. The citizens of Belgium elect the community government in Belgium. This government is elected by the people who belong to one linguistic community, no matter where they live.

73(B). Silk routes linking Asia with Europe and northern Africa.

The silk routes are a good example of vibrant pre-modem trade and cultural links between distant parts of the world. This route knitted together Asia, and linked Asia with Europe and North America. The name 'silk routes' points to the importance of west-bound Chinese silk cargoes along this route.

Historians have identified several silk routes, over land and by sea, knitting together vast regions of Asia and linking Asia with Europe and Northern Africa.

They are known to have existed since before the Christian era and thrived almost till the 15th century. Chinese pottery also travelled the same route, as did textiles and spices from India and South-East Asia. In return, precious metals gold and silver flew from Europe to Asia. Trade end cultural exchange always went hand in hand. Early Christian missionaries almost certainly travelled this route to Asia, as did early Muslim preachers a few centuries later. Buddhism emerged from Eastern India and spread in several directions through Intersecting points on the silk routes.

74(C). Ramachandra Guha said "It is the formation of linguistic states that has allowed India to escape what might have been a worse fate still".

Ramachandra Guha is a famous author and historian who supported linguistic formation of states in India. He said linguistic states help to strengthen Indian unity.

75(B). Concurrent List includes subjects of common interest to both the Union Government as well as the State Governments, such as education, forest, trade unions, marriage, adoption and succession. Both the Union as well as the State Governments can make laws on the subjects mentioned in this list.

"Trade" is in state list, whereas " trade and commerce" is in concurrent list.

76(C). The upper class in Victorian Britain preferred things produced by hand because they came to symbolise refinement and class. The products could be customised according to their choices and they could get these made according to their wishes and likes.

These are the following reasons:

- Handmade products came to symbolise refinement and class.
- They were better finished, individually produced, and carefully designed.
- Machine-made goods were for masses, for colonies, not for classes.
- Handmade goods were costlier, of better quality and fine threads.

77(C). Soil formed by intense leaching is Laterite soil.

Leaching is defined as the loss of water-soluble plants nutrients from the soil, which happens due to the rain or irrigation process. If leaching reaches its optimal level and starts contaminating the underground water, then it is called intensive leaching.

78(B). Over a hundred countries of the world today claim and practice some kind of democratic politics: they have formal constitutions, they hold elections, they have parties and they guarantee rights of citizens. While these features are common to most of them. These democracies are very much different from each other in terms of their social situations, their economic achievements and their cultures. The first step towards thinking carefully about the outcomes of democracy is to recognize that democracy is just a form of government. It can only create conditions for achieving something. The citizens have to take advantage of those conditions and achieve those goals.

79(C). On global situation and resources available in the country, economic development does not depend.
The four main factors of economic growth are land, labor, capital, and entrepreneurship. Factors that Influence the economic development of a country are:
- Capital Formation
- Natural Resources
- Marketable Surplus of Agriculture
- Conditions in Foreign Trade etc.

80(A). The effects of the Non-Cooperation movement On the economic front were that Foreign goods were boycotted, liquor shops picketed, foreign cloth burnt in huge bonfires, started wearing Indian clothes. The effects of non-cooperation on the economic front were dramatic. Foreign goods were boycotted, liquor shops picketed, and foreign cloth burnt in huge bonfires. The import of foreign cloth halved between 1921 and 1922, its value dropping from Rs 102 crore to Rs 57 crore.

81(B). Dadabhai Naoroji (4 September 1825 - 30 June 1917), also known as 'Grand Old Man of India' and "Unofficial Ambassador of India", was a British Zoroastrian scholar, businessman and politician from the Liberal Party of Parliament was a member (MP).

83(A). Fiscal deficit means Govt. expenditure minus Revenue receipts.
A fiscal deficit is a shortfall in a government's income compared with its spending. The government that has a fiscal deficit is spending beyond its means. A fiscal deficit is calculated as a percentage of gross domestic product (GDP), or simply as total dollars spent in excess of income. In either case, the income figure includes only taxes and other revenues and excludes money borrowed to make up the shortfall. A fiscal deficit is different from fiscal debt.

The latter is the total debt accumulated over years of deficit spending.

84(B). Nyaya Panchayat cannot send a person to jail.
A Nyaya panchayat is a system of dispute resolution at the village level in the panchayati raj system of India. Legislation to formalize these bodies and bring them within the ambit of organised justice in India was planned as part of the Panchayati Raj reforms of Rajiv Gandhi in the 1980s, but was put on hold to coincide with broader reform of the justice system, which was never carried out. Following the victory of the Congress Party-led United Progressive Alliance in the 2004 Indian general election, the National Advisory Council advised the Government of India to introduce legislation. To draft legislation in this regard a drafting committee, under the chairmanship of Professor Upendra Baxi, has been formed by the Ministry of Panchayati Raj, Government of India. The bill on the issue is proposed to be debated in the winter session of the Indian Parliament. Nyaya panchayat can only fine up to ₹100 and cannot send anyone to jail.

85(B). The term filament is used under the 'tidal hypothesis'. The tidal hypothesis was formulated by British scholar Sir James Jeans in 1919.

86(B). GSAT is Communication Satellite.
The full name is a Geosynchronous satellite. It is placed in a geosynchronous orbit on the earth. It provides support to telecommunication services (like- TV broadcasting, internet, weather forecasting, etc.)

87(C). The correct chronological order of the formation of the following states in India are Ngaland, Haryana, Sikkim and Arunachal Pradesh.
Nagaland on 1st December 1963.
Haryana on 1st November 1966.
Sikkim on 16th May 1975.
Arunachal Pradesh on 20th Feb 1987.

88(A). Kangra painting is a mixture of Rajasthan and Mughal. The pictorial art of Kangra is one of the finest gifts of India to the art world. It originated in a small hill state 'Guler' in lower Himalayas in 18th century when a family of Kashmiri painters trained in Mughal Style of painting sought shelter at the court of Raja Dalip Singh of Guler.

89(C). Salal Hydroelectric Power Station is a Chenab River run-of-the-river hydroelectric facility. Salal Hydroelectric Project is built on river Chenab in district of Jammu & Kashmir in India.

90(C). Peshawar and Mathura were the two major centers of power during the rule of the Kushans.
- The best-known of the rulers who controlled the Silk Route were the Kushanas, who ruled over central Asia and north-west India around 2000 years ago.
- Their two major centres of power were Peshawar and Mathura.
- Taxila was also included in their kingdom.
- During their rule, a branch of the Silk Route extended from Central Asia down to the seaports at the mouth of the river Indus, from where silk was shipped westwards to the Roman Empire.
- The Kushanas were amongst the earliest rulers of the subcontinent to issue gold coins.
- These were used by traders along the Silk Route.
- The most famous Kushana ruler was Kanishka, who ruled around 1900 years ago.

91(B). The Name of Shershah in childhood was farid.
Mughal Emperor Shershah was originally named Farid Khan at the time of his birth. He was the emperor who started the Suri dynasty in the year 1540 by defeating Humayun, the previous Mughal Emperor. Shershah was known to be one of the greatest administrators during the time of medieval India.

92(B). Jallianwala Bagh massacre took place on April 13, 1919.
Gandhiji called for a massive strike on April 6, 1919, in protest against the Rowlatt Act. On April 13, 1919, an unarmed but large crowd gathered at Jallianwala Bagh in Amritsar, Punjab, to protest the arrest of its popular leaders Dr. Saifuddin Kitchlu and Dr. Satyapal, where army commander Reginald Edward Harry Dyer opened fire on an unarmed peaceful crowd and killed about 1,000 people. Rabindranath Tagore returned his 'Knight' title in protest against this massacre.

93(C). Sardar Sarovar Dam is constructed on Narmada river.
The Sardar Sarovar Dam is a concrete gravity dam built on the Narmada river in Navagam near Kevadiya, Narmada District, Gujarat in India. Four Indian states, Gujarat, Madhya Pradesh, Maharashtra and Rajasthan, receive water and electricity supply from the dam.

94(C). The Governor of a State shall be appointed by the President by warrant under his hand and seal.

95(C). International Shooting Sport Federation (ISSF) Junior World Cup began on 9 May 2022 at Suhl in Germany. Manu Bhaker and Saurabh Chaudhary was lead the Indian contingent at the event. National Rifle Association of India (NRAI) has shortlisted as many as 51 shooters for the German World Cup, including shooters like

Anish Bhanwala, Naamya Kapoor, Vivaan Kapoor, etc.

96(C). Vikram Sarabhai was the first chairman of ISRO.

ISRO was formed by Vikram Sarabhai in the year 1969. Vikram Ambalal Sarabhai was an Indian physicist and astronomer who initiated space research and helped develop nuclear power in India. He was honored with Padma Bhushan in 1966 and the Padma Vibhushan in 1972.

He is internationally regarded as the Father of the Indian Space Program.

97(D). Electric power is defined as the rate, per unit time, at which electrical energy is transferred by an electric circuit.

The SI unit of power is the watt, one joule per second.

Ampere- Electric Current
Volt- Electric Potential (Voltage)
Coulomb- Electric Charge

98(A). Dioptre is unit of Power of a lens.

The SI unit of the focal length is the meter (m).

So the SI unit of power

$$= \frac{1}{(\text{SI unit of focal length})} = m^{-1} = \text{Dioptre (D)}.$$

$1 \text{ m}^{-1} = 1 \text{ D}$

99(C). Hitler is known as 'Fuehrer'.

Adolf Hitler was a German politician and leader of the Nazi party. He rose to power as Chancellor of Germany in 1933, and as Fuehrer in 1934. Fuehrer is a German word meaning "leader" or "guide". Adolf Hitler was the leader of Nazi Germany. His fascist agenda led to World War II and the deaths of at least 11 million people, including some six million Jews.

100(A). Former US President Barack Obama was awarded the Best Narrator Emmy for his work in Netflix's documentary series, Our Great National Parks. The five-part show, which features national parks from around the globe, is backed by Barack and Michelle Obama's production company, Higher Ground.

Mathematics

1. While computing mean of grouped data, we assume that the frequencies are _______.
   (a) centred at the class marks of the classes
   (b) evenly distributed over all the classes
   (c) centred at the upper limits of the classes
   (d) centred at the lower limits of the classes

2. The mean of following distribution is:

x_i	11	14	17	20
f_i	3	6	8	7

   (a) 15.6 (b) 17
   (c) 14.8 (d) 16.4

3. A solid sphere of radius $3cm$ is melted and then recast into small spherical balls each of diameter $0.6cm$. Find the number of small balls thus obtained.
   (a) 1100 (b) 1200
   (c) 1000 (d) 1300

4. To paint a solid cylinder whose radius is half of its height costs Rs. 2376. If it costs Rs. 14 per cm^2, find the height of the cylinder.
   (a) $8cm$ (b) $5cm$
   (c) $6cm$ (d) $3cm$

5. The altitude of a right triangle is 7 cm less than its base. If the hypotenuse is 13 cm, the other two sides of the triangle are equal to:
   (a) Base = 10 cm and Altitude = 5 cm
   (b) Base = 12 cm and Altitude = 5 cm
   (c) Base = 14 cm and Altitude = 10 cm
   (d) Base = 12 cm and Altitude = 10 cm

6. The sum of the reciprocals of Rehman's ages 3 years ago and 5 years from now is $\frac{1}{3}$. The present age of Rehman is:
   (a) 7 (b) 10
   (c) 5 (d) 6

7. Which of the following equations has 2 as a root?
   (a) $x^2 - 4x + 5 = 0$
   (b) $x^2 + 3x - 12 = 0$
   (c) $2x^2 - 7x + 6 = 0$
   (d) $3x^2 - 6x - 2 = 0$

8. Find the area of the shaded region in the given figure, if $ABCD$ is a square of side 14 cm and APD and BPC are semicircles.

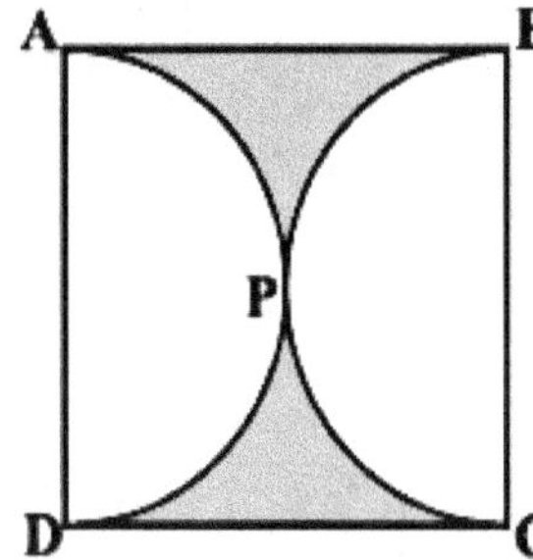

   (a) 42 cm^2 (b) 44 cm^2
   (c) 46 cm^2 (d) 48 cm^2

9. In the given figure, $ABCD$ is a square of side 14 cm. With centers A, B, C and D, four circles are drawn such that each circle touches externally two of the remaining three circles. Find the area of the shaded region.

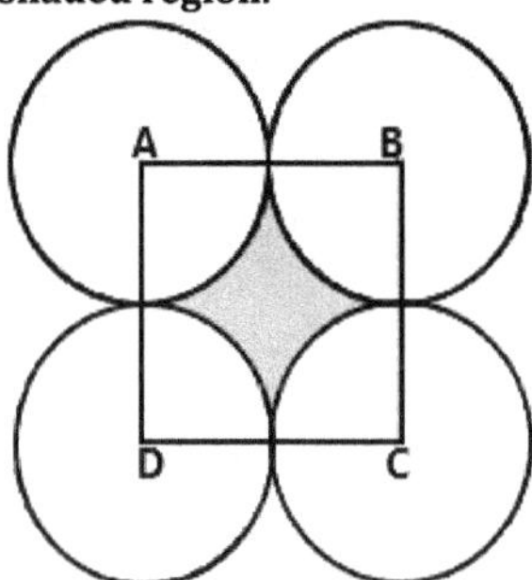

   (a) 42 cm^2 (b) 44 cm^2
   (c) 46 cm^2 (d) 48 cm^2

10. Which of the following is always true if $\sec A = \operatorname{cosec} B$?
   (a) $A + B = 45°$
   (b) $A = B$
   (c) $A + B = 90°$
   (d) $A + B = 180°$

11. Given $15 \cot A = 8$, find $\sin A$ and $\sec A$.
   (a) $\frac{15}{17}, \frac{17}{8}$ (b) $\frac{-15}{17}, \frac{17}{8}$
   (c) $\frac{17}{15}, \frac{1}{8}$ (d) $\frac{1}{17}, \frac{17}{8}$

12. What is the value of $\frac{\sin 75°}{\cos 15°} \div \frac{\operatorname{cosec} 60°}{\sec 30°} - 1$?
   (a) Not defined (b) 2
   (c) 1 (d) 0

13. The area of a rectangle gets reduced by 9 square units, if its length is reduced by 5 units and breadth is increased by 3 units. If we increase the length by 3 units and the breadth by 2 units, the area increases by 67 square units. Find the dimensions of the rectangle.
   (a) Length 10 units, Breadth 9 units
   (b) Length 12 units, Breadth 8 units
   (c) Length 17 units, Breadth 9 units
   (d) Length 19 units, Breadth 10 units

14. Solve the following pairs of equations by reducing them to a pair of linear equations:
   $$\frac{2}{\sqrt{x}} + \frac{3}{\sqrt{y}} = 2$$
   $$\frac{4}{\sqrt{x}} - \frac{9}{\sqrt{y}} = -1$$
   (a) $x = 2, y = 1$ (b) $x = 3, y = 6$
   (c) $x = 5, y = 8$ (d) $x = 4, y = 9$

15. The decimal expansion of the rational number $\frac{23}{2^3 5^2}$, will terminate after how many places of decimal?
   (a) 1 (b) 3
   (c) 4 (d) 5

16. $n^2 - 1$ is divisible by 8 if n is:
   (a) An integer
   (b) A natural number
   (c) An odd integer
   (d) An even integer

17. A real number $\frac{2^2 \times 3^2 \times 7^2}{2^5 \times 5^3 \times 3^2 \times 7}$ will have:
   (a) Terminating decimal
   (b) Non-terminating decimal
   (c) Non-terminating and non-repeating decimal
   (d) Terminating repeating decimal

18. If the HCF of 65 and 117 is expressible in the form 65 m – 117, then the value of m is:
   (a) 4 (b) 2
   (c) 1 (d) 3

19. If 1 is a zero of the polynomials $ay^2 + ay + 3$ and $y^2 + y + b$, then find the value of ab:
   (a) -2 (b) 2
   (c) -3 (d) 3

20. Which of the following is not graph of a quadratic polynomial?

(a)

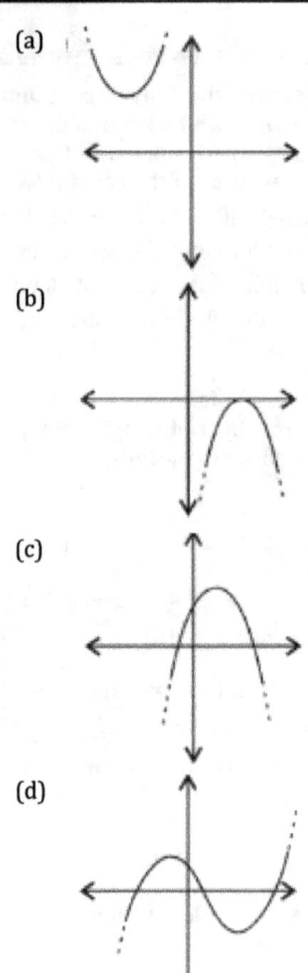

(b)

(c)

(d)

21. Three unbiased coins are tossed. What is the probability of getting at most two heads?

(a) $\frac{3}{4}$ (b) $\frac{1}{4}$

(c) $\frac{3}{8}$ (d) $\frac{7}{8}$

22. A card is drawn from a pack of 52 cards. The probability of getting a queen of club or a king of heart is:

(a) $\frac{1}{13}$ (b) $\frac{2}{13}$

(c) $\frac{1}{26}$ (d) $\frac{1}{52}$

23. Find the sum of odd numbers between 0 and 50.

(a) 425   (b) 525

(c) 625   (d) 725

24. Find the sum of those integers between 1 and 500 which are multiples of 2 as well as 5.

(a) 12250   (b) 12300

(c) 13250   (d) 13300

25. If TP and TQ are the two tangents to a circle with centre O so that $\angle POQ = 110°$, then $\angle PTQ$ is equal to:

(a) $60°$ (b) $70°$

(c) $80°$ (d) $90°$

26. The length of a tangent drawn from a point at a distance of $10\,cm$ of circle is $8\,cm$. The radius of the circle is:

(a) $4\,cm$ (b) $5\,cm$

(c) $6\,cm$ (d) $7\,cm$

27. In given figure, CP and CQ are tangents to a circle with centre O. ARB is another tangent touching the circle at R. If $CP = 11$ cm and $BC = 6$ cm then the length of BR is:

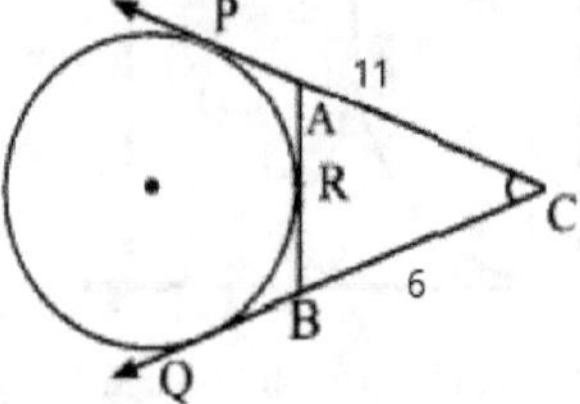

(a) 6   (b) 5

(c) 4   (d) 2

28. In the given figures the measures of $\angle P$ and $\angle R$ are respectively.

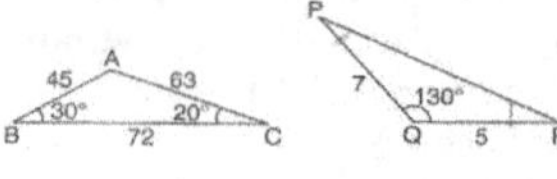

(a) $50°, 40°$ (b) $40°, 50°$

(c) $30°, 20°$ (d) $20°, 30°$

29. $\angle ADE = \angle ABC$, then CE is equal to:

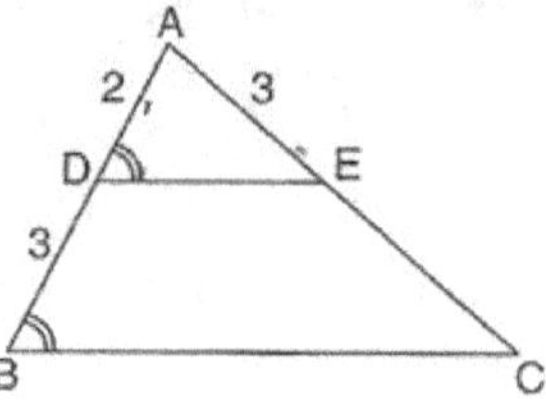

(a) 5   (b) 3

(c) 2   (d) 4.5

30. In $\triangle ABC$, given below, $AB = 8\,cm, BC = 10\,cm$ and $AC = 6\,cm$. If a point P lies on AB and Q on AC such that $PQ \| BC$ and $PQ = 5\,cm$, then find AP and AQ respectively.

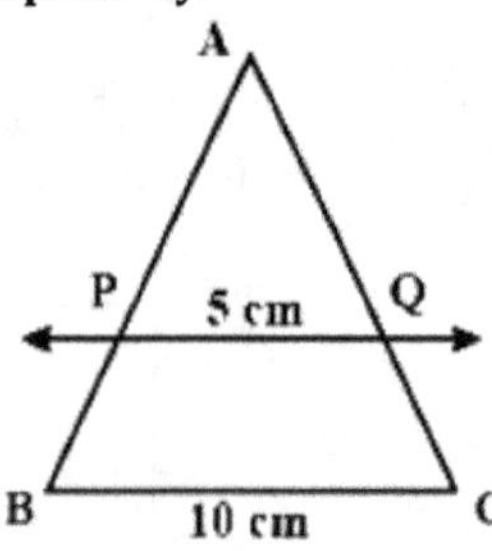

(a) $4\,cm$ and $3\,cm$

(b) $20\,cm$ and $3\,cm$

(c) $15\,cm$ and $10\,cm$

(d) $10\,cm$ and $5\,cm$

31. The functional unit of the environment:

(a) Ecosystem   (b) Nitrogen

(c) Carbon   (d) Oxygen

32. What percentage of sunlight is captured by plants to convert into food energy?

(a) 1%

(b) 10%

(c) 50%

(d) More than 50%

33. If copper is kept open in air, it slowly loses its shining brown surface and gains a green coating. It is due to the formation of:

(a) $CuSO4$ (b) $CuCO_3$

(c) $Cu(NO_3)2$ (d) CuO

34. Reacting with water, a metal produces:

(a) oxygen   (b) nitric acid

(c) a base   (d) water

35. A doctor advised a person to take an injection of insulin because:

(a) His blood pressure was low

(b) His heart was beating slowly

(c) He was suffering from goiter

(d) His sugar level in blood was high

36. Dwarfism results due to:

(a) Excess secretion of thyroxin

(b) Less secretion of growth hormone

(c) Less secretion of adrenaline

(d) Excess secretion of growth hormone

37. For the reaction $CuO + H_2 \rightarrow Cu + H_2O$ Which of the following statement is correct?

(a) CuO is being reduced and hydrogen is being oxidised

(b) CuO is being oxidised and hydrogen is being reduced

(c) Both CuO and H_2 are being reduced

(d) Both CuO and H_2 are being oxidised

38. Which of the following compounds is used for white-washing?

(a) $NaOH$ (b) KCl

(c) CaO (d) $CaCl_2$

39. Which type pf bond does hydrogen chloride molecule contains?

(a) Covalent bond
(b) Ionic bond
(c) Co-ordinate covalent bond
(d) Vander Waal bond

40. **Which of the following is the molecular formula of cyclobutane?**
(a) C_4H_{10}
(b) C_4H_6
(c) C_4H_8
(d) C_4H_4

41. **How many chromosomes are present in a ovum of human being?**
(a) 29
(b) 22
(c) 23
(d) 21

42. **Which vegetative part is used in the propagation of bryophyllum?**
(a) Stem
(b) Petal
(c) Root
(d) Leaf

43. **________ traits lead to evolution.**
(a) Acquired
(b) Inherited
(c) Evolutionary
(d) Natural

44. **Which phenomenon explains the formation of cauliflower from wild cabbage?**
(a) Natural selection
(b) Artificial selection
(c) Fossilisation
(d) Speciation

45. **A convex lens has a focal length of 40 cm. Calculate its power.**
(a) 3.5 D
(b) 2.5 D
(c) 6.6 D
(d) 4.5 D

46. **According to snell's law, $n_{21} \times n_{12} =$?**
(a) 0.0
(b) 1.0
(c) 2.0
(d) 1212

47. **The wire having a black plastic covering is a:**
(a) Live Wire
(b) Neutral Wire
(c) Earth Wire
(d) None of the above

48. **The strength of magnetic field around a current carrying conductor is:**
(a) Inversely proportional to the current but directly proportional to the square of the distance from wire.
(b) Directly proportional to the current and inversely proportional to the distance from wire.
(c) Directly proportional to the distance and inversely proportional to the current.
(d) Directly proportional to the current but inversely proportional the square of the distance from wire.

49. **Where does the filtration of blood occur in the kidneys?**
(a) Vasa recta
(b) Collecting duct
(c) Bowman's capsule
(d) Tubular part of nephron

50. **______ is generated as a 'waste' during photosynthesis in plants.**
(a) Water
(b) Oxygen
(c) Carbon dioxide
(d) Nitrogen

51. **Which of the following metals does not react with dilute sulphuric acid?**
(a) Zinc
(b) Sodium
(c) Silver
(d) Calcium

52. **Which of the following is(are) true when HCl (g) is passed through water?**
(i) It does not ionise in the solution as it is a covalent compound.
(ii) It ionises in the solution
(iii) It gives both hydrogen and hydroxyl ion in the solution
(iv) It forms hydronium ion in the solution due to the combination of hydrogen ion with water molecule
(a) (i) only
(b) (iii) only
(c) (ii) and (iv)
(d) (iii) and (iv)

53. **The angle through which a ray of light turns on passing through a prism is called:**
(a) Angle of emergence
(b) Angle of reflection
(c) Angle of incidence
(d) Angle of deviation

54. **Three resistances, each of 4Ω, are connected to form a triangle. The resistance between any two vertices of the triangle will be:**
(a) 12.4Ω
(b) 8.7Ω
(c) 6.1Ω
(d) 2.6Ω

55. **Observe the given circuit:**

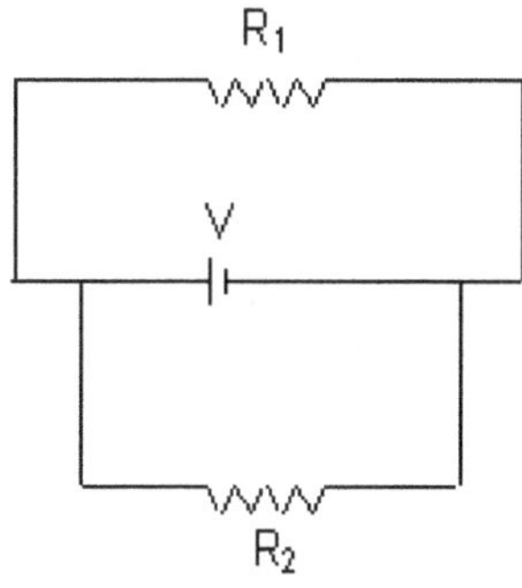

In this circuit, resistances R_1 and R_2 are in a________.
(a) parallel combination
(b) series combination
(c) mixed combination
(d) none of these

Social Science

56. **Which of the following is not correct with respect to drip irrigation?**
(a) It saves water wastage
(b) Fertilizers can be used with high efficiency
(c) It requires very less installation
(d) It prevents soil erosion

57. **Which factors have led to the decline in India's biodiversity?**
(a) Habitat destruction, hunting, poaching, over-exploitation, environmental pollution, poisoning and forest fires
(b) Mining
(c) Industry
(d) Large scale projects

58. **The highest quality of hard coal is:**
(a) Lignite
(b) Bituminous
(c) Peat
(d) Anthracite

59. **Banking is included in which of the following sectors of the Indian economy?**
(a) Tertiary sector
(b) Primary sector
(c) Secondery sector
(d) Government sector

60. **Different persons have:**
(a) same notion of country's development
(b) different notions of country's development
(c) conflicting nntions of country's develoment
(d) Both (B) and (C)

61. **When did Industrialization take place in France and parts of the**

German states?

(a) 18th century
(b) Later 18th century
(c) 19th century
(d) Mid 18th century

62. What are the features of primitive subsistence agriculture?

(a) Large amount of labour
(b) When the soil fertility decreases, the farmers shift and clear a fresh patch of land
(c) Canals were used
(d) Use of fertilisers

63. The RBI monitors the bank's:

(a) Cash books
(b) Cash balance
(c) Cash register
(d) None of the above

64. Gold mohar, a coin so named was brought in circulation by:

(a) Akbar
(b) Sher Shah Suri
(c) Ashok
(d) Shivaji

65. Fair globalisation refers to ensuring benefits to:

(a) Labourers   (b) Producers
(c) Consumers   (d) All the above

66. Globalisation has improved the living structure of which of the following?

(a) All the people
(b) People living in developing countries
(c) People living in developed countries
(d) None of the above

67. Marketing of goods and services which are hazardous to life and property is covered under:

(a) right to be protected
(b) right to be assured
(c) right to seek redressal
(d) right to be informed

68. Who shall be the Chairman of the Central Consumer Protection Council.

(a) The Minister incharge of consumer affairs in the Central Government
(b) The Minister incharge of consumer affairs in the State Government
(c) The Prime Minister
(d) The Speaker of Lok Sabha

69. In the 1920s in England, popular works were sold in cheap series, called the:

(a) Shilling Series
(b) Penny Series
(c) Yorkshire Series
(d) Oxford Series

70. How were the ancient handwritten manuscripts in India preserved?

(a) By binding
(b) Either pressed between wooden covers or sewn together
(c) Glued together
(d) Kept loose

71. Most of the Sinhala-speaking people are:

(a) Buddhists   (b) Hindus
(c) Muslims   (d) Christians

72. What was the most serious demand of the Sri Lankan Tamils which resulted in a civil war in Sri Lanka?

(a) Reservation of jobs for Tamils
(b) Recognition of Tamil as an official language
(c) Creation of an independent Tamil Eelam
(d) Creation of a federation with autonomy to Tamils

73. Which one of the following countries passed Corn Laws to restrict the import of corn?

(a) India   (b) France
(c) China   (d) Britaina

74. The basic idea of decentralization is _____________.

(a) To divide powers between central and state government
(b) To give powers to the local-self government
(c) To share power between two state governments
(d) To share power between different organs of government

75. Arunachal Pradesh was granted statehood in _______.

(a) 1972   (b) 1984
(c) 1985   (d) 1987

76. What was the possibility of getting a job with such abundance of labour in the cities?

(a) Jobs were given on the basis of merit and artistry of the jobseeker
(b) A job depended on existing networks of friendship and kin relations in the factory
(c) Jobs were given, if you were registered with a particular factory

(d) First come, first serve basis

77. Which one of the following type of resource is iron ore?

(a) Renewable
(b) Biotic
(c) Flow
(d) Non-renewable

78. In actual life, democracies do not appear to be very successful in:

(a) Reducing economic inequalities
(b) Maintaining dignity of each individual
(c) Ensuring equality to all
(d) All of the above

79. Democracy in India has strengthened the claims of the _________ castes for equal status and equal opportunity.

(a) Rich classes
(b) Middle classes
(c) Disadvantaged
(d) Aristocratic

80. When did the Non-Cooperation-Khilafat Movement begin?

(a) 1920   (b) 1919
(c) 1921   (d) 1922

General Awareness/ Knowledge

81. Who among the following poets wrote under the pen name 'Nirala' ?

(a) Jaishankar Prasad
(b) Ramdhari Singh Dinkar
(c) Maithili Sharan Gupta
(d) Suryakant Tripathi

82. Which one of the following is not included in the Fundamental Rights?

(a) Right to property
(b) Right to form association
(c) Right of assembly
(d) Right to move and stay in any part of the country

83. Match Column-A with Column-B and select the correct answer using the codes given below:

Column-A	Column-B
a. 1955	1. Export-Import Bank of India
b. 1964	2. Industrial Development Bank
c. 1982	3. Industrial Credit and Investment

d. 1987	4. Board of Industrial and Financial Reconstruction

(a) a-1, b-2, c-3, d-4
(b) a-2, b-3, c-1, d-4
(c) a-3, b-2, c-1, d-4
(d) a-4, b-1, c-2, d-3

84. **The guidelines for the police investigation are laid down by:**
(a) Supreme Court
(b) Judge
(c) Constitution
(d) None of these

85. **The series of lines connecting the vibrating places at the same time is called:**
(a) Homoacoustic lines
(b) Earthquake lines
(c) Covariance lines (coseismal lines)
(d) Isosomal lines

86. **Power of a lens is roughly dependent upon:**
(a) Curvature of the lens
(b) Height of the lens
(c) Size of the lens
(d) Width of the lens

87. **In which year, Goa was declared as India's 25th state?**
(a) 1987   (b) 1988
(c) 1989   (d) 1990

88. **The 'Gandhara' School of Art was influenced by the art from which of the following European countries?**
(a) Italy   (b) Belgium
(c) Hungary   (d) Greece

89. **In which of the following places AjantaEllora caves are situated?**
(a) Benguluru   (b) Delhi
(c) Aurangabad   (d) Lucknow

90. **In which of the following cities was the first Buddhist council held?**
(a) Nalanda   (b) Gaya
(c) Rajgir   (d) Bodhgaya

91. **Which of the following Sultan had maximum number of slaves in his court?**
(a) Balban
(b) Alauddin Khilji
(c) Muhammad bin Tughlaq
(d) Firoz Tughlaq

92. **Which of the following statements about the Deccan Riots Commission is/are correct?**
1. The Commission did not hold enquiries in the districts which were not affected.
2. The Commission did record the statements of ryots, sahukars and eye-witnesses.
Select the correct answer using the code given below:
(a) 1 only
(b) 2 only
(c) Both 1 and 2
(d) Neither 1 nor 2

93. **The percentage of carbon dioxide in our atmosphere is**
(a) 0.04%   (b) 0.03%
(c) 1%   (d) 3%

94. **Which of these is NOT a subject under Union List?**
(a) Public Health
(b) Atomic Energy
(c) Foreign Affairs
(d) War and Peace

95. **What is the name of the mascot for the 36th National Games Ahmedabad?**
(a) Sher   (b) Savaj
(c) Vikas   (d) Leo

96. **Who was the first man to reach the north pole in the world?**
(a) Robert Walpole
(b) Robert Peary
(c) Marco polo
(d) Edwin E. Aldrin

97. **Blindspot in the human eye can be located at:**
(a) Left end of Ciliary muscles
(b) Junction of the optic nerve and the retina
(c) Centre of eye Lens
(d) Both ends of Cornea

98. **A plant that grows in waters of high salinity is called____.**
(a) Halophytes
(b) Oxylophytes
(c) Psammophytes
(d) Chasmophytes

99. **The watchwords of the French Revolution-Liberty, Equality and _____ inspired the whole world.**
(a) Fraternity   (b) Justice
(c) Simplicity   (d) Freedom

100. **Which of the following web series won the Best Drama Series award at the 48 [th] International Emmy Awards 2020?**
(a) Ashram
(b) Made in Heaven
(c) Delhi Crime
(d) Mirjapur

// Hints and Solutions //

1(A). Mean is defined as the average of the given numbers. It is the sum of all the given data values divided by the total number of data values given in the set. In calculating the mean of grouped data, the frequencies are centred at the class marks of the classes.

2(D).

x_i	f_i	$f_j x_i$
11	3	33
14	6	84
17	8	136
20	7	140
	$\sum f_i = 24$	$\sum f_i x_i = 393$

$$x_{\text{mean}} = \frac{\sum f_i x_i}{\sum f_i} = \frac{393}{24} = 16.4$$

3(C). Given,
Radius of bigger sphere $(R) = 3cm$
Diameter of smaller spherical balls $= 0.6cm$
So, radius of small spherical balls $(r) = \frac{0.6}{2} = 0.3cm$
Let the number of small balls be n.
As we know,
Volume of sphere $= \frac{4}{3}\pi r^3$
According to the question,
$n\times$ Volumes of small spherical balls $=$ Volume of bigger sphere
$\Rightarrow n \times \frac{4}{3}\pi r^3 = \frac{4}{3}\pi R^3$
$\Rightarrow nr^3 = R^3$
$\Rightarrow n = \frac{R^3}{r^3}$
$\Rightarrow n = \left(\frac{R}{r}\right)^3$
$\Rightarrow n = \left(\frac{3}{0.3}\right)^3$
$\Rightarrow n = (10)^3$
$\Rightarrow n = 1000$
So, the number of small balls obtained is 1000.

4(C).

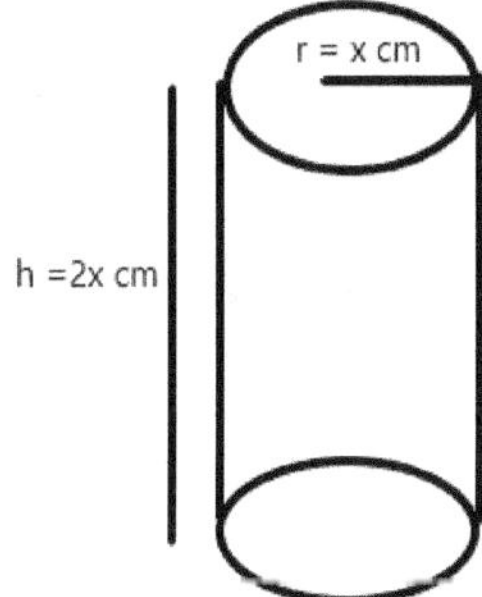

Given,
Radius $\times 2 = $ height
Let radius be xcm and height be $2xcm$.
The total cost of painting the whole cylinder $= $ Rs. 2376
Cost of painting per $cm^2 = $ Rs. 14
As we know,

Total surface area

$$= \frac{\text{Cost of painting whole surface}}{\text{Cost of painting per unit square}}$$

Total surface area of cylinder

$$= 2\pi rh + 2\pi r^2 = 2\pi r(h + r)$$

$$\Rightarrow 6\pi x^2 = \frac{1188}{7}$$

$$\Rightarrow 6 \times \frac{22}{7} \times x^2 = \frac{1188}{7}$$

$$\Rightarrow x^2 = \frac{1188 \times 7}{7 \times 22 \times 6}$$

$$\Rightarrow x^2 = \frac{54}{6}$$

$$\Rightarrow x^2 = 9$$

$$\Rightarrow x = 3$$

Radius of cylinder $= 3cm$

Height of cylinder $= 2x = 2 \times 3 = 6cm$

So, the height of the cylinder is $6cm$.

5(B). Let, the base be x cm

Altitude $= (x - 7)$ cm

In a right triangle,

Base^2 + Altitude^2 = Hypotenuse^2 (From Pythagoras theorem)

$$\therefore x^2 + (x - 7)^2 = 13^2$$

$$\therefore x^2 + (x - 7)^2 = 13^2$$

By using $(a - b)^2 = a^2 + b^2 - 2ab$

Now,

$$x^2 + x^2 + 49 - 14x = 169$$

$$\Rightarrow 2x^2 - 14x - 120 = 0$$

$$\Rightarrow 2(x^2 - 7x - 60) = 0$$

$$\Rightarrow x^2 - 7x - 60 = \frac{0}{2}$$

$$\Rightarrow x^2 - 7x - 60 = 0$$

$$\Rightarrow x^2 - 12x + 5x - 60 = 0$$

$$\Rightarrow x(x - 12) + 5(x - 12) = 0$$

$$\Rightarrow (x - 12)(x + 5)$$

$$\Rightarrow x = 12 \text{ or } x = -5$$

Since the side of the triangle cannot be negative.

Therefore, base $= 12$ cm and altitude $= 12 - 7 = 5$ cm

6(A). Let, x is the present age of Rehman

Three years ago his age $= x - 3$

Five years later his age $= x + 5$

Given, the sum of the reciprocals of Rehman's ages 3 years ago and after 5 years is equal to $\frac{1}{3}$.

$$\therefore \frac{1}{x} - \frac{3+1}{x-5} = \frac{1}{3}$$

$$\frac{(x+5+x-3)}{(x-3)(x+5)} = \frac{1}{3}$$

$$\frac{(2x+2)}{(x-3)(x+5)} = \frac{1}{3}$$

$$\Rightarrow 3(2x + 2) = (x - 3)(x + 5)$$

$$\Rightarrow 6x + 6 = x^2 + 2x - 15$$

$$\Rightarrow x^2 - 4x - 21 = 0$$

$$\Rightarrow x^2 - 7x + 3x - 21 = 0$$

$$\Rightarrow x(x - 7) + 3(x - 7) = 0$$

$$\Rightarrow (x - 7)(x + 3) = 0$$

$$\Rightarrow x = 7, -3$$

We know age cannot be negative, hence the answer is 7.

7(C). If 2 is a root then substituting the value 2 in place of x should satisfy the equation.

Let us verify the given options.

(a) $x^2 - 4x + 5 = 0$

$(2)^2 - 4(2) + 5 = 1 \neq 0$

So, $x = 2$ is not a root of $x^2 - 4x + 5 = 0$

(b) $x^2 + 3x - 12 = 0$

$(2)^2 + 3(2) - 12 = -2 \neq 0$

So, $x = 2$ is not a root of $x^2 + 3x - 12 = 0$

So, $x = 2$ is not a root of $x^2 + 3x - 12 = 0$

(c) $2x^2 - 7x + 6 = 0$

$2(2)^2 - 7(2) + 6 = 0$

Here, $x = 2$ is a root of $2x^2 - 7x + 6 = 0$

8(A).

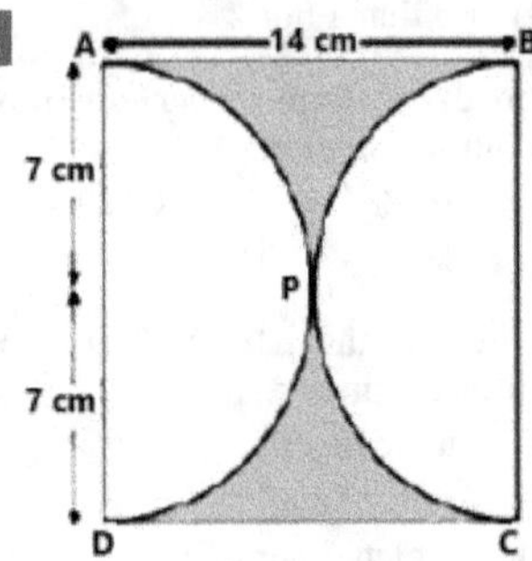

From the above figure it is evident that the radius of each semi-circle is $7cm$. For area of shaded region,

Area of each semi-circle $= \frac{1}{2}\pi r^2$

$$= \frac{1}{2} \times \frac{22}{7} \times (7)^2$$

$$= 77 \text{ cm}^2$$

Area of square $ABCD = $ (side)$^2 = (14)^2 = 196 \text{ cm}^2$

Area of the shaded region = Area of square $ABCD$ − Area of semi-circle APD − Area of semi-circle BPC

$$= 196 - 77 - 77 = 42 \text{ cm}^2$$

Therefore, the area of the shaded region in the given figure is 42 cm^2.

9(A).

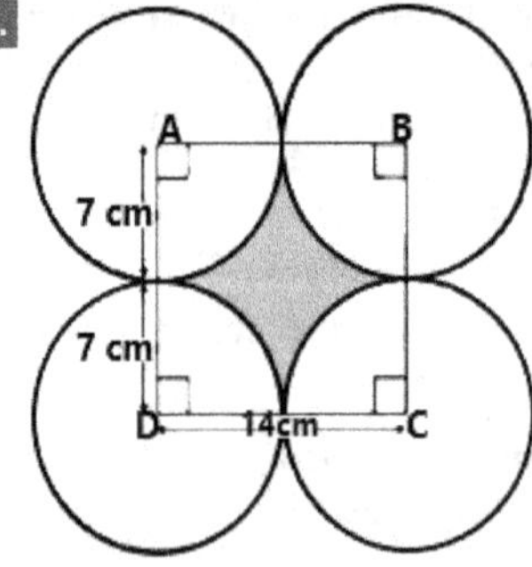

It is evident that,

Area of each of the 4 sectors is equal to each other

Sector of 90° in a circle of 7 cm radius.

For the area of shaded region,

Area of sector $= \frac{\theta}{360°} \times \pi r^2$

Area of each sector $= \frac{90°}{360°}\pi(7)^2$

$$= \frac{1}{4} \times \frac{22}{7} \times (7)^2$$

$$= \frac{77}{2} \text{ cm}^2$$

Area of square $ABCD = $ (side)^2

$= (14)^2 = 196 \text{ cm}^2$

Area of shaded portion = Area of square $ABCD - (4\times$ Area of each sector$)$

$$= 196 - \left(4 \times \frac{77}{2}\right)$$

$$= 196 - 154$$

$= 42$ cm^2

Therefore, the area of shaded portion is 42 cm^2.

10(C). By identity,

$\text{Sec } A = \text{Cosec}(90° - A)$

$\text{Sec } A = \text{Sec}(90° - B)$

Sec will be eliminated

$$= A = 90° - B$$

$$= A + B = 90°$$

11(A). Given,

$15 \cot A = 8$

$$\cot A = \frac{8}{15}$$

$$\Rightarrow \tan A = \frac{15}{8}$$

$$\left(\tan A = \frac{1}{\cot A}\right)$$

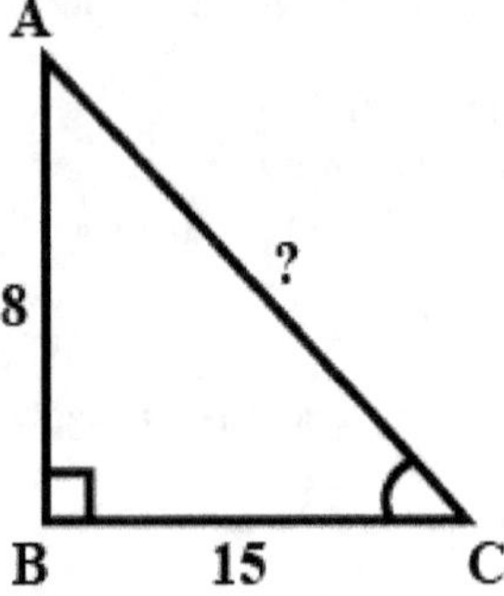

We know that,

$$\tan \theta = \frac{\text{opposite side}}{\text{adjacent side}}$$

Consider the attached figure, triangle ABC.

From Pythagoras theorem,

$$AC^2 = AB^2 + BC^2$$

$$AC^2 = 8^2 + 15^2$$

$$= 64 + 225$$

$$= 289$$

$$AC = 17$$

$$\cos A = \frac{\text{adjacent side}}{\text{Hypotenuse}}$$

$$= \frac{AB}{AC}$$

$$= \frac{8}{17}$$

$$\sec A = \frac{1}{\cos A}$$

$$= \frac{1}{\frac{8}{17}}$$

$$= \frac{17}{8}$$

$$\sin A = \frac{\text{opposite side}}{\text{Hypotenuse}}$$

$$= \frac{BC}{AC}$$

$$= \frac{15}{17}$$

12(D). Given,

$$\frac{\sin 75°}{\cos 15°} \div \frac{\text{cosec } 60°}{\sec 30°} - 1$$

So,

$$= \frac{\sin(90° - 15°)}{\cos 15°} \div \frac{\frac{2}{\sqrt{3}}}{\frac{2}{\sqrt{3}}} - 1$$

$$= \frac{\cos 15°}{\cos 15°} \div 1 - 1$$

$$= 1 - 1$$

$$= 0$$

13(C). Given,

Let Length of rectangle be x units
and Breadth of rectangle be y units
So,
Area = Length $\times$ Breadth
Area $= xy$
Given that,
Area gets reduced by 9 square units,
If length is reduced by 5 units and breadth increased by 3 units.
So,
New Area = New Length $\times$ New Breadth
Old Area $-9 = ($ Length $-5) \times ($ Breadth $+3)$
$xy - 9 = (x - 5)(y + 3)$
$xy - 9 = x(y + 3) - 5(y + 3)$
$xy - 9 = xy + 3x - 5y - 15$
$0 = xy + 3x - 5y - 15 - xy + 9$
$3x - 5y - 6 = 0$
$3x - 5y = 6 \qquad \ldots\ldots (1)$
Also,
Area increases by 67 square units,
If length is increased by 3 units and breadth increased by 2 units.
So,
New Area = New Length $\times$ New Breadth
Old Area $+67 = ($ Length $+3) \times ($ Breadth $+2)$
$xy + 67 = (x + 3)(y + 2)$
$xy + 67 = x(y + 2) + 3(y + 2)$
$xy + 67 = xy + 2x + 3y + 6$
$0 = xy + 2x + 3y + 6 - xy - 67$
$2x + 3y - 61 = 0$
$2x + 3y = 61 \qquad \ldots\ldots (2)$
So, our equations are
$3x - 5y = 6 \qquad \ldots\ldots (1)$
$2x + 3y = 61 \qquad \ldots\ldots (2)$
From (1),
$3x - 5y - 6 = 0$
$3x = 6 + 5y$
$x = \dfrac{6 + 5y}{3}$
Putting value of x in (2),
$2x + 3y = 61$
$2\left(\dfrac{6 + 5y}{3}\right) + 3y = 61$
Multiplying both sides by 3,
$3 \times 2\left(\dfrac{(6 + 5y)}{3}\right) + 3 \times 3y = 3 \times 61$
$2(6 + 5y) + 9y = 183$
$12 + 10y + 9y = 183$
$19y = 183 - 12$
$19y = 171$
$y = \dfrac{171}{19}$
$y = 9$
Putting $y = 9$ in equation (1),
$3x - 5y = 6$
$3x - 5(9) = 6$
$3x - 45 = 6$
$3x = 6 + 45$

$3x = 51$
$x = \dfrac{51}{3}$
$x = 17$
Therefore $x = 17, y = 9$ is the solution
So,
Length of rectangle $= x = 17$ units
Breadth of rectangle $= y = 9$ units

14(D). $\dfrac{2}{\sqrt{x}} + \dfrac{3}{\sqrt{y}} = 2 \qquad \ldots (1)$
$\dfrac{4}{\sqrt{x}} - \dfrac{9}{\sqrt{y}} = -1 \qquad \ldots (2)$
$\dfrac{1}{\sqrt{x}} = u$
$\dfrac{1}{\sqrt{y}} = v$
So, our equations become
$2u + 3v = 2 \qquad \ldots\ldots (3)$
$4u - 9v = -1 \qquad \ldots\ldots (4)$
Our equations,
$2u + 3v = 2 \qquad \ldots\ldots (3)$
$4u - 9v = -1 \qquad \ldots\ldots (4)$
From (3),
$2u + 3v = 2$
$2u = 2 - 3v$
$u = \dfrac{2 - 3v}{2}$
Putting value of u in (4),
$4u - 9v = -1$
$4\left(\dfrac{2 - 3v}{2}\right) - 9v = -1$
$2(2 - 3v) - 9v = -1$
$4 - 6v - 9v = -1$
$-6v - 9v = -1 - 4$
$-15v = -5$
$v = \dfrac{-5}{-15}$
$v = \dfrac{1}{3}$
Putting $v = \dfrac{1}{3}$ in (3),
$2u + 3v = 2$
$2u + 3\left(\dfrac{1}{3}\right) = 2$
$2u + 1 = 2$
$2u = 2 - 1$
$u = \dfrac{1}{2}$
So, $u = \dfrac{1}{2}$ and $v = \dfrac{1}{3}$
But, we need to find x and y,
$u = \dfrac{1}{\sqrt{x}}$
$\dfrac{1}{2} = \dfrac{1}{\sqrt{x}}$
$\sqrt{x} = 2$
Squaring both sides,
$(\sqrt{x})^2 = (2)^2$
$x = 4$
$v = \dfrac{1}{\sqrt{y}}$
$\dfrac{1}{3} = \dfrac{1}{\sqrt{y}}$
$\sqrt{y} = 3$
Squaring both sides,
$(\sqrt{y})^2 = (3)^2$
$y = 9$
Therefore, $x = 4, y = 9$ is the solution of the given equation.

15(B). Given,

$\dfrac{23}{2^3 5^2}$
$= \dfrac{23}{2(2)^2(5)^2}$
$= \dfrac{23}{2(2 \times 5)^2}$
$= \dfrac{23}{2(10)^2}$
$= \dfrac{11.5}{100} = 0.115$
Therefore, the decimal expansion of the rational number $\dfrac{23}{2^3 5^2}$ will terminate after three places of decimal.

16(C). As we know,
An odd number in the form $(2Q + 1)$ where Q is a natural number.
So, $n^2 - 1 = (2Q + 1)^2 - 1$
$= 4Q^2 + 4Q + 1 - 1$
$= 4Q^2 + 4Q$
Substituting $Q = 1, 2, \ldots$
When $Q = 1$,
$4Q^2 + 4Q = 4(1)^2 + 4(1) = 4 + 4 = 8$, it is divisible by 8.
When $Q = 2$,
$4Q^2 + 4Q = 4(2)^2 + 4(2) = 16 + 8 = 24$, it is also divisible by 8.
When $Q = 3$,
$4Q^2 + 4Q = 4(3)^2 + 4(3) = 36 + 12 = 48$, divisible by 8.
It is concluded that $4Q^2 + 4Q$ is divisible by 8 for all natural numbers.
So, $n^2 - 1$ is divisible by 8 for all odd values of n.

17(A). Given,
$\dfrac{2^2 \times 3^2 \times 7^2}{2^5 \times 5^3 \times 3^2 \times 7}$
$= 2^{2-5} \times 3^{2-2} \times 5^{-3} \times 7^{2-1}$
$= 2^{-3} \times 3^0 \times 5^{-3} \times 7^1$
$= \dfrac{7}{2^3 \times 5^3}$
$= \dfrac{7}{1000}$
$= 0.007$
$\therefore 0.007$ is a terminating non-repeating decimal.

18(B). Factors of 65 and 117 are:
$65 = 5 \times 13$
$117 = 3 \times 3 \times 13$
$\therefore$ HCF of 65 and 117 is 13.
Since, HCF $= 65m - 117$
$\therefore 65m - 117 = 13$
$\Rightarrow 65m = 13 + 117$
$\Rightarrow 65m = 130$
$\Rightarrow m = \dfrac{130}{65}$
$\Rightarrow m = 2$

19(D). Since, 1 is a zero of the given polynomials,
Then, $p(1) = 0$
Put $ay^2 + ay + 3 = 0$
$\Rightarrow a(1)^2 + a(1) + 3 = 0$
$\Rightarrow 2a + 3 = 0$
$\Rightarrow a = -\dfrac{3}{2}$
And $q(1)$
Put $y^2 + y + b$
$= (1)^2 + 1 + b = 0$

$\Rightarrow 2 + b = 0$

$\Rightarrow b = -2$

Now, $ab = \left(-\frac{3}{2}\right) \times (-2) = 3$

So, the value of ab is 3.

20(D). From the given options, only option (D) has more than two roots, so it cannot be graph of quadratic polynomial. For any quadratic polynomial $ax^2 + bx + c$, $a \neq 0$, the graph of the corresponding polynomial $ax^2 + bx + c$, has one of the two shapes: either open upwards like $\cup$ (parabolic shape) or open downwards like $\cap$ (parabolic shape), depending on whether $a > 0$ or $a < 0$ respectively. These curves are called parabolas. So, option (D) cannot be possible.

Also, the curve of a quadratic polynomial crosses the x-axis atmost two points but in option (D), the curve crosses the x-axis at three points, so it does not represent a quadratic polynomial.

Therefore, option (D) is not the graph of a quadratic polynomial.

21(D). Getting at most Two heads means 0 to 2 but not more than 2

Here $S = \{TTT, TTH, THT, HTT, THH, HTH, HHT, HHH\}$

Let $E =$ event of getting at most two heads

Then

$E = \{TTT, TTH, THT, HTT, THH, HTH, HHT\}$

$\therefore P(E) = \frac{n(E)}{n(S)} = \frac{7}{8}$

22(C). Here, $n(S) = 52$

Let $E =$ event of getting a queen of club or a king of heart

Then, $n(E) = 2$

$\therefore P(E) = \frac{n(E)}{n(S)}$

$= \frac{2}{52}$

$= \frac{1}{26}$

23(C). Odd numbers between 0 and 50 are $1, 3, 5, 7, \ldots, 49$.

These numbers form an AP with $a = 1, d = 2$ and $l = 49$.

Let the number of these numbers be n, then

$T_n = a + (n-1)d$

$a =$ first term

$d =$ common difference

$T_n = n^{\text{th}}$ term

$49 = 1 + (n-1) \times 2 \Rightarrow 48 = 2(n-1)$

$\Rightarrow 24 = n - 1 \Rightarrow n = 25$

$S_n = \frac{n}{2}(a + l)$

$a =$ first term

$l =$ last term

$S_n =$ Sum of nth term

$\therefore$ Sum of these numbers $= \frac{25}{2}(1 + 49) = \frac{25}{2} \times 50 = 25 \times 25 = 625$

24(A). The integers which are multiples of 2 as well as 5 must be multiples of 10. The integers between 1 and 500 which are multiples of 10 are $10, 20, 30, \ldots, 490$.

These numbers form an AP with $a = 10, l = 490$ and $n = 49$.

$S_n = \frac{n}{2}(a + l)$

$a =$ first term

$l =$ last term

$S_n =$ Sum of nth term

$\therefore$ Sum of these integers $= \frac{49}{2}(10 + 490)$

$= \frac{49}{2} \times 500 = 49 \times 250 = 12250$.

25(B). As per the given question:

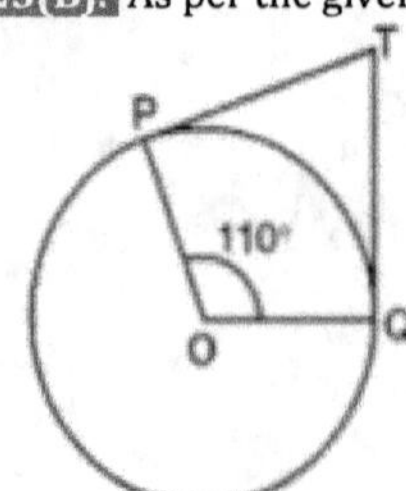

We can see, OP is the radius of the circle to the tangent PT and OQ is the radius to the tangents TQ.

So, $OP \perp PT$ and $TQ \perp OQ$

$\therefore \angle OPT = \angle OQT = 90°$

Now, in the quadrilateral $POQT$, we know that the sum of the interior angles is $360°$.

So,

$\angle PTQ + \angle POQ + \angle OPT + \angle OQT = 360°$

Now, by putting the respective values, we get,

$\angle PTQ + 90° + 110° + 90° = 360°$

$\therefore \angle PTQ = 70°$

26(C). According to the information given in the question, the diagram is as:

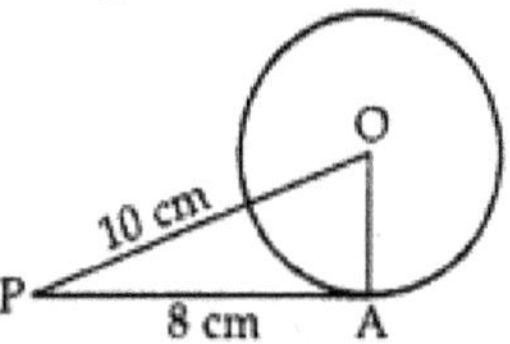

In right-angled triangle OAP, we have:

$OA^2 + AP^2 = OP^2$

$\Rightarrow OA^2 + (8)^2 = (10)2$

$\Rightarrow OA^2 + 64 = 100$

$\Rightarrow OA^2 = 100 - 64 = 36$

$\therefore OA = \sqrt{36} = 6$ cm

Thus, OA is the radius of the circle which is of 6 cm.

27(B). According to the question,

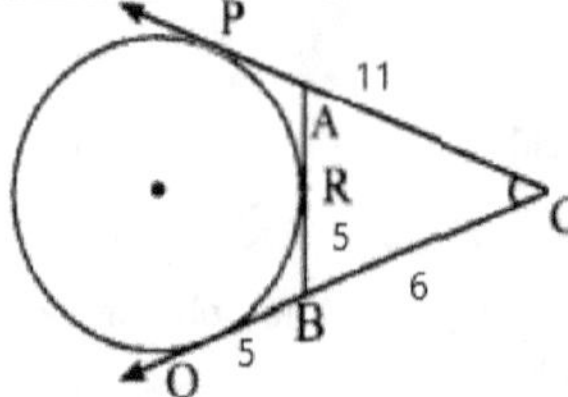

CQ and CP are the tangents to a circle.

So, $CQ = CP$ (Tangents to a circle from a common point (C) are equal in length).

$CP = CQ = 11$ cm

Also,

$BC + BQ = 11$ cm

$\Rightarrow BQ = CQ - BC$

$\Rightarrow 11 - 6$

$= 5$

$\therefore BQ = 5$ cm

So, $BR = BQ = 5$cm (Tangents to a circle from a common point (B) are equal in length.)

28(D). In $\triangle ABC$, $\angle A + \angle B + \angle C = 180°$

$\Rightarrow \angle A + 30° + 20° = 180°$

$\Rightarrow A = 130°$

Again, in $\triangle ABC$ and $\triangle QRP$,

$\frac{AB}{QR} = \frac{CA}{PQ}$

$\Rightarrow \frac{45}{5} = \frac{63}{7}$

$\Rightarrow \frac{9}{1} = \frac{9}{1}$

Since, Sides of $\triangle ABC$ and $\triangle QRP$ are proportional, and $\angle A = \angle Q$

Therefore, by SAS Similarity rule, $\triangle ABC \sim \triangle QRP$

$\therefore \angle A = \angle Q, \angle B = \angle R$ and $\angle C = \angle P$

$\Rightarrow \angle P = 20°$

and $\angle R = 30°$

29(D). In $\triangle ABC$ and $\triangle ADE$

$\angle ADE = \angle ABC$ [Given]

$\angle A = \angle A$ [Common]

$\therefore \triangle ABC \sim \triangle ADE$ [AA Similarity]

$\therefore \frac{AD}{DB} = \frac{AE}{EC}$

$\Rightarrow \frac{2}{3} = \frac{3}{EC}$

$\Rightarrow EC = 4.5$ cm

30(A). In $\triangle APQ$ and $\triangle ABC$,

line $PQ \parallel$ side BC ...given

$\therefore \angle APQ \cong \angle PBC$ ...corresponding angles

and $\angle AQP \cong \angle QCB$ ...corresponding angles

Also, $\angle PAQ \cong \angle BAC$ ...common angle

$\therefore \triangle APQ \sim \triangle ABC$ .... by AAA test of similarity

$\therefore \frac{AP}{AB} = \frac{AQ}{AC} = \frac{PQ}{BC}$ (In a pair of similar triangles, the corresponding sides are proportional)

$\therefore \frac{AP}{AB} = \frac{AQ}{AC} = \frac{5}{10} = \frac{1}{2}$

$\therefore AP = \frac{1}{2}AB$ and $AQ = \frac{1}{2}AC$

$\therefore AP = \frac{1}{2} \times 8$ and $AQ = \frac{1}{2} \times 6$

$\therefore AP = 4\,cm$ and $AQ = 3\,cm$

31(A). The structural and functional unit of the environment is the ecosystem.

The ecosystem is the structural and functional unit of the environment by which the different biotic and abiotic components interact with each other with respect to their environment.

32(A). 1 % percentage of sunlight is captured by plants to convert into food energy.

Most solar energy occurs at wavelengths unsuitable for photosynthesis. Between 98 and 99 percent of solar energy reaching Earth is reflected from leaves and other surfaces and absorbed by other molecules, which convert it to heat. Thus, only 1 to 2 percent is available to be captured by plants. The rate at which plants photosynthesize depends on the amount of light reaching the leaves, the temperature of the environment, and the availability of water and other nutrients such as nitrogen and phosphorus.

33(B). Step 1: Metal when exposed to air for a long time undergo corrosion. During corrosion, the metal on the surface undergoes a chemical reaction forming a new compound that changed the property of the metal at the surface. Rusting of iron is a common phenomenon of corrosion.
Step 2: Copper is a metal. Similarly. copper when kept open in air for a long time it slowly loses its shining brown surface and gains a green coating because of corrosion. During corrosion of copper, it reacts with carbon dioxide gas and moisture present in the air. This is called tarnishing of copper. The reaction is as follows.
$2Cu + H_2O + CO_2 + O_2 \rightarrow Cu(OH)_2 + CuCO_3$
Step 3: Different methods are available to prevent corrosion. Corrosion of copper can be protected by coating it with a thin layer of tin.

34(C). Reacting with water, a metal produces a base. Metals react with water and produce a metal oxide and hydrogen gas. Metal oxides that are soluble in water dissolve in it to further form metal hydroxide which are usually bases.

35(D). The person having high sugar level in blood is called a "Diabetic". Such persons are advised to take less sugar in diet, reduce weight, exercise regularly. Persons with severe diabetes (high sugar level in blood) are treated by giving injections of insulin. Pancreas secrete the hormone insulin. Its function is to regulate blood sugar level. Deficiency of insulin causes a disease known as diabetes that is characterized by large quantities of sugar in blood and even urine. Growth hormone secreted by the pituitary gland regulates growth and development of the body.

36(B). Dwarfism results due to less secretion of growth hormone. Deficiency of growth hormone in childhood cause dwarfism while excessive secretion causes gigantism. Deficiency of thyroxine cause goitre. Adrenaline is secreted in small amounts all the time but is secreted in large amount to prepare our body for action during fight or flight.
1. The anterior pituitary gland produces growth hormones.

2. Oversecretion of GH causes aberrant bodily growth, resulting in gigantism.
3. The inadequate secretion causes stunted growth, resulting in dwarfism.
4. The symptoms of dwarfism are short arms, legs, short neck, broad chest, etc.

37(A). Reduction reaction in simple terms means addition of Hydrogen or removal of Oxygen atom and Oxidation reaction in simple terms means addition of Oxygen or removal of Hydrogen atom.
CuO is being reduced and hydrogen is being oxidised. During this reaction, the copper(II) oxide is losing oxygen and is being reduced. The hydrogen is gaining oxygen and is being oxidised.
$CuO + H_2 \rightarrow Cu + H_2O$

38(C). The chemical substance which is used for whitewashing is Calcium oxide also known as quicklime or burnt lime or lime. The formula of substance X is CaO . It is a white or greyish white solid produced in large quantities by roasting calcium carbonate so as to drive off carbon dioxide.

39(A). Hydrogen chloride molecule contains covalent bond.
Hydrogen chloride (HCl) is a gas at atmospheric conditions. H–Cl bond is a covalent bond. A covalent bond is a chemical bond that involves the sharing of electron pairs between atoms.

40(C). The molecular formula of cyclobutane is C_4H_8.
Cyclobutane is a cycloalkane and organic compound with the formula $(CH_2)_4$. Cyclobutane is a colorless gas and commercially available as a liquefied gas. Derivatives of cyclobutane are called cyclobutanes. Cyclobutane itself is of no commercial or biological significance.

41(C). Ovum is the female sex cell or female gamete the male gamete is the sperm. A gamete, ovum or sperm, contains half the number of chromosomes found in the body cells of the parent, i.e., the gamete is haploid. In human there are total 46 chromosomes, so human ovum has only 23 chromosomes.

42(D). In the leaves of Bryophyllum meristematic marginal notches are present. From these meristematic tissues new plants can develop after coming in contact of soil. Bryophyllum is a group of plant species of the family Crassulaceae native to Madagascar. It is a section or subgenus within the genus Kalanchoe, and was formerly placed at the level of genus.

43(B). Evolution is the change in the inherited traits of a population from generation to generation. These traits are the expression of genes that are copied and passed on to offspring during reproduction.

44(B). In its uncultivated form, Brassica

oleracea is known as wild cabbage. The family includes cabbage, kale, collards, cauliflower, broccoli, kohlrabi, and Brussels sprouts, each variety is chosen for certain traits like flower buds, large leaves, and edible stems. Artificial selection is a process in which humans consciously select for or against particular features in organisms. Artificial selection has enabled the cultivation of new crops with desirable traits from one single common ancestor. Furthermore, once a plant with the combination of alleles for a desired phenotype is produced, it can be propagated asexually by taking cuttings, grafting and encouraging runners or through layering. By artificial selection, man has produced many crop plants like broccoli, cabbage, cauliflower, kohlrabi etc. from a common wild cabbage species by selective breeding and artificial selection.

45(B). The power of a lens is the reciprocal of its focal length. It is a measure of the degree of convergence or divergence of light rays achieved by a particular lens. The power of a convex lens is positive.
Power of lens $= \dfrac{1}{focallength}$
Given, focal length $= 40cm$ or $0.40m$
Therefore, the power of the given convex lens.
$= \dfrac{1}{focallength} = \dfrac{1}{0.40} = 2.5D$

46(B). According to Snell's law of refraction, the ratio of the sine of the angle of incidence to the sine of the angle of refraction is a constant for a given pair of media, and for the light of a given colour. If " i " is the angle of incidence and " r " is the angle of refraction, then:
$\dfrac{\sin i}{\sin r} = $ constant
$\therefore n_{21} \times n_{12} = 1$

47(B). The wire having a black plastic covering is a neutral wire.
During wiring in our houses, we use the traditional concept of using red colour wire as live, black as neutral and green for earth. These colour codes are used to distinguish between live, neutral and earth which is a standard way of colours coding for electric connections.

48(B). The strength of magnetic field around a current carrying conductor is directly proportional to the current and inversely proportional to the distance from wire. Magnetic field strength increases on increasing the current through the wire. Magnetic field strength decreases as the distance from the wire increases.

49(C). The filtration of blood occur in the kidneys Bowman's capsule.
Bowman's capsule surrounds the glomerular capillary loops and participates in the filtration of blood from the glomerular capillaries. Bowman's capsule

also has a structural function and creates a urinary space through which filtrate can enter the nephron and pass to the proximal convoluted tubule.

50(B). Oxygen is generated as a 'waste' during photosynthesis in plants.
To prepare one molecule of glucose, by the process of photosynthesis six molecules of carbon dioxide and six molecules of water is required. Six oxygen molecule is released as a waste product. This oxygen is produced due to splitting of water by the process of photolysis during light reaction.

51(C). Silver does not react with dilute sulphuric acid.
Silver will not react with sulphuric acid because it is least reactive metal to produce hydrogen by reacting with sulphuric acid.

52(C). HCl is a strong acid which ionizes completely in water to produce Hydrogen as well as Hydrogen and chlorine. Hydrogen produces combine with water molecules to give Hydronium ions.

$$HCl(g) \leftrightarrow H^+ + Cl^- \xrightarrow{\text{Aqueous sol}^n} H_3O^+ + Cl^-$$

53(D). A prism is a wedge-shaped portion of a transparent refracting medium bounded by two plane faces inclined to each other at a certain angle. The angle of deviation through a triangular prism is defined as the angle between the incident ray and the emerging ray. When a ray of light is refracted through a glass prism the sum of angle of incidence and angle of emergence is equal to the sum of angle of deviation produced and the angle of the prism. The minimum value of angle of deviation suffered by a ray on passing through a prism is called an angle of minimum deviation.

54(D). To find: the Resistance between any two terminals R
The two resistances are connected in series
$= R1 + R2$
$= 4 + 4 = 8\Omega$
The two resistances are connected in parallel (8Ω and 4Ω)
$\frac{1}{R} = \frac{1}{R_1} + \frac{1}{R_2}$
$\frac{1}{R} = \frac{R_1 + R_2}{R_1 \times R_2}$
$R = \frac{R_1 \times R_2}{R_1 + R_2}$
$R = \frac{8 \times 4}{8 + 4} = \frac{32}{12}$
$R = \frac{8}{3}\Omega$
$R = 2.6\Omega$

55(A). In this circuit, resistances R_1 and R_2 are in a parallel combination because the battery is connected between two resistance.

56(C). Drip irrigation requires very little installation is not true with respect to drip irrigation.
Drip irrigation is sometimes called trickle irrigation. It involves water dripping onto the soil at a very low rate (2–20 l/h) through a system of small diameter plastic pipes called emitters or drippers. Drip irrigation is a type of micro-irrigation system that has the ability to save water and nutrients from plants either above the soil surface or by slowly dripping water into buried roots below the surface.

57(A).
Factors which have led to the decline in India's biodiversity are as follow:
- Habitat destruction
- Hunting Poaching
- Over-exploitation
- Environmental pollution
- Poisoning Forest fires
- Habitat destruction.
- Hunting.
- Poaching.
- Over-exploitation.
- Environmental pollution.
- Poisoning.
- Forest fires.

58(D). The highest quality of hard coal is anthracite.
Anthracite is the highest rank of coal. It is a hard, brittle, and black lustrous coal, often referred to as hard coal, containing a high percentage of fixed carbon and a low percentage of volatile matter.
Coal is classified into four main types, or ranks:
- Anthracite
- Bituminous
- Subbituminous
- Lignite

59(A). Banking is included under service sector. The tertiary sector of the economy is the service sector. This sector provides services to the general population and to businesses. Activities associated with this sector include retail and wholesale sales, transportation and distribution, entertainment movies, television, radio, music, theatre, etc.

60(B). Different persons have different notions of country's development.
Different persons have different notions of development because life situations of persons are different. Development goals of a girl from a rich urban family will be surely different from a farmer in Rajasthan. It is because their situations, lifestyle and status are very different from each other. A goal which a person has entirely depends on his or her present life situation. Over a period of time if the situation changes, automatically goals of a person will also change.

61(C). In 19th century Industrialization take place in France and parts of the German states.
Britain met the criteria and industrialized starting in the 18th century. Britain exported the process to western Europe (especially Belgium, France and the German states) in the early 19th century.

62(B). When the soil fertility decreases, the farmers shift and clear a fresh patch of land is the feature of primitive subsistence agriculture.
Features of primitive subsistence agriculture in India are:
- It is practised on small patches of land with the help of primitive tools.
- Tools that are used are basically traditional tools such as hoe, dao and digging stick.
- This type of farming depends upon Monsoons, natural fertility of soil and environmental suitability.
- When the soil fertility decreases, the farmers shift to another plot of land.
- Electricity and irrigation facilities are not generally available to them which results in low productivity.

63(B). The RBI monitors the bank's Cash balance.
Banks have to submit information to the RBI on income and tax returns. The RBI sees that the banks give loans not just to profit-making businesses and traders but also to small cultivators. The RBI supervises the functioning of formal sources of loans. The Reserve Bank of India Act, 1934 requires the Central Government to entrust the Reserve Bank with all its money, remittance, exchange and banking transactions in India and the management of its public debt. The Government also deposits its cash balances with the Reserve Bank.

64(B). Gold Mohar was first introduced between 1540 and 1545 by Sher Shah Suri, as a way of uniting the different tribes in India under a single form of currency, thus encouraging trade and peace.

65(D). Fair globalisation refers to ensuring benefits to labourers, producers and consumers.
Fair globalisation refers to the status where the benefits of globalisation are equally distributed among the developing and developed nations. All positive and negatives aspects of development are enjoyed by both rich and the poor nations. Fair globalisation would create opportunities for all and also ensures that the benefits of globalization are shared by all. Government can play a major role in making this possible. Its policies must protect the interest of rich and poor both.

66(B). Globalisation has improved the living structure of People living in developing countries.
Globalization helps developing countries to deal with rest of the world increase their economic growth, solving the poverty problems in their country. Many developing

nations began to take steps to open their markets by removing tariffs and free up their economies. The volume and volatility of capital flows increases the risks of banking and currency crises, especially in countries with weak financial institutions. competition among developing countries to attract foreign investment leads to a "race to the bottom" in which countries dangerously lower environmental standards.

67(A). Marketing of goods and services which are hazardous to life and property is covered under right to be protected.
The Consumer Protection Act facilitates the consumers to complain against the qualities or prices of products and services they avail form traders. This law helps in preserving the interests of the consumer and redress the grievances accordingly by imposing a penalty on such violators or by other means.

68(A). The Minister incharge of Consumer Affairs in the Central Government who shall be the Chairperson of the Central Council. The Minister of State or Deputy Minister incharge of Consumer Affairs in the Central Government who shall be, the Vice-Chairperson of the Central Council.

69(A).
In 1920s England popular works were sold in cheap series called the shillings series.
Shilling series were books sold by traders in low cost to earn more monet in eighteenth century.
Shilling series were the books which were sold by the traders at a very low cost.
- Shilling series were books sold in low cost by traders to earn more money.
- Shilling series books were also called as chap man books in eighteenth century.

70(B).
Either pressed between wooden covers or sewn together the ancient handwritten manuscripts in India preserved.
The features of handwritten manuscripts before the age of print in India are as follows:
- Manuscripts were copied on Palm leaves or on handmade papers.
- In manuscripts sometimes pages were beautifully illustrated.
- The handwritten manuscripts were crushed between wooden covers or sewn together for preservation.
- Before the age of print in India Manuscripts were available in Vernacular languages.
- They were highly expensive and fragile.
- Handwritten manuscripts could not be read easily as script was written in different styles.

71(A). Most of the Sinhala-speaking people are Buddhist.

The Sinhalese people speak Sinhala, an Indo-Aryan language, and are predominantly Theravada Buddhists, although a small percentage of Sinhalese follow branches of Christianity. The Pali chronicles (e.g., the Mahavamsa) claim that the Sinhalese as an ethnic group are destined to preserve and protect Buddhism. In 1988 almost 93% of the Sinhala speaking population in Sri Lanka were Buddhist.

72(C). By 1980s several political organisations were formed demanding an independent Tamil Eelam (state) in northern and eastern parts of Sri Lanka.
The distrust between the Sinhala and Tamil turned into widespread conflict. It soon turned into a civil war. As a result thousands of people of both the communities have been killed.

73(D). The Corn Laws were tariffs and other trade restrictions on imported food and corn enforced in the United Kingdom between 1815 and 1846.
Under the aforementioned conditions, the landed groups pressurized to restrict import of corn. The laws which allowed the government to restrict the import of corn were commonly known as the Corn Laws. Soon, the corn laws had to be abolished as the urban dwellers who are industrialists were unhappy with the rising food prices. After this, food could be imported more cheaply than its production cost. British agriculture couldn't compete with the cheaper imports and rendered many people in the agricultural sector unemployed. They migrated to cities or other countries in search of work.
The food prices soon began to fall, and consumption in Britain rose. From the mid 19th century, rapid industrial growth led to higher incomes and more food imports. Lands were cleared for food production and railways were facilitated to connect agricultural regions with ports. New harbors were built and old ones were expanded to ship new cargos.

74(B). When power is taken away from Central and State governments and given to local government, it is called decentralization.
The basic idea behind decentralization is that there are a large number of problems and issues which are best settled at the local level. People have better knowledge of problems in their localities. They also have better ideas on where to spend money and how to manage things more efficiently.

75(D). Arunachal Pradesh was granted Statehood in 20th February 1987 following the 53rd Amendment of the Indian Constitution in 1986.
Arunachal Pradesh was known as the North-East Frontier Agency till 1972. On 20th January 1972, the area was renamed as "Arunachal Pradesh". In the same year

it was declared as a full-fledged Union Territory.

76(B). The possibility of getting a job with such abundance of labour in the cities depended on existing networks of friendship and kin relations in the factory. These are the following reasons:
- The abundance of labour in the market affected the lives of workers. As news of possible jobs travelled to the countryside, hundreds tramped to the cities.
- The actual possibility of getting a job depended on existing networks of friendship and kin relations.
- Many jobseekers had to wait weeks, spending nights under bridges or in night shelters. Some stayed in Night Refuges that were set up by private individuals; others went to the Casual Wards maintained by the Poor Law authorities.
- Seasonality of work in many industries meant prolonged periods without work. After the busy season was over, the poor were on the streets again.
- The fear of unemployment made workers hostile to the introduction of new technology. When the Spinning Jenny was introduced in the woolen industry.

77(D). Non renewable resources is the type of iron ore.
Non-renewable resources are natural resources. They are also known as finite resources as they cannot be replaced readily by natural means at a quick enough pace to keep up with the consumption. For example fossil fuels, groundwater, metal ores. Iron ore is also a non-renewable resource.Iron ore is a natural resource and is discovered in limited quantities. It is used up quicker than it can be formed again by natural processes. It is a mineral and minerals have definite chemical compositions.

78(A). In actual life, democracies do not appear to be very successful in reducing economic inequalities.
- The wealth and means are accumulated in hands of a few people and their share in the total income of the country has been increasing.
- However, the people at the bottom of society find it difficult to meet even their basic needs of life such as food, clothing, house, education and health.Not only that, their incomes have been declining.
- The deprived people are a large ratio of voters and no party will like to lose their votes.
- Yet democratically elected governments do not appear to be attentive to the cause of the poor. Thus democracies do not appear to be very successful in reducing economic inequalities.

79(C). Democracy in India has strengthened the claims of the disadvantaged castes for equal status and equal opportunity.

The fundamental right related to the statement is Right to Equality. All the citizens should be aware that equality in every walk of life is necessary for the development of the nation.

Equal status' and 'equal opportunity 'helps the society to restore back the dignity and freedom of the deprived sections of the society. It creates a sense of equality among the rather not too effective . People try to change their mindsets about the concept of upper and lower caste. Use of the words 'Equal status' and 'equal opportunity' can serve a lot in restoring the freedom and dignity of the people.

80(C). In 1921 the Non-Cooperation-Khilafat Movement begin.

The Khilafat movement or the Caliphate movement, also known as the Indian Muslim movement (1919–24), was a pan-Islamist political protest campaign launched by Muslims of British India led by Shaukat Ali, Maulana Mohammad Ali Jauhar, Hakim Ajmal Khan, and Abul Kalam Azad to restore the caliph of the Ottoman Caliphate, who was considered the leader of the Muslims, as an effective political authority. It was a protest against the sanctions placed on the caliph and the Ottoman Empire after the First World War by the Treaty of Sevres.

81(D). Suryakant Tripathi is known by his pen name "Nirala" was a renowned poet-novelist and story-writer.

Some of his Notable works are Saroj Smriti, Raam Ki Shaktipuja, Dhwani, Parimal, Priyatam, Anaamika, Prabhavati, Nirupama, Apsara, etc.

82(A). The Constitution of India does not recognize 'Right of Property' as Fundamental Right. 44th Constitutional Amendment, 1978, eliminated the right to acquire, hold and dispose of the property as a Fundamental Right. However, in another part of the Constitution, Article 300(A) was inserted to affirm that no person shall be deprived of his property by authority of law. Due to this, the Right of Property as a Fundamental Right is now substituted as 'Statuary Right' or constitutional Right.

83(C). The correct answer is a-3, b-2, c-1, d-4 .

84(A). The Supreme Court has laid down guidelines that the police must follow at the time of arrest, detention, and interrogation. The police are not allowed to torture or beat or shoot anyone during the investigation.

85(A). The series of lines connecting the vibrating places at the same time are called homoacoustic lines.

86(A). Focal length of a lens depends on its curvature and the medium outside the lens.

87(A). On 30 May 1987 Goa attained statehood (while Daman and Diu became a separate union territory), and Goa was reorganised into two districts, North Goa and South Goa.

Hence, the correct option is (C).

88(D). The 'Gandhara' School of Art was influenced by the art from Greece.

- Gandhara art, a style of Buddhist visual art that developed in what is now northwestern Pakistan and eastern Afghanistan between the 1st century BCE and the 7th century CE.
- The style, of Greco-Roman origin, seems to have flourished largely during the Kushan dynasty and was contemporaneous with an important but dissimilar school of Kushan art at Mathura (Uttar Pradesh, India).
- The Gandhara school incorporated many motifs and techniques from classical Roman art, including vine scrolls, cherubs bearing garlands, tritons, and centaurs. The basic iconography, however, remained Indian.

89(C). AjantaEllora caves are located near Aurangabad in Maharashtra. AjantaEllora caves are one of the finest examples of ancient rock-cut caves in India.

90(C). The first Buddhist council took place at the Saptaparna cave in Rajgir(Old name Rajagriha Mahakasyapa) just after the death of the Buddha.

91(D). Firoz Tughlaq had maximum number of slaves in his court. Firoz Tughlaq established a new department 'Diwan-i-Bandgan' for his Ghulams (slaves). He had 180,000 slaves.

92(C). The uprising began at Supa village in the district of Poona when moneylenders refused the farmer's loans.

- In 1875, farmers attacked a market place where many moneylenders lived.
- They burnt account books and looted grain shops.
- They also burnt the houses of sahukars.
- Sahukars were people who were both traders and moneylenders.
- When the revolt spread in the Deccan, the Government of India, worried by the memory of 1857, pressurised the Government of Bombay to set up a commission of enquiry to investigate into the causes of the riots.
- The commission produced a report that was presented to the British Parliament in 1878.
- The commission held enquiries in the districts where the riots spread, not in unaffected districts. So, statement 1 is correct.
- They recorded statements of ryots, sahukars and eyewitnesses, compiled statistical data on revenue rates, prices and interest rates in different regions, and collated the reports sent by district collectors. So, statement 2 is correct.

93(A). CO_2 makes up only about 0.04% of the atmosphere, and water vapor can vary from 0 to 4%. But while water vapor is the dominant greenhouse gas in our atmosphere, it has "windows" that allow some of the infrared energy to escape without being absorbed.

94(A). Public Health is not a subject under Union List. Atomic Energy, Foreign Affairs and War and Peace Association is the subject of the list. Public health is a state subject.

95(B). Union Home Minister Amit Shah launched the mascot and the anthem for the 36th National Games in Ahmedabad.

The mascot is named as 'Savaj' which means cub in Gujarati. The theme of the anthem is 'Ek Bharat Shreshtha Bharat'. The National Games will be organised from September 29 to October 12, across six cities in the state.

96(B). Robert Peary was the first man to reach the north pole in the world.

Robert Edwin Peary Sr. was an American explorer and officer in the United States Navy who made several expeditions to the Arctic in the late 19th and early 20th centuries. He is best known for, in April 1909, leading an expedition that claimed to be the first to have reached the geographic North Pole.

Hence the correct option is (B).

97(B). Blindspot in the human eye can be located at the junction of the optic nerve and the retina.

Blindspot: The eye lens focuses light on the back of the eye, on a layer called the retina. The retina contains several nerve cells. Sensations felt by the nerve cells are then transmitted to the brain through the optic nerve. At the junction of the optic nerve and the retina, there are no sensory cells, so no vision is possible at that spot. This is called the blind spot.

98(A). A halophyte is a plant that grows in waters of high salinity, coming into contact with saline water through its roots or by salt sprays, such as in saline semi-deserts, mangrove swamps, marshes and sloughs and seashores.

99(A). The watchwords of the French Revolution-Liberty, Equality and **Fraternity** inspired the whole world.

- The slogan "Liberté, Egalité, Fraternité" was initially used during the French Revolution and is a remnant of the Enlightenment.
- Despite being questioned numerous times, it was finally formed during the

Third Republic.

- It is currently part of the French national heritage, having been incorporated into the 1958 Constitution. "Liberty, Equality, and Fraternity" was one of the numerous mottos used during the French Revolution.

100(C). Delhi Crime web series won the Best Drama Series award at the 48 th International Emmy Awards 2020.

The 48 th International Emmy Awards 2020 was held in Hammerstein Ballroom, New York City. International Emmy Awards was formed in 1946 and in 1949 presented the first Emmys. The awards were made by the National Academy of Television Arts and Sciences. The awards are given in the following categories which are dramatic series, comedy series, special drama, limited series, and variety, music, or comedy. Delhi Crime became the 1 st Indian web series to receive an award in Drama-Series.

Practice Test 14

Mathematics

1. Mean of a data set is 22. If the ratio of the mode and median of the data set is $1:3$, then find the correct relation between mean, median and mode:
   (a) Mean > Median > Mode
   (b) Mode > Median > Mean
   (c) Median = Mode > Mean
   (d) Mean = Mode < Median

2. The marks obtained by 30 students of Class x of a certain school in a Mathematics paper consisting of 100 marks are presented in table below. Find the mean of the marks obtained by the students:

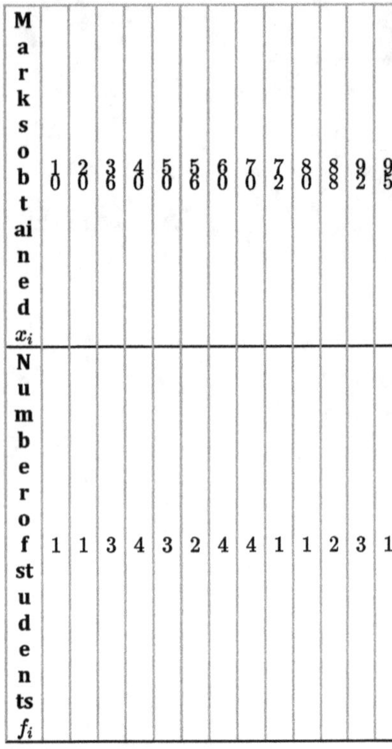

Marks obtained x_i	10	20	36	40	50	56	60	70	72	80	88	92	95
Number of students f_i	1	1	3	4	3	2	4	4	1	1	2	3	1

   (a) 59.3   (b) 59.4
   (c) 58.3   (d) 49.3

3. The curved surface area of a right circular cylinder of radius $1\,cm$ and height $1\,cm$ is:
   (a) $4\pi\,cm^2$ (b) $\pi\,cm^2$
   (c) $3\pi\,cm^2$ (d) $2\pi\,cm^2$

4. The total surface area of a solid right circular cylinder whose radius is half of its height h is equal to:
   (a) $\frac{3}{2}\pi h$ sq. units
   (b) $\frac{2}{3}\pi h^2$ sq. units
   (c) $\frac{3}{2}\pi h^2$ sq. units
   (d) $\frac{2}{3}\pi h$ sq. units

5. The roots of quadratic equation $2x^2 + x + 4 = 0$ are:
   (a) Positive and negative
   (b) Both Positive
   (c) Both Negative
   (d) No real roots

6. The product of two consecutive positive integers is 360. To find the integers, this can be represented in the form of quadratic equation as:
   (a) $x^2 + x + 360 = 0$
   (b) $x^2 + x - 360 = 0$
   (c) $2x^2 + x - 360$
   (d) $x^2 - 2x - 360 = 0$

7. The equation $(x+1)^2 - 2(x+1) = 0$ has:
   (a) two real roots
   (b) no real roots
   (c) one real root
   (d) two equal roots

8. Calculate the area of a sector of angle $60°$. When the circle has a radius of 6 cm.
   (a) $= \frac{135}{7}\,cm^2$ (b) $= \frac{136}{7}\,cm^2$
   (c) $= \frac{137}{7}\,cm^2$ (d) $= \frac{132}{7}\,cm^2$

9. If the sum of the areas of two circles with radii r_1 and r_2 is equal to the area of the circle of radius R, then:
   (a) $R^2 + r_1^2 = r_2^2$
   (b) $R^3 = r_1^2 + r_2^2$
   (c) $R^2 = r_1^2 - r_2^2$
   (d) $R^2 = r_1^2 + r_2^2$

10. What is $\cot A + \operatorname{cosec} A$ equal to?
    (a) $\tan\left(\frac{A}{2}\right)$
    (b) $\cot\left(\frac{A}{2}\right)$
    (c) $2\tan\left(\frac{A}{2}\right)$
    (d) $2\cot\left(\frac{A}{2}\right)$

11. What is the value of $\tan 75° + \cot 75°$?
    (a) 2   (b) 4
    (c) $2\sqrt{3}$ (d) $4\sqrt{3}$

12. If $\sin A + \sin^2 A = 1$, then find the value of $\cos^2 A + \cos^4 A$.
    (a) 1   (b) 0
    (c) 2   (d) 4

13. Ritu can row downstream 20 km in 2 hours, and upstream 4 km in 2 hours. Find her speed of rowing in still water and speed of the current.
    (a) Speed of boat in still water, $x = 6$ km/hr, Speed of stream, $y = 4$ km/hr
    (b) Speed of boat in still water, $x = 7$ km/hr, Speed of stream, $y = 3$ km/hr
    (c) Speed of boat in still water, $x = 10$ km/hr, Speed of stream, $y = 5$ km/hr
    (d) Speed of boat in still water, $x = 8$ km/hr, Speed of stream, $y = 3$ km/hr

14. 2 women and 5 men can together finish an embroidery work in 4 days, while 3 women 6 men can finish it in 3 days. Find the time taken by 1 woman alone to finish the work, and taken by 1 man alone.
    (a) Time taken by one woman to finish the work 28 days, Time taken by one man to finish the work 46 days
    (b) Time taken by one woman to finish the work 18 days, Time taken by one man to finish the work 36 days
    (c) Time taken by one woman to finish the work 10 days, Time taken by one man to finish the work 26 days
    (d) Time taken by one woman to finish the work 38 days, Time taken by one man to finish the work 36 days

15. Find the prime factorisation of the denominator of rational number expressed as $6.\overline{12}$ in simplest form:
    (a) 5×11 (b) 2×11
    (c) 4×11 (d) 3×11

16. The length, breadth, and height of a room are $8\,m\,50\,cm$, $6\,m\,25\,cm$ and $4\,m\,75\,cm$ respectively. Find the length of the longest rod that can measure the dimensions of the room exactly:
    (a) 25 cm   (b) 24 cm
    (c) 22 cm   (d) 20 cm

17. Dudhnath has two vessels containing 720ml and 405ml of milk respectively. Milk from these containers is poured into glasses of equal capacity to their brim. Find the minimum number of glasses that can be filled:
    (a) 20   (b) 25
    (c) 30   (d) 40

18. **Direction :** The following questions consist of two statements, one labelled as Assertion and the other Reason. Examine both the statements carefully and mark the correct choice according to the instructions given below.
Assertion : $\dfrac{13}{3125}$ is a terminating decimal fraction.
Reason : If $q = 2^n \cdot 5^m$ where n, m are non-negative integers, then $\dfrac{p}{q}$ is a terminating decimal fraction.

(a) Both Assertion and Reason are correct and Reason is the correct explanation for Assertion.

(b) Both Assertion and Reason are correct, but Reason is not the correct explanation for Assertion.

(c) Assertion is correct, but Reason is incorrect.

(d) Assertion is incorrect, but Reason is correct.

19. Which of the following polynomials when divided by $(x + 1)$ gives quotient $3x - 2$ and leaves remainder 3 ?

(a) $3x^2 + x + 1$ (b) $x^2 - x - 1$

(c) $3x^2 - x - 3$ (d) $3x^2 + x - 2$

20. If one zero of the polynomial $4x^3 - 4x^2 - x + 1$ is 1 , what are the other possible zeroes?

(a) $\dfrac{1}{2}, 4$ (b) $1, 3$

(c) $\dfrac{1}{2}, -1$ (d) $\dfrac{1}{2}, \dfrac{-1}{2}$

21. Two die are thrown find the probability of getting the sum of the numbers on their upper faces to be at most 3 .

(a) $\dfrac{1}{4}$ (b) $\dfrac{1}{6}$

(c) $\dfrac{1}{12}$ (d) $\dfrac{1}{36}$

22. If three coins are tossed then find the probability of the event of getting no tail.

(a) $\dfrac{1}{8}$ (b) $\dfrac{1}{4}$

(c) $\dfrac{3}{8}$ (d) $\dfrac{1}{2}$

23. The 17th term of an AP exceeds its 10th term by 7 . Find the common difference:

(a) 2   (b) 1

(c) 5   (d) 0

24. Subba Rao started work in 1995 at an annual salary of $Rs.\,5000$ and received an increment of $Rs.\,200$ each year. In which year did his income reach $Rs.\,7000$?

(a) 2006   (b) 2009

(c) 2008   (d) 2005

25. If tangents PA and PB from a point P to a circle with centre O are inclined to each other at angle of $80°$, then $\angle POA$ is equal to:

(a) $50°$ (b) $60°$

(c) $70°$ (d) $80°$

26. In the given figure, O is the centre of the circle, $AB = PQ = 6$ cm and $ON = 5$ cm . The length of $(OL + BL)$ is equal to:

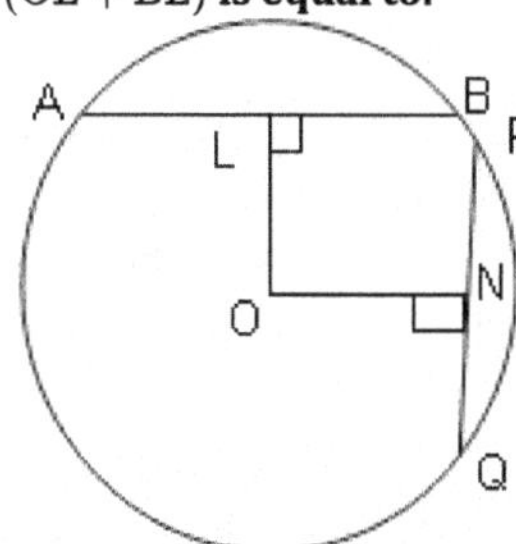

(a) 3 cm   (b) 5 cm

(c) 6 cm   (d) 8 cm

27. In the given figure, O is the centre of the circle, $AB = CD = 4$ units and $OL = 4.5$ units The value of $OM + MD$ is equal to:

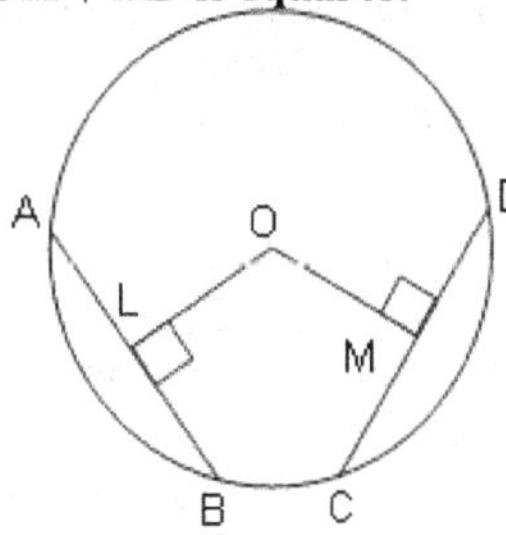

(a) 4.5 units   (b) 6.5 units

(c) 2 units   (d) 4.7 units

28. In a rectangle $ABCD$, E is middle point of AD . If $AD = 40$ m and $AB = 48$ m, then find EB .

(a) 52 m   (b) 56 m

(c) 62 m   (d) 66 m

29. The lengths of the diagonals of a rhombus are 16 cm and 12 cm. Then, the length of the side of the rhombus is:

(a) 9 cm   (b) 10 cm

(c) 8 cm   (d) 20 cm

30. If
$$\triangle ABC \sim \triangle QRP, \dfrac{ar(\triangle ABC)}{ar(\triangle PQR)} = \dfrac{9}{4},$$
$AB = 18$ cm and $BC = 15$ cm, then PR is equal to:

(a) 10 cm   (b) 12 cm

(c) $\dfrac{20}{3}$ cm   (d) 8 cm

31. If 100 J energy is available at the producer level in a food chain then the energy available to the secondary consumer will be:

(a) 0.1 J   (b) 1 J

(c) 0.01 J   (d) 10 J

32. Which of the following radiation is responsible for the conversion of atmospheric oxygen to ozone?

(a) Ultraviolet radiations

(b) Infrared radiations

(c) Cosmic radiations

(d) Gamma radiations

33. Which among the following elements cannot be turned into wire?

(a) Copper   (b) Platinum

(c) Carbon   (d) Aluminium

34. Which of the following is not malleable?

(a) Copper   (b) Graphite

(c) Silver   (d) Aluminium

35. Which one of the endocrine glands is known as the master gland?

(a) Pituitary   (b) Adrenal

(c) Thyroid   (d) Parathyroid

36. Neurons that carry information to an effector are called as _____ neurons.

(a) sensory neurons

(b) motor neurons

(c) interneurons

(d) spinal neurons

37. The following reaction describes the rusting of iron.
$$4Fe + 3O_2 \rightarrow 4Fe^{3+} + 6O^{2-}$$
Which one of the following statements is incorrect?

(a) This is an example of a displacement reaction.

(b) Metallic iron is reduced to Fe^{3+} .

(c) Fe^{3+} is an oxidising agent.

(d) Metallic iron is a reducing agent.

38. When the gases sulphur dioxide and hydrogen sulphide mix in the presence of water, the reaction is as shown:
$$SO_2 + 2H_2S \rightarrow 2H_2O + 3S$$
Here, hydrogen sulphide acts as:

(a) An oxidizing agent

(b) A dehydrating agent

(c) A reducing agent

(d) A catalyst

39. Which of the following statements

are correct for carbon compounds?

(a) Most carbon compounds are good conductors of electricity.

(b) Most carbon compounds are poor conductors of electricity.

(c) Force of attraction between molecules of carbon compounds is not very strong.

(d) Both (B) and (C)

40. Identify the product formed when methane reacts with chlorine in the presence of sunlight is:

(a) C_2Cl_6

(b) CH_3Cl

(c) $CHCl_4$

(d) None of these

41. Pollen grains do not germinate on the stigma of the same flower. The phenomenon is __________.

(a) Prepotency   (b) Embryo sac

(c) Self sterility   (d) Dichogamy

42. Which of the following birth control measure can be considered as the safest?

(a) The rhythm method

(b) The use of physical barriers

(c) Termination of unwanted pregnancy

(d) Sterilization techniques

43. There are ________ versions for each trait in an offspring;

(a) 2   (b) 3

(c) 4   (d) 5

44. Variations cannot occur due to:

(a) crossing over

(b) mutation

(c) effect of environment

(d) asexual reproduction

45. The focal length of a lens of power is -2.0 D. What type of lens is this?

(a) Concave lens

(b) Convex lens

(c) Plane lens

(d) None of these

46. An object is placed at 20 cm in front of a concave mirror produces three times magnified real image. What is focal length of the concave mirror?

(a) 15 cm   (b) 6.6 cm

(c) 10 cm   (d) 7.5 cm

47. By which instrument, the presence of magnetic field be determined ?

(a) Magnetic Needle

(b) Ammeter

(c) Galvanometer

(d) Voltmeter

48. Which of the following statement is not correct about the magnetic field?

(a) Magnetic field lines form a continuous closed curve.

(b) Magnetic field lines form a continuous closed curve.

(c) Direction of tangent at any point on the magnetic field line curve gives the direction of magnetic field at that point.

(d) Outside the magnet, magnetic field lines go from South to North pole of the magnet.

49. Veins have valves to:

(a) prevent back flow of blood

(b) prevent the collapse of the vein

(c) maintain its position in the body

(d) None of these

50. The xylem in plants are responsible for:

(a) transport of water.

(b) transport of food.

(c) transport of amino acid.

(d) transport of oxygen.

51. Calcium phosphate is present in tooth enamel. The nature of the calcium phosphate is:

(a) Acidic   (b) Basic

(c) Neutral   (d) Amphoteric

52. A sample of soil is mixed with water and allowed to settle. The clear supernatant solution turns the pH paper yellowish-orange. Which of the following would change the colour of this pH paper to greenish-blue?

(a) Lemon juice   (b) Vinegar

(c) Common salt (d) Antacid

53. The light enters our eye through the transparent ________, passes through the ______ and is focused on the _____.

(a) cornea, lens, retina

(b) retina, cornea, lens

(c) retina, optic nerve, lens

(d) lens, retina, optic nerve

54. A current of $30mA$ passes through a circuit for 10 minutes. If the potential difference within the circuit is $20V$, then the work done in moving the charges through the circuit is:

(a) $6J$ (b) $60J$

(c) $100J$ (d) $360J$

55. A $2.5V$ battery is connected across a resistor of 500Ω. If the battery voltage is changed to $5V$, what should be the resistance of a resistor which will draw the same amount of current?

(a) 500Ω (b) 750Ω

(c) 1000Ω (d) 1250Ω

Social Science

56. What is a barrier across flowing water that obstructs, directs or retards the flow, often creating a reservoir, lake or impoundment?

(a) Canal

(b) Embankment

(c) Dam

(d) Lake

57. ________ in third world countries is often cited as the cause of environmental degradation.

(a) Developmental projects

(b) Rural urban development

(c) Overpopulation

(d) Exploitation of resources

58. Which one of the following minerals is not obtained from the veins and lodes?

(a) Tin   (b) Zinc

(c) Lead   (d) Gypsum

59. Choose one correct statement from the following:
Underemployment occurs:

(a) When people are not willing to work.

(b) When people are working slowly.

(c) When people are working less than what they are capable of doing.

(d) When people are not paid for their jobs.

60. In the data for the Per capita income of Haryana, Kerala, Bihar- which state has the lowest per capita income?

(a) Haryana   (b) Kerala

(c) Bihar   (d) All equal

61. What is Liberalism?

(a) 'Liberalism' derives from the Latin root liber, meaning free-freedom for the individual and equality of all before the law

(b) End of autocracy

(c) Equal rules for all

(d) Liberty to the upper classes

62. The first source of irrigation in India is:

(a) Canals

(b) Pond
(c) Wells and tube wells
(d) Other sources

63. **Paper currency is known as 'fiat money' :**
(a) Because only a fraction of total currency is in coins
(b) Because it is decreed legal tender
(c) Because it cannot be used as payment for debts
(d) All of the above

64. **In urban India:**
(a) There are only urban co-operative banks
(b) Some state co-operative banks also operate
(c) some PACSs also operate.
(d) All of the above

65. **The most common route for MNC investments is to buy up ______.**
(a) Local resources
(b) Local technology
(c) Excess land for factories
(d) Local companies

66. **What are the key ideas behind understanding the process of globalisation and its impact?**
(a) Integration of production
(b) Integration of gross profits
(c) Integration of markets
(d) Both (A) & (C)

67. **When did United Nations adopt the UN Guidelines for Consumer Protection?**
(a) 1985 (b) 1990
(c) 1995 (d) 1999

68. **When was the 'Right to Information' Act passed?**
(a) In January 2002
(b) In March 2004
(c) In October 2005
(d) In July 2007

69. **When did the printing press first come to India?**
(a) With East India Company
(b) Much after the establishment of the British
(c) With Portuguese missionaries in the mid-sixteenth century
(d) With the Dutch merchants

70. **What began English printing in India?**
(a) James Augustus Hickey began to edit the Bengal Gazette
(b) East India Company started

printing for its administrative purposes
(c) English writers encouraged it in India
(d) Colonial government printed to build its image

71. **In which part of Sri Lanka are the Sri Lankan Tamils concentrated?**
(a) North and South
(b) North and East
(c) East and West
(d) South and East

72. **In Srilanka, a new constitution stipulated that the state shall protect and foster ______Tamil Indians.**
(a) Hindu (b) Buddhist
(c) Christain (d) Islam

73. **Who among the following was a well-known pioneer of mass production?**
(a) Jamshedji Tata
(b) G.D. Birla
(c) Henry Ford
(d) None of the above

74. **Under the Indian Constitution the residuary powers are enjoyed by the __________.**
(a) The Parliament
(b) The State Assembly
(c) The Local Government
(d) The District Administration

75. **The State Reorganization Commission was appointed by __________.**
(a) Mahatma Gandhi
(b) Sardar Patel
(c) Indira Gandhi
(d) Pt. Jawaharlal Nehru

76. **What happened when the Spinning Jenny was introduced in the woolen industry?**
(a) The women welcomed it very well
(b) It was not able to produce in competition to labour
(c) Women who survived on hand spinning began attacking the new machines
(d) There was no conflict over the introduction of the jenny

77. **Under which of the following type of resource can tidal energy be put?**
(a) Replenishable
(b) Human-made
(c) Abiotic
(d) Non-renewable

78. **Who is 'Sovereign' in a Democratic form of Government?**
(a) Government
(b) State
(c) People
(d) None of these

79. **Which one of the following is not the way to resolve a conflict in a democracy?**
(a) Mass mobilisation
(b) Using Parliament
(c) Doing justice
(d) Armed revolution

80. **What is the meaning of picket?**
(a) Foreign goods were burnt
(b) Non-financing of foreign imports
(c) Wearing only Indian clothes
(d) A form of demonstration or protest by which people block the entrance to a shop, factory or office

General Awareness/ Knowledge

81. **With which of the following was Kadri Gopalnath associated?**
(a) Sitar (b) Saxophone
(c) Tabla (d) Flute

82. **The phrase equality before law" used in Article-14 of the Indian Constitution has been borrowed from:**
(a) U.S.A. (b) Germany
(c) Britain (d) Greece

83. **The number of complaints with the Banking Ombudsman registered during 2018 increased by:**
(a) 10% (b) 15%
(c) 20% (d) 25%

84. **Which of the following is not matched correctly?**
(a) Article 145: salary of judges
(b) Article 143: Power of President to consult with the Supreme Court
(c) Article 141: orders of the Supreme Court is applicable to all courts of India
(d) Article 139: Power of Supreme Court to issue writ petition

85. **If the direction of rotation of the Earth is reversed, what will happen at IST when it is noon on the International Date Line?**
(a) 06: 30 pm (b) 05: 30 pm
(c) 18:30 pm (d) 17:30 pm

86. Which one of the following is India's heaviest rocket and referred to as 'Bahubali'?
(a) PSLV - C - 37 (b) RLV - TD
(c) GSLV MK - III (d) PSLV - XL

87. Which of the following pairs of "original state - the territory the new state was created from" is incorrect?
(a) Andhra Pradesh – from the state of Madras
(b) Arunachal Pradesh – from the state of Assam
(c) Goa – from the state of Maharashtra
(d) Meghalaya – from the state of Assam

88. 'Aloo Posto' is a traditional delicacy of which state of India?
(a) Haryana   (b) Uttarakhand
(c) Gujarat   (d) West Bengal

89. Srinagar is located at the bank of _____ river.
(a) Indus   (b) Jhelum
(c) Ravi   (d) Beas

90. In which state five inscriptions of the Rashtrakuta dynasty have been found in the twelfth century?
(a) Tamil Nadu (b) Karnataka
(c) Kerala   (d) Maharashtra

91. Where is the tomb of Akbar?
(a) Sikandra
(b) Agra
(c) Aurangabad
(d) Fatehpur Sikri

92. 'Who first used the word 'Pakistan'?
(a) Sir Syed Ahmed
(b) Mohammad Iqbal
(c) Mohammad Ali Jinnah
(d) Chaudhary Rahmat Ali

93. **Direction:** The following questions consist of two statements, one labelled as Assertion and the other Reason. Examine both the statements carefully and mark the correct choice according to the instructions given below.
Assertion : Abiotic components of an ecosystem involve the cycling of material and the flow of energy.
Reason : Abiotic components are essential to keep biotic factors alive.
(a) Both assertion and reason are correct and the reason is the correct explanation for assertion.
(b) Both assertion and reason are correct but the reason is not the correct explanation for assertion.
(c) Assertion is correct but the reason is incorrect.
(d) Assertion is incorrect but the reason is correct.

94. In which year was the national commission on Farmers set up?
(a) 2001   (b) 2004
(c) 2006   (d) 2007

95. Which among the following cup/trophy is awarded for women in the sport of Badminton?
(a) Webb Ellis Cup
(b) Wisden Trophy
(c) Uber Cup
(d) Derby Cup

96. Who was the first blind man to scale Mt. Everest?
(a) Jerrie Fredritz
(b) Maureen Cathreen
(c) Erik Weihenmayer
(d) Edwin E. Aldrin

97. Which one of the following elements is present in the green pigment of leaves?
(a) Magnesium (b) Iron
(c) Calcium   (d) Copper

98. Practically, the work output of a machine is _____ the work input due to the effect of friction.
(a) always more than
(b) opposite to
(c) always less than
(d) always zero to

99. World war II began with the German invasion of _____.
(a) Russia
(b) France
(c) United KIngdom
(d) Poland

100. Who has been conferred with the Order of the Rising Sun, Gold and Silver Star by the Govt of Japan in July 2022 ?
(a) Kushal Jain
(b) Ravi Parmar
(c) Narayanan Kumar
(d) Pramod Tomar

// Hints and Solutions //

1(A). Given,
Mean of a data set $= 22$
Ratio of mode and median $= 1 : 3$
As we know that,
Mode $= 3($ Median $) - 2($ Mean $)$

Now,
Ratio of mode and median be $1x : 3x$.
$x = 3 \times (3x) - (2 \times 22)$
$\Rightarrow 8x = 44$
$\Rightarrow x = \frac{44}{8}$
$\Rightarrow x = 5.5$
Since, the mode is x so, mode of the data is 5.5.
Median $= 3x$
Median $= 3 \times 5.5$
Median $= 16.5$
Mean $= 22$
Mode $= 5.5$
$\therefore$ The correct relation is Mean $>$ Median $>$ Mode.

2(A). Recall that to find the mean marks, we require the product of each x_i with the corresponding frequency f_i. So, let us put them in a column as shown in Table 14.1.

Marks obtained (x_i)	Number of students (f_i)	$f_i x_i$
10	1	10
20	1	20
36	3	108
40	4	160
50	3	150
56	2	112
60	4	240
70	4	280
72	1	72
80	1	80
88	2	176
92	3	176
95	1	95
Total	$\Sigma f_i = 30$	$\Sigma f_i x_i = 1779$

Now,
$\bar{x} = \frac{\Sigma f_i x_i}{\Sigma f_i} = \frac{1779}{30} = 59.3$
Therefore, the mean marks obtained is 59.3.

3(D). Given:
$r = 1\ cm$ and $h = 1\ cm$
A curved surface area of cylinder $= 2\pi r h$
$= 2\pi \times 1 \times 1$
$= 2\pi\ cm^2$

4(C). Given,
$h = h, r = \frac{h}{2}$
We know that the total surface area of the cylinder $= 2\pi r(h + r)$
So,
$= 2\pi \times \frac{h}{2}\left(h + \frac{h}{2}\right)$
$= \pi \times h\left(\frac{3h}{2}\right)$
$= \frac{3}{2}\pi h^2$ sq. units

5(D). $2x^2 + x + 4 = 0$
$\Rightarrow 2x^2 + x = -4$
Dividing the equation by 2, we get
$\Rightarrow x^2 + \frac{1}{2}x = -2$
$\Rightarrow x^2 + 2 \times x \times \frac{1}{4} = -2$

By adding $(\frac{1}{4})^2$ to both sides of the equation, we get

$\Rightarrow (x)^2 + 2 \times x \times \frac{1}{4} + (\frac{1}{4})^2 = (\frac{1}{4})^2 - 2$

$\Rightarrow (x + \frac{1}{4})^2 = \frac{1}{16} - 2$

$\Rightarrow (x + \frac{1}{4})^2 = \frac{-31}{16}$

So, The roots of quadratic equation $2x^2 + x + 4 = 0$ are no real roots because $(x + \frac{1}{4})^2$ is negative.

6(B). Let x and $(x+1)$ be the two consecutive integers.

According to the given question,

$\Rightarrow x(x+1) = 360$

$\Rightarrow x^2 + x = 360$

$\Rightarrow x^2 + x - 360$

7(A). Given,

$(x+1)^2 - 2(x+1) = 0$

$x^2 + 1 + 2x - 2x - 2 = 0$

$x^2 - 1 = 0$

$x^2 = 1$

$x = \pm 1$

8(D). Given,

The angle of the sector $= 60°$

$r = 6$ cm

Using the formula,

The area of sector $= \left(\frac{\theta}{360°}\right) \times \pi r^2$

$= \left(\frac{60°}{360}\right) \times \pi r^2$ cm^2

Put the value of r and θ

area of the sector $= 6 \times \frac{22}{7}$ cm^2

$= \frac{132}{7}$ cm^2

9(D). Given,

the radius of first circle$= r_1$

the radius of Second circle$= r_2$

According to the question

$\pi R^2 = \pi r_1^2 + \pi r_2^2$

$\pi R^2 = \pi(r_1^2 + r_2^2)$

$R^2 = r_1^2 + r_2^2$

10(B). As we know that:

$\cot A = \frac{\cos A}{\sin A}$ and $\operatorname{cosec} A = \frac{1}{\sin A}$

Therefore,

$\cot A + \operatorname{cosec} A = \frac{\cos A}{\sin A} + \left(\frac{1}{\sin A}\right)$

$= \frac{(\cos A + 1)}{\sin A}$

On solving the above equation using the half-angle formulas, we get

[Note: $\quad \cos A = 2\cos^2(\frac{A}{2}) - 1 \quad$ and

$\sin A = 2\sin(\frac{A}{2})\cos(\frac{A}{2})$]

$\cot A + \operatorname{cosec} A = \frac{\cos(\frac{A}{2})}{\sin(\frac{A}{2})}$

$= \cot(\frac{A}{2})$

So, the value of $\cot A + \operatorname{cosec} A = \cot(\frac{A}{2})$.

11(B). $\tan 75° + \cot 75° = ?$

$\tan 75° = \tan(30° + 45°)$

As we know that,

$\tan(A+B) = \frac{\tan A + \tan B}{1 - \tan A \times \tan B}$

$= \frac{\tan 30° + \tan 45°}{1 - \tan 30° \times \tan 45°} = \frac{\sqrt{3}+1}{\sqrt{3}-1}$

$[\because \tan 30° = \frac{1}{\sqrt{3}}, \tan 45° = 1]$

$\cot 75° = \frac{1}{\tan 75°} \quad [\because \cot x = \frac{1}{\tan x}]$

$= \frac{\sqrt{3}-1}{\sqrt{3}+1}$

$\therefore \tan 75° + \cot 75° = \frac{\sqrt{3}+1}{\sqrt{3}-1} + \frac{\sqrt{3}-1}{\sqrt{3}+1} = 4$

12(A). Given,

$\sin A + \sin^2 A = 1$

$\Rightarrow \sin A = 1 - \sin^2 A$

As we know that:

$\because 1 - \sin^2 \theta = \cos^2 \theta$

$\Rightarrow \sin A = \cos^2 A \ldots$ (i)

Squaring both sides

$\Rightarrow \sin^2 A = \cos^4 A \ldots$ (ii)

From equations (i) and (ii), we have

$\cos^2 A + \cos^4 A = \sin A + \sin^2 A = 1$

13(A). Given,

Let the speed of boat in still water be x km/hr

and let the speed of current be y km/hr\)

Now,

Speed downstream $= x + y$

Speed upstream $= x - y$

Ritu can row 20 km downstream in 2 hours

For downstream,

Distance $= 20$ km

Time $= 2$ hours

Speed $= x + y$

We know that,

Speed $= \frac{\text{Distance}}{\text{Time}}$

$x + y = \frac{20}{2}$

$x + y = 10 \qquad \ldots\ldots$ (1)

Ritu can row 4 km upstream in (2\) hours

For upstream,

Distance $= 4$ km

Time $= 2$ hours

Speed $= x - y$

We know that,

Speed $= \frac{\text{Distance}}{\text{Time}}$

$x - y = \frac{4}{2}$

$x - y = 2 \qquad \ldots\ldots$ (2)

So, our equations are

$x + y = 10 \qquad \ldots\ldots$ (1)

$x - y = 2 \qquad \ldots\ldots$ (2)

From (1),

$x + y = 10$

$x = 10 - y$

Putting $x = 10 - y$ in (2),

$x \quad y = 2$

$(10 - y) - y = 2$

$-2y = 2 - 10$

$-2y = -8$

$y = \frac{-8}{-2}$

$y = 4$

Putting $y = 4$ in (1),

$x + y = 10$

$x + 4 = 10$

$x = 10 - 4$

$x = 6$

Thus, $x = 6, y = 4$ is the solution

So,

Speed of boat in still water, $= x = 6$ km/hr

Speed of stream, $y = 4$ km/hr

14(B). Given,

Let time taken by 1 woman to finish the work $= x$ days

Work finished by 1 woman in 1 day $= \frac{1}{x}$

Similarly,

Let time taken by 1 man to finish the work $= y$ days

Work finished by 1 man in 1 day $= \frac{1}{y}$

Given that,

2 women and 5 men complete the work in 4 days

$\therefore$ Work finished by 2 women and 5 men in 1 day

$= \frac{1}{4}$ 2 $\times$ (Work finished by 1 woman in 1 day)

$+5 \times$ (Work finished by 1 man in 1 day)

$= \frac{1}{4}$

$2 \times \frac{1}{x} + 5 \times \frac{1}{y} = \frac{1}{4}$

$\frac{2}{x} + \frac{5}{y} = \frac{1}{4} \qquad \ldots\ldots$ (1)

Also,

3 women and 6 men complete the work in 3 days

$\therefore$ Work finished by 3 women and 6 men in 1 day $= \frac{1}{3}$

$3 \times$ (Work finished by 1 woman in 1 day)

$+6 \times$ (Work finished by 1 man in 1 day)

$= \frac{1}{3}$

$3 \times \frac{1}{x} + 6 \times \frac{1}{y} = \frac{1}{3}$

$\frac{3}{x} + \frac{6}{y} = \frac{1}{3} \qquad \ldots\ldots$ (2)

Solving, equation (1) $\times 3-$ equation 2) $\times 2$

$\frac{6}{x} + \frac{15}{y} = \frac{3}{4}$

$\frac{6}{x} + \frac{12}{y} = \frac{2}{3}$

$- \quad - \quad -$

$\frac{3}{y} = \frac{3}{4} - \frac{2}{3}$

$\therefore \frac{3}{y} = \frac{9-8}{12}$

$\therefore \frac{3}{y} = \frac{1}{12}$

$\Rightarrow y = 36$ days

Putting $y = 36$ in equation (1),

$\frac{2}{x} + \frac{5}{36} = \frac{1}{4}$

$\Rightarrow \frac{2}{x} = \frac{1}{4} - \frac{5}{36}$

$\Rightarrow \frac{2}{x} = \frac{9-5}{36}$

$\Rightarrow \frac{2}{x} = \frac{4}{36}$

$\Rightarrow x = 18$ days

So, $x = 18, y = 36$ is the solution of the given equation.

$\therefore$ Time taken by one woman to finish the work alone $= x = 18$ days

and Time taken by one man to finish the work alone $= y = 36$ days

15(D). Let $x = 6.\overline{12}\ldots$ (i)

$100x = 612.\overline{12}\ldots$ (ii) [Multiplying both sides by 100]

Subtracting (i) from (ii),

$99x = 606$

$x = \dfrac{606}{99} = \dfrac{202}{33}$

Denominator $= 33$

Prime factorisation $= 3 \times 11$

16(A). To find the length of the longest rod that can measure the dimensions of the room exactly, we have to find HCF.

L , Length $= 8$ m 50 cm $= 850$ cm $= 2^1 \times 5^2 \times 17$

B , Breadth $= 6$ m 25 cm $= 625$ cm $= 5^4$

H , Height $= 4$ m 75 cm $= 475$ cm $= 5^2 \times 19$

HCF of L, B and H is $5^2 = 25$ cm

Length of the longest rod $= 25$ cm

17(B). 1st vessel $= 720$ml ; 2nd vessel $= 405$ml

We find the HCF of 720 and 405 to find the maximum quantity of milk to be filled in one glass.

$405 = 3^4 \times 5$

$720 = 2^4 \times 3^2 \times 5$

HCF $= 3^2 \times 5 = 45$ml $=$ Capacity of glass

No. of glasses filled from 1st vessel $= \dfrac{720}{45} = 16$

No. of glasses filled from 2nd vessel $= \dfrac{405}{45} = 9$

Total number of glasses $= 25$

18(A). In a fraction, if the denominator is of the form $2^n \times 5^m$ then the fraction is always terminating.

In case of 3125, it can be written as,

$3125 = 2^0 \times 5^5$

So, it is terminating and the reason is the correct explanation to assertion.

19(A). Here, Divisor $= (x+1)$

Quotient $= 3x - 2$

Remainder $= 3$

Dividend $=$ Divisor $\times$ Quotient $+$ Remainder

$= (x+1) \times (3x - 2) + 3$

$= 3x^2 + 3x - 2x - 2 + 3$

$= 3x^2 + x + 1$

20(D). According to question

$4x^3 - 4x^2 - x + 1 = 0$

For the other possible zeroes, we will first take -1

So, we get $4x^3 - 4x^2 - x + 1 \neq 0$ (if we put -1 at the place of x).

This means that -1 could be one of the zeroes.

It also means that the number should be between -1 and 1 from which we can get the zeroes.

Therefore, we will try $-\dfrac{1}{2}$ at the place of x .

$4x^3 - 4x^2 - x + 1 = 0$

$= 4 \times \left(-\dfrac{1}{2}\right)^3 - 4 \times \left(-\dfrac{1}{2}\right)^2 - \left(-\dfrac{1}{2}\right) + 1$

$= 4 \times \left(-\dfrac{1}{8}\right) - 4 \times \left(\dfrac{1}{4}\right) + \left(\dfrac{1}{2}\right) + 1$

$= \left(-\dfrac{4}{8}\right) - 1 + \dfrac{1}{2} + 1$

$= -\dfrac{1}{2} - 1 + \dfrac{1}{2} + 1$ (all the numbers will get eliminated and we will receive a zero).

$= 0$

It means $-\dfrac{1}{2}$ is one of the zeroes.

like this for other zeroes, we will take one more number which is between -1 and 1 and check whether it is possible or not.

$\therefore 4x^3 - 4x^2 - x + 1 = 0$ (put $\dfrac{1}{2}$ as x)

Put $x = \dfrac{1}{2}$

$4x^3 - 4x^2 - x + 1 = 0$

$= 4\left(\dfrac{1}{2}\right)^3 - 4\left(\dfrac{1}{2}\right)^2 - \left(\dfrac{1}{2}\right) + 1$

$= 4 \times \dfrac{1}{8} - 4 \times \dfrac{1}{4} - \dfrac{1}{2} + 1$

$= \dfrac{1}{2} - 1 - \dfrac{1}{2} + 1$

$= 0$

After solving similarly as done above we get the zero.

Therefore, we can say that $\dfrac{1}{2}$ and $-\dfrac{1}{2}$ will be the other possible zeroes.

21(C). Sample space of nos obtained is $= 6 \times 6 = 36$ (As two dices are independent)

Sum of nos. obtained atmost $3 = (1,1), (1,2)(2,1) = 3$

Probability

$P = \dfrac{\text{Number of favorable outcomes}}{\text{Total number of outcomes}}$

probability of getting the event $= \dfrac{3}{36} = \dfrac{1}{12}$

22(A). A coin tossed three times sample space

$=$

$(H,H,H), (H,H,T), (H,T,H), (T,H,H)$ $, (H,T,T), (T,H,T), (T,T,H), (T,T,T)$

Favourable outcomes for No tail $= 1$

Probability

$P = \dfrac{\text{Number of favorable outcomes}}{\text{Total number of outcomes}}$

Probability $= \dfrac{1}{8}$

23(B). According to question,

Let a and d be the first term and common difference of the given AP.

The general or n^{th} term of an AP is given as,

$T_n = a + (n-1)d$

$a_{17} = a + (17-1)d = a + 16d$

$a_{10} = a + (10-1)d = a + 9d$

As per condition, $a_{17} - a_{10} = 7$

$\Rightarrow (a + 16d) - (a + 9d) = 7$

$\Rightarrow 7d = 7$

$\Rightarrow d = \dfrac{7}{7} = 1$

So, common difference is 1 .

24(D). It can be seen from the question, that the incomes of Subha Rao increase every year by $Rs.\,200$ and So, form an AP.

Therefore, after 1995 , the salaries for each year are:

$5000, 5200, 5400, \ldots$

Subba Rao's starting salary

Annual increment $= Rs.\,200$

Let n denote the number of years.

First term $= a = Rs.\,5000$

Common difference $= d = Rs.\,200$

$a_n = Rs.\,7000$

$\therefore 5000 + (n-1)200 = 7000$

$[\because a_n = a + (n-1)d]$

$\Rightarrow (n-1)200 = 2000$

$\Rightarrow n - 1 = \dfrac{2000}{200} = 10$

$\Rightarrow n = 10 + 1 = 11$

So, in the 11th year, his salary will become $Rs.\,7000$.

Now, in the case of the year, the sequence is 1995, 1996, 1997, 1998, $\ldots$

Let a_n a denote the required year.

$a_n = 1995 + (11-1)1 = 1995 + 10 = 2005$

So, in the year 2005 , Subba Rao's salary becomes $Rs.\,7000$.

25(A). According to the question,

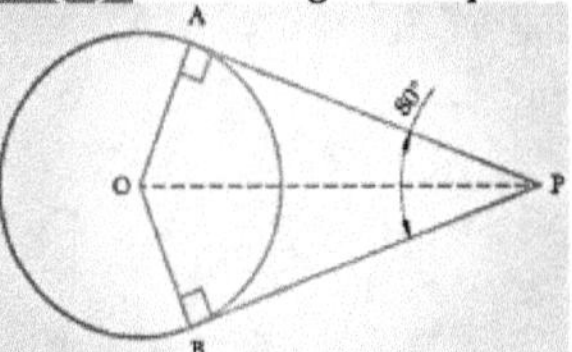

Now, in the above diagram, OA is perpendicular to PA and OB is perpendicular to PB i.e. $OA \perp PA$ and $OB \perp PB$

So, $\angle OBP = \angle OAP = 90°$

Now, in the quadrilateral AOBP ,

So,

$\angle AOB + \angle OAP + \angle OBP + \angle APB = 360°$

Putting their values, we get,

$\angle AOB + 260° = 360°$

$\angle AOB = 100°$

Now, consider the triangles $\triangle OPB$ and $\triangle OPA$.

$AP = BP$ (Since the tangents from a point are always equal)

$OA = OB$ (Which are the radii of the circle)

$OP = OP$ (It is the common side)

Now, we can say that triangles OPB and OPA are similar using SSS congruency.

So, $\angle POB = \angle POA$

$\angle AOB = \angle POA + \angle POB$

$2(\angle POA) = \angle AOB$

By putting the respective values, we get,

$\Rightarrow \angle POA = 100°/2 = 50°$

26(D). $\because AB = PQ = 6$ cm

and an angle bisects same through the center

$\therefore ON = OL = 5$ cm.

As we know that the angular bisector divides the chord into equal parts.

since OB = OP (radius of a circle)

Hence the angle subtended divides it into two equal parts.

$BL = \dfrac{1}{2}AB = \dfrac{1}{2} \times 6 = 3$ cm

$OL + BL = 5 + 3 = 8$ cm

27(B). $\because AB = CD = 4$ units

and an angle bisects same through the center

$\therefore OL = OM = 4.5$ units.

As we know that the angular bisector divides the chord into equal parts.

$OA = OD$ (radius of a circle)

Therefore, the angle subtended divides it

into two equal parts.
$MD = \frac{1}{2}CD = \frac{1}{2} \times 4 = 2$ units.
$OM + MD = 4.5 + 2 = 6.5$ cm

28(A).

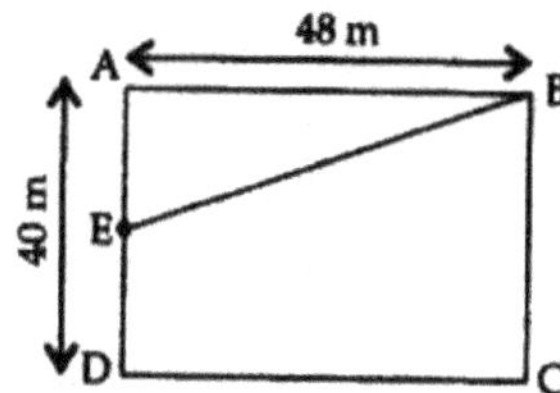

E is the mid-point of AD
Given,
$AE = \frac{40}{2} = 20$ m
$\angle A = 90° \dots$ [Angle of a rectangle
In rt. $\triangle BAE$,
$EB^2 = AB^2 + AE^2 \dots$ [Pythagoras theorem
$= (48)^2 + (20)^2$
$= 2304 + 400 = 2704$
$\therefore EB = \sqrt{2704} = 52$ m

29(B). We know that the diagonals of a rhombus are perpendicular bisectors of each other.
Given, $AC = 16$ cm
and $BD = 12$ cm
$\therefore AO = 8$ cm
$BO = 6$ cm
and $\angle AOB = 90°$

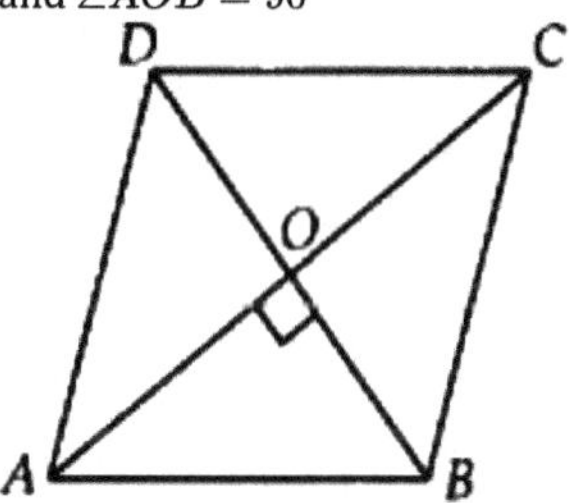

In right angled $\triangle AOB$,
$AB^2 = AO^2 + OB^2$ [by Pythagoras theorem]
$\Rightarrow AB^2 = 8^2 + 6^2 = 64 + 36 = 100$
$\therefore AB = 10$ cm

30(A). Given,
$\triangle ABC \sim \triangle QRP, AB = 18$ cm and $BC = 15$ cm

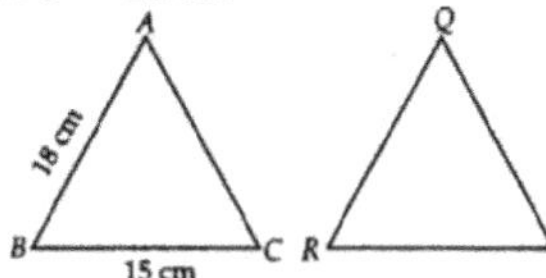

We know that, the ratio of area of two similar triangles is equal to the ratio of square of their corresponding sides.
$\therefore \frac{ar(\triangle ABC)}{ar(\triangle QRP)} = \frac{(BC)^2}{(RP)^2}$
But, $\frac{ar(\triangle ABC)}{ar(\triangle PQR)} = \frac{9}{4}$
Given,
$\Rightarrow \frac{(15)^2}{(RP)^2} = \frac{9}{4}$ [$\because BC = 15$ cm, given]
$\Rightarrow (RP)^2 = \frac{225 \times 4}{9} = 100$
$\therefore RP = 10$ cm

31(B). Food chain has trophic levels. These levels denotes type of organisms in a food chain. Transfer of energy through this food chain occurs, with only 10% passage of energy. This means 90% of energy is wasted at each trophic level. The sequence of trophic level is -
Producer, primary consumer, secondary consumer, tertiary consumer.
Producer to primary consumer -
100x10/100
Thus, 10 J of energy, out of 100 J reaches primary consumer.
Primary consumer to secondary consumer energy transferred is - 10x10/100
So, only 1 J of energy will reach secondary consumer.

32(A). Ultraviolet radiation is responsible for the conversion of atmospheric oxygen to ozone. When high-energy ultraviolet rays strike ordinary oxygen molecules (O2), they split the molecule into two single oxygen atoms, known as atomic oxygen. A freed oxygen atom then combines with another oxygen molecule to form a molecule of ozone.

33(C). Ductility is a physical property of matter, usually metals. It is the ability of metals to be drawn into thin wires. Non-metals are non-ductile in nature.
Out of the given elements platinum, aluminium and copper are metals while carbon is a non-metal. Therefore, carbon cannot be drawn into a wire.

34(B). Graphite is not malleable.
Malleability is the property of a metal by which it can be beaten into thin sheets without breaking or damaging it. Gold and silver are the most malleable metals on earth. Graphite is a non-metal, hence it is not malleable. Graphite is the only non-metal which conducts electricity.

35(A). The pituitary gland is sometimes called the "master" gland of the endocrine system because it controls the functions of many of the other endocrine glands. The pituitary gland is no larger than a pea, and is located at the base of the brain. Oxytocin, ADH/vasopressin hormone, prolactin hormone, growth hormone are secreted by this. These are collectively called pituitary hormones.

36(B). There are two types of neurons, motor neurons and sensory neurons. Motor neurons carry signals from the brain to the peripheral body parts. Sensory neurons carry signals from the peripheral body parts to the brain. In the reflex action, there are two body parts involved effector and affector. The effector is the organ that responds once the motor neuron brings the interpreted response from the brain to the effector organ.

37(B). The following reaction describes the rusting of iron:

$4Fe + 3O_2 \rightarrow 4Fe^{3+} + 6O^{2-}$
Here, metallic iron loses electrons to form Fe^{3+}. Hence, it has been oxidised. It is an example of redox reaction not just oxidation reaction. Iron is oxidised and oxygen is reduced in this reaction.

38(C). When the gases sulphur dioxide and hydrogen sulphide mix in the presence of water, then hydrogen sulphide acts as a reducing agent.
A chemical which donates electrons to other then it is called a reducing agent because the chemical undergoes oxidation and reduces other chemicals. The given reaction is:
$SO_2 + 2H_2S \rightarrow 2H_2O + 3S$
In the above reaction one mole of sulphur dioxide reacts with two moles of hydrogen sulphide and forms two moles of water and three moles of sulphur as the products. The sulphur dioxide got reduced by accepting electrons from hydrogen sulphide. Means sulphur dioxide is a oxidizing agent and hydrogen sulphide is a reducing agent.

39(D). Carbon compounds form covalent bonds, and they do not give rise to free electrons because all electrons are used to create the covalent bond. Also carbon compound does not dissociate itself into ions, so carbon compounds are poor electrical conductors. They do not have strong force of attraction between molecules of carbon compounds because covalent bond is weaker than ionic bond.

40(B). The product formed when methane reacts with chlorine in the presence of sunlight is CH_3Cl.
When a mixture of methane and chlorine is exposed to ultraviolet light typically sunlight a substitution reaction occurs and the organic product is chloromethane.
$CH_4 + Cl_2 \longrightarrow CH_3Cl + HCl$

41(C). When a pistil having functional female gametes fails to set seeds with viable and fertile pollen, which can bring about fertilisation in another pistil, the pistil and pollen are said to be incompatible and this is known as incompatibility.
When the sexual incompatibility is between individuals of different species, it is interspecific.
When the sexual incompatibility is between individuals of same species, it is intraspecific. This intraspecific incompatibility is also called as self-incompatibility which may include many reasons like pollen fail to germinate on the surface of the stigma of the same flower, which is also known as self-sterility.

42(D). Sterilization method: It is a very effective and permanent method of contraception. Sterilization techniques can be considered as the safest among the options as the side-effects are less among others in the long run of time.

Rhythm method: The biggest drawback is that it is not as effective in preventing pregnancy as other methods of birth control.

Failure rates for barrier contraception are much higher than those of long acting reversible contraception.

Termination of unwanted pregnancy after specific time is quiet risky for mother.

43(A). There are usually at least two forms (called alleles) of most genes, and the effect they have when expressed in the individual, i.e. the characteristic they produce, varies according to the form of the other gene they are combined with in each body cell. Alleles show their effect only if both genes are of this type.

44(D). Low genetic variation is seen in asexual reproduction unlike sexual reproduction as asexually reproducing organisms produce identical copies of themselves, they pass on the maximum quantity of their own genetic material to each offspring.

45(A). The power of the lens is known as the inverse of the focal length of the lens measured in meter(m).

$$\text{Power of lense} = \frac{1}{\text{focal length in meter}}$$

$$\text{Power of lens (P)} = \frac{1}{f}$$

$$P = -2D$$

$$f = \frac{-1}{2}$$

$$= -0.5m$$

A concave lens has a negative focal length. Therefore, it is a concave lens.

46(A). Given,

Object distance, $u = -20$ cm

A concave mirror forms a real magnified image only when the image to be formed is inverted i.e. $m = -3$

Magnification $m = \frac{-v}{u}$

$$\therefore -3 = \frac{-v}{-20}$$

$$\Rightarrow v = -60 \text{ cm}$$

As we know,

$$\frac{1}{v} + \frac{1}{u} = \frac{1}{f}$$

$$\therefore \frac{1}{-60} + \frac{1}{-20} = \frac{1}{f}$$

$$\Rightarrow f = \frac{-60}{4}$$

$$= -15 \text{ cm}$$

Thus focal length of the mirror is 15 cm.

47(A). By Magnetic Needle instrument, the presence of magnetic field be determined. Any origin of magnetism, an electromagnet or magnet, is enclosed by a magnetic field. That field can be recognized by various devices, giving information about the field direction and its strength.

A compass is commonly a thin magnet or magnetized iron pin balanced on a pivot. It can be utilized to detect tiny magnetic fields. The needle will turn to point toward the opposing pole of a magnet. It can be extremely sensitive to small magnetic fields. A simple compass can discover a magnetic field and explain its direction. Iron filings can be utilized to show the magnetic field shape. A gaussmeter can detect a field at the sophisticated level and indicate its strength, as measured in gauss units.

48(D). Outside the magnet, magnetic field lines go from south to north pole of the magnet is not the correct statement regarding magnetic field.

The two magnetic field lines never intersect each other. The tangent drawn to the field lines then it will have two direction of magnetic field at the same point of intersection which is not possible, since magnetic field line have only one direction at a particular point. Magnetic field lines are continuous curves.It originate from north pole and terminate on south pole. But inside the magnet it moves from south pole to north pole forming a closed loop. So, there is no any origination or termination point like electric field. Magnetic field are connecting the arrows gives continuous magnetic field lines. Small compasses used to test a magnetic field will not disturb it.

49(A). Veins have valves to prevent the back flow of blood.

Veins are blood vessels which bring blood from the body back to the heart. They are larger and hold more blood than the arteries. The blood passing through the veins is deoxygenated (except in pulmonary veins) and flows at a low pressure. It flows slow and steady against the direction of gravity. Therefore, veins have valves to prevent the backflow of blood.

50(A). Xylem is a type of tissue in vascular plants that transports water and some nutrients from the roots to the leaves. Phloem is the other type of transport tissue; it transports sucrose and other nutrients throughout the plant. The main function of the xylem is to transport water and some soluble nutrients, including minerals and inorganic ions, upwards from the roots to the rest of the plant. Xylem is made up of several types of cells. Tracheids are long cells that help transport xylem sap and also provide structural support. Vessel elements are shorter than tracheids but also help conduct water. The first xylem that develops in a growing plant is called protoxylem, and it contains narrow vessels as the plant is not yet big.

51(B). Calcium phosphate is present in tooth enamel. The nature of the calcium phosphate is basic.

Calcium phosphate is basic salt since it is a source of weak phosphoric acid and a slightly stronger base of calcium hydroxide. Calcium phosphate is a mineral comprising calcium ion $\left(Ca^{2+}\right)$ and phosphate ion which is inorganic in nature. It is present in the crown area of the tooth and also in bones.

52(D). According to the question the solution of water and soil is acidic in nature as it is able to turn the litmus paper into yellow-orange colour. As we know lemon is a rich source of vitamin C, which is known as citric acid. Being a weak acid it will be able to turn the litmus to red. Vinegar is a combination of water and acetic acid. It acts as a mild acid and it also turns the litmus paper to red. Common salt includes the sodium and chloride ions and is not able to turn the litmus to blue as it is not a basic compound.

Antacid has its neutralizing property for acidsand it reduces the acidity with the alkaline nature of its compounds such as aluminium and sodium carbonate. So antacid would change the pH paper from yellow-orange to greenish-blue while others are acidic in nature.

53(A). The light enters our eye through the transparent cornea, passes through the lens and is focused on the retina.

Light enters our eye through the cornea, the clear, curved layer in front of the iris and pupil. After passing through the cornea, light travels through the pupil which is surrounded by iris and behind the iris sits the lens which changes the shape and focuses light onto the retina then the photoreceptors in the retina convert the image into electrical signals, which are carried to the brain by the optic nerve.

54(D). Given, $i = 30mA, t = 10min$

$V = 20V$

So, we know $Q = it$

$Q = 30 \times 10^{-3}(A) \times (10 \times 60)S$

$Q = 600 \times 30 \times 10^{-3} \Rightarrow 18.0C$

Now from $w = Q \times V$

$= 18.0 \times 20 \Rightarrow 360J$

55(C). First, let's find the current for the first situation:

$$I = \frac{V}{R}$$

$$= \frac{2.5}{500}$$

$$= 0.005 \text{ A}$$

So, since the current won't change, therefore:

$$R = \frac{V}{I}$$

$$= \frac{5}{0.005}$$

$$= 1000 \ \Omega$$

56(C). A dam is a barrier across flowing water that obstructs, directs or retards the flow, often creating a reservoir, lake or impoundment.

"Dam" refers to the reservoir rather than the structure. Most dams have a section called a spillway or weir over which or through which it is intended that water will flow either intermittently or continuously. Dams are classified according to structure, intended purpose or height. Based on structure and the materials used, dams are classified as timber dams, embankment dams or masonry dams, with several subtypes. According to the height, dams can be categorised as large dams and major dams or alternatively as low dams, medium height dams and high dams.

57(C).
Overpopulation in third world countries is often cited as the cause of environmental degradation.
Overpopulation cause many problems such as Habitat destruction, hunting, poaching, over-exploitation, environmental pollution, poisoning and forest fires are factors, which have led to the decline in biodiversity. Other environmental destruction are unequal access, inequitable consumption of resources and differential sharing of responsibility for environmental well-being.

58(D). Gypsum mineral is not obtained from the veins and lodes.
In igneous and metamorphic rocks, minerals occur in Veins and Lodes. Veins-Smaller occurrences of minerals in cracks, faults, joints, and crevices of the igneous and metamorphic rocks are Veins. Lodes-Larger occurrences of minerals in cracks, faults, joints, and crevices of the igneous and metamorphic rocks are Lodes. Minerals found in Veins and Lodes are- Lead, Copper, Tin, and Zinc.

59(C). Underemployment occurs when people are working less than what they are capable of doing.
Underemployment is a condition in which workers are employed in less than full-time or regular jobs or insufficient jobs for their training or economic needs. Also, underemployment is a worker's underuse because a job does not use the skills of the worker, i.e., part-time, or leaves the worker idle.

60(C). Bihar has the lowest per capita income.
Per capita income is a measure of the amount of money earned per person in a nation or geographic region. Per capita income for a nation is calculated by dividing the country's national income by its population. Goa is the Highest per capita income state in India with a per capita income of Rs. 4,22,149. The per capita income of Goa is three times of National Per Capita. Per capita income is often used to measure a sector's average income and compare the wealth of different populations. Per capita income is also often used to measure a country's standard of living. This helps to ascertain a country's development status.

61(A). Liberalism is derives from the Latin root liber, meaning free- freedom for the individual and equality of all before the law.

Liberalism, political doctrine that takes protecting and enhancing the freedom of the individual to be the central problem of politics. Liberals typically believe that government is necessary to protect individuals from being harmed by others, but they also recognize that government itself can pose a threat to liberty.

62(C). Wells and tube wells are the first sources of irrigation in India. Irrigation by the canal is the most important means of irrigation in India and it is second after tube well, but this means of irrigation is more prevalent in North India than South India, because this system is widespread in those areas, where there are large flat plains. And the soil is deep and fertile and the ever-flowing rivers flow.

63(B). Paper currency is known as 'fiat money' because it is decreed legal tender.
Fiat money is a government-issued currency that is not backed by a commodity such as gold . Fiat money gives central banks greater control over the economy because they can control how much money is printed. This means most coin and paper currencies that are used throughout the world are fiat money. This includes the U.S. dollar, the British pound, the Indian rupee, and the euro. The value of fiat money is not determined by the material with which it is made.

64(A).
In urban India there are only urban cooperative banks.
The term Urban Co-operative Banks (UCBs), though not formally defined, refers to primary cooperative banks located in urban and semi-urban areas . These banks were traditionally centred around communities, localities work place groups. They essentially lent to small borrowers and businesses.
Hence, the correct option is (B).

65(D). The most common route for MNC investments is to buy up Local companies.
Benefit to local companies lure them to seek investment by MNCs:
- MNCs can provide money for additional investments, like buying new machines for faster production.
- MNCs might bring with them the latest technology for production.
- MNCs also buy some local companies to expand production, since they have wealth exceeding the entire budgets of some of the developing countries.

66(D). Globalisation involves integration of production and integration of markets.
Globalization decreases the cost of manufacturing . This means that companies can offer goods at a lower price to consumers. The average cost of goods is a key aspect that contributes to increases in the standard of living. Consumers also have

access to a wider variety of goods. At the same time, global economic growth and industrial productivity are both the driving force and the major consequences of Globalization. They also have big environmental consequences as they contribute to the depletion of natural resources, deforestation and the destruction of ecosystems and loss of biodiversity.

67(A). United Nations adopted the UN Guidelines for Consumer Protection in 1985.
The United Nations Guidelines for Consumer Protection (UNGCP) are "a valuable set of principles for setting out the main characteristics of effective consumer protection legislation, enforcement institutions and redress systems and for assisting interested Member States in formulating and enforcing domestic and regional laws, rules and regulations that are suitable to their own economic and social and environmental circumstances, as well as promoting international enforcement cooperation among Member States and encouraging the sharing of experiences in consumer protection."

68(C). The 'Right to Information' Act was passed in October 2005.
This law empowers Indian citizens to seek any accessible information from a Public Authority and makes the Government and its functionaries more accountable and responsible. Under the provisions of the Act, any citizen may request information from a "public authority" (a body of Government or "instrumentality of State") which is required to reply expeditiously or within thirty days.

69(C).
With Portuguese missionaries in the mid-sixteenth century the printing press first come to India.
The printing press was brought to India by the Jesuit missionaries. They came to Goa in the 19th century, who learnt Konkani and printed many tracts. But in 1674, about 50 books were printed in Konkani and Kanarese languages. The Catholic priests published the first book in Tamil in 1579, at Cochin and in 1713 the first book in Malayalam was printed by them. The Dutch Protestant missionaries had already printed 72 Tamil books by 1710, most of them translations of earlier texts. By the end of the 18 th century, newspapers began to appear in various Indian languages.

70(A).
James Augustus Hickey began to edit the 'Bengal Gazette', a weekly magazine in India.
It was a private English magazine, not having British influence on it, which introduced English printing in India. Hickey

published a lot of advertisements, on import and sale of slaves. He also published gossips about the company's senior officials in India. Enraged by this, Governor General Warren Hastings persecuted Hickey.

71(B). Sri Lankan Tamils constitute an overwhelming majority of the population in the Northern Province and are the largest ethnic group in the Eastern Province.
According to the 2012 census there were 2,270,924 Sri Lankan Tamils in Sri Lanka, 11.2% of the population. They are minority in other provinces. 70% of Sri Lankan Tamils in Sri Lanka live in the Northern and Eastern provinces.

72(B). A new constitution stipulated that the state shall protect and foster Buddhism, thus disregarding the Tamils.
- In 1956, an Act was passed to recognise Sinhala as the only official language, thus disregarding Tamil.
- The governments followed preferential policies that favoured Sinhala applicants for university positions and government jobs.
- A new constitution stipulated that the state shall protect and foster Buddhism.

73(C). A well-known pioneer of mass production was the car manufacturer Henry Ford. He adapted the assembly line production to his new car plant in Detroit.
On December 1, 1913, Henry Ford installs the first moving assembly line for the mass production of an entire automobile. His innovation reduced the time it took to build a car from more than 12 hours to one hour and 33 minutes.

74(A). Residuary powers are those powers which can be made by the parliament only.
It is different from 3 lists, union list, state list, and concurrent list. These powers are neither under the legislative powers of the State nor the Union. Parliament has exclusive power to make any law with respect to any matter not enumerated in the Concurrent List or State List. Such power shall include the power of making any law imposing a tax not mentioned in either of those Lists.

75(D). The State Reorganization Commission was appointed by Pandit Nehru in 22 December 1953.
In 1955, after nearly two years of study, the Commission recommended that India's state boundaries should be reorganised to form 14 states and 6 territories.
States Reorganisation Commission consisted of Fazal Ali, K. M. Panikkar and H. N. Kunzru. Some of its recommendations were implemented in the States Reorganisation Act of 1956.

76(C). When the Spinning Jenny was introduced in the woolen industry women who survived on hand spinning began attacking the new machines.
The spinning jenny allowed more threads and yarns to be produced by fewer spinners. The early spinning jenny also produced a weaker thread than could be produced by hand so there was a decrease in quality until improvements were made to the machines and a dependable power source became available.

77(A). Tidal energy is a renewable or replenishable source of energy as it is inexhaustible in nature.
It is generated when tidal barrages or dams are constructed across a narrow opening to the sea. Water rushes into the dam as the sea level rises, which moves the blades of the turbines attached at the opening of the dam. Tidal energy can prove to be very advantageous. It is environmentally friendly, provides a long term economy as, once, a tidal-power system is up and running, it's comparatively cheaper to maintain. It is energy efficient. Tidal power is called a green energy source, as it emits zero greenhouse gases. It also doesn't take up a lot of space. It happens to be very reliable. As the sea currents are very predictable, with well-known cycles, it is easier to construct tidal energy systems with the correct dimensions, thus making the source of energy very reliable. The lifespan is very long. For instance, La Rance tidal barrage power plant, constructed in 1966, still generates large amounts of electricity up to this day.

78(C). People is 'Sovereign' in a Democratic form of Government.
In any state, sovereignty is assigned to the person, body, or institution that has the ultimate authority over other people in order to establish a law or change an existing law. In political theory, sovereignty is a substantive term designating supreme legitimate authority over some polity. In modern democracies, sovereign power rests with the people and is exercised through representative bodies such as Congress or Parliament. The Sovereign is the one who exercises power without limitation. Sovereignty is essentially the power to make laws, even as Blackstone defined it.

79(D). The following which is not a way to resolve a conflict in a democracy is Armed revolution. As the word sounds an armed revolution is a group of people that are armed and are protesting against something or the ongoing ruling government.
- These groups are armed and usually try to carry out revolutions.
- The basic concept of democracy and the constitution states that no person is allowed to use arms or any sort of weapons to resolve something or to carry out something.
- Peaceful protest and resolution to an ongoing conflict are allowed that is peaceful marching, rallies, etc.
- Nonviolence is promoted in a democratic country.

80(D). The meaning of picket is a form of demonstration or protest by which people block the entrance to a shop, factory, or office.
Picketing is a type of protest where individuals obstruct entry to a store, factory, or office. Standing in front of or around a workplace by workers to draw attention to their concerns, discourage patronage, and, during strikes, dissuade strikebreakers.

81(B). Kadri Gopalnath was associated with Carnatic music, specifically with the saxophone, which he popularized in this genre of Indian classical music.

82(C). Article 14 of the Indian Constitution, which provides for equality before the law has been borrowed from the British constitution. So, Britain is the correct answer.

84(A). Article 145 is not related to the salary of judges.
Article 145 was debated on 6th June 1949. It authorized the Supreme Court to make rules for its functioning.

85(A). If the Earth's direction of rotation is reversed, the time when it is noon (12:00) on the International Date Line will be 06:30 Indian Standard Time (IST-India Standard Time).
The chronological line determined on the earth's surface leaving the land segments almost simultaneously 180° east and west meridian is called the international date line.

86(C). GSLV MK - III is India's heaviest rocket and referred to as 'Bahubali'.
GSLV Mk-III weighs 3,423kg and is the heaviest launcher in India. It is taller than a 13-story building (43 meters, to be precise) and even then, it is the shortest Indian launcher.

87(C). Goa was carved out of the earlier state of Bombay.

88(D). 'Aloo Posto' is a traditional delicacy of West Bengal.
- Bengali Aloo Posto is a simple dish made with spiced potatoes and cooked in chillies, turmeric, and poppy seeds. A great side dish or meal for any occasion.
- Some other famous dishes of West Bengal- Luchi-Alur Dom, Kosha Mangsho, Daab Chingri, Keemar Doi Bora, Bhetki Macher Paturi, Shukto etc.

89(B). Srinagar is located in the Kashmir Valley and is situated on the banks of the Jhelum River, a tributary of the Indus. The city is famous for its gardens, lakes and houseboats.

90(B). The Rashtrakuta dynasty was founded by Dantidurga (650-670) AD in 650 AD. The last ruler of this dynasty was Karka-II (972-974 AD).E.).

91(A). Akbar's tomb at Sikandra is an excellent example of assimilation of different styles of architecture and it represents a significant departure from the earlier Mughal buildings. The tomb carries the characteristic flavor of the airy tiered pavilions of the Agra Fort and Fatehpur Sikri.

92(D). Chaudhary Rahmat Ali was one of the first supporters to demand Pakistan. On 28 January 1933, the word Pakistan came to the world and the word was given by Chaudhary Rahmat Ali.

93(A). The assertion is correct because plants can synthesize food due to the presence of abiotic components like carbon dioxide and sunlight, due to which energy is produced. This energy is transferred at each trophic level.
The reason is correct because due to energy obtained, organisms at each trophic level sustain.
So, both assertion and reason are correct and the reason is the correct explanation for assertion.

94(B). The national commission on Farmers was set up in 2004.
National Commission on Farmers:
- It was constituted on November 18, 2004, under the chairmanship of Professor M.S. Swaminathan.
- The aim of the commission was to address the nationwide calamity of farmers suicides in India.
- The commission also contained:
- Full-time Members – Ram Badan Singh, Y.C. Nanda
- Part-time Members – R. L. Pitale, Jagadish Pradhan, Chanda Nimbkar (yet to join), Atul Kumar Anjan
- Member Secretary – Atul Sinha
- Based on the studies the NCF submitted four reports in December 2004, August 2005, December 2005 and April 2006.
- The fifth report was submitted in October 2006 it suggested achieving the goal of "faster and more inclusive growth" as envisaged in the Approach to 11th Five Year Plan.

95(C). Uber Cup is awarded for women in the sport of Badminton.
The Uber Cup, sometimes referred to as the Women's World Team Championship, is a major international badminton competition contested by national women's badminton teams from various countries. It was first organized in 1956–1957 at an interval of three years. Then from 1984 it started happening at an interval of every two years.

96(C). Erik Weihenmayer was the first blind man to scale Mt. Everest.
Erik Weihenmayer is an American athlete, adventurer, author, activist, and motivational speaker. He was the first blind person to reach the summit of Mount Everest, on May 25, 2001.
Hence, the correct answer is (C).

97(A). In the green pigment of leaves magnesium is present. Magnesium is needed during photosynthesis for chlorophyll to capture sun energy, i.e., magnesium is required to give green colour to leaves.

98(C). In practice, the work output of a machine is always less than the work input due to the effect of friction.
The work output of a machine is never equal to the work input because some of the work done by the machine is used to overcome the friction created by the use of the machine.
This is the reason why the efficiency of a machine can never be 100%. The efficiency is the work output, divided by the work input, and expressed as a percentage.

99(D). World war II began with the German invasions of Poland.
- German forces under the control of Adolf Hitler bombed Poland on 1st September 1939.
- One week after the Molotov-Ribbentrop Pact was signed between Germany and the Soviet Union, and one day after the Supreme Soviet of the Soviet Union accepted the pact, the German invasion began.
- On 17 September, the Soviet Union invaded Poland.

100(C). Vice-Chairman of the Chennai-based Sanmar Group, Narayanan Kumar has been conferred with the Order of the Rising Sun, Gold and Silver Star by the Govt of Japan in July 2022 .
He has been awarded for his contribution to strengthening economic relations between Japan and India Mr. Kumar is also the Chairman of the Indo-Japan Chamber of Commerce and Industry.

Mathematics

1. The mean of the data: $4, 10, 5, 9, 12$ is:
   (a) 8 (b) 10
   (c) 9 (d) 15

2. The median of the data $13, 15, 16, 17, 19, 20$ is:
   (a) $\frac{30}{2}$ (b) $\frac{31}{2}$
   (c) $\frac{33}{2}$ (d) $\frac{35}{2}$

3. The length, breadth and height of a solid cuboid is $14cm$, $12cm$ and $8cm$ respectively. If cuboid is melted to form identical cubes of side $2cm$, then what will be the number of identical cubes?
   (a) 168 (b) 144
   (c) 156 (d) 128

4. The base of the pyramid is circular whose radius is $14cm$ and the slant height is $20cm$. Find the curved surface area of the cylinder.
   (a) $870cm^2$ (b) $880cm^2$
   (c) $860cm^2$ (d) $850cm^2$

5. Choose the quadratic equation with roots 7 and -1.
   (a) $x^2 - 7x + 6 = 0$
   (b) $x^2 + 8x + 7 = 0$
   (c) $(x + 7)(x - 1) = 0$
   (d) $x^2 - 6x - 7 = 0$

6. The equation $(x + 1)^2 - 2(x + 1) = 0$ has:
   (a) Two real roots
   (b) No real roots
   (c) One real root
   (d) Two equal roots

7. Which of the following is the set of roots of the equation $25n^2 = 9$?
   (a) $\frac{3}{5}, \frac{-3}{5}$ (b) $\frac{3}{5}, \frac{3}{5}$
   (c) $\frac{3}{8}, \frac{-3}{5}$ (d) $\frac{1}{3}, \frac{1}{5}$

8. Find the area of the shaded region in the given figure, if radii of the two concentric circles with center O are 7 cm and 14 cm respectively and $\angle AOC = 40°$.

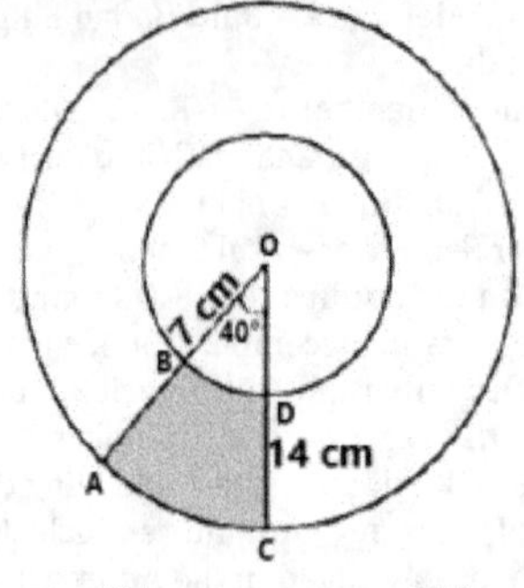

   (a) $\frac{154}{3}$ cm^2 (b) $\frac{144}{3}$ cm^2
   (c) $\frac{134}{3}$ cm^2 (d) $\frac{124}{3}$ cm^2

9. In the given figure, AB and CD are two diameters of a circle (with center O) perpendicular to each other and OD is the diameter of the smaller circle. If $OA = 7$ cm, find the area of the shaded region.

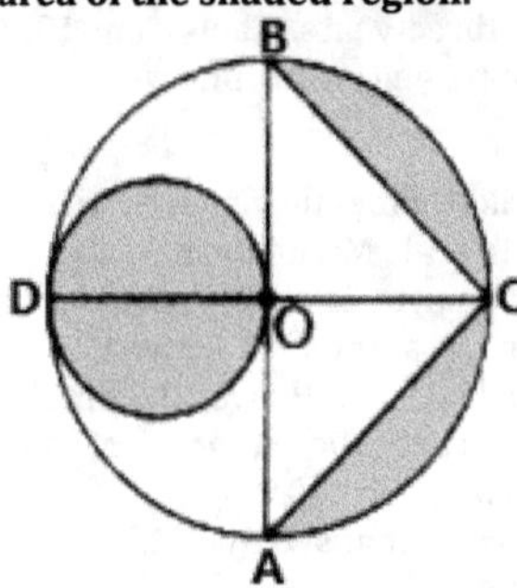

   (a) 66.5 cm^2 (b) 76.5 cm^2
   (c) 86.5 cm^2 (d) 96.5 cm^2

10. Simplify: $\cos 55° \cdot \operatorname{cosec} 35° - 1$
    (a) 2 (b) 1
    (c) -2 (d) 0

11. If
    $\cos(90° - \theta) \cdot \sec\theta \cdot \tan(90° - \theta) \cdot \operatorname{cosec}\theta = x$
    , what is the value of x?
    (a) $\sin\theta$ (b) $\cot\theta$
    (c) $\operatorname{cosec}\theta$ (d) $\tan\theta$

12. What is the value of $\frac{\cos 0° \cdot \sin 25° \cdot \sec 85° \cdot \tan 45°}{\operatorname{cosec} 5° \cdot \cos 65° \cdot \sin 90°}$?
    (a) 0
    (b) $\sin^2 25° \cdot \sec^2 85°$
    (c) 1
    (d) $\sin^2 25° \cdot \cos^2 85°$

13. The ages of two friends Ani and Biju differ by 3 years. Ani's father Dharam is twice as old as Ani and Biju is twice as old as his sister Cathy. The ages of Cathy and Dharam differ by 30 years. Find the ages of Ani and Biju respectively.
    (a) Age of Ani $= 19$ years and age of Biju $= 16$ years.
    (b) Age of Ani $= 16$ years and age of Biju $= 15$ years.
    (c) Age of Ani $= 21$ years and age of Biju $= 16$ years.
    (d) Age of Ani $= 18$ years and age of Biju $= 12$ years.

14. If $2x + y = 23$ and $4x - y = 19$, find the values of $5y - 2x$.
    (a) 31 (b) 22
    (c) 65 (d) 10

15. Using Euclid's division algorithm, find the HCF of 56, 96 and 404.
    (a) 4 (b) 5
    (c) 6 (d) 7

16. The length, breadth, and height of a room are 8 m 50 cm, 6 m 25 cm and 4 m 75 cm respectively. Find the length of the longest rod that can measure the dimensions of the room exactly:
    (a) 25 cm (b) 24 cm
    (c) 22 cm (d) 20 cm

17. A bag contains 4 blue and 12 red balls. One ball is drawn at random. What is the probability that the ball drawn is red?
    (a) $\frac{1}{4}$ (b) $\frac{3}{4}$
    (c) $\frac{1}{8}$ (d) $\frac{3}{7}$

18. In a simultaneous throw of two coins, the probability of getting at least one head is:
    (a) $\frac{1}{2}$ (b) $\frac{1}{3}$
    (c) $\frac{2}{3}$ (d) $\frac{3}{4}$

19. If α, β are real and $\alpha^2, -\beta^2$ are the roots of $a^2 x^2 + x + 1 - a^2 = 0; (a > 1)$, then $\beta^2 = ?$
    (a) a^2 (b) 1
    (c) $1 - a^2$ (d) $1 + a^2$

20. If the roots of the given equation $2x^2 + 3(\lambda - 2)x + \lambda + 4 = 0$ be equal in magnitude but opposite in sign, then value of λ is:
    (a) 1 (b) 2
    (c) 3 (d) $\frac{2}{3}$

21. If the roots of $x^2 - bx + c = 0$ are each decreased by 2, then resulting equation is $x^2 - 2x + 1 = 0$, if and only if:
    (a) $b = 6, c = 9$

(b) $b = 3, c = 5$
(c) $b = 2, c = 1$
(d) $b = -4, c = 3$

22. If α, β be the zeros of the quadratic polynomial $2x^2 + 5x + 1$, then the value of $\alpha + \beta + \alpha\beta =$
(a) -2
(b) -1
(c) 1
(d) None of these

23. An AP consists of 37 terms. The sum of the three middle most terms is 225 and the sum of the last three terms is 429. Find the the sum of all the 37 terms.
(a) 2775 (b) 2875
(c) 3775 (d) 4775

24. Find the:
Sum of those integers from 1 to 500 which are multiples of 2 as well as 5
.
(a) 12750 (b) 13750
(c) 14750 (d) 15750

25. From a point P which is at a distance of 13 cm from centre O of a circle of radius 5 cm , in the same plane, a pair of tangents PQ and PR are drawn to the circle. Area of quadrilateral $PQOR$ is:
(a) $65 \, \text{cm}^2$ (b) $60 \, \text{cm}^2$
(c) $30 \, \text{cm}^2$ (d) $90 \, \text{cm}^2$

26. In the given figure, AB and AC are tangents to the circle with centre O such that $\angle BAC = 40°$, then $\angle BOC$ is equal to:

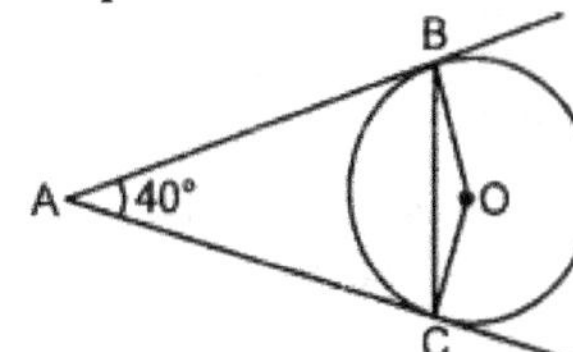

(a) $50°$ (b) $85°$
(c) $140°$ (d) $155°$

27. The length of the tangent from an external point P on a circle with centre O is:
(a) Always greater than OP
(b) Equal to OP
(c) Always less than OP
(d) Cannot be estimated

28. In the given figure $XY \| BC$. If $AX = 3$ cm, $XB = 1.5$ cm and $BC = 6$ cm , then XY is equal to:

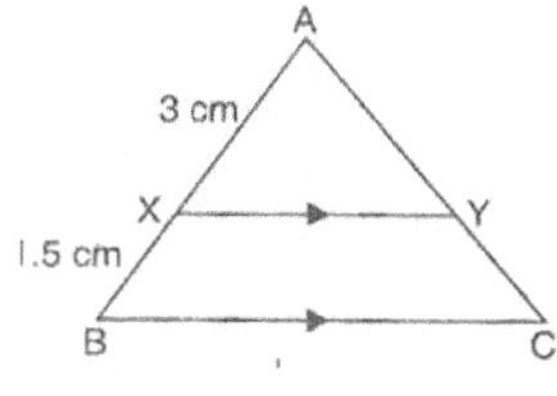

(a) $4 \, cm$ (b) $3 \, cm$
(c) $6 \, cm$ (d) $4.5 \, cm$

29. In the adjoining figure P and Q are points on the sides AB and AC respectively of $\triangle ABC$ such that $AP = 3.5$ cm, $PB = 7$ cm, $AQ = 3$ cm, $QC = 6$ cm and $PQ = 4.5$ cm . The measure of BC is equal to:

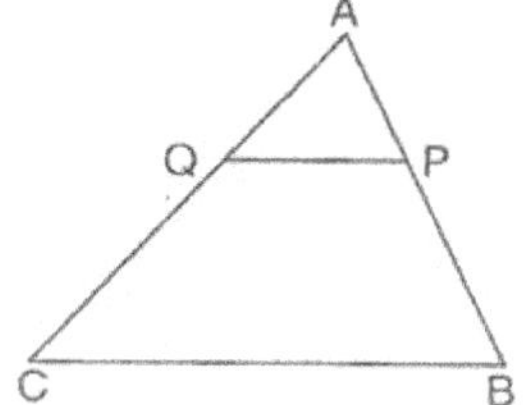

(a) $9 \, cm$ (b) $12.5 \, cm$
(c) $15 \, cm$ (d) $13.5 \, cm$

30. If ABC is an equilateral triangle with side $12 \, cm$ and AD is the median. Find the length of DG if G is the centroid of $\triangle ABC$.
(a) $6\sqrt{3}$ (b) $4\sqrt{3}$
(c) $3\sqrt{3}$ (d) $2\sqrt{3}$

Science

31. ________belongs to the category of primary consumers.
(a) Snakes
(b) Cattle
(c) Eagle
(d) None of these

32. Which of the following organisms can synthesise their food by the process of photosynthesis?
(a) Algae
(b) Fungi
(c) Viruses
(d) Zooplanktons

33. Which of the following can undergo a chemical reaction?
(a) $MgSO_4 + Fe$ (b) $ZnSO_4 + Fe$
(c) $MgSO_4 + Pb$ (d) $CuSO_4 + Fe$

34. During electrolytic refining of zinc, pure zinc gets:
(a) deposited at cathode
(b) deposited at anode
(c) deposited at cathode as well at anode
(d) remains in the solution

35. The growth of tendrils in pea plants is due to ________.
(a) effect of light
(b) effect of gravity
(c) rapid cell division in tendrilled cells in contact with the support
(d) rapid cell divisions in tendrilled cells that are away from the support

36. Name the hormone responsible for ripening of fruits.
(a) Ethylene
(b) Abscisic acid
(c) Auxin
(d) None of these

37. The odour of SO_2 gas is:
(a) Odourless
(b) Foul-smelling
(c) Pungent
(d) Sweet smelling

38. Which of the following solution is obtained by reacting zinc metal with $NaOH$ solution?
(a) Na_2ZnO_2 (b) Na_32NO_3
(c) $2NO$ (d) $Zn(OH)_2$

39. The gas used in the hydrogenation of oils in presence of nickel as a catalyst is:
(a) Methane (b) Ethane
(c) Oxygen (d) Hydrogen

40. When ethanol react with sodium, which gas will produce?
(a) Hydrogen
(b) Oxygen
(c) Sodium ethoxide
(d) Carbon dioxide

41. The mode of reproduction that depends on the involvement of two individuals to create a new generation is called:
(a) Sexual reproduction
(b) Asexual reproduction
(c) Budding
(d) None of the above

42. The primary sex organ found in human males is:
(a) Ovary
(b) Testis
(c) Urethra
(d) None of the above

43. Name the organ analogous to the wings of birds.
(a) Forelimb of human

(b) Fore-leg of horse

(c) Wings of insect

(d) None of these

44. What are the carriers of factor?

(a) Alleles

(b) Chromosomes

(c) DNA

(d) None of these

45. According to snell's law, $n_{21} \times n_{12} =$?

(a) 0.0   (b) 1.0

(c) 2.0   (d) 12.12

46. An object, 4.0 cm in size, is placed at 25.0 cm in front of a concave mirror of focal length 15.0 cm . At what distance from the mirror should a screen be placed in order to obtain a sharp image?

(a) 34.5 cm   (b) 35.5 cm

(c) 37.5 cm   (d) 33.5 cm

47. The force on a current-carrying conductor when placed perpendicular in a uniform magnetic field.

(a) $F = BIL$

(b) $\dfrac{B}{IL}$

(c) $\dfrac{L}{BI}$

(d) None of the above

48. Breathing is a _________ process.

(a) chemical   (b) mechanical

(c) physical   (d) biochemical

49. Energy released during respiration is stored in the form of:

(a) ATP   (b) NADP

(c) ADP   (d) FAD

50. Acids are stored in containers made of:

(a) Plastic

(b) Glass

(c) Both (A) and (B)

(d) None of the above

51. Which of the following signs is usually printed on containers of acids or bases to warn people about the dangerous corrosive nature of acid or base?

(a) A hazard warning sign

(b) A bird sign

(c) A lion sign

(d) None of the above

52. When do we say a person is colour blind?

(a) When person cannot see in the dark

(b) When person cannot see in the light

(c) When person cannot differentiate between colours

(d) All of these

53. If $500\,\Omega$ of resistance is made by adding five $100\,\Omega$ resistance of tolerance 4%, then the tolerance of the combination is:

(a) 5%   (b) 4%

(c) 20%   (d) 10%

54. Two $5.0\,\Omega$ resistors are connected as shown in the diagram.

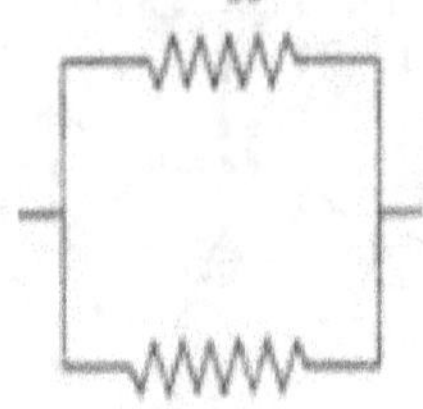

What is the total resistance of the combination?

(a) less than $5.0\,\Omega$

(b) $5.0\,\Omega$

(c) more than $5.0\,\Omega$

(d) $10.0\,\Omega$

55. The current flowing through a lamp marked as $50\,W$ and $250\,V$ is:

(a) $5\,A$ (b) $2.5\,A$

(c) $2\,A$ (d) $0.2\,A$

Social Science

56. The uses of multi-purpose projects is _________.

(a) Rain water harvesting

(b) Scenic beauty

(c) Electricity generation

(d) All of the above

57. The biological loss is strongly correlated with the loss of______.

(a) Agricultural production

(b) Industrial production

(c) Cultural diversity

(d) Loss of resources

58. Which one of the following is not true regarding the importance of manufacturing industries?

(a) They generate jobs in the secondary and tertiary sectors

(b) Export of manufactured goods brings in foreign exchange

(c) Manufacturing industries encourage trade and commerce

(d) The economic strength of a country is measured in terms of the raw material it possesses

59. How do big private companies contribute in the development of a nation?

(a) By increasing the demands for their products through advertisements.

(b) By increasing their profits.

(c) By increasing productivity of the country in the manufacturing of industrial goods.

(d) By providing private hospital facilities for the rich.

60. According to Human Development Report 2020 which of the following neighbouring countries has better performance in terms of human development than India?

(a) Bangladesh   (b) Sri Lanka

(c) Nepal   (d) Pakistan

61. When did the Treaty of Vienna take place and who were the participants?

(a) 1816, Britain, Russia, Prussia

(b) 1815, Britain, Russia, Prussia, Austria

(c) 1820, Britain and Russia

(d) 1817, Russia, Prussia, Austria

62. Which of the following is the staple food crop of the majority of Indian people?

(a) Maize   (b) Jowar

(c) Rice   (d) Wheat

63. In which year was the RBI nationalised?

(a) 1971   (b) 1956

(c) 1949   (d) 1935

64. Which of the following is not a formal source of credit?

(a) Banks

(b) Cooperative

(c) Employer

(d) All of the above

65. Goods are placed in________that can be loaded intact onto ships, railways, planes and trucks.

(a) Vessels   (b) Containers

(c) Receptacles   (d) Tanks

66. What are disadvantages of Globalisation?

(a) Causes job displacement

(b) Exploits cheaper labor markets

(c) Increases potential global recessions

(d) All of the above

67. How many consumer groups are there in the country?
(a) Over 700   (b) Over 900
(c) Over 800   (d) Over 1000

68. Why is it that rules have been made so that the manufacturer displays information?
(a) Consumers need to know
(b) For the convenience of the consumer
(c) To protect the producer
(d) Consumers have the right to be informed

69. When did the first printed edition of the Ramcharitmanas of Tulsidas, a sixteenth-century text, come out?
(a) 1810   (b) 1910
(c) 1815   (d) 1812

70. What was the Vernacular Press Act of 1878 about?
(a) No rights for Indians to write
(b) It provided the government with extensive rights to censor reports and editorials in the vernacular press
(c) Indian writers to be banished
(d) Only English writings to be published

71. Power can be shared in modern democracies _____.
(a) Among different organs of government
(b) Among governments at different levels
(c) Among different social groups
(d) All of the above

72. When did the Civil War of Sri Lanka end?
(a) 2010   (b) 2009
(c) 2005   (d) 2011

73. In which of the following years Rinderpest arrived in Africa?
(a) 1880   (b) 1882
(c) 1876   (d) 1885

74. The State created on the basis of culture, ethnicity or geography, out of the following is _________.
(a) Manipur   (b) Nagaland
(c) Tripura   (d) Mizoram

75. Which among the following is an example of the Unitary system of Government?
(a) Belgium
(b) Sri Lanka
(c) Both (A) and (B)
(d) None of these

76. Before the age of the machine industry, where did the finer varieties of silk and cotton goods come from?
(a) Egypt   (b) India
(c) Persia   (d) Rome

77. Which one of the following is the main cause of land degradation in Punjab?
(a) Intensive cultivation
(b) Deforestation
(c) Over-irrigation
(d) Overgrazing

78. 'Equal treatment of women' is a necessary ingredient of a democratic society. This means that:
(a) Women are actually always treated with respect
(b) It is now easier for women to legally wage struggle for their rights
(c) Most societies across the world are now increasingly women dominated
(d) None of the above

79. Democracy is seen to be good in principle:
(a) But felt to be not so good in its practice
(b) But wide in practice
(c) And much better in practice
(d) None of the above

80. Why did the Non-Cooperation movement slow down?
(a) Lack of unity amongst the people
(b) The British overpowered it
(c) Handmade Indian goods like Khadi worked out more expensive and time-consuming than mill-made goods
(d) People did not give up on foreign goods

General Awareness/ Knowledge

81. Aryabhata was a famous-
(a) Doctor   (b) Painter
(c) Astronomer   (d) Scientist

82. Article 19 of the Indian Constitution includes which rights?
(a) Right to constitutional remedies
(b) Right to freedom of speech and expression
(c) Right against exploitation
(d) Right to freedom of religion

83. Which of the following Indian companies had become one of the top three most-valuable brands in the information technology (IT) service sector of the world?
(a) Wipro
(b) Infosys
(c) HCL Technologies
(d) Tata Consultancy services

84. In which case did the Supreme Court rule that protection under Article 21 is available only against arbitrary executive action and not from arbitrary legislative action?
(a) Maneka Gandhi case
(b) First Judges case
(c) Kesavananda Bharati Case
(d) A. K. Gopalan case

85. Consider the following pairs:

Hills	State
1. Lushai Hills	Mizoram
2. Erramalla Hills	Kerala
3. Javadi Hills	Tamil Nadu
4. Satmala Hills	Madhya Pradesh

Which of the pairs given above are correctly matched?
(a) 1 and 2   (b) 3 and 4
(c) 1 and 3   (d) 2 and 4

86. What is the name of the new commercial arm of ISRO?
(a) NSIL   (b) VSSC
(c) DRDO   (d) SDSC

87. The old name of which of the following states/union territories is wrongly given?
(a) Karnataka - Mysore
(b) Tamil Nadu - Madras
(c) Lakshadweep - Laccadive, Minicoy and Amindivi Islands
(d) Meghalaya - Eastern Hill Province

88. Which of the following is correctly matched?
Nautanki: Uttar Pradesh
Tamasha: Maharashtra
Bhavai: Gujarat
(a) 1 and 2
(b) 2 and 3
(c) 1 and 3
(d) All of the above

89. Which of the following place is not connected by National Highway No. 15?
(a) Jaisalmer
(b) Barmer

(c) Hanumangarh

(d) Bikaner

90. After the death of King Ashoka the _____ declined rapidly.

(a) Maurya Dynasty

(b) Chola Dynasty

(c) Chalukya Dynasty

(d) Gupta Dynasty

91. Tulsidas wrote Ramcharitmanas in the reign of:

(a) Babar   (b) Akbar

(c) Aurangzeb   (d) Jahangir

92. After the battle of Buxar the East India Company agreed to pay _____ every year to the Mughal Emperor.

(a) Rs. 82 lakh   (b) Rs. 26 lakh

(c) Rs. 44 lakh   (d) Rs. 68 lakh

93. Sustainable development can be achieved by:

(a) Judicious use of natural resources

(b) Misuse of natural resources

(c) Recovery of natural resources

(d) Not using the natural resources

94. Britishers established Fort St. George as a trading outpost of East India Company in:

(a) Varanasi   (b) Chandigarh

(c) Chennai   (d) Jaipur

95. Who is the first Indian woman cricketer to hit a century in T20 International cricket by scoring 103 runs in 51 balls?

(a) Anjali Bhagwat

(b) Harmanpreet Kaur

(c) Anju Bobby George

(d) Anuradha Biswal

96. Who was the first women prime minister of India?

(a) Mrs. Unnnati Sharma

(b) Mrs. Indira Gandhi

(c) Sarojini Naidu

(d) Rekha Saini

97. Which one of the following is NOT decomposed by bacterial action?

(a) Vegetable remains

(b) Plastic materials

(c) Animal carcasses

(d) Wastes of flowers

98. _____ are the connective tissue that connects two bones to each other.

(a) Tendons   (b) Muscles

(c) Cartilages   (d) Ligaments

99. The Soviet Union broke down in the year _____.

(a) 1991   (b) 1880

(c) 2000   (d) 1900

100. Which movie has won the Best Feature Film award at the $68th$ National Film Awards announced in July 2022 ?

(a) Tanhaji

(b) KGF Chapter-1

(c) Badhaai Do

(d) Soorarai Pottru

// Hints and Solutions //

1(A). Mean
$$= \frac{(4+10+5+9+12)}{5} = \frac{40}{5} = 8$$

2(C). For the given data, there are two middle terms, 16 and 17.

So, median $= \frac{(16+17)}{2} = \frac{33}{2}$

3(A). Given,

Length of cuboid $(l) = 14cm$

Breadth of cuboid $(b) = 12cm$

Height of cuboid $(h) = 8cm$

Side of cube $(a) = 2cm$

After melting and reformation volume remains same.

As we know,

Volume of cuboid $= l \times b \times h$

Volume of cube $= (\text{side})^3$

Number of cubes $= \dfrac{\text{Volume of cuboid}}{\text{Volume of cube}}$

$\therefore$ Number of cubes $= \dfrac{(14 \times 12 \times 8)}{(2 \times 2 \times 2)}$

$= 7 \times 6 \times 4$

$= 168$

4(B). Given,

Radius $(r) = 14cm$

Slant height $(l) = 20cm$

As we know,

Perimeter of Base $= 2\pi r$

The curved surface area of cylinder $= \frac{1}{2} \times$ Perimeter of Base $\times$ Slant height

$\therefore$ The curved surface area of cylinder

$= \frac{1}{2} \times 2\pi r \times 20$

$= \frac{22}{7} \times 14 \times 20$

$= 22 \times 40$

$= 880 cm^2$

$\therefore$ The curved surface area of the cylinder is $880 cm^2$.

5(D). To find the quadratic equation that has roots 7 and -1 we will put one of the values in the equations.

If the equations will be equal to zero then that equation has roots 7 and -1.

(A). $x^2 - 7x + 6 = 0$

first, we will put $x = 7$

$(7)^2 - 7 \times 7 + 6 = 0$

$49 - 49 + 6 = 0$

$6 = 0$

So, we get that it is not equal to zero.

$\therefore$ this equation can't have roots 7 and -1.

Similarly, we will put the values 7 and -1 in other equations and see which one gets to zero.

Options B and C don't satisfy as the equation is not equal to zero.

Whereas if we put the value of $x = 7$ in the equation:

$x^2 - 6x - 7 = 0$

we get,

$(7)^2 - 6(7) - 7 = 0$

$49 - 42 - 7 = 0$

$7 - 7 = 0$

Now we will put $x = -1$

$x^2 - 6x - 7 = 0$

$(-1)^2 - 6(-1) - 7 = 0$

$1 + 6 - 7$

$7 - 7 = 0$

Therefore, we can say that this equation has roots 7 and -1.

6(A). Given equation is:

$(x + 1)^2 - 2(x + 1) = 0$

$\Rightarrow x^2 + 1 + 2x - 2x - 2 = 0$

$\Rightarrow x^2 - 1 = 0$

$\Rightarrow x^2 = 1$

$\Rightarrow x = \pm 1$

The x has two values $+1$ and -1. So the equation $(x + 1)^2 - 2(x + 1) = 0$ has two real roots.

7(A). The given equation is:

$25n^2 = 9$

$\Rightarrow 25n^2 - 9 = 0$

$\Rightarrow (5n)^2 - (3)^2 = 0$

We know that, $(a)^2 - (b)^2 = (a + b)(a - b)$

$\Rightarrow (5n - 3)(5n + 3) = 0$

$\Rightarrow (5n - 3) = 0$ or $(5n + 3) = 0$

$\Rightarrow n = \frac{3}{5}, \frac{-3}{5}$

So the set of roots of the equation $25n^2 = 9$ is $\frac{3}{5}, \frac{-3}{5}$.

8(A).

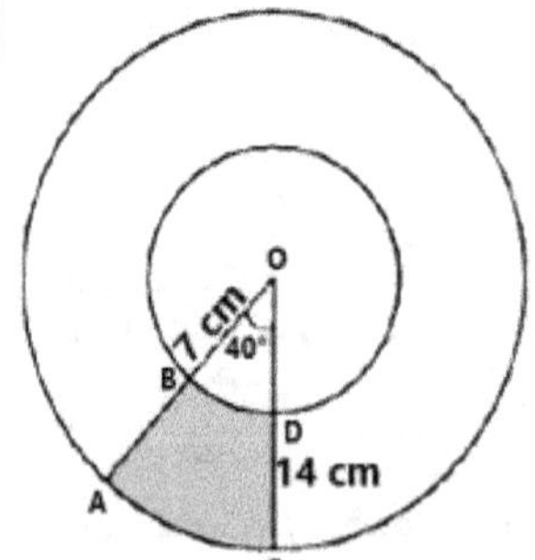

Given,

Radius of inner circle $= 7$ cm

Radius of outer circle $= 14$ cm

Angle subtended is $40°$

Now,

Area of shaded region $=$ Area of sector $AOC -$ Area of sector BOD

Area of sector $= \frac{\theta}{360°} \times \pi r^2$

$= \frac{40°}{360°} \times \pi(14)^2 - \frac{40°}{360°} \times \pi(7)^2$

$= \frac{40°}{360°} \times \frac{22}{7} \times (14)^2 - \frac{40°}{360°} \times \frac{22}{7} \times (7)^2$

$= \dfrac{616}{9} - \dfrac{154}{9}$

$= \dfrac{462}{9}$ cm ^{2}

$= \dfrac{154}{3}$ cm ^{2}

Therefore, the area of the shaded region in the given figure is $\dfrac{154}{3}$ cm ^{2}.

9(A).

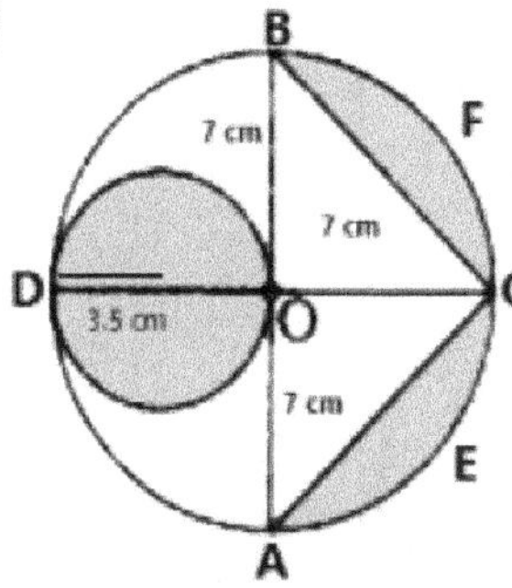

Given,

Radius of larger circle $= r_1 = 7$ cm

Radius of smaller circle $= r_2 = \dfrac{7}{2}$ cm

For area of shaded region,

Area of smaller circle $= \pi r_2^2$

$= \dfrac{22}{7} \times \left(\dfrac{7}{2}\right)^2$

$= \dfrac{77}{2}$ cm ^{2}

Area of semi-circle $AECFB$ of larger circle

$= \dfrac{1}{2} \pi r_1^2$

$= \dfrac{1}{2} \times \dfrac{22}{7} \times (7)^2$

$= 77$ cm ^{2}

Area of $\triangle ABC = \dfrac{1}{2} \times AB \times OC$

$= \dfrac{1}{2} \times 14 \times 7$

$= 49$ cm ^{2}

Area of the shaded region = Area of smaller circle + Area of semi-circle $AECFB$ − Area of $\triangle ABC$

$= \dfrac{77}{2} + 77 - 49$

$= 28 + 38.5 = 66.5$ cm ^{2}

Therefore, the area of shaded region is 66.5 cm ^{2}.

10(D). Given:

$\cos 55° \cdot \operatorname{cosec} 35° - 1$

Now,

$\Rightarrow \cos(90° - 35°) \cdot \operatorname{cosec} 35° - 1$

$\Rightarrow \sin 35° \cdot \dfrac{1}{\sin 35°} - 1$

$\Rightarrow 1 - 1$

$\Rightarrow 0$

11(C). Given:

$\cos(90° - \theta) \cdot \sec \theta \cdot \tan(90° - \theta) \cdot \operatorname{cosec} \theta = x$

By applying properties of trigonometry we get,

$\sin\theta \cdot \dfrac{1}{\cos\theta} \cdot \cot\theta \cdot \dfrac{1}{\sin\theta} - x$

$\Rightarrow \dfrac{\cot\theta}{\cos\theta} = \dfrac{\frac{1}{\tan\theta}}{\cos\theta}$

$\Rightarrow \dfrac{\frac{1}{\frac{\sin\theta}{\cos\theta}}}{\cos\theta} = \dfrac{\frac{\cos\theta}{\sin\theta}}{\cos\theta}$

$\Rightarrow \dfrac{\cos\theta}{\cos\theta \times \sin\theta} = \dfrac{1}{\sin\theta}$

$\Rightarrow \operatorname{cosec}\theta$

12(B). Given:

$\cos 0° \cdot \sin 25° \cdot \sec 85° \cdot \tan 45° \cdot \operatorname{cosec} 5° \cdot \cos 65° \cdot \sin 90°$

Now,

$\Rightarrow \cos 0° \cdot \sin 25° \cdot \sec 85° \cdot \tan 45° \operatorname{cosec}(90° - 85°) \cdot \cos(90° - 25°) \cdot \sin(90° - 90°)$

$\Rightarrow \cos 0° \cdot \sin 25° \cdot \sec 85° \cdot \tan 45° \cdot \sec 85° \cdot \sin 25° \cdot \cos 0°$

$\Rightarrow 1 \cdot \sin 25° \cdot \sin 25° \cdot \sec 85° \cdot \sec 85° \cdot 1 \cdot 1$

$\Rightarrow \sin^2 25° \cdot \sec^2 85°$

13(A). Let the age of Ani and Biju be x and y respectively.

Then according to the question

$x - y = 3 \ldots\ldots\ldots$ (i)

Dharam is twice the age of Ani

Hence, age of Dharam $= 2x$

Age of Cathy is half the age of Biju

Then age of Cathy $= \dfrac{y}{2}$

Then according to the question

$2x - \dfrac{y}{2} = 30$

$\Rightarrow 4x - y = 60 \ldots..$ (ii)

Subtracting (ii) from (i)

$\Rightarrow x - y - 4x + y = 3 - 60$

$\Rightarrow -3x = -57$

$\Rightarrow x = \dfrac{-57}{-3} = 19$

Substitute the vale of x in (i)

$\Rightarrow 19 - y = 3$

$\Rightarrow -y = -16$

$\Rightarrow y = 16$

$\therefore$ Age of Ani $= 19$ years and age of Biju $= 16$ years.

14(A). The given equations are

$2x + y = 23 \quad \ldots$ (i)

$4x - y = 19 \quad \ldots$ (ii)

On adding (i) and (ii), we get

$6x = 42 \Rightarrow x = 7$

On putting $x = 7$ in (i), we get

$14 + y = 23 \Rightarrow y = 9$

Now,

$5y - 2x = 5 \times 9 - 2 \times 7 = 31$

15(A). Using Euclid's division algorithm,

$96 = 56 \times 1 + 40$

$56 = 40 \times 1 + 16$

$40 = 16 \times 2 + 8$

$16 = 8 \times 2 + 0$

H.C.F of $(56, 96) = 8$

$404 = 8 \times 50 + 4$

$8 = 4 \times 2 + 0$

$\therefore$ H.C.F of $(56, 96, 404) = 4$

16(A). To find the length of the longest rod that can measure the dimensions of the room exactly, we have to find HCF.

L , Length $= 8$ m 50 cm $= 850$ cm $= 2^1 \times 5^2 \times 17$

B , Breadth $= 6$ m 25 cm $= 625$ cm $= 5^4$

H , Height $= 4$ m 75 cm $= 475$ cm $= 5^2 \times 19$

HCF of L, B and H is $5^2 = 25$ cm

Length of the longest rod $= 25$ cm

17(B). Total number of balls $n(S) = (12 + 4)$

$\Rightarrow 16$

Number of red balls $n(A) = 12$

P (drawing a red ball) $= \dfrac{n(A)}{n(S)}$

$= \dfrac{12}{16} = \dfrac{3}{4}$

18(D). Here $S = \{HH, HT, TH, TT\}$

Let $E =$ event of getting at least one head $= \{HT, TH, HH\}$

$\therefore P(E) = \dfrac{n(E)}{n(S)} = \dfrac{3}{4}$

19(B). $\alpha^2, -\beta^2$ are the roots of $a^2 x^2 + x + 1 - a^2 = 0$

$\Rightarrow \alpha^2 - \beta^2 = -\dfrac{1}{a^2}$,

And

$\Rightarrow \alpha^2(-\beta^2) = \dfrac{1 - a^2}{a^2}$

$(\alpha^2 + \beta^2)^2 = (\alpha^2 - \beta^2)^2 + 4\alpha^2\beta^2$

$= \dfrac{1}{a^4} + 4\left(\dfrac{a^2 - 1}{a^2}\right) = \dfrac{1}{a^4} + 4 - \dfrac{4}{a^2}$

$= \left(2 - \dfrac{1}{a^2}\right)^2 \Rightarrow \alpha^2 + \beta^2 = 2 - \dfrac{1}{a^2}$

$\beta^2 = \dfrac{1}{2}\left[(\alpha^2 + \beta^2) - (\alpha^2 - \beta^2)\right]$

$= \dfrac{1}{2}\left[2 - \dfrac{1}{a^2} + \dfrac{1}{a^2}\right] = 1$

20(B). Given equation is $2x^2 + 3(\lambda - 2)x + \lambda + 4 = 0$

We know that equation $ax^2 + bx + c = 0$

Then sum of roots $= \dfrac{-b}{a}$

Let α, β be the roots of the given equation

$\therefore \alpha + \beta = -\dfrac{3(\lambda - 2)}{2}$

But it is given that

$\alpha = -\beta$

Therefore, $-\beta + \beta = -\dfrac{3(\lambda - 2)}{2}$

$0 = -\dfrac{3(\lambda - 2)}{2}$

$0 \times 2 = -3(\lambda - 2)$

$\dfrac{0}{-3} = (\lambda - 2)$

$0 = (\lambda - 2)$

$\lambda - 2 = 0$

$\therefore \lambda = 2$

21(A). We know that equation $ax^2 + bx + c = 0$

Then sum of roots $= \dfrac{-b}{a}$ and product of roots $= \dfrac{c}{a}$

For the given equation,

Let the roots be α and β

$\alpha + \beta = b$ and $\alpha\beta = c \quad \ldots$ (i)

As per the given condition,

$(\alpha - 2 + \beta - 2) = 2 \quad \ldots$ (ii)

$\therefore \alpha + \beta = 6$

$\therefore b = 6 \quad \ldots$ from (i) & (ii)

Also, $(\alpha - 2)(\beta - 2) = 1 \quad \ldots$(iii)

$\therefore \alpha\beta - 2(\alpha + \beta) + 4 = 1$

$\therefore c - 2(6) = -3$

$\therefore c = 9$

22(A). We know that equation $ax^2 + bx + c = 0$

Then sum of roots $= \dfrac{-b}{a}$ and product of roots $= \dfrac{c}{a}$

Let α, β are the zeros of the quadratic equation.

Therefore,

$\alpha + \beta = -\frac{5}{2}$ and $\alpha\beta = \frac{1}{2}$

Now,

$\alpha + \beta + \alpha\beta = -\frac{5}{2} + \frac{1}{2}$

$= \frac{-4}{2}$

23(A). Let a be the first term and d be the common difference of the AP.

As the AP has 37 terms, so the three middle most terms are a_{18}, a_{19}, a_{20} and the last three terms are a_{35}, a_{36}, a_{37}

Given,

$a_{18} + a_{19} + a_{20} = 225$

$T_n = a + (n-1)d$

$a = $ first term

$d = $ common difference

$T_n = n^{\text{th}}$ term

$\Rightarrow (a + 17d) + (a + 18d) + (a + 19d) = 225$

$\Rightarrow 3a + 54d = 225 \Rightarrow a + 18d = 75 \quad \dots \dots (i)$

and $a_{35} + a_{36} + a_{37} = 429$

$\Rightarrow (a + 34d) + (a + 35d) + (a + 36d) = 429$

$\Rightarrow 3a + 105d = 429 \Rightarrow a + 35d = 143 \quad \dots \dots (ii)$

Subtracting (i) from (ii), we get

$17d = 68 \Rightarrow d = 4$

Substituting $d = 4$ in (i), we get

$a + 18 \times 4 = 75 \Rightarrow a = 3$

$\therefore$ The AP is $3, 7, 11, 15, \dots$

Sum of all the 37 terms

$S_n = \frac{n}{2}[2a + (n-1)d]$

$a = $ first term

$d = $ common difference

$S_n = $ Sum of nth term

$= \frac{37}{2}(2a + 36d) = 37(a + 18d)$

$= 37(3 + 18 \times 4) = 37 \times 75 = 2775$

24(A). The integers from 1 to 500 which are multiples of 2 as well as 5 are $10, 20, 30, \dots, 500$

These numbers form an AP with $a = 10, l = 500$ and $n = 50$

$S_n = \frac{n}{2}(a + l)$

$a = $ first term

$l = $ last term

$S_n = $ Sum of nth term

$\therefore$ Sum of these numbers $= \frac{50}{2}(10 + 500) = 25 \times 510 = 12750$.

25(B). According to the information given in the question, the diagram is as:

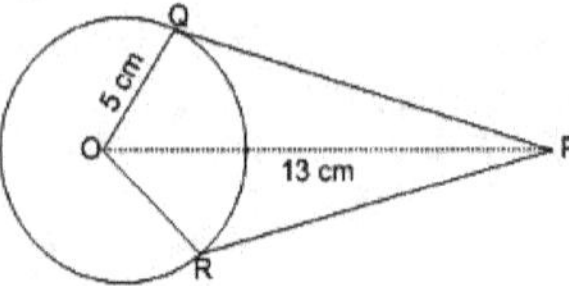

$\angle OQP = \angle ORP = 90°$ (Angle at point of contact of tangent)

Now,

In $\triangle OQP$,

$\Rightarrow QP = \sqrt{OP^2 - OQ^2}$

$\Rightarrow QP = \sqrt{(13)^2 - (5)^2}$

$\Rightarrow QP = \sqrt{169 - 25}$

$\Rightarrow QP = \sqrt{144}$

$\Rightarrow QP = 12$ cm

$\therefore$ Area of $\triangle OQP = \frac{1}{2} \times 12 \times 5$

$= 30$ cm^2

$\therefore$ Area of $PQOR = 2 \times 30$

$= 60$ cm^2

26(C). As we know that,

Tangent is perpendicular to the radius at point of contact.

So, $\angle ABO = \angle ACO = 90°$

In a quadrilateral, the sum of the angles is $360°$.

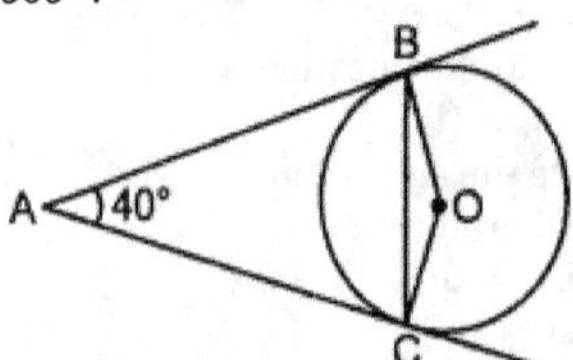

$\Rightarrow \angle BAC + \angle BOC + \angle ABO + \angle ACO = 360°$

$\Rightarrow 90° + \angle BOC + 90° + 40° = 360°$

$\Rightarrow \angle BOC + 220° = 360°$

$\Rightarrow \angle BOC = 360° - 220°$

$\therefore \angle BOC = 140°$

27(C). According to the information given in the question, the diagram is as:

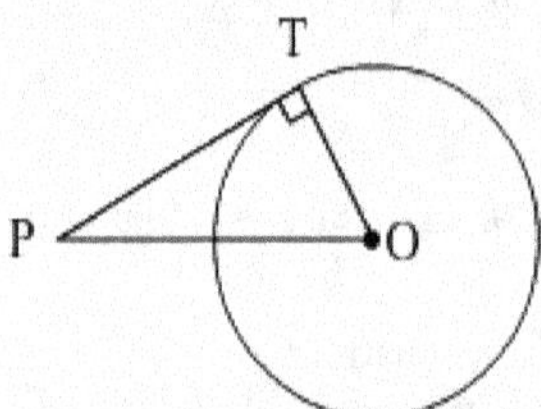

PT is a tangent drawn from an external point P on the circle with centre O.

$\angle OTP = 90°$ (Radius is perpendicular to the tangent at the point of contact)

So, $\triangle OPT$ is a right triangle. OP is the hypotenuse of the right $\triangle OPT$.

$\therefore$ OP > PT (In a right triangle, hypotenuse is the longest side).

Or, PT < OP

Thus, the length of the tangent from an external point P on the circle with centre O is always less than the hypotenuse OP.

28(A). Since $XY \| BC$, then using Thales theorem,

$\Rightarrow \frac{AX}{AB} = \frac{XY}{BC}$

$\Rightarrow \frac{3}{4.5} = \frac{XY}{6}$

$\Rightarrow XY = 4$ cm

29(D). In $\triangle ABC$

$\Rightarrow \frac{AQ}{QC} = \frac{AP}{PB} \Rightarrow \frac{3}{6} = \frac{3.5}{7} \Rightarrow \frac{1}{2}$

since $\frac{AQ}{QC} = \frac{AP}{PB}$

therefore, $QP \| BC$

$\therefore \frac{AQ}{AC} = \frac{QP}{BC}$

$\Rightarrow \frac{3}{9} = \frac{4.5}{BC}$

$\Rightarrow BC = 13.5$ cm

30(D). Given:

ABC is an equilateral triangle.

$AB = BC = CA = 12\, cm$

AD is the median of $\triangle ABC$

We know that,

The point at which three medians of a triangle intersect is called the centroid of the triangle.

The centroid of a triangle divides medians in the ratio of $2 : 1$.

In an equilateral triangle median and perpendicular bisector of the triangle coincide with each other.

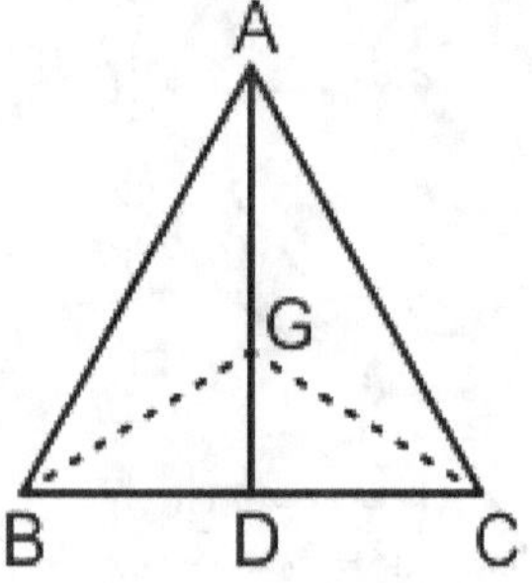

According to the question,

$\triangle ABC$ is an equilateral triangle.

So, AD is a perpendicular bisector of $\triangle ABC$.

So, $BD = CD = \frac{BC}{2}$ and $\angle ADB = 90°$

Now, according to the Pythagoras theorem,

$AD^2 = AB^2 - (\frac{BC}{2})^2$

$\Rightarrow AD^2 = 12^2 - (\frac{12}{2})^2$

$\Rightarrow AD^2 = 144 - 36$

$\Rightarrow AD = 6\sqrt{3}$

Now, we have to find DG,

$DG = (\frac{1}{3}) \times AD$

$\Rightarrow DG = (\frac{1}{3}) \times 6\sqrt{3}$

$\Rightarrow DG = 2\sqrt{3}$

$\therefore$ The length of DG is $2\sqrt{3}$.

31(B). The consumers in an ecosystem are heterotrophs, mostly animals which feed on other organisms. Consumers are also called as phagotrophic, as they ingest food. Consumers can be first-order consumers, e.g., herbivores, cattle, rabbits, deer, insects like grasshopper, etc. They feed on producers. Primary carnivores are second-order consumers. They feed on herbivores. Secondary carnivores are third-order consumers that feed on primary carnivores. For example, Small fish and water insects like scavenger beetles that feed on the crustaceans.

32(A). Algae, along with plants and some bacteria and fungi, are autotrophs. Autotrophs are the producers in the food chain, meaning they create their own nutrients and energy. Kelp, like most autotrophs, creates energy through a process called photosynthesis.

33(A). The Reactivity series is an arrangement of metals in the order of decreasing reactivities. We can infer that a more reactive metal displaces a less

reactive metal from a solution of its salt.
$K > Na > Ca > Mg > Al > Zn > Fe > Pb > H > Cu > Hg > Ag > Au$
From the reactivity series, it is clear that F e is more reactive than Cu and can replace Cu . But in the case of Mg and Zn , we find that they are more reactive than F and same in the case of Mg and Pb where Mg is more reactive than Pb .

34(A). In the electrolytic refining process, the impure metal is made the anode and a thin strip of pure metal is made the cathode.
A solution of the metal salt is used as an electrolyte.
On passing the current through the electrolyte, the pure metal from the anode dissolves into the electrolyte.
An equivalent amount of pure metal is deposited on the cathode.

35(D). The growth of tendril in pea plants is due to rapid cell divisions in tendril cells that are away from the support. A tendril is a slender stem- or petiole-like structure that is used by vines and lianas (climbing plants) to wrap around or to hook a support.

36(A). Ethylene stimulates ripening of fruit such as tomatoes, lemons, oranges etc.
- It also increases the rate of respiration.
- It also regulate abscission and senescence.
- It is also responsible for breaking dormancy.

37(C). Sulfur dioxide (also sulphur dioxide) is a chemical compound with the formula SO_2 . It is a toxic gas with a pungent, irritating smell. It is released naturally by volcanic activity and is produced as a by-product of the burning of fossil fuels contaminated with sulfur compounds.

38(A). $Zn + 2NaOH \rightarrow Na_2ZnO_2 + H_2$
Zinc metal with sodium hydroxide to produce zincate sodium and hydrogen. This reaction takes place at a temperature near $550°C$ Zinc is a transition metal that shows moderate reactivity. Zinc reacts with NaOH to form sodium zincate with the evolution of hydrogen gas.

39(D). The gas used in the hydrogenation of oils in the presence of nickel as a catalyst is hydrogen.
Unsaturated hydrocarbon adds hydrogen in the presence of catalysts, such as nickel, to form saturated hydrocarbon.

40(A). If a small piece of sodium is dropped into some ethanol, it reacts steadily to give off bubbles of hydrogen gas and leaves a colourless solution of sodium ethoxide, CH_3CH_2ON and hydrogen gas is evolved.
$2C_2H_5OH + 2Na \rightarrow 2C_2H_5ONa + H_2$

41(A). Sexual reproduction is the mode of reproduction that requires gametes from both male and female organisms. These gametes fertilize and develop to form a new individual.
It is the mode of reproduction in which gamete cells from two organisms, one male and one female, combine to form a singular zygote. This zygote shares half of its genetic information with the father and the other half with the mother.

42(B). The primary sex organ found in human males is the testis. Testis produces sperms and hormones that are responsible for the control and onset of the whole reproduction process. To help the process of sperm production and transport to the respective site accessory sex organs help.

43(C). Wings of bird and wings of insect both are analogous as both of them perform the same function of flight while structures and origin are different. Feathers of birds originate from their forelimbs, the wings of insects originate from the inner or outer surface of the insect's body.

44(B). The carriers of factor are chromosomes and transfer hereditary information from one generation to another. Genetic information is passed from generation to generation through inherited units of chemical information (in most cases, genes). Organisms produce other similar organisms through sexual reproduction, which allows the line of genetic material to be maintained and generations to be linked.

45(B). According to Snell's law of refraction, the ratio of the sine of angle of incidence to the sine of angle of refraction is a constant for a given pair of media, and for the light of a given colour. If " i " is the angle of incidence and " r " is the angle of refraction, then:
$\frac{\sin i}{\sin r} = $ constant
$\therefore n_{21} \times n_{12} = 1$

46(C). Object-size, $h = +4.0$ cm
Object-distance, $u = -25.0$ cm
Focal length, $f = -15.0$ cm
$\frac{1}{v} + \frac{1}{u} = \frac{1}{f}$
or,
$\frac{1}{v} = \frac{1}{f} - \frac{1}{u} = \frac{1}{-15.0} - \frac{1}{-25.0} = -\frac{1}{15.0} + \frac{1}{25.0}$
or, $\quad \frac{1}{v} = \frac{-5.0+3.0}{75.0} = \frac{-2.0}{75.0}$ or,
$v = -37.5$ cm
The screen should be placed at 37.5 cm in front of the mirror.

47(A). When the current carrying conductor is placed perpendicular to the magnetic field, magnetic field produces maximum force on the conductor. when the current carrying conductor is placed parallel or anti parallel with magnetic field then magnetic field produces no force on the conductor.
Length of the wire which remain in magnetic field andAngle between the current carrying conductor and magnetic field.In the question conductor is placed perpendicular to the magnetic field i.e $\theta = 90°$ that means $\sin\theta = 1$ that is maximum possible value of $\sin\theta$. When the current carrying wire is placed perpendicular to the magnetic field then magnetic force acting on the conductor is maximum i.e $F = ILB$.

48(B). Breathing is a mechanical process. Breathing (or pulmonary ventilation) has two phases - inspiration (or inhalation) and expiration (or exhalation). It is a mechanical process that depends on volume changes in the chest cavity. The volume changes result in pressure changes, which lead to the flow of gases to equalise the pressure.

49(A). Energy released during respiration is stored in the form of Adenosine Triphosphate (ATP). During cellular respiration, glucose is broken down in the presence of oxygen to produce carbon dioxide and water. The energy released during the reaction is captured by the energy-carrying molecule ATP (adenosine triphosphate). Adenosine triphosphate is the primary energy carrier in living things. The removal of one phosphate group releases 7.3 kilocalories per mole, or 30.6 kilojoules per mole, under standard conditions.

50(B). Acids are typically stored in glass containers because some acids will destroy plastics or react with them forming inedible products as these plastics are modified petroleum products and hence, corrode the plastic vessels easily. Glass on the other hand is not corroded by these acids so they are a good option.

51(A). A hazardous sign is usually printed on containers of acids or bases to warn people about the dangerous corrosive nature of acid or base.

52(C). Colour blindness is said to occur when a person cannot differentiate between colours although his vision may otherwise be normal. The most common type of color blindness makes it hard to tell the difference between red and green.

Another type makes it hard to tell the difference between blue and yellow. People who are completely color blind don't see color at all, but that's not very common.

53(B). We know that,
Individual resistors are having resistance:
$R = 100 \pm 4$
Now,
On combining 5 similar resistors we get:
$5R = 500 \pm 20$
So, tolerance of the combination is also 4%

54(A). As we can see that both resistance are connected in parallel.
For parallel combination:
$R_{eq} = \dfrac{R_1 R_2}{R_1 + R_2}$
$R_{eq} = \dfrac{5 \times 5}{5 + 5} = 2.5 \, \Omega$
Thus, Equivalent resistance is less than $5.0 \, \Omega$

55(D). We know that,
The power dissipated is given by $P = Vi$
where,
V = voltage across lamp
i = current flowing through lamp
Now,
$i = \dfrac{P}{V}$
$= \dfrac{50}{250}$
$= 0.2 \, A$

56(D). All of the above are uses of multi-purpose projects.
Today, dams are built not just for irrigation but for electricity generation, water supply for domestic and industrial uses, flood control, recreation, inland navigation and fish breeding. So, dams are now referred to as multi-purpose projects where the many uses of the impounded water are integrated with one another.
Advantages of multi-purpose projects:
- Helps in the generation of electricity.
- Water stored in the reservoirs is provided to farmers to irrigate their lands.
- Dams supply water for domestic and industrial uses.
- Reservoirs in multipurpose projects are used for inland navigation, Recreational activities and Fish breeding.

57(C). The biological loss is strongly correlated with the loss of Cultural Diversity.
Because it has increasingly affected many indigenous and other forest dependent people that directly depend upon various components of forest and wildlife for food, drink, medicine, culture, spiritualism etc

58(D). The economic strength of a country is measured in terms of the raw material it possesses not true regarding the importance of manufacturing industries.
Importance of Manufacturing:
- Manufacturing sector is considered the backbone of development in general and

economic development.
- Manufacturing industries helps in modernising agriculture.
- It reduce the heavy dependence of people on agriculture income by providing them jobs.
- Helps in eradication of unemployment & poverty.
- Helps in bringing down regional disparities.
- Exports of manufactured goods expand trade & commerce.

59(C). Big private companies contribute in the development of a nation by increasing productivity of the country in the manufacturing of industrial goods. It promotes rapid economic development through creation and expansion of infrastructure. It creates employment opportunities.

60(B). Sri Lanka has better performance in terms of human development than india.

Country	Gross National Income (GNI) per capita (2011 PPP $)	Life Expectancy, at birth	Mean Years of Schooling of People aged 25 and above	HDI Rank in the world. (2018)
Sri Lanka	12,707	77	10.6	73
India	6,681	69.7	6.5	130
Myanmar	4,961	67.1	5.0	148
Pakistan	5,005	67.3	5.2	154
Nepal	3,457	70.8	5.0	143
Bangladesh	4,976	72.6	6.2	134

61(B). In 1815 the Treaty of Vienna take place Britain, Russia, Prussia, Austria were the participants.
The Treaty of Vienna of 25 March 1815 was the formal agreement of the allied powers — Austria, Great Britain, Prussia and Russia — committing them to wage war against Napoleon until he was defeated.

62(C). Our country is the second largest producer of rice in the world after China. It is a kharif crop which requires high temperature, (above 25°C) and high humidity with annual rainfall above 100 cm.

63(C). RBI was nationalised in year 1949.
The Reserve Bank of India (RBI) is the central bank of India, which was established on April 1, 1935, under the Reserve Bank of India Act. The Reserve Bank of India uses monetary policy to

create financial stability in India, and it is charged with regulating the country's currency and credit systems. In 1926, the Hilton Young Commission recommended the setting up of the Reserve Bank of India. At the time of establishment, the authorized capital of the Reserve Bank of India was Rs. 5 crores.

64(C). "Employer" is not a formal source of credit.
Formal source of credit include capacity, capital, conditions, character, and collateral. There is no regulatory standard that requires the use of the formal source of credit, but the majority of lenders review most of this information prior to allowing a borrower to take on debt.

65(B). Goods are placed in containers that can be loaded intact onto ships, railways, planes and trucks.
Container terminals or container ports (used interchangeably) are the terms designated for the intermediate destination facilities that enable shipping containers to switch methods of transport in route to their final destination. Efficient and well-connected container ports enabled by frequent and regular shipping services are key to minimizing trade costs, including transport costs, linking supply chains and supporting international trade. Thus, port performance is a critical factor that can shape countries' trade competitiveness.

66(D). All the above options are disadvantages of Globalisation.
Globalization is defined as the increase in the flow of goods, services, capital, people, and ideas across international boundaries. There are some grim sides of Globalisation too. They are as: (i) Unequal economic growth (ii) Lack of local businesses (iii) Increases potential global recessions(iv) Exploits cheaper labor markets (v) Causes job displacement.

67(A). The consumer movement in India has made some progress in terms of numbers of organised groups and their activities. There are today more than 700 consumer groups in the country of which only about 20-25 are well organised and recognised for their work. However, the consumer redressal process is becoming cumbersome, expensive, and time-consuming. Many a time, consumers are required to engage lawyers. These cases require time for filing and attending the court proceedings etc.

68(D). Manufacturer displays information because consumers have the right to be informed.
A manufacturer is a person or company that produces finished goods from raw materials by using various tools, equipment, and processes, and then sells the goods to consumers. The Consumer

Protection Act, 1986, defines Right to Information as 'the right to be informed about the quality, quantity, potency, purity, standard and price of goods so as to protect the consumer against unfair trade practices'.

69(A). The first printed edition of the Ramcharitmanas of Tulsidas, a sixteenth-century text, come out in 1810.
Name the first edition of Indian religious text published in vernacular. It was Ramcharitmanas of Tulsidas, a sixteenth-century text, which came out from Calcutta in 1810 which was the first edition of an Indian religious text published in vernacular.

70(B). The Vernacular Press Act of 1878 it provided the government with extensive rights to censor reports and editorials in the vernacular press.
Vernacular Press Act, in British India, law enacted in 1878 to curtail the freedom of the Indian-language (i.e., non-English) press. Proposed by Lord Lytton, then viceroy of India (governed 1876–80), the act was intended to prevent the vernacular press from expressing criticism of British policies—notably, the opposition that had grown with the outset of the Second Anglo-Afghan War (1878–80). The act excluded English-language publications. It elicited strong and sustained protests from a wide spectrum of the Indian populace.

71(D). All of the above option are true regarding power shared in modern democracies.
In modern democracies, power sharing arrangements can take many forms.
- Power is shared among different organs of government, such as the legislature, executive and judiciary.
- Power can be shared among governments at different levels i.e a general government for the entire country and governments at the provincial or regional level.
- Power may also be shared among different social groups, such as the religious and linguistic groups.

72(B). After a 26-year military campaign, the Sri Lankan military defeated the Tamil Tigers in May 2009, bringing the civil war to an end.
The Sri Lankan civil war fought in Sri Lanka from 1983 to 2009. Beginning on 23 July 1983, there was an intermittent insurgency against the government by the Velupillai Prabhakaran-led Liberation Tigers of Tamil Eelam (LTTE, also known as the Tamil Tigers). The LTTE fought to create an independent Tamil state called Tamil Eelam in the north-east of the island, due to the continuous discrimination and violent persecution against Sri Lankan Tamils by the Sinhalese dominated Sri Lankan Government.

73(A). Rinderpest arrived in Africa in the late 1880s.
In Africa, in the 1890s, a fast-spreading disease of cattle plague or rinderpest had a terrifying impact on peoples livelihoods and the local economy. This is a good example of the widespread European imperial impact on colonised societies. It shows how in this era of conquest even a disease affecting cattle reshaped the lives and fortunes of thousands of people and their relations with the rest of the world. Rinderpest arrived in Africa in the late 1880s. It was carried by infected cattle imported from British Asia to feed the Italian soldiers invading Eritrea in East Africa. Entering Africa in the east, rinderpest moved west like forest fire, reaching Africas Atlantic coast in 1892.It reached the Cape (Africas southernmost tip) five years later. Along the way rinderpest killed 90 per cent of the cattle. The loss of cattle destroyed African livelihoods. Planters, mine owners and colonial governments now successfully monopolised what scarce cattle resources remained, to strengthen their power and to force Africans into the labour market. Control over the scarce resource of cattle enabled European colonisers to conquer and subdue Africa.

74(B). The State created on the basis of culture, ethnicity or geography, is Nagaland.
It is a predominantly tribal state on the eastern border. It is mostly hilly and enjoys the reputation of being a home to Nagas, a brave group of people in the region. In April 1962, the Nagaland Security Regulation, 1962, for the suppression of subversive activities, maintenance of essential supplies and services and control of military requirements was passed. In August 1962, a bill was moved in the Indian Parliament for creating a state of Nagaland.

75(B). Sri Lanka is an example of the Unitary system of Government.
Sri Lanka has a unitary form of government. In a unitary state, the central government is the supreme power and the different units of the government work under its direction. Federalism has long been advocated as a means of resolving the ethnic issues and unbalanced development in Sri Lanka. As the unitary state has resulted in uneven development across Sri Lanka, the Western Province dominates over the other eight provinces.

76(B). Before the age of machine industries, silk and cotton goods from India dominated the international market in textiles. Coarser cottons were produced in many countries, but the finer varieties often came from India.
The Armenian and Persian merchants took these goods from Punjab to Afghanistan. Persia and Central Asia. Though most of the trade was carried through land routes, but the sea route was and Hoogly were the most important pore which were used for trade.
A complex and complete market before the arrival of the outsiders, the Dade was handled by a variety of Indian merchants and bankers.
The whole process of Dade basically involved three steps:
- Financing production
- Carrying or transporting goods
- Supplying goods to the exporters

77(C). Over-irrigation is the main cause of land degradation in Punjab.
Over irrigation: Since a large number of farmers now use tubewells for the irrigation of their fields, they potentially over irrigate the land to save the frequency of irrigation and also to make the soil suitable for higher moisture required crops. This leads to an increased level of salinity in the soil which degrades the quality of soil.
Over irrigation is a result of increased stress on the land to produce more quantity of crops in a limited area to feed the huge population of India. Hence, more scientific practices need to be followed.

78(B). 'Equal treatment of women' is a necessary ingredient of a democratic society. This means that it is now easier for women to legally wage struggle for their rights. This statement can be justified in following ways:
(i) In a non-democratic country, the principle of individual freedom and dignity have no legal and moral power. But in democracy this is recognized
(ii) Recognized human rights help the women to wage a struggle against the inequality
(iii) Women are given all fundamental rights as men. This opens the autonomy and freedom for women.
(v) Economic independence or access to livelihood as equal to men is the main means of empowering women. In democracy there is no discrimination between men and women regarding the opportunity and status in work place

79(A). Democracy is seen to be good in principle but felt to be not so good in its practice.
The reasons for this:
- The decision-making process in democracy is delayed.
- Democracies often frustrate the needs of the people.
- It often ignore the demands of majority of its population.
- The routine tales of corruption associated with it.
- Most democracies fall short of elections that provide fair chance to everyone and in subjecting every decision to public debate.

80(C). The Non-Cooperation movement

slow down because handmade Indian goods like Khadi worked out more expensive and time-consuming than mill-made goods.

The reasons were:

(i) Some leaders within Congress were reluctant to participate in Non-Cooperation Movement as they feared in might lead to popular violence.

(ii) Khadi cloth was more expensive than mass-produced mill cloth and poor people could not afford to buy it.

(iii)For the movement to be successful, alternate Indian institutions had to be set up so that they could be used in place of the British ones. These were slow to come up. So students and teachers began trickling back to government schools and lawyers joined back work in government courts.

81(C). Aryabhata was a great astronomer, astrologer and mathematician of ancient India. He wrote 'Aryabhattiyam Granth' at the age of just 23. Aryabhata developed the decimal system and also told that the earth revolves around the sun while rotating on its axis. He threw light on the real reason for the occurrence of solar eclipse and lunar eclipse. Due to his unprecedented contribution in astronomy, India's first satellite was named Aryabhata.

82(B). Article 19 of the Indian Constitution includes "Right to freedom of speech and expression".

83(D). Tata Consultancy services had become one of the top three most valuable brands in the information technology (IT) service sector of the world.

Tata Consultancy Services (TCS) is an Indian multinational information technology (IT) services and consulting company headquartered in Mumbai, Maharashtra, India with its largest campus located in Chennai, Tamil Nadu, India. It is a subsidiary of the Tata Group and operates in 149 locations across 46 countries.

84(D). In A. K. Gopalan case, the Supreme Court rule that protection under Article 21 is available only against arbitrary executive action and not from arbitrary legislative action.

Life and personal liberty have been mentioned under Article 21 of the Constitution of India. In the case of Maneka Gandhi, a detailed discussion was held regarding life and personal liberty and the right mentioned under Article 21 was made a very important right. The Supreme Court of India has interpreted in the context of this article that Article 21 is the essence of the Right to Freedom. All the rights related to freedom under the Constitution of India are mentioned in Article 21 as well. Similarly article 22 is also related to article 21. Article 22 cannot be considered as a single article in itself, but the importance of this article is included with article 21 of the

constitution, so article 21 article 20 should be read together.

85(C). **Lushai Hills:** The Lushai Hills are a mountain range in Mizoram and Manipur, India. The range is part of the Patkai range system and its highest point is 2,157 m high Phawngpui, also known as 'Blue Mountain'.

Erramalla Hills: It is a range of hills in western Andhra Pradesh state. The hills, which trend northeast to southwest, are situated on the eastern edge of the Deccan plateau, between the basins of the Krishna River (north) and the Penneru River (south).

Javadi Hills: They are an extension of the Eastern Ghats spread in the northern part of the state of Tamil Nadu. Javadi Hills is home to spectacular waterfalls.

Satmala Hills : Satmala is a mountain range which runs across Nashik District, Maharashtra. They are an integral part of the Sahyadris range within Nashik.

86(A). NSIL is the name of the new commercial arm of ISRO. It was founded on 6 March 2019. It is the commercial arm of ISRO with the primary responsibility of enabling Indian industries to take up high technology space-related activities.

87(D). Meghalaya is a state in North-East India. Meghalaya was earlier a part of Assam.

88(A). A theatre is a great form for story-telling in which one or more actors using the skills of dancing, acting, singing, talking, miming, etc. Theatre crafts like masks, make-up, and costumes are used to create a story. Theatre is a composite art form in which many skills, arts, and crafts are brought together. Lightweight jewellery, sceneries and stages, music with drums and trumpets, manjiras are a part of Theatre.

Every corner of India has its own unique form of folk theatre.

- Nautanki of Uttar Pradesh often draws on romantic Persian literature for its themes. So, pair 1 is correct.
- Raw vigour and bawdy humour characterize the Tamasha of Maharashtra. So, pair 2 is correct.
- The Bhavai is related to Rajasthan. So, pair 3 is incorrect.

89(C). National Highway Authority of India:

- The NHAI is responsible for developing, managing, and maintaining the highways of the country.
- It comes under the Ministry of Road Transport & Highways.
- It came into the picture in the year 1988 and began its work in 1995.
- NH 15 passes through Pathankot-Amritsar-Bhatinda-Ganganagar-Bikaner-Jaisalmer-Barmer-Samakhiali
- It is 1526km long and passes through Rajasthan, Punjab & Gujarat.

So, we conclude that NH 15 does not pass through Hanumangarh.

90(A). After the death of King Ashoka, the Maurya Dynasty declined rapidly.

- The later Mauryas ruled from 232 BC-185 BC .
- Ashoka's death was followed by the division of the Mauryan Empire into two parts– Western and Eastern regions .

91(B). Tulsidas wrote Ramcharitmanas in the reign of Akbar.

92(B). After the battle of Buxar, the East India Company agreed to pay Rs. 26 lakh every year to the Mughal Emperor Shah Alam - II.

93(A). Sustainable development can be achieved by judicious use of natural resources.

Sustainable development stands for meeting the needs of the current generation without jeopardizing the ability of futures generations to meet their own needs. In other words, a better quality of life for everyone, now and for generations to come. It offers a vision of progress that integrates immediate and longer-term objectives, local and global action and regards social, economic and environmental issues as inseparable and interdependent components of human progress. This can be brought about only by using the existing resources wisely.

95(B). Harmanpreet Kaur is the first Indian woman cricketer to hit a century in T20 International cricket by scoring 103 runs in 51 balls.

Harmanpreet Kaur was named India's captain for the T20 World Cup in the Caribbean.

In the opening match of the tournament against New Zealand, Harmanpreet became the first woman for India to score a century in T20 as she slammed 103 off just 51 balls.

96(B). Mrs Indira Gandhi was the first women prime minister of India.

Indira Priyadarshini Gandhi (19 November 1917 – 31 October 1984) was an Indian politician and a central figure of the Indian National Congress. She was the 3rd prime minister of India and was also the first and, to date, only female prime minister of India. Hence the correct option is (B).

97(B). Plastic is non degradable thing so it cannot be decomposed by any method or it cannot be decomposing by bacterial action.

98(D). Ligaments are the connective tissue that connects two bones to each other. Ligaments are a short band of tough flexible connective tissues which connect two bones. Ligaments connect bones to other bones.

99(A). The Soviet Union was officially known as the Union of Soviet Socialist

Republics (USSR). It was established in 1922 and lasted till 1991. It was a group of 15 Soviet Socialist Republics. The Soviet Union has its origins in the Russian Revolution of 1917.

100(D). The winners of the 68*th* National Film Awards- 2022 were announced by Information & Broadcasting Ministry on 22 July 2022 in New Delhi.

Additional Information:

Best Feature Film: Soorarai Pottru

Best Actor: Suriya for Soorarai Pottru & Ajay Devgn for Tanhaji

Madhya Pradesh won the 'Most Film Friendly State' award.

Best Actress: Aparna Balamurali for Soorarai Pottru.